ADJUDICATING OVER ANARCHY

Without access to state-backed enforcement measures, international adjudicators must rely on their authority to influence real-world outcomes. In this book, Geraldo Vidigal thoroughly examines the judicial powers of international courts and tribunals and how these powers are used in practice. The author reviews, and offers a comprehensive theory for, the various social mechanisms that explain why and how international judicial pronouncements affect the behaviour of states, influencing the views of individuals within states as well as changing states' mutual expectations of cooperative and sanction-worthy behaviour. The book considers how judicial remedies can induce compliance by targeting specific areas of disagreement, interpreting obligations, declaring violations and establishing how wrongdoer states must offset unlawful injury. An often untapped type of remedy relies on the ability of courts to determine permissible responses to breach: what measures other actors may take to respond to violations, compelling wrongdoers to comply with their obligations and provide redress for injury.

GERALDO VIDIGAL is Associate Professor at the University of Amsterdam. He holds a PhD in Law (Cambridge), LLM (Sorbonne) and LLB (University of São Paulo). He has worked as Dispute Settlement Lawyer at the World Trade Organization and as Senior Research Fellow at the Max Planck Institute (Luxembourg).

CAMBRIDGE STUDIES IN INTERNATIONAL AND COMPARATIVE LAW: 195

Established in 1946, this series produces high quality, reflective and innovative scholarship in the field of public international law. It publishes works on international law that are of a theoretical, historical, cross-disciplinary or doctrinal nature. The series also welcomes books providing insights from private international law, comparative law and transnational studies which inform international legal thought and practice more generally.

The series seeks to publish views from diverse legal traditions and perspectives, and of any geographical origin. In this respect it invites studies offering regional perspectives on core *problématiques* of international law, and in the same vein, it appreciates contrasts and debates between diverging approaches. Accordingly, books offering new or less orthodox perspectives are very much welcome. Works of a generalist character are greatly valued and the series is also open to studies on specific areas, institutions or problems. Translations of the most outstanding works published in other languages are also considered.

After seventy years, Cambridge Studies in International and Comparative Law sets the standard for international legal scholarship and will continue to define the discipline as it evolves in the years to come.

Recent books in the series can be found at the end of this volume.

ADJUDICATING OVER ANARCHY

Judicial Remedies, Compliance, and Enforcement in International Law

GERALDO VIDIGAL

University of Amsterdam

CAMBRIDGE
UNIVERSITY PRESS

CAMBRIDGE
UNIVERSITY PRESS

Shaftesbury Road, Cambridge CB2 8EA, United Kingdom

One Liberty Plaza, 20th Floor, New York, NY 10006, USA

477 Williamstown Road, Port Melbourne, VIC 3207, Australia

314–321, 3rd Floor, Plot 3, Splendor Forum, Jasola District Centre, New Delhi – 110025, India

103 Penang Road, #05–06/07, Visioncrest Commercial, Singapore 238467

Cambridge University Press is part of Cambridge University Press & Assessment, a department of the University of Cambridge.

We share the University's mission to contribute to society through the pursuit of education, learning and research at the highest international levels of excellence.

www.cambridge.org
Information on this title: www.cambridge.org/9781107160255

DOI: 10.1017/9781316673072

When citing this work, please include a reference to the DOI 10.1017/9781316673072

First published 2026

Cover image: © Rene Magritte, The Battle of Argonne, 1959 c/o Pictoright Amsterdam 2024.

A catalogue record for this publication is available from the British Library

Library of Congress Cataloging-in-Publication Data
Names: Vidigal, Geraldo, author.
Title: Adjudicating over anarchy : judicial remedies, compliance, and enforcement in international law / Geraldo Vidigal, University of Amsterdam.
Description: Cambridge, United Kingdom ; New York, NY : Cambridge University Press, 2025. | Series: Cambridge studies in international and comparative law | Includes bibliographical references and index.
Identifiers: LCCN 2025011447 (print) | LCCN 2025011448 (ebook) | ISBN 9781107160255 (hardback) | ISBN 9781316613337 (paperback) | ISBN 9781316673072 (epub)
Subjects: LCSH: International courts. | Jurisdiction (International law) | Arbitration (International law)
Classification: LCC KZ6115 .V53 2025 (print) | LCC KZ6115 (ebook) | DDC 341.5/5–dc23/eng/20250602
LC record available at https://lccn.loc.gov/2025011447
LC ebook record available at https://lccn.loc.gov/2025011448

ISBN 978-1-107-16025-5 Hardback

But should I supplicate to be released
Or give such order, then, with added cords
Be it your part to bind me still the more.

Odyssey (transl. William Cowper), Book 12, 163–164

Words, words, words.

Hamlet, Act II, Scene II

CONTENTS

PREFACE

This book has had many beginnings. Its first version was a traditional legal investigation into how international courts approach the prospect, and the occasional fact, of non-compliance with their rulings. My initial hunch, which developed into a PhD dissertation, was that there was something wrong with the common view that compliance, enforcement and implementation are 'political' matters. And, while the World Trade Organization had developed a highly regulated system for compliance adjudication, culminating in an authorisation for sanctions (or, as I came to call them, 'permissible responses') to be applied against the wrongdoer, most international courts seemed to stop at the establishment of consequences for breach. Much of the classical legal scholarship, supported by statements by the International Court of Justice, seemed to accept the assumptions that an international court 'neither can nor should contemplate the contingency of the judgment not being complied with'[1] and that 'the use which the successful party makes of the judgment is a matter which lies on the political and not on the judicial plane'.[2]

My PhD dissertation – *Judicial Remedies for Non-compliance with International Law* – was dedicated to showing that this assumption is incorrect, either conceptually or in adjudicatory practice. This research, available as originally submitted in Cambridge University Library, now informs Parts II and III of this book, which focus on judicial practice.

The second beginning took place when two reviewers of the book proposal found this approach overly positivistic. They remarked,

[1] *Nuclear Tests (New Zealand/France)*, [1974] ICJ Reports, p. 477; *Nuclear Tests (Australia/France)*, [1974] ICJ Reports, p. 272; *Military and Paramilitary Activities in and against Nicaragua (Nicaragua* v. *United States)*, Jurisdiction, [1984] ICJ Reports, p. 392, 437; *Continental Shelf (Tunisia/Libya) (Revision and Interpretation)*, [1985] ICJ Reports, p. 192, 229. This is a quotation from *Chorzów Factory (Merits)* (1928) PCIJ Ser A No 17, p. 63. See *Wimbledon* (1923) PCIJ Ser A No 1, p. 15, 32.

[2] *Northern Cameroons*, [1963] ICJ Reports, p. 15, 37.

correctly, that there was a lot more to be said about the topic of judicial remedies and compliance than a legal analysis can offer, and one could usefully illuminate it by integrating insights from the interdisciplinary scholarship on international adjudication and compliance with international law. I agreed, believing that doing this would be a matter of a few months, perhaps a year, in which I would simply integrate, as a throat-clearing exercise, much of the compliance scholarship I had purged from the original thesis to ensure a manageable focus and adherence to university word limits. I could then move on to the legal analysis.

This proved to be a naïve belief. Achieving a version of the book that was true to my view of why international judicial rulings matter, and what courts can do with the limited powers available to them, would take me another ten years and five cities. As I went through the international relations literature on state compliance, incentives and constructed identities, it became clear that this scholarship had its own concerns and internal struggles. Much of it seemed to treat law itself with a broad brush. I would have to find a solution in the field of law.

This was when I was introduced to two key works. First, Robert Ellickson's book *Order Without Law* provided a conceptual framework, if not outright answers, to the question of how a horizontal social order, without a distinction between coercion-wielding authorities and their subjects, can operate and maintain a normative system. Second, Tom Ginsburg and Richard McAdams' article 'Adjudicating in Anarchy: An Expressive Theory of International Dispute Resolution' offered something most theories of adjudication are lacking: an explanation for how adjudication can be relevant to behaviour even where the adjudicator can neither wield the prospect of overwhelming coercion nor rely on a particularly strong recognition of the adjudicator's legitimacy by the addressees of its pronouncements. Integrating these insights into the previous work allowed me to overcome the paralysis generated by the excess of theories of international adjudication and (two years later) complete the book. Though the title for this book was the product of trying out various combinations of the key terms that animate the argument, the coincidental homage to 'Adjudicating in Anarchy' is a fortuitous outcome.

Part I of this book is thus a long response to the reviewers' concerns. It is an exploration, informed by international relations literature but not seeking to become international relations scholarship, of international law's five layers of compliance control. The five layers identify the different actors that can ensure a state's compliance with international commitments, or sanction breaches, making violations less attractive in the first place. These actors include not only agents within the addressee state (Layer 1, or 'voluntary compliance', whether by the government or by the wider bureaucracy) but also agents of other states, whether injured states acting through the heavily regulated Layer 2 ('inter-state enforcement') or all states acting through the little-regulated Layer 3 ('diffuse enforcement'). In the highly institutionalised international society of the twenty-first century, sanctions can also be determined by international institutions, acting through Layers 4 ('institutional enforcement') or 5 ('authorised enforcement'). Identifying these different layers of compliance control permits understanding what forces adjudicators can mobilise through their different judicial remedies.

Explaining how adjudicators mobilise these forces required developing a second typology. A common assumption in interdisciplinary scholarship is that international adjudication is a blunt instrument whereby international courts establish norms, or, alternatively, identify or 'monitor' breaches. And, while adjudicators themselves do far more than that, the great flexibility of international judicial remedies in practice makes taking their variety into account understandably difficult for other fields. I therefore established two axes for remedy classification, depending on their function – to define norms or to sanction breaches – but also on their focus: whether they concern the normative order as it exists in general or the legal consequences of a state's disturbance of this order. The outcome was a fourfold classification of international judicial remedies, explored in Part II: Mere Adjudication, Declaration of Breach, Consequential Duties and Permissible Responses.

This typology, as well as the classification of strategic uses of remedies explored in Part III – remedy repetition, remedy escalation, remedy withholding and remedy foreshadowing – came late in the writing process but proved extremely helpful. These classifications provide structure to a study that does not concern itself with how a specific international court employs its remedial powers, or how uses of remedial authority compare between a few different adjudicators, but with *international adjudication in general.* International courts are defined by their lack of a connection to a state, that is, to a hierarchical social apparatus with control over political and economic resources that it is expected to mobilise, at the orders of the court, to apply coercion against recalcitrant addressees of the court's pronouncements. Without this connection, which I call *potestas*, international courts must rely on the coercion-less authority of their pronouncements – their *auctoritas* – to influence outcomes. Put otherwise, international courts rely on the distinctive power of the word alone. A key question the book seeks to answer is how through different types of pronouncements, amounting to different uses of their judicial authority, international courts are able to influence the behaviour of states, and enhance the enforceability of international legal norms, even without a connection to coercive power.

The core contention linking the various parts, and perhaps the core argument of the book, is this: that international courts, having no direct access to the coercive apparatus of a state, can only produce effects on state behaviour to the extent that their pronouncements can mobilise the layers of compliance control that lead states to behave (mostly) according to international norms in the first place. By employing different remedies, international courts may seek to mobilise different elements of international law's compliance control system. Their choice of remedies depends on whether they aim to facilitate the restoration of lawful relations, condemn law-breaking conduct with symbolic redress for aggrieved parties, or provide substantive redress and material reparation for injury. These uses of the power of the word show the limits, but also explain the potential, of adjudication as an instrument to induce behavioural change in the horizontal international order. To these I have added a fourth, little-explored use of judicial authority: to determine not what a wrongdoer must to in order to provide redress for unlawful action, but what other actors – states and, increasingly, international organisations and bodies – are entitled to do to respond to the unlawful conduct and enforce legal norms vis-à-vis the wrongdoer.

These three key moments – choosing international judicial remedies as a topic, accepting to step beyond traditional legal scholarship to illuminate it, and identifying works that offered a conceptual ground for the argument – have guided both the writing of the book and its ultimate form. The themes I explore, however, have long been significant to me. These themes appear in my Master's dissertation, where I sought to outline a distinctive concept of 'sanctions' in international law linked to institutional authorisation. They also appear in my Bachelor's final paper, in which I reflect upon the impact of authoritative international institutions over the conception of states as the preeminent actors in international law and international relations. Thinking of when I started writing this book in fact reminds me of a high school Chemistry teacher who, whenever asked about topics for her next exam, would answer, only half in jest: 'Everything – everything you have learned since you were born.'

Ultimately, I may have been writing this book my entire academic life. The main challenge, as those who have known me for the past decade will know, has been to accept to stop writing it. It is now done. With it, I can say that, if nothing else, I have added my small brick to the edifice of international law.

ACKNOWLEDGEMENTS

This book grew out of my PhD thesis, supervised at Cambridge by Lorand Bartels, whose general scepticism of broad claims I hope can still be found here, in the cautious language I used to ultimately make my broad claims. The reflections that became Part I draw on ideas about the international society and the role of institutions that were first sketched out in my Bachelor's thesis, written under Celso Lafer, and Master's thesis, supervised by Hélène Ruiz Fabri. Additionally, at the University of São Paulo, Alberto do Amaral Jr. and Tercio Sampaio Ferraz Jr. were major influences. In Paris, Pierre-Michel Eisemann, Brigitte Stern, Geneviève Bastid-Burdeau and Yves Daudet provided great insights into the practice of states and international institutions. I will always be thankful to James Crawford for arranging my PhD defence at lightning speed, and to Petros Mavroidis for engaging with this first version of the manuscript and providing essential guidance over the years.

This is the first time the argument of the book, regarding the role, relevance, potential and limitations of international adjudication, appears in its entirety. Over the years, many sparring partners have, sometimes unwittingly, helped me to test and refine the underlying ideas. I include here Daniel Arbix, Fernando Bordin, Kathleen Claussen, Andreas Kulick, Harlan Cohen, Ben Heath, Cecily Rose, Federica Paddeu, Niamh Dunne, Orla Lynskey, Julian Arato, Vladislav Lanovoy, Túlio di Giacomo Toledo, Leonardo Borlini, Jelena Beaumler, Peter-Tobias Stoll, Wolfgang Alschner, Stephanie Forrest, Neil Rogachevsky, Martins Paparinskis, Victor do Prado, Graham Cook, Rodd Izadnia, Carlo Cantore, Shashank Kumar, Gabrielle Marceau, Beatriz Stevens, Celso de Tarso Pereira, Michel Erpelding, Manuel Devers and Tomer Broude. In Amsterdam, Pola Cebulak, Stephan Schill, Yvonne Donders, Kiki Bröllman, Andrea Leiter, Christina Eckes, Kevin Jon Heller and Nataša Nedeski have all given me entry points into parts of international law

I was less familiar with. Special thanks are owed to Ingo Venzke for not letting me get away with never publishing The Book.

I must also thank those who, through the years, offered their mentorship, and sometimes crucial infrastructure and funding, allowing me to progress with various points of the project. Here I include Georgio Sacerdoti, Petros Mavroidis, Bernard Hoekman, Joost Pauwelyn, Theresa Carpenter, Valerie Hughes, Marisa Goldstein, Vera Thorstensen, Michelle Badin, Heike Krieger, Andreas Zimmerman, Krzysztof Pelc, and Andrew Hurrell. At Amsterdam, my colleagues Vid Prislan, Johanna Aleria Lorenzo, Hege Elisabeth Kjos, Rosanne van Alebeek, Eliana Cusato, Pieter Jan Kuijper, Jim Mathis, and Johannes Fahner have all helped create the kind of intellectual community from which a book is born. For final proof-read of such extensive materials as the final book covers, I was fortunate to be able to enlist the expertise of leading scholars Lauge Poulsen and Kostiantyn Gorobets (for *A Theory of International Adjudication*), Marco Longobardo (for *A Typology of Judicial Remedies*), and Graham Cook and Juliette McIntyre (for *Remedies and Compliance in International Judicial Practice*). The usual caveat applies.

On the final steps of the journey, I received invaluable help from a number of research assistants in Amsterdam. Adam Di Simine and Ola Ruzikowska conducted thorough reviews of earlier versions of the text, while Alexandru Spătaru, Anna Kitz, Carolina Saad, Phoebe Griffin and Witold Marynowski helped me update the jurisprudence and references. Tejas Rao helped me finalise the text and Allan Vidigal conducted a thorough final review. The infinite patience of my successive contact points at Cambridge University Press should be noted. Auropradeepa Rajapriyan and her eagle-eyed team were essential to turn a dozen electronic files into a nicely designed book.

Final thanks go to my parents, Geraldo and Heloisa, who heard promises about the book being *almost* finished longer than anyone else; to Marianna, for never once doubting that it would be finished one day; and to Caroline, who made sure that I crossed the finish line so we would have weekends again. Let this be one more of the many we will cross together.

ABBREVIATIONS

ACHR	American Convention on Human Rights
ACJ	Andean Court of Justice
AfCHPR	African Court on Human and Peoples' Rights
ARSIWA	Articles on Responsibility of States for Internationally Wrongful Acts
ASEAN	Association of Southeast Asian Nations
ASP	Assembly of States Parties
ATPS	American Treaty on Pacific Settlement (Pact of Bogotá)
BIT	Bilateral Investment Treaty
BIVAC	Bureau of Inspection, Valuation, Assessment and Control
CACJ	Central American Court of Justice
CARICOM	Caribbean Community
CCJ	Caribbean Court of Justice
CCSBT	Convention for the Conservation of Southern Bluefin Tuna
CERD	International Convention on the Elimination of All Forms of Racial Discrimination
CITES	Convention on International Trade in Endangered Species of Wild Fauna and Flora
CJEU	Court of Justice of the European Union
CMS	CMS Gas Transmission Company
CoE	Council of Europe
CoM	Committee of Ministers (Council of Europe)
DRC	Democratic Republic of the Congo
DSB	Dispute Settlement Body
DSU	Dispute Settlement Understanding
EACJ	East African Court of Justice
EC	European Communities
ECCJ	ECOWAS Community Court of Justice
ECHR	European Convention on Human Rights
ECOWAS	Economic Community of West African States
ECR	European Court Reports
ECtHR	European Court of Human Rights
ECT	Energy Charter Treaty

EEC	European Economic Community
EU	European Union
EWCA	England and Wales Court of Appeal
EWHC	England and Wales High Court
FSIA	Foreign Sovereign Immunities Act
FYROM	Former Yugoslav Republic of Macedonia
G7	Group of Seven
GATS	General Agreement on Trade in Services
GATT	General Agreement on Tariffs and Trade
HCA	High Court of Australia
IACtHR	Inter-American Court of Human Rights
IC(s)	international court(s)
ICAO	International Civil Aviation Organization
ICC	International Criminal Court
ICJ	International Court of Justice
ICSID	International Centre for Settlement of Investment Disputes
IEBL	Inter-Entity Boundary Line
ILC	International Law Commission
ILO	International Labour Organization
ILOAT	ILO Administrative Tribunal
IO(s)	international organisation(s)
IP	intellectual property
ISDS	investor-state dispute settlement
ITLOS	International Tribunal for the Law of the Sea
IUCT	Iran–US Claims Tribunal
LG&E	LG&E Energy Corp.
MEA(s)	Multilateral Environmental Agreement(s)
Mercosur	Common Market of the South
MFN	most-favoured nation
MOP	Meeting of the Parties
NAFTA	North American Free Trade Agreement
NCP(s)	Non-compliance Procedures and Mechanisms
OAS	Organization of American States
OASAT	OAS Administrative Tribunal
OECD	Organization for Economic Co-operation and Development
PCA	Permanent Court of Arbitration
PCIJ	Permanent Court of International Justice
PLO	Palestine Liberation Organization
RIAA	Reports of International Arbitral Awards
RPT	Reasonable Period of Time
RTA	Regional Trade Agreement
SADC	Southern African Development Community

SCM	Agreement on Subsidies and Countervailing Measures
SGS	Société Générale de Surveillance
SICA	Central American Integration System
TRIPS	Trade-Related Aspects of Intellectual Property Rights
TRUDS	Tokyo Round Understanding on Dispute Settlement
UK	United Kingdom of Great Britain and Northern Ireland
UN	United Nations
UNCIO	United Nations Conference on International Organization
UNCITRAL	United Nations Commission on International Trade Law
UNCLOS	United Nations Convention on the Law of the Sea
UNEP	United Nations Environment Programme
UNFCCC	United Nations Framework Convention on Climate Change
UNGA	United Nations General Assembly
UNRIAA	United Nations Reports of International Arbitral Awards
UNSC	United Nations Security Council
US	United States of America
USMCA	United States-Mexico-Canada Agreement
USTR	United States Trade Representative
VCLT	Vienna Convention on the Law of Treaties
WAEMU	West African Economic and Monetary Union
WTO	World Trade Organization
ZASCA	Supreme Court of Appeal of South Africa

1

Introduction

The Paradox of International Adjudication

1.1 Adjudication and the International Order

The term 'international adjudication' embodies an inherent tension. Adjudication can be defined as the intervention of an external actor – a 'third party' – to settle an interpretative dispute between two or more other actors. Under international law, adjudicators are those provided with delegated authority to establish the meaning of an international normative instrument or framework and determine the legal effects of its application to facts or events. As the Permanent Court of International Justice (PCIJ) put it in *Chorzów Factory (Interpretation)*, for the purposes of the international legal system, final judicial pronouncements 'ensure recognition of a situation at law, once and for all and with binding force as between the Parties; so that the legal position thus established cannot again be called in question so far as the legal effects ensuing therefrom are concerned'.[1] When exercising this delegated authority, international courts (ICs) perform the role that Martin Shapiro describes as that of adjudicators in general: to 'impose [a] solution on both parties even if one or both do not voluntarily consent to the solution'.[2] Adjudicators

[1] *Factory at Chorzów (Interpretation of Judgments Nos. 7 and 8)* (1925) PCIJ Ser. A No. 11, p. 20. See Richard B. Bilder, 'International Third Party Dispute Settlement' (1989) 17 *Denver Journal of International Law & Policy* 471. On the different ways lawyers and political scientist see adjudication, see Mark A. Pollack, 'Political Science in International Adjudication', in Cesare P.R. Romano, Karen J. Alter, and Yuval Shany (eds.), *The Oxford Handbook of International Adjudication* (Oxford: Oxford University Press, 2014), 388–387.

[2] Martin Shapiro, *Courts: A Comparative and Political Analysis* (Chicago: University of Chicago Press, 1981), 4. This is labelled the arbitrator's 'legal authority'. Judges' authority is wholly consent-independent: 'judges may impose a final resolution independent of the consent of the parties' (Shapiro, *Courts*, 7).

'resolve interpretative questions',[3] 'issue binding rulings',[4] or, even more succinctly, 'decide cases'.[5]

International adjudicators, however, perform their role within a highly specific environment: the international order. Legal scholars often describe it as a 'decentralised' or 'horizontal' order, one characterised by the absence of a legal hierarchy between its main subjects – states – as well as by the lack of an authority hierarchically superior to states, capable of establishing, adjudicating upon, and enforcing rules without the concurrence of states themselves.[6] As the Charter of the United Nations (UN) puts it, a fundamental normative tenet of the international order – distant as it may be from its material reality – is the 'sovereign equality' of its component states.[7]

In international relations scholarship, Hedley Bull assimilated the international order to an 'anarchical society'.[8] This is a society in which 'all states, in their dealings with one another, are bound by the rules and institutions of the society they form'[9] but where, at the same time, 'there is no central authority able to interpret and enforce the law, and thus individual members of the society must themselves judge it and enforce it'.[10] International adjudication somewhat calls into question this sharp

[3] Duncan Kennedy, *A Critique of Adjudication (fin de siècle)* (Cambridge, MA: Harvard University Press, 1998), 1.

[4] Karen Alter, *The New Terrain of International Law: Courts, Politics, Rights* (Princeton, NJ: Princeton University Press, 2014), 8.

[5] William Lucy, *Understanding and Explaining Adjudication* (Oxford: Oxford University Press, 1999), 2.

[6] The metaphors of 'decentralisation' and 'horizontality' are pervasive in international legal scholarship. See, for example, Hans Kelsen, *Principles of International Law* (New York: Rinehart, 1952), 22; International Law Commission (ILC), 'Fragmentation of International Law: Difficulties Arising from the Diversification and Expansion of International Law – Report of the ILC Study Group Finalized by Martti Koskenniemi', A/CN.4/L.682 (2006), 486; James Crawford, 'Multilateral Rights and Obligations in International Law' (2006) 319 *RdC* 325–482, at 345.

[7] Charter of the United Nations, signed 26 June 1945, in force 24 October 1945, 1 UNTS 16 Article 2(1). On the notion of equality between states, see Andreas Osiander, 'Sovereignty, International Relations, and the Westphalian Myth' (2001) 55 *International Organization* 251–287. On the effects of material inequality among states over global norm-setting, see Daniel W. Drezner, *All Politics Is Global: Explaining International Regulatory Regimes* (Princeton, NJ: Princeton University Press, 2007), at 8–9.

[8] Hedley Bull, *The Anarchical Society: A Study of Order in World Politics*, 2nd edn (Basingstoke: Macmillan, Ed 1977/1995), 25.

[9] Ibid.

[10] Ibid., 46. See also Barry Buzan, Charles Jones, and Richard Little, *The Logic of Anarchy: Neorealism to Structural Realism* (New York: Columbia University Press, 1993).

duality. ICs issue adjudicatory rulings on legal interpretation and application that rely, for their operation and effectiveness, not on the mobilisation of coercive power (what I will term *potestas*) but on authority (or *auctoritas*).[11] As Karen Alter noted, while international adjudicators 'may not be able to call upon centralized tools of coercion to enforce their rulings', adjudication 'remove[s] from governments and domestic judges the monopoly power to define what international law requires'.[12]

This book is an investigation into the tension between these two elements: power and authority. It examines the role, possibilities, and limits of adjudicators' authority in an international society in which they are kept at a distance from the mobilisation of material resources that is usually identified with power. Significant scholarship has examined this tension from the viewpoint of states and their decisions to negotiate, adjudicate, or pursue their interests unilaterally.[13] I take the perspective of adjudicators, focusing not on the desirability of adjudication for states or their legitimacy challenges[14] but on their instruments, or, as I will label them collectively, their judicial remedies: the different tools available to ICs to perform their adjudicative task and influence developments in the international society.

[11] Karen J. Alter, Emilie M. Hafner-Burton, and Laurence R. Helfer, 'Theorizing the Judicialization of International Relations' (2019) 63 *International Studies Quarterly* 449–463, 450–451.

[12] Alter, *The New Terrain of International Law*, 9–10.

[13] Alter et al., 'Theorizing the Judicialization of International Relations'. Christina L. Davis, *Why Adjudicate? Enforcing Trade Rules in the WTO* (Princeton, NJ: Princeton University Press, 2011). On self-interested states' decisions in creating and designing tribunals in the first place, see John C. Yoo and Eric Posner, 'Judicial Independence in International Tribunals' (2005) 93 *California Law Review* 1; Laurence R. Helfer and Anne-Marie Slaughter, 'Why States Create International Tribunals: A Response to Professors Posner and Yoo' (2005) 93 *California Law Review* 899; Andrew T. Guzman, 'International Tribunals: A Rational Choice Analysis' (2008) 157 *University of Pennsylvania Law Review* 171; Leslie Johns, *Strengthening International Courts: The Hidden Costs of Legalization* (Ann Arbor, MI: University of Michigan Press, 2015).

[14] For debates regarding international adjudicators' legitimacy and authority, see Cesare P.R. Romano, 'Legitimacy, Authority, and Performance: Contemporary Anxieties of International Courts and Tribunals' (2020) 114 *American Journal of International Law* 149–163; Nienke Grossman, Harlan Grant Cohen, Andreas Føllesdal, and Geir Ulfstein (eds.), *Legitimacy and International Courts* (Cambridge: Cambridge University Press, 2018); Robert Howse, Hélène Ruiz Fabri, Geir Ulfstein, and Michelle Q. Zang (eds.), *The Legitimacy of International Trade Courts and Tribunals* (Cambridge: Cambridge University Press, 2018); Theresa Squatrito, Oran R. Young, Andreas Føllesdal, and Geir Ulfstein (eds.), *The Performance of International Courts and Tribunals* (Cambridge: Cambridge University Press, 2018).

The object of the book is how international adjudicators – including but extending beyond those formally termed 'international courts'[15] – can, and do, perform the role of interpreting the law and settling legal disputes in the decentralised international society. ICs hear claims against states, pronounce reasoned legal rulings, and issue judicial remedies. At the same time, they lack enforcement powers: they are not connected to anything akin to the modern state, in the sense of a centralised social apparatus tasked with mobilising, at the orders of the adjudicator, political and economic resources to apply coercion in order to secure the implementation of judicial rulings.[16] This means that translating judicial interpretations into what Michael Reisman has termed 'controlling reality'[17] depends on the mobilisation of forces other than those of a centralised social apparatus. What these forces are in the international society and how they can be mobilised by adjudicators who do not control any material resources are the central themes of this book.

This chapter outlines the core elements of the theory of international judicial authority, judicial remedies, and their compliance/enforcement challenges, which will animate the subsequent chapters. The central argument I introduce here, unpack in the rest of this chapter, and develop in the rest of the book involves three steps. First, since international adjudicators lack control over political and economic resources, they rely exclusively on authority: the ability to influence the perception and behaviour of other actors, in particular those who do have control over these resources. Second, ICs exercise their adjudicative authority entirely by issuing communications regarding the international normative framework and the characterisation of facts under this framework. Third, the instruments available to adjudicators

[15] Throughout the book, 'adjudicator' and 'international court/IC' are used interchangeably and in a broad sense, encompassing any actor performing adjudication on the so-called international plane, that is, detached from the legal hierarchy of any particular state. The actor may formally be termed 'court', 'tribunal', or have any other name. Although I am primarily concerned with ICs, insights in this book may apply to, and sometimes use as examples, actors in similar positions, such as human rights committees, compliance bodies within multilateral environmental agreements, or arbitrators in transnational legal disputes not involving states.

[16] In Max Weber's famous definition, the modern state is 'a human community that (successfully) claims the monopoly of the legitimate use of physical force within a given territory' (H.H. Gerth and C. Wright Mills (translated and edited), *From Max Weber: Essays in Sociology* (Oxford: Oxford University Press, 1946), 78.

[17] W. Michael Reisman, 'The Enforcement of International Judgments' (1969) 63 *AJIL* 1–27, at 6.

to influence party behaviour – which I will term 'judicial remedies' – are all different forms of the same two communications: those establishing the content of international rights and obligations within an applicable normative framework and those characterising conduct under this framework.[18]

As a corollary, effective judicial remedies are communications of an adjudicator regarding the international normative framework that are able to mobilise the forces that cause actors with control over economic and political resources – essentially, states and their agents – to adjust their perception and behaviour in function of this normative framework. This adjustment can happen for reasons internal to the actor, such as the recognition of the adjudicator's legitimacy and a desire or impulse to behave lawfully or appropriately. It can equally, or additionally, stem from an actor's awareness that the adjudicator's statements influence how other observers understand permissible and prohibited actions, prompting adjustments in the first actor's own behaviour. As discussed below, a crucial feature of authoritative pronouncements is their ability to reshape each actor's expectations about the likely beliefs and actions of others.[19] In this manner, the adjudicator's pronouncements can alter the strategic landscape in which even actors unwilling to follow the adjudicator's determinations make their decisions.

The remainder of this chapter is organised as follows. Section 1.2 examines the means and mechanisms by which the decentralised international normative framework influences state conduct and induces compliance, borrowing from Robert Ellickson's theory of 'order without law'. Section 1.3 introduces into the framework the problem of uncertainty in a decentralised normative system and explains how it is mitigated by the establishment of focal points for norm interpretation and legal characterisation. Section 1.4 considers the content of normative authority dissociated from control over coercive resources, laying down a fourfold typology of remedies that international adjudicators can employ to mobilise international law's compliance-inducing forces. Section 1.5 summarises the argument and outlines the structure of the book.

[18] Adjudicators may influence state conduct and the international normative framework beyond the confines of the dispute before them. But this is not what their judicial remedies are for.

[19] See on this Arash Abizadeh, 'The Grammar of Social Power: Power-To, Power-With, Power-Despite and Power-Over' (2023) 71 *Political Studies* 3.

1.2 Compliance, Persuasion, and Enforcement

1.2.1 Compliance as Politics and Enforcement: The Legal Scholarship

The question of why state agents change their behaviour in response to statements that international lawyers consider authoritative, final, or binding used to elide international legal scholars. Over much of the twentieth century, international lawyers concentrated their efforts on the expansion of judicial dispute settlement, without much heed to the question of compliance. One author has observed that major international law textbooks traditionally did not even include entries for 'compliance' or 'enforcement'.[20] A survey of the literature on the topic indicates that the most widely used definition for compliance – 'a state of conformity or identity between an actor's behavior and a specified rule'[21] – does not have its roots in international legal thinking but in the literature on international relations.[22]

[20] Jutta Brunée, 'Enforcement Mechanisms in International Law and International Environmental Law', in Ulrich Beyerlin, Peter-Tobias Stoll, and Rüdiger Wolfrum (eds.), *Ensuring Compliance with Multilateral Environmental Agreements* (Leiden: Martinus Nijhoff, 2006), 1–23, at 1.

[21] Kal Raustiala and Anne-Marie Slaughter, 'International Law, International Relations and Compliance', in Walter Carlsnaes, Thomas Risse, and Beth A. Simmons (eds.), *The Handbook of International Relations* (Thousand Oaks, CA: Sage Publications, 2002), 538–558, at 539.

[22] Comprehensive accounts of this scholarship are provided in Ingrid Wuerth, 'Compliance', in Jean d'Aspremont and Sahib Singh (eds.), *Concepts for International Law: Contributions to Disciplinary Though* (Cheltenham: Elgar, 2019), 117–126; Jana von Stein, 'The Engines of Compliance', in Jeffrey L. Dunoff and Mark A. Pollack (eds.), *Interdisciplinary Perspectives on International Law and International Relations: The State of the Art* (Cambridge: Cambridge University Press, 2013), 477–501; Anne-Marie Slaughter Burley, 'International Law and International Relations: A Dual Agenda' (1993) 87 *AJIL* 205–239; Markus Burgstaller, *Theories of Compliance with International Law* (Leiden: Brill, 1995); Harold Hongju Koh, 'Why Do Nations Obey International Law?' (1997) 106 *Yale Law Journal* 2599–2659; Beth A. Simmons, 'Compliance with International Agreements' (1998) 1 *Annual Review of Political Science* 75–93; Ronald B. Mitchell, 'Compliance Theory: An Overview', in James Cameron, Jacob Werksman, and Peter Roderick (eds.), *Improving Compliance with International Environmental Law* (London: Earthscan, 1996), 3–28; Raustiala and Slaughter, 'International Law, International Relations and Compliance'; Andrew Guzman, *How International Law Works: A Rational Choice Theory* (Oxford: Oxford University Press, 2008), 33; David Armstrong, Theo Farrell, and Hélène Lambert, *International Law and International Relations* (Cambridge: Cambridge University Press, 2012); Joel P. Trachtman, *The Economic Structure of International Law* (Cambridge: Harvard University Press, 2008). See also Robert Howse and Ruti G. Teitel, 'Beyond Compliance: Rethinking Why International Law Really Matters' (2010) 1 *Global Policy* 127–136, at 128.

As regards lawyers and legal scholars, they have traditionally set aside the question of compliance, usually taking one of three paths.[23] Many devoted their attention to the process leading to binding judgments, assuming for the purposes of their scholarship that compliance should follow essentially because the tenet *pacta sunt servanda* so requires. This approach can be associated with the idea that international law constitutes a form of 'compelling morality' for states[24] and, especially once clarified by an adjudicator, triggers a 'compliance pull',[25] or 'propensity to comply',[26] based on 'legal legitimacy'.[27] This view is largely echoed in a statement by the PCIJ in *Chorzów Factory*, repeated multiple times by the International Court of Justice (ICJ): the Court 'neither can nor should contemplate the contingency of the judgment not being complied with'.[28] Among those who sought to justify the assumption of states' inclination to comply with a rule once it is clarified, perhaps the most striking statement came from Hersch Lauterpacht: 'The moral and political effect of the judgment of a judicial tribunal is so tremendous that its legal finality has a tendency to approach actual finality'.[29]

Others have acknowledged that problems of non-compliance, including voluntary non-compliance with clear, adjudicated commitments, exist, while claiming that these problems are political rather than legal. The ICJ itself stated, in *Northern Cameroons*, that 'the use which the

[23] Significantly, much of this scholarship is principally concerned with the PCIJ and ICJ, which for long and until the 'proliferation' of ICs in the 1990s held a central place in international adjudication. See Cesare P.R. Romano, 'The Proliferation of International Judicial Bodies: The Pieces of the Puzzle' (1999) 31 *N.Y.U. Journal of International Law & Policy* 709.

[24] Elihu Root, 'The Sanction of International Law' (1908) 2 *ASIL Proceedings* 14, 16–17.

[25] Thomas M. Franck, *The Power of Legitimacy among Nations* (Oxford: OUP, 1990), 45–46.

[26] Abram Chayes and Antonia Handler Chayes, *The New Sovereignty: Compliance with International Regulatory Agreements* (Cambridge, MA: Harvard University Press, 1998), 3.

[27] Jutta Brunnée and Stephen J. Toope, *Legitimacy and Legality in International Law: An Interactional Account* (Cambridge: Cambridge University Press, 2010), 20.

[28] *Chorzów Factory (Merits)* (1928) PCIJ Ser. A No. 17, p. 63. See *Wimbledon* (1923) PCIJ Ser. A No. 1, p. 15, 32; *Nuclear Tests (New Zealand/France)*, [1974] ICJ Reports, p. 477; *Nuclear Tests (Australia/France)*, [1974] ICJ Reports, p. 272; *Military and Paramilitary Activities in and against Nicaragua (Nicaragua. United States)*, Jurisdiction, [1984] ICJ Reports, p. 392, 437; *Continental Shelf (Tunisia/Libya) (Revision and Interpretation)*, [1985] ICJ Reports, p. 192, 229.

[29] Hersch Lauterpacht, *The Function of Law in the International Community* (Oxford: OUP, 2011 [1933]), at 276. Or see James Brierly: 'Law is by its very nature imperative; there must exist an *obligation* to obey it' (James Brierly, *The Law of Nations* (Oxford: Clarendon Press, 1928), 37).

successful party makes of the judgment is a matter which lies on the political and not on the judicial plane'.[30] Shabtai Rosenne argued that 'both compliance with a decision and the enforcement of a decision is in each case a political operation'.[31] Laurence Boisson de Chazournes and Antonella Angelini asserted that 'the enforcement of judgments … acquires a political rather than a legal character'.[32] Constanze Schulte concurred that 'the efficacy of the post-adjudicative phase will not be determined by another judicial examination, but by immediate political action'.[33]

As regards the ICJ, this view aligns with the conclusion of the Committee of Jurists that drafted the Court's Statute. The 'execution of the decisions of the Court', the Committee reasoned, 'was not the business of the Court itself' but 'concern[ed] rather the Security Council' of the UN.[34] This view is reflected in subsequent ICJ statements regarding compliance. In *Haya de La Torre*, responding to a request for clarification regarding the implementation of a prior ruling, the Court stated that a judgment entails for the parties 'only the obligation of compliance therewith', and 'it is not part of the Court's judicial function to make … a choice' among the various paths available to the parties following its rulings. Such a choice 'could not be based on legal considerations, but only on considerations of practicability or of political expediency'.[35] This echoes the approach adopted by Edvard Hambro, perhaps the first among modern scholars concerned with implementation of

30 *Northern Cameroons*, [1963] ICJ Reports, p. 15, 37.

31 Shabtai Rosenne, *The Law and Practice of the International Court, 1920–2005* (Leiden: Martinus Nijhoff, 2006), 195.

32 Laurence Boisson de Chazournes and Antonella Angelini, 'After "The Court Rose": The Rise of Diplomatic Means to Implement the Pronouncements of the International Court of Justice' (2012) 11 *Law and Practice of International Courts and Tribunals* 1, fn. 5.

33 Constanze Schulte, *Compliance with Decisions of the International Court of Justice* (Oxford: OUP, 2004), 19. See also Mary Ellen O'Connell, *International Dispute Resolution: Cases and Materials* (Durham, NC: Carolina Academic, 2012), 374–383; Per Magid, 'The Post-Adjudicative Phase', in Connie Pack and Roy S. Lee (eds.), *Increasing the Effectiveness of the International Court of Justice – Proceedings of the ICJ/UNITAR Colloquium to Celebrate the 50th Anniversary of the Court* (Leiden: Martinus Nijhoff, 1997), 324–347, at 326 ('[t]he post-adjudicative phase is not – as the word itself reveals – a judicial phase').

34 Proceedings of the Committee of Jurists, 14 *United Nations Conference on International Organization* 853 (1945) (in response to a proposal to include in the statute 'means for assuring' the implementation of the Court's judgments).

35 *Haya de La Torre*, [1951] ICJ Reports, p. 71, 78–79.

adjudicators' rulings, whose conclusion was that states must 'execute judgments in good faith' but are otherwise 'free with regard to execution'.[36] Perhaps not coincidentally, Hambro was the Registrar of the Court during the *Haya de la Torre* case.

A third strand of scholars sought to follow the traditional domestic law approach to the issue of compliance: to examine, or develop, means to ensure 'implementation', 'enforcement', or 'execution' of judgments. Michael Reisman pointed out that the mere reference to 'enforcement' should not serve to shield questions of implementation from legal considerations. The distinction between adjudication and enforcement, he argued, 'has tended to put the latter into a nonlegal category . . . [and] to insulate the crucial problem of the realization of authority pronouncement from lawyers. By implication, courts and lawyers are not concerned with postadjudicative processes'.[37]

Discussion of such post-adjudicative processes, however, is usually limited by the notion that international adjudicators lack control over material resources.[38] Rather than seeking judicial responses at the international level, scholars have often looked to domestic courts and political bodies for means of enforcement. A 1960 article by Oscar Schachter provided the tone for much of the subsequent scholarship. Schachter divided the 'remedial measures' available to a successful party, in case of non-compliance with a judicial decision, into two branches. First were 'methods of enforcement by the successful party', including diplomatic and economic pressures, unilateral attachment of property belonging to the debtor state, enforcement through the debtor's municipal courts, and use of armed force. Second was 'enforcement through international organization'.[39] This collective enforcement involved essentially recourse to the UN Security Council, with a subsidiary role for other UN bodies and UN agencies. This enforcement, then, was essentially

[36] Edvard Hambro, *L'Exécution des Sentences Internationales* (Liège: Vaillant-Carmanne, 1936), 60.

[37] William Michael Reisman, *Nullity and Revision – The Review and Enforcement of International Judgments and Awards* (New Haven: Yale University Press, 1971), 645–657.

[38] Christine Gray, *Judicial Remedies in International Law* (Oxford: Clarendon, 1987), at 210 ('any proposal to extend the use of judicial settlement to new areas, and any discussion of its present role, must take account of the limitations of judicial remedies').

[39] Oscar Schachter, 'The Enforcement of International Judicial and Arbitral Decisions' (1960) 54 *AJIL* 1, 6, 17.

a matter for states and international organisations, not for international adjudicators.[40]

The idea that ICs should themselves be concerned with compliance, which would gain traction from the 1990s, was perhaps first expressed in 1981 by Roger Fisher. In *Improving Compliance with International Law*, Fisher proposed not recourse to sanctions ('the basic technique . . . of the criminal law') but 'legal machinery'.[41] First, international law needs 'ways of obtaining authoritative determinations with respect to alleged non-compliance'.[42] Second, there must be means of assessing 'compliance with an authoritative decision . . . where there has been a dispute'.[43]

Fisher divided compliance into 'first-order compliance', that is, states' overall compliance with international commitments, and 'second-order compliance', that is, compliance in situations where there is disagreement regarding what the law requires. As Section 2.2 will clarify, there is little dispute that overall state compliance with international law is high. But 'the weakness in the international legal system lies in its lack of an orderly and lawful way of coping with alleged departures from what the law provides'.[44] Thus, he concluded, the key objective of those seeking to improve compliance with international law should be to develop the set of responses to the eventuality of non-compliance.[45]

Assessing what legal responses to non-compliance are available and may improve compliance, however, requires understanding what motivates states to comply with their commitments in the first place. This question, often set aside by traditional international lawyers focusing on adjudication,[46] has been examined in depth by a literature adjacent to traditional legal scholarship – 'international law and international relations'. This literature examines the role and application of international law through an interdisciplinary lens, adopting concepts, methods, and

[40] See, for example, Reisman, *Nullity and Revision*, 674–844; E.K. Nantwi, *The Enforcement of International Judicial Decisions and Arbitral Awards in Public International Law* (Leiden: Sijthoff, 1966); Schulte, *Compliance with Decisions*, 19. See however Mutlaq Al-Qahtani, 'The Role of the International Court of Justice in the Enforcement of Its Judicial Decisions' (2002) 15 *Leiden Journal of International Law* 781, 804 (acknowledging the issue and proposing a new approach 'at least, in some derivative matters').

[41] Roger Fisher, *Improving Compliance with International Law* (Charlottesville, VA: University Press of Virginia, 1981), 30.

[42] Ibid., 29.

[43] Ibid., 25.

[44] Ibid., 29.

[45] Ibid., 8.

[46] But see the discussion regarding Georges Scelle and Hans Kelsen in Section 2.3.3.

language from economics, political science, psychology, or sociology, and applying these disciplines' insights to ascertain and explain the influence of norms on state behaviour.

1.2.2 *Compliance as Behaviour: The International Relations Scholarship(s)*

The study of the motives for state compliance with international law is often traced back to Louis Henkin's 1968 book, *How Nations Behave.*[47] Henkin's project was to bridge the gap between international lawyers' view of international law as something to be complied with at all costs and the perception of international law as largely irrelevant for state behaviour, popular in the 'realist' strand of international relations scholarship inaugurated by Hans Morgenthau. In his 1948 book *Politics among Nations*, Morgenthau had summarised the realist attitude to norms with a quote: 'You may cover whole skins of parchment with limitations, but power alone can limit power'.[48]

Henkin's central claim was condensed in what came to be known as the *Henkin formula*: '[i]t is probably the case that almost all nations observe almost all principles of international law and almost all of their obligations almost all of the time'.[49] In itself, this assessment was shared by Morgenthau, who acknowledged that 'the great majority of the rules of international law are generally observed by all nations without actual compulsion'.[50] However, Morgenthau and other political realists saw compliance with scepticism, arguing that it occurs essentially when it coincides with states' national interests.[51] Henkin, on the other hand,

[47] Louis Henkin, *How Nations Behave: Law and Foreign Policy*, 2nd edn (New York: Columbia University Press, 1979 [1968]). See Harold Hongju Koh, 'The Future of Lou Henkin's Human Rights Movement' (2007) 38 *Columbia Human Rights Law Review* 487.

[48] Hans J. Morgenthau, *Politics among Nations: The Struggle for Power and Peace*, 5th edn (New York: Alfred A. Knopf, 1978), 189 (quoting John Randolph of Roanoke, 19th Century Member of the US Congress).

[49] Henkin, *How Nations Behave*, at 47.

[50] Morgenthau, *Politics among Nations*, at 29.

[51] See Edward H. Carr, *Twenty Years' Crisis, 1919–1939: An Introduction to the Study of International Relations* (London: MacMillan, 1939/1946), 87 ('supposedly absolute and universal principles were not principles at all, but the unconscious reflections of national policy based on a particular interpretation of national interest at a particular time'); George W. Downs, David M. Rocke, and Peter N. Barsoom, 'Is the Good News about Compliance Good News about Cooperation?' (1996) 50 *International Organization* 379, 386, 399 ('the high level of compliance and the marginality of enforcement result from

affirmed the existence of a causal link between rule and conduct, of 'forces which induce nations to observe law'.[52] States would prefer compliance, first, for 'psychological' internal reasons[53] and, second, to avoid damaging their relations with other states. 'Internal impulsions and international inducements ... promote the observance of law and obligation'.[54]

The Henkin formula would later be referred to as 'the sentence that launched a thousand articles'.[55] Over the next decades, a sophisticated compliance scholarship developed around the questions of why, when, and how international legal rules may influence state conduct.[56] Contrasting with the somewhat sweeping statements sometimes made in previous contributions, the post-Henkin compliance scholarship provided nuance and considered with method the various elements that may affect a state's decision to comply.

Its sophistication notwithstanding, the key debate within the compliance scholarship concerns the principal motive for state compliance. Some, following Morgenthau, emphasise the coercive element and reject outright any claims that norms have an independent effect on behaviour.[57] Others seek to demonstrate how international norms are internalised by states, guiding their behaviour and delineating, or 'constructing', their identity and interests.[58] Yet others seek to establish that states, though remaining essentially self-interested actors – or focal points for

the fact that most treaties require states to make only modest departures from what they would have done in the absence of an agreement').

52 Henkin, *How Nations Behave*, at 49.

53 Ibid., at 60.

54 Ibid., at 315.

55 Koh, 'The Future of Lou Henkin's Human Rights Movement', 488.

56 See note 21.

57 See, for example, Jack L. Goldsmith and Eric A. Posner, *The Limits of International Law* (Oxford: Oxford University Press, 2005), at 13 ('international law does not pull states toward compliance contrary to their interests, and the possibilities for what international law can achieve are limited by the configuration of state interests and the distribution of state power'); George W. Downs, 'Enforcement and the Evolution of Cooperation' (1997) 19 *Michigan Journal of International Law* 319.

58 See, for example, Beth A. Simmons, *Mobilizing for Human Rights: International Law in Domestic Politics* (Cambridge: Cambridge University Press, 2009), 127; Oran R. Young, *International Governance: Protecting the Environment in a Stateless Society* (Ithaca, NY: Cornell University Press, 1994), 195 ('arrangements featuring enforcement as a means of eliciting compliance are not of much use in international society'); Brunnée and Toope, *Legitimacy and Legality*, 55 ('shared understandings and rules that adhere to the criteria of legality must be reinforced through a continuing practice of legality').

decision-making by domestic polities[59] – have a rational self-interest in complying with rules. Once they reach normative understandings, concerns with retaliation, reciprocal non-compliance and reputational costs could lead to rational compliance.[60]

For present purposes, there is no need to choose one strand of the scholarship over the others, nor to devise 'compliance metrics' as a benchmark for the significance of international law and its various subfields.[61] More relevant than the question of who is 'correct' is the articulation that each strand provides of the different factors contributing to compliance with international rules. Authors in the various strands at the end of the day recognise some merit in others' arguments. Thus, realist George Downs acknowledges that 'wrongheaded' realism sometimes prevents sophisticated analysis, noting that enforcement has strengths and limitations[62] and recognising a (limited) value in the concept of reputational costs.[63] On the other hand, legitimacy-focused Thomas Franck sees rational choice as useful, arguing, however, that long-term national interests include strengthening the rule of law.[64]

The divergences between the strands often boil down to emphasis. As Beth Simmons notes, 'the less one is willing to strawman the arguments of the major proponents, the clearer become the numerous points of overlap'.[65] As Daniel Drezner points out (regarding the debate about the relevance of non-state actors), in explaining why their theories work

[59] Andrew Guzman, 'A Compliance-Based Theory of International Law' (2002) 90 *California Law Review* 1823, at footnote 68 ('institutionalists recognize that state decisions are the product of a domestic political process in which different interests compete for influence ... institutionalists usually model the state as a single actor to simplify the analysis').

[60] See, for example, Guzman, *How International Law Works*, 33–36; Trachtman, *The Economic Structure*, 81–83. Rational choice assessments tend to rely on regime theory and game theory. For these, see Robert O. Keohane, *After Hegemony: Cooperation and Discord in the World Political Economy* (Princeton, NJ: Princeton University Press, 1984); Robert Axelrod, *The Evolution of Cooperation* (New York: Basic, 1984).

[61] See Monica Hakimi, 'The Work of International Law' (2017) 58 *Harvard International Law Journal* 1, at 46 ('conflict is part of what international law is for – and not just a perversion or problem for international law to overcome').

[62] Downs, 'Enforcement and the Evolution of Cooperation', at 344.

[63] George W. Downs and Michael A. Jones, 'Reputation, Compliance, and International Law' (2002) 31 *The Journal of Legal Studies* S95.

[64] Thomas M. Franck, 'The Power of Legitimacy and the Legitimacy of Power' (2006) 100 *AJIL* 88, at 98.

[65] Simmons, 'Compliance with International Agreements', 75, 76.

'[b]oth sides tend to generalize from their most favorable cases'.[66] Analysing the different strands of thought in this field, Benedict Kingsbury finds that they can be viewed as rationalisations of different conceptions of international law, with different scholarly theories relating closely to a scholar's views on the role international law *should* play in the domestic and international order.[67]

In short, their disagreements notwithstanding, the various authors in the compliance scholarship elaborate on elements that are complementary in explaining compliance with international legal rules, within an international system characterised by the absence of an authority superior to that of states and capable of ensuring that legal commands are 'armed with a sanction'.[68] The different elements emphasised by the different schools essentially match the two forces identified by Henkin as motivating compliance: internal impulsions within states and external inducements produced by the prospect of other actors' responses to their behaviour.

Importantly for present purposes, the compliance scholarship usually focuses on the internal perspective of states and their bilateral relations with other states. In so doing, it often collapses into the category of 'external' motives forces within the international society that are of very different characters, emanating from injured states, third states, and international organisations. For the purposes of understanding the instruments at the disposal of adjudicators to influence state conduct, it is helpful to consider in more detail the various types of external forces that promote norm-conforming and sanction non-conforming behaviour.

[66] Drezner, *All Politics is Global*, at 88.

[67] Benedict Kingsbury, 'The Concept of Compliance as a Function of Competing Conceptions of International Law' (1998) 19 *Michigan Journal of International Law* 345, at 346; Howse and Teitel, 'Beyond Compliance'. See also Hakimi, 'The Work of International Law'.

[68] See John Austin, *The Province of Jurisprudence Determined* (London: John Murray, 1832), 148–149, arguing that the lack of coercive sanctions makes international law 'law improperly so called'. Even in H.L.A. Hart's more communication-oriented theory, the lack of 'organised sanctions' is seen as problematic for international law and an obstacle to its operation, making it a 'legal system' only by analogy. See H.L.A. Hart, *The Concept of Law* (Oxford: Clarendon, 1961), 194.

1.2.3 Compliance as System: Five Layers of Social Control

Seeing compliance as a single phenomenon with a principal cause can obscure the variety of forces that impel states (or any actors) to adopt certain behaviour in function of norms. Rather than having a single motive, compliance usually relies on the application of, and interaction between, various levels of self-imposed and externally imposed constraints. This may be all the more so with regard to states, whose conduct is rarely determined by a single individual. Even where a single state agent appears to make a decision, her being in a position to make this decision is itself the product of a series of social processes. And the decision, besides reflecting the agent's own beliefs and preferences, is subject to various political and legal constraints at the domestic level; is influenced by the expectations of the decision-maker regarding the responses of other actors (domestic and foreign); and is subject to these actors' reactions once the decision is announced or the relevant conduct carried out.[69] An understanding of compliance and its relationship to judicial rulings demands an examination of the various layers of forces that may lead to what observers ultimately perceive as norm compliance and of the articulation between them.

An assessment of the articulation of these forces in an international setting can be developed on the basis of the typology outlined by Robert Ellickson in *Order without Law: How Neighbors Settle Disputes*, a study of a community of ranchers and farmers in the relatively isolated Shasta County, California.[70] Ellickson found that the community's members interacted primarily on the basis of informal social norms rather than state-enforced norms. Indeed, calling upon state agents to interfere with a dispute was considered a sanction under the ranchers' informal normative order.[71] To explain the operation of this order, Ellickson developed a typology of classes, or 'levels', of norms that constitute 'a comprehensive system of social control', going beyond 'law' (a term he reserves to state-enforced, government-created norms) and encompassing an array of other social processes, or 'sanctions', that are mobilised or available to promote norm-conforming behaviour.

[69] See Helen V. Milner, *Interests, Institutions, and Information: Domestic Politics and International Relations* (Princeton, NJ: Princeton University Press, 1997).

[70] Robert Ellickson, *Order without Law: How Neighbors Settle Disputes* (Cambridge: Harvard University Press, 1991).

[71] Ibid., at 57.

Table 1.1 *Elements of a Comprehensive System of Social Control*[72]

Controller	*Rules*	*Sanction*	*Combined System*
1. First-Party Control Actor	Personal ethics	Self-sanction	Self-control
2. Second-Party Control Person Acted Upon	Contracts	Personal self-help	Promise-enforced contracts
3. Third-Party Control Social Forces	Norms	Vicarious self-help	Informal control
Organisation	Organisation rules	Organisation enforcement	Organisation control
Government	Law	State enforcement	Legal system

These processes range from 'Level 1' control by self-sanction (with 'sanctions' such as shame or guilt) to 'Level 5' control by government authorities, under the threat of enforcement by the state apparatus. Besides these, Ellickson identifies three other processes. Level 2 or bilateral enforcement prevails in 'contractual' rules, in the sense of promises made bilaterally between actors, sanctioned by means of self-help through various forms of retaliation. Besides bilateral sanctioning, norms are also subject to diffuse 'Level 3' enforcement by actors in the community, with sanctions such as gossip, and consequential harm to the violator's reputation, or active third-party sanctions by other community members ('vicarious self-help'). Finally, operating at Level 4 are organisations with voluntary participation, which often set up their own norms, applicable to their participants and controlled by the organisations themselves. Table 1.1 presents Ellickson's typology.

Ellickson's account of a comprehensive normative order (or 'system of social control') provides a useful starting point for the analysis of international law compliance for three key reasons. First, by presenting four levels of social control alternative to the 'law' enforced by the state under Level 5, this account offers a meaningful disaggregation of the forces that motivate actors' compliance with norms besides, and regardless of, the intervention of a centralised coercive apparatus. Second, rather than seeking a main driving force behind compliance, it acknowledges that norm-oriented behaviour occurs for a multiplicity of reasons. For the purposes of understanding how adjudication can impact state

[72] Reproduced from Ellickson, *Order without Law*, 131.

compliance with international law, identifying the various layers of motives for compliance and having an account of the relevant compliance-inducing mechanisms is far more valuable than seeking ways to scientifically determine their relative importance. Third, it does away with the binary distinction between 'legal sanctions' applied by state agents and 'social sanctions' applied by other actors. Ellickson's reconstruction of a comprehensive normative order still identifies sanctions as the distinctive element characterising a normative order.[73] At the same time, it not only acknowledges that self-applied, interpersonal, and organisational sanctions can be more effective at shaping behaviour than state-administered sanctions[74] but also accords to this diverse array of sanctioning actors the character of norm enforcers.[75]

In short, the five levels provide an account of how a society without a centralised organisation of an authority structure and enforcement apparatus, and in this sense 'anarchical', may not be anarchical in the sense of being 'devoid of rules'.[76] Chapter 2 will develop a variation of the five-level system framework, applicable to the international society, using the term 'layers of compliance control'. There, Table 2.1 synthesises the five layers of compliance-inducing forces of international law, each corresponding to one type of controller or enforcer. Together, these layers form international law's compliance control system. The disaggregation of international law's compliance control system illuminates the diversity of forces that prevent this horizontal social order, without a hierarchically organised legal order enforced through coercion by state agents, from being lawless. In the international society as in other social orders without a centralised enforcer, norms remain pervasive. They observably frame and guide social relations and, in cases of violation, are regularly upheld through decentralised sanctions, imposed by the various actors both on themselves and on each other.

73 Ellickson, *Order without Law*, 128.

74 See, on interpersonal sanctions, Lisa Bernstein, 'Opting out of the Legal System: Extralegal Contractual Relations in the Diamond Industry' (1992) 21 *The Journal of Legal Studies* 115–157.

75 Ellickson still reserves the term 'law' for state-enforced norms. Without assuming a preeminence of Level 5 over the others, however, the distinction between broad and narrow understandings of 'legal system' becomes terminological rather than substantive. See Section 2.2.3.

76 Hedley Bull, *The Anarchical Society: A Study of Order in World Politics* (Houndmills: Palgrave Macmillan, 2002).

The resulting normative framework is no doubt distinct from one in which an organised state apparatus, whose authorities have overwhelming control over the community's material resources, is tasked with hierarchically interpreting and applying rules, as well as with enforcing them against vis-à-vis all actors. It is nonetheless characterised by sanctions, once the concept of 'sanctions' is extended beyond the sanctions applied centrally by such authorities. It then becomes clear that in horizontally organised societies a normative framework also exists, and that is constantly referred to, applied, and enforced through sanctions by its various participating actors.

1.3 The Problem of Interpretation and the Role of Authority

1.3.1 Normative Indeterminacy and Semantic Struggles

The existence of a variety of institutions claiming distinctive normative authority challenges the picture of international law as a wholly horizontal legal order. Indeed, as a matter of its normative make-up, international law has become highly and diversely institutionalised over the past century.[77] Through treaties and within international bodies, states have established and developed a number of fora where they can publicly exchange views and keep records of common understandings, establish procedures for collective decision-making, create agencies for independent scrutiny of conduct, and set up bodies with the ability to adjudicate disputes. As a matter of its means of social control, however, international law remains heavily reliant on decentralised sanctions by its component states. Though international institutions and bodies may provide interpretative guidance and occasionally condemn unlawful or undesirable conduct, states retain quasi- if not fully monopolistic control over the political and economic resources that can be mobilised to meaningfully affect other states' interests.

As Ellickson's framework clarifies, even complete decentralisation does not prevent a normative order from operating, guiding behaviour, or structuring interactions. A horizontal normative order operating in a wholly decentralised manner functions largely through self-regulation

[77] For an early assessment, see R.R. Baxter, 'International Law in "Her Infinite Variety"' (1980) 23 *International and Comparative Law Quarterly* 549. See, more recently, Danae Azaria, 'The Legal Significance of Expert Treaty Bodies Pronouncements for the Purpose of the Interpretation of Treaties' (2020) 22 *International Community Law Review* 33.

and self-enforcement.[78] Indeed, in the international order, there is little doubt that states are overwhelmingly able to agree on the applicable rights and obligations and behave accordingly, settling most emerging disagreements through consultations and negotiation. Thus, international aviation depends on concordant interpretation of complex legal provisions and agreement by a multitude of actors regarding the permissible trajectories of thousands of aircraft; yet, tens of thousands of flights cross the Earth without incident every day. International trade depends on port workers applying rules and procedures agreed to in a dozen different international fora, which are consulted, argued about at the domestic level, and complied with (in the sense of not leading to interstate disputes regarding compliance) in the overwhelming majority of cases. Even state borders enjoy the respect of virtually all states at virtually all times. A state that avowedly breaches another's widely recognised borders (usually, by asserting a diverging interpretation of the applicable normative framework) will likely, at this very point, be respecting 'almost all' of its internationally recognised borders rather than rejecting the overall territoriality principle and the duty of states to respect borders.

As a result, if compliance is defined as state conduct being unopposed by other actors, international law is observed by 'almost all nations . . . almost all the time'.[79] However, by the same token, it is probably the case that almost all states are, almost all of the time, engaged in at least one interpretative struggle with at least one other state regarding their borders, their mutual trade obligations, or their duties with respect to one another's citizens – or their own citizens.

This is to be expected. In any normative order, due to either genuine belief or self-interest (often, a mixture of both), different actors hold different interpretations of what norms require, permit, or prohibit. And, in the horizontal international legal order, a state's 'norm entrepreneurship'[80] is kept in check solely by the ability of others – in particular, other states – to respond with claims of violation, demands for redress, and,

[78] For an account of this system grounded on 'practices of legality' rather than sanctions, see Brunnée and Toope, *Legitimacy and Legality*.

[79] Henkin, *How Nations Behave*, 47.

[80] Scholars have used the concept of 'norm entrepreneurs' to describe 'people interested in changing social norms' (Cass R. Sunstein, 'Social Norms and Social Roles' (1996) 96 *Columbia Law Review* 903–968, at 909). In international law and international relations scholarship, these are those who 'attempt to convince a critical mass of states (norm leaders) to embrace new [social] norms' (Martha Finnemore and Kathryn Sikkink,

ultimately, measures capable of compelling a change of heart in those determining the conduct of the norm entrepreneur state. Each state is able not only to state its own interpretations of international commitments and assessments of how facts fit under these commitments but also to act upon these self-interpretations. As Carmen Wunderlich notes, even a state disputing an overwhelming normative consensus (a 'rogue state') can be thought of, in a horizontal order with no commonly recognised norm interpreter, as a particularly strident norm entrepreneur, acting on its own understanding of the desirable normative framework, against other states', equally valid, understandings.[81]

This is not a mere academic construction. The Arbitral Tribunal in *Air Service Agreement* noted:

> Under the rules of present-day international law . . . each State establishes for itself its legal situation vis-à-vis other States. If a situation arises which, in one State's view, results in the violation of an international obligation by another State, the first State is entitled, within the limits set by the general rules of international law pertaining to the use of armed force, to affirm its rights through 'counter-measures'.[82]

It is on these occasions, in which states with conflicting interpretations are under no special obligations to follow an institution's pronouncements, that the international legal order faces some of its greatest difficulties. Whenever a dispute emerges between states regarding the lawfulness of a specific conduct, the horizontality of international law becomes patently clear. All states being equally sovereign, none has the authority to impose their interpretation of the applicable legal framework on another. Contrary to hierarchical legal systems, in which a distinction between 'authorities' and 'subjects' can be drawn so that the former's interpretation prevails (in principle and until a contradictory interpretation is pronounced by a hierarchically higher authority), in international law there is (in principle) no criterion for determining whose interpretation, among those voiced by the different sovereign participants in an

'International Norm Dynamics and Political Change' (1998) 52 *International Organization* 887–917, at 895).

81 Carmen Wunderlich, *Rogue States as Norm Entrepreneurs: Black Sheep or Sheep in Wolves' Clothing?* (Cham: Springer, 2020), 4 (they 'attempt to establish (alternative) norms or to promote normative meanings that fundamentally deviate from the prevailing liberal perspective').

82 *Air Service Agreement Arbitration (France* v. *United States)*, 18 RIAA (1978) 417, at 443 (The Tribunal caveats that this is true 'unless the contrary results from special obligations arising under particular treaties').

interaction, should prevail. When faced with horizontal interpretative disputes, states are locked in what Ingo Venzke termed 'semantic struggles in which actors craft legal interpretations in an attempt to implement meanings of legal expressions that are aligned with their convictions or interests'.[83]

It is of course possible to seek to increase the clarity or specificity of legal rules and 'narrow[] the scope for reasonable interpretation'.[84] However, the authors of the leading article conceptualising legalisation in international relations go too far when they state that '[a] precise rule specifies clearly and unambiguously what is expected of a state or other actor . . . in a particular set of circumstances'.[85] Semantic struggles are an inevitable consequence of the indeterminacy of normative text, in the sense that, while text can be informative, it is never exhaustive. It is impossible to establish that a certain conduct is a violation of legal commitments merely by considering the text of a treaty provision (or a pattern of conduct allegedly generating norms). Sentences (or patterns of conduct) may be vague or ambiguous, sometimes in ways that only become clear once an event occurs whose characterisation is disputed. There are no complete contracts.

The impossibility of full contractual precision arises, first, because a term's meaning is inextricable from its context and from the purpose of the communication. This embeddedness of terms in their linguistic ecosystem is reflected in Article 31.1 of the Vienna Convention on the Law of Treaties (VCLT): 'A treaty shall be interpreted in good faith in accordance with the ordinary meaning to be given to the terms of the treaty in their context and in the light of its object and purpose'.[86] Similarly, with regard to customary law, the objective of 'ascertain[ing] whether there is a general practice that is accepted as law'[87] raises all

83 Ingo Venzke, *How Interpretation Makes International Law: On Semantic Change and Normative Twists* (Oxford: Oxford University Press, 2012), 58.

84 Kenneth W. Abbott, Robert O. Keohane, Andrew Moravcsik, Anne-Marie Slaughter, and Duncan Snidal, 'The Concept of Legalization' (2000) 54 *International Organization* 401, 412.

85 Ibid.

86 VCLT, Article 31(1). The indeterminacy is all but confirmed by the ILC. See ILC, 'Report of the International Law Commission on the Work of its 18th Session', ILC *Ybk* 1966/II, 172, 219–220. See also Alexander Orakhelashvili, 'Political Life of Treaties: Indeterminacy, Interpretation and Political Consequences' (2021) 20(3) *Chinese Journal of International Law* 545–560.

87 ILC, 'Draft Conclusions on Identification of Customary International Law', ILC Ybk 2018/II.2, 124.

forms of questions, which the literature has explored in depth.[88] Even seemingly clearly worded rules invariably contain exceptions, sometimes provided for in other provisions of a treaty or in special practice, often inferred from a preamble, document or practice that exists in connection with the rule.

Additionally, even if a treaty provision – usually, the most easily identifiable source of a 'rule' – appears to establish an obligation unambiguously when read in isolation, a variety of treaty and extra-treaty instruments and legal mechanisms may render this obligation inapplicable, in general or to a particular situation. The provision may be subject to an exception under the treaty or a related instrument. Interpretation of the treaty or broader normative framework may need adjustments to reflect subsequent practice, subsequent agreement, systemic integration, and normative evolution.[89] An obligation may have ceased to exist or be inapplicable to a situation due to *lex posterior* (desuetude or subsequent treaty), *lex specialis* (a more specific treaty rule), or *lex superior* (*jus cogens* or a norm deriving from the UN Charter).[90] Finally, even an ostensibly clear violation may be justified if a circumstance precluding wrongfulness applies. The International Law Commission's (ILC) Articles on State Responsibility[91] feature six of them: consent,

[88] See, for example, Jörg Kammerhofer, 'Uncertainty in the Formal Sources of International Law: Customary International Law and Some of Its Problems' (2004) 15 *European Journal of International Law* 523–553.

[89] Julian Arato, 'Subsequent Practice and Evolutive Interpretation: Techniques of Treaty Interpretation Over Time and Their Diverse Consequences' (2010) 9 *The Law & Practice of International Courts and Tribunals* 443–494; Campbell McLachlan, 'The Principle of Systemic Integration and Article 31(3)(C) of the Vienna Convention' (2005) 54 *International & Comparative Law Quarterly* 279–319.

[90] Joost Pauwelyn, *Conflict of Norms in Public International Law: How WTO Law Relates to Other Rules of International Law* (Cambridge: Cambridge University Press, 2003); Ralf Michaels and Joost Pauwelyn, 'Conflict of Norms or Conflict of Laws: Different Techniques in the Fragmentation of Public International Law' (2012) 22 *Duke Journal of Comparative & International Law* 349; Thomas Weatherall, *Jus Cogens: International Law and Social Contract* (Cambridge: Cambridge University Press, 2015); Jose E. Alvarez, *International Organizations as Law-Makers* (Oxford: Oxford University Press, 2006), especially 184–198.

[91] ILC, 'Articles on the Responsibility of States for Internationally Wrongful Acts', ILC Ybk 2001, II.2, 1. The Articles, approved on second reading by the International Law Commission (ILC) in 2001, were noted by the UN General Assembly and annexed to GA Resolution 56/83 (12 December 2001).

self-defence, countermeasures, force majeure, distress, necessity, and compliance with peremptory norms.[92]

In short, each of the key stages of the legal assessment of a situation – the interpretation of a provision, the consideration of its surrounding normative context, the assessment of justifications and circumstances precluding wrongfulness, and the application of the interpretative outcome to the facts of a case – involves interpretation. Together, they provide plenty of room for the emergence of multiple, sometimes equally defensible, assertions regarding the content of obligations and the characterisation of conducts. And, even if states can agree on the applicable legal interpretation and on the characterisation of conduct, they may still disagree on a violation's legal consequences for the affected parties.

International law thus operates under a fundamental difficulty: the lack of legal certainty in the application of its layers of social control. As Leslie Johns put it, '[f]or states to cooperate, they must first have common expectations about appropriate behavior and the consequences for inappropriate behavior'.[93] This is not to say that decentralised interpretation impedes the operation of a normative system. In Ellickson's community of cattle ranchers, sanctioning seemed to be applied by the various actors on the basis of their self-interpretation of the rules. However, while Ellickson downplays the relevance of uncertainty for the operation of an informal normative framework,[94] a core difficulty for international law is the uncertainty inherent to the application of norms in the many complex and overlapping areas in which this horizontal normative order applies. It is on this point that the intervention of adjudicators qualitatively changes the operation of international law.

1.3.2 Settling Interpretative Disputes: The Role of Adjudication

The function of international adjudication is often described as that of settling interpretative disputes.[95] It is true that, as a matter of their current set of functions in the international society, ICs have come to

[92] Ibid., Articles 20–26. See Federica Paddeu, *Justification and Excuse in International Law: Concept and Theory of General Defences* (Cambridge: Cambridge University Press, 2018).

[93] See Johns, *Strengthening International Courts*, 13.

[94] Ellickson, *Order without Law*, at 253.

[95] John G. Collier and Vaughan Lowe, *The Settlement of Disputes in International Law: Institutions and Procedures* (Oxford: Oxford University Press, 2000); Natalie Klein, *Dispute Settlement in the UN Convention on the Law of the Sea* (Cambridge:

do far more than that. Armin von Bogdandy and Ingo Venzke noted that 'dispute settlement' suggests a state-oriented, bilateralist framing of the role of ICs. This framing leaves aside key functions performed by contemporary international adjudicators, including acting as organs of the international community and developing and shaping international legal regimes.[96] Their broader formulation of the role of adjudication is that ICs 'generate and stabilize normative expectations and control and legitimize other institutions'.[97] At the same time, international adjudication continues to operate essentially according to the model of third-party dispute settlement. Even international criminal courts seek to organise their procedure as a series of 'disputes' between the prosecution and the accused, to be adjudicated impartially by the IC.[98] The broader norm-setting authority of ICs depends, as a matter of procedural rules governing the exercise of jurisdiction, on their ability to hear and adjudicate upon an underlying, fact-laden, and usually bilateral, dispute.[99]

A dispute was famously defined by the PCIJ as 'a disagreement on a point of law or fact, a conflict of legal views or of interests between two persons'.[100] The settlement of the dispute by an adjudicator implies the end of valid disagreement for the purposes of the relevant legal order. It is, as a number of constitutive instruments of international

Cambridge University Press, 2004); Jonathan Charney, 'Third Party Dispute Settlement and International Law' (1998) 36 *Columbia Journal of Transnational Law* 65.

96 Armin von Bogdandy and Ingo Venzke, *In Whose Name? A Public Law Theory of International Adjudication* (Oxford: Oxford University Press, 2012), 28–94. See also David D. Caron, 'Towards a Political Theory of International Courts and Tribunals' (2006) 24 *Berkeley Journal of International Law* 401; Karen J. Alter, 'Agents or Trustees? International Courts in Their Political Context' (2008) 14 *European Journal of International Relations* 33.

97 von Bogdandy and Venzke, *In Whose Name?*, 101. For assessments of various functions of adjudication, see Joshua Paine, *The Functions of International Adjudication and International Environmental Litigation* (Cambridge: Cambridge University Press, 2024); Rosa Möhrlein, *The Multiplicity of Judicial Functions of International Courts and Tribunals. An Inquiry with a Focus on the International Court of Justice* (Groningen: Chimaira, 2024).

98 For a deeper treatment, see Kai Ambos, 'International Criminal Procedure: "Adversarial", "Inquisitorial" or Mixed?' (2003) 3 *International Criminal Law Review* 1, 3. Judicial (Advisory) Opinions are more clearly an exception in this regard.

99 Admittedly, this leaves out the significant, and perhaps increasing, role of advisory opinions, in which ICs can and do lay down rules and interpretations in the abstract.

100 *Mavrommatis Palestine Concessions (Greece* v. *United Kingdom),* Objection to the Jurisdiction of the Court, Judgment (1924) PCIJ Ser. A No. 2, p. 7, 11.

adjudicators state, 'final',[101] 'binding on the parties',[102] and 'without appeal'.[103] As explained by the ICJ, 'a judicial decision . . . has the force of *res judicata* and clarifies the rights and obligations of the parties'.[104]

From a legal standpoint, ICs are thus in a position to eliminate lawful disagreement. In a wholly horizontal order, sovereign equals' claims regarding the applicable norms and the characterisation of facts are of equal value. This absolute horizontality disappears once an adjudicator validly exercises jurisdiction. As a matter of law, binding adjudicatory pronouncements perform what Robert Cover called a 'jurispathic' or 'law-killing' function.[105] The adjudicator's pronouncements set aside, for the purposes of the legal system, all but one of the competing claims regarding the normative framework, and its application to acts and events, put forward by the various actors in their interpretative struggles. Rosalyn Higgins described the judicial function as 'to subject such disputes as the parties request to an authoritative legal process' and 'not finding "the correct rule" but rather making a choice between alternatives – and alternatives which . . . are often each meritorious'.[106]

At the same time, the decentralisation of the international order means that ICs lack a key element usually presumed in conceptualisations of adjudication developed having in mind domestic legal orders: the connection between adjudication and coercion. Shapiro considers this the distinctive feature of judges when compared to arbitrators: 'having means to tap the organized forces of coercion in the society to enforce their

[101] Statute of the International Court of Justice (ICJ Statute), San Francisco, 26 June 1945, in force 24 October 1945, Article 60; United Nations Convention on the Law of the Sea (UNCLOS), Montego Bay, 10 November 1986, in force 16 November 1994, 1833 UNTS 397, Article 296; European Convention on Human Rights (ECHR), 4 November 1950, in force 3 September 1953, Article 44; Protocol to the Association of Southeast Asian Nations (ASEAN) Charter on Dispute Settlement Mechanisms, 8 April 2010, in force 28 July 2017, Article 15(1).

[102] Convention on the Settlement of Investment Disputes between States and Nationals of Other States (ICSID Convention), Washington, in force 14 October 1966, 575 UNTS 159, Article 53; Revised Treaty of the Economic Community of West African States (ECOWAS), 24 July 1993, in force 28 August 1994, Article 15(4).

[103] ICJ Statute, Article 60; UNCLOS, Annex VII, Article 11; American Convention on Human Rights (ACHR), 22 November 1969, in force 18 July 1978, Article 67.

[104] *Arbitral Award of 3 October 1899 (Guyana* v. *Venezuela)*, Jurisdiction of the Court, Judgment, [2020] ICJ Reports, p. 455, 479.

[105] Robert M. Cover, 'The Supreme Court, 1982 Term-Foreword: Nomos and Narrative' (1983) 97 *Harvard Law Review* 1–306, at 28.

[106] Rosalyn Higgins, 'Policy Considerations and the International Judicial Process' (1968) 17 *International and Comparative Law Quarterly* 58, 61.

solution'.[107] In domestic legal orders, as Cover noted, '"interpretation" suggests a social construction of an interpersonal reality',[108] but *judicial* interpretation is marked by the shadow of violence: 'as the judge interprets . . . she also acts – through others – to restrain, hurt, render helpless, even kill'.[109]

Assessments of the role and effects of adjudication usually connect judicial interpretation to the use, or at least threat or 'shadow', of coercion by the state apparatus to enforce judicial decisions.[110] The characterisation of courts as 'jurispathic' thus extends beyond the symbolic plane in which claims to normativity are made and proposed interpretations are offered. As Franklin Snyder explained, it means that 'the judge will select one of the squalling brood of conflicting legal meanings to elevate and to enforce with the violence of the state – and will slay the rest'.[111] Cover observes: 'Legal interpretive acts signal and occasion the imposition of violence upon others'.[112]

International adjudicators cannot rely on such a connection. Their rulings bind states as collective entities and establish their rights and obligations under international law. For the purposes of each state's internal legal hierarchy, however, the determinative views will emerge not from adjudicators but from domestically authoritative persons and bodies – in particular, those within that polity who control the deployment of coercion by the state apparatus. Of course, states may choose to accord value in thei domestic legal hierarchy to international judicial rulings. As the Caribbean Court of Justice (CCJ) put it in *TCL* v. *Guyana*, '[i]ncorporation into domestic law may make it possible to invoke the coercive powers of the State in support of orders made by the Court and give efficacy to its orders'. By the same token, however, this incorporation

107 Shapiro, *Courts: A Comparative and Political Analysis*, 7.

108 Robert M. Cover, 'Violence and the Word' (1986) 95(8) *Yale Law Journal* 1601–1629, at 1602.

109 Ibid., 1609.

110 Robert M. Cover, 'The Bonds of Constitutional Interpretation: Of the Word, the Deed, and the Role' (1986) 20 *Georgia Law Review* 815, 833 ('Interpretation always takes place in the shadow of coercion'.)

111 Franklin G. Snyder, 'Nomos, Narrative, and Adjudication: Toward a Jurisgenetic Theory of Law' (1999) 40(5) *William and Mary Law Review* 1623, at 1624.

112 Cover, 'Violence and the Word', 1601. Although one can connect any form of interpretative overruling with violence, Cover notes that what he considers 'the violence of judges' is not the same as 'the violence that exists in literature or in the metaphoric characterization of literary critics and philosophers' (Cover, 'Violence and the Word', 1610).

determines the extent of the recognition of the IC's authority domestically. If a dispute arises, 'a court (presumably a local court) may be called upon to decide'.[113]

Ultimately, the impact of ICs' rulings depends on their influence on states' domestic legal-political orders. It is the assessment of the situation by those within the domestic hierarchical structure, interacting under domestic political and legal processes, that will lead the various individuals acting on behalf of the polity to adopt the measures that international lawyers interpret as 'state conduct', and international relations scholars as 'state behaviour'. The ability to influence these assessments, without being able to rely on a coercive apparatus, can be characterised as an IC's authority.

1.4 Judicial Authority and Judicial Remedies in Horizontality

1.4.1 Authority in Horizontality: Auctoritas Without Potestas

Authority is an essentially contested concept, 'an object of dispute and political contestation'[114] wherever it has emerged. Its very existence as a separate element from power is sometimes challenged.[115] The contemporary term, as used in Latin-influenced languages with various shades of meaning, descends from the Roman *auctoritas*. *Auctoritas* is usually associated with an ineffable notion of moral authority, the 'possession of something more than power',[116] and stands in contrast with *potestas*, the more determinable legal authority within an organised legal/societal hierarchy. *Potestas* in Roman society has been described as 'a legal power or authority to which a person was entitled'.[117] *Auctoritas*, by contrast, eludes a unified definition, and has been employed in a variety of

[113] CCJ, *Trinidad Cement Limited and TCL Guyana Incorporated* v. *Guyana (Non-compliance/Contempt)*, CCJ App No 2 of 2009 (Original Jurisdiction), Judgment, 29 March 2010, para. 49. This statement applies even in contexts of high institutionalisation, such as the law and institutions of the European Union. See Section 2.2.1.

[114] Frank Furedi, *Authority: A Sociological History* (Cambridge: Cambridge University Press, 2013), 3. See W.B. Gallie, 'Essentially Contested Concepts' (1956) 56 *Proceedings of the Aristotelian Society* 167.

[115] Gregory Rowe, 'Reconsidering the *Auctoritas* of Augustus' (2013) 103 *Journal of Roman Studies* 115; Rafael Domingo, 'Das Binom auctoritas-potestas im römischen und modernen Recht' (1998) 4 *Orbis Iuris Romani* 7.

[116] Rowe, 'Reconsidering the *Auctoritas* of Augustus', 1.

[117] William Smith (ed.), *Dictionary of Greek and Roman Antiquities* (Boston: Little Brown, 1870), 351.

expressions and occasions, conveying the notion that something 'enlarges, confirms, or gives to a thing its completeness and efficient form'.[118]

When referring to international judicial authority, I will use the term *auctoritas* where useful to avoid the association between authority and hierarchy, domination, subordination, and reflexive obedience. This association is pervasive in modern investigations of the concept. Max Weber stated, with regard to the state as a hierarchical order, that '[i]f the state is to exist, the dominated must obey the authority claimed by the powers that be'.[119] Hannah Arendt saw in the concept of authority two elements: an individual's freedom to decide, on the one hand, and this individual's voluntary surrendering of this freedom to another, on the other hand. She noted that authority exists 'in contradistinction to both coercion by force and persuasion through arguments'.[120] The authoritative relationship (she uses 'authoritarian relation') is therefore one characterised by obedience that 'rests neither on common reason nor on the power of the one who commands' but on 'the hierarchy itself, whose rightness and legitimacy both recognize and where both have their predetermined stable place'.[121]

Herbert Marcuse's outline of the concept goes in a similar direction: authority is 'the tying of will (indeed of thought and reason) to the authoritative will of an Other', in a manner 'which is not based purely on coercion' but involves a degree of 'voluntariness', so that the authority relationship involves both 'a certain measure of freedom' and 'the surrender of autonomy' by the subordinate, a 'tying of the subject's reason and will to pre-establish[ed] contents . . . as the obligatory norms for his (sic) reason and will'.[122] Joseph Raz's conception draws from the same dissociation between coercion and authority: 'the justified use of coercive power is one thing and authority is another'.[123] Authority exists, as Ingo Venzke put it, 'between power and persuasion'.[124] An authoritative pronouncement is

118 Ibid., 246.

119 Gerth and Mills, *From Max Weber*.

120 Hannah Arendt, 'What Is Authority?', in Hannah Arendt (ed.), *Between Past and Future* (New York: Penguin,1968), 91–141, at 93.

121 Ibid.

122 Herbert Marcuse, *A Study on Authority*, translated by Joris de Bres (London: Verso, 2008), 7.

123 Joseph Raz, 'Authority and Justification' (1985) 14 *Philosophy & Public Affairs* 3–29, at 5.

124 Ingo Venzke, 'Between Power and Persuasion: On International Institutions' Authority in Making Law' (2013) 4(3) *Transnational Legal Theory* 354–373.

one to which the addressee feels bound without needing to be rationally persuaded but also without the need for externally inflicted coercion (or, in some accounts, even the prospect of coercion).

These reflections on authority integrate, and in a sense assume, an underlying hierarchy recognised by both parties. This is not only the particular and circumstantial hierarchy between the two parties to the authoritative relationship. It is also a broader hierarchy, on which the particular hierarchy stands: a hierarchical ordering of society, where the authoritative actor's instructions cause the addressees of its pronouncements to reflexively surrender their decision-making autonomy and comply with determinations made by the authoritative actor.[125] As Kostiantyn Gorobets notes, the 'standard view of authority . . . assumes that authority is necessarily *somebody*'.[126]

Raz's notion of 'practical authority' aims to avoid assuming this underlying hierarchical structure, drawing a distinction between voluntary 'surrender of judgment' and 'blind obedience'. Raz describes the role of practical authority as to 'mediate between ultimate reasons and the people to whom they apply'.[127] An authority examines an actor's already-applicable reasons to act one way or the other and determines how these reasons will apply in a specific context. An authority can thus direct another person's actions not due to the latter's 'blind obedience' but because, and when, 'it is better to conform . . . than to decide for oneself, unaided by authority'.[128] As Raz explains, 'all authoritative directives should be based, in the main, on reasons which already independently apply to the subjects of the directives and are relevant to their action in the circumstances covered by the directive'.[129] The 'point and purpose of authorities . . . is to preempt individual judgment on the merits'.[130]

Raz's conception elides the question of how precisely the authoritative person or body elicits compliance with its determinations, reasoning

125 Arendt, 'What Is Authority?', 93 ('Against the egalitarian order of persuasion stands the authoritarian order, which is always hierarchical').

126 Kostiantyn Gorobets, 'Peaks and Valleys: Contemplating Authority of International Law', in Kostiantyn Gorobets, Andreas Hadjigeorgiou, and Pauline Westerman (eds.), *Conceptual (Re)Constructions of International Law* (Cheltenham: Edward Elgar, 2022), 171–87, 175.

127 Joseph Raz, 'Authority, Morality and Law' (1985) 68(3) *Monist* 195–324, at 299–300.

128 Joseph Raz, 'The Problem of Authority: Revisiting the Service Conception' (2006) 90(4) *Minnesota Law Review* 1003–1044, at 1014.

129 Raz, 'Authority and Justification', 15.

130 Ibid.

solely that '[a] person can have authority over another only if there are sufficient reasons for the latter to be subject to duties at the say-so of the former'.[131] Explanations for what these sufficient reasons are tend to fall into either coercion or accepted legitimacy. Thus, an entity with authority is one that 'is effective in imposing its will on many over whom it claims authority, perhaps because its claim to legitimacy is recognized by many of its subjects'.[132] Raz does consider the potential non-compliance with an authoritative ruling – in this case, an arbitral award – by a recalcitrant actor. However, he contends solely that compliance should be expected, since the very point of an arbitration is to require the renunciation by each party of the reasons they previously advanced for their actions, once these reasons are rejected by an arbitrator: '[i]f the disputants do not then reject these reasons as possible bases for their own action, they defeat the very point and purpose of the arbitration'.[133]

The example inevitably prompts the question: why would a dissatisfied litigant not seek to defeat the very point and purpose of an arbitration she has lost? Raz's findings stop short of examining the social mechanisms through which an authoritative entity's authority can be effective, even when (or rather, especially when) a party would prefer not to comply with the authority's determinations and instead insists on the already-rejected reasons for action. In other words, Raz, whose central concern is with the legitimacy of authority, assumes authority itself, in the sense of the voluntary subordination of the will: 'Raz's conception of authority depends for its cogency on the thought that as long as the subject does better by reason overall by obeying certain classes of commands, the subject has a duty to obey every one of the commands: the correct as well as the incorrect'.[134]

The concept of authority relevant for present purposes – the authority of ICs – does not necessarily involve a subordination of the will in the sense that an international judicial authority's pronouncements will be

[131] Raz, 'The Problem of Authority', 1013.

[132] Raz, 'Authority, Morality and Law', 296 (emphasis added).

[133] Raz, 'Authority and Justification', 10. For a deeper treatment of Raz's conception and the relationship between 'authority' and 'authorities', see Gorobets, 'Peaks and Valleys', 173–175.

[134] Tom Christiano, 'Authority', in Edward N. Zalta (ed.), *The Stanford Encyclopedia of Philosophy* (Palo Alto, Cal.: Stanford University, 2020). There is of course abundant scholarship seeking to challenge, affirm, or re-interpret Raz's conception of authority. See, for example, Evan Fox-Decent, 'Fiduciary Authority and the Service Conception', in Andrew S. Gold and Paul B. Miller (eds.), *Philosophical Foundations of Fiduciary Law* (Oxford: Oxford University Press, 2014).

obeyed by others. After all, a key feature of the 'sovereign equality'[135] of states is the preservation of each state's ability to remain the key focal point for decision-making even after expressing a commitment to one among the various available courses of action. States are not subject to each other's authority or compelled to submit to a hierarchically superior authority, retaining the ultimate ability not to follow through on international commitments. Nor does international judicial authority match Raz's alternative concept of 'theoretical authority', which is focused on the heightened persuasive value, a 'reason for belief', that authority grants to a person's or an entity's advice.[136] A more illuminating parallel is the remark by Theodor Mommsen regarding the *auctoritas* of the Roman Senate, whose pronouncements he deemed 'more than advice and less than a command, an advice which one may not safely ignore'.[137] Similarly, international adjudicators hold authority in that their pronouncements may be *disobeyed* by their addresses but not *disregarded* without consequences.

This formulation, however, appears to equally beg the question. Why may states 'not safely ignore' an IC's pronouncements? A claim to adjudicative authority is a claim to be able to influence perceptions regarding the content of its normative framework merely by issuing communications regarding norms and facts, without a connection to the coercive apparatus of the state.[138] To affirm the possibility of ICs' authority is to assert that their mere pronouncements, unaccompanied by the threat of coercion, can produce such a meaningful effect on sovereign states that they cannot be disregarded by their addressees.

Chapter 3 investigates this question, arguing that IC *auctoritas* derives from two related but distinguishable processes. One involves the adjudicator's legitimacy or authority as traditionally considered, in the sense that an actor may have a propensity to comply with, or at least believe that she has a 'rebuttable duty' to implement, a ruling.[139] This requires, as Laurence Helfer and Anne-Marie Slaughter put it, 'convincing domestic

135 UN Charter, Article 2(1).

136 Raz, 'Authority, Morality and Law', 296 ('the advice of a theoretical authority is a reason for belief for those regarding whom that person or institution has authority').

137 In Arendt, 'What Is Authority?', 123 (citing Theodor Mommsen's, *Romisches Staatsrecht*, 3rd edn (Leipzig: S. Hirzel, 1888), 1034, 1038–1039).

138 Guzman, 'International Tribunals', 179 ('Whatever impact international tribunals have, then, must be the result of the ruling itself and the information in that ruling').

139 Başak Çali, *The Authority of International Law: Obedience, Respect, and Rebuttal* (Oxford: Oxford University Press, 2015), at 73.

government institutions ... to use their power on [the tribunal's] behalf'.[140] The second process operates at the inter-state or, more broadly, interactional level, as what Thomas Ginsburg and Richard McAdams have termed the 'expressive' effect of adjudication.[141] The common recognition of the distinctive character of judicial pronouncements by the various participants means that, even where a specific actor would rather not recognise the adjudicator's authority, each actor's expectation is that other actors' expectations will be affected by the pronouncement. The result is a self-fulfilling prophecy, in which common recognition of the adjudicator's special status leads each actor to adjust its perceptions and conduct following the adjudicator's ruling, not out of individual recognition of the adjudicator's legitimacy to rule but owing to its expectation that other actors will adjust their perceptions and conduct.[142] Thus, an individual actor may *disobey* the adjudicator's pronouncements and even declare its intention not to implement them or not to recognise their effects. However, because each of the actors in the international order knows the adjudicator's pronouncements will anchor the expectations of the others, it is impossible for an individual actor to *disregard* them without consequence.

1.4.2 Using Auctoritas: Four Categories of Judicial Remedies

Authors considering adjudicative authority often portray it as a single phenomenon: the ability to issue communications that influence social perception of appropriate or required conduct. Adjudicators, however, act through specific communications, which I will refer to generally as 'remedies'. Douglas Laycock defines remedies as 'anything a court can do for a litigant who has been wronged or is about to be wronged'.[143] A metaphor originating in English law, 'remedies' is now widely used to designate, in both common law and civil law jurisdictions, '[t]he means by which a right is enforced or the violation of a right is prevented, redressed, or compensated'.[144]

[140] Laurence R. Helfer and Anne-Marie Slaughter, 'Toward a Theory of Effective Supranational Adjudication' (1997) 107 *Yale Law Journal* 273, 278.

[141] Tom Ginsburg and Richard H. McAdams, 'Adjudicating in Anarchy: An Expressive Theory of International Law' (2004) 45 *William and Mary Law Review* 1229–1339.

[142] The distinction between this expressive effect and legitimacy-based accounts of authority is explored in Section 3.3.2.

[143] Douglas Laycock, *Modern American Remedies*, 4th edn (New York: Aspen, 2010), 1.

[144] Henry Campbell Black, *Black's Law Dictionary*, 6th edn (St. Paul, MN: West, 1991), 1294. See the literature referred in Section 4.1.1.

The notion that judicial remedies involve a court 'doing' something would seem to put remedies beyond the reach of international adjudicators. If ICs are defined by their lack of connection to a coercive apparatus, they are unable to directly affect controlling reality. They operate entirely through *auctoritas*. Accordingly, their remedies amount exclusively to communications regarding international law.

The multiple possibilities of these communications, on the one hand, and their lack of connection to coercive apparatuses, on the other, have led some to caution against attempts to develop extensive typologies in this area. As regards the ICJ, Ian Brownlie counselled that 'there is no great profit in seeking to erect internal partitions within the sphere of judicial remedies'.[145] Examining the question in light of the multiplication of ICs and tribunals, Christine Gray found that '[t]he diversity of tribunals is clearly reflected in the diversity of their practice on remedies'.[146] The ICJ has affirmed a broad freedom to award remedies.[147] Providing more detail, the European Court of Human Rights (ECtHR) has repeatedly asserted that its judgments are 'essentially declaratory in nature',[148] including in this category its legal interpretations,[149] findings of violation,[150] and determinations of conduct required from wrongdoers.[151]

However, it is possible to classify judicial remedies not on the basis of the practice of the various courts – an exercise in which one inevitably ends up concentrating on what courts themselves are prepared to award as remedies – but on the focus and function of the various potential types of authoritative communication an actor may issue. In Chapters 4 and 5, I offer and develop a fourfold typology of international judicial remedies,

145 Ian Brownlie, 'Remedies in the International Court of Justice', in Vaughan Lowe and Malgosia Fitzmaurice (eds.), *Fifty Years of the International Court of Justice* (Cambridge: Cambridge University Press, 1996), 566.

146 Christine Gray, 'Remedies in International Dispute Settlement', in Cesare P.R. Romano, Karen J. Alter, and Yuval Shany (eds.), *The Oxford Handbook of International Adjudication* (Oxford: Oxford University Press, 2014), 871–896, at 896.

147 *LaGrand*, [2001] ICJ Reports, p. 466, 485 ('Where jurisdiction exists over a dispute on a particular matter, no separate basis for jurisdiction is required by the Court to consider the remedies a party has requested for the breach of the obligation').

148 *Assanidze* v. *Georgia*, Application No. 71503/01, Judgment of 8 April 2004, para. 202.

149 *Fabris* v. *France*, Application No. 16574/08, Judgment of 7 February 2013 (Merits), para. 75.

150 *Cyprus* v. *Turkey*, Application No. 25781/94, Judgment of 12 May 2014 (Just Satisfaction), para. 27.

151 *Marckx* v. *Belgium*, Application No. 6833/74, Judgment of 13 June 1979, para. 38; *Lyons and Others* v. *United Kingdom*, Application No. 15227/03, Decision of 8 July 2003 (Admissibility).

capitalised to facilitate identification: Mere Adjudication, Declaration of Breach, Consequential Duties, and Permissible Responses concern the new legal relations that emerge.

This typology is based on two divides. As regards their *focus*, remedies may focus on the ordinarily applicable rules of international law or on the new legal relations that arise following a violation.[152] The focus of Mere Adjudication and Declaration of Breach is the interpretation and application of the normative framework that applies to the parties independently of any alleged breach. Through Mere Adjudication, an adjudicator settles disputes regarding the applicable normative framework: the existence of certain disputed rules, their scope, applicability in a case, and interpretation. A Declaration of Breach settles a dispute regarding the legal characterisation of conduct under the adjudicated rules (as does its negative form – an express declaration that no violation has taken place).

The other two categories of remedies, Consequential Duties and Permissible Responses, focus on the new legal relations that emerge from a breach. Having identified a breach, an adjudicator may establish Consequential Duties. This covers both specifying the conduct required for cessation and determining the reparation that is adequate to offset the injury caused by the violation. Additionally, though less commonly, adjudicators may determine Permissible Responses, which focus not on the obligations that arise for a wrongdoer but on the permissible conduct for other actors in the face of the breach. In awarding the remedy of Permissible Responses, an IC employs its judicial authority to establish that certain measures are warranted (and, in some cases, required) and can (or must) lawfully be adopted by other actors, owing either to the violation or following the wrongdoer's failure to provide redress for it.

On a different axis, it is possible to classify the four types of remedies according to the primary purpose of the remedy: clarifying obligations or imposing sanctions. A judicial pronouncement is useful for a complainant for two distinct reasons. It may provide authoritative interpretations

[152] The former can be thought of as the interpretation of 'primary rules', 'substantive rules', or 'rules of conduct', as per the division used by the International Law Commission in its Articles on State Responsibility; the latter, as concerning the 'secondary rules' (ILC Yearbook 1970, vol. II, p. 306, para. 66 (c)). A dispute, however, can concern the violation of 'secondary' or 'procedural' rules, if the dispute emerged after one party decided not to follow the initially applicable primary rules. See, for example, *Gabčíkovo-Nagymaros Project (Hungary* v. *Slovakia)*, Judgment, [1997] ICJ Reports, p. 7, 31–34.

of rules and clarifications of obligations, directly serving the interests of the complainant. But a complainant resorting to adjudication may have a different primary goal: harming the interests of the wrongdoer. Indeed, in many disputes brought to international adjudication, legal interpretation is incidental to the primary purpose of the complainant, which is to obtain a ruling that harms the interests of the alleged wrongdoer. This can be done either symbolically by the adjudicator itself, by creating for the wrongdoer embarrassment or stigma, or by a pronouncement that enables or enjoins others – those in control of political and economic resources – to adopt measures against the wrongdoer.[153] In different ways, issuing a Declaration of Breach and determining Permissible Responses serve the latter purpose. These remedies trigger international law's compliance-inducing mechanisms, and in this sense sanction, or enable the sanctioning of, violations.

Gathering on two different axes these two divides, and anticipating the detailed examination of remedies and judicial practice in Chapters 4 and 5, Table 1.2 categorises the various remedies that can be awarded by international adjudicators.

1.5 Argument and Structure of the Book

From a legal standpoint, a key argument of this book is that adjudication does not sit on a 'legal' plane outside the compliance-inducing process of international law but is part of this compliance-inducing process, by means of which the international normative framework governing state conduct is continuously formed, interpreted, and applied (chiefly) by states. In the framing used here, 'compliance' goes beyond a unidirectional assessment of conduct in the light of applicable legal rules, even if this is how courts, which are usually tasked with performing this very operation, often portray compliance.[154] Likewise, compliance does not belong to a 'post-adjudicative stage' of disputes. Instead, compliance is

[153] For recent discussions of the relevance and limits of stigmatisation, see Oona Hathaway and Scott J. Shapiro, 'Outcasting: Enforcement in Domestic and International Law' (2011) 121 *Yale Law Journal* 252; Adrian Rogstad, 'When Stigmatization Fails: Russia and Aggression in Ukraine' (2022) 7(4) *Journal of Global Security Studies* 1.

[154] See, for example, *Mavrommatis Jerusalem Concessions (Readaptation)* (1927) PCIJ Ser. A No. 11, p. 12; *Haya de La Torre*, [1951] ICJ Reports, p. 71, 78–79; Appellate Body Report, *US – Continued Suspension*, adopted 14 November 2008 (WT/DS320/AB/R), para. 328; Inter-American Court of Human Rights, *Apitz Barbera et al.* v. *Venezuela (Compliance with Judgment)*, 23 November 2012; European Court of Human Rights,

Table 1.2 *A Typology of Judicial Remedies*

Function of the Remedy / Focus of the Remedy	Interpreting Obligations	Sanctioning Violations
Ordinary Legal Framework	**Mere Adjudication** • Existence/applicability of rules • Interpretation of rules • Application of rules to conduct/situation	**Declaration of Breach** • Recording of events • Declaration of breach • Satisfaction
Legal Relations Emerging from a Breach	**Consequential Duties** *Prospective* • Cessation • Guidance on implementation ('specific performance') • Prospective restitution • Guarantees of non-repetition *Retrospective* • Restitution (retrospective) • Measures of satisfaction • Compensation (obligation)	**Permissible Responses** • Authorised/ required response • non-cooperation • reciprocal non-performance • self-defence • Authorised or declared termination/ suspension of treaty • entirely • of specific rights/ benefits • Compensation (enforceability)

continuously created and contested in interactions between actors in the international order. The notion of compliance is inseparable from the constant flow of communications about, and struggles over, the normative framework within which states and other actors are given existence, pursue objectives, and make decisions. The various judicial remedies available to ICs are part of these communications. They amount to different uses of the specific authority held by adjudicators in this communicative network – their judicial *auctoritas*. The different remedies mobilise in different manners the forces that exist within, and

Lyons and Others v. *United Kingdom (Fourth Decision on Admissibility)*, 8 July 2003 (Application No. 15227/03) (2003).

structure, these communicative interactions, seeking to curtail interpretative divergences so as to enhance the ability of these forces to induce the various actors to behave in ways that amount to compliance with international law.

The book has two main aims: to explore the nature and extent of the authority of international adjudicators, and to examine the ways in which adjudicators use (and might use) this authority to influence outcomes. It does not address the 'compliance question' in terms of establishing specific tests to assess compliance or applying interdisciplinary tools to calculate 'rates of compliance'.[155] Although Chapter 2 develops a theory explaining why, how, and when states comply with the rulings of international adjudicators, the rest of the book does not focus on empirically testing this theory – such as by analysing specific courts, identifying patterns in state behaviour, or consulting with current and former state officials about their motivations for compliance. Instead, the book examines the role of adjudication, the different communicative instruments (remedies) available to adjudicators, and the ability of these instruments to influence differently the communications and interactions that constitute international law.

In this regard, the remainder of the book is divided into three parts. Part I, entitled *A Theory of International Adjudication*, examines how adjudicators hold and exercise authority in the international society. Chapter 2 takes a step back from questions involving adjudication and examines the broader issue of how norms operate within an a-hierarchical, or horizontal, social order. Building on insights by Lon Fuller and Robert Ellickson, I develop on the social mechanisms by which participants in a horizontal order, devoid of governmental laws sanctioned by a centralised enforcer, maintain this order. This normative order is grounded, on the one hand, on its ability to infuse in the various actors a sense of the legitimacy of their (and others') actions, and on the other hand on various sanctioning mechanisms that actors employ vis-à-vis each other to respond to perceived violations.

Chapter 3 introduces into this order the authorities established by states to provide authoritative statements regarding its normative

[155] For challenges to this approach to compliance, see Lisa L. Martin, 'Against Compliance', in Jeffrey L. Dunoff and Mark A. Pollack (eds.), *Interdisciplinary Perspectives on International Law and International Relations: The State of the Art* (Cambridge: Cambridge University Press, 2013), 591–610; Wuerth, 'Compliance'; Kingsbury, 'The Concept of Compliance'; Howse and Teitel, 'Beyond Compliance'.

framework and, to a certain extent, to enforce it. It examines adjudicative authority itself, as well as ways in which adjudication interacts with other institutions tasked with enforcing international commitments: the United Nations Security Council and General Assembly, regional international organisations, political bodies under multilateral environmental agreements, or the World Trade Organization (WTO). An adjudicator's rulings may influence outcomes through its legitimacy, by affecting state agents inclined to recognise its authority and seek to comply with their states' obligations. It may also influence outcomes 'expressively', by affecting collective perceptions regarding permissible, prohibited, and required behaviour.

Part II of the book, entitled *A Typology of Judicial Remedies*, explores the typology of remedies introduced in Section 1.4. Chapter 4 considers the role, impact, and availability of the three traditional remedies ICs employ to intervene in disputes: Mere Adjudication, Declaration of Breach, and Consequential Duties. For each of these, I examine the remedy's defining elements, categorise its sub-types, and investigate how various ICs have applied these remedies. I also consider how they relate to, and mobilise, international law's compliance-inducing mechanisms, before analysing the conditions under which the different ICs are prepared to issue these remedies – that is, their 'remedial jurisdiction'.

Chapter 5 explores the fourth, and least studied, type of remedy available to ICs: Permissible Responses. A number of ICs have adjudicated, *ex post*, on the lawfulness of measures adopted by states in response to perceived unlawful conduct by other states: retorsions, countermeasures, suspension and termination of treaties, the *exceptio non adimpleti contractus*, and self-defence. Two questions thus arise: first, whether and when ICs are permitted to determine Permissible Responses *ex ante*, as prospective judicial remedies; and, second, the extent of permissible adjudication in this regard, in particular when it comes to self-help measures used not to press for voluntary compliance but to secure direct enforcement, seizing a wrongdoer's property or constraining its nationals. An expansive interpretation of judicial remedies may give international adjudicators the ability to determine whether, in certain cases, seizing property (and, in rarer cases, arresting individuals) is a permissible response to a prior violation. Although this interpretation is subject to significant obstacles, I argue that, if it were to prevail in even a limited number of cases, the position of international adjudicators would change qualitatively. While still holding solely *auctoritas*, ICs would acquire means to, indirectly, mobilise state *potestas*, that is, the *potestas* of states other than the wrongdoer.

Part III of the book, entitled *Judicial Remedies and Compliance in International Judicial Practice*, shifts from a conceptual examination of the remedial authority of international adjudicators and its relationship to the compliance-inducing forces of international law to an assessment of judicial practice regarding non-compliance with rulings. Put differently, how can, and how do, international adjudicators deploy judicial remedies in cases of alleged non-compliance? Without the ability to determine the application of coercive measures, ICs may employ two strategies to address non-compliance: *remedy repetition* and *remedy escalation*.

Through remedy repetition, an IC may reaffirm or refine a prior Mere Adjudication, issue a new Declaration of Breach in response to non-compliance or repeated violations, or reiterate a finding of Consequential Duties. Remedy escalation, by contrast, involves awarding remedies that are more severe or intrusive than those previously granted. This may include Mere Adjudication over points previously left undecided; a Declaration of Breach where none was previously issued; a more emphatic finding of non-compliance with the prior rulings; or the determination of new Consequential Duties, potentially relating to additional facts or injuries that have arisen since the initial rulings (including non-compliance itself). An IC with the appropriate jurisdiction might also determine Permissible Responses to ongoing violations, though judicial practice in this regard is limited outside the field of trade.

The availability of remedy repetition and remedy escalation casts a shadow over a state's post-ruling decision-making, ensuring that decisions at this stage are influenced not only by 'considerations of practicability or of political expediency'[156] but also by the potential for new unfavourable adjudicatory rulings. The prospect of remedy escalation, in particular, may motivate a state to comply with earlier rulings (or settle the matter) to avoid the imposition of a more severe remedy. The decision not to provide certain remedies, or to postpone consideration of their appropriateness to a subsequent procedural stage, can be thought of as *remedy withholding*. Occasionally, both procedural rules and judicial rulings expressly foreshadow certain remedies, indicating the potential scope for remedy escalation in case of continued breach or non-compliance.

[156] *Haya de La Torre*, [1951] ICJ Reports, p. 71, 78–79.

Chapter 6 begins by examining the unique system of remedies developed over decades in the field of international trade and consolidated in the WTO Dispute Settlement Understanding. The WTO's system of remedies, often termed 'prospective' or 'compliance-oriented', expressly sets aside issues of compensation for injury and seeks to mobilise, over time, the various layers of forces that lead to state compliance with international commitments. For this purpose, it employs two main strategies: remedy repetition, with repeated uses of Mere Adjudication, Declaration of Breach, and (prospective) Consequential Duties; and remedy escalation, with persistent non-compliance leading to an authoritative determination of Permissible Responses. This system is also characterised by built-in remedy withholding, since permissible responses cannot be determined at the 'original' adjudication stage, but only once the violating member has been identified and afforded an opportunity to comply.

Chapters 7, 8, and 9 employ this typology of remedies, and the concepts of remedy repetition, remedy escalation, remedy withholding, and remedy foreshadowing, to examine the law and practice of other ICs and tribunals faced with the prospect and the fact of non-compliance with their rulings, from the ICJ to the Inter-American Court of Human Rights to arbitral tribunals in investment disputes. Most ICs lack specific procedures for examining compliance and providing remedies for non-compliance with their rulings. Over time, however, functionally equivalent mechanisms have been developed in various adjudicatory systems and settings, often ad hoc or through judicial interpretation.

Chapter 7 analyses cases in which specific post-judgment procedures are available, or have been devised by courts themselves, permitting judicial assessment of 'compliance', 'execution', or 'implementation' of rulings. Chapter 8 discusses cases in which, in the absence of dedicated legal provisions, parties seek remedies for alleged non-compliance through new claims of breach, examining potential objections to adjudication at this stage, as well as the techniques developed by different ICs to engage in compliance adjudication and remedy escalation. Chapter 9 examines a particular form employed by adjudicators to allow compliance adjudication and remedy escalation: the issuing of partial rulings, which allows ICs to withhold more grievous remedies while retaining the entitlement to issue them as options in subsequent stages of the dispute. This allows ICs not only to retain influence over the dispute but, in some cases, expressly to foreshadow future remedies, employing them as sanctions for non-compliance. Chapter 10 offers an overall conclusion.

PART I

A Theory of International Adjudication

2

Law without Hierarchy

Sanctions, Shared Understandings, and Compliance in Horizontal Legal Orders

2.1 Introduction

This chapter and the next take a step back from examining how international adjudicators exercise their powers in practice to consider where these powers originate. In other words, why should we expect an international adjudicator's determinations to have any influence over the surrounding social order?

The starting point for answering this question, and the focus of this chapter, is an assessment of the broader social setting within which international adjudicators operate: the international order. This state-centric or 'Westphalian'[1] order is defined, on the one hand, by a plurality of states, that is, hierarchically organised social apparatuses that act as focal points for collective decision-making and, crucially, for the mobilisation of social coercion; and, on the other hand, by the absence of a central hierarchical structure capable of imposing on the various state apparatuses compliance with judicial determinations, or of determining the application of coercive measures against them. An analysis of the ability of international adjudicators to influence the behaviour of states in such an order – conducted in Chapter 3 – must be built on an assessment of how this order operates in the first place and how the normative

[1] This order operates not because the 'Westphalian myth' is historically accurate but because it is the dominant mental model that guides the decisions of relevant actors, in particular those capable of mobilising material resources. See Andreas Osiander, 'Sovereignty, International Relations, and the Westphalian Myth' (2001) 55 *International Organization* 251–287. For accounts of this order see Hedley Bull, *The Anarchical Society: A Study of Order in World Politics*, 2nd edn (Basingstoke: Macmillan, 1995); Andrew Hurrell, *On Global Order: Power, Values, and the Constitution of International Society* (Oxford: Oxford University Press, 2007).

framework that we term 'international law', following Jeremy Bentham,[2] operates and affects state behaviour.

Section 2.2 begins by setting aside common assumptions regarding norms and adjudicators and examining the operation of norms within a-hierarchical, or horizontal, social orders. Building on insights by Lon Fuller and Robert Ellickson, I provide an account of how norms operate in a horizontal social order. Section 2.3 surveys the various theories that scholars in the fields of international law and international relations have developed to explain the influence of international legal norms on state behaviour. Section 2.4 considers how international law may influence state behaviour even under the assumption that states act as rational, utility-maximising unitary actors. Section 2.5 assesses the challenges to these assumptions and examines three reasons why state compliance with international norms may exceed the predictions of the rational states model: behavioural explanations, explanations based on disaggregating the state, and constructivist explanations. Section 2.6 concludes.

2.2 Reframing the Legal Order: From Hierarchy to Horizontality

2.2.1 Adjudicating in Horizontality: Law, Hierarchy and Coercion

International adjudicators intervene within the 'decentralised' or 'horizontal' international order, composed by a variety of mutually recognised sovereigns.[3] In contemporary international law, the exercise of sovereignty is tempered by a variety of domestic and international institutions

[2] Jeremy Bentham, *An Introduction to the Principles of Morals and Legislation* (London: T. Payne and Son, 1780), p. 6 ('Principles of legislation in matters betwixt between nation and nation, or, to use a new though not inexpressive appellation, in matters of *international* law'). Note that Hugo Grotius, for example, did not think in terms of a specific set of rules that apply between nations as much as of general human rights and duties, deriving from 'the law of nature' and 'divine voluntary law', which *also* apply to sovereigns. See Hugo Grotius, *The Rights of War and Peace*, translated by A.C. Campbell (Clark, NJ: Lawbook Exchange, 1901), book 1, chapters 1–2.

[3] This order is of course constructed. See James G. March and Johan P. Olsen, 'The Institutional Dynamics of International Political Orders' (2005) 52 *International Organization* 943–969, at 944 ('This Westphalian nation-state order makes a fundamental distinction between domestic political spheres characterized by institutional density, hierarchical relationships, shared interests, and strong collective identities, and an international political sphere characterized by a lack of strong institutions, few rules, conflicting interests, and conflicting identities').

and practices capable of establishing obligations for states through voting or adjudicative processes.[4] However, in principle, it remains the case, as the Permanent Court of International Justice (PCIJ) stated in its 1928 *S.S. Lotus* Judgment, that '[i]nternational law governs relations between independent States'.[5] Put otherwise, at its core, international law is horizontal law.

The horizontal structure of the international order means that international courts (ICs) are structurally different from their domestic counterparts. In the organisational model that underlies contemporary legal systems, a domestic court is defined (at least in part) by its place within the hierarchy of the state, which gives it the ability to determine the application of coercive measures against recalcitrant parties.[6] Domestic adjudication can produce concrete effects, regardless of its perceived legitimacy to the parties, through the threat of mobilisation of political and economic resources of the state, either forcing compliance or imposing sanctions against non-compliance.

However, a domestic judge or tribunal does not directly apply force. The source of their coercive power is not the physical force of the holders of positions in the Judiciary but the overall legal hierarchy on which the state is built. Those with objective control over the coercive apparatus of the state, capable of directly mobilising irresistible force against individuals, deem themselves a part of, and bound by, this legal hierarchy, and – in a functioning modern state – will respond to judicial decisions by applying or refraining from applying coercive measures as determined by courts.

Contrary to their domestic counterparts, ICs have (in principle) no place within the internal legal hierarchy of states. They are, as developed in Chapter 1, endowed with *auctoritas* but deprived of *potestas*.[7] Operating entirely on the international plane, judicial interpretation is thus severed from its corollary in domestic law: the threat of mobilisation of the political and economic resources of the state apparatus. Without a

[4] See Christian Tomuschat, 'Obligations Arising for States without or against Their Will' (1993) 241 *RdC* 269.

[5] *S.S. Lotus* (1927) PCIJ Ser. A No. 9, p. 5, 18.

[6] This is subject to familiar objections: the sanctions-centric model of adjudication does not apply well to, for example, cases concerning the constitutionality in the abstract of a law or policy, or in which the state itself is required to change conduct. And the hierarchical element becomes rarified when rulings are directed at those at the highest echelons of government or of the coercive apparatus of the state.

[7] See Section 1.4.

place in the internal legal hierarchy of states, ICs are unable to mobilise resources to secure implementation of their decisions.

Within a hierarchically organised social order, courts intervene in disputes between other actors and are able to 'impose [a] solution on both parties even if one or both do not voluntarily consent to the solution'.[8] This ability depends fundamentally on the connection between courts and the coercive apparatus of the state, or rather, on the embeddedness of courts within this apparatus. As Robert Cover notes, although one can seek to portray (domestic) judicial interpretation as 'a voice of reason'[9] intervening to prevent social conflict, within a hierarchically ordered society there is an 'unseverable connection between legal interpretation and violence'.[10] Judicial interpretation takes place, at the bare minimum, in the shadow of coercion. It carries the weight of the coercive measures that the state apparatus can apply against the addressees of the court's pronouncements, either as a response to previous conduct or in case of non-compliance with the court's determinations.

To be sure, the constitutive instruments of the various ICs usually establish, side by side with an assertion of the final and binding nature of their decisions, an obligation to comply with judicial rulings. Each UN Member 'undertakes to comply with the decision of the International Court of Justice in any case to which it is a party'.[11] Parties to the European Convention on Human Rights (ECHR) 'undertake to abide by the final judgment of the Court in any case to which they are parties'.[12] Parties to the American Convention on Human Rights (ACHR) 'undertake to comply with the judgment of the Court in any case to which they are parties'.[13] Pursuant to the United Nations

[8] Martin Shapiro, *Courts: A Comparative and Political Analysis* (Chicago: University of Chicago Press, 1981), p. 4. In Shapiro's framework, this is labelled the arbitrator's legal authority. Judges' authority is depicted as wholly consent-independent: 'judges may impose a final resolution independent of the consent of the parties' (Shapiro, *Court: A Comparative and Political Analysis*, p. 7).

[9] Robert M. Cover, 'Violence and the Word' (1986) 95 *The Yale Law Journal* 1601–1629, at 1628.

[10] Ibid., 1610.

[11] Charter of the United Nations, 26 June 1945, in force 24 October 1945, 1 UNTS XVI, Article 94.

[12] European Convention on Human Rights, 4 November 1950, in force 3 September 1953, Art. 46(1).

[13] Inter-American Convention on Human Rights, 22 November 1969, in force 18 July 1978, Article 68(1).

Convention on the Law of the Sea (UNCLOS), any decision by a court or tribunal under UNCLOS 'shall be complied with by all the parties to the dispute'.[14] The WTO Dispute Settlement Understanding (DSU) provides that adopted reports of the Appellate Body 'shall be ... unconditionally accepted by the parties to the dispute'.[15]

However, no shift in the internal legal hierarchies of states accompanies these commitments. In the so-called Westphalian international order, international obligations fall on the state as a whole and produce effects on the international plane, without having an established place in each state's internal legal hierarchy.[16] This means that those within a state who employ violence to ensure compliance with its legal order – and, by extension, with the decisions of domestic courts that determine the content of this legal order in political arrangements characterised by a separation of powers – are not similarly called upon to ensure compliance with the rulings of ICs binding upon the state.

States may decide, of course, to give automatic or 'direct' effect within their legal order to the decisions of certain international adjudicators. This can be done via the legislature, as Members of the European Union have done by incorporating into their legal orders the Treaties of the European Union that require them to integrate judgments of the Court of Justice of the European Union (CJEU) within their legal order.[17] It can also be done by adjudicators. Thus, some constitutional courts in Latin America have accorded a form of 'direct effect' not only to the ACHR as a text but also to the judgments of the Inter-American Court of Human Rights by which this Court determines the ACHR's interpretation, establishes violations, and specifies duties that arise for states found responsible for human rights violations.[18]

[14] United Nations Convention on the Law of the Sea, Montego Bay, 10 November 1986, in force 16 November 1994, 1833 UNTS 397, Article 296(1).

[15] Dispute Settlement Rules: Understanding on Rules and Procedures Governing the Settlement of Disputes, Marrakesh Agreement Establishing the World Trade Organization, 1994, 1869 U.N.T.S. 401, Article 17.14.

[16] As discussed below, a state may determine in its own legal order a different arrangement. The same state may, however, seek to revise this arrangement; its organs may overrule it, or simply disregard it. In this case, the underlying Westphalian structure of the international order re-emerges. See also Section 5.5, on judicial determination that coercive measures are permissible as responses to violations.

[17] Paul Craig and Gráinne De Búrca, *EU Law, Texts, Cases and Materials*, 6th edn (Oxford: Oxford University Press, 2015), 180 ff.

[18] Alexandra Huneeus, 'Constitutional Lawyers and the Inter-American Court's Varied Authority' (2016) 79 *Law & Contemporary Problems* 179–207; Jorge Contesse,

International agreements and bodies can seek to establish direct applicability. The Revised Treaty of the Economic Community of West African States (ECOWAS) provides that 'Judgements of the Court of Justice shall be binding on the Member States, the Institutions of the Community and on individuals and corporate bodies'.[19] Some ICs, like the Andean Court of Justice (ACJ), have concluded that domestic courts must accept their rulings as domestically enforceable orders.[20] However, even where the relevant treaties specify this and this is determined by an international adjudicator, in each case direct effect must ultimately be accepted by the state's domestic organs. The same organs, or other organs operating within the hierarchical structure of the state, are able to revoke or modify this acceptance, or make it subject to certain, domestically established (and ultimately, given the underlying control over the coercive apparatus of the state, domestically determined) conditions.[21]

Due to its structural horizontality, international law is unable to perform one of the functions most closely associated with law. The international normative framework may – perhaps, inevitably will – have a role in the psychological and political processes that lead to the formation of a state's positions and underlie state conduct. But, should the outcome of this view-formation processes be a position that conflicts with that adopted by the institutions established to provide international law with a voice, these institutions are unable to impose their view on states. Using a duality sketched out by Lon Fuller, international law cannot directly operate as 'an instrument of social control', in the sense of control exercised by a hierarchical superior with the ability to mobilise material resources to impose on other actors compliance with its determinations or sanctions for non-compliance.[22] The operation

'Contestation and Deference in the Inter-American Human Rights System' (2016) 79 *Law & Contemporary Problems* 123–145.

[19] Revised Treaty of the ECOWAS, signed 24 July 1993, in force 23 August 1995, 2373 U.N.T.S. 233, Article 15(4).

[20] ACJ, *Case No. 02-AI-2019 (SugarLatam* v. *Ecuador)*, Judgment, 18 July 2023, para. 6.4. This is based on Articles 25 and 30 of the Treaty Creating the Court of Justice of the Cartagena Agreement, adopted 28 May 1979, in force 19 May 1983, as amended.

[21] Regarding domestic courts' resistance to the supremacy of EU law as interpreted by the CJEU, see Sára Kiššová, 'An Overview of the Doctrine of *Ultra Vires* from the Perspective of the German Federal Constitutional Court and the Polish Constitutional Court' (2022) 2 *Slovak Yearbook of European Union Law* 33–48.

[22] Lon L. Fuller, 'Law as an Instrument of Social Control and Law as a Facilitation of Human Interaction' (1975) 1 *BYU Law Review* 89–96.

and influence of international law rely on the ability of international legal rules and institutions to perform Fuller's second function of the law: to act as 'a means for facilitating human interaction'.[23] For international law as interpreted by international institutions to have an effect on outcomes, these institutions must influence, without being able to rely on hierarchical superiority, those acting in the role of agents of states, whose ultimate allegiance is not to international law but to their state's institutions. It is in this sense that international law is interactional rather than hierarchical.

2.2.2 Horizontal Law as Interactional Law: Lon Fuller and Robert Ellickson

Broadly speaking, all law can be described as 'interactional'.[24] Law is both the product of social interactions and an element that informs these interactions. In legal philosophy, the notion that all law involves a degree of horizontality is associated with the work of Fuller and his account of law as an 'interactional process' rather than 'a unidirectional exercise of authority'.[25] Adapting Fuller's account to international law, Jutta Brunée and Stephen Toope have developed 'an interactional theory of international legal obligation',[26] grounded on Fuller's idea of an 'internal morality of law', on the one hand, and on constructivist scholarship on international relations on the other.[27] Following this scholarship, Brunée and Toope argue that 'the power of international law rests in a felt sense of obligation, rooted in a specific form of legal legitimacy'.[28]

The concept of interactional or horizontal law employed here draws partly on Lon Fuller's insights, but does not require committing to the

[23] Ibid. Note that the latter function does not necessarily imply positive connotations. The rule according to which one may kill in self-defence and even the rule that permits 'blood feuds' to uphold a certain society's moral code are in Fuller's view rules 'facilitating human interaction'. (Lon L. Fuller, 'Human Interaction and the Law' (1969) 14 *American Journal of Jurisprudence* 1–36, at 21).

[24] See, in the same vein, Jeremy Webber, 'The Grammar of Customary Law' (2009) 54 *McGill Law Journal* 579–626, at 579 ('All law is customary').

[25] Lon L. Fuller, *The Morality of Law*, Revised Edition (New Haven: Yale University Press, 1969), 223.

[26] Jutta Brunnée and Stephen J. Toope, *Legitimacy and Legality in International Law: An Interactional Account* (Cambridge: Cambridge University Press, 2010), 20. On constructivist scholarship, see Section 2.5.3.

[27] Ibid., 14.

[28] Ibid., 124.

constructivist idea that international law produces a 'felt sense of obligation' for decision-makers within states. The roles of both international law and judicial authority can be explained by less demanding theories of how states behave.[29] More importantly, the concept of interactional law differs from Fuller's account in that his most developed account of law – his outline of a theory of law in *The Morality of Law* – remains essentially an account of *hierarchical law*.

It is only in a post-scriptum to *The Morality of Law* that Fuller infers, from the non-hierarchical legal phenomena of international law and (domestic) customary law, the idea that, in every legal system, there is a 'horizontal element in what positivism views as vertically imposed law'.[30] He thus proposes viewing legal norms 'as providing guideposts for human interaction' rather than 'a one-way projection of authority'.[31] The core of his account of the law assumes a law that operates within the hierarchical structure of the state. Thus, Fuller proposes that 'the functioning of a legal system depends upon a cooperative effort – an effective and responsible interaction – between law-giver and subject'.[32] Despite highlighting the horizontal component in any human relation, this account maintains separate roles for 'law-giver' and 'subject', a separation that assumes that an authority relationship exists between them that harks from a broader hierarchical structure.[33] Thus, even if conceptually this structure is not seen as unilaterally imposed but as a product of mutual interaction, it remains a hierarchical structure. In this sense, Fuller's 'interactional account' of the legal phenomenon offers a glimpse of law's inner horizontality, in the sense that legal hierarchies ultimately rely on their operation between equally human individuals. But it remains fundamentally an account of the operation of a hierarchical legal order.

[29] As discussed below, other strands of scholarship either take the opposite route from constructivism, assuming that states will generally act as self-interest rational actors (rational choice theories), or are agnostic on the matter of commitment to obligations, demanding evidence for the existence of such commitment as well as an explanation for its operating mechanism (behavioural theories).

[30] Fuller, *The Morality of Law*, 233.

[31] Ibid., 223.

[32] Ibid., 209.

[33] Fuller developed on and sophisticated the interactional account, and its foundational character for state-enforced (or 'enacted') law, noting that 'enacted law itself depend for its existence on the development of "stable interactional expectancies" between lawgiver and subject' (Fuller, 'Human Interaction and the Law', 25).

A similar challenge arises with regard to H. L. A. Hart's *The Concept of Law*. Although the theory developed in this work seeks to challenge John Austin's coercion-based account of the law by taking as a starting point, rather than the coercive element in law enforcement, a shared understanding of obligation between enforcer and subject, Hart ultimately concludes that state 'officials' are the ones whose understanding of the law determines its existence and content. Contrasted with these officials, who must 'accept[] secondary rules as critical common standards of behaviour', 'ordinary citizens' are subject to the test of 'obedience' only.[34] It is ultimately this authority-based conception of the law that grounds Hart's much-discussed opposition to characterising international law a legal system. There is 'some analogy', he concedes, between this decentralised self-help system, where 'resort to war or forceful retaliation' may be lawful responses to legal violations, and the 'use of force, legally regulated and officially administered, as a sanction in municipal law'. But 'the facts are undeniably different'.[35] In this regard, Hart sees the lack of authoritative determination of the lawfulness of decentralised sanctions as a fundamental challenge, if not for international law to exist, for it to operate as a legal system: 'whereas a municipal court has a compulsory jurisdiction to investigate the rights and wrongs of "self help", and to punish a wrongful resort to it, no international court has a similar jurisdiction'.[36]

More fertile ground for understanding international law as an interactional, a-hierarchical normative system may be found in the work of Robert Ellickson. In *Order without Law*, Ellickson developed a theory of an interactional normative order from his observation of social interactions among cattle ranchers in a rural county in the United States. He observed that in this community, where state agents were largely absent,[37] 'informal control norms emerge to help people achieve order without law'.[38] These informal control norms, he concluded, constitute an essentially interactional normative system, with norms and sanctions operating without legal hierarchy between its participants.

[34] H.L.A. Hart, *The Concept of Law* (Oxford: Clarendon Press, 1961), 113.

[35] Ibid., 233.

[36] Ibid. For an assessment of whether Hart's assessment still holds, see Carmen E. Pavel, 'Is International Law a Hartian Legal System?' (2018) 31 *Ratio Juris* 307–325.

[37] More precisely, calling upon agents of the state to intervene in a local dispute was seen as a violation of the local, informal normative order.

[38] Robert Ellickson, *Order without Law: How Neighbors Settle Disputes* (Cambridge: Harvard University Press, 1991), 127.

Ellickson's work is particularly relevant to an understanding of international law because, contrary to Fuller's account of the law, it does not take as a starting point a hierarchically organised order, broadly recognised as normative, featuring relations of authority and subordination, and enforced by a coercive apparatus, to then identify the elements of horizontality that exist within this verticalised, hierarchical order.[39] Instead, *Order without Law* takes the opposite route, identifying, within a community organised around the principle of equality, a normative system that applies horizontally among its members to control and sanction undesirable behaviour.

Ellickson's chosen title, 'Order without Law', highlights how the informal normative system developed within this rural community operates in isolation from, and even against the norms of, the vertical legal system in force in the same territory and for the same persons. Ellickson's choice of terminology suggests that, like Hart and possibly more than Fuller, he is ambivalent about the 'legal' character of an a-hierarchical normative framework.[40] His detained analysis of this framework nonetheless provides significant insights relevant to an examination of the operation of other non-hierarchical normative systems – including international law.

2.2.3 *The Five Layers of the International Normative Order*

An interactional normative system is similar to a hierarchical system in its basic elements: expressed or implied norms, normatively assessed behaviour, and sanctions for non-conforming behaviour. The norms that govern relations among participants are 'evidenced by patterns of sanctions, patterns of primary behavior, and aspirational statements'.[41] The relevance of a norm, and to an extent its very existence as a norm within a community, depends on its ability to influence the conduct of its addressees. Thus, a 'guideline for human conduct' is a norm (or 'rule') to the extent that it 'influences the behavior either of those to whom it is addressed or of those who detect others breaching the guideline'.[42]

[39] Fuller, *The Morality of Law*, 93 ('we have generally taken the viewpoint of the conscientious legislator').

[40] See on this note 46 and accompanying text.

[41] Ellickson, *Order without Law*, 183.

[42] Ibid., 128.

Ellickson follows legal theorists, political scientists, and sociologists who concluded that, among these elements, the application of sanctions is a normative order's particular and identifying element.[43] Verbal and textual statements that identify desirable and undesirable behaviour may be relevant to communicate a rule but, for Ellickson, are in themselves 'weak evidence' of its normative value within the community. Basing the identification of a norm on the conduct of the rule's primary addressees – those performing the conduct to which the norm refers – is also problematic. Regularity of behaviour can take place for a number of reasons. There is no guarantee that stated norms cause or influence even highly regular behaviour. Conversely, the application of sanctions both identifies a norm and provides evidence of its relevance for the sanctioning agent. As Ellickson put it, 'the best, and always sufficient, evidence that a rule is operative is the routine (though not necessarily inevitable) administration of sanctions – whether rewards or punishments – upon people detected breaking the rule'.[44]

This raises the question of who applies sanctions in a horizontal legal order, which is defined by the absence of the characteristic sanctioning agents of domestic, hierarchically organised legal systems: the representatives of the organised community, that is, the state. Here again Ellickson's work proves insightful. Going beyond the state-enforced rules that he classifies as 'law', he identifies five forms of 'social control', of which enforcement by the state is only one.[45]

The first noteworthy aspect of Ellickson's typology is that it reserves the term 'law' to rules enforced by the state. This is a terminological rather than a substantive issue. Whether to call 'law' the entire spectrum of normative phenomena governing human behaviour, or to reserve the term to those norms that are enforced by the coercive apparatus of the state, is largely a matter of focus. In a hierarchical domestic legal order, from the viewpoint of those operating within the apparatus of the state, it

[43] Ibid. He cites Herbert Hart, Emile Durkheim, Robert Axelrod, and George Homans. Many others could be added. The opposite view, argued by Brunée and Toope on the basis of a reading of Fuller, emphasises a 'practice of legality' over sanctions. See Jutta Brunnée and Stephen J. Toope, 'International Law and the Practice of Legality: Stability and Change' (2018) 49(4) *Victoria University of Wellington Law Review* 429–445. As discussed in this chapter, the two elements are complementary. Just as a system purely based on coercion would not be a legal system in the sense we think of 'law' today, a system where no sanctions are applied would not qualify as 'legal'.

[44] Ellickson, *Order without Law*, 128.

[45] For the table summarising the five forms or levels, see Table 1.1 in Chapter 1.

is the state's own rules that determine whether and to what extent to take into account, and possibly incorporate and enforce, norms made within religious or professional communities, or applied between neighbours.[46] From the viewpoint of the individuals affected by norms of a religious or professional community – or, as in the case of the close-knit, geographically determined community that Ellickson studied (Shasta County, California) – violating communal norms may lead to sanctions perceived as more grave, and more certain in their application, than those that might be imposed by the largely absent state.

A similar distinction between 'law' and 'non-law' in the international order is less clear.[47] If an overarching 'supra-governmental' apparatus tasked with international rule enforcement existed, it would be required to determine which among the various norms promoted within the community are 'legal' from the perspective of its enforcement activities. As it stands, international law is an amalgamation of customary norms, treaties and treaty-based norms, norms issued by international organisations, and a few fundamental norms, compliance with which is deemed of interest to all states.[48]

As an interactional system lacking a centralised rule enforcer, international law is left in principle with Ellickson's remaining four non-government-based levels of enforcement. However, as I will argue, a fifth level (referred to as '[5]') has been developed which seeks to emulate the structure of state enforcement of norms of collective concern, though only in selected instances and dependent on the application of sanctions by the various states' coercive apparatuses. Enforcement of norms under these five levels constitutes a multi-layered system of compliance control.

[46] This – enforceability by the organised apparatus of the state – is arguably the key distinctive element of the legal system when compared to 'primitive' horizontal systems, even to those who, like Hart, look for a less sanctions-centric approach. See, for example, Hart, *Concept of Law*, 2–3. Others do challenge this sharp distinction entirely (Jutta Brunée and Stephen J. Toope, *Legitimacy and Legality in International Law: An Interactional Account* (Cambridge: Cambridge University Press, 2010), 20).

[47] See Dinah Shelton, 'Introduction: Law, Non-Law and the Problem of "Soft Law"', in Dinah Shelton (ed.), *Commitment and Compliance: The Role of Non-Binding Norms in the International Legal System* (Oxford: Oxford University Press, 2000).

[48] These are not only those known as *jus cogens* norms, but *erga omnes* norms, that is, those for which, '[i]n view of the importance of the rights involved, all States can be held to have a legal interest in their protection' (*Barcelona Traction, Light and Power Company, Limited (Belgium* v. *Spain)*, Judgement, ICJ Rep. 1970, p. 3, 32). See Priya Urs, 'Obligations *Erga Omnes* and the Question of Standing before the International Court of Justice' (2021) 34 *Leiden Journal of International Law* 505–525. On the possible 'centrally enforced' norm against the use of force, see footnotes 56–57.

These means of enforcement do not apply in isolation but may be combined; different types of sanctions may be applied jointly, or sequentially.[49] These five social mechanisms promoting compliance, as they apply to state conduct, will henceforth be referred to as *layers* of compliance control.

Table 2.1 summarises the five layers of control mechanisms that impel states to comply with international law. These layers are:

Layer 1 – Voluntary compliance by states with the system's norms, enforced through self-control (including compliance by domestic bureaucracy or governmental decisions, or 'self-sanctions' such as a state's domestic judiciary ordering compliance or reparation);[50]

Layer 2 – Bilateral control by the 'second party', that is, the state whose interests a violation harms directly. Bilateral self-help measures include retorsions, countermeasures and, in case of the violation of the norm against the use of force, self-defence;

Layer 3 – Decentralised third-party control, that is, control by third states acting as 'nonhierarchically organised social forces',[51] including through merely discursive sanctions. Layer 3 applies in case of norms that protect a collective interest, though the assessment of this collective character is determined by states individually;

Layer 4 – Institutional control by organisations capable of sanctioning their members. This layer covers all manners of sanctions that are determined and can be implemented by an international organisation or through a multilateral treaty system, such as loss of voting rights, suspension or expulsion of an organisation;

[49] Ibid., 127. Ellickson mentions that 'leaders of the kibbutzim of Israel gradually escalate the forcefulness of their organisational responses against antisocial members – from informal negative gossip, to official rebuke at a group meeting, to the ultimate punishment of expulsion' (Ellickson, *Order without Law*, 219). Escalation of sanctions is a common technique used, for example, in multilateral environmental agreements and by human rights bodies. See Jutta Brunée, 'Compliance Control', in Geir Ulfstein, Thilo Marauhn, and Andreas Zimmermann (eds.), *Making Treaties Work: Human Rights, Environment and Arms Control* (Cambridge: Cambridge University Press, 2007), 373–390.

[50] In international law, a 'self-sanction' can be the shame or guilt a state representative feels when their state is in non-compliance with what it views as a legal obligation of the state. It can also imply the imposition of a sanction, or even an order for the relevant state agents to comply with an international obligation, issued by the state's own administrative of judicial authorities.

[51] Ellickson, *Order without Law*, 127.

Table 2.1 *International Law's Layers of Compliance Control*

Layer	*Controller*	*Rule*	*Sanction Type*	*Term*
			First-Party Control	
1	Domestic actors	All	Self-control (bureaucratic, governmental, political, judicial)	Voluntary compliance
			Second-Party Control	
2	Injured or specially affected state	Bilateral obligation	Condemnation, adjudication, bilateral self-help (retorsions, countermeasures, termination or suspension of treaty, self-defence)	Inter-state enforcement
			Third-Party Control	
3	Third states	Collective obligation (*erga omnes /erga omnes partes*)	Condemnation, adjudication, third-party self-help (retorsions, third-party countermeasures, suspension or termination of interdependent treaty, collective self-defence)	Diffuse enforcement
4	International organisation (IO) or multilateral body	IO or treaty rules	Institutional sanctions (condemnation, loss of voting rights, suspension or expulsion)	Institutional enforcement
[5]	IO or multilateral body/ states	IO or treaty rules	Authorised sanctions (suspension of treaty rights, suspension of economic relations, military sanctions)	Authorised enforcement

Layer [5] – Control via institutionally authorised coercive measures. Layer [5] involves the combined activity of international institutions and states, with institutions determining the lawfulness and appropriateness of sanctions and states being tasked with mobilising the resources necessary to implement them vis-à-vis the sanctioned state.

To each layer corresponds a type of violated rule and a sanction type. Note that the term 'sanctions' is used here in a broad sense, including (i) what could be called 'merely social' sanctions, including self-restraint by various organs of the state and verbal condemnation; (ii) the horizontal bilateral responses often identified with international law's sanctions, including non-performance of obligations, whose permissibility is primarily determined by the sanctioning state itself; and (iii) sanctions applied or authorised by institutions and organs formally empowered, usually by treaty, to determine sanctions for unlawful conduct.[52] The square brackets indicate the inexact nature of the analogy between Layer [5], on the international plane, and Ellickson's Level 5, encompassing government-established domestic norms enforced by the coercive apparatus of the state.

Three clarifications are in order. It can be highlighted upfront that, within the interdisciplinary scholarship assessing the effects of international law on state behaviour, there is controversy on the significance of Layer 1. For some realist and rational choice theory authors, as a matter of methodology, the notions of 'voluntary compliance' and 'self-sanction' invite the question whether this is actual rule compliance or merely the action that a state would take in any case. Thus, in their analysis of state conduct, two of the fiercest proponents of a realist approach to international law declare to 'consistently exclude one preference from the state's interest calculation: a preference for complying with international law'.[53]

However, state compliance with norms in the absence of sanctions is pervasive in, and central to, international law. Some conceptualise this as the product of internal mechanisms: voluntary compliance, internalised compliance, or 'self-sanctioning'. Others see it as a rational response to uncertainty regarding future sanctioning, or even as less-than-rational behaviour by state representatives failing to act rationally in accordance

[52] In Ellickson's framework, not only is self-enforcement meaningful but gossip also counts as a sanction: ['t]he mildest form of self-help is truthful negative gossip' (Ellickson, *Order without Law*, 57).

[53] Jack L. Goldsmith and Eric. A. Posner, *The Limits of International Law* (Oxford: Oxford University Press, 2005), 9.

with their state's aggregate self-interests.[54] However, accounts of the operation of international law that seek to set aside Layer 1 entirely – and, once institutions are established, Layers 4 and [5] – inevitably end up providing a distorted picture, which assigns to the inter-state Layers 2 and 3 a level of influence over state conduct that cannot be explained by the operation of these layers alone.

Likewise, it may be noted in advance that the deployment of sanctions pertaining to each of these layers is uneven and, in this sense, 'political'. At the same time, in any legal order uniform rule enforcement is an aspiration rather than a fact. States regularly invoke international norms and condemn their violation by other states. They also often follow up by responding and, through discourse or action, sanctioning perceived wrongdoers for their violation of rules. Whether one calls this horizontal normative system 'law' or seeks a different term, to differentiate it from governmental law, is a matter of terminological preference and analytical focus rather than a substantively relevant position. Put otherwise, calling a horizontal normative system 'law' does not imply misunderstanding it for a hierarchical normative system.

Finally, the addition of Layer [5] to the list may demand clarification. Its archetypal example is problematic from a rule-of-law perspective. This is the enforcement by the United Nations Security Council (UNSC) of the prohibition of threats to the peace, breaches of the peace, and acts of aggression, using its powers under Chapter VII of the UN Charter. When deliberating and voting at the UNSC, state representatives overtly act as political operators rather than independent adjudicators. Equally worryingly for a law-enforcing institution, the UNSC's composition and procedure de facto exempt a few states from being sanctioned. Relatedly, there is the question of whether these 'prohibitions' pass a legality test if the UNSC can determine case by case, even retrospectively, what was prohibited. As a result, the 'legal' status of these prohibitions has often been discussed.[55]

[54] Those who maintain an overly deterministic view of the relationship between domestic politics and international norm compliance would do well to consider the aftermath of the ICJ's *Avena* Judgment ([2004] ICJ Reports, p. 12) and the ultimately unsuccessful efforts by the George W. Bush administration to secure compliance with it. See Jesse Townsend, '*Medellin* Stands Alone: Common Law Nations Do Not Show a Shared Postratification Understanding of the ICJ' (2009) 34 *Yale Journal of International Law* 463.

[55] See, for example, James Crawford, 'The Relationship between Sanctions and Countermeasures', in Gowlland-Debbas (ed.), *United Nations Sanctions and International Law* (The Hague: Kluwer Law, 2007), 57–68, at 57 ('the response to them is authorised in virtue of their character as threats to or breaches of peace and not in virtue of their character as internationally wrongful acts'); *Contra*, Jean Combacau, 'Le chapitre VII de la Charte des Nations Unies: résurrection ou métamorphose?', in Rafâa Ben Achour and Slim Laghani

As a matter of the operation of the international normative system as a 'system of social control', there is little question that norms against unwarranted uses of force exist in the sense that they are regularly, if unevenly, enforced. Thus, though plainly deficient from a rule-of-law perspective, this blanket prohibition is a norm in the technical Kelsenian sense: sanctions are attached to violations, established by an authority empowered to determine when the norm has been violated.[56] Besides being subject to sanctions administered by the UNSC, violations of these norms can be, and have been, enforced under Layer 2 (individual self-defence) or Layer 3 (collective self-defence).[57] Additionally, the UN General Assembly has occasionally sought to enforce them, both acting under Layer 4 (condemnation) and purporting to act under Layer [5] (demanding sanctions).[58] Finally, these norms can be (and have been) enforced by regional organisations, such as the African Union or the Organization of American States.[59]

Once identified, Layer [5] should not be restricted to UNSC sanctions or the norms they (unevenly) enforce. Rather than focusing on its content, Layer [5] may be considered from the perspective of its

(eds.), *Les nouveaux aspects du droit international – Colloque des 14, 15 et 16 avril 1994* (Pedone, 1994), 139–158, identifying as the Council's task 'to make concrete the obligation, imprecise but included in the Charter, of abstaining from all acts constituting a threat to peace or a breach of peace, and of all acts of aggression' ('*concrétiser l'obligation, imprécise mais incluse dans la Charte, de s'abstenir de tout acte constitutif d'une menace pour la paix ou une rupture de la paix, et de tout acte d'agression*'). See also Mary Ellen O'Connell, 'Debating the Law of Sanctions' (2002) 13 *European Journal of International Law* 63–79; Jeremy Matam Farrall, *United Nations Sanctions and the Rule of Law* (Cambridge: CUP, 2007). The 'legality' test here seems reminiscent of a Fullerian view that there is a necessary 'internal morality' to the law. See Fuller, *The Morality of Law*, 33 ff.

56 Hans Kelsen, *The Law of the United Nations: A Critical Analysis of Its Fundamental Problems* (Clark: Lawbook Exchange, 2011), 735–737. See Olivier Corten, *The Law against War: The Prohibition on the Use of Force in Contemporary International Law*, 2nd edn (Oxford: Hart, 2021); Christine Gray, *International Law and the Use of Force*, 4th edn (Oxford: Oxford University Press, 2018). These norms have been invoked – both by the Security Council and by individual states – as applying not only vis-à-vis states but vis-à-vis all members of the international community, regardless of their legal status, international legal personality, or UN Membership. Michael Byers, 'Terrorism, the Use of Force and International Law after 11 September' (2002) 51 *International & Comparative Law Quarterly* 401–414.

57 Murray Colin Alder, *The Inherent Right of Self-Defence in International Law* (Dordrecht: Springer, 2012); James A. Green, *Collective Self-Defence in International Law* (Cambridge: Cambridge University Press, 2024).

58 See Section 3.4.2.

59 In this case, regional IOs may act under a UNSC mandate or seek to act as Layer [5] decision-makers themselves. See Ademola Abass, *Regional Organisations and the Development of Collective Security* (London: Hart Publishing, 2004).

structure. Layer [5] involves enforcement through the combined actions of an institutional decision-maker and one or more implementing states. It emerges when states delegate to an international institution the authority not only to identify violations but also to determine that inter-state sanctions are warranted in the face of these violations. Since international institutions lack control over political and economic sources to apply sanctions beyond the institutional sanctions of Layer 4, they rely on states for implementation of the relevant sanctions.

In other words, Layer [5] is characterised by institutionally authorised sanctions. These are sanctions whose permissibility is determined by an international institution but whose application depends on action by those in control of means of coercion, that is, states. Layer [5] can be said to enforce norms of 'collective concern'. The collective character of this concern, however, is not determined by the content of the relevant norms but by the very fact that states, *ex ante*, endow an institution with the authority to determine that sanctions having a coercive character are warranted in case of their violation.

The remainder of this chapter examines the operation of international law as a wholly horizontal, that is, inter-state legal order. Layers 2 and 3 will thus feature prominently, while Layers 4 and [5] will be discussed more thoroughly in Chapter 3.

2.3. International Law and State Behaviour: Realism, Rationalism, and Constructivism

2.3.1 International Relations Theory and Compliance: Realists, Institutionalists and Constructivists

Among international relations scholars, the interest in norms in inter-state relations arose from the observation that states often do abide by their commitments when, objectively, it would have been open to them to disregard these commitments in the pursuit of their short-term interest.[60] To explain this discrepancy, two main theoretical schools emerged that challenged the realist paradigm. Although the sharp theoretical debates of the 1990s are now less prominent, a survey of the key schools of thought helpfully highlights their different points of emphasis.

[60] For comprehensive accounts of the compliance scholarship, see note 20 in Chapter 1.

Scholars such as Oran Young,[61] Stephen Krasner,[62] and Robert Keohane,[63] while retaining the assumption that states are primarily rational actors, considered that states' mutual commitments and patterns of behaviour lead to the development of certain mutual expectations for permissible and prohibited behaviour, which they termed 'international regimes' – usefully defined as the 'principles, norms, rules, and decision-making procedures around which actor expectations converge in a given issue-area'.[64] Although powerful states may contribute disproportionately to the creation of regimes (a proposition that can itself be challenged),[65] once a regime is in place it acquires not only the ability to modify conduct that would be expected from a self-interested state acting rationally[66] but also 'stickiness', that is, the ability to endure even after the conditions that led to their creation have changed.[67]

A third group of scholars, labelled 'constructivists', seeks to explain institutions as the product of 'collective understandings' which 'provide people with reasons why things are as they are and indications as to how they should use their material abilities and power'.[68] In international relations scholarship, a strand of this group was led by Emanual Adler,[69] Alexander Wendt,[70] Kathryn Sikkink, and Martha Finnemore.[71] Another strand was championed by Nicholas Onuf[72] and Friedrich

61 Oran R. Young, *Governance in World Affairs* (Ithaca: Cornell University Press, 1999).

62 Stephen D. Krasner, *International Regimes* (Ithaca: Cornell University Press, 1983).

63 Robert O. Keohane, *After Hegemony: Cooperation and Discord in the World Political Economy* (Princeton, NJ: Princeton University Press, 1984).

64 Krasner, *International Regimes*, 2.

65 See Adam Bower, *Norms without the Great Powers: International Law and Changing Social Standards in World Politics* (Oxford: Oxford University Press, 2017).

66 Stephen D. Krasner, 'Structural Causes and Regime Consequences: Regimes as Intervening Variables' (1982) 36(2) *International Organization* 185–205.

67 See Michael Lipson, 'Transaction Cost Estimation and International Regimes: Of Crystal Balls and Sheriff's Posses' (2004) 6(1) *International Studies Review* 1–20.

68 Emanuel Adler, 'Seizing the Middle Ground: Constructivism in World Politics' (1997) 3(3) *European Journal of International Relations* 319–363, at 322.

69 Ibid. See also Emanuel Adler, *Communitarian International Relations: The Epistemic Foundations of International Relations* (New York: Routledge, 2005).

70 Alexander Wendt, *Social Theory of International Politics* (Cambridge: Cambridge University Press, 1999).

71 Kathryn Sikkink and Martha Finnemore, 'Taking Stock: The Constructivist Research Program in International Relations and Comparative Politics' (2001) 4 *Annual Review of Political Science* 391–416.

72 Nicholas Onuf, *World of Our Making: Rules and Rule in Social Theory and International Relations* (New York: Routledge, 1989/2012).

Kratochwil.[73] Constructivists point out that the international order, constituted by entities we call 'states', is itself a product of communicative processes both within and among states. Constructivists do not operate with fixed assumptions of 'states' as units of analyses, interacting on the basis of predetermined state interests in what is sometimes labelled the 'black boxes' or 'billiard balls' model of international relations.[74] Instead, constructivists postulate that international relations, like other types of human relations, involve various levels of interpersonal interaction. These interactions are largely shaped by ideational factors, including the postulate that a person is an 'agent of' state A or state B.[75] Thus, the international order does not have pre-existing rules but is 'what states make of it'.[76] The basic elements underlying realist and rationalist theories – states' identities, interests, and array of potential actions – are constituted and modified over time through economic, social, political, and cultural developments within states, as well as by states' inter-relations.

Prior to examining how the different elements of the international legal order may engender compliance, it should be noted that much of the compliance scholarship is concerned with 'cooperation' and 'commitments' rather than compliance with 'international law' as understood by positivist lawyers. The *legal* element – the binding or non-binding character of the commitments conveyed in legal documents, the legal status of decision-making bodies, and the procedural mechanisms designed to assess these legal questions, all that which international lawyers traditionally recognise as making up their discipline and providing legal answers to normative questions[77] – is dealt with superficially, when not quietly set

[73] Friedrich V. Kratochwil, *Rules, Norms, and Decisions: On the Conditions of Practical and Legal Reasoning in International Relations and Domestic Affairs* (Cambridge: Cambridge University Press, 1991).

[74] Vendulka Kubálková, 'Foreign Policy, International Politics, and Constructivism', in Vendulka Kubálková (ed.), *Foreign Policy in a Constructed World* (New York: M.E. Sharpe, 2001), 15–37, at 28.

[75] Sikkink and Finnemore, 'Taking Stock', 392–393: 'constructivism is an approach to social analysis that asserts the following: (a) human interaction is shaped primarily by ideational factors, not simply material ones; (b) the most important ideational factors are widely shared or intersubjective beliefs, which are not reducible to individuals; and (c) these shared beliefs construct the interests and identities of purposive actors'.

[76] Alexander Wendt, 'Anarchy Is What States Make of It: The Social Construction of Power Politics' (1992) 46(2) *International Organization* 391–425. See also Onuf, *World of Our Making*.

[77] See Prosper Weil, 'Towards Relative Normativity in International Law?' (1983) 77 *AJIL* 413–442, at 424 (arguing against the 'multiplication of … degrees of normative intensity').

aside. As the authors of a comprehensive review of this literature note, 'most theories of compliance with international law are at bottom theories of the behavioral influence of legal rules'.[78] It is not clear that the legal status of the norms in question matters for these theories. At best, what lawyers view as the binding character of a rule translates into a signal of 'sincere and deeply held expectations of compliance' on the part of the actors involved in an interaction.[79] Within the conceptual framework of this scholarship, there is little room for an ontological distinction between law and non-law. Instead, compliance scholars usually consider state commitments in various forms, seeing what lawyers view as binding rules as a specific category of commitments within 'a spectrum of commitment along which states choose to locate their promises'.[80] A political commitment made at a high-level summit, or acquiescence to a threat made by another state, might be behaviourally as relevant as, or more relevant than, a fully ratified treaty, a final judicial decision, or a *jus cogens* norm.

Additionally, or perhaps as a consequence, this literature often provides little clarity on what exactly it means for a rule to be 'complied with'. As Benedict Kingsbury explains, the underlying assumption of much of this literature – in particular, of those who resort to the billiard-ball model – is that a well-defined and unambiguous body of rules exists that can be contrasted to 'behavior' and lead to a numerical figure reflecting the 'rate' of compliance with said rules.[81] But, even assuming for a moment that a unified body of rules of international law can be agreed upon (or a subset of rules isolated from the rest of the international legal system), this would at most show a level of correlation between the examined behaviour and the rules in question. And, as many will point out, even a high correlation in one issue-area does not guarantee that the legal rule is responsible for, or even a relevant factor in, states' decision to adopt a certain conduct.[82]

78 Kal Raustiala and Anne-Marie Slaughter, 'International Law, International Relations and Compliance', in Walter Carlsnaes, Thomas Risse, and Beth A. Simmons (eds.), *The Handbook of International Relations* (London: Sage, 2002), 539.

79 Shelton, 'Introduction: Law, Non-Law and the Problem of "Soft Law"', 17.

80 Andrew T. Guzman, 'A Compliance-Based Theory of International Law' (2002) 90 *California Law Review* 1823–1887, at 1828.

81 Benedict Kingsbury, 'The Concept of Compliance as a Function of Competing Conceptions of International Law' (1998) 19 *Michigan Journal of International Law* 345–372, at 346.

82 See, for example, Daniel W. Drezner, *All Politics is Global: Explaining International Regulatory Regimes* (Princeton, NJ: Princeton University Press, 2007), 11–25; Thomas M. Franck, *The Power of Legitimacy among Nations* (Oxford: Oxford University Press, 1990), 47.

These difficulties are not unknown to the compliance literature and are acknowledged by the very authors of the most widely used definition for compliance – 'a state of conformity or identity between an actor's behavior and a specified rule'.[83] Kal Raustiala and Anne-Marie Slaughter explain that compliance may well 'occur for reasons entirely exogenous'[84] to the rule being complied with. In other words, compliance does not, or not necessarily, stem from legal rules.[85] The binding or non-binding character of a rule is of little import in the question of whether it will be complied with. This will mean, when it comes to assessing the role of adjudicators, that the binding/non-binding divide, crucial as it is for the proceedings before most ICs, to their reasoning and their rulings, cannot itself be used to explain the subsequent step of compliance with these rulings. The effect of these rulings will depend not on their bindingness or lack thereof but on their ability to mobilise the 'external inducements and internal impulsions'[86] that lead states to comply with their international commitments.

This brief outline of the basic literature barely scratches the surface of the engagement of the discipline of international relations with compliance. It nonetheless provides context for an analysis of the different elements that, according to compliance theorists of different strands, may induce states to comply with their international commitments. On one end of the spectrum, those adopting a realist outlook focus entirely on states as interest-maximising, rational actors, constrained only by the prospect of sanctions by other states. On the other end of the spectrum are those who emphasise the role of norms and domestic internalisation processes in engendering the regular patterns of behaviour that regime participants identify as compliance. In between are scholars of various stripes who, while taking the basic set-up of realism as a starting point, believe that norms are complied with because they allow actors to reduce complexity and facilitate state interaction. These

83 Raustiala and Slaughter, 'International Law, International Relations and Compliance', 539.

84 Ibid.

85 For this reason, some prefer to distinguish 'compliance', which implies conscious adjustment of conduct to legal obligations, from 'conformity', which implies a mere absence of non-conforming behaviour. See Michelle Madden Dempsey, 'Authority, Obedience, and Justification' (2021) 90(2) *University of Cincinnati Law Review* 408–453, at 423.

86 Louis Henkin, *How Nations Behave: Law and Foreign Policy*, 2nd edn (New York: Columbia University Press, 1979 [1968]), 45 ff.

scholars either focus on the ability of norms and institutions to reduce transaction costs inherent to repeated interactions ('rationalists', 'neoliberals', or 'institutionalists')[87] or on the limitations to 'rational' behaviour on the part of states and their agents (behavioural theorists).[88]

2.3.2 *Externally Induced Compliance: Sanctions, Mutual Expectations, and Rational Choices*

Realism in international relations emerged in large measure as a counterpoint to a perceived excessive optimism with regard to the ability of international law to restrain states. For realists, the lack of a centralised, hierarchically organised coercive apparatus in the international order means that compliance with ostensibly binding legal norms is entirely conditional upon the relevant norms matching the interests of powerful states. If a state's representatives wish to adopt a certain course of action and believe that other states will not stop them from adopting it, any legal norms that purportedly stand in their way will be interpreted as allowing this conduct or will be ignored entirely. A more recent reference for the realist paradigm is Jack Goldsmith and Eric Posner's *The Limits of International Law*, whose central claim is that, outside of limited opportunities for cooperation, 'international legal rhetoric is used to mask or rationalize behaviour driven by self-interest factors that have nothing to do with international law'.[89]

Pursuant to this view, neither international legal rules nor the institutions that apply them meaningfully constrain the conduct of states. At most, they provide a veneer of legitimacy to decisions made by the representatives of the most powerful states on the basis of their perceived self-interest. What we call 'international law' does little more than provide states with a means to coordinate their behaviour to avoid inefficiencies. They may, for example, agree on air traffic rules, which, once established, no state has an interest in violating. However, whenever the expected benefits of a violation would seem to outweigh the expected

[87] A foundational author for this strand is Douglass North, in particular Douglass C. North, *Institutions, Institutional Change and Economic Performance* (Cambridge: Cambridge University Press, 1990/2012).

[88] Foundational texts for this strand are collected in Daniel Kahneman, Paul Slovic, and Amos Tversky (eds.), *Judgment under Uncertainty: Heuristics and Biases* (Cambridge: Cambridge University Press, 1982/2013).

[89] Goldsmith and Posner, *The Limits of International Law*, 226.

benefits of complying in the eyes of state agents, legal rules would not prevent the state from violating its obligations.[90]

Although many scholars identified with realism accept the fact of significant overall conformity of state behaviour to legal norms, they follow Hans Morgenthau in arguing that this conformity is not related to international norms themselves but takes place merely because (and to the extent that) legal compliance matches a state's perceived interests: 'compliance and the norms themselves emerge from the states' pursuit of self-interested policies on the international stage'.[91] High levels of compliance can occur essentially because the rules themselves enshrine power relations, giving legal form to arrangements and actions that would take place in any case, due to the interest of the states involved in the interaction and the correlation of forces between them. George Downs, David Rocke, and Peter Barsoom, for example, argue that the high level of observed compliance is due to states entering into 'shallow' agreements, which merely require them to adopt the conduct that they would have preferred to adopt even in the absence of an agreement.[92]

In sum, for realists, states generally comply with (or rather, conform to) international legal rules because these rules largely provide for behaviour which states would have adopted in the absence of rules.[93] Although states offer legal arguments to justify their conduct, these arguments are provided mainly to ensure continued relations with other states, and have no bearing on the behaviour itself.[94] Limitations on state behaviour depend not on the existence of legal rules but on the underlying prospect of a sanction. It is this prospect, rather than the rules, that can deter unlawful behaviour.

2.3.3 *Sanctions in International Law and the Horizontal Legal Order*

The notion that reactions from other states provide the sanctions that make international law into a legal system is not alien to international

90 Ibid., 226.

91 Jack L. Goldsmith and Eric A. Posner, 'A Theory of Customary International Law' (1999) 66 *University of Chicago Law Review* 1113–1177, at 1113.

92 George W. Downs, David M. Rocke, and Peter N. Barsoom, 'Is the Good News About Compliance Good News About Cooperation?' (1996) 50(3) *International Organization* 379–406; George W. Downs and Michael A. Jones, 'Reputation, Compliance, and International Law' (2002) 31(S1) *The Journal of Legal Studies* S95–S114.

93 Downs et al., 'Is the Good News about Compliance Good News about Cooperation?', 380.

94 Goldsmith and Posner, *The Limits of International Law*, 224.

lawyers. Two well-known proponents of this idea are Hans Kelsen and Georges Scelle. For Kelsen, sanctions are the distinctive element of a *legal* normative system. Thus, for international law to be such a legal system, it should 'provide for coercive acts (enforcement actions) as the consequence of a certain conduct of states determined by international law'.[95] Due to its decentralised character, he concluded, international law leaves the application of coercive acts to individual states. Writing in 1952, Kelsen viewed inter-state reprisals (which later evolved into countermeasures) and war as the sanctions of international law: '[i]f reprisals and war – typical measures of self-help – are not considered as legal sanctions because a minimum of centralization is considered to be an essential element of the law, the social order we call general international law cannot be regarded as law in the true sense of the term'.[96] In Kelsen's sanctions-based conception, international law can be considered a legal order because (and to the extent that) states are willing to respond to perceived violations with coercive measures.[97]

Georges Scelle's concept of '*dédoublement fonctionnel*' ('split role') performed a similar role. Its core idea was that state agents play a dual role when acting on the international stage. Although seeking to address a different question – that of the different allegiances that characterise state officials when interacting with international law – Scelle also saw in agents of individual states the key enforcers of the international legal order. Despite deriving their competences from a domestic legal order, state agents often employ their powers (i.e. their *potestas* under the domestic legal order) to 'ensure the efficacy of another legal order deprived of the organs necessary for this realisation, or possessing these organs only insufficiently'.[98]

[95] Hans Kelsen, *Principles of International Law* (New York: Rinehart, 1952), 22.

[96] Ibid., 36. See Francois Rigaux, 'Hans Kelsen on International Law' (1998) 9 *European Journal of International Law* 381–408.

[97] Note that willingness to adopt coercive measures is 'signaled' far more often than the relevant measures are deployed. See Daniel W. Drezner, *The Sanctions Paradox: Economic Statecraft and International Relations* (Cambridge: Cambridge University Press, 1999), 14–16.

[98] Georges Scelle, 'Le phénomène juridique du dédoublement fonctionnel', in Walter Schätzel (ed.), *Rechtsfragen der Internationalen Organisation – Festschriftfir H. Wehberg* (Frankfurt: Klostermann, 1956), 331 ('les agents dotés d'une compétence institutionnelle ou investis par un ordre juridique utilisent leur capacité "fonctionnelle" telle qu'elle est organisée dans l'ordre juridique qui les a institués, mais pour assurer l'efficacité des normes d'un autre ordre juridique privé des organes nécessaires à cette réalisation, ou n'en possédant que d'insuffisants').

Thus, the so-called realist position is not entirely divorced from legal scholarship on international law. Both Kelsen and Scelle would likely agree that it is the prospect of a sanction that gives international legal rules their normative character.[99] On the other hand, the claim that, because there are no centralised sanctions, international law is *irrelevant* appears to throw out the baby with the bath water. Even if one acknowledges that the lack of a centralised social apparatus tasked with enforcing rules and judgments makes international law distinct from domestic law, the logical response is not to assume the irrelevance of legal norms but to consider how they operate in this different setting. In other words, one must consider how a horizontal or interactional legal system can exist and, potentially at least, hold influence over state behaviour.

Richard Steinberg has argued that the supposed realist claim that 'international law does not matter' is a 'straw-man claim', used by international lawyers 'as the perfect foil for arguments that international law is important'.[100] Indeed, it is noteworthy that the oft-cited idea that international relations realists deem international law 'epiphenomenal' (an euphemism for 'irrelevant') appears to have spread among critics of realism. Although some critics even use the word between quotation marks,[101] it does not seem to appear in the actual work of key realists. A quotation often invoked in this context is John Mearsheimer's statement that 'institutions have minimal influence on state behavior, and thus hold little promise for promoting stability in the post-Cold War world'.[102] This claim, however, concerns only core issues of world order and military affairs. Despite military affairs being a core area – occasionally, a literally vital area – of inter-state relations, a significant logical jump is required to apply this claim to international trade or investment

[99] Scelle also looked into how then young international organisations, in particular the United Nations and the International Labour Organization, could replace this arrangement with agents fully committed to the international legal system. See Antonio Cassese, 'Remarks on Scelle's Theory of "Role Splitting" (Dédoublement Fonctionnel) in International Law' (1990) 1 *EJIL* 210–231.

[100] Richard Steinberg, 'Wanted – Dead or Alive: Realism in International Law', in Jeffrey L. Dunoff and Mark A. Pollack (eds.), *Interdisciplinary Perspectives on International Law and International Relations: The State of the Art* (Cambridge: Cambridge University Press, 2013).

[101] David J. Bederman, 'Constructivism, Positivism, and Empiricism in International Law' (2001) 89(2) *Georgetown Law Journal* 469–500, at 473.

[102] John J. Mearsheimer, 'The False Promise of International Institutions' (1995) 19(3) *International Security* 5–49, at 7.

treaties, environmental conservation obligations, human rights commitments, or the law of the sea.

In this regard, the realist claim may be understood as an international relations version of the Kelsenian view that, in order for a normative phenomenon to be considered 'law', a violation of its prescriptions must entail sanctions, including, at some point along the logical chain of events, coercive sanctions.[103] The challenge with the subsequent step – considering that international law is of little import – is that the behavioural influence of sanctions does not require their deployment. Ostensibly voluntary compliance, taking place at Layer 1, if often motivated by external forces, as the *prospect* of sanctions leads states' representatives to adjust their conduct accordingly. By focusing on cases in which sanctions have been deployed, one risks losing sight of the situations in which they are most useful: when, upon considering the prospect of an external response to their actions, states modify their conduct in order to avoid sanctions.[104]

If this pre-sanctions effect of international commitments is set aside, one is often left only with the most intractable situations, those in which the influence of the prospect of coercion over Layer 1 has been judged insufficient to induce rule-compliant behaviour. Through its domestic decision-making processes, a state has weighed the foreseeable scenarios for its conduct and determined that the foreseeable sanctions are a price worth paying for a certain action. In these cases, in which the cost of sanctions has already been found acceptable, their deployment may add little to the incentive structure perceived by those who opted for a violation. Nonetheless, this deployment may, seemingly paradoxically, be perceived as necessary by states seeking to uphold the normative order, not in order to change the present behaviour of the perceived wrongdoer but to assure to this and other potential wrongdoers that they will be subject to sanctions – even sanctions that impose high costs to their adopters without being matched by changes in behaviour.[105] As a result, insights into how international law can 'work' through external inducements, even in the absence of an organised law enforcement apparatus, depend on understanding how rational, self-interested states

[103] Hans Kelsen, 'The Pure Theory of Law and Analytical Jurisprudence' (1941) 55 *Harvard Law Review* 44, 57–58.

[104] Daniel Drezner, 'The Hidden Hand of Economic Coercion' (2003) 57 *International Organization* 643–659, at 645.

[105] Drezner, *The Sanctions Paradox*, 27.

modify their behaviour in response to the prospect, and in some cases the threat, of responses from other states.

2.4 External Inducements to Comply: Rational Choice Theories

2.4.1 External Inducements and Rational Choice Theory: Law as Focal Points for Interaction

The supposed realist claim that 'international law does not matter', though possibly a strawman, provides a useful starting point – a 'null hypothesis', as Steinberg put it[106] – to examine how the interactional normative framework we refer to as 'international law' may affect state behaviour. The effect of norms can be examined on two levels: that of inter-state relations and that of the decisions of the individuals responsible for 'state behaviour'.

Accordingly, the remainder of this section considers how legal norms might make a difference to state behaviour even if one assumes the basic model of international relations adopted by realists, based solely on external inducements. Next, Section 2.5 will consider how international legal norms intervene 'internally' in the decision-making processes that determine state behaviour, leading to conformity with international law beyond that which might be expected if agents were acting pursuant to the proclaimed tenets of full rationality and entirely in the service of what they perceive as the aggregate self-interest of their states.

In the 'billiard balls', or 'black boxes', model of international relations, states are presumed to act as unitary agents, each acting rationally to maximise its own self-interest, in particular the security of its existence, its economic welfare and power, and perhaps its glory or prominence among nations.[107] Internal pro-compliance forces, which Henkin termed 'internal impulsions' for compliance,[108] are assumed away. The question then becomes how, and to what extent, external forces might nonetheless lead a rational, interest-maximising state to act differently than it would in the absence of legal rules.

[106] Steinberg, 'Wanted – Dead or Alive: Realism in International Law', 146.

[107] The latter element already sits in tension with an extreme version of the idea of 'rational' states, since glory or prominence are non-instrumental objectives. See Richard Ned Lebow, *A Cultural Theory of International Relations* (Cambridge: Cambridge University Press, 2009).

[108] Henkin, *How Nations Behave*, 46.

The adoption of self-interest-based models does not imply that international legal norms are irrelevant to state behaviour, merely that they lack independent explanatory power. Jack Goldsmith and Eric Posner state that their core claim in *The Limits of International Law* is that 'the best explanation for when and why states comply with international law is . . . simply that states act out of self-interest'.[109] As a result, for them, '[i]nternational law refers to equilibrium outcomes in games of cooperation and coordination among rational, self-interested states . . . International law can be, and often is, effective and stable because once cooperation begins, it is in the rational self-interest of states to maintain it'.[110] Considering specifically the question of compliance, a set of authors usually regarded as international law sceptics – George Downs, David Rocke, and Peter Barsoom – equally argue that 'the high level of compliance and the marginality of enforcement result from the fact that most treaties require states to make only modest departures from what they would have done in the absence of an agreement'.[111]

Putting the question in terms of whether a state would act differently in the absence of 'an agreement', however, somewhat misses the point. The setting within which each state makes choices is itself shaped by legal rules. It makes little sense to dismiss the relevance of international law of the sea on the grounds that state A's compliance with the rule assigning to state B a certain portion of the sea, as its territorial waters or exclusive economic zone, is self-interested. This largely amounts to accusing international law of being an interactional, rather than a hierarchical, legal order. The partition of competences over the various portions of the sea has been negotiated and renegotiated, on various occasions and through different means. Its purpose is not to impose from above a certain set of rules but to allow states, as entities with different interests operating on a shared planet, to interact, empowering each one to pursue its own objectives and minimising friction between them. To return to Lon Fuller's duality, the claim that international law operates only weakly, if at all, as a top-down 'instrument of social control', does not prevent it from acting quite successfully horizontally, as 'a means for facilitating human interaction'.[112]

109 Goldsmith and Posner, *The Limits of International Law*, 225.

110 Ibid., 4.

111 Downs et al., 'Is the Good News about Compliance Good News about Cooperation?', 396.

112 Fuller, 'Law as an Instrument of Social Control'. Recall that this does not imply viewing positively all the interactions that law facilitates.

Developing this view to its full potential, the so-called 'rational choice theories' of international law consider that norms are relevant for inter-state interaction insofar as their negotiation and existence allow coordination and cooperation.[113] As Joel Trachtman puts it, pursuant to this view 'international law is produced in order to allow states to achieve their preferences with greater effectiveness'.[114] In some areas requiring mostly 'coordination', having *some* set of rules is in each state's self-interest and, once the rules are in place, so is complying with them. In these areas – the obvious example being, once more, air traffic rules – having rules allows self-interested states to better coordinate their actions and avoid conflict. Areas requiring mostly 'cooperation', on the other hand, are those in which conduct that maximises a state's self-interest may be detrimental to the interests of other states, either immediately (as often happens in international trade) or over time (as in pollution with transboundary effects).

2.4.2 External Pro-Compliance Forces: Andrew Guzmán's 'three Rs' of Compliance

The reasons for compliance with coordination rules are relatively straightforward: once a set of rules exists, it is in each state's self-interest to comply with it.[115] The more challenging puzzle emerges in cooperation-type scenarios: those which require states to do something that is not in their immediate self-interest, refraining, for example, from adopting self-serving economic policies that harm other states' interests or environment, from exploiting oil in a neighbouring state's territorial waters, or from invading the territory of a militarily weaker state. In these cases, compliance (or 'cooperation') depends on 'the shadow of the future' – the responses a state might expect from others in case of violation.[116]

[113] Andrew Guzman, *How International Law Works: A Rational Choice Theory* (Oxford: Oxford University Press, 2008); George Norman and Joel P. Trachtman, 'The Customary International Law Game' (2005) 99 *AJIL* 541–580, at 541.

[114] Joel P. Trachtman, *The Economic Structure of International Law* (Cambridge: Harvard University Press, 2008), 11.

[115] This raises the question of whose interests the rules themselves serve. In many cases, a self-interested state may have an interest in complying with an existing normative arrangement but might gain more from an alternative normative arrangement. In these cases, a high level of compliance may be combined with attempts to change the normative arrangement by states that believe they have the ability to do so.

[116] Trachtman, *The Economic Structure of International Law*, 7.

These responses can involve international institutions or non-governmental actors. Given that states retain overwhelming control over material resources, the literature on these responses focuses on inter-state mechanisms of compliance control, whether bilateral (Layer 2) or diffuse (Layer 3). Andrew Guzmán explains compliance with norms in these cases through the 'three Rs of compliance': the risk of 'retaliation' from other states, that is, of purposeful harm towards violators; the risk of 'reciprocity' by other states, that is, of reciprocal non-compliance with the rules violated; and the risk of a cost to the wrongdoer's 'reputation' of violating its commitments.[117]

The 'retaliation' element corresponds to what Ellickson called 'second person' enforcement in his theory of horizontal normative systems, that is, a purposeful response by affected states resulting in direct and identifiable harm to the interests of the violator.[118] Although there are distinctions between the precise concepts in international law and in political science, international law expressly incorporates a form of bilateral response to a violation through the concept of countermeasures. A state injured by a violation may respond by taking countermeasures, that is, by refraining from performing some of its own obligations towards the wrongdoing state.[119] Other forms of expressly authorised bilateral retaliation are retorsions (unfriendly responses that do not involve disregarding any legal obligation) and, in case of violations of norms relating to the use of force, self-defence.[120]

In the political science literature, retaliation is considered an effective means by which actors in repeated interactions are able to sustain a mutually desirable arrangement, requiring them to act in certain ways, even when an alternative course of conduct is available that brings an immediate benefit to the actor adopting it while disadvantaging other actors (which one may call a norm violation or, in political science-speak,

[117] Guzman, 'A Compliance-Based Theory of International Law'.

[118] See also the 'second-party mode of reasoning' in Kratochwil, *Rules, Norms and Decision*, 35–36.

[119] ILC Articles, Art. 49, 52. Under the ILC Articles, countermeasures (contrary to the notion of reprisals) must be adopted and designed not as punishment for the violation but as means of obtaining cessation of the unlawful act and provision of reparation for the injury it caused. See Elizabeth Zoller, *Peacetime Unilateral Remedies: An Analysis of Countermeasures* (Dobbs Ferry: Transnational, 1984); Serena Forlati, 'Reactions to Non-Performance of Treaties in International Law' (2012) 25 Leiden Journal of International Law 759–770.

[120] On the controversy around armed reprisals in contemporary international law, see Section 5.2.5.

'non-cooperation' or 'defection'). Robert Axelrod famously used game theory to model situations where non-cooperation can bring short-term gains to self-interested players. He examined how 'cooperation can emerge among egoists without central authority' if participants in the interaction employ a 'tit-for-tat' strategy, 'starting with cooperation, and thereafter doing what the other player did [cooperating or not] on the previous move'.[121] In other words, the threat of retaliatory non-compliance acts as a deterrent, fostering high levels of overall compliance.

A second reason for states to comply with their commitments is the prospect of reciprocity. To distinguish it from retaliation, which is a purposive response causing harm to the interests of the wrongdoer, reciprocity can be seen as the prospect of weakened compliance with the violated norm itself. In other words, each instance of non-compliance leads to the weakening of the perception among actors that a norm requires a certain behaviour. Significant non-compliance by all actors, or a few cases of egregious non-compliance, could lead to the perception that the rule no longer applies and has fallen into desuetude.

Here again international law features mechanisms that incorporate this social phenomenon into legal interaction. Customary international law can emerge from any behaviour, including behaviour that contradicts existing treaty rules.[122] Thus, if states repeatedly violate a rule of international law (whether customary or not), a new customary rule may emerge that displaces the previous rule. International law also provides an instrument through which states can actively apply reciprocity to treaty rules: under the Vienna Convention on the Law of Treaties, a material violation of a treaty allows other parties to respond by terminating or suspending the treaty.[123]

These legal mechanisms may seem paradoxical. They allow states to engage in conducts that objectively violate international law as a means to engender the evolution or dismantling of the violated rule. Realists might argue this underscores their claim that international law is

[121] Robert Axelrod, *The Evolution of Cooperation*, Revised Edition (New York: Basic Books, 2006), viii.

[122] Mark Eugen Villiger, *Customary International Law and Treaties: A Manual on the Theory and Practice of the Interrelation of Sources*, 2nd edn (Hague: Kluwer, 1997), 206 ff.

[123] Vienna Convention on the Law of Treaties, Vienna, 23 May 1969, in force 27 January 1980, 1155 UNTS 331, Article 60. See Forlati, 'Reactions to Non-Performance of Treaties'.

susceptible to manipulation by self-interested states. By the same token, however, these mechanisms create a deterrent against legal violations, especially when states derive significant benefits from the continued observance of the rule. In other words, the risk that customary or treaty rules may fall into desuetude – whether or not formally recognised as such by an adjudicator – should prompt self-interested states to act carefully in pursuing 'norm entrepreneurship' by disregarding rules or asserting exceptions. This is particularly true when they value the protection provided by this rule in other contexts. Other states, even if they cannot or do not retaliate, are likely to mimic the norm entrepreneur's behaviour by ignoring the rule or invoking the same exception in the future.

This dynamic may explain, for example, why even powerful states hesitate to infringe otherwise easily violable rules, such as those granting small coastal states control over their territorial sea or exclusive economic zone. While a powerful state might breach such a rule in a specific instance without facing immediate repercussions, doing so would undermine the broader framework of generally applicable rules. This would create uncertainty about territorial and maritime control for all states, including the powerful one, ultimately hampering its ability to advance its own interests. Without widely accepted norms governing the allocation of control over resources, states and companies would face the burden of repeatedly assessing complex power dynamics and risks whenever organising resource access or supply chains. Such arrangements would lack stability and be perpetually vulnerable to challenges driven by states' shifting self-interests. To avoid this costly and potentially volatile scenario, even dominant states have a vested interest in respecting and upholding rules that empower smaller and weaker states to govern resources within their designated territorial and maritime zones.

The third of the 'three Rs' of compliance with international law identified by Guzmán is reputation. The concept of reputation is relatively straightforward: states that comply with their obligations develop a 'reputation for compliance', while those that violate their obligations develop a reputation for non-compliance. As Guzmán puts it, a 'good reputation is valuable because it makes promises more credible and, therefore, makes future cooperation both easier and less costly'.[124] Within this framework, a state's reputation functions like a political

[124] Guzman, *How International Law Works*, 33.

credit score, influencing how other states approach negotiations. A state perceived to have a poor reputation for compliance faces difficulties entering into new agreements, as other states will likely view it as untrustworthy. Even if negotiations proceed, the low-reputation state will probably be required to accept more onerous commitments than those imposed on a state with a stronger compliance record. These heightened demands serve to offset the perceived risk of non-compliance and may include additional guarantees that would not be required from a high-reputation state. From this perspective, reputation incentivises states to honour their obligations, even in the absence of immediate retaliation or reciprocal consequences, as maintaining a good reputation ultimately aligns with their long-term self-interest.

2.4.3 The Challenge of Reputation and the Limits of External Inducements

The concept of reputation is controversial, in part, due to how much work it is supposed to do. Theoretical frameworks that maintain that states modify their behaviour to comply with international commitments while also assuming away all internal motivations to comply must postulate that *some* external sanction prevents self-interested, rational states from ignoring their obligations. However, a significant portion of observed compliance with norms is not plausibly explained either by foreseeable retaliation or by particularly consequential reciprocity. Reputational loss vis-à-vis other states might fill this gap and explain this additional compliance, but can do so only if one expands its scope in ways that can become implausible.

Thus, if a reputational cost is to deter a purely materially self-interested state from violating its human rights obligations, such a state must believe that this violation will harm its prospects of obtaining some material benefit. However, it is not clear that a state's reputation for respecting the human rights of its population is relevant for other, equally materially self-interested, states dealing with that state in the economic field. Indeed, a state with a reputation for prioritising the rights of workers, local communities, indigenous peoples, or the environment, over the material self-interest of companies – domestic or foreign – may take a 'reputational hit' in its economic dealings with other states.

For example, New Zealand's recognition of its Maori population's rights means that its trade agreements with its most important partners contain an exception clause allowing non-compliance with its economic obligations, if this is required to comply with its obligations towards the Maori.[125] Many of New Zealand's trade partners may praise its commitments towards the Maori and even consider as legitimate the ensuing obstacles to trade and investment. But, if they are negotiating as self-interested states, these trade partners will consider these obstacles as such, that is, as potential hurdles against New Zealand complying with its trade and investment commitments. In this case, the 'reputational credit score' of New Zealand vis-à-vis its trading partners might decrease, rather than increase, through New Zealand's compliance with its obligations towards its Maori population.

In other words, the difficulty with the notion of reputation as a deterrent to breach is not that it is not a consideration at all. Instead, the issue lies in the enormity of the task it is meant to perform in an interaction among entirely rational, self-interested states, lacking any internal (Layer 1) motivation to comply. A key shortcoming of retaliation and reciprocity as international law's sanctions is how poorly they perform in multilateral contexts, where obligations are owed to a diffuse group, or where a treaty promotes an environmental or human rights objective (a 'public good'), so that no specific actor has an incentive to be a 'second-party enforcer'.[126] Reputation, Guzmán asserts, is 'capable of explaining the multilateral cooperation that we observe, even in the public good areas'.[127] This wholly external version of reputation would thus be required to cause calculating, self-interested states to comply with their international obligations, even in the absence of foreseeable retaliation or reciprocity, out of a generic concern with uncertainty surrounding other states' future reactions.

This seems implausible. At a minimum, a 'thicker' concept of reputation — one that incorporates less rationalist considerations such as state pride, the personal shame of state officials, or politicians' concern with their legacy — seems necessary to plausibly explain compliance in

[125] Comprehensive and Progressive Agreement for Trans-Pacific Partnership, 8 March 2018, in force 30 December 2018, Article 29.6; EU-New Zealand FTA, 30 June 2022, Article 25.6. UK-New Zealand FTA, 22 February 2022, chapter 22. New Zealand's obligations originate from the 1840 Waitangi Treaty, which is now, as a matter of international law, part of New Zealand's domestic legal system.

[126] Alexander Thompson, 'The Rational Enforcement of International Law: Solving the Sanctioners' Dilemma' (2009) 1 *International Theory* 307–321.

[127] Guzman, *How International Law Works.*

these cases.[128] A more refined account would recognise that reputation does not function solely as an external sanction but rather conflates two related but distinguishable mechanisms of social control. In addition to operating at Layer 3, as a diffuse 'compliance score' maintained by other states, reputation (or rather, the prospect of reputational loss) acts by triggering feelings of shame, guilt or concern in individual state agents, regarding their own actions or those of their state, thus operating at Layer 1.[129] Without the latter component, the effects of reputation on state agents, and as a consequence its explanatory power for state behaviour, are likely severely limited.[130]

With their wholly external conception of reputation, rational choice theorists aim to assume away all of a state's internal motives to comply with international obligations, only to replace them with an externalised but generic and undefinable state-wide concern for reputation. It is no wonder that, for those who adopt a strict rational choice view of international law, this aspect of Guzmán's theory appears unsatisfactory.[131] On the other hand, most of those who do believe that there is a 'propensity to comply'[132] with international obligations, beyond compliance that can be explained by prospects of harmful retaliation or reciprocity at the inter-state level, will usually seek justifications for this tendency outside the framework of a theory whose very assumptions seem to deny this possibility.

2.5 Internal Impulsions for Compliance: Behavioural Theory, Two-Level Games, and Constructivism

Those who view compliance as more than a strategic choice made by self-interested states, and international law as more than the aggregate of

[128] See Wim Zimmerman, *Beyond Indeterminacy: On Reputation and Interpretation in International Law* (PhD Thesis defended at the University of Amsterdam, 2023, on file with author), 40–45.

[129] See on this Harlan Grant Cohen, 'Can International Law Work? A Constructivist Expansion' (2009) 27 *Berkeley Journal of International Law* 636–674, at 640 ('Guzman's Reputation-based account is much more than a rational choice theory. Rather, it is the beginning of a bridge between constructivist, liberal, and rational choice accounts').

[130] See Fuad Zarbiyev, 'International Law in an Age of Post-Shame' (2020) 9(3) *ESIL Reflections*.

[131] Downs et al., 'Is the Good News about Compliance Good News about Cooperation?'.

[132] Abram Chayes and Antonia Handler Chayes, *The New Sovereignty: Compliance with International Regulatory Agreements* (Cambridge, MA: Harvard University Press, 1998), 3–4.

strategic choices, must look within states for non-strategic reasons for complying with rules. Admitting non-strategic compliance significantly expands the range of possibilities for international rules to influence the behaviour of states.

In Ellickson's individual-oriented model of levels of social control, internal motivations to comply are lumped together as 'personal ethics' under Level 1. In states, Layer 1 of international social control encompasses a plurality of political, social, and psychological processes. Scholars have taken three main, non-mutually exclusive, theoretical pathways to explain the 'internal' effects that international legal rules produce over state conduct. These 'internal' effects lead to compliance in cases where rational consideration of a state's material interests and possibilities, and the foreseeable consequences of its actions, might suggest a breach as the rational course of action. The first pathway involves departing from perfect rationality and integrating into the 'billiard balls' model of the international order insights from the field of behavioural studies. These insights suggest that individuals, including those in positions of institutional responsibility, do not act rationally in the sense of exploring every conceivable option and calculating costs and benefits. They act instead with *bounded rationality* and decide on the basis of *heuristics*. The second pathway involves departing from the assumption of the unitary state and applying rational choice theory to the *internal struggles* within the state, disaggregating the state into its component political coalitions. The third pathway departs the furthest from the assumptions of rational choice theory, proposing that human decisions often do not follow a 'logic of consequences' but a 'logic of appropriateness'. International norms, once internalised, inform individual views of what actions are appropriate, shaping both the objectives of states in their international relations (their 'self-interest') and the range of conducts they deem permissible to pursue these objectives.

2.5.1 Behavioural Theory: States as Actors with Bounded Rationality

Behavioural theorists have made key contributions to the field of economics, demonstrating empirically that – and, importantly, how – humans do not act rationally in the pursuit of calculable self-interest. Instead, humans act with bounded rationality and are guided by mental shortcuts ('heuristics').[133] Their insights have been brought to research in international law relatively recently, chiefly by Anne van Aaken[134] and Tomer Broude,[135] and have found fertile ground in international legal scholarship.[136] The empirical research methods used by behavioural theorists to assess decision-making by individuals are difficult to transpose to states or even to state leaders.[137] However, their findings – and how insightful they appear, once articulated – should at least put the burden on those continuing to use unbounded rationality as the basis for their theoretical framework to explain why demonstrable patterns in human decision-making and behaviour would not apply to the behaviour of state agents.

Empirical research on the role of heuristics in states' foreign policy is still embryonic.[138] Nonetheless, a number of heuristics present in human decision-making, demonstrated by behavioural theorists, can explain compliance with international law in situations in which such an explanation would be difficult in a model in which state agents act with unbounded rationality. Three important examples are loss aversion, the anchoring effect, and fairness-based judgment.

Loss aversion is an inherent human aversion to a decrease in utility, welfare, or status when compared to a perceived status quo. Amos Tversky and Daniel Kahneman demonstrated the phenomenon through experiments showing that individuals assign a higher value to a loss than to an equivalent gain.[139] This engenders the so-called endowment effect, or status quo bias: 'people view the existing state of affairs as an endowment that they value more than possibly improved conditions, which they associate with risk and uncertainty'.[140] And, as Daniel Peat notes, 'action which involves the loss of property, such as territory or arms,

133 Kahneman et al., *Judgment under Uncertainty*, 3 ff.

134 Anne van Aaken, 'Behavioral International Law and Economics' (2014) 55 *Harvard International Law Journal* 421–482.

135 Tomer Broude, 'Behavioral International Law' (2015) 163 *University of Pennsylvania Law Review* 1099–1157.

136 See the symposium following Daniel Peat, Veronika Fikfak, and Eva van der Zee, 'Behavioural Compliance Theory' (2022) 13 *Journal of International Dispute Settlement* 167–178. More broadly, see Benjamin van Rooij, 'Behavioral Jurisprudence: The Quest for Knowledge about the Ex-ante Function of Law and Behavior' (2020) 22(1) *Jerusalem Review of Legal Studies* 57–77.

137 van Aaken, 'Behavioral International Law and Economics', 481.

138 Both Broude and van Aaken conclude by proposing that empirical research be undertaken.

139 Amos Tversky and Daniel Kahneman, 'The Framing of Decisions and the Psychology of Choice' (1981) 211(4481) *Science* 453–458.

140 Broude, 'Behavioral International Law', 1140.

might be particularly difficult to take'.[141] If compliance is seen as part of the status quo, a state agent is likely to view it as preferable, all else being equal, to a violation that may lead to gains but is also a potential source of loss. For a state representative considering a course of action that might lead to retaliation or a reputational loss for their state (or, if disaggregating the state, for themselves), the prospective gain from non-compliance would need to be significantly larger than the prospective loss, from retaliation, reciprocity, or reputational damage, to be considered worth risking a loss in relation to the status quo.

The anchoring effect operates at the level of cognition rather than preferences. Given human difficulties with making objective assessments of reality, in particular but not solely a changing reality, individuals tend to evaluate new information on the basis of information they already possess: 'different starting points generate different evaluations'.[142] Information tends to be incorporated insofar as it is compatible with previously acquired information. And, when asked to make an assessment of reality, individuals previously provided with some information will use it as a 'reference point' and consider to what extent their assessment should deviate from it.[143] In terms of compliance, this suggests that decision-makers, having been informed that norms require or prohibit certain action, will consider not what the most rational course of action is, in light of a comprehensive assessment of their interests and existing possibilities, but whether there is reason to deviate from the reference point. Even a deviation, that is, non-compliance, is likely to remain partial. Rather than considering the full range of possible courses of action and their foreseeable outcomes, actors are likely to consider whether and how far to deviate from the parameters embodied in the available rule.

Finally, individuals, even those operating within a negotiation, rarely adopt wholly self-interested behaviour. Instead, individuals reason and act on the basis of elements such as altruism (some concern for the well-being of others), fairness (treating like cases alike), and justice (beyond-

[141] Daniel C. Peat, 'Perception and Process: Towards a Behavioural Theory of Compliance' (2022) 13 *Journal of International Dispute Settlement* 179–209, at 191.

[142] van Aaken, 'Behavioral International Law and Economics', 430 (citing Amos Tversky and Daniel Kahneman, 'Judgment under Uncertainty: Heuristics and Biases' (1974) 185 (4157) *Science* 1124–1131).

[143] Ibid., 429–430 (citing Edward J. Joyce and Gary C. Biddle, 'Anchoring and Adjustment in Probabilistic Inference in Auditing' (1981) 19 *Journal of Accounting Research* 120–145, at 125).

rational punishment of 'bad actors').[144] Rule compliance, additional to what could be expected from a set of rational, self-interested actors, may thus arise, first, out of less-than-self-interested behaviour by the complying actor. It may also arise from an assessment by a self-interested actor that its conduct will be sanctioned, beyond that which would be rational, by other actors, acting out of altruism towards the injured parties or the impulse for justice against a 'bad actor'.

These heuristics all operate within each state, as part of Layer 1 of compliance control. Even considering the billiard-ball model of state interaction, incorporating the insights from behavioural theory into models of human behaviour thus tends to produce a higher level of compliance with norms than that supposed by a model assuming wholly rational, purely self-interested unitary state actors. This tendency becomes even more acute once we take the next steps away from the rational choice model and challenge the assumption of the unitary state, as an actor with its own interests making decisions that it deems rational. This can be done by considering that domestic actors: (a) have their own interests and agendas; and (b) do not act entirely out of personal self-interest, but pursue their objectives in accordance with prevailing norms. These considerations are reflected, respectively, in the analysis of international politics as a two-level game and in so-called constructivist approaches to international relations.

2.5.2 State Conduct and Domestic Actors: Compliance and the Two-Level Game

Analysing state behaviour as that of actors with bounded rationality and subject to the same heuristics as individuals leaves intact the basic realist model of inter-state interaction, in which states interact as 'billiard balls', unitary actors pursuing their aggregate self-interest and seeking to act in ways that they believe will serve this self-interest. In reality, each state is constituted by a multitude of individuals, who split into factions and form coalitions according to political and economic interests, personal

[144] van Aaken, 'Behavioral International Law and Economics', 432–435. See also Tom R. Tyler, *Why People Obey the Law* (Princeton, NJ: Princeton University Press, 2006), 112 ('findings of [empirical] research [show that] compliance with the law is influenced by judgments about the legitimacy of legal authority'); Kim Richard Nossal, 'International Sanctions as International Punishment' (1989) 43 *International Organization* 301–322.

allegiances (including ethnic or religious), or societal preferences. One way to explain the higher-than-rational level of compliance with international legal norms is to analyse what international law interprets as 'state conduct' not as the product of decisions by unitary entities acting in pursuit of certain goals, whether rationally or not, but as the product of domestic struggles.

Disaggregating the state into its component coalitions allows perceiving state policy relevant for international law as not a separate 'foreign policy' but as a form of domestic policy. From this perspective, rule-formation, interpretation, and compliance are decisions made by agents of states not only in the pursuit of goals of the state as an objective aggregator of citizens' preferences but in the pursuit of goals of one or another of its component coalitions, including in their disputes with each other.

The result is a version of Robert Putnam's 'two-level game' of foreign policy, which takes as its starting point 'the inevitability of domestic conflict about what the "national interest" requires'.[145] Helen Milner has addressed in depth the question of how domestic actors influence state behaviour on the international plane.[146] Beth Simmons has investigated the other side of the equation – how international agreements influence domestic political dynamics – with respect to human rights agreements.[147] She considers three ways in which human rights treaties can affect domestic political dynamics. They allow elites to bring specific issues into national political debates; they permit litigation of issues in domestic courts; and they catalyse political mobilisation, allowing actors to circumvent substantive debate by framing their position as a demand for compliance with international commitments.[148]

There are therefore two different directions in which this version of the two-level game operates. Domestic coalitions may, on the one hand, seek to enshrine their preferences in international legal instruments and the

[145] Robert D. Putnam, 'Diplomacy and Domestic Politics: The Logic of Two-Level Games' (1988) 42 *International Organization* 427–460, at 460. Putnam is more interested in the ability of those sitting at the intersection between national politics and international negotiations to use the existence of each arena as an asset when negotiating in the other one.

[146] Helen V. Milner, *Interests, Institutions, and Information: Domestic Politics and International Relations* (Princeton, NJ: Princeton University Press, 1997).

[147] Beth A. Simmons, *Mobilizing for Human Rights: International Law in Domestic Politics* (Cambridge: Cambridge University Press, 2009).

[148] Ibid., 14–15.

practice of bodies operating at the international level. On the other hand, they may, concomitantly or successively, seek to enshrine compliance with the relevant norms within the domestic legal and political order. The Ottawa Convention Banning Landmines,[149] probably the most striking success case of civil society influence over international law, was itself the result of intense work by organised civil society. Many of the organisations involved worked against the interests of landmine producers in their own countries.[150] The adoption of the Convention, in turn, allowed these same organisations to push for internalisation – thus creating legal norms within the domestic hierarchy of the state, enforceable through its coercive apparatus – on grounds that prohibiting landmines was no longer a matter of domestic policy-making only but one of compliance with international obligations.[151]

This example highlights another aspect of the two-level game that may promote compliance: the internationalisation of coalitions.[152] Not only can promotion of objectives go beyond the jurisdiction where a coalition operates primarily but, in many cases, internationalisation is key. Internationalisation may assist a coalition in promoting its objectives in three manners. First, if one takes a behavioural or a constructivist perspective, internationalisation may itself produce effects on state conduct by inducing the perception that there is a 'gold standard' for conduct, which would demand affirmative justification for non-compliance. Second, a transnational coalition pressing for compliance with certain norms everywhere can counter the argument, common in domestic politics, that a state's agreement to self-limitation will harm it to the benefit of other states. Third, if one takes a more realist approach, and believes that only external sanctions change state behaviour, internationalisation allows coalitions to mobilise other jurisdictions to pressure for fulfilment of their objectives in their home jurisdiction. The result is that domestic coalitions, in pursuit of their agenda or to isolate certain

[149] Convention on the Prohibition of the Use, Stockpiling, Production and Transfer of Anti-Personnel Mines and on Their Destruction (the 'Ottawa Convention'), entered into force 1 March 1999, 36 ILM (1997) 1507.

[150] Kenneth Anderson, 'The Ottawa Convention Banning Landmines, the Role of International Non-Governmental Organizations and the Idea of International Civil Society' (2000) 11 *European Journal of International Law* 91–120.

[151] Oriol Costa, 'The Unexpected EU Leadership on Landmines: The Influence of the Ottawa Convention on the EU' (2009) 18 *European Security* 245–261.

[152] See Nina Reiners, *Transnational Lawmaking Coalitions for Human Rights* (Cambridge: Cambridge University Press, 2021).

decisions from the political process, may use their political influence domestically to empower international law and its institutions in manners that might seem irrational if the state's overall interests, in particular its interest in retaining the ability to change policies at will, were the controlling motive for state conduct.[153]

Two well-documented developments offer particularly striking examples of internationalisation being used to further a coalition's interests and objectives. First is the extraordinary rise of international investment law, applied by arbitral tribunals dissociated from the domestic legal systems. Second is the transformation of the Law of the European Union from a body of interactional inter-state law into a dominant element in the domestic legal hierarchy of each European Union (EU) member state. In both cases, coalitions operating transnationally have not only established an international, interactional legal regime but enmeshed the regime's norms into domestic legal hierarchies. In both cases, the outcome was to make the international regime enforceable directly by the domestic courts of each participating state – and, subsidiarily, by the courts of other participants of the regime – thus strengthening both internal and external compliance-inducing forces, including against states' subsequent change of heart (or government).

The contemporary treaty-based international investment law regime was built slowly, starting from the late 1950s.[154] Rather than featuring a single overarching treaty, international investment law is constituted by a patchwork of bilateral and regional agreements, which together provide bases for transnational investors to bring, before arbitral tribunals operating at the international level, claims against participating states that investors believe discriminated against them or treated them unfairly.[155] These agreements do not simply bind participating states in the traditional sense of establishing obligations binding at the international level. They also allow investors to obtain awards for damages from international investment tribunals that may be enforced in the domestic courts of the state found in breach without the need for a decision by

153 Xinyuan Dai, 'Why Comply? The Domestic Constituency Mechanism' (2005) 59 *International Organization* 363–398.

154 Taylor St John, *The Rise of Investor-State Arbitration: Politics, Law, and Unintended Consequences* (Oxford: Oxford University Press, 2018). For earlier origins, see Kate Miles, *The Origins of International Investment Law: Empire, Environment and the Safeguarding of Capital* (Cambridge: Cambridge University Press, 2013).

155 Stephan W. Schill, *The Multilateralization of International Investment Law* (Cambridge: Cambridge University Press, 2009).

the government to comply.[156] Additionally, under the applicable conventions, investment awards can usually be enforced in the courts of third states, removing from individual states the ability to prevent enforcement by changing their domestic law.[157] Finally, there is ample record of sanctions for non-compliance with international investment awards being sought, often successfully, from other states and the international financial institutions which provide, especially to developing countries, a crucial financial lifeline in times of crises and key funding for infrastructure projects.[158]

The international investment regime was not a product of states acting rationally to maximise their aggregate self-interest. It was an outcome, on the one hand, of the decisions of foreign policy professionals seeking to 'depoliticise' investment disputes which previously had to be taken up by the governments of investors' home states, leading to high-level political tensions (and occasional kinetic confrontation).[159] On the other hand, it was also the product of intense lobbying with governments, by a mix of well-funded lobbyists defending the interests of transnational investors and true believers in the economic growth and development benefits of governmental respect for (international) contracts and property rights.[160] Finally, it is impossible to ignore the objectives, beliefs, and interests of the public international lawyers and commercial arbitration lawyers who make up the bulk of the investment arbitration community in expanding

[156] Susan Choi, 'Judicial Enforcement of Arbitration Awards under the ICSID and New York Conventions' (1995) 28 *NYU Journal of International Law & Politics* 175–216.

[157] ICSID Convention, Arts 53–54; New York Convention on the Recognition and Enforcement of Foreign Arbitral Awards, Art. III. See Claudia Priem, 'International Investment Treaty Arbitration as a Potential Check for Domestic Courts Refusing Enforcement of Foreign Arbitration Awards' (2013) 10 *NYU Journal of Law & Business* 189–221.

[158] See Jorge E. Viñuales and Dolores Bentolila, 'The Use of Alternative (Non-Judicial) Means to Enforce Investment Awards against States', in Laurence Boisson de Chazournes, Marcelo Kohen, and Jorge E. Viñuales (eds.), *Diplomatic and Judicial Means of Dispute Settlement* (2012), 247–277; Peat, 'Perception and Process', 195–196.

[159] Michael Waibel, *Sovereign Defaults before International Courts and Tribunals* (Cambridge: CUP, 2011), 29–42.

[160] St John, *The Rise of Investor-State Arbitration*; Filip Batselé, 'Foreign Investors of the World, Unite! The International Association for the Promotion and Protection of Private Foreign Investments (APPI) 1958–1968' (2023) 34(2) *European Journal of International Law* 415–447; Ursula Kriebaum, 'Evaluating Social Benefits and Costs of Investment Treaties: Depoliticization of Investment Disputes', in Katia Fach Gómez, Anastasios Gourgourinis, and Catherine Titi (eds.), *International Investment Law and the Law of Armed Conflict* (Cham: Springer, 2020).

the reach of the protection offered by investment agreements – expanding their own intellectual and political influence as a by-product.[161] Once the interests and objectives of these coalitions are taken into account, the seemingly irrational investment regime can be seen as a product of essentially rational decisions made by the individuals that built it, shaped it, and continue to promote and enforce it, in developed and developing countries alike.[162]

A similar reasoning can be (and has been) used to explain the development of what is arguably the most constraining, and most complied with, international legal regime: the law of the EU.[163] EU law, which in its infancy relied on the compliance mechanisms and sanctions common to public international law regimes, acquired features over time that make it a *sui generis* legal regime that in some ways has left the field of public international law to constitute a 'new legal order'.[164] Three of these features are crucial: (i) the power of the CJEU to hear individual complaints and order monetary compensation from EU member states to individuals, including their own nationals, injured by violations of EU law; (ii) the direct effect of instruments of EU law, including EU regulations and CJEU rulings, which domestic judges in EU member states must apply irrespective of implementation by governments or parliaments; and

[161] Malcolm Langford, Daniel Behn, and Runar Hilleren Lie, 'The Revolving Door in International Investment Arbitration' (2017) 20 *Journal of International Economic Law* 301–331; Juan J. Garcia Blesa, 'Indeterminacy, Ideology and Legitimacy in International Investment Arbitration: Controlling International Private Networks of Legal Governance?' (2022) 35(5) *International Journal for the Semiotics of Law* 1967–1194.

[162] One could take this to an extreme and see the entirety of international law as the product of self-interested behavior by national coalitions seeking to promote their own interests domestically and abroad, mediated by states. The Marxist perspective on (international) law sometimes comes close to this view. See, for example, China Miéville, *Between Equal Rights: A Marxist Theory of International Law* (Leiden: Brill, 2005), 317–318 ('Law is a relation between subjects abstracted of social context, facing each other in a relationship predicated on private property, dependent on coercion'; 'internecine battles between the "warring brothers" of the ruling class make up a great swathe of the international legal structure').

[163] Joseph H.H. Weiler, 'The Transformation of Europe' (1991) 100 *Yale Law Journal* 2403–2483; Alec Stone Sweet, *The Judicial Construction of Europe* (Oxford: Oxford University Press, 2004); André Nollkaemper, 'The Role of National Courts in Inducing Compliance with International and European Law: A Comparison', in Marise Cremona (ed.), *Compliance and the Enforcement of EU Law* (Oxford: Oxford University Press, 2012).

[164] CJEU, Case 26/62 NV *Algemene Transport- en Expeditie Onderneming van Gend en Loos* v. *Nederlandse administratie der belastingen* [1963] ECR (English Spec Ed) 1, 12.

(iii) the doctrine of supremacy of EU law, which requires domestic courts of Members States to 'disapply' their own domestic law when inconsistent with EU law, and simultaneously requires domestic courts to apply the CJEU's interpretation of EU law – and, in case of doubt, to request such an interpretation from the CJEU. Combined, these three features make EU law the 'new legal order' that the CJEU has proclaimed it to be,[165] one that pervades the domestic legal order of EU member states and prevails, under their domestic legal order, over the rules and determinations made at the national level.[166]

With hindsight, it is possible to consider this system as being in the rational self-interest of EU member states. The 'pooling of sovereignty' that EU law enshrines allows EU member states to combine their political and economic resources to exert a level of influence over global affairs beyond the reach of any individual member state. It also allows them to resist pressures from non-members to act in certain ways that would be difficult for a government of an EU member state, even a large member state, to resist alone. By forcing joint decision-making, empowering EU institutions, and making non-compliance with EU law by state agents an uphill battle against their own legal order, EU law arguably enhances the political power and economic welfare of each EU member state. The many applications for EU membership, from virtually all countries with a defensible claim to being 'European',[167] and the willingness of candidate countries to engage in deep legal reforms for this purpose,[168] suggest that states see it as a rational move to join the EU.

It is far less clear that building up this strong legal regime was a rational decision for EU countries in the 1960s–1980s, at least if by 'rational' one means decisions that increase the ability of a state's decision-makers to decide independently from external constraints.

[165] Ibid.; also CJEU, *Case 6/64 Flaminio Costa* v. *ENEL [1964] ECR (English Spec Ed) 585 Summary No. 3.*

[166] Monica Claes, 'The Primacy of EU Law in European and National Law', in Anthony Arnull and Damian Chalmers (eds.), *Oxford Handbook of European Union Law* (Oxford: Oxford University Press, 2015); Dorota Leczykiewicz, 'Effectiveness of EU Law before National Courts: Direct Effect, Effective Judicial Protection, and State Liability', in Damian Chalmers and Anthony Arnull (eds.), *Oxford Handbook of European Union Law* (Oxford: Oxford University Press, 2015), 212–248.

[167] Eli Gateva, *European Union Enlargement Conditionality* (New York: Palgrave, 2015).

[168] Frank Schimmelfennig and Ulrich Sedelmeier, 'Governance by Conditionality: EU Rule Transfer to the Candidate Countries of Central and Eastern Europe' (2004) 11 *Journal of European Public Policy* 661–679.

As research has shown, the transformation of EU law into today's *sui generis* legal regime was conducted largely by its courts. The strong EU law was the product of an alliance between a CJEU willing to make decisions that increased the relevance of EU law vis-à-vis domestic laws (and, by extension, the relevance of its own decisions vis-à-vis those of domestic courts and politicians) and domestic courts willing to use EU law as a means of promoting their own roles in formulating domestic policy vis-à-vis the elected branches of government.[169] Whether or not the outcome is seen as rational for member states when considered as a whole, the actions of the CJEU and domestic courts were highly strategic in contributing to it.

Investment Law and EU Law are among the international legal regimes that engender the highest levels of compliance, certainly if one considers as compliance the payment of compensation ordered by international adjudicators. Both regimes would be difficult to explain through a fully realist lens, or even a fully rationalist lens, since they go beyond 'cooperation' and imply objective constraints, ingrained in domestic law, on the ability of states to alter their behaviour. Although human rights law is the branch of law usually associated with a state tying its own hands with respect to the ability of future political actors to modify domestic law, the rulings of human rights courts remain largely restricted to the international plane, requiring an active decision to comply, usually on the part of elected branches of government.[170] By contrast, investment law and EU law are embedded in the legal fabric (or, in the language of this chapter, legal hierarchy) of states themselves. As a result, rulings by the CJEU and awards of investment arbitrators are often complied with not by an actor considering a state's, or government's, interests or preferences, rational or otherwise, but by bureaucrats and judges performing their daily tasks within the legal hierarchy within which they operate. In the case of investment law, this may in fact lead a judge in state A to enforce obligations owed by state B vis-à-vis (an investor from) state C.[171]

[169] See, most recently, Tommaso Pavone and R. Daniel Kelemen, 'The Evolving Judicial Politics of European Integration: The European Court of Justice and National Courts Revisited' (2019) 25 *European Law Journal* 352–373; Weiler, 'The Transformation of Europe'; Karen Alter, 'The European Court's Political Power' (1996) 19 *West European Politics* 458–487.

[170] Courtney Hillebrecht, *Domestic Politics and International Human Rights Tribunals: The Problem of Compliance* (Cambridge: Cambridge University Press, 2014).

[171] See on this Section 5.5.3.

The pervasiveness of such bureaucratic or judicial compliance in one regime would seem to contradict not only the 'billiard balls' model of the international order but also any model based on a mere combination of preferences and instrumental rationality (unless, that is, this model is stretched so thin that it infers from any action taken that this was the preferred and rational action for the relevant actor). In reality, in a functioning hierarchical state, judges and bureaucrats do not act on the basis of case-specific considerations of their own interests or those of their state but seek to perform their tasks according to the laws and regulations that govern their conduct and provide for the issue at hand (possibly, but irrelevantly for present purposes, because they believe this is in their own long-term self-interest).

Contemplating the possibility of bureaucratic or judicial compliance does not serve only to demonstrate that pure rational calculation on behalf of state interests offers an insufficient account of reasons for compliance. It also opens the door for considering that not all state agents are driven by the desire to serve certain material interests, be it their states' or their own, by conducting constant assessments of how best to achieve this self-serving purpose. Hierarchically minded bureaucrats and judges will usually (though not always) ask instead what it is that they *should* do in a particular instance: enforce an arbitral award, apply a certain legal rule, grant a certain certification, or approve a certain legal act. And, while this may seem like a relatively unremarkable assessment of how judges and bureaucrats behave, it raises the question of why one should automatically assume that higher-level bureaucrats, politicians, and government leaders should be impervious to this rationale. If such bureaucratic compliance exists, then the assessment of reasons for compliance must contemplate the possibility that not only rank-and-file civil servants but also the actors we normally associate with 'political' decision-making by states sometimes act in the same way. They may comply with international rules and decisions not following an evaluation of self-interest but due to an assessment that applicable norms mandate a certain course of action, and there are no particularly strong reasons not to comply in a particular case.[172]

[172] This assessment matches the concept of 'rebuttable duties' in Basak Çali, *The Authority of International Law – Obedience, Respect, and Rebuttal* (Oxford: Oxford University Press, 2015), 80–84.

2.5.3 Constructivism: International Law as Shared Understandings

Mechanisms for compliance that operate at the domestic or intra-state level are sometimes set aside in explanations for state compliance with international law. In most cases, this is due to the underlying grand theories used by international relations scholars. Many of these theories take state preferences (the objectives and the preferred course of action of each state, and its starting position in its interactions with other states) as given, and only consider as significant compliance a choice of conduct that does not conform to these initial preferences.[173] This excludes from the analysis, by definition, the possibility that international legal rules may shape the state's very preferences or starting positions. This kind of analysis is useful in that it explains how external constraints affect a state's decision once domestic actors have settled their internal struggle to determine that state's preferences. But the theory's own blindness to the internal processes that lead to conforming behaviour should not be taken to mean that these processes do not exist.

Some scholars considering how states behave outright reject the model of the state as a rational actor. These scholars, who fall under the broad category of 'constructivists', argue that the 'behaviour' of states cannot be analysed in isolation from the social structures, including rules and institutions, that shape both their interests and their identities, in a 'process of signaling, interpreting and responding' that creates 'intersubjective meanings'.[174] Against the practice of seeking to understand state behaviour as a function of interests – be it those of the state as a whole or those of individuals – and then devising a role for a set of externally imposed 'international norms', constructivists argue that neither state interests nor norms are given. The social processes through which a state establishes its identity, together with the interaction between this collective self and other states, constitute what a state will perceive as its interests at any given point.[175]

The constructivist strand of the compliance scholarship emphasises the communicative function of rules in the international society, finding

[173] Goldsmith and Posner, *The Limits of International Law*; Downs et al., 'Is the Good News about Compliance Good News about Cooperation?'.

[174] Wendt, 'Anarchy Is What States Make of It', 391–425.

[175] Martha Finnemore and Kathryn Sikkink, 'International Norm Dynamics and Political Change' (1998) 52 *International Organization* 887–917; Alexander Wendt, *Theory of International Politics* (Cambridge: Cambridge University Press, 1999).

that, although coercive rule enforcement may be significant, it does not constitute the main drive behind compliance even in domestic societies, and is ultimately 'not of much use in international society'.[176] In the case of individuals, compliance with rules prevails when, and because, once a norm is internalised and perceived as legitimate, following it becomes the preferred option – and non-conformity a source of shame.[177] States are abstract entities, but the process of rule internalisation occurs in international law as well. Harold Koh argued that the interaction between states and the constant interpretation of rules 'leads to reconstruction of national interests, and eventually national identities'.[178] This strand of the scholarship emphasises the often informal nature of rule enforcement, through negative reactions from the community and, in extreme cases, ostracism of the offender.[179] Norms are seen not as elements external to state behaviour but as the shared understandings that allow states to interact in the first place. The interactions are based on a myriad underlying, quasi-unconscious, assumptions: what 'states' are, who can represent them, what they should strive for, and the roles of the various individuals involved in, and affected by, each interaction.

This conceptual framework erodes the distinction between a state acting 'in its own interests' and acting 'in compliance with international law'. The entire setting within which the question of compliance is relevant becomes communication-dependent, and the very distinction between 'interest' and 'norm' becomes blurry. Does a US military vessel captain respect Canadian or Cuban territorial waters out of self-interest or of compliance with norms? When the EU adopts a regulation banning imports of products causing deforestation, is this norm compliance due to internalisation or self-interested behaviour to protect local producers? Do member states of the Organization for Economic Co-operation and Development (OECD) incorporate soft norms produced within the organisation out of specific self-interest, as a means of generating a norm that they believe will benefit them, or out of an internalised belief that

176 Oran R. Young, *International Governance: Protecting the Environment in a Stateless Society* (Ithaca: Cornell University Press, 1994), 74, 195. See also Oran R. Young, *Compliance and Public Authority: A Theory with International Application* (Baltimore: John Hopkins University Press, 1979).

177 Cass R. Sunstein, 'On the Expressive Function of Law' (1996) 144 *University of Pennsylvania Law Review* 2021–2053, at 2030.

178 Harold Hongju Koh, 'Why Do Nations Obey International Law?' (1997) 106 *Yale Law Journal* 2659.

179 Sunstein, 'On the Expressive Function of Law', 2030.

this organisation is the appropriate forum for setting out common standards and avoiding friction? Constructivist explanations, despite not offering reproducible models for state interaction, often provide more plausible, multi-causal explanations for compliance in each particular case.

For the same reason, however, constructivist scholarship has a more challenging time proposing means for addressing non-compliance. Scholars often postulate a 'compliance pull'[180] or 'propensity to comply',[181] assuming that a desire to comply will emerge from the communicative processes between relevant actors. For example, Thomas Franck notes that compliance should increase with a 'community's perception of a rule's legitimacy' and 'that rule's claim to fairness'[182] but has little to say about how to address purposeful non-compliance.[183] Abram Chayes and Antonia Handler Chayes identify three main sources of non-compliance. They mention, first, ambiguities in normative text and indeterminacy in the content of norms; second, the limited capacity of states to comply; and, third, the time needed for social, economic, and political changes conveyed by international norms to enter the social fabric of states.[184] The solution to these sources of non-compliance must accordingly be 'managerial': determining a meaning for the rules and persuading states to comply. Breaches are seen as the product of miscommunication rather than wilful intent.

This feature marks the limits of the constructivist strand of scholarship as a tool for improving compliance with norms. Constructivism offers useful insights for when compliance occurs, when rational choice theory would expect it not to occur, and calls into question many of the assumptions underlying the various compliance models. It also provides a strong basis for considering that, in many cases, compliance arises not from concerns by 'the state' with external sanctions and threats but from action, by a variety of agents within the state, withing a logic of

180 Franck, *The Power of Legitimacy among Nations*, 43.

181 Chayes and Chayes, *The New Sovereignty*, 3–4.

182 Thomas M. Franck, *Fairness in International Law and Institutions* (Oxford: Oxford University Press, 1998), 8.

183 Franck's considerations in *The Power of Legitimacy among Nations* seem to merge the deontological and sociological meanings of 'norms': a 'rule' (which may be unrelated to legal text) is defined as a 'depiction and prediction of state conduct and of the pressure to comply felt by the state, even when it fails to comply' (Franck, *Fairness in International Law*, 43); this would seem to define away non-compliance.

184 Chayes and Chayes, *The New Sovereignty*, 9–17.

appropriateness.[185] Constructivism thus highlights elements of the tool-box for improving compliance that those focusing on sanctions and state-wide incentives might overlook: the training of state agents on how to identify, interpret, and incorporate international norms; the organisation of meetings and debates between these agents, and between them and those operating on the international level, to exchange experiences and views, and to form communication networks and personal and professional bonds; and the establishment of mechanisms to consolidate knowledge and adopt guidelines for action (whatever their legal status), be it through consensus, voting, or adjudication. These actions all tackle challenges for greater compliance by agents who would otherwise be willing to comply.

What this conceptual framework misses is how to deal with the remaining non-compliance. Even assuming that a large measure of observed non-compliance is due to miscommunication, interpretation mismatches, and a lack of capacity to comply, there remains the issue of how to address strategic, self-interested non-compliance. The image of humans as inherently well-meaning actors, who act selfishly due to misunderstandings or poor socialisation, is difficult to reconcile with any objective account of human interaction across history. And, like the other false image of the human being against which it is directed – that of the purely self-interested, fully rational actor – it misses a crucial part of the compliance tool-box.

In the decentralised international system, in which states operate as the primary focal points for decision-making – and, crucially, for decision-making regarding the application of coercion on individuals – a functioning normative system cannot depend solely on the internal processes taking place within each state. These Layer 1 internal processes, involving inter-individual interaction as well as intra-individual psychological processes, are the functional equivalent for states of 'personal ethics' in Ellickson's classification of systems of social control. Although a normative system without any degree of normative internalisation would be difficult to maintain, internalisation alone cannot produce such a system.[186]

[185] This can also be seen as an effect of the challenge of entirely disentangling rational choice analysis from constructivist and behavioural elements, once one is willing to open up the black box of the state and consider the individuals making the relevant decisions. See Cohen, 'Can International Law Work?, 667–673.

[186] In fact, internalisation itself is strongly connected to diffuse enforcement by social forces, including through mere discourse and condemnation of the failure by others to abide by normative standards. See Judith van Erp, 'Shaming and Compliance', in Benjamin van Rooij and Daniel Sokol (eds.), *The Cambridge Handbook of Compliance* (Cambridge:

Additionally, to remain effective, internalisation depends on the perception of fairness in the application of rules.[187] This means not solely that an actor must perceive the application of norms to its own conduct as fair, when considered in isolation, but also that it must perceive the norm as being valid for all members of the relevant society.[188] If no consequence ensues from one actor's violations of the relevant norm, other actors' perception of the norm as being applicable within that society will likely wither. Thus, the view of law as shared understandings that guide behaviour, on the basis of the logic of appropriateness, depends on these understandings remaining shared. Sanctions are the instruments through which actors, including states, uphold these shared understandings in the face of violations. In other words, the continued social applicability of what Henkin termed 'internal impulsions' to comply depends on the application of 'external inducements' against non-compliance, that is, sanctions. This is regardless of measurable effectiveness of these sanctions in the sense of changing the wrongdoer's specific behaviour. A sanction targets future conduct, and the conduct of other, similarly positioned actors, at least as much as it targets the specific wrongdoer and conduct against which it is ostensibly directed.

2.6 Conclusion

International law affects and influences state behaviour despite the lack of a centralised rule enforcer. The supposed realist view, which would consider international law 'epiphenomenal', is reflected in the work of legal scholars who consider that international law needs a functional equivalent to state-enforced sanctions to be a legal system. Although those taking an extreme sceptical view of international law are arguably

Cambridge University Press, 2021), 438–450; Christina Boyes, Cody D. Eldredge, Megan Shannon, and Kelebogile Zvobgo, 'Social Pressure in the International Human Rights Regime: Why States Withdraw Treaty Reservations' (2023) 54(1) *British Journal of Political Science* 241–259.

[187] Franck, *Fairness in International Law.*

[188] The norm itself may, of course, incorporate different treatment for different members. Examples in international law are the concepts of Common but Differentiated Responsibilities, in international environmental law, and that of Special and Differential Treatment favouring developing countries and least-developed countries, in international trade law. See Nicolas Lamp, 'How Some Countries Became "Special": Developing Countries and the Construction of Difference in Multilateral Trade Lawmaking' (2015) 18 *Journal of International Economic Law* 743–771.

overstating the effects of any legal system on behaviour, their view, which assumes away voluntary compliance and norm internalisation, provides a useful starting point for an assessment of how international law influences state behaviour.

The so-called compliance scholarship of international relations has, over the past decades, debated the influence of international law over the conduct, or 'behaviour', of states. Some of this scholarship has focused precisely on how forces external to a state, chiefly the responses or the prospect of responses by other states, may influence the decisions of state agents, leading international norms to have effects over their decision-making. These forces are particularly relevant to those who take a sceptical view of the inherent value of international norms for the decision-making process that leads to state behaviour, who instead consider states as interest-maximising, unitary rational actors. I have argued that, even if one is to accept this viewpoint, international norms remain relevant to the extent that they (a) determine expectations of behaviour against which actual behaviour can be contrasted, allowing a system entirely based on state perceptions of 'compliance' and 'violation' to operate with less uncertainty; and (b) provide a focal point for other states' decision-making, allowing the operation of the various compliance-inducing mechanism of international law.

Three factors by which observable reality deviates from the 'billiard balls' model of unitary, rational states, help explain state compliance with norms that exceed the predictions of this model. First, as observed and demonstrated by behavioural scholars, humans do not behave fully rationally but operate according to mental shortcuts ('heuristics'). These shortcuts allow them to reduce complexity and make decisions in the face of complex reality and the limits of information and rationality. Even if agents within a state seek to act fully rationally, the prospect that those in other states might operate irrationally (and 'oversanction' them) should lead them to greater compliance than the rational state model assumes. Second, states are not unitary actors. A version of the 'two-level game' of international and domestic politics suggests that domestic coalitions will try to use international norms, and the prospect of sanctions by other states, in their domestic struggles. On the one hand, they may push at the international level for the development of norms that benefit their own domestic agendas. On the other hand, they may use international norms to increase their influence and promote their interests and values at the domestic level. The third explanation considers the 'constructivist' explanations for human behaviour that may lead state agents to comply with international legal rules, acting based on a logic of appropriateness rather than a logic of consequences.

None of these models, taken alone, offers a complete account of how and when states comply with international norms. Highlighting different aspects of the normative phenomenon, together they support the assessment that, once a norm emerges and is recognised as such by state agents (whether one sees this as a consolidation of a power configuration, a reflex of reciprocal expectations, a focal point for coordination, or a shared sense of appropriate conduct), it activates intra- and inter-state social mechanisms that favour compliant behaviour. Although, as illustrated by the many examples discussed throughout this book, these mechanisms are far from fail-proof, they give international law its sociological normativity. They account for the generally high levels of compliance with international law observed across issue areas – and for the costs and risks incurred by agents and states that pursue non-compliance, even when no central, hierarchically organised apparatus can determine the application of coercion against them.

3

Courts without Power

Judicial Authority in International Law

3.1 Introduction

Chapter 2 examined how international law may operate and influence state behaviour within a wholly decentralised, horizontal social order, lacking both a centralised law enforcer and authoritative decision-making. This chapter considers how this normative landscape and its operation can be changed through the addition of a hierarchical element: authoritative decisions, and international adjudication in particular. International adjudication operates within the structurally decentralised international order. In this structure, ICs cannot rely for influence on power, understood as a connection between their pronouncements and a coercive social apparatus tasked with enforcing them. Instead, the influence of adjudicators in the international order must derive entirely from judicial authority.[1]

Although there is an inevitable overlap between the legal and sociological meanings of authority, it is useful to distinguish them conceptually. Legally speaking, authority is coterminous with jurisdiction or competence. It can be described as the feature of an actor's pronouncements on legal questions that, within the legal system, distinguishes these pronouncements from those made by other actors, giving them a higher claim to legal truth and, in case of decisions not subject to appeal, finality. A final judicial decision from an authoritative court establishes conclusively the meaning of the rights and obligations in dispute for the parties involved. As the International Court of Justice (ICJ) put it in *Haya de la Torre*, adjudication amounts to 'defining the legal relations ... established between the parties', whether they emerge from a legal text or from

[1] For the distinction between power (as *potestas*) and authority (as *auctoritas*), see Section 1.4.1.

patterns of conduct accepted as binding, entailing 'the obligation of compliance therewith'.[2]

As a matter of law, authority may be thought of as binary: an actor either has or lacks the legal competence to issue an authoritative pronouncement on an issue.[3] An international adjudicator has judicial authority when it is empowered to exercise jurisdiction, that is, to pronounce on a legal issue, determining for other legal subjects their rights and obligations with binding effect. This ability rests on the consent of states to accept the IC's jurisdiction.[4] In Hugh Thirlway's definition, in international law 'jurisdiction means the power, conferred by the consent of States, to hear and determine with binding force a dispute between those States'.[5] As the ICJ has consistently affirmed, its 'jurisdiction is always based on the consent of the parties'.[6] Treaties that establish ICs usually specify the extent to which ratification of the treaty implies acceptance of an adjudicator's jurisdiction, usually by stating that its rulings on the interpretation and application of a treaty are 'without appeal' and 'final' or 'binding' for parties to a dispute.[7] Consent to jurisdiction can also be nuanced and contain exceptions[8]

[2] *Haya de La Torre*, [1951] ICJ Reports, p. 71, 79.

[3] This does not preclude disputes regarding whether an actor has authority under the law to make a final pronouncement on a specific issue. These disputes can be taken to actors within the legal system that are empowered to make this determination; decisions can be challenged or resisted. Challenges tend to be equally binary, in the sense of being claims that a body has *no* authority, rather than *less* authority, over an issue.

[4] This is of course a general description. Each IC's jurisdiction depends on its constitutive instrument(s). Thus, the ICJ, ITLOS and the IACtHR are empowered to issue Advisory Opinions, which do not have binding effect; and the reports of WTO panels and of the Appellate Body only produce their legal effects once adopted by the WTO Dispute Settlement Body.

[5] Hugh Thirlway, 'The Law and Procedure of the International Court of Justice 1960–1989' (2011) 81(1) *British Yearbook of International Law* 13–170, at 90.

[6] *Armed Activities on the Territory of the Congo (New Application: 2002) (Democratic Republic of the Congo* v. *Rwanda)*, Jurisdiction and Admissibility, [2006] ICJ Reports, p. 6, 32; *East Timor (Portugal* v. *Australia)*, Judgment, [1995] ICJ Reports, p. 90, 101; *Corfu Channel (United Kingdom* v. *Albania)*, Preliminary Objections, Judgment, [1947–1948] ICJ Reports, pp. 27–28.

[7] See Section 1.1.

[8] In the case of the ICJ, for example, consent to jurisdiction may be given in a variety of manners, including *ex ante* for all legal disputes (in the case of an unqualified declaration under Article 36(2) of the ICJ Statute) or *ex post* after a claim is filed (*forum prorrogatum*). It is also highly customisable, so that states are able to exclude from their consent to jurisdiction entire classes of disputes.

or be inferred from a joint reading of two or more legal instruments.[9]

Asserting an entity's authority under the law, however, is not the same as asserting its authority in a sociological sense. Legal assessments of authority allow actors to identify whether an entity may pronounce with authority on a particular subject, binding certain actors as a matter of the legal order. It is in this binary sense that lawyers argue over the extent of the authority of advisory opinions[10] or provisional measures.[11] It is also in this sense that, for example, the United States argued that the Inter-American Court of Human Rights (IACtHR) did not have the authority to declare the Inter-American Declaration of Human Rights a binding document,[12] or that China claimed that the Arbitral Tribunal in *South China Sea* had 'no jurisdiction', and its award, 'no binding force'.[13]

These debates, however, do not relate to why any of these ICs' determinations, in disputes over which they do have authority in the sense of jurisdiction, are authoritative in the sense of affecting decision-making within states.[14] In other words, judicial authority in the sense of formal

[9] In investment law, jurisdiction of arbitral tribunals is commonly constituted through a plurality of legal instruments. See Jan Paulsson, 'Arbitration without Privity' (1995) 10 *ICSID Review – Foreign Investment Law Journal* 232–257.

[10] See, for example, Roberto Ago, 'Binding Advisory Opinions of the International Court of Justice' (1991) 85 *American Journal of International Law* 439–451; Niccolò Lanzoni, 'The Authority of ICJ Advisory Opinions as Precedents: The Mauritius/Maldives Case' (2022) 2 *Italian Review of International and Comparative Law* 1–27.

[11] Cameron A. Miles, *Provisional Measures before International Courts and Tribunals* (Cambridge: Cambridge University Press, 2017), 4 ('the authority to grant interim relief may be seen as one of the inherent powers of international courts and tribunals'); Cameron Miles, 'Provisional Measures and the "New" Plausibility in the Jurisprudence of the International Court of Justice' (2018) 88 *British Yearbook of International Law* 1–46.

[12] *Interpretation of the American Declaration of the Rights and Duties of Man*, Advisory Opinion OC-10/89, 14 July 1989, Ser. A No. 10, para. 12 ('The American Declaration of the Rights and Duties of Man represents a noble statement of the human rights aspirations of the American States. Unlike the American Convention, however, it was not drafted as a legal instrument').

[13] See Chinese Society of International Law, 'The South China Sea Arbitration Awards: A Critical Study' (2018) 17(2) *Chinese Journal of International Law* 207–748, at 709.

[14] In addition to influencing outcomes, judicial interpretations of the applicable legal framework become reference points for subsequent legal debates. See on this Ingo Venzke, *How Interpretation Makes International Law: On Semantic Change and Normative Twists* (Oxford: Oxford University Press, 2012). Karen Alter, Laurence Helfer and Mikael Madsen term this element 'extensive authority', contrasting it with the 'narrow authority' over a specific dispute. See Karen J. Alter, Laurence R. Helfer, and Mikael Rask Madsen, 'How Context Shapes the Authority of International Courts' (2016) 79(1) *Law and Contemporary Problems* 1–36, at 6. See also Harlan Grant Cohen,

jurisdiction over a dispute or issue is not the same as judicial authority in the sense of ability to influence outcomes.[15]

This chapter considers how adjudication can affect the operation of the international normative framework by introducing an authoritative element. It examines the social processes through which authoritative pronouncements enhance the compliance-inducing mechanisms of international law, how adjudication interacts with the limited forms of centralised sanctioning authority, and what limits restrict its operation in a social order that remains structurally decentralised. Section 3.2 considers how international adjudication operates in general by addressing two key obstacles to the operation of a purely interactional, horizontal normative order: linguistic uncertainty and normative indeterminacy. Section 3.3 examines how adjudicators, merely by stating their interpretation of the law, trigger and enhance the internal and external motivators for compliance described in Chapter 2. Section 3.4 considers the operation of authority in the instances in which international law goes beyond its decentralised enforcement mechanisms and features forms of centralised sanction – often, but not always, within the framework of international organisations (IOs) – pointing equally to the limits of authority in a setting in which control over material resources remains decentralised. Section 3.5 concludes.

3.2 Horizontality, Uncertainty, and Authority in International Law

3.2.1 Decentralised Normative Orders and the Problem of Uncertainty

As discussed in Chapter 2, international law operates as a structurally horizontal and decentralised normative order. Despite the absence of a centralised interpreter or enforcer of norms, states often comply with their international obligations owing to a combination of internal and

'Theorizing Precedent in International Law', in Andrea Bianchi, Daniel Peat, and Matthew Windsor (eds.), *Interpretation in International Law* (Oxford: Oxford University Press, 2015), 268–289, at 275 ('Precedent might best be understood as the burden prior interpretations of a particular rule put on future arguments about the content or meaning of the rule').

15 There is yet a third meaning of authority, which Scott Shapiro describes as 'the moral right to rule'. Scott J. Shapiro, 'Authority', in Jules L. Coleman, Kenneth Einar Himma, and Scott J. Shapiro (eds.), *The Oxford Handbook of Jurisprudence and Philosophy of Law* (Oxford: Oxford University Press, 2012), 386. Although the question of the rightfulness or legitimacy of authority is not the focus of this book, actors' perception of rightfulness or legitimacy of authority will, of course, influence the extent to which they adjust their behaviour in response to authoritative pronouncements.

Table 3.1 *Layers of Compliance Control – Summary*

Layer	*Controller*	*Rule*	*Sanction Type*	*Term*
		First-Party Control		
1	Domestic actors	All	Self-control	Voluntary compliance
		Second-Party Control		
2	Affected state	Bilateral	Bilateral sanctioning	Inter-state enforcement
		Third-Party Control		
3	Third states	Collective	Diffuse sanctioning	Diffuse enforcement
4	IO/multilateral body	IO/treaty	Institutional sanctions	Institutional enforcement
[5]	IO/body plus states	IO/treaty	Authorised sanctions	Authorised enforcement

external social processes. These processes function across five layers, discussed in Section 2.2.3 and summarised in Table 2.1, of which Table 3.1 is a simplified version:

When international law operates through wholly decentralised enforcement (Layers 1, 2, and 3), it is subject to significant uncertainty regarding the content of norms. Whether the norms that state agents are seeking to apply arise from legal texts or patterns of conduct, their content is not self-evident: they must be interpreted and applied to the dispute. And, in the horizontal international order, states possess in principle what the ICJ has termed 'equal rights of qualification'.[16] Absent an agreed recognition of authority, states hold equal authority to interpret norms and situations, assess conduct, and determine which responses to norm violations are warranted. As the arbitral tribunal in *Lac Lanoux* put it, 'it is incumbent on each state to assess, reasonably and in good faith, the situations and the rules in which it is involved; its assessment may be contradicted by that of another state; in this case, a

[16] *Asylum (Colombia* v. *Peru) (Judgment)* [1950] ICJ Reports, p. 266, 275. See also *Air Service Agreement Arbitration (France* v. *United States)*, 18 RIAA (1978) 417, at 443. See Eirik Bjorge, 'Opposability and Non-Opposability in International Law' (2021) *British Yearbook of International Law* [forthcoming].

dispute arises'.[17] And, unless a commonly recognised authority can intervene, actions and responses based on divergent normative perceptions coexist on equal footing.[18]

In this fully horizontal, or 'interactional', normative order, the various actors taking part in, or observing, international relations, must themselves interpret the relevant rules before determining how to act. These actors include not only state agents seeking to assess whether their own behaviour complies with their state's international obligations or will be perceived as a violation (whether or not they ultimately decide, or even aim, to comply). It also includes the states directly affected, or rather, their agents, who must assess the normative framework to determine whether, and how, to respond to or sanction the former state's conduct. And, importantly, it includes the agents of third parties not directly involved in the interaction, especially agents of third states, who are themselves in control of coercive social apparatuses. All of these actors must assess whether any of the interacting states' actions should cause them to express a negative reaction, condemning actions incompatible with their view of the existing norms or, as the case may be, adopting sanctions of their own in response.

The wholly de-institutionalised framework – decentralised at the level of *auctoritas* as well as of *potestas* – therefore imposes significant hurdles to the effectiveness and very operation of the international normative order. As a matter of voluntary (Layer 1) compliance, the lack of firm legal grounds deprives actors within states of certainty as regards which conduct to pursue. Likewise, agents of potentially sanctioning actors lack clarity as to whether other states' actions are permitted or prohibited, and therefore lack certainty regarding how their own responses will be interpreted by other actors. The acute indeterminacy of norms in a de-institutionalised, horizontal interactional law, a direct consequence

[17] *Lac Lanoux (Spain* v. *France)* (1957) UNRIAA 12 281, 310 ('il appartient à chaque Etat d'apprécier, raisonnablement et de bonne foi, les situations et les règles qui le mettent en cause; son appréciation peut se trouver en contradiction avec celle d'un autre Etat; dans ce cas, apparaît un différend').

[18] Ibid. ('l'une d'elles n'est jamais obligée de suspendre, du fait du différend, l'exercice de sa compétence, sauf engagement de sa part'). But see the ILC Commentary on ARSIWA Article 49(1): 'A State which resorts to countermeasures based on its unilateral assessment of the situation does so at its own risk and may incur responsibility for its own wrongful conduct in the event of an incorrect assessment' (ILC *Ybk* 2001, II.2, p. 130). Absent an authoritative decision-maker, however, this formulation begs the question. The claim that an assessment was incorrect is itself subject to normative uncertainty.

of the sovereign equality of states, thus hampers the horizontal legal framework's ability to operate and influence behaviour.[19] It is to address this uncertainty – not overall uncertainty arising from the indeterminacy of language but the specific structural normative uncertainty that afflicts horizontal orders – that states establish international institutions, such as international adjudicators, and endow them with authority.

3.2.2 *Uncertainty, Self-Interpretation, and Sanctions in the International Legal Order*

Equality among states is a normative construct rather than a reflection of objective inter-state relations. What we call the horizontal international order never entirely matched the model of an egalitarian, fully informal, and fully de-institutionalised normative order. Since its usual postulated origin in the 1648 Peace of Westphalia,[20] the ostensibly egalitarian international normative order has coexisted with religious authority, changing political and dynastic configurations among its central political entities, as well as widespread imperial arrangements and colonial domination in their relations with peripheral entities. Even after the stabilisation of the state system following the decolonisation wave of the 1960s to 1980s,[21] vast differences in political and economic power exist among the various formally equal sovereigns.

Despite not corresponding to objective reality, the conceptual framework of an international society composed of sovereign equals has grounded international legal thinking for the past two centuries. To the extent that international law can be said to be a horizontal legal system grounded in equality among its members, for much of its existence it did correspond to a significant extent to Ellickson's depiction of an informal, horizontal normative system. In such a system, sanctions are

[19] See, most famously, H.L.A. Hart, *The Concept of Law* (Oxford: Clarendon Press, 1961), 233 (considered in Section 2.2.2).

[20] For the argument that this order did not emerge in 1648 and is a product of eighteenth- and nineteenth-century projection, see Andreas Osiander, 'Sovereignty, International Relations, and the Westphalian Myth' (2001) 55 *International Organization* 251–287. International lawyers often consider international law to pre-date the Westphalian order, dating it back to Spanish scholasticism following Spain's maritime expansion and colonisation of the Americas, and perhaps even earlier. See Wilhelm G. Grewe, *The Epochs of International Law – Translated and Revised by Michael Byers* (New York: de Gruyter, 2000) [first edition originally published in 1984], 7–11.

[21] Umut Özsu, *Completing Humanity: The International Law of Decolonization, 1960–82* (Cambridge: Cambridge University Press, 2024).

decentralised and norms are the product of repeated social interactions, crystallising into the reciprocal expectations of behaviour that lawyers term 'customary international law'.[22] This decentralised system featured, as its principal enforcement mechanism, Layer 2 bilateral sanctions, that is, reciprocity and other bilateral responses to violations affecting specifically one state. Layer 2 sanctions are given specific legal forms under international law, such as countermeasures, suspension of treaties, and self-defence, all of which are legal instruments subject to notification requirements and limitations of form and proportionality.[23]

Besides these bilateral legal responses, the international normative order has always featured diffuse and often little-regulated decentralised third-party (Layer 3) responses to behaviour perceived by states as disturbing, or threatening to disturb, the international order more broadly. Many scholars did not even ascribe a legal character to these decentralised third-party responses. Dionisio Anzilotti, one of the great early systematisers of international law, made a distinction between an injured state's responses to violations of that state's rights (*diritto sogettivo*), which were legally regulated, and responses to violations of general legal duties (*diritto oggettivo*). The only states with a *right* to respond to unlawful conduct, as part of their general right to invoke the responsibility of an offender, were those states injured by the violation. Injured states would have the legal entitlement to adopt bilateral enforcement measures (Layer 2) against the responsible state.

By contrast, for Anzilotti, if a state were to react to another state's conduct contrary to a general legal duty, it could not be acting to defend its 'inter-national' right vis-à-vis the offender. Due to the absence of delegated authority to act on behalf of the international legal order or international community, a state purporting to defend the legal order in general as diffuse enforcer, that is, under Layer 3, would be acting upon a mere *interest*.[24] Although this third state could have a legitimate

[22] The classic formulation appears in *North Sea Continental Shelf*, [1969] ICJ Reports, p. 3, 45. On the view of custom as reciprocal expectations, see Monica Hakimi, 'Making Sense of Customary International Law' (2020) 118 *Michigan Law Review* 1487–1537. See also George Norman and Joel P. Trachtman, 'The Customary International Law Game' (2005) 99 *American Journal of International Law* 541.

[23] See Section 2.4.2.

[24] The reference to 'interest' should be understood in the context of German legal theory, for which the very definition of a right is a 'legally protected interest' (Rudolf von Jhering, *L'esprit du droit romain dans ses diverses phases de son développement*, 3rd edn (Paris: A. Marescq, 1878), vol. 4, p. 326 (§§ 70–71)). Anzilotti does not refer to Jhering but cites

interest in defending the international legal order, this interest would be extra-legal:

> Once we exclude the right of states to act, whether individually or collectively, against the author of a violation of the right of another, all that remains is the possibility of action founded on the interest of all states and each of them in that the principles of international law be respected . . . states that act to prevent or repress a violation of another's right are therefore exercising neither a legal right nor a legal duty, but simply a lawful activity.[25]

This view of third-party intervention to repress a violation, which considers it a largely unregulated activity, predates the legal regulation of the use of force, in particular in the Charter of the United Nations.[26] It is nonetheless compatible with a horizontal social order with a low level of institutionalisation. In such an order, in which no authorised institutions are able to interpret rights and obligations, establish violations, and specify the appropriate sanctions, these determinations are left to individual actors. The use of force is now subject to a significant degree of legal regulation, with the UNSC being 'confer[red] primary responsibility for the maintenance of international peace and security' and being authorised by UN Members to make decisions in this area 'on their behalf'.[27] Outside of this and other fields in which institutions are empowered to make decisions, to this day there is significant legal uncertainty as regards the permissibility of decentralised third-party enforcement under Layer 3.

This is reflected, for example, in the regulation of permissible third-party responses to unlawful conduct in the International Law Commission (ILC) Articles on State Responsibility. Article 54 provides that states not specifically injured or affected by a violation may adopt

other German authors who employ this right/interest distinction. Note, too, that this lack of a legitimate law enforcer for diffuse interests of all states is the difficulty that Scelle addresses with the concept of *dédoublement fonctionnel* (see Section 2.3.3).

[25] Dionisio Anzilotti, *Teoria generale della responsabilità dello stato nel diritto internazionale* (Firenze: F. Iumachi, 1902), 92–93 ('Escluso il diritto degli stati ad agire, sia individualmente sia collettivamente, contro l'autore di una violazione del diritto altrui, non rimane che la possibilità di un'azione fondata sull'interesse di tutti gli stati e di ciascuno di essi a che sieno rispettati i principî del diritto internazionale . . . Gli stati che agiscono per impedire o reprimere una violazione del diritto altrui non esercitano dunque nè un diritto nè un dovere giuridico, ma semplicemente un'attività lecita').

[26] See Christine Gray, *International Law and the Use of Force*, 4th edn (Oxford: Oxford University Press, 2018); Olivier Corten, *The Law against War: The Prohibition on the Use of Force in Contemporary International Law*, 2nd edn (Oxford: Hart, 2021).

[27] UN Charter, Article 24(1).

'lawful measures ... to ensure cessation of the breach and reparation' to injured parties.[28] The ILC Commentary to Article 54, however, describes various instances of what it terms an 'embrionary' practice of responses to perceived unlawful conduct by states other than an injured state.[29] This collected practice mentions drastic measures, including economic embargoes and freezing of state assets. Rather than declaring these third-party responses unlawful in the absence of an authoritative decision by an adjudicator or authorised decision-making body, the ILC concludes that 'the current state of international law of countermeasures taken in the general or collective interest is uncertain'.[30]

A cautious approach to the enforcement of obligations by third states is understandable. Interaction in a fully horizontal normative order takes place in an indeterminate legal universe, in which one sovereign state's assessment of the relevant rights and obligations is as authoritative as any other state's. From the viewpoint of those seeking a functioning normative system in which violations are punished and rule-compliant behaviour is not, this indeterminacy leads both to under-sanctioning, with even blatant violations of general norms going unpunished, and over-sanctioning, with opportunistic invocation of the duty to sanction by actors merely pursuing their self-interest. In these horizontal normative orders, as Ellickson noted, third-party sanctioning by 'nonhierarchically organized social forces' is predictably inconsistent.[31]

It is logically concerning that a state might take advantage of normative indeterminacy to under-interpret its international obligations in such a way that allows it to deviate from these obligations in pursuit of its own interests. An equally pressing concern, however, is that a state might over-interpret another's obligations and, under the pretext of responding to a prior breach, pursue spurious interests in manners which would ordinarily not be permissible. As Bruno Simma noted, subjecting the defence of the legal order 'to the mercy of individual auto-determination [i.e., self-interpretation] and self-enforcement'[32] by each state may appear like an elegant solution to the absence of a centralised enforcer. In practice, however, it leads to the risk that self-interested actors will

[28] ILC Articles, Art. 54.

[29] ILC *Ybk* 2001, II.2, p. 137.

[30] Ibid., p. 139.

[31] Robert Ellickson, *Order without Law: How Neighbors Settle Disputes* (Cambridge: Harvard University Press, 1991), 127.

[32] Bruno Simma, 'From Bilateralism to Community Interests' (1994) 250 *RdC* 217, at 331.

pursue their self-interested goals, and empower themselves to ignore legal constraints, under the guise of enforcing international law.[33] Accordingly, the international legal norms governing third-party sanctioning focus less on requiring *some* sanctioning of unlawful conduct than on preventing unwarranted or abusive sanctioning.[34]

3.2.3 Delegated Interpretative Authority and the Establishment of (Legal) Hierarchy

This depiction – of a decentralised and largely informal international normative system in which state relations take place essentially bilaterally, written rules are comparatively rare when compared to customary law, and adjudication depends on specific consent, making all claims by individual states with regard to the interpretation of their commitments equally authoritative – corresponds reasonably accurately to the international order of the nineteenth century. In the twenty-first century, despite this remaining the core conceptual model for many international lawyers and state agents conducting international relations, it has become increasingly inaccurate as a description of the international normative system. Throughout the twentieth century, states have constituted, through treaties and sometimes other arrangements, a variety of political bodies and institutions within which states, and increasingly other actors, can articulate and debate interpretative claims.

Many of these institutions, in particular political organs of IOs, feature decision-making procedures that allow majorities to, through a vote, give greater weight to certain interpretations. More importantly for present purposes, other bodies – international adjudicators – are entrusted by states, *ex ante*, with interpreting and applying their engagements in a manner that states commit to consider 'binding', 'final', and 'without appeal'.[35] Although these bodies' decisions are ultimately grounded in

[33] Shabtai Rosenne recalls it being common practice in Nazi Germany the 'repeated, flagrant and at times violent instances of deliberate breaches of treaty' in response to alleged breaches by other states, terming this practice 'Sportpalast Diplomatie' from 'the place in Berlin from which this kind of diplomacy was regularly practiced' (Shabtai Rosenne, *Breach of Treaty* (Cambridge: Grotius, 1985), 11).

[34] See Martin Dawidowicz, *Third-Party Countermeasures in International Law* (Cambridge: Cambridge University Press, 2017); Priya Urs, 'The Elusiveness of "Interdependent Obligations" and the Invocation of Responsibility for Their Breach' (2024) *British Yearbook of International Law* [forthcoming].

[35] For examples, see Section 1.3.2.

this initial state consent, once in place, they are empowered to issue statements that, for the purposes of the normative system, prevail over conflicting interpretations by individual states. These institutions fundamentally change what one may call the 'authority landscape' of the international order. As José Alvarez put it, '[t]he contemporary international system no longer consists of completely autonomous nations free to act independently in the pursuit of their self-interest'.[36]

Although the creation and empowerment of institutions occurred incrementally, with regard to adjudication a major milestone took place at the turn of the twentieth century. At the two Hague Peace Conferences of 1899 and 1907, a plurality of the then-recognised states, including most European states, agreed to compulsory arbitration of disputes.[37] More important than this agreement in the abstract was the establishment of a standing institution – the Permanent Court of Arbitration (PCA) – and the conferral on this institution of procedural and material means to overcome the non-cooperation of recalcitrant states. Contrary to earlier arbitral arrangements, the PCA could produce an adjudicatory ruling following the unilateral submission of a dispute by a party, as long as the two parties had previously entrusted the PCA with administering arbitrations regarding the interpretation or application of the relevant commitments.

The Hague Peace Conferences produced many major legal texts establishing core rules of conduct, codifying existing custom, and developing new rules for armed conflict. One instrument, the Hague Convention for the Pacific Settlement of International Disputes, signed in 1899 and revised in 1907, was of a different character. It set up procedures and institutions for the settlement of disputes. The PCA, while not itself conducting arbitrations, could act as a registry for disputes and, crucially, ensure the appointment of arbitrators in cases in which a state that had consented to arbitration subsequently failed to cooperate in the composition of the arbitrator or arbitral tribunal. Through PCA arbitration, for the first time a state's own interpretations of its rights and obligations could be overridden by an adjudicator, without that state's *ex post* consent or cooperation to have the dispute settled, grounded in its *ex*

[36] Jose E. Alvarez, *International Organizations as Law-Makers* (Oxford: Oxford University Press, 2006), 74.

[37] The 1899 Convention had twenty-six original signatories, nineteen of which European; the 1907 Convention had forty-three original signatories, twenty-four of which non-European.

ante consent to have a dispute, or a category of disputes, settled by a PCA-established Arbitral Tribunal.

This fundamental change did not go unnoticed. The establishment of the PCA in the 1899 Convention was marked by the concern, expressed by the Russian diplomat who wrote its first draft, Frederic de Martens, that arbitration was inadequate for disputes touching upon the 'vital interests, or national honour of States'.[38] The 1899 Convention set up a number of safeguards to ensure that PCA arbitration would remain limited to 'questions of a legal nature'.[39] Article 19 foresaw the possibility of *ex ante* agreement to compulsory adjudication, through 'general or private Treaties expressly stipulating recourse to arbitration as obligatory on the Signatory Powers'. Article 31, however, limited the extent of the authority shift. It conditioned states' obligation 'to submit loyally to the award' of a PCA Arbitral Tribunal to an *ex post* act, to take place once the dispute was known to the parties: the signature of 'a special Act (*compromis*), in which the subject of the difference is clearly defined, as well as the extent of the Arbitrators' powers'.[40] Refusing to sign this special act would be potentially unlawful. However, by refusing to sign it, a state would prevent the tribunal from exercising valid jurisdiction over the dispute in the first place.[41] Under the 1899 Hague Convention, then, states retained the ability to prevent, *ex post*, the deployment of arbitration in disputes that they did not consider to be 'of a legal nature', by refusing to sign the special act.

The second step of the shift, taken in the 1907 Hague Convention, was to permit truly compulsory, unilaterally established adjudication. Besides the *ex post compromis*, Article 53(1) of the 1907 Convention foresaw a second source of jurisdiction for a PCA Arbitral Tribunal: an *ex ante* 'general Treaty of Arbitration ... providing for a "*Compromis*" in all disputes' of a specified kind.[42] The principle of *ex post* consent was

[38] James B. Scott (ed.), *Reports to the Hague Conferences of 1899 and 1907* (Carnegie Endowment for International Peace, 1917), 98.

[39] 1899 Hague Convention on the Pacific Settlement of International Disputes, adopted 29 July 1899, in Force 4 September 1900, Article 16.

[40] Ibid., Article 31.

[41] *Interpretation of Peace Treaties (Second Phase)*, Advisory Opinion, [1950] ICJ Reports, p. 221, 229 ('The failure of machinery for settling disputes by reason of the practical impossibility of creating the Commission provided for in the Treaties is one thing; international responsibility is another').

[42] Convention for the Pacific Settlement of International Disputes, adopted 18 October 1907, in force 26 January 1910, Article 53(1).

partially safeguarded by the provision empowering a state to 'declare[] that in its opinion the dispute does not belong to the category of disputes which can be submitted to compulsory arbitration'. The same provision, however, provided for the relinquishment of this entitlement by the state, if 'the Treaty of Arbitration confers upon the Arbitration Tribunal the power of deciding this preliminary question'.[43]

Inherent in the reformulation of the jurisdictional provision was a fundamental transformation: a transfer of ultimate normative authority over legal disputes from states to arbitrators. Arbitration had been a part of modern international law since the 1794 Jay Treaty arbitrations, and arbitration among political entities far precedes that.[44] The shift operated by the Hague Conventions was to provide a path, and a procedural framework, for states to go beyond agreeing *ex post* to have specific disputes heard by a specific adjudicator. Although expressed in the negative, Article 53(1) of the 1907 Convention allowed states to agree, *ex ante*, to authorise another actor – a PCA-constituted Arbitral Tribunal without access to a coercive apparatus – to override their own interpretation of their rights and obligations under international law.[45]

The Hague Conventions were followed by innumerable other authority-creating treaties. The two key institution-building treaties establishing general-purpose adjudicators – the 1920 Permanent Court of International Justice (PCIJ) Statute, connected to the 1919 Covenant of the League of Nations, and the 1945 UN Charter which established the ICJ – permitted the compulsory settlement of disputes by political bodies (the Council of the League of Nations and the UNSC), while retaining the requirement of consent for the PCIJ and ICJ respectively to have jurisdiction over disputes. Other treaties took a more incisive approach. Some included, by default but subject to reservation or withdrawal, the parties' *ex ante* consent to an adjudicator's jurisdiction regarding interpretation and application of the treaty. Others went beyond this and made consent

43 Ibid.

44 See Jackson H. Ralston, *International Arbitration from Athens to Locarno* (Stanford: Stanford University Press, 1929); Tamar Meshel, '225 Years to the Jay Treaty: Interstate Arbitration between Progress and Stagnation' (2020) 3 *International Comparative, Policy & Ethics Law Review* 1.

45 Another adjudicator, with significantly broader jurisdictional powers, was created in 1907: the (first) Central American Court of Justice. It lasted until 1918. See Manley O. Hudson, 'The Central American Court of Justice' (1932) 26 *American Journal of International Law* 759–786; Charles Ripley, 'The Central American Court of Justice (1907–1918): Rethinking the World's First Court' (2018) 19 *Diálogos* 47–68.

to adjudication over the treaty an inextricable part of the agreement: no state could become a party to the treaty, or a member of the IO it established, without accepting the compulsory jurisdiction of an adjudicator over disputes regarding its interpretation and application.

In the latter category are treaties, such as the United Nations Convention on the Law of the Sea (UNCLOS), the World Trade Organization (WTO) Agreements, the European Convention on Human Rights (ECHR), or the African Court of Human and People's Rights (AfCHPR), that require states parties to consent to the jurisdiction of an adjudicator over treaty obligations, sometimes including jurisdiction to hear disputes brought by private parties. In the former category are treaties that establish frameworks within which jurisdiction can be exercised by a specific adjudicator, such as the ICJ, while either retaining the requirement that dispute-specific consent to jurisdiction be given or allowing parties to withhold such consent.[46]

The prospect of adjudication qualitatively changes the character of the underlying rules, which shift from being what Harlan Cohen termed 'negotiated law' to 'adjudicated law'.[47] Even where adjudicatory interpretation is formally binding only on parties to each dispute, if the adjudicator's rulings are publicly available they will inevitably produce authoritative effects on the perception of all actors participating in the regime regarding their rights and obligations.[48] Thus, in a sense, these treaties permit adjudicatory interpretations to affect or even determine, de facto, the rights and obligations of all states parties, whether or not they subscribe to the jurisdictional clause.[49]

[46] Some treaties that feature optional or derogable jurisdictional clauses have an eminently procedural character. Examples include the Hague Convention on the Pacific Settlement of International Disputes, 18 October 1907, in force 26 January 1910; Statute of the International Court of Justice, San Francisco, 26 June 1945, in force 24 October 1945. Others set out substantive obligations while endowing an IC with jurisdiction over their interpretation, such as the ACHR; human rights treaties such as the Genocide Convention and the Convention on the Elimination of All Forms of Racial Discrimination; the Vienna Conventions on Diplomatic Relations and on Consular Relations; or the ICSID Convention. Treaties featuring a derogable or optional jurisdictional clause preserve to an extent the right of states to self-interpretation, while engendering a dynamic that often results in generalised resort to adjudication, sometimes leading to IC jurisdiction over virtually all states parties (as the IACtHR has over states parties to the ACHR).

[47] Harlan Grant Cohen, 'International Law's Erie Moment' (2013) 34 *Michigan Journal of International Law* 249, 252.

[48] See on this Venzke, *How Interpretation Makes International Law.*

[49] See, for example, Krzysztof J. Pelc, 'The Politics of Precedent in International Law: A Social Network Application' (2014) 108 *American Political Science Review* 547–564.

This shift from a de-institutionalised to an institutionalised normative system may be understood through the conceptual lens of a legalisation of international relations, as articulated by Kenneth Abbott, Robert Keohane, Andrew Moravcsik, Anne-Marie Slaughter, and Duncan Snidal. Their conceptual framework is useful insofar as it separates the question of the use of legal form to convey commitments from that of the locus of authority to interpret these commitments. This framework permits avoiding 'a narrow view of law as requiring enforcement by a coercive sovereign' and allows speaking of legalisation as 'a particular form of institutionalization'.[50]

The authors propose that the degree of legalisation of commitments can be measured on the basis of three dimensions. The first is *obligation*, involving both the decision to enshrine commitments in formal treaties, rather than in memoranda of understandings, communiqués or guidelines, and the choice to word commitments as obligations, rather than exhortations or pledges to 'take steps towards' an objective. Expressing a commitment as a legal obligation allows other states (and non-state actors) to 'assert legal claims . . ., engage in legal discourse, invoke legal procedures, and resort to legal remedies' not warranted in the case of explicitly political, non-binding commitments.[51]

The second dimension of legalisation is *precision*. A precise rule 'specifies clearly and unambiguously what is expected of a state or other actor . . . in a particular set of circumstances', covering 'both the intended objective and the means of achieving it'.[52] Precision is particularly relevant where the third dimension – delegation – is lacking. In this context, the norms being conveyed will be 'interpreted and applied by the very actors whose conduct they are intended to govern', without institutions empowered either to de-legitimise interpretations or to change the legal text to curtail undesirable interpretations. Without delegation of either adjudicatory or rule-making powers, the five authors contend, norms are more legalised if they are formulated as precise rules, rather than general standards of conduct, precluding 'inappropriate, self-serving interpretations' by the different states.[53]

[50] Kenneth W. Abbott, Robert O. Keohane, Andrew Moravcsik, Anne-Marie Slaughter, and Duncan Snidal, 'The Concept of Legalization' (2000) 54 *International Organization* 401–419, at 402.

[51] Ibid., 411.

[52] Ibid., 412.

[53] Ibid., 414.

The third dimension of legalisation is *delegation*. Delegation involves the establishment or designation of third parties to interpret and apply norms.[54] This concept is broad, covering delegation of all three traditional functions of government: (i) to adjudicate upon disputes and interpret norms; (ii) to establish new norms, either specifying how broad standards apply to certain cases or developing new rules on the basis of delegated competences; and (iii) to apply in a centralised manner the agreed norms and, for example, determine the allocation of the resources assigned to an international financial institution.[55]

Of the three dimensions, obligation and precision facilitate the operation of the international normative framework without calling into question its horizontal structure. All else being equal, a promise framed as an obligation will carry more weight than one framed as a commitment to 'give positive consideration to' a course of action or similar formulation. Likewise, a provision establishing a detailed rule – such as UNCLOS Article 3, which sets up a limit to each state's territorial sea of 12 nautical miles from the coastal state's shore – is simpler to follow, and makes identifying violations less controversial, than a vague standard, such as coastal states having jurisdiction over those portions of the sea that they can militarily defend from land.[56]

At the same time, in a horizontal normative order, even a precise commitment worded as an absolute obligation within a binding document remains subject to unresolvable interpretative struggles: disputes may concern the meaning of the text itself, the relevance of other instruments and events for its interpretation and possible subsequent modification, or the applicability of exceptions and particular circumstances to the case in which the commitment is invoked.[57] In a horizontal normative framework, the dispute must be solved by a mix of persuasion – with one party assenting to an interpretation other than that which it had initially advanced, and which was likely more favourable to its interests – and coercion, with the application by other states of

[54] Ibid., 418.

[55] A degree of delegation exists even if the possibility of individual veto remains. See Dan Sarooshi, *International Organizations and Their Exercise of Sovereign Powers* (Oxford: Oxford University Press, 2005).

[56] For the latter standard, see Hugo Grotius, *The Law of War and Peace* (Indianapolis: Liberty Fund, 2005), book. 2, chapter III, §13.2 ('Jurisdiction or Sovereignty over a Part of the Sea is acquired ... In Regard to Territory, when those that sail on the Coasts of a Country may be compelled from the Land').

[57] These elements are explored in Section 1.3.

measures to force a state advancing a certain interpretation, with which the former states disagree, to back down and accept, or at least acquiesce to, the interpretation advanced by these other states.

Delegation, and in particular the delegation of interpretation, qualitatively transforms the framework of interaction. A state that commits to considering 'final and binding' a third party's interpretations of its commitments renounces the entitlement to self-interpret its rights and obligations. It would be unwise of course to overstate the extent of such renunciation: sovereign states always retain, de facto, the power not to follow an adjudicator's rulings, and states of all sizes occasionally seek to de-legitimise unfavourable rulings.[58] The delegation of interpretation is nonetheless transformative in that it establishes legal authority: it adds to a state's obligations, as they are perceived by all other states participating in or observing the interaction, the duty to accept as final the authoritative interpreter's determinations with respect to that state's rights and obligations.

In twenty-first-century international law, enforcement capabilities remain overwhelmingly in the hands of states and their agents. Nevertheless, the international legal system has evolved from a largely informal and de-institutionalised framework into one that is both highly formalised and heavily institutionalised. At the turn of the century, scholars were less concerned with the absence of international adjudicators to pronounce on disputes and interpret rules than with their 'proliferation' and 'multiplication' without any overarching coordination mechanism.[59]

This shift operates not at the level of *potestas* but at the level of *auctoritas*. State agents continue to hold the key levers of power in the

[58] Conceivably, international adjudicators might act ultra vires. An entitlement to declare judicial interpretations ultra vires could however be abused by states that are simply dissatisfied with the outcome of a dispute. See Ineta Ziemele, 'International Courts and *Ultra Vires* Acts', in Caflisch et al. (eds.), *Droits de l'Homme – Regards de Strasbourg. Liber Amicorum Luzius Wildhaber* (Kehl am Rhein: N.P. Engel, 2007), 537–556.

[59] Benedict Kingsbury, 'Foreword: Is the Proliferation of International Courts and Tribunals a Systemic Problem' (1999) 31 *New York University Journal of International Law and Politics* 679–696; Karin Oellers-Frahm, 'Multiplication of International Courts and Tribunals and Conflicting Jurisdiction – Problems and Possible Solutions' (2001) 5(1) *Max Planck Yearbook of United Nations Law Online* 67–104; Thomas Buergenthal, 'Proliferation of International Courts and Tribunals: Is It Good or Bad?' (2001) 14(2) *Leiden Journal of International Law* 267–275. See, more recently, Robert Howse, Hélène Ruiz-Fabri, Geir Ulfstein, and Michelle Q. Zhang (eds.), *The Legitimacy of International Trade Courts and Tribunals* (Cambridge: Cambridge University Press, 2018).

sense that the mobilisation of material resources takes place through the internal legal hierarchies of states. But the assertions by state agents regarding their entitlement to pull these levers coexist with assertions by an array of international institutions, with various degrees of independence from states themselves. Often, states have expressly consented to consider these institutions' assertions as prevailing over their own statements. To return to the metaphor of the landscape, there is no longer a 'flat' authority landscape, in which states' claims are all equally plausible. At the same time, the pyramid structure often used to represent domestic law[60] does not exist in international law, since states are not subject to an overarching sovereign that can make rules for them. Instead, this authority landscape is characterised by 'peaks' of legalisation and institutionalisation and 'valleys' in which sovereign equality and the absence or weakness of authoritative institutions continue to prevail.[61]

This raises the question of the mechanisms through which statements made by these legally authoritative bodies can indeed be sociologically authoritative. If those representing sovereign states retain control over the political and economic resources that can be used to deploy coercive measures, why would they relinquish their beliefs and accept a powerless adjudicator's pronouncements on the conduct required from them, let alone adjust their behaviour to comply with its rulings? It is to this question that Sections 3.3 and 3.4 are dedicated.

3.3 *Auctoritas*, Compliance and Sanctions in a Decentralised Normative Order

3.3.1 Internally Motivated Compliance through Semantic and de facto Authority

When a state's internal political and legal processes drive compliance with international law without requiring external enforcement, this is referred to as internally motivated compliance, or Layer 1 of the compliance system outlined in Chapter 2. Wholly internally motivated compliance with judicial pronouncements may arise when individuals,

[60] Though often associated with Hans Kelsen, the pyramid metaphor was developed by his disciple Adolf Julius Merkl. See Rafael Domingo, *The New Global Law* (Cambridge: Cambridge University Press, 2010), 147.

[61] I owe this metaphor to Kostia Gorobets. See Kostiantyn Gorobets, 'Peaks and Valleys: Contemplating the Authority of International Law', in Pauline Westerman et al. (eds.), *Conceptual (Re)Constructions of International Law* (Cheltenham: Elgar, 2022), 171–187.

previously holding divergent or contrary positions, revise their beliefs and adjust their behaviour out of a sense of legal or moral duty.

Voluntary compliance need not be wholly internally motivated. External pressures – such as the anticipation of responses from other actors, the risk of weakening a particular norm, or the threat of reputational harm – influence decisions that may seem purely internal. The prospect of such external responses can prompt private actors to react negatively to non-compliance, effectively transforming a potential future external response into an immediate, real market response. Compliance-interested actors often cite these external factors to justify their own compliance, or persuade others to comply.[62] Thus, while voluntary compliance is observable, it is also inextricably linked to the implied or express possibility of social or material sanctions.

It is nonetheless useful to consider when internally motivated compliance may occur. Adopting a constructivist or 'legitimacy-oriented' view of decision-making, internally motivated compliance is enforced through self-sanctioning by state agents who have internalised the duty to comply with international norms.[63] From this viewpoint, adjudicators influence state behaviour simply by articulating what is prohibited, permitted, and obligatory. To the extent that actors are understood to act not purely strategically but following a logic of appropriateness, an adjudicator's pronouncements can function as authoritative statements traditionally conceived. They operate through the recognition of 'hierarchy itself'[64] or internal 'psychological' motivations,[65] whereby actors acknowledge a societal hierarchy that allows statements from authoritative figures to shape not only their actions but also their worldviews. From this perspective, adjudicators' decisions establish the boundaries of permissible and impermissible behaviour, providing a shared framework and language for advancing claims and resolving interpretative divergences, thereby influencing how actors evaluate their own conduct and that of others.

62 Beth A. Simmons, 'Compliance with International Agreements' (1998) 1 *Annual Review of Political Science* 75–93.

63 Harold Hongju Koh, 'Why Do Nations Obey International Law?' (1997) 106 *Yale Law Journal* 2599; Harold Hongju Koh, 'Internalization through Socialization' (2005) 54 *Duke Law Journal* 975. On this perspective, see Section 2.4.

64 Hannah Arendt, 'What Is Authority?', in Hannah Arendt, *Between Past and Future* (New York: Penguin,1968), 91–141, 93. See Section 1.4.1.

65 Louis Henkin, *How Nations Behave: Law and Foreign Policy*, 2nd edn (New York: Columbia University Press, 1979 [1968]), 60.

This effect is captured by Ingo Venzke's concept of 'semantic authority', defined as 'an actor's capacity to influence and shape meanings as well as the ability to establish its communications as authoritative reference points in legal discourse'.[66] Within this conceptual framework, international law is understood to condition and shape the behaviour of the various actors operating within it, who all purport to act within its normative framework, and, in doing so, each advance their preferred views of what this framework permits, requires, and prohibits. Legal disputes are seen as instances of what Pierre Bourdieu has termed 'symbolic struggles over the power to produce and to impose the legitimate vision of the world'.[67] Within these struggles, the various actors advance diverging interpretations of the applicable normative framework, aiming to exert a form of interpretative power that operates at the symbolic or linguistic level, 'by making others believe in the rightness of interpretations'.[68] Actors 'make interpretative claims that are aligned with their interests or convictions' and 'seek to tap the law's force to their advantage'.[69]

Following this constructivist perspective, international adjudicators hold authority and affect legal discourse because their pronouncements affect other actors' perceptions of the applicable normative framework. As Venzke writes, 'judicial institutions shift meanings and can establish their own interpretations as new reference points for legal discourse ... participants in legal discourse can simply not avoid relating their argument to earlier judicial decision'.[70] In Bourdieusian terminology, adjudicative authority can be framed as 'symbolic capital', the social imprint that endows an agent's perspective with 'an absolute, universal value, thus snatching it from a relativity that is by definition inherent in every point of view, as a view taken from a particular point'.[71] Symbolic capital is what makes the interpretations contained in an authority's

[66] Venzke, *How Interpretation Makes International Law*, 61, 63 (citing Dietrich Busse, 'Semantic Strategies as a Means of Politics: Linguistic Approaches to the Analysis of "Semantic Struggles"', in Pertti Ahonen (ed.), *Tracing the Semiotic Boundaries of Politics* (Berlin: de Gruyter, 1993), 121–128).

[67] Pierre Bourdieu, 'Social Space and Symbolic Power' (1989) 7(1) *Sociological Theory* 14–25, at 20. See Matthew Eagleton-Pierce, *Symbolic Power in the World Trade Organization* (Oxford: Oxford University Press, 2013).

[68] Venzke, *How Interpretation Makes International Law*, 61, 58.

[69] Ibid., 62, 61.

[70] Ibid., 71.

[71] Bourdieu, 'Social Space and Symbolic Power', 22.

pronouncements prevail, in the minds of other actors, over their own previously advanced interpretations.

A similar symbolic conceptualisation of adjudicative authority is inherent in the concept of '*de facto* authority' of ICs developed by Karen Alter, Laurence Helfer and Mikael Rask Madsen, which breaks down international judicial authority into a range of levels of influence held by an adjudicator over various audiences. As they explain, a court holds de facto authority when 'one or more audiences recognize, by their words, actions, or both, that IC rulings are legally binding and engage in actions that push towards giving full effect to those'.[72] The level of authority of an IC varies with the breadth and nature of the audiences that recognise the binding character of its pronouncements over their own conduct and normative environment. An IC can hold 'narrow' authority when only the litigants in a case perceive the ruling as relevant for their conduct. It can reach 'intermediate' authority when a court's pronouncements 'affect[] the behavior and decisions of other similarly situated actors'. And it can attain 'extensive authority' when its adjudicative pronouncements affect the perceptions of 'a broader legal field of, for example, attorneys, government officials, and scholars'.[73] An institution's pronouncements can thus carry variable degrees of de facto authority, corresponding to their effects over audiences beyond the direct addressees of the pronouncements.

These two constructivist conceptualisations of international judicial authority emphasise its operation at the internal level, not only of states but of individuals themselves. Semantic or de facto authority would seem to constrain state action by foreclosing some types of argument in the interaction between state officials (whether within a state or among states). The underlying assumption is that state behaviour is determined by actors whose perception of permissible – or appropriate – conduct and justification is shaped and constrained by norms that each actor enforces vis-à-vis not only other actors but also herself. The idea that authority operates by establishing a meaning for language and foreclosing the availability of certain arguments thus relies on self-enforcement of norms by individuals. In Michael Reisman's expression, authority here

[72] Alter et al., 'How Context Shapes the Authority'. See, more broadly, Karen J. Alter, Laurence R. Helfer, and Mikael Rask Madsen, *International Court Authority* (Oxford: Oxford University Press, 2018).

[73] Ibid., 10. They also refer to the potential for 'popular' authority, when recognition of IC rulings extends beyond the legal field to 'encompass the public in general' (Ibid.).

acts as a 'determinant of individual or group behavior' by indicating a course of action 'with a degree of clarity sufficient to excite internal tension or psychic dysphoria if an incompatible course is followed'.[74]

For the same reason, however, this version of the operation of adjudicative authority will appear unpersuasive to some. As discussed in Chapter 2, for different reasons various authors reject or doubt the proposition that states act pursuant to a logic of appropriateness or are, in their ultimate patterns of behaviour, affected by the sort of 'internal tension' or 'psychic dysphoria' that an individual might suffer when presented with an authoritative determination. These authors would demand a different explanation for the operation of judicial pronouncements, one which does not rely on the ability of ICs to constrain the minds and actions of particular individuals by the mere fact of being termed a 'court' and employing judicial language.

For those who are suspicious of the relevance of internal compliance control mechanisms in the international order, an external justification for the effects of adjudication would be required, even if its effects could be produced without actual deployment of coercion. Authoritative pronouncements would have to influence the interaction between individuals in such a manner that even a state agent seeking to behave rationally, maximising their (or their state's) perceived self-interest without regard for normative constraints, would have her perceived potential range of action affected by the authoritative pronouncement. Put otherwise, to those who reject or doubt the constructivist perspective, in order to be convincingly authoritative, judicial pronouncements cannot operate within the psyche of rule-abiding individuals.[75] To have an effect upon state behaviour, they must affect the strategic landscape within which state agents seeking to act in their states' self-interest make decisions.

3.3.2 Bilateral Relations and Expressive Authority – Changing Games through Statements

For those who view states as unitary, self-interest actors operating strategically and unaffected by the Layer 1 constraint of self-enforcement,

[74] William M. Reisman, *Nullity and Revision – The Review and Enforcement of International Judgments and Awards* (New Haven: Yale University Press, 1971), 645.

[75] Usually, scepticism regarding the sanction-independent effect of international courts (holding *auctoritas*) on individual decision-making of state agents does not extend to rulings of domestic courts (holding *potestas*). See, for example, Jack L. Goldsmith and Eric A. Posner, *The Limits of International Law* (Oxford: Oxford University Press, 2005), 93–94.

and international law as lacking Layer 5 (governmental) enforcement, the role of adjudication must be understood through its capacity to activate compliance mechanisms at the inter-state level: Layers 2 (bilateral enforcement) and 3 (decentralised third-party enforcement).[76] This explanation must account for the influence of adjudicators over state behaviour, as Thomas Ginsburg and Richard McAdams put it, 'independent of their perceived legitimacy and the sanctions they wield'.[77] To explain this influence, these authors developed an 'expressive theory' of adjudication, grounded in game theory, which explores how adjudication facilitates coordination in bilateral inter-state relations.[78] McAdams has further expanded this framework, examining how expressive adjudication strengthens the role of law in multi-party settings by galvanising third-party sanctioning mechanisms.[79]

Building on these insights, this section develops a theory of the expressive influence of international adjudicators. Expressive influence extends beyond traditional conceptions of authority, which depend on the authority's legitimacy in the eyes of the addressees of their rulings. Additionally, as conceptualised by Ginsburg and McAdams, expressive influence shapes behaviour independently from the adjudicator's ability to impose sanctions. Its source lies in the recognition, among all participants in a social interaction, that the authority's statements about what is prohibited, permitted, or required are distinct from those of other actors.

The distinctiveness of adjudicatory statements lies in their ability to 'stand out' among the myriad communications regarding the normative framework, creating a focal point for interaction and grounding mutual expectations of behaviour.[80] This quality, described as 'salience' rather than authority, separates expressive influence from individual recognition of legitimacy. Salience derives from the shared understanding

[76] Layers 4 (institutional enforcement) and [5] (authorised enforcement) involve decisions by international organisations and other bodies. For those for whom 'power alone can limit power' (See Chapter 1, note 47 [Roanoke] and accompanying text), explanations must involve *potestas*. Layers 4 and [5] ultimately matter solely to the extent that they affect inter-state relations (on which see Section 3.4).

[77] Tom Ginsburg and Richard H. McAdams, 'Adjudicating in Anarchy: An Expressive Theory of International Law' (2004) 45 *William and Mary Law Review* 1229–1339, at 1047. McAdams notes that his aim is to supplement, not displace, theories that rely on sanctions and legitimacy (Ibid., 1046).

[78] Ibid., at 1266.

[79] Richard H. McAdams, 'The Expressive Power of Adjudication' (2005) 2005 *University of Illinois Law Review* 1043.

[80] Ginsburg and McAdams, 'Adjudicating in Anarchy', 1329.

among actors of the adjudicator's unique position in the normative framework. Crucially, this recognition is not merely individual but social: '[w]hat makes an outcome focal is not merely that it stands out to each individual, but that each individual believes that it stands out to others, that each individual believes that each individual believes that it stands out to others, and so forth'.[81]

This component of authority may be termed expressive. Cass Sunstein has defined the expressive function of law as 'the function of law in "making statements" as opposed to controlling behavior directly'.[82] Expressive authority emerges when each actor in the interaction recognises that the adjudicator's statements, whatever that actor's individual beliefs and preferences, will produce an effect over other actors' beliefs. This effect is to create, in each actor, expectations regarding that actor's own behaviour as well as the behaviour this actor can expect from others. In other words, expressive authority influences not individual perceptions of permissible and expected behaviour but mutual expectations of permissible, prohibited, and required behaviour.

An expressive approach to authority in the international order is helpful insofar as it may take as a starting point the state-centric social order that state agents usually understand themselves to be operating in. Through repeated interactions and deliberate law-making, states develop rules and conventions regarding their respective entitlements and duties, allowing them to coordinate behaviour, avoid conflict, and reduce the costs of interaction, including conflictual interaction. However, this normative framework is marked by indeterminacy. States may usually be able to agree on how the normative framework guides their actions, including by permitting responses in case of violation. However, states will occasionally, and often on important matters, advance diverging interpretations of the relevant rules, or diverging accounts of facts. In these cases, the undecidability among the various views and interpretations advanced by equally sovereign states prevents the normative order from guiding behaviour.

Against this indeterminacy, international adjudicators may influence behaviour merely by making statements regarding the normative framework and its application to the participants. Adjudicators' expressive influence then operates by affecting states' mutual expectations.

[81] Ibid., 1268.

[82] Cass R. Sunstein, 'On the Expressive Function of Law' (1996) 144(5) *University of Pennsylvania Law Review* 2021–2053, at 2024.

The salience of the adjudicator's statements means that, rather than being undecidably diverging, actors' expectations can converge around the adjudicator's statements. The various actors will feel empowered to base their conduct on the adjudicator's statements regarding the content of the normative framework and their entitlements within it, and emboldened to condemn and sanction those who fail to do so.

Thus, under an expressive theory of authority, salient statements do not in and of themselves induce behaviour.[83] What they do is provide the various states, as well as other actors, with discernible unifying statements on the behaviour expected of each actor under the normative framework. Informed of these statements and other actors' knowledge of them, each actor can then determine how to behave and establish benchmarks for others' expected behaviour. In this framework, then, the influence of adjudicators does not depend on individual recognition of the adjudicator's technical prowess, superior judgment, or hierarchical ascendancy. The mere common knowledge of the adjudicator's statements is sufficient to alter the strategic landscape in which state agents make decisions.

To explain the operation of expressive authority, this model takes as a starting point a bilateral relationship in which two constantly interacting states have both common and competing objectives. In each interpretative dispute regarding their respective entitlements and obligations, 'each nation prefers to gain ... by having the other side defer to its claim, but each considers the worst possible outcome to be a military conflict'.[84] Even if military conflict is not immediately foreseeable, if the loss of benefits of cooperation, mutually harmful retaliation, and the prospect of escalation are credible, each party can anticipate a dispute evolving into a highly costly conflict for both. This risk may lead both parties to prefer coordination, with some wins and some losses, to self-interested action that increases the possibility of conflict.[85] At the same

[83] This can also be termed the 'expressive component' of authority. Rather than competing with theories that attribute the influence of authoritative pronouncements to their perceived legitimacy, it offers a complementary explanation for this influence.

[84] Ginsburg and McAdams, 'Adjudicating in Anarchy', 1235–1236. As they explain, this leaves out disputes in which either side, or both, prefer conflict to accepting a loss.

[85] See Daniel W. Drezner, *The Sanctions Paradox: Economic Statecraft and International Relations* (Cambridge: Cambridge University Press, 1999), 16 ('Because of imperfect information, states frequently engage in signaling techniques to demonstrate credibility ... economic sanctions are ineffective as coercive tools, but may be useful as signals').

time, if these states lack any means of determining, for each dispute, whether they should pursue their claim forcefully or back down in the name of long-term cooperation, each party is likely to pursue its claim in every dispute, thus increasing the risk of undesirable conflict.

In these cases, Ginsburg and McAdams argue, 'someone who is not a player [may] influence the players in the game merely by communicating in favor of a particular outcome'.[86] Given the parties' distaste for conflict, they note, even a third party that solved every divergence by randomly stating an expected result would improve coordination. This random decision-maker would be an instrument that both parties could rely on to determine when each of them is meant to back down. Such a randomising decider might guide fruitful cooperation between two parties to a long-term interaction on the conditions that (1) each party that loses believes that it had a fair chance of winning and will have a fair chance of winning in the future; and (2) on balance, each party believes that it is better off maintaining the relationship with the other party than entering into conflict over the decided issue. This allows international adjudicators to contribute to coordination 'expressively, without sanctions, by clarifying the convention and the state of the world to which it applies'.[87]

The main condition Ginsburg and McAdams pose for the adjudicator (or any speaker) to be effective in this scenario is that its expressed views be 'salient'. The concept of salience, which forms the basis for expressive authority, differs from that of 'legitimacy' of the adjudicator/speaker as usually considered in discussions regarding authority. While authority in the sense of legitimacy implies voluntary delegation by each actor of its judgment to the authoritative speaker, 'salience' implies solely that both parties recognise the authoritative speaker's statements as distinct from the plethora of other statements on the conduct required for coordination. A salient actor can be, as the authors explain (quoting Thomas Schelling), 'the bystander who jumps into an intersection and begins to direct traffic' during a blackout, provided that all relevant actors can see the bystander's actions and know that others are also seeing her actions.[88] The resulting improved coordination, and observed compliance with the bystander's directions, is not the result of each driver's

[86] Ginsburg and McAdams, 'Adjudicating in Anarchy', 1266.

[87] Ibid., 1329.

[88] Ibid., 1267 (quoting Thomas Schelling, *The Strategy of Conflict* (Cambridge, MA: Harvard University Press, 1960), 144).

individual assessment of the bystander's legitimacy but of the alignment of expectations among the various, equally self-interested, drivers.

Under a purely expressive approach to adjudication, the elements usually thought to contribute to an adjudicator's legitimacy – expertise, independence, impartiality – are meaningful in their ability to preclude a predictable strategy by the players in case of randomised decisions: the manufacturing of interpretative disputes to play the odds. If an adjudicator is perceived to decide randomly, each player has an incentive to challenge all the entitlements claimed by the other player, including those it does not genuinely believe are in dispute, simply on the expectation that a random decision-maker will give victory to the claimant in half of the cases. This is why, Ginsburg and McAdams reason, 'players will only agree to accept an adjudicator who appears to be accurate, meaning perceptive and unbiased'.[89] Conversely, if adjudicators value receiving further appointments to adjudicate, they can be expected to adopt accuracy as an objective in their rulings: 'an adjudicator will want to adopt a strategy that maximizes her chances that players will ask her to serve as an adjudicator again in the future'.[90]

The key benefit of the expressive theory of adjudication is its ability to provide a morally agnostic theory of the influence of adjudication. Expressive authority does not depend on any actor's belief in the legitimacy of an adjudicator or the 'right to rule' of any actor,[91] or on actors' 'surrender of autonomy' and abandonment of self-interested behaviour.[92] Purely self-interested states, and a purely self-interested adjudicator, may be able to produce a counter-intuitive outcome: a high degree of cooperation, and a high degree of compliance with the adjudicator's statements, without the need to assume the legitimacy of the adjudicator in the eyes of the contenders, or a preference by any of the relevant actors for rule-abiding or ethical behaviour.

3.3.3 *Introducing Sanctions: Expressive Authority in Bilateral and Multi-Party Settings*

Once one accepts the expressive influence of authority, the reasoning above can be extended beyond single-issue, bilateral relations, to the

[89] Ibid., 1274.
[90] Ibid.
[91] Shapiro, 'Authority', 386.
[92] Herbert Marcuse, *A Study on Authority* (transl. Joris de Bres) (London: Verso, 2008), 7.

multi-issue, multilateral setting that is the international order. In this order, a variety of sanctioning mechanisms operate simultaneously to induce compliance. Self-enforcement (Layer 1) and bilateral sanctioning (Layer 2) are complemented by third-party (Layer 3) decentralised enforcement by other states, through reputational harm, reciprocity, and, on select occasions, third-party retaliation. Additionally, as examined in Section 3.4, the prospect of enforcement carried out by IOs and other international bodies at Layer 4, or coordinated by them at Layer [5], can induce compliance.

Layer 2 sanctions can be considered largely within the context of a bilateral relation as described in Section 3.3.2. Adjudicators may be significant in their ability to determine whether an actor has committed a violation and whether a sanction is or was warranted. Subject to the same conditions as above, adjudication can usefully be employed to assess the lawfulness of sanctions, so that an unwarranted sanction can then be treated as a violation, while a warranted one can be accepted. With the interpretative conflict resolved, the participants in the interaction can then move on and avoid the costs of conflict. With regard to diffuse enforcement by third states (Layer 3), the ability of an adjudicator to align expectations may be even more significant than it is in bilateral relations. This is due to the overall disincentive for non-involved actors, that is, those who have no immediate interest in a dispute, to incur the cost of applying sanctions.

In any setting, applying sanctions requires the sanctioner to expend resources.[93] Even merely discursive sanctions are likely to mar relations between sanctioner and sanctioned. In a decentralised setting in which sanctioners employ their own resources rather than collective ones, this means that all sanctions hinge on the relative power of the actors involved. If only bilateral sanctions matter, powerful actors face limited disincentives to act against less powerful ones. Diffuse third-party sanctions may create additional disincentives for violation in multi-party settings. However, to the extent that these sanctions depend on a conscious decision to sanction, they involve an additional challenge when compared to bilateral sanctions.

[93] Lisa L. Martin, 'Credibility, Costs, and Institutions: Cooperation on Economic Sanctions' (1993) 45 *World Politics* 406, 416 ('sanctions are valuable tools in international politics, precisely because they force those who impose them to bear some costs'); Daniel W. Drezner, 'Bargaining, Enforcement, and Multilateral Sanctions: When Is Cooperation Counterproductive?' (2000) 54 *International Organization* 73–102.

The literature on third-party sanctions has often noted that third-party sanctions tend to be undersupplied due to the so-called sanctioner's dilemma,[94] including economic sanctions[95] and reputational ones.[96] A prospective third-party sanctioner's cost-benefit analysis involves not solely the costs of the sanctioning act but also those of the collective action problem. A collective action problem arises because a state sanctioning a violation that does not affect it specifically must bear the full cost of this sanction, while the benefits of norm compliance will be diffuse and not uniquely enjoyed by the sanctioning state. As Alexander Thompson puts it, 'all states that are parties to [a multilateral] treaty or that benefit from the customary rule stand to gain from compliance', and thus 'all actors would be better off finding a way to punish a violator, thereby inducing compliance'. However, 'no single state has an incentive to do so', because the gains from compliance for each actor are smaller than the cost of sanctions. This is likely to result in under-sanctioning of violations of obligations owed to groups rather than individuals, 'leaving all . . . worse off'.[97]

A second aspect of the problem arises, for any sanctioner, 'in the relative anarchy of international politics',[98] due to the horizontal structure of the international order and the consequential uncertainty regarding the interpretation of norms and characterisation of conduct. In this horizontal structure, states considering whether to sanction what they deem to be violations must not only consider the costs of deploying resources to sanction the violation but also what Thompson terms 'potential political costs' of sanctioning. These costs derive from uncertainty regarding the character of the sanction, that is, whether they are both warranted and appropriate. Both in bilateral relations and for third-party sanctioning, a sanctioner state must 'convince other states that its actions are a form of enforcement in defense of legal rules rather than an

94 Alexander Thompson, 'The Rational Enforcement of International Law: Solving the Sanctioners' Dilemma' (2009) 1(2) *International Theory* 307–321. See also William H. Kaempfer and Anton D. Lowenberg, 'Unilateral Versus Multilateral International Sanctions: A Public Choice Perspective' (1999) 43 *International Studies Quarterly* 37–58.

95 Lisa L. Martin, *Coercive Cooperation: Explaining Multilateral Economic Sanction* (Princeton, NJ: Princeton University Press, 1992), 8–10.

96 Andrew T. Guzman, 'A Compliance-Based Theory of International Law' (2002) 90(6) *California Law Review* 1823–1887, at 1863.

97 Thompson, 'The Rational Enforcement of International Law', 311.

98 Ibid.

aggressive pursuit of more selfish goals' or risk being itself the subject of sanctions.[99]

The risk of being perceived as a wrongdoer decreases the willingness of states to consider sanctioning in the first place, including against bilateral violations, unless the sanctioner is independently interested in adopting the sanctions. The collective action problem makes third states even less likely to adopt sanctions in which they are not independently interested. Independent interest may exist if a sanction fulfils a foreign policy objective of the sanctioner, such as isolating a rival economically or politically, but also if it fulfils a domestic policy objective, such as advantaging domestic economic actors vis-à-vis a foreign competitor. The independent interest a potential sanctioner could have in the sanction in turn leads to suspicion that any sanctioner is covertly applying a self-interested measure, further decreasing the likelihood that a non-self-interested state will adopt sanctions, even discursive ones.

Adjudication can reduce the costs arising from the uncertainty element in the sanctioner's dilemma.[100] As McAdams explains, 'third-party enforcement requires that third parties form beliefs about what the norm requires and whether a particular individual has met those requirements'.[101] This is also the case with respect to Layer 2 enforcement, if it takes place in a multi-party setting in which the parties are being observed by other states and considering these others' beliefs and potential sanctioning behaviour. Thus, a sanctioner state's beliefs do not form in isolation but depend on a calculation of how the sanctioned state, as well as third states, will respond to the sanction. If there is uncertainty regarding whether sanctioning is justifiable, each potential sanctioner is likely to avoid the risk of an unjustified sanction, reducing the prospect of a violation being sanctioned.

99 Ibid., 312.

100 In a decentralised system, individual actors adopting sanctioning measures for a public good (rule enforcement) incur costs which adjudication cannot address. See however sanctions under Layers 4 and [5] in Section 3.4. From this perspective, the entire enforcement apparatus of the state can be seen as a device to make the cost of sanctioning violations bearable by entrusting them to collectively funded specialised agents, who adopt sanctions both at a low cost to themselves and (due to the legal authority structure and their position within it) with negligible costs deriving from the uncertainty element in the sanctioner's dilemma.

101 McAdams, 'The Expressive Power of Adjudication', 1094.

On the other hand, 'the dilemma disappears if there is widespread agreement on the situation at hand'.[102] A consensus can be fostered by entrusting the decision to a third party, which then assumes the role of the authoritative (or 'salient') adjudicator. By issuing a ruling that establishes the existence of a violation and specifies what can be demanded from the wrongdoer, the adjudicator enables potential third-party sanctioners, as well as observing actors, to align their expectations and resolve the sanctioner's dilemma. This alignment increases the likelihood of sanctions being adopted – even if, often, these will be low-cost discursive sanctions – where legal debates, uncertainty, and concerns about accusations of unwarranted sanctioning might otherwise deter responses entirely.

Addressing the third-party sanctioner's dilemma is another way in which expressive authority makes international adjudication authoritative, without requiring the adjudicator to be perceived as a legitimate ruler, or its reasoning as particularly persuasive to an addressee of its pronouncements.[103] In this regard, state agents of third-party sanctioners do not need to 'comply' with the adjudicator's rulings by acting against their perception of state interests. Within the rational choice framework of expressive adjudication theory, the adjudicator's role is to offer a unifying, salient interpretation of the normative framework. This shared understanding enables actors to coordinate their actions without the structural uncertainty characteristic of horizontal systems. This function is particularly important in the common scenario where only a subset of states – or even a single state – is motivated to sanction a violation, in what Lisa Martin terms 'asymmetry of interests among potential sanctioners'.[104] A judicial finding of breach provides states with the necessary licence to impose sanctions, reassured that other states are unlikely to penalise them for unwarranted or excessive sanctioning.

Similarly, states without self-interest in sanctioning can be expected to accept third-party sanctions – and sometimes even participate in

[102] Thompson, 'The Rational Enforcement of International Law', 317.

[103] Martin proposes an alternative effect arising from the very act of seeking an international institution's decision: 'states can use self-imposed costs and international institutions to increase audience costs and thus make credible commitments' (Martin, 'Credibility, Costs and Institutions', 421).

[104] Ibid., at 408 ('The process of organizing multilateral sanctions typically occurs under conditions of significant asymmetry of interests among potential sanctioners, with one state having a strong interest in seeing sanctions imposed and thus assuming an entrepreneurial role in organizing the multilateral effort').

them – without affirmatively recognising the adjudicator's legitimacy to determine conduct or the persuasiveness of its reasoning in the particular case. Once state agents collectively expect an adjudicator's interpretation of the normative framework to be salient, they are likely to accept its validity and, in many cases, engage in sanctioning when the adjudicator establishes a violation, unless they have strong countervailing reasons. This reasoning mirrors the previous scenario, where parties in a bilateral relationship comply with an adverse ruling to avoid conflict, provided they expect to benefit from future rulings. Once the adjudicator has declared a violation, an observer state, or more precisely its agents, may support and participate in third-party sanctions imposed by other states, to avoid conflict with the sanctioning parties. The observing state will likely do so if (1) it expects to be the one seeking to sanction a violation in the future and does not want others to challenge the adjudicator's authority then, and (2) the benefits it gains from maintaining the integrity of the normative framework outweigh the costs it may incur by condoning, or participating in, sanctioning.

In other words, an adjudicator's expressive authority allows states to coordinate not only reciprocal 'first-order' behaviour but also 'second-order' behaviour, that is, sanctioning behaviour. Adjudication lowers the costs of, and thus enables and facilitates, both Layer 2 sanctioning by the injured state and Layer 3 decentralised sanctions by third parties. The mere fact that the violation is established by the actor considered 'saliently' authoritative, rather than being unilaterally determined by each party and subject to uncertainty and contestation by others, decreases a potential sanctioner's disincentives to sanction. It does so by reducing the likelihood that the sanctioner will itself be subject to third-party sanctions for unwarranted sanctioning.

Expressive authority is usually considered to be behind the success of adjudicatory panels under the 1947 General Agreement on Tariffs and Trade (GATT), which were not empowered to make binding decisions and did not even adjudicate on a formally binding agreement. Robert Hudec concluded that, in the GATT's early years, panel findings of violation led to 'at least partial correction' in 100 per cent of the cases. In the more contentious 1980s, this number was still 83 per cent, with 'full satisfaction' in 57 per cent of cases.[105] This level of compliance was

[105] Robert E. Hudec, *Enforcing International Trade Law: The Evolution of the Modern GATT Legal System* (Salem, NH: Butterworth, 1991), 344–351. Robert E. Hudec, Daniel L.M. Kennedy, and Mark Sgarbossa, 'A Statistical Profile of GATT Dispute

observed even though Layer 2 retaliatory sanctions were rarely applied and Layer 3 sanctions were largely discursive and reputational.

Hudec identified 'the force of community pressure' as '[t]he ultimate "remedy" which made the GATT dispute settlement procedure as successful as it was'.[106] GATT Panels contributed merely by informing the perception of the GATT's contracting parties regarding the content of the GATT normative framework and expressing panellists' views on whether a violation had taken place. Even though GATT contracting parties failed to adopt many panels' reports, which were thus not recognised as having formal legal value, these panels' pronouncements still guided the application, between the GATT's contracting parties, of the decentralised sanctioning mechanisms of international law.

As Hudec concluded, '[c]ommunity pressure is something that can be generated without an elaborate structure of remedial procedures'.[107] It can be generated especially, he could have added, where the community has a means to 'speak with one voice' and the various states that compose it can apply pressure, even if merely discursive or symbolic, on the basis of a unifying statement of the applicable norms and violations. Adjudicative *auctoritas* is thus the ability to make pronouncements that the relevant actors recognise as salient, that is, as tendentially unifying statements of the normative framework and of the characterisation of conduct under it.

3.4 Legalisation and Authority: Centralisation, Delegation and the Limits of *Auctoritas* in a Decentralised Social Order

3.4.1 Delegation of Sanctioning Authority: International Organisations and Quasi-Organisations

The mechanisms for adjudicative influence considered above apply even within a wholly decentralised normative framework, in which states decide individually on whether and how to comply and to sanction

Settlement Cases: 1948–1989' (1993) 2 *Minnesota Journal of International Law* 1, 96. Petros Mavroidis, however, questions the extent to which Hudec's analysis may be influenced by selection bias, since established panels were those which defendants allowed to be established in the first place. See Petros C. Mavroidis, 'Remedies in the WTO Legal System: Between a Rock and a Hard Place' (2000) 11 *EJIL* 763, 810.

106 Robert E. Hudec, 'Broadening the Scope of Remedies in WTO Dispute Settlement', in Friedl Weiss and Jochem Wiers (eds.), *Improving WTO Dispute Settlement Procedures* (London: Cameron May, 2000), 345, 400.

107 Ibid.

violations, operating under Layers 1, 2, and 3. This section examines the role of adjudicators in the increasing set of instances in which, using treaties and other arrangements, states agree to establish institutions through which they are able to decide collectively. States delegate to these institutions the authority to determine institutional (Layer 4) sanctions, as well as to authorise, or require, states to apply certain sanctions that involve the mobilisation of resources (which I have termed Layer [5]).

Besides interpretative authority, treaties that establish international institutions sometimes delegate sanctioning authority.[108] Sanctioning authority empowers the international institution to go beyond interpreting the agreed rules of conduct and to emulate the function of sanctions in a domestic legal order: creating material, political, or reputational disadvantages for the actor found in breach. In game-theoretical terms, this means going beyond guiding mutual expectations and seeking to 'impose costs . . . to pressure the target of sanctions to adjust internal or external policies'.[109] By grounding sanctions on agreed collective decision-making processes, states replicate the distinction that exists in domestic social orders between legal sanctions – those imposed following a decision by an authority – and 'mere' social sanctions, which arise from reputational concerns or are applied independently of the legal system.[110] Hans Kelsen articulated the relevance of this distinction: '[t]he legal norm refers to the conduct of two entities: the citizen, against whose delict the coercive measure of the sanction is directed; and the organ that is to apply the coercive measure to the delict'.[111]

Layers 4 and [5] appear when states delegate to a decision-making body the authority to determine, in particular instances, what sanctions are permissible or obligatory for a breach. Decisions made by international institutions that establish rights and obligations, or even

[108] Dan Sarooshi draws a distinction between 'delegations' and 'transfers' of powers, the latter taking place when the conferral of a power is framed as irrevocable. Sarooshi, *International Organizations and Their Exercise of Sovereign Powers*, 54, 65.

[109] Martin, *Coercive Cooperation*, 1.

[110] Hans Kelsen, 'The Pure Theory of Law and Analytical Jurisprudence' (1941) 55 *Harvard Law Review* 44, 57–58 ('psychic coercion is not a specific element of the law. Moral and religious norms as well are coercive in this psychological sense . . . the law sets up coercive measures as sanctions that are to be directed under definite conditions against definitive individuals').

[111] Ibid., 58.

identify a violation, ordinarily serve as catalysts for regular inter-state sanctioning mechanisms under Layers 2 and 3. The two additional layers emerge when the institution itself is empowered to determine the appropriate sanctions. Institutional sanctions (Layer 4) are decided and implemented by the institutions themselves, and may include verbal or written condemnations, the suspension of participation or voting rights, or even expulsion from an organisation or organ.[112] Authorised sanctions (Layer [5]), on the other hand, can be determined by an institution (using its *auctoritas*) but involve, in their deployment, the use *potestas*, requiring material resources. An IO or institution can establish the permissibility or even the obligation to sanction under Layer [5], but its implementation relies on further action by states – usually, parties to the treaty or arrangement that created the institution. In essence, the institution lends its *auctoritas* to the sanction, but the sanction itself necessitates the deployment of coercive power, which only states have at their disposal.[113]

Delegation of sanctioning authority does not need to involve international adjudicators as traditionally understood, that is, bodies composed of individuals, tasked with making impartial decisions and given resources to decide with independence from governments. In fact, most bodies tasked with determining the applicability of sanctions are 'political' bodies, composed of government representatives whose decisions are based at least as much on foreign policy preferences of governments as on the pursuit of accurate legal interpretation and legal characterisation.

Imposing sanctions requires interpreting a legal text or practice, characterising the conduct of (usually) a state in light of this interpretation, and determining whether applicable sanctions are warranted. However, though the sanctioning institution must interpret a normative framework, the focus of a sanction is not to facilitate social interaction but to impose social control.[114] For sanctioning bodies,

[112] In this regard, one can think of institutions as exercising a degree of *potestas*, for example, preventing a state delegate from attending a certain meeting or not counting her vote in decision-making. The application of Layer 4 sanctions is usually entrusted to organs composed of states. As long as the decision is a collective one and its application is entrusted to a collective body rather than to states deciding individually, the relevant sanction is no longer inter-state or dependent solely on a sanctioning state's willingness and ability to apply it.

[113] I thank J. Benton Heath for helping me think through this topic.

[114] On this distinction, based on Lon Fuller's work, see Section 2.2.

adjudication takes place not as the primary focus of attention but incidentally.[115]

The adjudicatory function implied in institutional sanctioning may be subject to contestation. In many cases, the sanctioned party may challenge the well-foundedness of sanctions, claiming that they are unwarranted, purely politically motivated, or excessive. This opens the possibility for adjudication by a body with *auctoritas* derived from its features of independence, impartiality, and duty to interpret and apply legal norms – an IC. Thus, though international adjudicators do not normally engage in sanctioning activity,[116] ICs can be involved in institutional sanctioning by ensuring that there is a check on unwarranted or disproportionate sanctions – and, conversely, by backing the deployment of warranted and proportionate sanctions with their *auctoritas*. As the remainder of this section shows, not all institutional sanctioning involves ICs. Where it does, however, adjudicative *auctoritas* adds to the relevant sanctioning mechanism, potentially lowering the costs of decision-making as well as those of sanction deployment.

3.4.2 Delegated Sanctioning Authority and (Lack of) Adjudication at the United Nations

The UN Charter features sanctions at layers 4 and [5]. The United Nations General Assembly (UNGA) is empowered to apply Layer 4 sanctions, sometimes called 'institutional' or 'corporative', that is, those that United Nations organs both adopt and implement.[117] Articles 5 and

[115] See Oscar Schachter, 'The Quasi-Judicial Role of the Security Council and the General Assembly' (1964) 58 *AJIL* 962. See also Alvarez, *International Organizations as Law-Makers*, 174 ('the [Security] Council has acted in a "quasi-judicial" capacity even though, as a political body whose members do not abstain on matters raised under Chapter VII, it is not capable of granting states the independent, impartial and even-handed judicial consideration that some would argue underpins article 1(1) of the Charter').

[116] International adjudicators may engage in sanctioning activity in specific contexts, in the context of the deployment of their authority rather than the deployment of coercive measures. They may, for example, refuse to consider arguments submitted outside of specific time frames and formats, or evidence produced using fraud. They may also respond to breach or non-compliance with a prior ruling by adopting symbolic sanctions, such as formal condemnations or declarations of breach or non-compliance, or, as discussed in Chapter 5, by authorising others to deploy coercive sanctions.

[117] Jean Combacau, *Le pouvoir de sanction de l'ONU: étude théorique de la coercition non militaire* (Paris: A. Pedone, 1974); Charles Leben, *Les sanctions privatives de droits ou de qualité dans les organisations internationales spécialisées: recherches sur les sanctions internationales et l'évolution du droit des gens* (Bruxelles: Bruylant, 1979).

6 permit, respectively, suspension and expulsion of a member by the UNGA, in either case upon the recommendation of the United Nations Security Council (UNSC).[118] Additionally, Article 19 provides for an 'automatic' sanction: the loss of voting rights for Members whose financial contribution payments remain in arrears for two years. Though this sanction is considered to arise *ipso facto* from a state falling in arrears, Article 19 gives the UNGA authority to permit the member to continue voting, a right it has exercised on a number of instances.[119]

The UNGA's Layer 4 powers to suspend or expel any member have been used only once, and atypically. In 1971, a General Assembly Resolution asserted 'the lawful rights of the People's Republic of China ... as the only legitimate representatives of China to the United Nations', and in the same breath decided 'to expel forthwith the representatives of Chiang Kai-shek from the place which they unlawfully occupy at the United Nations and in all the organizations related to it'.[120] The UNGA has used institutional sanctions in other contexts. It has twice suspended states from the Human Rights Council (Libya in 2011[121] and Russia in 2022)[122] using its power, under the resolution that established the Council, to 'suspend the rights of membership in the Council of a member of the Council that commits gross and systematic violations of human rights'.[123] In both cases, it grounded the sanction in its own determinations that gross and systematic violations of human rights had occurred, rather than seeking or relying on adjudicatory rulings.

The UNSC is principally entrusted under Chapter VII of the UN Charter with the adoption of Layer [5] enforcement, authorising – usually, requiring – the deployment of sanctions whose application depends on states mobilising economic or political resources. The Council may, under Article 39, characterise a situation as one giving rise to sanctions: a

[118] See on this Hans Kelsen, 'Sanctions under the Charter of the United Nations' (1946) 12 *Canadian Journal of Economics and Political Science* 429–438.

[119] Christian Tomuschat, 'Article 19', in Bruno Simma et al. (eds.), *The Charter of the United Nations: A Commentary, Volume I*, 3rd edn (Oxford: Oxford University Press, 2012).

[120] UNGA Res. 2758/XXVI of 25 October 1971 ('Restoration of the lawful rights of the People's Republic of China in the United Nations').

[121] UNGA Res. 65/265 of 1 March 2011 ('Suspension of the rights of membership of the Libyan Arab Jamahiriya in the Human Rights Council').

[122] UNGA Res. ES-11/3 of 7 April 2022 ('Suspension of the rights of membership of the Russian Federation in the Human Rights Council').

[123] UNGA Res. 60/251 of 3 April 2006 ('Human Rights Council'), para. 8.

threat to the peace, a breach of the peace, or an aggression. Under Articles 41 and 42, it may determine economic and military sanctions.[124] Under Article 25 of the Charter, UN Members are required to 'accept and carry out the decisions of the Security Council' adopted in accordance with the Charter. Though the Council's approach to the application of sanctions has evolved and now ensures some degree of procedural legality, in particular insofar as individuals are targeted,[125] as regards sanctions against states its decisions remain grounded in its own determinations that a threat to the peace or a breach of the peace has occurred.

Despite the UNGA not being given Layer [5] sanctioning authority under the Charter, it has made incursions into Layer [5] enforcement. It first did so when it offered its authority to the use of force in Korea. The 1950 'Uniting for Peace' resolution authorises the UNGA to adopt resolutions in case the UNSC 'fails to exercise its primary responsibility for the maintenance of international peace and security'. The UNGA may then 'mak[e] appropriate recommendations to Members for collective measures, including in the case of a breach of the peace or act of aggression the use of armed force'.[126] A subsequent UNGA resolution termed the People's Republic of China's involvement in Korea 'aggression', calling upon states to 'lend every assistance to the United Nations action in Korea' as well as to 'refrain from giving any assistance to the aggressors in Korea'.[127] In the 1980s, the UNGA declared South Africa's apartheid policies legal violations and recommended the adoption by members of a variety of economic sanctions against it.[128] In both cases, it adopted a similar attitude to the UNSC, making itself the determination that sanctions were warranted.

[124] UN Charter, Articles 39–42.

[125] See Devika Hovell, *The Power of Process: The Value of Due Process in Security Council Sanctions Decision-Making* (Oxford: OUP, 2016); Bardo Fassbender, 'Targeted Sanctions Imposed by the UN Security Council and Due Process Rights' (2006) 3 *International Organizations Law Review* 437; Thomas Dörfler, *Security Council Sanctions Governance: The Power and Limits of Rules* (Oxford: Routledge, 2019).

[126] UNGA Res. 377 (V) ('Uniting for Peace'), 3 November 1950.

[127] UNGA Res. 498 (V) ('Intervention of the Central People's Government of People's Republic of China in Korea'), 1 February 1951, paras. 1, 3, 4, 5.

[128] See, for example, the multiple sanctions proposed in UNGA Resolutions A/RES/36/172, of 17 December 1981 ('Policies of Apartheid of the Government of South Africa') and lifted in A/RES/48/1, of 12 October 1993 ('Lifting of sanctions against South Africa'). See Rebecca Barber, 'An Exploration of the General Assembly's Troubled Relationship with Unilateral Sanctions' (2021) 70 *International and Comparative Law Quarterly* 343–378.

The role of legal assessments in the discussion and adoption of sanctions by the UNGA and UNSC is complex. Within both organs, delegates' discussions tend to be openly political, and their votes are understood to be guided primarily by foreign policy considerations of their respective governments. At the same time, their decisions are legal decisions, and they, unavoidably, must interpret rules and characterise facts prior to adopting sanctions. The prevalent rationale of UNSC decisions has been called a 'political operation *within* the law, rather than decision according *to* the law',[129] and law's role in security debates, that of 'a handmaid to state power and interest, a facilitator for politics to take its natural course'.[130] Neither the UNSC nor the UNGA have ever requested an adjudicator's opinion or referred to an adjudicator's views when determining whether and how to apply sanctions. Providing the ICJ with compulsory jurisdiction to interpret and apply the UN Charter would logically have permitted it to determine whether a sanction decided by the UNSC (or UNGA) was unwarranted or excessive. However, a proposal to establish this compulsory jurisdiction was rejected in San Francisco.[131]

The one instance in which Layer [5] sanctions were challenged at the ICJ was the *Lockerbie* case, brought by Libya, which ended inconclusively and with various ICJ judges providing diverging accounts of the ability of the Court to review the legality of UNSC resolutions.[132] Instead, it seems that a form of 'decentralised' control of legality emerges, with various actors making their own determinations of the legality of sanctions under the Charter. This matches José Alvarez's view that, in the design of the Charter, '[i]f the [Security] Council goes too far, the anticipated remedy is political, not legal: members should exercise their right of civil disobedience and fail to comply with the Council's demands, even in breach of the Charter'.[133] In other words, in the absence of a structured legal system for compliance control by an

[129] See Rosalyn Higgins, 'The Place of International Law in the Settlement of Disputes by the Security Council' (1970) 64 *American Journal of International Law* 1, 16.

[130] Martti Koskenniemi, 'The Place of Law in Collective Security', (1996) 17 *Michigan Journal of International Law* 455, 488.

[131] See Mohamed Sameh M. Amr, *The Role of the International Court of Justice as the Principal Judicial Organ of the United Nations* (The Hague: Kluwer, 2003), 300–301. See, however, Mutlaq Al-Qahtani, 'The Role of the International Court of Justice in the Enforcement of Its Judicial Decisions' (2002) 15 *Leiden Journal of International Law* 781.

[132] Ibid.

[133] Alvarez, *International Organizations as Law-Makers*, 266.

independent authoritative body, decentralised control emerges: 'institutional practice and the general acceptability of what IOs do provide the ultimate test for legality'.[134]

Coincidentally perhaps, the two most prominent instances of open contestation of the legality of UNSC sanctions came not from individual states but from regional IOs. One was the *Kadi* case, in which the Court of Justice of the European Union determined that EU member states should not enforce certain sanctions against individuals, due to their shortcomings in terms of fundamental rights standards.[135] The other was termed by Tshibangu Kalala the 'civil disobedience' determined by the Organisation of African Unity regarding the sanctions against Libya.[136] Although mere non-compliance with UN sanctions is a common occurrence, civil disobedience grounded in the *auctoritas* of an international institution (adjudicatory or political) presents a challenge of a different nature. This disobedience targets sanctions not only at the political level but at the level of their lawfulness – of the exercise by the sanctioning bodies of their *auctoritas* within the limits of their state-granted competences.[137]

3.4.3 Ex Post Adjudication of Delegated Sanctions: Collective Sanctions by Regional International Organisations

Significant scholarly attention has been given to sanctioning by United Nations bodies, and especially to Layer [5] sanctions determined by the UNSC. However, most sanctioning activity by IOs has taken place in the context of regional organisations or other treaties, such as multilateral

[134] Ibid. See also Antonios Tzanakopoulos, *Disobeying the Security Council: Countermeasures against Wrongful Sanctions* (Oxford: Oxford University Press, 2011).

[135] CJEU, Joined cases C-402/05P & C-415/05P, *Kadi & Al Barakaat International Foundation* v. *Council and Commission*, Judgment (Grand Chamber), 3 September 2008. See Samantha Besson, 'European Legal Pluralism after Kadi' (2009) 5 *European Constitutional Law Review* 237.

[136] Tshibangu Kalala, 'La décision de l'O.U.A. de ne plus respecter les sanctions décrétées par l'O.N.U. Contre la Libye: désobéissance civile des États africains à l'égard de l'O.N.U.' (1999) 32 *Revue Belge de Droit International* 545.

[137] See Enzo Canizzarro and Paolo Palchetti, '*Ultra Vires* Acts of International Organizations', in Jan Klabbers and Asa Wallendahl (eds.), *Research Handbook on the Law of International Organizations* (Cheltenham: Elgar, 2011), 365–397. Importantly, in *Kadi* the CJEU ultimately did not pronounce on the UNSC's exercise of *auctoritas* but isolated it from the lawful exercise of *potestas* under EU law.

environmental agreements (MEAs), which permit the adoption of sanctions against states that fail to live up to certain standards. Although these sanctions – at both Layer 4 and Layer [5] – are often determined by political bodies, they tend to have a very different relationship to adjudication than the UNGA and UNSC.

Treaties establishing regional integration organisations tend to permit their members, usually gathered as the highest decision-making body of the organisation, to adopt sanctions against members who fail to abide by certain standards.[138] In any case, under the Vienna Convention on the Law of Treaties (VCLT) Article 60(2)(a), a material breach of a multilateral treaty by one of its parties allows 'the other parties by unanimous agreement to suspend the operation of the treaty in whole or in part or to terminate it', either entirely or with respect to the wrongdoer, in practice expelling it from the treaty.[139]

Under the VCLT as well as most regional agreements that permit sanctions, the parties to the treaty adopt the sanctioning decision. However, the question whether a violation of the treaty (or its material breach) has been committed remains a legal question. And many of the regional agreements that delegate sanctioning authority to a political body also delegate to an adjudicator the authority to settle disputes regarding the interpretation and application of the agreement. Thus, contrary to the ICJ in relation to sanctions adopted by the UNSC or the UNGA, adjudicators under regional sanction-permitting agreements

[138] See, on sanctions by regional international organisations, Namira Negm, 'The Sanctions Regime of the African Union in Response to Unconstitutional Changes of Government', in Ian Johnstone and Steven Ratner (eds.), *Talking International Law: Legal Argumentation Outside the Courtroom* (New York: OUP, 2022), 218–236; Stefano Palestini, 'Regional Organizations and the Politics of Sanctions against Undemocratic Behaviour in the Americas' (2021) 42 *International Political Science Review* 469–483; Elin Hellquist, 'Regional Organizations and Sanctions Against Members: Explaining the Different Trajectories of the African Union, the League of Arab States, and the Association of Southeast Asian Nations', (2014) *KFG Working Paper Series*, No. 59, Kolleg-Forschergruppe (KFG) "The Transformative Power of Europe", Freie Universität Berlin; Konstantinos D. Magliveras, 'Legal and Procedural Issues Arising from the Expulsion of the Russian Federation from the Council of Europe' (2023) 23 *International and Comparative Law Review* 95–116.

[139] VCLT, Article 62(2)(a). See Geraldo Vidigal, 'Enforcing Democracy at the Regional Level: Paraguay's Suspension Before the Mercosur Court' (2013) 2 *Cambridge International Law Journal* 337–349, at 343; Maïmouna Diakité and Zoé Baize, 'Sanctions by International Organizations and Judicial Review: The Case of Mali vs the Conference of Heads of States and Government of the WAEMU' (2024) 51 *Legal Issues of Economic Integration* 171–194.

may have compulsory jurisdiction over disputes regarding the applicable normative framework. A sanctioned state may therefore seise an adjudicator – and one whose rulings bind the sanctioning authority, or at least the states that compose it – with the question of whether a sanction is or was warranted.

In recent years, there have been two challenges before adjudicators with respect to sanctions decided by political organs of regional organisations. First, Paraguay challenged, before the Mercosur Permanent Review Tribunal, the decision by the other three Mercosur member states to suspend its right to take part in Mercosur decision-making due to a 'breakdown of democracy' in Paraguay.[140] The Tribunal considered that it did have jurisdiction to determine whether a breakdown of democracy – which triggers the application of sanctions under Mercosur's Democratic Commitment Protocol – had taken place. However, it dismissed the case on grounds that the 'emergency procedure' to which Paraguay resorted was reserved for disputes regarding perishable goods.[141] This emergency procedure was the only manner to seise the Tribunal directly, rather than on appeal from an arbitral award by an Ad Hoc Arbitral Tribunal. Thus, although adjudication of sanctions is available under Mercosur law, due to the temporal delay to obtain a final decision, an adjudicatory ruling will only be obtained by a highly persistent sanctioned member.

A second instance of adjudicatory review of collective sanctioning was the challenge by Mali to sanctions imposed on it by its West African regional partners. This was less straightforward because the challenge took place before the Court of the West African Economic and Monetary Union (WAEMU), whose political body had merely implemented sanctions to mirror those determined by the Economic Community of West African States (ECOWAS). And, while the revised ECOWAS Treaty provides for sanctions '[w]here a Member fails to fulfil its obligations to the Community',[142] no similar provision is found in the WAEMU Treaty.[143] Mali brought up the issue before the WAEMU Court, obtaining an Order

[140] *Decisión sobre la Suspensión del Paraguay en el Mercosur en Aplicación del Protocolo de Ushuaia sobre Compromiso Democrático*, MERCOSUR/CMC/DEC. No 28/12, 29 June 2012.

[141] Laudo No 01/2012 (Award 1/2012), Tribunal Permanente de Revisión del Mercosur, 21 July 2012, paras. 34–35, 40. See Vidigal, 'Enforcing Democracy at the Regional Level'.

[142] ECOWAS Revised Treaty, dated 24 July 1993, Article 77(1).

[143] Diakité and Baize, 'Sanctions by International Organizations and Judicial Review'.

from its President. The sanctions were subsequently suspended by ECOWAS, before Mali withdrew from the organisation.

Unsurprisingly given the complexities involved, the seising of adjudicators with disputes regarding institutional or authorised sanctions occurs only in a small subset of the cases in which these sanctions are adopted. At the Council of Europe, the Committee of Ministers declared in February 2022 a 'serious violation by the Russian Federation of its obligations under Article 3 of the Statute of the Council of Europe' as a result of Russia's invasion of Ukraine, and 'agreed to suspend the Russian Federation from its rights of representation in the Council of Europe'.[144] The next month, after the procedure for expulsion, when the Committee of Ministers decided 'that the Russian Federation cease[d] to be a member of the Council of Europe as from 16 March 2022', the Committee of Ministers acknowledged that its decision arrived one day after Russia itself had communicated its withdrawal from the Council of Europe.[145] Although one might debate whether the reason for Russia's expulsion fit appropriately as a violation of Article 3 (whose focus is the rule of law),[146] Russia did not challenge the measure before any adjudicator.

3.4.4 *Ex Ante Adjudication of Delegated Sanctions: Multilateral Environmental Agreements and Trade Agreements*

A different form of relationship of adjudication to delegated sanctioning authority emerges when the delegating text requires the sanctioning body – which usually remains a political organ – to ground its rulings on an assessment of the situation by an impartial decision-maker. Many MEAs provide for measures and procedures to be adopted in response to non-compliance by contracting parties with certain commitments or established targets.[147] These 'non-compliance procedures and mechan-

[144] Committee of Ministers. Consequences of the aggression of the Russian Federation against Ukraine, CM/Del/Dec(2022)1426ter/2.3, 25 February 2022.

[145] Committee of Ministers. Resolution CM/Res(2022)2 on the cessation of the membership of the Russian Federation to the Council of Europe. CM/Res(2022)2, 16 March 2022.

[146] See Magliveras, 'Legal and Procedural Issues', 99.

[147] The concept of 'non-compliance' is used as a softer alternative to 'breach'. It might suggest that the regular rules of state responsibility do not apply. See Malgosia A. Fitzmaurice and Catherine Redgwell, 'Environmental Non-Compliance Procedures and International Law' (2000) 31 *Netherlands Yearbook of International Law* 35–65.

isms'[148] (NCPs) aim for a '"carrot-stick" approach … to encourage compliance',[149] establishing both rewards for compliance and an array of measures that can adopted in response to persistent or egregious non-compliance.

Given the variety of subject matters of MEAs and the various negotiation trajectories, each NCP is unique. However, some regularities exist, including their key organs and available measures. There is often a separation between two organs. On the one hand, a 'compliance committee' or 'implementation committee', with certain features of an impartial adjudicatory body, is tasked with producing reports, assessing compliance by MEA contracting parties with the MEA's rules, as well as the attainment of MEA targets. Compliance committee activity has led in some cases to 'the development of quasi-jurisprudence sometimes referred to as "case law"'.[150] On the other hand, a more clearly political body – typically, one composed of state representatives, such as the Conference of the Parties or Meeting of the Parties – is usually given the legal authority to determine responses to non-compliance. These responses may include, in serious cases, the impositions of 'measures', referred to with a sufficient degree of generality to encompass both institutional Layer 4 and authorised Layer [5] sanctions.

Ostensible sanctions under NCPs are rare. NCPs operate largely based on dialogue, publication of reports, and issuing of general recommendations.[151] In 2008 and 2009, the Enforcement Branch of the Kyoto Protocol's Compliance Committee determined that Greece and Croatia

[148] Tullio Treves et al. (eds.), *Non-Compliance Procedures and Mechanisms and the Effectiveness of International Environmental Agreements* (The Hague: TMC Asser, 2009).

[149] Francesca Romanin Jacur, 'The Non-Compliance Procedure of the 1987 Montreal Protocol to the 1985 Vienna Convention on Substances That Deplete the Ozone Layer', in Tullio Treves et al. (eds.), *Non-Compliance Procedures and Mechanisms*, 11–32.

[150] Simon Marsden, 'Non-Compliance Procedures', (2016) 27 *Yearbook of International Environmental Law* 131–136, 133.

[151] See Jutta Brunnée, 'Promoting Compliance with Multilateral Environmental Agreements' in Jutta Brunnée, Meinhard Doelle, and Lavanya Rajamani (eds.), *Promoting Compliance in an Evolving Climate Regime* (Cambridge: Cambridge University Press, 2011), 38–54. The exception is perhaps CITES, under whose auspices a significant practice has emerged of trade embargoes for non-compliance with its provisions. See Peter H. Sand, 'Enforcing CITES: The Rise and Fall of Trade Sanctions' (2013) 22 *Review of European, Comparative & International Environmental Law* 251–263; Tanya Wyatt, *Is CITES Protecting Wildlife? Assessing Implementation and Compliance* (Abingdon: Routledge, 2021).

were in non-compliance with their Kyoto Protocol obligations.[152] In both cases, the parties were 'declared to be in non-compliance', required to 'develop a plan' to restore compliance, and prevented from participating in emissions trading 'pending the resolution of the question of implementation'.[153] In both cases, the Enforcement Branch, composed of representatives of a number of parties to the Protocol, was empowered to adopt these decisions without reference to a prior ruling of a separate compliance body. Once an internal procedure before the Enforcement Branch results in a final decision, condemned parties are permitted to appeal from this decision to the protocol's plenary organ: the Conference of the Parties serving as Meeting of the Parties.[154]

The closest to a case in which, under an NCP, country-specific sanctions were determined with the participation of a separate 'compliance body' and 'political body' was that of measures taken against Russia for non-compliance with the Montreal Protocol on Substances that Deplete the Ozone Layer.[155] Among the 'Indicative List of Measures' that a Meeting of the Parties may determine in case of non-compliance are facilitative measures ('[a]ppropriate assistance'), discursive sanctions ('[i]ssuing cautions') and withdrawal of treaty rights ('[s]uspension . . . of specific rights and privileges under the Protocol').[156] These determinations are made after a submission on non-compliance is examined by an Implementation Committee, which issues a 'report to the Meeting of the Parties, including any recommendations it considers appropriate'.[157]

In 1995, the Montreal Protocol Implementation Committee took up a communication by Russia, requesting a grace period for implementing its

[152] Helga Jónsdóttir, 'The Kyoto Protocol Compliance System: Is the System Effective Enough to Ensure Compliance?', Thesis, Stockholm universitet, 2013; Sebastian Oberthür and René Lefeber, 'Holding Countries to Account: The Kyoto Protocol's Compliance System Revisited after Four Years of Experience' (2010) 1 *Climate Law* 133–158.

[153] UNFCCC, Enforcement branch of the Compliance Committee. CC-2009-1-6/Croatia/EB (13 October 2009) Preliminary finding, para. 23; UNFCCC. Enforcement branch of the Compliance Committee. CC-2007-1-6/Greece/EB (6 March 2008) Preliminary finding, para. 18. Both findings were later converted into final decisions.

[154] Croatia appealed from its final ruling, then withdrew the appeal (Jónsdóttir, 'The Kyoto Protocol Compliance System', at 23).

[155] Montreal Protocol on Substances That Deplete the Ozone Layer, adopted 16 September 1987, in force 1 January 1989, 1522 UNTS 3 (1987).

[156] Meeting of the Parties to the Montreal Protocol, Decision IV/5 (25 November 1992), Annex V.

[157] Ibid., Annex IV, para. 9.

commitments, as a communication of likely future non-compliance.[158] Following an assessment of the matter, the Implementation Committee found that Russia had not provided sufficient information for it to make a recommendation at that point, but that future recommendations 'could include ... the adoption of restrictions on trade in new or recycled substances between the Russian Federation and [non-developing] countries'.[159] The Meeting of the Parties subsequently adopted a decision in the negative: '[t]o allow ... the Russian Federation to export substances controlled under the Montreal Protocol to Parties ... members of the Commonwealth of Independent States, including Belarus and Ukraine'.[160] The decision to 'allow' continued trade was followed by a proviso: 'In doing so, the Russian Federation will undertake the necessary action to secure that no re-exports will be made from the Commonwealth of Independent States, including Belarus and Ukraine, to any Party to the Montreal Protocol.'[161] The Meeting of the Parties also recommended that international assistance be provided to Russia to enable compliance with its commitments, 'contingent on the settlement of [reporting] problems with the Implementation Committee'.[162]

At the Meeting of the Parties, Russia responded harshly to this proposed decision. Russia stated that, rather than the facilitative and progressive approach that the Montreal Protocol implied, the decision proposed 'immediately to take measures under item C of the indicative list' and 'to apply sanctions that would harm the Russian Federation's commercial and economic interests and undermine the efforts of the Government aimed at compliance with the Protocol'.[163] Following adoption of the decision by consensus (or 'consensus minus one', with Russia having unsuccessfully called for a vote on the relevant paragraphs), Russia claimed that '[t]he decision in question was tantamount to a revision of the Montreal Protocol'.[164] These developments, and their uniqueness in the field, are

[158] See O. Yoshida, 'Soft Enforcement of Treaties: The Montreal Protocol's Noncompliance Procedure and the Functions of Internal International Institutions' (1999) 10 *Colorado Journal of International Environmental Law and Policy* 95–142.

[159] UNEP, *Report of the Implementation Committee under the Non-Compliance Procedure for the Montreal Protocol on the Work of Its Tenth Meeting*, UN Doc. UNEP/OzL.Pro/ImpCom/lO/4 (30 August 1995), para. 38(c).

[160] Meeting of the Parties to the Montreal Protocol, *Decision VII/18: Compliance with the Montreal Protocol by the Russian Federation* (27 December 1995), para. 8.

[161] Ibid.

[162] Ibid., para. 9.5.

[163] UNEP, *Report on the Seventh Meeting of the Parties to the Montreal Protocol*, UN Doc. UNEP/OzL.Pro.7/12 (27 December 1995), para. 128.

[164] Ibid., para. 133. See paras. 129–132. See also Ibid., para. 130: 'the Secretariat clarified that the practice followed in Meetings of the Parties to the Montreal Protocol was that, when

evidence of both the potential and the limitations of NCPs. Where facilitative action and institutional sanctions fail, even contemplating authorised (Layer [5]) sanctions may be perceived as an unwarranted interference by collective bodies with states' interests.

A contrasting case is that of authorised sanctions under trade agreements, of which the most active has been the WTO, at least as it operated between 1995 and 2020.[165] The WTO dispute settlement system evolved from the dispute settlement clause of the 1947 GATT, which delegated to a collective political body – the GATT Contracting Parties – not only adjudicative authority but also Layer [5] sanctioning authority. Pursuant to GATT Article XXIII:2, if 'the circumstances are serious enough', the Contracting Parties 'may authorize a contracting party or parties to suspend the application to any other contracting party or parties of . . . concessions or other obligations under this Agreement'. The practice of the GATT Contracting Parties quickly became to delegate to an adjudicatory body – first, 'working parties' composed of representatives of three contracting parties, then 'panels' composed of three individuals – the task of drafting a report. The Contracting Parties could then decide whether to adopt the report, giving it the imprint of a decision of the Contracting Parties, or to reject it. Given that the Contracting Parties made all their decisions by consensus, a condemnatory report required the concurrence of the party being condemned. Nonetheless, over forty-eight years of GATT Era disputes, the Contracting Parties adopted 96 out of 136 reports issued by panels and other GATT adjudicators.[166]

A key element in the transformation of the GATT into the WTO was the adoption of the Dispute Settlement Understanding (DSU), by which decision-making is de facto delegated to adjudicatory bodies. In principle, the DSU kept in place the previous interplay between adjudicatory bodies (panels, the newly established Appellate Body, and arbitrators) and the political body composed of all WTO Members, the Dispute Settlement Body (DSB). It is the DSB that formally makes

only one Party objected to a draft decision, that decision would be carried by consensus and the position of the dissenting Party would be clearly reflected in the report of the Meeting'.

165 A number of regional trade agreements reproduce in some measure the WTO mechanism of trade sanctions. In many of these mechanisms, however, the authorised sanctions are not conditional on explicit authorisation *ex ante*, but permissible and subject to *ex post* adjudication. See Section 7.3.

166 WTO, *GATT Disputes: 1948–1995 Volume 1: Overview and One-Page Case Summaries* (Geneva: WTO, 2018), 26.

all the key decisions regarding dispute settlement. In practice, however, the decision-making authority rests with the adjudicatory bodies. At the adjudication stage, the adjudicators' reports are adopted quasi-automatically, that is, 'unless the DSB decides by consensus not to adopt' the report.[167] Consensus not to adopt a report has never been achieved. Upon adoption, the findings made by the panel or Appellate Body are converted into rulings of the DSB, requiring 'prompt compliance' from WTO members found in breach.[168]

In case of condemnatory findings, the adoption of a dispute settlement report by the DSB opens the door for Layer [5] sanctions in case of non-compliance. Under the DSU, if a member does not comply with a DSB report within a reasonable period of time,[169] the DSB may authorise the complainant to adopt sanctions against the wrongdoer, in the form of reciprocal non-performance of WTO obligations. The most common form of WTO sanctions sought by complainants is the adoption of retaliatory tariffs; occasionally, developing countries have sought the right to suspend, in their territory, intellectual property rights held by the wrongdoer's nationals.[170]

While WTO-authorised sanctions are very different from UNSC-mandated sanctions, they are structurally similar in that they are both Layer [5] authorised sanctions. And, while the WTO dispute settlement system reserves to a political body the sanctioning authority, the political body can only use this authority based on adjudicatory findings of breach, subject to further findings that proposed sanctions are warranted and not disproportionate. It is the DSB – a political body composed of all WTO members – that, following a multi-stage procedure, authorises a member to 'suspend concessions or other obligations' vis-à-vis a recalcitrant wrongdoer.[171] However, at every stage of this procedure, an adjudicatory ruling is either required (e.g. to ground the original condemnatory report) or is available to the wrongdoer (e.g. to curtail excessive sanctioning).

167 DSU, Article 17.14. See also Ibid., Article 16.4.

168 DSU, Article 21.1. Article 21.3 provides that a reasonable period of time for compliance is permissible if 'it is impracticable to comply immediately with the recommendations and rulings'. Under Article 21.3(c), an arbitrator can be called upon to determine this reasonable period of time.

169 The reasonable period of time may be determined by arbitration. See Article 22.3.

170 See Section 6.4.3.

171 DSU, Article 22.3.

As discussed in Section 7.3, many other trade agreements feature similar procedures. In many of them, permissible retaliation depends on an original finding of breach but can be adopted on the basis of a unilateral assessment of non-compliance with the original ruling. The targeted state is nonetheless expressly authorised to challenge the measures selected, on the basis of them being unwarranted or excessive, leading to a new ruling authorising or precluding lawful retaliation. A unique role in this regard is that of the Andean Court of Justice, which has a consistent jurisprudence by which it not only authorises but sometimes encourages trade retaliation, by all other Andean Community states, against a persistent wrongdoer.[172]

The relationship between the 'adjudicative' and 'political' bodies in non-compliance procedures and trade agreements is thus not one in which the adjudicative body controls compliance by the political body with legal requirements. Instead, it is the political body that benefits from adjudicative *auctoritas* and, especially when determining sanctions, adds to the adjudicator's findings its own political *auctoritas*. In so doing – and in particular where it consistently follows the guidance provided by the adjudicatory bodies – the political body significantly weakens claims that its decisions are the product of interests or convenience. Conversely, adjudicatory bodies are spared the task of being decision-makers and determining sanctions whose implementation they are unable to ensure.

Adjudication may thus provide greater authority to Layer 4 sanctions, such as suspension from voting, which are usually applied by political bodies. It may also enhance the effectiveness of Layer [5] sanctions, such as interruption of trade, which require implementation by individual states. The latter sanctions, formally authorised by a political body, become clearly distinguished from self-judging sanctions subject to legal uncertainty, and perhaps even from sanctions determined by the political body alone, since it is grounded in the adjudicative *auctoritas* of an adjudicator. At the WTO, whenever Layer [5] sanctions have been authorised, they have been treated seriously and led to significant negotiations and concessions.[173] Although one should not fall under the illusion that an institutional authorisation nullifies

[172] See Section 8.4.2.2.

[173] See Geraldo Vidigal, 'Remedies and Compliance', in Daniel Bethlehem, Donald McRae, Rodney Neufeld, and Isabelle Van Damme (eds.), *The Oxford Handbook of International Trade Law*, 2nd edn (Oxford: Oxford University Press, 2022), 967–992.

political realities, no member against which WTO sanctions have been authorised – be it the United States, the European Union, or China – has sought to challenge the conclusion that the sanctions were warranted as a consequence of their violation of WTO law.

3.5 Conclusion: Affecting Outcomes through *Auctoritas*

Adjudication addresses a key deficiency in a purely interactional, horizontal normative order: uncertainty. Both the internal and the external social mechanisms that lead to state compliance with international law depend on an understanding of what norms require from states. In a wholly decentralised order, however, this understanding is subject to self-interpretation by each agent, or each state, of the written texts and fact patterns from which norms are inferred. In the absence of authoritative decision-making, therefore, decentralised normative systems are subject to a high degree of uncertainty, compounded by the impossibility of differentiating between genuine disagreement over the interpretation of texts and the characterisation of facts, on the one hand, and self-serving, opportunistic interpretation on the other. Adjudication addresses this uncertainty, equipping the relevant normative framework with a mechanism for reaching a unified interpretation.

Given the lack of hierarchy that characterises the international legal order, international judicial authority cannot rely on a connection to a coercive apparatus to influence outcomes. Moreover, as long as state agents feel bound primarily by the state's internal legal hierarchy, neither can ICs rely on reflexive obedience of their authority. Judicial authority thus depends on the adjudicator's ability to influence perceptions with respect to the normative framework within which decisions and actions take place. However, an IC cannot rely on binding the will of the individuals whose action its pronouncements would require. International judicial authority operates by reaching an audience beyond these individuals. Put otherwise, the authority of an international adjudicator lies in the capacity of its pronouncement to shape the perception of actors in the international order broadly defined regarding the norms that apply to their conduct, so that these actors come to expect from the addressees of an authoritative pronouncement the adoption of certain conducts and respond negatively to attempts to resist to or dismiss these pronouncements. It is thus the conduct of other actors in the international order – chiefly, but not solely, those representing states – that prevents the pronouncements of international authoritative actors from being disregarded.

In this regard, what international judicial remedies can 'do' is to influence audiences' perceptions of (i) the interpretation of norms and (ii) the character of conducts as legal violations. An authoritative international adjudicator can, through expressive action alone, eliminate the scope for legitimate disagreement regarding the applicable normative framework, the interpretation of its norms, and their applicability to a certain situation. In so doing, adjudication enables the operation of the mechanisms, internal and external, through which the international legal order ordinarily influences state conduct. By eliminating reasons for legitimate divergence regarding the interpretation and application of rules, adjudicators allow the horizontal international normative system to operate unimpaired by interpretative uncertainty.

Adjudicators' interpretation of commitments may thus increase the potency of international law's various layers of compliance-inducing mechanisms. Domestically at Layer 1, adjudication may trigger a perception that there is a duty to comply, empower domestic groups demanding compliance, and sharpen concerns over reputational harm and retaliation. Externally at the inter-state level (Layers 2 and 3), besides triggering reputational harm, adjudication enables the application on surer footing of horizontal sanctions requiring deployment of resources, such as countermeasures, setting aside otherwise legitimate concerns with the equal value of the various legal positions expressed by states. Finally, adjudication may induce IOs to determine sanctions, at Layers 4 and [5], unimpeded by legitimate disagreement among their members over whether a sanction is being lawfully applied or is an abusive act of economic coercion.[174]

Eliminating interpretative uncertainty does not ensure compliance, which still depends on the ability of the international order's various layers of compliance control to lead to a change in state behaviour. By removing interpretative uncertainty, however, adjudication significantly reinforces these layers' operation. In particular, adjudication mobilises the operation of these layers when it would not ordinarily be in the interest of, or a priority for, particular actors to perform their compliance-inducing role.

[174] In *Military and Paramilitary Activities*, the ICJ examined a specific case of unlawful coercion, 'intervention', which it held to be 'wrongful when it uses methods of coercion' to interfere in a state's 'choice of a political, economic, social and cultural system, and the formulation of foreign policy'. *Military and Paramilitary Activities in and against Nicaragua (Nicaragua* v. *United States of America)*, Judgment (Merits), [1986] ICJ Reports, p. 14, 108. The recent concerns with economic coercion seem to pose far greater challenges. See on this Antonios Tzanakopoulos, 'The Right to Be Free from Economic Coercion' (2015) 4(3) *Cambridge Journal of International and Comparative Law* 616–633.

Faced with an authoritative interpretation, a domestic bureaucrat, judge, or parliament member who might ordinarily choose to defer to the political branches of government on the interpretation of the law will be to a greater extent (though not necessarily) inclined to pursue compliance. An injured state may with more certitude pursue its rights through measures of response to an act identified as unlawful by an adjudicator. Third states have a diminished ability to declare themselves neutral with regard, at least, to the legal situation at hand, and those that are interested in a solution that coincides with the adjudicator's rulings will feel buttressed in their ability to call for a change of behaviour. Organs of IOs may feel empowered, or even required, to deploy certain procedures and sanctions against a wrongdoer. In extreme cases involving the use of force, the UNSC may be empowered to act through sanctions – even though the change here is less likely to be significant, given both its decision-making procedure and the fact that it is usually the very adjudicator of the rules that it enforces through sanctions.

Chapters 4 and 5 consider these possibilities in more detail. They examine the different uses of judicial authority as four types of judicial remedies. Deploying different remedies allows international adjudicators to trigger different effects of their authority, and mobilise different layers of international law's system of compliance control.

PART II

A Typology of Judicial Remedies

4

Judicial Remedies in International Law

Adjudicating, Declaring Breaches, Establishing Consequences

4.1 Judicial Remedies in the International Order

4.1.1 Introduction

'Remedies' is a blanket term used to designate the set of responses a legal system authorises to cure an illegality. A metaphor originating in Roman law, 'remedies' is now widely used to designate, in both common law and civil law jurisdictions, '[t]he means by which a right is enforced or the violation of a right is prevented, redressed, or compensated'.[1] In its broadest sense, the notion of remedies encompasses a variety of instruments, practices, powers, and prerogatives that serve the function of giving effectiveness to the rights and obligations provided for in a legal system. In a stricter definition, the term is often employed to refer only, or essentially, to *judicial* remedies – determinations, injunctions, and orders issued by courts (and other agencies performing an adjudicatory function) with a view to redressing an illegality or providing some form of reparation to injured parties.[2]

[1] Henry Campbell Black, *Black's Law Dictionary*, 6th edn (Saint Paul: West, 1991), 1294. See also Jonathan Law and Elizabeth A. Martin (eds.), *Oxford Dictionary of Law*, 7th edn (Oxford: Oxford University Press, 2009), 467; John Burke (ed.), *Jowitt's Dictionary of English Law*, 2nd edn (London: Sweet & Maxwell, 1977), 1540. Pierre Bourdon and Pauline Marcou, 'Aux Origines de la Notion de Remède pour Traiter les Vices de la Formation des Contrats Civils et Administratifs' (2022) 4 *Revue des Contrats* 92; Samuel Sales Fonteles, *Remédios Constitucionais*, 5th edn (Salvador: Juspodivm, 2023); María Luisa Palazón Garrido, *Los Remedios Frente al Incumplimiento en el Derecho Comparado* (Navarra: Aranzadi, 2014); Martin Ebers, *Rechte, Rechtsbehelfe und Sanktionen im Unionsprivatrecht* (Tübingen: Mohr Siebeck, 2016).

[2] Douglas Laycock, 'How Remedies Became a Field: A History' (2008) 27 *Review of Litigation* 161, 165.

When considering international judicial remedies, much of the literature pragmatically starts by assessing the powers of adjudicators under the relevant adjudicatory system[3] or, more commonly given the overall paucity of regulation of remedies in international adjudication, by the concrete uses adjudicators make of their adjudicatory powers.[4] Some scholars start from the question of what would be the best, or 'optimal', system of remedies.[5] These approaches often bracket the logically precedent question of what effects international judicial remedies *can* produce. This chapter considers this question, starting from the conclusion of Chapter 3: separated from the hierarchical structure of states and thus unable to determine the mobilisation of coercive force by the organised community, ICs must rely entirely on their authority (*auctoritas*) for the influence of their rulings over the conduct of various actors.

This chapter examines how international adjudicators may intervene within the international order, employing their interpretative authority to produce effects over the perceptions and incentives of states. I refer to the different uses of this interpretative authority as 'judicial remedies' and employ the term broadly, in two different senses. First, as discussed in this chapter and in the ones that follow, the term 'judicial remedies' as

[3] R. Rajesh Babu, *Remedies under the WTO Legal System* (Leiden: Martinus Nijhoff, 2012); René Barents, *Remedies and Procedures before the EU Courts*, 2nd edn (Alphen aan den Rijn: Wolters Kluwer, 2016).

[4] Christine Gray, *Judicial Remedies in International Law* (Oxford: Clarendon, 1987); Dinah Shelton, *Remedies in International Human Rights Law*, 2nd edn (Oxford: Oxford University Press, 2005); Martins Paparinskis, 'Investors' Remedies under EU Law and International Investment Law' (2016) 17 *Journal of World Investment & Trade* 919–941; Victor Stoica, *Remedies before the International Court of Justice: A Systemic Analysis* (Cambridge: Cambridge University Press, 2021); Helen Keller, Corina Heri, and Réka Piskóty, 'Something Ventured, Nothing Gained? – Remedies before the ECtHR and Their Potential for Climate Change Cases' (2022) 22 *Human Rights Law Review* 1–36.

[5] Petros C. Mavroidis, 'Remedies in the WTO Legal System: Between a Rock and a Hard Place' (2000) 11 *European Journal of International Law* 763–813; Alan O. Sykes, 'Public Versus Private Enforcement of International Economic Law: Standing and Remedy' (2005) 34(2) *Journal of Legal Studies* 631–666; Joost Pauwelyn, *Optimal Protection of International Law: Navigating between European Absolutism and American Voluntarism* (Cambridge: Cambridge University Press, 2008); Anne van Aaken, 'Primary and Secondary Remedies in International Investment Law and National State Liability: A Functional and Comparative View', in Stephan W. Schill (ed.), *International Investment Law and Comparative Public Law* (Oxford: Oxford University Press, 2010); Sergio Puig, 'No Right without a Remedy: Foundations of Investor-State Arbitration' (2014) 35(3) *University of Pennsylvania Journal of International Law* 829–861; Kent Roach, *Remedies for Human Rights Violations: A Two-Track Approach to Supra-National and National Law* (Cambridge: Cambridge University Press, 2021).

used here encompasses determinations made by *all* international adjudicators – whether termed a 'court', 'tribunal', 'arbitrator', 'panel', or 'commission' – provided that these determinations are considered final as a matter of the international legal system.[6] On the one hand, this terminological broadness helps avoid theoretical discussions regarding what constitutes an 'international court'.[7] On the other hand, it distinguishes remedies issued by international adjudicators from two other types of remedies considered below: unilateral and bilateral remedies. Alternative terms, such as 'adjudicatory remedies' or 'third-party remedies', might be more precise. 'Judicial remedies' has the virtue of sounding natural.

Second, and more substantively, the term 'judicial remedies' as it is used here encompasses *all* legally final determinations issued by international adjudicators. The concept thus goes beyond a strict definition of judicial remedies that would encompass solely the judicial establishment of consequences of internationally wrongful acts, in particular as compiled and codified by the International Law Commission (ILC) in its Articles on State Responsibility (ARSIWA).[8] Indeed, as explained below, this aspect of decisions, which ICs themselves sometimes term 'remedies',[9] is a subset of the remedies available to international adjudicators it is the category that I label Consequential Duties.[10]

[6] By 'final' I do not mean 'immutable' or 'irresistible'. See *Application for Revision and Interpretation of the Judgment of 24 February 1982 in the Case concerning the Continental Shelf (Tunisia/Libyan Arab Jamahiriya)*, Judgment, [1985] ICJ Reports, p. 192, 219.

[7] For this discussion, see Hervé Ascensio, 'La notion de juridiction internationale en question', in Société Française de Droit International, *La Juridictionnalisation du Droit International* (Paris: Pedone, 2003).

[8] ILC, 'Draft articles on Responsibility of States for Internationally Wrongful Acts, with commentaries', ILC Ybk 2001, II.2, p. 116.

[9] *Application of the Interim Accord of 13 September 1995 (the former Yugoslav Republic of Macedonia* v. *Greece)*, [2011] ICJ Reports, p. 644, 692; *Jurisdictional Immunities of the State*, [2012] ICJ Reports, p. 99, 152; *Whaling in the Antarctic*, [2014] ICJ Reports, p. 226, 298; *Certain Iranian Assets (Islamic Republic of Iran* v. *United States of America)*, Judgment (Merits), 30 March 2023, para. 224; *Assadnidze* v. *Georgia*, Application No. 71503/01, Judgment of 8 April 2004, para. 202; *Ivanţoc and Others* v. *Moldova and Russia*, Application No. 23687/05, Judgment (Merits and Just Satisfaction), Judgment of 15 November 2011, para. 83; Appellate Body Report, *US – Cotton (21.5)*, adopted 20 June 2008 (WT/DS267/AB/RW), fn. 494; *RWE Innogy GmbH and RWE Innogy Aersa S.A.U.* v. *Kingdom of Spain*, ICSID Case No. ARB/14/34, Decision on Jurisdiction, Liability, and Certain Issues of Quantum (30 December 2019), para. 681.

[10] Conversely, this choice leaves out the remedies of 'provisional' or 'interim' measures, at least as a specific category. They are instruments to deliver, provisionally, the four categories of remedies. This does not mean that states do not see them as remedies.

Section 4.2 explores the concept of judicial remedies in international law. International judicial remedies must be understood within the context of a broader horizontal social order, where they coexist with, rather than replace, unilateral and transactional remedies. In this framework, the role of judicial remedies is not to mobilise coercive force but to provide authoritative determinations regarding, first, the content of the normative framework and, second, the characterisation of conduct and facts within this framework. Since ICs are not part of a hierarchically organised, coercive apparatus, their remedies cannot directly trigger the deployment of coercive measures.

4.1.2 *Remedies in Horizontality: Bilateral and Unilateral Remedies*

In a wholly horizontal normative order, that is, one in which no authorities are available to provide remedies against wrongful conduct, a breach of norms is enforced by its participants in two different manners. The wrongdoer may self-enforce norms by providing redress for injury it caused, in what I have termed Layer 1 compliance; or other parties can enforce norms vis-à-vis the wrongdoer, either reciprocally (Layer 2) or diffusely as third parties (Layer 3). References among international lawyers to these almost intuitive possibilities can be traced back to Grotius' remark that 'injuries done might be considered in a twofold Respect, either as they may be repaired or punished'.[11] In a horizontal

From the viewpoint of a complainant, Malcolm Shaw noted, the mere filing of a claim may constitute a remedy '[i]n the broadest sense', as it 'may assist, stimulate or engage bilateral or multilateral negotiations or regional or global settlement mechanisms'. Malcolm N. Shaw, 'A Practical Look at the International Court of Justice', in Malcolm D. Evans (ed.), *Remedies in International Law: The Institutional Dilemma* (Oxford: Hart Publishing, 1998), 23. On provisional measures, see Cameron A. Miles, *Provisional Measures before International Courts and Tribunals* (Cambridge: Cambridge University Press, 2017).

11 Hugo Grotius, *The Rights of War and Peace: Including the Law of Nature and of Nations* (transl. A.C. Campbell) (Charleston: Nabu, 2011), bk. 2, ch. 20, para. 1(1). See also Vattel: 'Reprisals are used from Nation to Nation, to make justice to themselves, when it cannot be obtained otherwise. If a Nation seizes what belongs to another, if she refuses to pay a debt, to repair an injury, or to give to it just satisfaction; the latter may seize something belonging to the former, and apply it to its profit, until achieving what is owed to it with damages & interests, or keep it, until it is given full satisfaction. In this latter case, it is more a Seizure ['*Arrêt ou Saisie*'] than Reprisals' (Emmerich de Vattel, *Le Droit des Gens ou Principes de la loi naturelle, appliqués à la conduite et aux affaires des Nations et des Souverains* (Neuchâtel: A. Londres, 1758), 531 (author's translation)).

normative order, the wrongdoer may remedy violations bilaterally, or transactionally, vis-à-vis each injured party, providing them with redress in some form. Alternatively, other actors may respond to a breach by engaging in harmful conduct vis-à-vis the wrongdoer, to demand the provision of acceptable redress or simply as a response to the violation.[12]

Horizontal normative enforcement continues to exist within hierarchically organised states, which incorporate them as permissible transactional and unilateral remedies. In William Blackstone's 1765 *Commentaries to the Laws of England*, transactional and unilateral remedies appear as means 'to accomplish the redress of private injuries' without (or preceding) the intervention of a public authority.[13] Transactional or bilateral remedies 'arise from the joint act of all the parties together',[14] involving some form of redress that the responsible party voluntarily provides to those aggrieved by a violation. Unilateral remedies arise 'from the sole act of the injured party'[15] and include various means of vindication available to aggrieved parties in the face of unlawful conduct without (or before) resorting to a court or obtaining voluntary redress from the offender.[16] In permitting unilateral remedies, 'the law allows a man to be his own avenger, or to minister redress for himself'.[17]

Traditionally in international law, the primary responsibility for addressing unlawful conduct lies with states acting horizontally. Transactional, or bilateral, and unilateral remedies are reflected in two types of consequences of unlawful acts codified in the ILC ARSIWA. Part Two of ARSIWA codifies the consequences of wrongful conduct in terms of *bilateral* remedies expected from a wrongdoer, setting out the duties

[12] The legal regulation of measures of response has historically sought to set aside the punishment element in measures of response and interpret them as directed at the target's future compliance with duties. This approach does not always match state practice. See the debates regarding armed reprisals mentioned in Section 5.2.5.

[13] Wayne Morrisson (ed.), *Blackstone's Commentaries on the Laws of England* (London: Cavendish, 2013), bk. 3, para. 4. Blackstone also identifies remedies that occur 'by operation of law'.

[14] Ibid., p. 13. For Blackstone, '[transactional remedies] are only two, accord, and arbitration' (Ibid., bk 3, para. 26).

[15] Ibid., bk 3, para. 6.

[16] Blackstone's unilateral remedies include the right to self-defence; the right to 'lawfully claim and retake' one's property without 'breach of the peace'; the right to engage in 'abatement, or removal, of nuisances'; and the 'taking of a personal chattel out of the possession of the wrongdoer into the custody of the party injured, to procure a satisfaction for the wrong committed' (Ibid., bk 3, para. 10).

[17] Ibid., bk 3, para. 11.

that arise from a violation. Part Three governs unilateral remedies under the law of responsibility – the means by which other states may respond to unlawful conduct and demand cessation of the violation and reparation of injuries.[18]

Scholars and adjudicators often refer to transactions between states as remedies. Wolfgang Alschner refers to mutually agreed solutions as the 'preferred remedy' under World Trade Organization (WTO) law.[19] Michael Schmitt notes that 'a request for the responsible State to remedy the internationally wrongful act must precede the [counter]-measure'.[20] The rule requiring exhaustion of local remedies, prior to filing a claim before an international adjudicator, can be thought of as a bilateral remedy. As Antonio Cançado Trindade explained, this rule gives a state the 'opportunity to redress the alleged wrong within the framework of its own domestic legal system'.[21] In the *SRFC* Advisory Opinion, the International Tribunal for the Law of the Sea (ITLOS) noted that a coastal state may report that another state's flag is being used in illicit fishing, creating for the latter 'an obligation to investigate the matter and, if appropriate, take any action necessary to remedy the situation'.[22]

Similarly, both scholarship and ICs have referred to unilateral measures taken in response to a breach as remedies, from Elizabeth Zoller's concept of 'peacetime unilateral remedies'[23] to Jonathan Charney's

[18] ARSIWA, Articles 28–41 (Part Two) and 42–54 (Part Three). Note that the articles both codify more than these matters (e.g. Articles 40 and 41 establish obligations for states other than the wrongdoer) and do not exhaust available remedies. The possibility of suspending or terminating of a treaty in response to its material breach, for example, is governed by the law of treaties.

[19] Wolfgang Alschner, 'Amicable Settlements of WTO Disputes: Bilateral Solutions in a Multilateral System' (2014) 13 *World Trade Review* 65–102, at 69.

[20] Michael N. Schmitt, 'Below the Threshold Cyber Operations: The Countermeasures Response Option and International Law' (2014) 54 *Virginia Journal of International Law* 697–732, at 716.

[21] A.A. Cançado Trindade, 'Exhaustion of Local Remedies in International Law and the Role of National Courts' (1986) 17 *Archiv des Völkerrechts* 333–370, at 334. While, from the viewpoint of a state's domestic law, this rule includes domestic *judicial* remedies, under international law a domestic judicial remedy is a bilateral remedy: an organ of one state acknowledges a violation of international law caused by that state to another state or one of its nationals, offering them a remedy for the injury. If the aggrieved party accepts this remedy, the outcome is a (perhaps implied) transaction.

[22] *Request for Advisory Opinion submitted by the Sub-Regional Fisheries Commission*, Advisory Opinion, 2 April 2015, ITLOS Reports 2015, p. 463.

[23] Elizabeth Zoller, *Peacetime Unilateral Remedies: An Analysis of Countermeasures* (Dobbs Ferry: Transnational, 1984).

reference to 'third state remedies'.[24] The ILC refers to countermeasures as 'a feature of a decentralized system by which injured States may seek to vindicate their rights and to restore the legal relationship with the responsible State which has been ruptured by the internationally wrongful act'.[25] In *Tehran Hostages*, the International Court of Justice (ICJ) found that Iran had 'remedies placed at its disposal by diplomatic law' for abuses of the diplomatic functions.[26] A WTO panel condemned the United States for having 'unilaterally determined that it had the right to take remedial action'.[27] Both scholarly debate and judicial practice thus use 'remedies' to refer, sometimes indistinctly, to judicial, transactional, and unilateral remedies. A proper understanding of the concept requires keeping in mind that different types of phenomena are referred to as 'remedies'.

4.1.3 *Judicial Remedies without Enforcement Powers*

Scholarly discussion of judicial remedies usually presumes hierarchy and a domestic legal environment, characterised by a coercive apparatus at the orders of the adjudicator. Douglas Laycock defines judicial remedies as 'anything a court can do for a litigant who has been wronged or is about to be wronged'.[28] In Dinah Shelton's account, the 'remedial task is to convert the law into results'.[29] Once courts are available for

[24] Jonathan I. Charney, 'Third State Remedies in International Law' (1989) 10 *Michigan Journal of International Law* 57–101. See also John Norton Moore, 'Enhancing Compliance with International Law: A Neglected Remedy' (1999) 39(4) *Virginia Journal of International Law* 881–1016.

[25] ILC, 'Draft Articles on Responsibility of States for Internationally Wrongful Acts, with Commentaries', ILC Ybk 2001, II.2, p. 128.

[26] *United States Diplomatic and Consular Staff in Tehran (United States of America* v. *Iran)*, [1980] ICJ Reports, p. 3, 40–41. Among these remedies, the ICJ mentioned the right to 'notify the sending State that any particular member of its diplomatic mission is "persona non grata" or "not acceptable"' and 'the power which every receiving State has, at its own discretion, to break off diplomatic relations with a sending State and to call for the immediate closure of the offending mission'.

[27] Panel Report, United *States – Import Measures on Certain Products from the European Communities*, adopted 10 January 2001 (WT/DS165/R), para. 6.106. Ibid., para. 100 (finding 'a unilateral determination by the United States that a WTO violation had occurred for which the United States determined that a remedial action was needed').

[28] Douglas Laycock, *Modern American Remedies*, 3rd edn (New York: Aspen, 2002), cited in Brian A. Garner (eds.), *Black's Law Dictionary*, 9th edn (Saint Paul: West, 2004), 1407.

[29] Shelton, *Remedies in International Human Rights Law*, 54.

'expounding and enforcing' laws, Blackstone notes, 'remedy is . . . principally to be sought by application to these courts of justice'.[30]

In a functioning state, instructions by a state's courts lead those in the state apparatus who have direct control over material resources, economic as well as political, to apply coercive measures to *enforce* judicial rulings against recalcitrant parties. This enforcement amounts, as Michael Reisman put it, to 'transformation, by community means, of authoritative pronouncement into controlling reality'.[31] Enforcement permits judicial remedies to be superimposed to horizontally applied transactional and unilateral remedies. A domestic court, as an organ hierarchically superior to the parties, imposes state law by replacing bilateral or unilateral remedies with judicially determined ones. As Douglas Laycock put it, '[t]he remedy is the practical payoff – what the court can do *for* you if you win, and what the court can do *to* you if you lose'.[32] He concludes: '[a] right with no effective remedy is unenforceable and largely illusory'.[33]

This sets up a challenge for international adjudicators. As Robert Jennings noted, ICs lack 'the principal weapons of enforcement used by domestic courts . . . restraints on the person, or restraints upon assets or real property'.[34] Judith Bello observed that even the WTO, sometimes credited with having enforcement capabilities, 'has no jailhouse, no bail

[30] Morrisson, *Blackstone's Commentaries*, 2.

[31] W. Michael Reisman, 'The Enforcement of International Judgments' (1969) 63 *American Journal of International Law* 1, 6.

[32] Laycock, 'How Remedies Became a Field, 161, 165.

[33] Ibid. This has long been the position of common law courts. In the 1703 Judgment in *Ashby* v. *White*, Lord Chief Justice Holt held that '[i]f the plaintiff has a right, he must of necessity have a means to vindicate and maintain it, and a remedy if he is injured in the exercise or enjoyment of it, and, indeed it is a vain thing to imagine a right without a remedy' (*Ashby* v. *White* (1703) 92 ER 126, 137–139). Lord Holt's dissent was upheld by the House of Lords (17 *House of Lords Journal* 526–536 (27 March 1704)). In *Marbury* v. *Madison*, the US Supreme Court held that 'where a specific duty is assigned by law, and individual rights depend upon the performance of that duty . . . the individual who considers himself injured has a right to resort to the laws of his country for a remedy' (*Marbury* v. *Madison*, 5 US 137 (1803), at 137). And, in *Kendall* v. *United States*, the same Supreme Court held that it would be 'a monstrous absurdity' if 'in a well-organized government . . . there should be no remedy, although a clear and undeniable right should be shown to exist', since 'the power to enforce the performance of the act must rest somewhere' (*Kendall* v. *United States*, 37 US 524 (1838), at 624).

[34] Robert Jennings, 'The Judicial Enforcement of International Obligations' (1987) 47 *Zeitschrift für ausländisches öffentliches Recht und Völkerrecht* 3, at 8.

bondsmen, no blue helmets, no truncheons or tear gas'.[35] There is therefore nothing international adjudicators can 'do for a litigant'[36] beyond issuing legal rulings that define and characterise prohibited, permissible, and required behaviour. The role of judicial remedies must be conceptualised accordingly.

Lacking enforcement capabilities, ICs often use the term 'remedies' to refer to the portion of their rulings in which they determine legal consequences for the violations identified.[37] In *Croatia* v. *Serbia*, the ICJ stated that 'remedies might appropriately be ordered by the Court . . . dependent upon the findings that the Court may in due course make of breaches'.[38] In the Commentary to ARSIWA, the ILC refers to the consequences of breach as 'secondary rules relating to remedies'.[39] In the same vein, Chittharanjan Amerasinghe defines 'remedial jurisdiction' as 'the jurisdiction to settle disputes about, and to determine, secondary rights and obligations'.[40] James Crawford notes that 'restitution, compensation and satisfaction cover a field which might be described as "judicial remedies"'.[41] In this strand of scholarship, judicial remedies are framed as judicial determinations that replace bilateral remedies – or rather, determine their applicability and required content – establishing what is required from a wrongdoer following a violation.

This conception of judicial remedies in international law, however, is doubly limited. First, those restricting remedies to adjudicated consequences of breach seem to derive from the absence of judicial control over a coercive apparatus an absence of adjudicatory authority over the primary means of external enforcement of international law. This authority is widely accepted, at least *ex post* – as a means of condemning

[35] Judith H. Bello, 'The WTO Dispute Settlement Understanding: Less is More' (1996) 90 *American Journal of International Law* 416–418, at 416–417.

[36] Laycock, *Modern American Remedies*, 1407.

[37] See note 9.

[38] *Application of the Convention on the Prevention and Punishment of the Crime of Genocide (Croatia* v. *Serbia)*, Preliminary Objections, Judgment, [2008] ICJ Reports, p. 412, 465. See also Ibid., p. 463.

[39] ILC Ybk 2001, II.2, p. 89. See also the term 'remedies' used to refer to satisfaction (p. 105) and compensation (p. 106).

[40] Chittharanjan F. Amerasinghe, *Jurisdiction of International Tribunals* (The Hague: Kluwer, 2003), 390. See also Chester Brown, *A Common Law of International Adjudication* (Oxford: Oxford University Press, 2007), 9 (remedies 'are governed by secondary rules of international law which are treated as part of the law of state responsibility').

[41] James Crawford, *The Law of State Responsibility: The General Part* (Cambridge: Cambridge University Press, 2013), 506.

Table 4.1 *A Typology of Judicial Remedies*

Focus of the Remedy \ Function of the Remedy	Interpreting Obligations	Sanctioning Violations
Ordinary Legal Framework	**Mere Adjudication** • Existence/applicability of rules • Interpretation of rules • Application of rules to conduct/situation	**Declaration of Breach** • Recording of events • Declaration of breach • Judicial/declaratory satisfaction

Framework Emerging from a Breach	**Consequential Duties**
	Prospective
	• Cessation
	• Guidance on implementation ('specific performance')
	• Prospective restitution
	• Guarantees of non-repetition
	
	Retrospective
	• Restitution (retrospective)
	• Measures of satisfaction
	• Compensation (obligation)
		Permissible Responses
		• Authorised/required response
		• non-cooperation
		• reciprocal non-performance
		• self-defence
		• Authorised or declared termination/ suspension of treaty
		  • entirely
		  • of specific rights/ benefits
		• Compensation (enforceability)

unlawful deployment of unilateral remedies.[42] It is the ability of international adjudicators to determine the permissibility of responses *ex ante* that is rarely considered outside of fields in which it is specifically provided for, in particular WTO law.[43] Second, this conception limits international judicial remedies to the settlement of disputes regarding consequences of breach. As the remainder of this chapter will show, even setting aside the possibility of *ex ante* judicial determination of permissible responses, the remedial value of international adjudication extends far beyond this.

[42] See Section 5.2.
[43] See Section 6.3.

The definition of remedies adopted here includes all final adjudicatory pronouncements that authoritatively interpret and apply international law. All IC pronouncements involve these two core operations – interpretation and application. It is nonetheless possible to classify judicial remedies based on two axes: their *object or scope* and their *central function*. This framework yields a fourfold categorisation of judicial remedies. Accordingly, this chapter and the next examine the four categories of judicial remedies introduced in Chapter 1 and summarised in Table 4.1: Mere Adjudication, Declaration of Breach, Consequential Duties, and Permissible Responses.[44]

Remedies can be categorised according to their *object or scope*. Their primary focus can be either (1) the normative framework applicable to – typically between – the parties, independently of any alleged violation; or (2) the legal consequences of an alleged violation for these legal relations. Remedies focusing on the first element (the existing normative framework) include the identification and interpretation of the normative framework, termed here Mere Adjudication, and the determination of whether certain conduct constitutes a violation of this framework, labelled Declaration of Breach. As discussed below, although sometimes considered 'pre-remedial', these determinations are frequently requested by complainants – often as stand-alone remedies – highlighting their perceived remedial value.

Beyond Mere Adjudication and Declaration of Breach, adjudicators can issue remedies that focus on element (2), addressing the new legal relations arising from a breach. These remedies include adjudicatory pronouncements on two key matters. First, adjudicators may specify the Consequential Duties of the wrongdoer, determining the conduct required to cease the breach and provide redress for the injury caused. Second, adjudicators may establish Permissible Responses, identifying measures that other parties are entitled to adopt in response to the breach. This involves determining whether a wrongdoer's breach of international law – and potentially its subsequent conduct – justifies responses by other actors, who would otherwise rely on unilateral interpretations of the situation, norms, and permissible reaction. The judicial remedy of Permissible Responses is explored at length in Chapter 5.

The second aspect of remedies according to which they can be classified is their primary function: this can be to determine applicable rights

[44] Table 4.1 is a reproduction of Table 1.3.

and obligations or to sanction violations. Mere Adjudication and Consequential Duties primarily interpret obligations. Through these remedies, an IC establishes the conduct required from the parties under international law, clarifying their rights and obligations. In terms of adjudication's expressive function,[45] these remedies create a focal point for restoration of cooperative relations, authoritatively defining what the applicable norms demand and providing a foundation for subsequent negotiations. While Mere Adjudication focuses on the normative framework independently of any breach, Consequential Duties address the new obligations arising from a breach and the resulting injury.

By contrast, Declaration of Breach and Permissible Responses are primarily designed to sanction violations. A Declaration of Breach operates mainly at a symbolic level, eliminating uncertainty about the existence of a violation and triggering the reputational and other negative consequences that emerge from being formally identified as a wrongdoer. By determining Permissible Responses, an adjudicator legitimises resort by other states to the more tangible sanctions available to them, which the adjudicator cannot directly deploy. The central purpose of these remedies is to, within the limits of an international adjudicator's *auctoritas*, impose costs on the wrongdoer for its legal violation.

4.2 Mere Adjudication and Declaratory Remedies

4.2.1 Concept and Practice

Mere Adjudication is at once the most straightforward of the four types and that which can involve the most varied findings. Through Mere Adjudication, an adjudicator states its understanding of the normative framework governing a certain matter, authoritatively interpreting the texts or conducts whose normative value or normative content is in dispute. As discussed in Chapter 3, in the absence of authoritative determinations, norm-creating texts and conducts suffer from inherent indeterminacy, meaning that different states and non-state actors may always hold diverging views of what the normative framework requires, even when they can agree on the applicable normative sources; often, actors will diverge regarding not only the normative implications of documents or conducts but also their normative value.

[45] See Section 3.3.2.

A judicial determination establishing the applicable normative framework and determining its content is thus a significant remedy. A judgment in which a court restricts itself, whether by its own choosing or at the request of the parties, to establishing the meaning of primary obligations is often termed a declaratory judgment,[46] and this portion of a broader ruling, a declaratory remedy. Declaratory remedies have great flexibility and, as their main scope is to determine legal rights and obligations, may be used to 'respond to a wide variety of disputes'.[47] Additionally, other than in disputes involving solely questions of fact, or avowed non-compliance,[48] Mere Adjudication is a necessary step in the adjudicatory process, providing the basis for all further remedies.

In a purely declaratory judgment, an adjudicator's task is to perform Mere Adjudication and 'declare the law'.[49] This involves settling the question of the existence and applicability of certain rules (or a whole legal regime) to the case and determining the content of any obligations these rules impose upon the parties. Once determined by judicial pronouncement, 'the obligation then appears not as a proposition of general law, but is applied to particular parties in the circumstances of a particular case'.[50]

Depending on the scope of the disagreement between the parties, Mere Adjudication may involve one or more of four elements or steps: existence, applicability, interpretation, and application. The adjudicator may, first, establish whether some or all of the norms invoked exist as legal norms and are subject to its adjudicatory authority. This may involve assessing questions of normative existence: whether the text or conduct invoked has the correct 'pedigree' – a manner of adoption or

[46] Edwin M. Borchard, 'Editorial Comment – Declaratory Judgments in International Law' (1935) 29(3) *American Journal of International Law* 488–492, at 489. I avoid labelling the remedy of Mere Adjudication as 'Declaratory Remedy' because, arguably, all remedies are declaratory of rights and obligations. Admittedly, they are also all exercises of mere adjudication.

[47] Juliette McIntyre, 'Declaratory Judgments of the International Court of Justice' (2012) 25 *Hague Yearbook of International Law* 107–158, at 156.

[48] See, for example, *US – Anti-Dumping Measures on PET Bags*, adopted 18 February 2010, WT/DS383/R. See also *Sovereignty over Pedra Branca/Pulau Batu Puteh, Middle Rocks and South Ledge* (*Malaysia* v. *Singapore*), Judgment, [2008] ICJ Reports, p. 12.

[49] *Free Zones*, PCIJ Reports Ser. A/B No. 46, 138 ('it cannot lightly be admitted that the Court, whose function it is to declare the law, can be called upon to choose between two or more constructions determined beforehand by the Parties, none of which may correspond to the opinion at which it may arrive').

[50] Jennings, 'The Judicial Enforcement of International Obligations'.

development which gives them normative value and makes them binding on the parties under the relevant legal framework.[51] In *Obligation to Negotiate Access to the Pacific*, for example, the ICJ concluded that the obligation Bolivia requested the Court to establish did not 'arise[] for Chile from any of the invoked legal bases'.[52] In *Qatar* v. *Bahrain*, the ICJ determined that the exchanges of letters between the parties constituted 'international agreements creating rights and obligations',[53] and would therefore serve as a basis for the judgment.

The question of pedigree may be context-specific, and its determination may be affected by the IC's jurisdiction. Since ICs often have limited jurisdiction and may only adjudicate on limited issues, a key decision is whether a certain norm can be adjudicated on by the adjudicator in question.[54] The key rulings by the ICJ in *Military and Paramilitary Activities*, by ITLOS in *M/V 'SAIGA' (No. 2)*, and by the UNCLOS Tribunal in *Guyana* v. *Suriname*, were not so much that the respondent had used force unlawfully as that the adjudicator was empowered to adjudicate on whether an unlawful use of force had taken place.[55]

Conversely, a finding that an IC cannot apply a certain rule, or the rule does not have the claimed legal pedigree within the legal framework that

[51] Ronald Dworkin, 'The Model of Rules I' (1967) 35(1) *University of Chicago Law Review* 14–46, at 17 (Dworkin uses the word 'pedigree' to describe what he sees as the positivist model of rules espoused by H.L.A. Hart).

[52] See, for example, *Obligation to Negotiate Access to the Pacific (Bolivia* v. *Chile)*, Judgment, [2018] ICJ Reports, p. 507, 563 ('no obligation to negotiate Bolivia's sovereign access to the Pacific Ocean has arisen for Chile from any of the invoked legal bases').

[53] *Maritime Delimitation and Territorial Questions between Qatar and Bahrain*, Jurisdiction and Admissibility, [1994] ICJ Reports, p. 112, 126–127. See Elihu Lauterpacht, 'Partial Judgments and the Inherent Jurisdiction of the International Court of Justice', in Vaughan Lowe and Malgosia Fitzmaurice (eds.), *Fifty Years of the International Court of Justice – Essays in Honour of Sir Robert Jennings* (Cambridge: Cambridge University Press, 1996).

[54] See Lorand Bartels, 'Jurisdiction and Applicable Law Clauses in International Law: Where Does a Tribunal Find the Principal Norms Applicable to the Case Before It?', in Tomer Broude and Yuval Shany (eds.), *Multi-Sourced Equivalent Norms in International* (Oxford: Hart, 2011), 115–141.

[55] *Military and Paramilitary Activities in and against Nicaragua*, Merits, Judgment, [1986] ICJ Reports, p. 14; *Guyana* v. *Suriname*, PCA Case No. 2004-04, Award, 17 September 2007, para. 445; *M/V 'SAIGA' (No. 2) (Saint Vincent and the Grenadines* v. *Guinea*), Judgment, ITLOS Reports 1999, p. 10, 61. The grounds for these assertions of jurisdiction were different in each case. See Fabian Simon Eichberger, 'Give a Court an Inch and It Will Take a Yard? The Exercise of Jurisdiction over Incidental Issues' (2021) 81 *ZaöRV* 235.

the IC applies, can be a victory. The key substantive ruling made by the UNCLOS Tribunal in *South China Sea* was arguably that UNCLOS' regulation of the matter in dispute 'leaves no space for an assertion of historic rights'.[56] In *EC – Hormones*, the WTO Appellate Body drew a distinction between 'a general principle of customary international *environmental* law' and 'a principle of *general* or *customary international law*', implying that only the latter would affect the WTO rights and obligations it was empowered to apply.[57] In *Mexico – Soft Drinks*, the United States' key victory was the Appellate Body's finding that it did not have jurisdiction to assess the breach of North American Free Trade Agreement (NAFTA) obligations by the United States.[58] In *Kadi*, the Court of Justice of the European Union considered the legal value of a binding UN Security Council Resolution and, while recognising 'the primacy of that resolution in international law',[59] determined that 'an international agreement cannot affect the allocation of powers fixed by the [European Union] Treaties'.[60]

Second, the adjudicator may determine whether the norms invoked, once it is established that they are valid norms applicable between the parties, apply to the situation at hand and are thus liable for interpretation in the context of the dispute before it. This step concerns whether the norms in question, though existing, valid and binding, are disconnected from the situation in which the adjudicator is asked to interpret

[56] UNCLOS Tribunal, *The South China Sea Arbitration (The Republic of Philippines* v. *The People's Republic of China)*, PCA Case No. 2013-19, Award, 12 July 2016, para. 261. A similar ruling was made in the GATT Panel Report, *EEC – Quantitative Restrictions Against Imports of Certain Products from Hong Kong*, adopted 12 July 1983 (L/5511 – 30S/129), paras 19, 27 (finding that 'economic, social and historical aspects [without] corresponding GATT provision in justification . . . lay outside its consideration').

[57] Appellate Body Report, *EC – Hormones*, adopted 13 February 1998 (WT/DS26/AB/R, WT/DS48/AB/R), para. 123. This is a different question from whether the adjudicator would have jurisdiction to apply the relevant norms.

[58] Appellate Body Report, *Mexico – Soft Drinks*, adopted 26 March 2006 (WT/DS308/AB/R), para. 78 and fn. 174. The Appellate Body concluded that its only alternative was to disregard Mexico's allegation that its WTO-inconsistent measure was a response to the United States' breach of NAFTA and examine the question in light of WTO law.

[59] CJEU, Joined Cases C-402/05P and C-415/05P, *Yassin Abdullah Kadi and Al Barakaat International Foundation* v. *Council of the European Union and Commission of the European Communities* [2008] ECR I-6351, para. 288.

[60] Ibid., para. 282. See also Ibid., paras. 315 ff. Resolutions of the UN Security Council adopted under Chapter VII of the UN Charter are binding, by virtue of Article 25 of the Charter; pursuant to its Article 103, they 'prevail' over 'obligations under any other international agreement'. The EU Treaties are international agreements.

them. This inevitably involves an interpretation of the scope of the relevant norms and may even lead to a finding of lack of jurisdiction *ratione materiae* of the adjudicator. If this threshold is not passed, all that the adjudicator will issue is a negative interpretation, in the sense of a determination that the relevant normative framework does not apply to the situation or arguments brought to its attention. Thus, in *Application of the International Convention on the Elimination of All Forms of Racial Discrimination* (CERD), the ICJ found that 'the measures complained of by Qatar in the present case ... do not fall within the scope of CERD'.[61] In *Ecuador* v. *United States*, the Arbitral Tribunal found that, while Ecuador invoked 'general obligations of good faith in the performance of treaties and the principle of *pacta sunt servanda*', its request did not concern 'the interpretation or application of the treaty' over which the Tribunal had jurisdiction.[62] And, in *Nuclear Tests (Examination)*, the ICJ rejected New Zealand's request after concluding that the situation brought before the Court 'd[id] not fall within the provisions' of the normative instrument invoked.[63]

The third step, norm interpretation, is the core of Mere Adjudication as a remedy. If norms exist that apply to the situation of the dispute, the adjudicator can establish the content of these norms and clarify the obligations that they impose on the parties. The outcome for the parties is a set of pronouncements, within the adjudicator's judgment, award, ruling, or report, interpreting the relevant legal norms and determining their scope, content, and effects. Rather than two or more competing interpretations, the parties (and all those who read the judgment) will have access to the adjudicator's interpretation of these elements.

A final possible component of Mere Adjudication is application: an assessment of the facts presented by the parties in light of the norm as interpreted by the adjudicator. If the consequence of this application is a

[61] *Application of the International Convention on the Elimination of All Forms of Racial Discrimination (Qatar* v. *United Arab Emirates)*, [2021] ICJ Reports, p. 71, 106. For the converse ruling, see *Application of the International Convention on the Elimination of All Forms of Racial Discrimination (Armenia v. Azerbaijan)*, ICJ, Judgment of 12 November 2024, para. 90 (finding that 'the acts alleged are capable of constituting violations of CERD, and thus fall within the scope of the Convention').

[62] *Republic of Ecuador* v. *The United States of America*, PCA Case No. 2012-05, Award, 29 September 2012, para. 227.

[63] *Request for an Examination of the Situation in Accordance with Paragraph 63 of the Courts Judgment of 20 December 1974 in the Nuclear Tests (New Zealand* v. *France) Case*, [1995] ICJ Reports, p. 288, 307. The instrument was the ICJ Judgment in *Nuclear Tests (New Zealand* v. *France), Judgment*, [1974] ICJ Reports, p. 457.

finding of violation, this already enters the scope of the logically subsequent remedy – Declaration of Breach. If it is a consequential obligation, it can be thought of as a Consequential Duty. However, in many cases adjudicators will spell out the consequences of their normative interpretation for the situation at hand without making any finding of breach or determining new consequent obligations. In *Territorial and Maritime Dispute*, the ICJ stated that '[t]he consequence of the Court's Judgment is that the maritime boundary between Nicaragua and Colombia throughout the relevant area has now been delimited as between the Parties'.[64] In *Arbitral Award Made by the King of Spain*, the ICJ, having found that the Award whose validity Nicaragua contested was 'valid and binding', found that 'Nicaragua is under an obligation to give effect to it' but ignored Honduras' request for a declaration that Nicaragua's prior failure to give effect to the Award was a breach of international law.[65]

Parties on occasion expressly request an adjudicator to offer solely Mere Adjudication in a dispute, refraining from requesting further remedies. This is particularly common when the adjudicator is seised by agreement between the parties. For example, in *Savarkar*, the parties asked a Permanent Court of Arbitration (PCA) Arbitral Tribunal to determine merely whether Great Britain was required to return a certain prisoner to France in order to be 'in conformity with the rules of international law'.[66] In *North Sea Continental Shelf*, the ICJ noted that 'the Court is requested by each of the two Special Agreements to decide what are the applicable "principles and rules of international law". The Court is not asked actually to delimit the further boundaries'.[67]

Alternatively, an adjudicator may reject a request for further remedies, on the understanding that they are unwarranted and solving the interpretative dispute is a sufficient remedy. In *Cameroon* v. *Nigeria*, the ICJ issued a declaratory judgment, settling the border dispute, and rejected Cameroon's claims regarding Nigeria's responsibility for unlawful occupation of Cameroonian territory. The ICJ affirmed that the judgment determining the respective territories of the parties 'sufficiently addressed' the injury suffered by Cameroon, and stated that it would not 'seek to

64 *Territorial and Maritime Dispute (Nicaragua* v. *Colombia)*, Judgment, Merits, [2012] ICJ Reports, p. 624, 718. See note 71.

65 *Arbitral Award Made by the King of Spain on 23 December 1906*, Judgment of 18 November 1960: [1960] ICJ Reports, p. 192, 195–197, 217.

66 *Arrest and Return of Savarkar (France* v. *Great Britain)*, PCA Case No. 1910-03, Award, 23 February 1911, para. 1.

67 *North Sea Continental Shelf*, Judgment, [1969] ICJ Reports, p. 3, 13.

ascertain' the existence or the extent of Nigeria's responsibility for the occupation.[68] Quoting this jurisprudence, the PCA Arbitral Tribunal in *Guyana* v. *Suriname*, stated, in response to Guyana's request that Suriname's responsibility be engaged, that 'Guyana now has undisputed title to the area where the incident occurred – the injury done to Guyana has thus been "sufficiently addressed"'.[69]

Similarly, in *Territorial and Maritime Dispute*, the ICJ rejected Nicaragua's request for a declaration that Colombia had violated international law 'by stopping and otherwise hindering Nicaragua from accessing and disposing of her natural resources' in the disputed area, reasoning that, even if these were objective violations, a Declaration of Breach was unwarranted because 'the Judgment d[id] not attribute to Nicaragua the whole of the area which it claim[ed]'.[70] In *Ghana* v. *Côte d'Ivoire*, ITLOS developed this reasoning further when it rejected Ghana's request for a declaration that Côte d'Ivoire had violated its sovereignty by conducting hydrocarbon activities in a disputed area. ITLOS concluded that, in case of overlapping continental shelf areas, '[o]nly a decision on delimitation establishes which part of the continental shelf under dispute appertains to which of the claiming States', with the consequence that activities do not amount to violations if 'carried out before the judgment was delivered and if the area concerned was the subject of claims made in good faith by both States'.[71]

4.2.2 Remedial Value and Effects

The remedial utility of Mere Adjudication is in the interpretation of the applicable legal framework by an authoritative third party. An authoritative declaration regarding the extent of rights and obligations of the parties eliminates – at least for the purposes of the legal system – the scope for legitimate dispute regarding the interpretation of the rules. It substitutes the plurality of possible interpretations for a single one, valid over and above those previously asserted by the parties.[72]

[68] *Land and Maritime Boundary between Cameroon and Nigeria (Cameroon* v. *Nigeria: Equatorial Guinea Intervening)*, Judgment, [2002] ICJ Reports, p. 303, 317–321, 452.

[69] *Guyana* v. *Suriname*, PCA Case No. 2004-04, Award, 17 September 2007, para. 451.

[70] *Territorial and Maritime Dispute (Nicaragua* v. *Colombia)*, Judgment, Merits, [2012] ICJ Reports, p. 624, 718.

[71] *Delimitation of the Maritime Boundary between Ghana and Côte d'Ivoire in the Atlantic Ocean (Ghana* v. *Côte d'Ivoire)*, Judgment, ITLOS Reports 2017, p. 4, 158.

[72] *Factory at Chorzów (Interpretation)* (1925) PCIJ Ser. A No. 11, p 20. It is beyond the scope of this book to discuss the problems associated with applying the tenet *res judicata*

This is distinct from not permitting parties to hold or even express disagreement. The WTO DSU distinguishes between, on the one hand, the obligation of the parties to the dispute to 'unconditionally accept[]' the conclusions of an adopted Appellate Body report and the entitlement of WTO Members to 'express their views' regarding the report, even within the WTO Dispute Settlement Body.[73] This chimes well with Joseph Raz's remark that, following an authoritative determination, 'there is no reason for anyone to restrain their thoughts or their reflections'; the effect of the authoritative determination is that 'reasons that could have been relied upon to justify action before [an adjudicator's] decision cannot be relied upon once the decision is given'.[74]

The explanation for this seeming dissonance, between a party's entitlement to express disagreement with an authoritative decision and its inability to disregard the decision in its actions, is found in the fact that the authoritative decision operates a change in the expectations of legitimate behaviour of, at a minimum, the parties to whom it is addressed – and, likely, other parties, too.[75] This change is relatively simple to integrate into a constructivist model of international relations, in which actors cannot help but follow the logic of appropriateness. Following an authoritative decision, an actor that has 'internalized the duties and obligations that define an institutional identity' will adjust her conduct accordingly, since her motivations for action are grounded on

in the international legal system or the extent to which legal interpretations contained in judgments produce effects for third parties. On res *judicata*, see *Genocide Convention (Bosnia* v. *Serbia)*, Judgment, [2007] ICJ Reports, p. 43, 95; Ian Scobbie, 'Res Judicata, Precedent and the International Court: A Preliminary Sketch' (1999) *Australian Yearbook of International Law* 299–317; Vaughan Lowe, 'Res Judicata and the Rule of Law in International Arbitration' (1996) 8 *African Journal of International and Comparative Law* 38. Regarding effects for third parties, courts themselves have noted that effects do exist, especially when states have engaged in joint conduct and when the rules interpreted are not bilateral but multilateral treaties or customary rules. See *Certain Phosphate Lands in Nauru (Nauru* v. *Australia)*, Preliminary Objections, Judgment, [1992] ICJ Reports, p. 240, 261–262 ('a finding by the Court ... might well have implications for the legal situation' of non-parties to the dispute); *US – Stainless Steel (Mexico)*, adopted 20 May 2008 (WT/DS344/AB/R), para. 161 ('the relevance of clarification contained in adopted Appellate Body reports is not limited to the application of a particular provision in a specific case').

73 DSU, Article 17(14).

74 Joseph Raz, 'Authority and Justification' (1985) 14 *Philosophy & Public Affairs* 3–29, at 10.

75 On this perspective, see Section 2.3.1.

'the concepts of duties and obligations'.[76] To the extent that these duties and obligations comprise not only those arising under the domestic legal hierarchy but also those arising from a broader notion of doing one's duties for the common good,[77] the authoritative determination of an international adjudicator regarding prohibited, permissible, and obligatory conduct for a state will affect what state agents within the state perceive as the appropriate conduct for themselves.[78]

Explaining the value of Mere Adjudication from a more rationalist perspective is more challenging. The answer here, following the expressive theory of international adjudication developed in Chapter 3, lies in the ability of the adjudicator to express an interpretation of the relevant normative framework that is perceived as 'salient' or 'unique'. The adjudicator's distinctive position as a salient or unique interpreter, rather than being one among many interpreters, is grounded in part on the consent of the parties, in part on the elements usually associated with international adjudication – independence, impartiality, and expertise. Following an insight by Thomas Schelling, Tom Ginsburg and Richard McAdams define 'salience' or 'uniqueness' as a feature of a certain statement of an outcome that 'for some psychological, historical, or cultural reason . . . draws special mental attention from all the players ... causing the players to expect others to focus on it'.[79] This effect in turn produces what I have termed the expressive element of *auctoritas*:

> The ability of a third party, someone who is not a player in the coordination game, to influence the players in the game merely by communicating in favor of a particular outcome. By endorsing a particular outcome in the common view or hearing of the players, the third party makes that equilibrium *stand out* from the rest, which may then create self-fulfilling expectations that others will play the strategy associated with that equilibrium. In this way, third-party cheap talk *constructs* a focal point.[80]

[76] Ole Jacob Sending, 'Constitution, Choice and Change: Problems with the "Logic of Appropriateness" and Its Use in Constructivist Theory' (2002) 8 *European Journal of International Relations* 443–470, at 449.

[77] Ibid., 445.

[78] For the argument that international law does have this ability, see Başak Çali, *The Authority of International Law: Obedience, Respect, and Rebuttal* (Oxford: Oxford University Press, 2014).

[79] Tom Ginsburg and Richard H. McAdams, 'Adjudicating in Anarchy: An Expressive Theory of International Law' (2004) 45 *William and Mary Law Review* 1229–1339, at 1265.

[80] Ibid., 1266–1267.

Mere Adjudication is an interpretation of the applicable legal framework, issued by a third party that, as part of the applicable normative framework, is empowered to express the parties' rights and obligations. An adjudicator's statement regarding the correct interpretation of the legal framework changes the perceived normative setting. A normatively ambiguous setting, in which diverging interpretations of what the applicable norms require are equally legitimate, is replaced with a setting in which one interpretation stands out. Thus, the mere utterance of the required outcome by the adjudicator may prevent a situation of irresolvable conflict between two actors – what Ginsburg and McAdams term the 'Hawk/Hawk' conflict scenario.[81] The adjudicator's statement makes both parties, as well as observers assessing their behaviour, aware that one of the parties is entitled to a certain action (to play 'Hawk'), while the other is to refrain, with respect to this particular matter, from taking the action that would benefit it the most (and thus to play 'Dove'). From a rational choice perspective, then, if both parties perceive the Hawk/Hawk outcome as the worst possible one – the one leading to mutually harmful conflict and possibly third-party sanctions – the mere expression by the adjudicator of who must 'play Dove' in a particular respect (e.g. by not exploiting resources in a portion of the sea) allows disputing parties to coordinate their behaviour and act pursuant to their assigned role, complying with their international obligations as a consequence.[82]

4.2.3 *Legal Limits of Mere Adjudication*

As a matter of jurisdiction, the authority to award Mere Adjudication is generally implied in the decision to entrust an adjudicator with interpreting or applying a certain term to a dispute or a class of disputes. The ability of adjudicators to award this remedy is usually limited by the overarching requirement that adjudication be employed to settle disputes rather than make judicial pronouncements in the abstract. A dispute, as famously defined by the PCIJ, is 'a disagreement on a point of law or fact, a conflict of legal views or interests between two persons'.[83] Reference to

[81] Ibid., 1259 ('While the ambiguity lasts, the nations may fail to coordinate and end up in a Hawk/Hawk fight.').

[82] See Section 3.3.2. It may be worth repeating at this point that state-wide rationality, besides being a theoretical construction, is neither the only deterrent to violations nor a guarantee of compliance.

[83] *Mavrommatis Palestine Concessions*, Judgment, (1924) PCIJ Ser. A No. 2, p. 7, 11.

'interests' suggests that, even if a respondent professes not to have an interpretative dispute with a claimant, the claimant may still be able to obtain adjudication if the respondent's actions objectively harm or have harmed its legal interests. Although this definition leaves some room for interpretation,[84] its essence is that the judgment must produce 'a concrete effect in the relations between the parties'.[85]

In the disputes in which the ICJ refused to adjudicate on grounds that no dispute existed, its reasoning was precisely that adjudication requires a concrete dispute regarding the law applicable between the parties. In *Northern Cameroons*, the Court reasoned that the entire legal framework over which it was called upon to exercise jurisdiction had expired. The absence of effects of the ICJ's decision upon future legal relations between the parties, the Court reasoned, made legal questions 'only [of] an academic interest',[86] rendering adjudication 'devoid of purpose'.[87] In *Nuclear Tests*, having found that an out-of-court statement by the respondent regarding its future conduct (but not the legality of its previous conduct) entailed the termination of the dispute, the ICJ concluded that there was no longer utility in its pronouncement. The Court held:

> It does not enter into the adjudicatory functions of the Court to deal with issues *in abstracto*, once it has reached the conclusion that the merits of the case no longer fall to be determined. The object of the claim having disappeared, there is nothing on which to give judgment.[88]

A significant question in this regard concerns the ability of ICs to issue declaratory rulings *preventively*, with a view to determining the parties' rights and obligations before conduct subject to legal uncertainty takes place. The jurisprudence on this issue, discussed in Section 5.3.2, will be particularly relevant to establishing whether and when ICs are empowered to award Permissible Responses as prospective remedies.

[84] See, for example, the inconclusive statements by the ICJ in *Request for Interpretation of the Judgment of 31 March 2004 in the Case concerning Avena and Other Mexican Nationals (Mexico* v. *United States of America)*, Judgment, [2009] ICJ Reports, p. 3, 12–17.

[85] Shabtai Rosenne, *The Law and Practice of the International Court 1920–2005*, 4th edn, Vol. III (Leiden: Martinus Nijhoff, 2006), 1580.

[86] *Case concerning the Northern Cameroons (Cameroon* v. *United Kingdom)*, Preliminary Objections, Judgment, [1963] ICJ Reports, p. 15, 35.

[87] Ibid., 38.

[88] *Nuclear Tests (Australia* v. *France)*, Judgment, [1974] ICJ Reports, p. 253, 271–272; *Nuclear Tests (New Zealand* v. *France)*, Judgment, [1974] ICJ Reports, p. 457, 476–477.

4.3 Declaration of Breach

4.3.1 Concept and Practice

In cases where the main objective of the parties is to obtain Mere Adjudication – a judicial determination regarding the substantive rights and obligations of the parties – it may be said that 'the Court's task is completed the moment it has declared the law'.[89] In most cases, however, states have recourse to ICs not merely with the objective of settling a legal dispute but with the aim of establishing that another state has violated its obligations. A judicial Declaration of Breach is thus the next logical step in the adjudication process, opening the door for remedies that only become available in case of a legal breach. As the Commentary to ARSIWA notes, '[s]uch a declaration may be a preliminary to a decision on any form of reparation, or it may be the only remedy sought'.[90]

A judicial Declaration of Breach is an authoritative statement, by an impartial and independent organ, that international law is being, or has been, violated. In terms of its legal significance, a Declaration of Breach is a means for a court or tribunal to go beyond merely settling a legal dispute on interpretation and application of rules and send a clear, public condemnatory message, while not (or not at this stage) establishing for the offender any additional legal obligations. While with Mere Adjudication the adjudicator interprets the normative framework and, in so doing, establishes a focal point for lawful interactions, through a Declaration of Breach the adjudicator authoritatively declares that one of the actors has crossed the line separating lawful from unlawful conduct.

Scholars have hinted at the distinct character of this remedy when compared to Mere Adjudication. Hans Kelsen argued that 'the most important and essential stage in any legal procedure' is not the impartial determination of the content of the law but '[t]he objective examination and unbiased decision of the question whether or not the law has been violated'.[91] Christine Gray found that declarations of breach take a different form when compared to declaratory judgments that simply state the content of the law, but considered that this was a difference of form rather than substance.[92] In *Chorzów Factory*, the PCIJ implied that

89 Jennings, 'The Judicial Enforcement of International Obligations', 15.
90 ILC Ybk 2001, II.2, p. 107.
91 Hans Kelsen, 'Compulsory Adjudication of International Disputes' (1943) 37 *American Journal of International Law* 397–406, at 397.
92 Gray, *Judicial Remedies in International Law*, 97–98.

declaring a breach involves a different, 'more important jurisdiction' than determining reparation.[93]

A Declaration of Breach performs a distinct function from Mere Adjudication. Through Mere Adjudication, an IC establishes focal points for the operation of the international legal order. In awarding a Declaration of Breach, the adjudicator goes one step further and assigns to one of the parties (and sometimes to both) the label of wrongdoer. This seemingly purely symbolic act may amount not only to a form of symbolic reparation but also, in terms of the operation of the international legal order, to a *sanction* that an international adjudicator is able to deploy through its own actions. The significance of the sanctioning function of adjudication becomes clear when considering the disputes sometimes brought before international adjudicators in which the ostensible subject-matter of the legal dispute appears to play a minor role in a broader conflict or tension between the parties. The complaint's goal seems to be to obtain a Declaration of Breach, invoking for this purpose whichever legal instrument can provide a path to jurisdiction and an obligation whose violation can be attributable to the respondent.[94]

This sanctioning function of Declarations of Breach may have been first articulated in an adjudicatory decision by the Arbitral Tribunals in the 1913 *Carthage* and *Manouba* cases, concerning French vessels captured by Italy during the Turkish–Italian war. The Tribunals held that, in addition to compensation for material damages:

> for cases in which one Power would have breached its obligations, whether general or specific, vis-à-vis another Power, the establishment of this fact, especially in an arbitral award, constitutes already a serious sanction.[95]

This statement includes and conflates three conceptually separable elements of the Declaration of Breach. First, the recording, in the

[93] *Factory at Chorzów*, Jurisdiction, Judgment, (1927) PCIJ Ser. A No. 9, p. 23.

[94] See, for example, *Application of the International Convention on the Elimination of All Forms of Racial Discrimination* (*Qatar* v. *United Arab Emirates*), Preliminary Objections, Judgment, [2021] ICJ Reports, p. 71; *Application of the International Convention on the Elimination of All Forms of Racial Discrimination* (*Georgia* v. *Russian Federation*), Preliminary Objections, Judgment, [2011] ICJ Reports, p. 70.

[95] *Manouba (France* v. *Italy)* (1913) 11 UNRIAA 463, 475; *Carthage (France* v. *Italy)* (1913) 11 UNRIAA 449, 460 ('pour le cas où une Puissance aurait manqué à remplir ses obligations, soit générales, soit spéciales, vis-à-vis d'une autre Puissance, la constatation de ce fait, surtout dans une sentence arbitrale, constitue déjà une sanction sérieuse').

decision of an adjudicator, of the facts that amounted to a violation. Second, the express declaration by the adjudicator that such a violation has taken place. Third, the decision by the adjudicator to assign to this declaration the value of a symbolic sanction, sometimes setting aside requests for other forms of legal sanction (and in particular the provision of what these Tribunals termed 'pecuniary sanctions').[96] Each element deserves further examination.

The recording of the facts of a violation, unaccompanied by a formal declaration of its occurrence, may seem like the most underwhelming of sanctions. An assessment of international practice, however, suggests that states assign significant value to recording conducts that might be considered breaches of international obligations, even when decoupled from a formal statement declaring a breach. Not only do states dedicate significant energy to avoiding such records, but they also recognise the sanctioning value of these records when designing legal mechanisms and procedures.

Thus, at the United Nations Human Rights Commission and Human Rights Council, those seeking to debate an issue must sometimes start by defeating a 'no-action motion' proposed by the state being scrutinised and which, if approved, prevents all further discussion of the matter.[97] Within non-compliance procedures of multilateral environmental agreements, reports are often issued, first, to the party concerned. For example, in the Barcelona Convention, among the possible measures 'to bring about full compliance' is the decision to 'publish cases of non-compliance'.[98] The decision to publish is made only after a technical organ (the Non-Compliance Committee) has presented a confidential report to, and engaged with, the state concerned, and must be approved by a political organ, the Meeting of the Parties (MOP).[99] The decision to publish is also distinct from, and less grievous than, a 'caution' to the

[96] Ibid. ('sanctions pécuniaires').

[97] Elvira Domínguez Redondo, 'The Universal Periodic Review of the UN Human Rights Council: An Assessment of the First Session' (2008) 7 *Chinese Journal of International Law* 721–734. Approval of no-action motions at the Human Rights Council is rare. See Eric Tistounet, *The UN Human Rights Council: A Practical Anatomy* (Cheltenham: Edward Elgar, 2020), 244–245.

[98] Convention for the Protection of the Marine Environment and the Coastal Region of the Mediterranean and its Protocols, Decision No. IG.17/2 ('Procedures and mechanisms on compliance under the Barcelona Convention and its Protocols'), 18 January 2008 (doc. UNEP(DEC)/MED IG. 17/10), para. 33.

[99] Ibid., para. 32.

state concerned or the 'issu[ing of] a report of non-compliance regarding that Party'.[100] Irini Papanicolopulu laments that 'the Decision does not provide for the publication of the findings of the Committee ... bearing in mind that the publication of such findings may constitute a sanction imposed by the MOP'.[101]

Overall, the recording by an international body of a state's actions that are likely to be considered objectionable engenders to some degree the negative reputational effects of a declaration of breach, due solely to its placement in a public, official, permanently accessible document. A recording of the facts, even when unaccompanied by a formal Declaration of Breach, can thus be considered a toned-down version of this remedy. In fact, the refusal to issue a formal Declaration of Breach is often justified by the reasoning that the state's good faith renders a recording of the events sufficient.[102]

Most commonly, a Declaration of Breach includes a formal determination by the adjudicator that a state has breached its international obligations. This declaration is often issued solemnly in the operative part of a judicial ruling, including where the main remedy requested by a complainant is distinct, such as monetary compensation or the performance of specific conduct. It is also often requested independently of Consequential Duties.[103] In *Nicaragua (Contras)*, *M/V 'SAIGA' (No. 2)*, and *Guyana* v. *Suriname*, claimants sought and obtained, in addition to a declaration of specific breaches leading to consequential duties of reparation, formal judicial declarations that the respondents had breached the rule prohibiting the use of force in international relations.[104]

[100] Ibid., para. 34.

[101] Irini Papanicolopulu, 'Procedures and Mechanisms on Compliance under the 1976/1995 Barcelona Convention on the Protection of the Mediterranean Sea and Its Protocols', in Tullio Treves et al. (eds.), *Non-Compliance Procedures and Mechanisms and the Effectiveness of International Environmental Agreements* (Cambridge: Cambridge University Press, 2009), 165–167.

[102] *Territorial and Maritime Dispute* (*Nicaragua* v. *Colombia*), Judgment, [2012] ICJ Reports, p. 624, 717–718; *Land and Maritime Boundary between Cameroon and Nigeria* (*Cameroon* v. *Nigeria*: *Equatorial Guinea intervening*), Judgment, [2002] ICJ Reports, p. 303, 452.

[103] In *Ireland* v. *United Kingdom*, Ireland explicitly clarified to the ECtHR that its complaint 'ha[d] not as an object the obtaining of compensation for any individual person' (*Ireland* v. *United Kingdom (Merits and Just Satisfaction)*, Application No. 5310/71, Judgment of 18 January 1978, para. 245).

[104] *Military and Paramilitary Activities in and against Nicaragua*, Merits, Judgment, [1986] ICJ Reports, p. 14; *Guyana* v. *Suriname*, PCA Case No. 2004-04, Award,

A further possibility for adjudicators, within the scope of the Declaration of Breach, is to award symbolic satisfaction. ICs often state that their judicial Declarations of Breach are awarded 'as satisfaction'.[105] Although usually categorised as a form of reparation (and thus most akin to the Consequential Duties examined below), a judicial declaration awarding satisfaction as a remedy operates functionally as a heightened form of the Declaration of Breach. Satisfaction traditionally consisted of symbolic gestures by a wrongdoing state, such as a salute to the flag of the aggrieved state, indicating formal recognition of its wrongful conduct.[106] While, in some rare cases, judicially awarded satisfaction has included a Consequential Duty to perform some conduct – these cases are examined in Section 4.3 – it has become common practice for ICs to consider that their own rulings 'constitute appropriate satisfaction'.[107] In the *San Juan River* Judgment, the ICJ responded to a variety of requests for remedies, by both parties, by stating that 'the declaration of the breach . . . provides adequate satisfaction for that breach'.[108] Spelling out the general principle, the Eritrea-Ethiopia Claims Commission stated that 'where injury is non-material and hence not compensable by restitution or compensation, the appropriate form of reparation for a State's wrongful act is satisfaction'.[109]

The attribution of this function to judicial rulings dates back to the statements by the 1913 *Carthage* and *Manouba* Tribunals, that 'the establishment of [a breach], especially in an arbitral award, constitutes already *a serious sanction*'.[110] The same reasoning was applied by the ICJ in *Corfu Channel*, in which the Court declared that the United Kingdom's minesweeping operations in Albanian waters 'violated the

17 September 2007; *M/V 'SAIGA' (No. 2) (Saint Vincent and the Grenadines* v. *Guinea)*, Judgment, ITLOS Reports 1999, p. 10, 61.

105 See, for example, *Corfu Channel case*, Judgment of 9 April 1949: [1949] ICJ Reports, p. 4, 36.

106 ILC Ybk 2001, II.2, p. 106–107.

107 *Corfu Channel case*, Judgment of 9 April 1949: [1949] ICJ Reports, p. 4, 36.

108 *Certain Activities Carried Out by Nicaragua in the Border Area and Construction of a Road in Costa Rica along the San Juan River (Merits), Costa Rica* v. *Nicaragua and Nicaragua* v. *Costa Rica*, [2015] ICJ Reports 665, p. 717, 739.

109 Eritrea-Ethiopia Claims Commission, *Final Award – Eritrea's Damages Claims* (2009) 26 RIAA 505, 619. See also Ibid., 620 (recording that 'Ethiopia has appropriately conceded, with its expression of regret at the hearing, that Eritrea is entitled to satisfaction in the form of a declaration of the serious wrongfulness of Ethiopia's actions').

110 *Manouba* (*France* v. *Italy*) (1913) 11 UNRIAA 463, 475; Carthage (France v. *Italy)* (1913) 11 UNRIAA 449, 460. See note 101.

sovereignty of the People's Republic of Albania, and that this declaration by the Court constitutes in itself appropriate satisfaction'.[111] The ICJ has subsequently issued similar remedies for various violations, including breaches of procedural provisions[112] and minor breaches of a treaty,[113] but also the violation of diplomatic immunity from jurisdiction[114] and – more controversially – for a failure to prevent and punish genocide.[115]

This practice is not exclusive to the ICJ. In *Rainbow Warrior*, the Arbitral Tribunal concluded that it could not issue an order for cessation of the expired obligation, lamented that no request for monetary compensation had been made, and awarded a declaration of breach 'as satisfaction'.[116] ITLOS has sometimes awarded Declarations of Breach in conjunction with awards for compensation, asserting that the former covers non-pecuniary damage. In *M/V 'SAIGA' (No 2)*, ITLOS considered that its declarations of breach 'constitute[d] adequate reparation' for the unlawful use of force against the ship.[117] In *M/V 'Virginia G'*, the claimant withdrew a claim for moral damages and requested instead 'satisfaction or an apology'. Observing that 'satisfaction can take the form of a judicial declaration', the Tribunal declared that Guinea-Bissau had violated Panama's rights under the United Nations Convention on the Law of the Sea (UNCLOS) and considered that these declarations 'constitute[d] adequate reparation'.[118]

111 *Corfu Channel case*, Judgment of 9 April 1949: [1949] ICJ Reports, p. 4, 36. The Court drew a distinction between the actions of the two parties. Albania was 'responsible under international law for the explosions . . . in Albanian waters' that caused deaths, injuries, and material damages, entailing a duty to pay compensation (Ibid.).

112 *Mutual Assistance in Criminal Matters (Djibouti* v. *France)*, [2008] ICJ Reports, p. 177, 245, 247; *Pulp Mills (Argentina* v. *Uruguay)*, [2010] ICJ Reports, p. 14, 102, 106.

113 *Application of the Interim Accord of 13 September 1995 (FYROM* v. *Greece)*, Judgment of 5 December 2011, p. 644, para. 169.

114 *Arrest Warrant (Democratic Republic of the Congo* v. *Belgium)*, [2002] ICJ Reports, p. 3, 31.

115 *Bosnian Genocide (Bosnia* v. *Serbia)*, [2007] ICJ Reports, p. 43, 234, 239. See notes 134–138.

116 *Rainbow Warrior (New Zealand* v. *France)* (1990) 20 RIAA 215, 270, 272. Examining France's non-compliance with its obligation to detain an individual for a period of time, the tribunal concluded that it could not demand fulfilment of the original obligation because, had it been fulfilled, it would have expired.

117 *M/V 'SAIGA' (No. 2) (Saint Vincent and the Grenadines* v. *Guinea*), Judgment, ITLOS Reports 1999, p. 10, para. 176.

118 *M/V 'Virginia G' (Panama* v. *Guinea-Bissau)*, Judgment, ITLOS Reports 2014, p. 4, paras. 447–448.

As a means of adding to the Declaration of Breach, an alternative to satisfaction seems to be the formal engagement of the responsibility of the wrongdoer, in which the existence of legal consequences is asserted but these consequences are not (or not yet) judicially determined. Thus, in *Hostages*, after pointing to the 'repeated and multiple breaches' of diplomatic and consular law committed by Iran, the ICJ made a formal finding that Iran 'ha[d] incurred responsibility towards the United States', without developing on its content.[119] More broadly, the ICJ, the European Court of Human Rights (ECtHR), and the Inter-American Court of Human Rights (IACtHR) have all adopted the practice of expressly engaging state responsibility and leaving to a subsequent stage of the proceedings the determination of the precise consequences arising from this engagement.[120]

While this practice reveals a common reliance by ICs in the symbolic power of their rulings, it should not be inferred from this that this reliance has led to a consistent use of remedial powers or even a consistent vocabulary. In *Cameroon* v. *Nigeria*, the ICJ appears to have accepted Nigeria's argument that it was acting under 'reasonable mistake' or 'honest belief' that the territory in question belonged to it.[121] However, neither reasonable mistake nor honest belief constitutes a circumstance precluding wrongfulness. Statements that a Declaration of Breach was reparation were made by the arbitral tribunal in *Rainbow Warrior*[122] and by ITLOS in *M/V 'SAIGA' (No. 2)*.[123] In *Suriname* v. *Guyana*, the PCA Arbitral Tribunal referred to *Nigeria* v. *Cameroon* and *M/V 'SAIGA' (No. 2)* in its decision to declare that the threat to use force against a private ship was a violation of Guyana's international obligations, but stopped short of considering that this declaration constituted a means of reparation.[124]

119 *United States Diplomatic and Consular Staff in Tehran* (*United States of America* v. *Iran*), Judgment, [1980] ICJ Reports, p. 3, 41.

120 This practice is examined in Section 4.3.1.3.

121 *Land and Maritime Boundary between Cameroon and Nigeria* (*Cameroon* v. *Nigeria: Equatorial Guinea intervening*), Judgment, [2002] ICJ Reports, p. 303, 451.

122 *Rainbow Warrior (New Zealand* v. *France)* (1990) 20 RIAA 215, 274.

123 *M/V 'SAIGA' (No. 2) (Saint Vincent and the Grenadines* v. *Guinea*), Judgment, ITLOS Reports 1999, p. 10, para. 176 (stating that its declaration that the use of force by Guinea had been unlawful 'constitute[d] adequate reparation' to Saint Vincent and the Grenadines).

124 *Guyana* v. *Suriname*, PCA Case No. 2004-04, Award, 17 September 2007, paras. 438–440. The Tribunal did nonetheless state that 'Guyana now has undisputed title to the area where the incident occurred – the injury done to Guyana has thus been "sufficiently addressed"' (Ibid., para. 451).

And the ECtHR, which usually interprets its power to provide 'just satisfaction'[125] as an entitlement to award pecuniary damages, has sometimes provided satisfaction as a stand-alone remedy instead of such damages.[126]

The problematic nature of the purely judicial award of satisfaction as a heightened Declaration of Breach, in particular as a response to a request for Consequential Duties, was highlighted in the *Rainbow Warrior* arbitration. The Arbitral Tribunal lamented that no request for monetary compensation had been put forward. It then awarded, *proprio motu*, a Declaration of Breach 'as satisfaction';[127] and issued a 'recommendation' for the parties to establish a 'fund to promote close and friendly relations between the citizens of the two countries', proposing that France contribute US$2 million to this fund.[128] This ruling, which Gray termed 'bizarre',[129] suggests that the Tribunal itself understood the unsatisfactory character of even a heightened Declaration of Breach.

Another case in which judicial satisfaction, as a mere heightened form of the Declaration of Breach, constituted a seemingly unsatisfactory remedy was *Bosnian Genocide*. Having found that Serbia had 'failed to comply both with its obligation to prevent and its obligation to punish genocide deriving from the [Genocide] Convention' (as well as with ICJ provisional measures), the ICJ engaged Serbia's responsibility, then stated that Bosnia was 'entitled to reparation in the form of satisfaction'.[130] The operative part of the Judgment stated that the case was 'not one in which an order for payment of compensation, or ... a direction to provide assurances or guarantees of non-repetition, would be appropriate'.[131]

This may have had to do with Bosnia only having claimed compensation for 'financially assessable damage',[132] precluding any consideration regarding payment of moral damages. However, as Andrea Gattini suggests, the Court 'could have shown more creativity and

[125] ECHR, Article 41.

[126] See, for example, *Scopelliti* v. *Italy (Merits and Just Satisfaction)*, Application No. 15511/89, Judgment of 23 November 1993, para. 31.

[127] *Rainbow Warrior (New Zealand* v. *France)* (1990) 20 RIAA 215, 272.

[128] Ibid., 274.

[129] Gray, *Judicial Remedies in International Law*, 420.

[130] *Bosnian Genocide (Bosnia* v. *Serbia)*, [2007] ICJ Reports, p. 43, 233–234.

[131] Ibid., p. 239.

[132] Ibid., p. 72. See however note 247. For an award of compensation based on the ascertainable facts and 'extreme seriousness of the violation', even in the absence of documentation quantifying material damages, see Eritrea-Ethiopia Claims Commission, *Final Award – Eritrea's Damages Claims* (2009) 26 RIAA 505, 620–621.

sensitivity', establishing alternative forms of redress, inspired for example by the jurisprudence of the IACtHR[133] and by a UN General Assembly Resolution that recommends remedies and forms of reparation for victims of gross violations of human rights.[134] The ICJ's decision not to establish any Consequential Duty may have been guided (and this may be the heart of the problem) by a desire to provide the two parties with a favourable environment for subsequent reconciliation.[135] This is an understandable concern. However, the contrast between a condemnation for breach of a *jus cogens* rule and the provision of an entirely abstract consequence understandably 'gives the whole judgment a flavour of half-heartedness'.[136]

4.3.2 *Remedial Value and Effects*

A sceptic might classify Declarations of Breach among what F.A. Mann labelled 'esoteric means of redress', a category comprising 'such remedies as intervention, reprisals, satisfaction or apology' (and, seemingly, anything other than pecuniary compensation).[137] If considered as a means of providing redress for injury, a Declaration of Breach, even one given the heightened form of satisfaction, may indeed appear unsatisfactory, especially when used to respond not to symbolic or procedural but to immeasurable injury.[138]

The true value of Declarations of Breach and satisfaction seems to be not a reparatory function but a sanctioning effect. Following the trail of *Carthage* and *Manouba* Tribunals, which termed the Declaration of Breach 'a serious sanction',[139] Juliette McIntyre interprets these declarations as being 'directed to *penalising* the responsible State and not to *repairing* any injury'.[140] In *Corfu Channel*, Judge Azevedo considered the 'purely declaratory' judicial establishment of the breach as a

133 See Section 2.4.4.

134 Andrea Gattini, 'Breach of the Obligation to Prevent and Reparation Thereof in the ICJ's Genocide Judgment' (2007) 18 *European Journal of International Law* 695–713, at 711.

135 Ibid.

136 Ibid.

137 F. A. Mann, 'The Consequences of an International Wrong in International and National Law' (1976) 48 *British Yearbook of International Law* 1, at 2.

138 See, in regard to the *Bosnian Genocide* case, Marko Milanovic, 'State Responsibility for Genocide: A Follow-Up (2007) 18 *European Journal of International Law* 669–694; Gattini, 'Breach of the Obligation to Prevent and Reparation'.

139 See note 53.

140 McIntyre, 'Declaratory Judgments of the International Court of Justice', 153.

'moral sanction', issued to 'give satisfaction' to Albania and replace 'the familiar mediaeval procedure [of] apologies, flag saluting, etc'.[141] This use of satisfaction echoes Federico García-Amador's view that satisfaction, addressing not the injury but the unlawful act itself, is punitive in scope.[142] In issuing a Declaration of Breach, an IC in fact deploys a form of sanction – a symbolic, Layer 4 institutional sanction. In *TCL* v. *Guyana*, the Caribbean Court of Justice (CCJ) found that, '[w]hen one transplants civil contempt of court into the international arena among nation states, the primary sanction is a declaratory finding of contempt or noncompliance with the Court's order'.[143] Against Guyana's objection, the CCJ concluded that 'Guyana failed to comply promptly with the Order and so was in breach of Article 215 of the Revised Treaty [establishing the obligation to comply with CCJ judgments]'.[144]

How to explain this punitive or sanctioning value of a Declaration of Breach? International lawyers have long noticed that, as Hersch Lauterpacht put it, a judicial condemnation engenders 'the charge of bad faith', in which the state 'appears as a law-breaker' and incurs 'the odium of having violated the law'.[145] Hudec argued that the General Agreement on Tariffs and Trade's (GATT's) 'ultimate remedy' was 'the force of community pressure"[146] while Joost Pauwelyn stated that an identified violation engenders 'community costs' for as long as it remains unaddressed, impinging especially upon the reputation of the wrongdoer.[147]

To understand the mechanisms through which a Declaration of Breach operates, and may be considered a sanction, it is useful to think back in terms of international law's compliance-inducing mechanisms explored in Chapter 2. If one accepts that there are internal reasons for a state to comply with obligations, a Declaration of Breach triggers Layer

[141] *Corfu Channel*, Judgment of 9 April 1949: [1949] ICJ Reports, p. 4, 114 (Dissenting opinion of Judge Azevedo).

[142] F.V. García-Amador, *The Changing Law of International Claims*, vol. 575 (Dobbs Ferry: Oceana, 1984).

[143] CCJ, *Trinidad Cement Limited and TCL Guyana Incorporated* v. *Guyana (Non-Compliance/Contempt)*, CCJ Application No. 2 of 2009 (Original Jurisdiction), Judgment, 29 March 2010, para. 43.

[144] Ibid., para. 25.

[145] Hersch Lauterpacht, *The Function of Law in the International Community* (Oxford: Oxford University Press, 2011 [1933]), 276.

[146] Robert E. Hudec, 'Broadening the Scope of Remedies in WTO Dispute', in Friedl Weiss and Jochem Wiers (eds.), *Improving WTO Dispute Settlement Procedures* (London: Cameron May, 2000), 400.

[147] Pauwelyn, *Optimal Protection of International Law*, 44.

1 enforcement mechanisms ('self-sanction'), empowering domestic political actors to pursue compliance unencumbered by charges of legal uncertainty.[148] State agents responsible for the relevant conduct may respond directly to a Declaration of Breach, if they are seeking to act in accordance with the relevant normative framework; or they may be required to do so by a hierarchically superior agent, including an independent judiciary. As discussed in Chapter 2, these actors may change their conduct following the logic of appropriateness or because, under the logic of consequences, they believe causing the state to continue committing acts flagged as internationally unlawful will lead to negative consequences for them or their states.

A Declaration of Breach produces effects over other layers of international law's compliance-inducing system, affecting even a state considered as a unitary, self-interested actor. With regard to Layer 2 (bilateral enforcement), an assessment of the expressive function[149] of a Declaration of Breach would consider a pre-adjudicatory situation in which both states parties to an interaction hold opposing views on whether a violation has occurred. Both may seek to apply sanctions. The state that felt aggrieved will sanction what it sees as a violation; the other state will sanction what it sees as an unlawful response to a non-violation. Even setting aside the possibility of escalation, mutual sanctioning under legal indeterminacy will produce negative effects for both states.[150] In these cases, merely by expressing its view on whether there has been a violation, an adjudicator can produce an alignment of normative assessments.[151] The party found in breach then suffers any reputational and reciprocity effects that being flagged as a violator produces. Equally importantly, while the party found in breach may discursively protest the finding, the authoritative settlement of the matter provides an opportunity for both parties to put the normative struggle behind them, restoring their regular relations and preventing harmful mutual sanctions.

These expressive effects are of course subject to constraints. For parties to be affected by the adjudicator's statement and adjust their expectations

[148] See Section 2.5.

[149] See Section 3.3.1.

[150] Ginsburg and McAdams, 'Adjudicating in Anarchy', 1272 ('the resulting sanctioning behavior could make both sides worse off').

[151] Leslie Johns, *Strengthening International Courts: The Hidden Costs of Legalization* (Ann Arbor, MI: University of Michigan Press, 2015), 16.

(including as third-party reputational sanctioners), they must believe that the adjudicator's assessment is authoritative (i.e. salient). Additionally, the more vital a party deems its interests in the disputed matters, the less it will be willing to adjust its expectations and behaviour following an adverse determination by the adjudicator. This expressive effect nonetheless explains both (1) why a Declaration of Breach can, even in a purely bilateral dispute, lead the party found in breach to accept its violation and change behaviour; and (2) why a mere Declaration of Breach, unaccompanied by Consequential Duties, will sometimes constitute a sufficient remedy for an aggrieved party. This will be the case whenever its priority is to obtain a discursive victory and restore relations with the wrongdoer, rather than to obtain redress additional to this restoration to address the injury the violation has caused.

Furthermore, few violations of international law are of concern solely to the disputing parties. Even in ostensibly bilateral disputes, third states act as involuntary enforcers through Layer 3 enforcement: their consideration of the reputation of the wrongdoer, their involuntary tendency to apply norms on the basis of reciprocity, and – in serious cases – their ability to retaliate against a wrongdoer.[152] Thus, even if a third state finds no reason to be involved in a dispute, its beliefs regarding the disputing states, their trustworthiness, and the ways in which it should interact with them are constantly adjusted to account for these states' actions and responses in disputes with other actors.

Declarations of Breach, then, operate well where diffuse (Layer 3) enforcement is a powerful promoter of compliance but is significantly affected by uncertainty, as well as by the sanctioner's dilemma.[153] If the adjudicator's statements are seen to be genuine and more accurate than those the parties themselves make (put otherwise, if the adjudicator has *auctoritas*), its statements will 'cause individuals to update their beliefs about the state of the world'.[154]

While, between the disputing parties, legal indeterminacy is problematic in that it risks leading to over-sanctioning, as regards third parties indeterminacy tends to lead to under-sanctioning. In the absence of an impartial determination, regardless of the private views of state agents, third states are likely to treat the situation as a disputed one. States may

[152] See Section 3.3.2.
[153] See Section 3.3.2.
[154] Ginsburg and McAdams, 'Adjudicating in Anarchy', 1274.

side with either party; most are likely to remain indifferent to avoid marring their relations with each of the disputing parties.

Once a Declaration of Breach is issued, it is clear to the community who the wrongdoer is. Involuntary Level 3 sanctions arise, and voluntary ones become more likely to be applied. Third states that had sided with the state found in breach become more likely to press it to comply. International law relies on third-party sanctioning, usually through reputation and reciprocity, occasionally through retaliation. A Declaration of Breach provides a focal point around which third parties can coordinate their sanctioning decisions. As a result, third parties may act, if not in unison, with mutual knowledge that a breach was flagged and without sanctioning each other on grounds of wrongful sanctioning.[155] If the adjudicator is trusted by third states to make accurate rulings, it engenders coordinated involuntary sanctions, permits coordinated voluntary sanctioning, and, because third states are likely to avoid sanctioning until the adjudicator has pronounced a violation, deters both voluntary and involuntary over-sanctioning.

As regards the added value of satisfaction, two views are possible. Seen in a good light, this remedy operates as a heightened form of Declaration of Breach, providing the parties to the dispute and third states with an instrument to align their views that a wrongful act was committed. This remedial value becomes particularly clear in its occasional appearance in investment arbitration – a regime usually known for its focus on monetary compensation. In *Quiborax* v. *Bolivia*, the International Centre for Settlement of Investment Disputes (ICSID) Arbitral Tribunal disagreed with the respondent that satisfaction was unavailable due to being 'punitive in nature'. It found that, 'as part of the process of settling the dispute', it could have awarded a 'declaration of breach of the duty to arbitrate in good faith'.[156] The Tribunal in *Cementownia* v. *Turkey* went further, acceding to the respondent state's request for satisfaction against the investor and 'declar[ing] formally that the Claimant ha[d] filed a fraudulent claim against the Republic of Turkey'.[157]

[155] Ibid., 1095.

[156] *Quiborax S.A.* v. *Bolivia*, ICSID Case No. ARB/06/2, Award, 16 September 2015, para. 561, 564. See however *CMS* v. *Argentina*, ICSID Case No. ARB/01/8, Award (12 May 2005), para. 399 (finding that, where the dispute does not concern 'reparation due to an injured State, satisfaction can be ruled out at the outset').

[157] *Cementownia* v. *Turkey (I)*, ICSID Case No. ARB(AF)/06/2, Award, 17 September 2009, paras. 162–163.

At the same time, one may also see satisfaction through a negative lens. In awarding a Declaration of Breach as satisfaction, an adjudicator often implicitly determines that no further consequential duties emerge for a wrongdoer from its violation. In so doing, the adjudicator prevents the aggrieved party from demanding the fulfilment of consequential duties before it ceases sanctioning, and requesting third states to sanction, the wrongdoer. By awarding satisfaction as a form of reparation, thus, adjudicators are able to provide certainty not only with regard to the existence of the breach but also with regard to the inexistence of further conditions to be fulfilled by the wrongdoer to address the breach.[158]

4.3.3 *Jurisdiction and Applicability*

Jurisdiction to issue a Declaration of Breach is generally seen as an inherent part of adjudicator's jurisdiction to adjudicate on a dispute, unless an agreement specifically limits the powers of an adjudicator. The *Rainbow Warrior* Arbitral Tribunal had 'no doubt that this power exists and that it is seen as a significant sanction'.[159] In *Corfu Channel*, the ICJ went as far as claiming that, when faced with as grave a breach as military intervention, 'to ensure respect for international law, of which it is the organ, the Court must declare that the action … constituted a violation'.[160]

Once the relevant law has been interpreted, the essential formal requirement for a declaration of breach is that the court must be capable of interpreting the conduct of the relevant state. In *Tehran Hostages*, the ICJ formulated the question in terms of an assessment in 'two phases':

> First it must determine how far, legally, the acts in question may be regarded as imputable to the Iranian State. Second, it must determine the compatibility or incompatibility with the obligations of Iran under treaties in force or any other rules of international law that may be applicable.[161]

[158] This may have been the case in *Bosnian Genocide*, in which the ICJ rejected the complainant's request for monetary compensation. The Court found, however, that the respondent was under an obligation to transfer to the ICTY certain persons accused of genocide (*Bosnian Genocide (Bosnia* v. *Serbia)*, Judgment, [2007] ICJ Reports, p. 43, 234–235).

[159] *Rainbow Warrior (New Zealand* v. *France)* (1990) 20 RIAA 215, 273, 275.

[160] *Corfu Channel case*, Judgment of 9 April 1949: [1949] ICJ Reports, p. 4, 35.

[161] *United States Diplomatic and Consular Staff in Tehran* (*United States of America* v. *Iran*), Judgment, [1980] ICJ Reports, p. 3, 29. The Court in fact refers to 'responsibility' in the sense of determination of blame for the breach. See also *Phosphates in Morocco (Preliminary Objections)*, (1938) PCIJ Ser. A/B No. 74, p. 28.

Although these elements may be conceptually distinct,[162] they are difficult to separate in practice: conduct may be attributable to a state without being unlawful, but conduct which is not attributable to the state cannot constitute a breach of its international obligations. This was first noted in *Dickson Car Wheel Co*, in which the Mexican–US General Claims Commission noted that 'in order that a State may incur responsibility under international law it is necessary that an unlawful international act be imputed to it, *that is*, that there exists a violation of a duty imposed by an international juridical standard'.[163] This duty may be a negative duty not to act in certain ways or so as to produce certain outcomes; it may also be a duty to prevent certain conduct from taking place within a state's territory or wherever it has jurisdiction.[164] Although separable for purposes of analysis, the two elements, of conduct contrary to international obligations and its attribution to a state, constitute aspects of the same occurrence – a breach of the law. It is the existence of this breach that an adjudication identifies, with legal effects, in a Declaration of Breach.

4.4 Consequential Duties

4.4.1 Concept and Practice

Many authors and adjudicators, when referring to 'remedies' in international adjudication, mean the remedy of Consequential Duties: judicial findings that a legal breach entails certain new obligations for the wrongdoer. This is the sense in which the ICJ employed the term 'remedies' in *LaGrand*, stating that, '[w]here jurisdiction exists over a dispute on a particular matter, no separate basis for jurisdiction is required by the

[162] See ILC Ybk 2001, II.2, p. 39.

[163] *Dickson Car Wheel Co (USA)* v. *United Mexican States* (1931) 4 RIAA 669, 678 (emphasis added).

[164] See, for example, *Pulp Mills (Argentina* v. *Uruguay*), [2010] ICJ Reports, p. 14, para. 197 (duty of due diligence over private parties); *Bosnian Genocide (Bosnia* v. *Serbia)*, [2007] ICJ Reports, p. 43, paras. 429–430 (obligation to prevent genocide); *Armed Activities in the Territory of the Congo (Democratic Republic of the Congo* v. *Uganda) (Merits)*, [2005] ICJ Reports, p. 168, 281–282; *Argentina – Hides and Leather*, adopted 16 February 2001, WT/DS155/R, paras. 11.19–11.21; *Loizidou* v. *Turkey*, Application No. 153118/89, Judgment of 23 March 1995, paras. 59–64 (potential duties in relation to territories over which the state has jurisdiction); *Commission* v. *France* (1997) C-265/95, para. 31, and Mercosur Ad Hoc Tribunal, Award No 9/2006 (*Roadblocks*), 6 September 2006, para. 149 (duty to adopt measures to prevent obstacles to the free movement created by actions of private individuals).

Court to consider the remedies a party has requested for the breach of the obligation'.[165] In *Whaling in the Antarctic*, the ICJ referred to remedies as 'measures that go beyond declaratory relief'.[166] In *China – Raw Materials*, the Appellate Body found that, in order to help secure a positive resolution of the dispute, it was required to go beyond providing 'merely declaratory' relief.[167]

Part Two of ARSIWA codifies, from state and judicial practice, two types of duties arising from a violation. First are so-called prospective duties, including the obligations to cease the wrongful conduct and, in certain circumstances, to offer guarantees of non-repetition. Second is the obligation to offer reparation for the injury caused by the violation. Indeed, in many cases consequential duties operate horizontally: states acknowledge a legal violation and recognise, and seek to perform, the prospective and retrospective obligations that arise for them following the breach.[168] As with other remedies, in issuing Consequential Duties an international adjudicator does not establish otherwise inexistent obligations but determines, in the context of a dispute, rights and obligations that could have arisen and been recognised between the parties without its intervention.

4.4.1.1 Prospective Consequential Duties – Cessation and Guarantees of Non-Repetition

Prospective Consequential Duties amount to a specification by the adjudicator of the conduct required to cease the violation, and, in some cases, to provide guarantees of non-repetition. Cessation, as codified in ARSIWA Article 30(a), is the 'first requirement' for a state to discharge its responsibility following a breach.[169] This duty may be coupled, 'if the circumstances so require', with an obligation to offer assurances and guarantees of non-repetition.[170] As the ARSIWA Commentary notes, the duty of cessation is 'future-looking';[171] it is the prospective portion

[165] *LaGrand (Germany* v. *United States of America)*, Judgment, [2001] ICJ Reports, p. 466, 516.

[166] *Whaling in the Antarctic (Australia* v. *Japan)*, Judgment, [2014] ICJ Reports, p. 226, 298.

[167] *China – Measures Related to the Exportation of Various Raw Materials*, adopted 30 January 2012, WT/DS395/AB/R, paras. 264–265.

[168] ILC Ybk 2001, II.2, p. 89.

[169] Ibid.

[170] ILC Articles, Article 30.

[171] ILC Ybk 2001, II.2, p. 90.

of the consequences arising out of unlawful conduct, in the sense that it addresses the wrongful conduct itself rather the injury it has caused.

The key obligation that arises for a wrongdoer in this regard is the cessation and non-repetition of the violation. Thus, although adjudicators sometimes frame prospective remedies as 'orders' for states to engage in specific conduct,[172] any conduct that results in a cessation of the violation may fulfil the order. This point is articulated most clearly by the ECtHR, whose traditional position is that the means by which a state will cease a violation are a matter of its choice.[173] In *Assanidze* v. *Georgia*, after having ruled that the claimant was unlawfully detained, the ECtHR held that 'its judgments are essentially declaratory in nature and that, in general, it is primarily for the State concerned to choose the means to be used in its domestic legal order in order to discharge its legal obligation' to comply.[174] However, it added, 'by its very nature, the violation found in the instant case does not leave any real choice as to the measures required to remedy it'. As a result, the ECtHR concluded that 'the respondent State must secure the applicant's release at the earliest possible date'.[175]

The ICJ has often acknowledged a similar distinction. In *LaGrand*, *Avena* and *Jadhav*, the Court found that the United States and Pakistan, having criminally condemned foreigners without regard for the rights secured by the Vienna Convention on Consular Relations, were required to 'allow the review and reconsideration' of convictions and sentences to implement their rights under the Convention but could do so 'by means of [their] own choosing'.[176] In *Arrest Warrant*, by contrast, Belgium had

172 *Whaling in the Antarctic (Australia* v. *Japan)*, Judgment, [2014] ICJ Reports, p. 226, 298 ('The Court therefore will order that Japan shall revoke any extant authorization, permit or licence to kill, take or treat whales in relation to JARPA II, and refrain from granting any further permits under Article VIII, para. 1, of the Convention, in pursuance of that programme'). Some call this 'specific performance'. See Stoica, *Remedies before the International Court of Justice*, 46 ('specific performance means that a state has to fulfil its obligations').

173 *Scopelliti* v. *Italy (Merits and Just Satisfaction)*, Application No. 15511/89, Judgment of 23 November 1993, para. 31.

174 *Assanidze* v. *Georgia (Merits)*, Application No. 71503/01, Judgment of 8 April, paras. 202–203.

175 Ibid. See also *Ilascu* v. *Moldova and Russia*, Application No. 48787/99, Judgment of 9 July 2004. See generally Philip Leach, 'Beyond the Bug River: A New Dawn for Redress before the European Court of Human Rights?' (2005) 10 *European Human Rights Law Review* 148.

176 *LaGrand (Germany* v. *United States of America)*, Judgment, [2001] ICJ Reports, p. 466, 516; *Avena and Other Mexican Nationals (Mexico* v. *United States of America)*, [2004]

issued an arrest warrant disregarding the immunity from criminal jurisdiction of a Minister for Foreign Affairs. Although Belgium could comply with the ensuing obligation 'by means of its own choosing', this obligation was not to reconsider but to 'cancel the warrant in question and so inform the authorities to whom it was circulated'.[177] In *Alleged Violations*, the ICJ followed the declaration that provisions of Colombia's domestic law infringed upon Nicaragua's sovereign rights and Exclusive Economic Zone with the statement that Colombia had 'the obligation, by means of its own choosing, to bring the provisions … into conformity with customary international law' as previously determined by the Court.[178]

Other ICs have, like the ECtHR, occasionally concluded that in the dispute at hand cessation required specific conduct, so that the choice of means was reduced or, in their view, non-existent. In *Whaling in the Antarctic*, the ICJ, having found that Japan's programme permitting certain types of whaling was incompatible with its obligations, determined that Japan 'shall revoke any extant authorization, permit or licence granted … and refrain from granting any further permits in pursuance of that programme'.[179] At the same time, the Court left it to Japan to 'take account of the reasoning and conclusions contained in [its] Judgment as it evaluates the possibility of granting any future permits'.[180] In *Enrica Lexie*, having concluded that Italy's marines benefited from immunity from prosecution, the UNCLOS Arbitral Tribunal determined that 'India must take the necessary steps in order to cease to exercise its criminal jurisdiction over the Marines'.[181] In *Noudehouenou* v. *Benin*, the African Court of Human and People's Rights (AfCHPR) ordered Benin

ICJ Reports, p. 12, 72. Note that, in *Avena* (but not in *LaGrand*), the ICJ framed these remedies as 'reparation' (Ibid.). *Jadhav (India* v. *Pakistan)*, Judgment, [2019] ICJ Reports, p. 418, 460.

177 *Arrest Warrant (Democratic Republic of the Congo* v. *Belgium)*, Judgment, [2002] ICJ Reports, p. 3, 32–33. Although the individual in question had left office, the warrant was 'still extant, and remain[ed] unlawful' (Ibid., p. 32). Compare with the finding of the arbitral tribunal in *Rainbow Warrior* that it could not issue an order for cessation due to the chronological expiry of the original obligation (*Rainbow Warrior (New Zealand* v. *France)* (1990) 20 RIAA 215, 270).

178 *Alleged Violations of Sovereign Rights and Maritime Spaces in the Caribbean Sea (Nicaragua* v. *Colombia)*, Judgment of 21 April 2022, p. 69.

179 *Whaling in the Antarctic (Australia* v. *Japan)*, Judgment, [2014] ICJ Reports, p. 226, 300.

180 Ibid., p. 298.

181 *The 'Enrica Lexie' Incident (Italy* v. *India)*, PCA Case No. 2015-28, Award, 21 May 2020, para. 888.

to remove members of the Executive branch from its High Judicial Council to ensure the independence of the judiciary.[182] In *Fuel Price Differences*, the Andean Court of Justice ordered Bolivia and Ecuador to 'adopt the measures necessary and appropriate to cease the conduct declared in breach of Andean Community law'.[183]

The prospective character of cessation also means that solely obligations that continue into the future can be targeted with cessation. In *Certain Iranian Assets*, the ICJ rejected Iran's request that United States decisions 'infringing the rights of Iran and of Iranian companies . . . cease to have effect . . . and that no steps are taken against the assets or interests of Iran or any Iranian entity or national that involve or imply the recognition or enforcement of such acts'.[184] The ICJ noted that, since the United States had denounced the treaty under which the acts being challenged were unlawful, the duty of cessation no longer applied.[185]

At the WTO, the main Consequential Duty afforded in a dispute settlement report is a recommendation for cessation of the unlawful conduct within a reasonable period of time.[186] Recommendations generally target the specific measures that a complainant has identified and brought to the WTO dispute settlement system for adjudication. In *China – Raw Materials*, the Appellate Body reasoned that, to avoid 'merely declaratory' findings of inconsistency, it made sense for the panel to articulate the ensuing 'implementation obligations'.[187] This panel had found that China's WTO-inconsistent measure was made effective through annually recurring legal instruments. The panel concluded that China was required 'to bring its measures into conformity with its WTO

[182] AfCHPR, *Application 028/2020 (Houngue Eric Noudehouenou* v. *Republic of Benin)*, Judgment, 1 December 2022, para. 203(xvi).

[183] *Fuel Price Differences (Peru* v. *Bolivia)*, Case No. 02-AI-2020, Judgment, 17 July 2023, p. 50; ACJ, *Fuel Price Differences (Peru* v. *Ecuador)*, Case No. 05-AI-2021, Judgment, 17 July 2023, p. 48–49.

[184] *Certain Iranian Assets (Islamic Republic of Iran* v. *United States of America)*, Judgment of 30 March 2023, para. 225.

[185] Ibid., paras. 227–229. With regard to the improper application of this reasoning to restitution, see *Rainbow Warrior (New Zealand* v. *France)* (1990) 20 RIAA 215, 274.

[186] Despite their label, 'recommendations' in WTO dispute settlement are binding, at the very least, in the sense that not implementing them within the allotted reasonable period of time entails the possibility of certain legal consequences (WTO-authorised retaliation).

[187] Appellate Body Report, *China – Raw Materials*, adopted 22 February 2012, WT/DS395/AB/R, para. 264.

obligations such that the "series of measures" does not operate to bring about a WTO-inconsistent result'.[188] Put more generally, a WTO recommendation identifies the measure ostensibly causing the violations and specifies the duty to 'bring the measure found to be inconsistent with a [WTO] agreement into compliance therewith'.[189] The true obligation remains to cease the unlawful conduct as a whole and ensure substantive compliance with the applicable commitments.[190]

The second element of prospective consequences are so-called guarantees of non-repetition. In the Commentary to the ILC Articles, the ILC stated that these guarantees are 'sought when the injured State has reason to believe that the mere restoration of the pre-existing situation does not protect it satisfactorily'.[191] As regards its use as a judicial remedy, in *LaGrand*, the ICJ affirmed (offering little in the way of reasoning) that its remedial jurisdiction included the entitlement to order a state to provide guarantees of non-repetition.[192] The Court ultimately found solely that 'the commitments undertaken by the United States' to implement its obligations 'must be regarded as meeting the ... request for a general assurance of non-repetition'.[193] The ICJ employed the same procedure in *Avena*, but neither in these[194] nor in subsequent judgments[195] has the Court followed through and issued this remedy, or fleshed out its possible contents.

By contrast, the IACtHR has developed a versatile tool-box of Consequential Duties under the label 'guarantees of non-repetition'.

188 Panel Report, *China – Raw Materials*, adopted 22 February 2012, WT/DS395/R, paras. 8.8, 8.15, 8.22.

189 WTO Dispute Settlement Understanding, Article 22.2.

190 See also Appellate Body Report, *EC – Continued Suspension*, adopted 14 November 2008, WT/DS320/AB/R, para. 316 ('Even if the European Communities should be presumed to have acted in good faith when adopting the implementing measure, that does not mean that the measure has achieved substantive compliance'). More broadly, Geraldo Vidigal, 'Re-Assessing WTO Remedies: The Prospective and the Retrospective' (2013) 16 *Journal of International Economic Law* 505–534.

191 ILC Ybk 2001, II.2, p. 89–91.

192 *LaGrand (Germany* v. *United States of America)*, Judgment, [2001] ICJ Reports, p. 466, 485.

193 Ibid., 516.

194 Ibid., 513, 516; *Avena and Other Mexican Nationals (Mexico* v. *United States of America)*, [2004] ICJ Reports, p. 12, 69.

195 *Dispute regarding Navigational and Related Rights (Costa Rica* v. *Nicaragua)*, Judgment, [2009] ICJ Reports, p. 213, 217; *Pulp Mills (Argentina* v. *Uruguay)*, Judgment, [2010] ICJ Reports, p. 14, 105; *Jurisdictional Immunities (Germany* v. *Italy: Greece intervening)*, Judgment, [2012] ICJ Reports, p. 99, 154.

IACtHR guarantees of non-repetition are, together with 'measures of satisfaction' (examined below), at the core of what has been called the Court's 'remedial activism'.[196] In *Gutiérrez-Soler* v. *Colombia*, the IACtHR described guarantees of non-repetition as 'positive measures that the State must adopt to prevent repetition of the harmful events' found to have taken place in the individual case judged.[197]

These measures vary significantly. In *Gutiérrez* v. *Colombia*, the IACtHR determined that Colombia was required, among others, to investigate the events reported and identify, try, and punish the perpetrators; provide psychological and psychiatric treatment to the victims; publish the factual findings in the judgment; and establish training programs in human rights to the police.[198] In *Aloeboetoe* v. *Suriname*, involving a massacre committed by military officers in a village populated by an ethnic minority, the IACtHR ordered Suriname to create trust funds and a foundation, reopen a local school, and ensure its functioning, as well as that of the local medical clinic.[199] In *YATAMA* v. *Nicaragua*, the Court ordered Nicaragua not only to reform its electoral law to allow for universal participation as required by the American Convention on Human Rights (ACHR) but also to publicise the decision of the Court and to 'adopt, within a reasonable time, the necessary legislative measures to establish a simple, prompt and effective recourse to contest the decisions of the Supreme Electoral Council that affect human rights, such as the right to participate in government'.[200] In *Marc Chang* v. *Guatemala*, a case involving the killing, by Guatemalan security forces, of an anthropologist researching internally displaced peoples, the IACtHR ordered Guatemala to create a scholarship bearing the name of the victim, and to 'name a well-known street or square in Guatemala City after Myrna Mack Chang, and place a plaque in her memory where she died, or nearby, with reference to the activities she carried out'.[201]

196 Thomas M. Antkowiak, 'Remedial Approaches to Human Rights Violations: The Inter-American Court of Human Rights and Beyond' (2008) 46 *Columbia Journal of Transnational Law* 351–419, at 366.

197 *Gutiérrez-Soler* v. *Colombia*, Merits, Reparations and Costs, Judgment, 12 September 2005, IACHR Ser. C No. 132, para. 63.

198 Ibid., para. 127.

199 *Aloeboetoe* v. *Suriname*, Reparation and Costs, Judgment, 10 September 1993, IACHR Ser. C No. 11, paras. 96, 99–108.

200 *YATAMA* v. *Nicaragua*, Preliminary Objections, Merits, Reparations and Costs, Judgment, 23 June 2005, IACHR Ser. C No. 127, para. 275(9).

201 *Mack Chang* v. *Guatemala*, Merits, Reparation and Costs, Judgment, 25 November 2003, IACHR Ser. C No. 101, para. 301.

4.4.1.2 Retrospective Consequential Duties – Restitution and Satisfaction

The retrospective portion of Consequential Duties corresponds to those pronouncements aimed at giving effect to the principle that any unlawful act gives rise to a duty of reparation for injury caused by the breach.[202] In *Chorzów Factory*, the PCIJ established the canonical formulation of this principle, stating that it is 'a principle of international law, and even a general conception of law, that any breach of an engagement involves an obligation to make reparation'.[203] This has since been reaffirmed by various ICs[204] and held by ITLOS, in *M/V 'SAIGA' (No. 2)*, to constitute 'a well-established rule of international law'.[205] As codified by the ILC in ARSIWA Article 31, this rule provides that a state responsible for a violation must 'make full reparation for the injury caused by the internationally wrongful act'.

Despite the affirmation of the principle of full reparation as 'even a general conception of law',[206] it is often the case that disputes, especially

202 The principle itself long predates ICs. As expressed by Grotius, legal breaches give rise to 'an Obligation by the Law of Nature to make Reparation for the Damage, if any be done' (Grotius, *The Rights of War and Peace*, bk. 2, ch. 17, para. 1). See Dionisio Anzilotti, *Teoria generale della responsabilità dello stato nel diritto internazionale* (Florence: Lumachi, 1902), 12–15.

203 *Factory at Chorzów*, Merits, Judgment, (1928) PCIJ Ser. A No. 17, p. 5, 29.

204 *Phosphates in Morocco (Preliminary Objections)*, (1938) PCIJ Ser. A/B No. 74, p. 10, 28; *Reparation for Injuries*, Advisory Opinion, [1949] ICJ Reports, p. 184; *Peace Treaties (Second Phase)*, Judgment, [1950] ICJ Reports, p. 221, 228; *Gabčíkovo-Nagymaros (Hungary* v. *Slovakia)*, [1997] ICJ Reports, p. 7, 80; *Arrest Warrant (Democratic Republic of the Congo* v. *Belgium)*, [2002] ICJ Reports, p. 3, 31; *Armed Activities in the Territory of the Congo (Democratic Republic of the Congo* v. *Uganda) (Merits)*, [2005] ICJ Reports, p. 168, 257; *Application of the Genocide Convention (Bosnia* v. *Serbia)*, [2007] ICJ Reports, p. 43, 233; *Aloeboetoe* v. *Suriname*, Reparation and Costs, Judgment, 10 September 1993, IACHR Ser. C No. 11, para. 43; *Francovich* v. *Italy* [1991] Case No. C-6/90, ECR I-5357, paras. 33–36; *Papamichalopoulos and Others* v. *Greece (Article 50)*, Application No. 14556/89, Judgment of 31 October 1995, para. 34; Eritrea-Ethiopia Claims Commission, *Final Award – Ethiopia's Damages Claims* (2009) 26 RIAA 631, 633. The key exception are adjudicators in the field of international trade. See James Crawford, *Brownlie's Principles of Public International Law*, 8th edn (Oxford: Oxford University Press, 2012), 540; Malcolm N. Shaw, *International Law*, 6th edn (Cambridge: Cambridge University Press, 2008), 778.

205 *M/V 'SAIGA' (No. 2) (Saint Vincent and the Grenadines* v. *Guinea)*, Judgment, ITLOS Reports 1999, p. 10, para. 170.

206 *Factory at Chorzów (Indemnity)* (1928) PCIJ Ser. A No. 17, p. 29. In the case of investment arbitration, the very possibility of a court granting remedies other than pecuniary compensation is contested (Christoph Schreuer, 'Non-Pecuniary Remedies in ICSID Arbitration' (2004) 20 *International Arbitration* 325–332).

inter-state disputes, focus on Declaration of Breach and prospective Consequential Duties. As the thorough analysis undertaken by Massimo Iovane shows, the primacy of restitution and compensation in principle and in court statements is not always reflected in the remedies actually granted in disputes.[207] In *Ireland* v. *United Kingdom*, Ireland clarified to the ECtHR that its complaint 'ha[d] not as an object the obtaining of compensation for any individual person'.[208] The Arbitral Tribunal in *Rainbow Warrior* lamented that no request for monetary compensation had been put forward and awarded a declaration of breach 'as satisfaction'.[209] Gray noted this disconnect and concluded that '[f]or international tribunals it may be true enough that responsibility once established involves a duty to make reparation, but generally reparation and responsibility have a limited role in international relations'.[210]

Under the ILC Articles, reparation may take three different forms: *restitutio in integrum*, involving the reversal of the breach and the restoration, as far as possible, of the *status quo ante*; financial compensation, to cover any financially assessable damage that restitution cannot redress; and satisfaction, a category that encompasses a variety of symbolic measures whose unifying element is the public recognition of the breach as such.[211] Truly retrospective Consequential Duties would seem to require conduct going beyond that which is required to resume compliance with the wrongdoer's substantive obligations. As traditionally awarded, restitution and satisfaction rarely imply Consequential Duties in the sense of requiring from a state conduct additional to that required to cease the violation, leaving much of the work of offsetting material and moral injury to compensation.

As regards restitution, conduct required to provide it usually coincides with the cessation of the wrongful conduct. This is particularly the case for restitution in the narrow sense codified in the ILC Articles, that is, the duty to 're-establish the situation which existed before the wrongful act was committed'.[212] This contrasts with the formula used by the PCIJ in

[207] Massimo Iovane, *La Riparazione nella Teoria e nella Prassi dell'Illecito Internazionale* (Milan: Giuffrè, 1990), 61–142.

[208] *Ireland* v. *United Kingdom (Merits and Just Satisfaction)*, Application No. 5310/71, Judgment of 18 January 1978, para. 245.

[209] *Rainbow Warrior (New Zealand* v. *France)* (1990) 20 RIAA 215, 272.

[210] Christine Gray, 'Is There an International Law of Remedies?' (1985) 56 *British Yearbook of International Law* 25–47, at 29.

[211] ILC Articles 31, 34–37. See ILC Ybk 2001, I.2, p. 95–105.

[212] ILC Articles, Article 35.

Chorzów Factory, that 'reparation must, as far as possible, wipe out all the consequences of the illegal act and reestablish the situation which would, in all probability, have existed if that act had not been committed'.[213] In the case of a claim of violation of territory or other dispute regarding entitlement, there is no meaningful difference between restoring the situation and ceasing the wrongful conduct (or indeed complying with the substantive obligations as interpreted by the adjudicator).

Other canonical examples of restitution, such as the release of unlawfully detained persons or ships,[214] equally imply the same conduct required for the cessation of the violation. The ICJ Judgment in *Tehran Hostages*, sometimes cited as an example of restitution,[215] ostensibly provided that Iran was under an obligation to 'take all steps to redress the situation resulting' from the breach; the concrete duties established by the Court, however, were for Iran to cease the unlawful detention of hostages and to allow them to leave Iranian territory.[216] As a matter of its effects, this remedy was less one of restitution than an elaboration on the duty of cessation, identifying the wrongful conduct that should cease and specifying actions required to meet this duty.

By contrast, in *Temple of Preah Vihear*, the ICJ determined that Thailand, besides being required to 'withdraw any military or police forces, or other guards or keepers, stationed by her at the Temple' (which the Court had found to be in Cambodian territory), was under the 'obligation to restore to Cambodia any objects ... removed from the Temple or the Temple area by the Thai authorities'.[217] Although one could potentially infer the latter obligation from the overall obligation not to interfere with Cambodian sovereignty,[218] the judicial determination that full compliance with the Judgment required more than simply prospective withdrawal of troops from Cambodian territory seems like a clearer case of truly retrospective restitution.

213 *Factory at Chorzów*, Merits, Judgment, (1928) PCIJ Ser. A No. 17, p. 5, 47.

214 Crawford, *Brownlie's Principles of Public International Law*, 570–571.

215 ARSIWA Commentary, ILC Ybk 2001, II.2, p. 97; Gray, *Judicial Remedies in International Law*, p. 96.

216 *United States Diplomatic and Consular Staff in Tehran* (*United States of America* v. *Iran*), Judgment, [1980] ICJ Reports, p. 3, 44–45.

217 *Temple of Preah Vihear (Cambodia* v. *Thailand)*, Judgment, [1962] ICJ Reports, p. 6, 37.

218 See *Request for Interpretation of the Judgment of 15 June 1962 in the Case concerning the* Temple of Preah Vihear *(Cambodia* v. *Thailand)*, Judgment, [2013] ICJ Reports, p. 281, 316 (concluding that both obligations arose 'as a consequence of th[e] finding' of Cambodian sovereignty over the Temple area).

The distinction between cessation and restitution could appear most clearly in cases where, as in *Certain Iranian Assets*, the violated obligation has ceased to apply.[219] In this case, a determination of restitution could have required the wrongdoer to restore the *status quo ante* and annul or offset the unlawful acts, that is, the 'judicial decisions [that] ordered the attachment, execution, turnover or distribution of assets of certain Iranian companies'.[220] Since Iran only requested the ICJ to establish the United States' duty of cessation, the Court was able to point to the termination of the treaty by the United States and reject the requested remedy. On the other hand, a request for restitution can prove challenging. In *Rainbow Warrior*, the Arbitral Tribunal confused the two, interpreting (in Gray's words, 'perversely interpreting')[221] New Zealand's request for unlawfully released officers to be returned to detention as a request for prospective cessation, then rejected it because the original obligation would have expired had it been fulfilled.[222]

As regards satisfaction, the ordinary award of the remedy of judicial Declaration of Breach as satisfaction is best classified as a heightened version of the Declaration of Breach, since no actual duty arises for the wrongdoer from this remedy. This is different from a judicial remedy such as that awarded in the *S.S. 'I'm Alone'* case, in which the Arbitral Tribunal required the United States to offer satisfaction by its own acts. Having declared the sinking of the *I'm Alone* 'an unlawful act', the Tribunal ruled that the United States, besides paying financial compensation for the damage, 'ought formally to acknowledge its illegality, and to apologize'.[223]

This raises the question of how far an IC can demand the fulfilment of various Consequential Duties under the heading of satisfaction. The ECtHR is expressly empowered to 'afford just satisfaction' in case domestic law permits 'only partial reparation'[224] and has interpreted this provision to mean it has a power to award pecuniary damages (examined

219 *Certain Iranian Assets (Islamic Republic of Iran* v. *United States of America)*, Judgment, [2023] ICJ Reports, p. 51, 126.
220 Ibid., para. 113.
221 Christine Gray, 'The Choice between Restitution and Compensation' (1999) 10(2) *European Journal of International Law* 413–423, at 420.
222 *Rainbow Warrior (New Zealand* v. *France)* (1990) 20 RIAA 215, 270.
223 *S.S. 'I'm Alone'* (1935) 3 RIAA 1616, 1618.
224 ECHR, Article 41.

in Section 4.4.1.3).[225] The ECtHR has, however, stopped short of awarding other measures of satisfaction, although these have sometimes been issued by governments regardless.[226] By contrast, the IACtHR has adopted the practice of demanding from states 'measures of satisfaction', of a non-pecuniary character, as a means to overcome the limitations of restitution, compensation, and purely declaratory satisfaction. In *Gutiérrez-Soler* v. *Colombia*, the IACtHR described measures of satisfaction as 'measures to be ordered to protect the rights that were affected, as well as to make reparations [for] the consequences the infringements brought about'.[227] The underlying reasoning is that reparations should not 'involve enrichment or impoverishment of the victim[s] or [their] heirs', and 'any reparations ordered must be consistent with the violations established'.[228]

The rationale underlying the IACtHR's 'measures of satisfaction' seems logical. If the remedy of judicially awarded satisfaction is a means of symbolic redress to injured parties, its appropriate content should carry symbolic value for the victims, as well as represent a symbolic loss to those who perpetrated and supported the violation. In *Gómez Palomino* v. *Peru*, the IACtHR issued a number of measures of satisfaction, establishing for Peru the duty to investigate the events that resulted in violations; the prosecution and punishment of those responsible; the 'obligation to conduct a search for the mortal remains of the victim and to deliver them to his next of kin'; the obligation to fund the education of the victim's child, including secondary and higher education; and the duty to 'amend ... [Peru's] criminal law in order to render it consistent with the international standards on forced disappearance of persons'.[229]

[225] See, for example, *Scopelliti* v. *Italy (Merits and Just Satisfaction)*, Application No. 15511/89, Judgment of 23 November 1993, para. 31.

[226] *El-Masri v. The Former Yugoslav Republic of Macedonia*, Application No. 39630/09, Judgment of 13 December 2012, paras. 175–178. See Daniella Stoltz and Beth Van Schaack, 'It's Never Too Late to Say "I'm Sorry": Sovereign Apologies over the Years', *Just Security* (2021).

[227] *Gutiérrez-Soler* v. *Colombia*, Merits, Reparations and Costs, Judgment, 12 September 2005, IACHR Ser. C No. 132, para. 63.

[228] *Juvenile Reeducation Institute* v. *Paraguay*, Preliminary Objections, Merits, Reparations and Costs, Judgment, 2 September 2005, IACHR Ser. C No. 112, para. 261.

[229] *Gómez-Palomino* v. *Peru*, Merits, Reparations and Costs, Judgment, 22 November 2005, IACHR Ser. C No. 136, paras. 136–149. See David C. Baluarte, 'Strategizing for Compliance: The Evolution of the Compliance Phase of Inter-American Court Litigation and the Strategic Imperative for Victims' Representatives' (2012) 27(2) *American University International Law Review* 263–321, at 308–309.

Laurence Burgorgue-Larsen has termed the IACtHR's approach to reparations 'to say the least, innovative and forward-looking'.[230] In *Armed Activities*, the ICJ accepted in principle their availability under international law but stopped short of stating that they could be awarded as a judicial remedy.[231] Peculiar as these measures may seem, they are more consistent with the breaches that usually give rise to claims before the IACtHR, and with the general objectives of the American Convention on Human Rights, than either translating moral injury into pecuniary damages or relabelling ordinary Declarations of Breach as satisfaction. While most international adjudicators may have difficulties adopting as proactive an approach to remedies as the Inter-American Court, measures of satisfaction (together with guarantees of non-repetition) might have been useful to avoid the sense of injustice in decisions like the ones in *Rainbow Warrior* and *Bosnian Genocide*. After both the ICJ and the ECtHR have adopted the practice of issuing specific determinations of conduct required to comply with primary obligations being violated (as 'orders'),[232] making similarly specific determinations of conduct to be followed to comply with a state's Consequential Duties seems less of a challenge.[233]

4.4.1.3 Retrospective Consequential Duties – Compensation

While fully retrospective restitution and measures of satisfaction are only occasionally employed by most international adjudicators, awards of monetary compensation have become a mainstay of international adjudication and are the main remedy employed by ICs to provide redress for past injury. In the terminology established in this chapter, the remedy of compensation is a judicial determination that a Consequential Duty arises for a wrongdoer to, as Article 35 of the ILC Articles puts it, 'cover

[230] Laurence Burgorgue-Larsen, 'The Right to Determine Reparations', in Laurence Burgorgue-Larsen and Amaya Ubeda de Torres (eds.), *The Inter-American Court of Human Rights – Case Law and Commentary* (Oxford: Oxford University Press, 2011), 224.

[231] *Armed Activities on the Territory of the Congo (Democratic Republic of the Congo v. Uganda) (Reparations)*, [2022] ICJ Reports, p. 13, 132–133.

[232] See Section 4.4.1.1.

[233] Arguably, however, a state is likely to find it more acceptable to comply with primary obligations, which it had an input in formulating, than to engage in conduct an adjudicator has unilaterally formulated and determined is appropriate to offset the symbolic portion of the injury caused by its violation.

any financially assessable damage' caused by the breach and 'not made good by restitution'.[234]

Historically, awards of compensation in inter-state relations were rare, on grounds that 'many sovereign interests do not lend themselves to quantification'.[235] Up until the development of permanent international adjudicators, monetary compensation in international law was principally granted in the context of claims commissions or ad hoc tribunals, following an agreement in principle between states that nationals of one state were entitled to compensation for personal or financial loss wrongfully caused by another state.[236] Early attempts to codify the law of responsibility, such as the one by Louis Sohn and Richard Baxter, were restricted to the 'field of pecuniary claims, more strictly legal in its nature than many of the other departments of international law'.[237] Federico García Amador, the first ILC Special Rapporteur on the Law of Responsibility, having received a broad mandate from the General Assembly to codify the law of responsibility, argued that it was 'not possible to proceed immediately with the codification of the entire topic', and restricted his reports to the issue of 'responsibility of States for damage caused to the person or property of aliens'.[238] It was the Second ILC Special Rapporteur, Roberto Ago, who expanded the focus of the Articles to cover '[e]very internationally wrongful act of a State',[239] in what one commentator has termed 'the Ago Revolution'.[240] This

[234] ILC Articles, Article 35.

[235] John Barker, 'The Different Forms of Reparation: Compensation', in James Crawford, Alain Pellet, and Simon Olleson (eds.), *The Law of International Responsibility* (Oxford: Oxford University Press, 2010), 603; Oscar Schachter, 'Compensation for Expropriation' (1984) 78 *American Journal of International Law* 121–130; Gray, 'Is There an International Law of Remedies?', 29.

[236] Frédéric Mégret, 'Mixed Claim Commissions and the Once Centrality of the Protection of Aliens', in Ignacio De la Rasilla and Jorge Viñuales (eds.), *Experiments in International Adjudication: Historical Accounts* (Cambridge: Cambridge University Press, 2019); Hélène Ruiz Fabri and Michel Erpelding, *The Mixed Arbitral Tribunals, 1919–1939 – An Experiment in the International Adjudication of Private Rights* (Baden-Baden: Nomos, 2023).

[237] Harvard Research on 'Responsibility of States for Damage Done in Their Territory to the Person or Property of Foreigners' (1929) 20 *American Journal of International Law Special Supplement* 133, 218. See also Edwin M. Borchard, *Diplomatic Protection of Citizens Abroad* (New York: Banks Law, 1928), 863.

[238] F.V. García-Amador, 'First Report on State Responsibility', ILC Ybk 1956, II.2, p. 221.

[239] ILC Articles, Article 1.

[240] Alain Pellet, 'The ILC's Articles on State Responsibility for Internationally Wrongful Acts and Related Texts', in James Crawford, Alain Pellet, and Simon Olleson (eds.), *The*

expansion enshrined a much more important role for legal claims – and adjudication – in international disputes, not only consolidating the idea of remedies beyond pecuniary compensation but also codifying the main features of the remedy of compensation in inter-state disputes.

Judicial practice regarding actual awards of compensation has been uneven. Early awards of pecuniary compensation issued by the PCIJ, ICJ, and ITLOS concerned the destruction of ships (S.S. '*Wimbledon*', *Corfu Channel* and *M/V 'SAIGA' (No. 2)* respectively).[241] The PCIJ never granted a similar order again, and the ICJ only did so six decades later, in a case involving an individual specifically injured by the violation (*Diallo*).[242] ITLOS and UNCLOS Tribunals, due to their case law concerning material injury to vessels and their owners, instead developed a more extensive jurisprudence on compensation,[243] as did the ECtHR, IACtHR, and investment tribunals, which deal essentially with claims brought by individuals and corporations for injuries to their person and property.

The hesitancy of some permanent adjudicators to award compensation for injury to what Lauterpacht termed 'general State interests', as opposed to direct 'injury to private interests',[244] contrasted with the practice of adjudicators, such as the *Trail Smelter* Arbitral Tribunal and the Eritrea-Ethiopia Claims Commission, both of which awarded compensation in cases affecting interests other than those of identifiable private persons.[245]

Both the ICJ and the ECtHR appear to have changed their stance on this issue. In *Certain Activities* and *Armed Activities*, the ICJ agreed to award compensation for injury suffered by entire communities or the environment.[246] The Court built on the findings of the *Trail Smelter*

Law of International Responsibility (Oxford: Oxford University Press, 2010), 75–76. See Roberto Ago, 'Le délit International' (1939) 68 *Hague Recueil* 415–554.

241 See Gray, *Judicial Remedies in International Law*, 77, 83.

242 *Ahmadou Sadio Diallo (Republic of Guinea* v. *Democratic Republic of the Congo)*, Merits, Judgment, [2010] ICJ Reports, p. 639, 691–692.

243 *M/V 'Virginia G' (Panama* v. *Guinea-Bissau)*, Judgment, ITLOS Reports 2014, p. 4, 125–126; *Duzgit Integrity Arbitration (Malta* v. *São Tomé and Príncipe)*, PCA Case No. 2014-07, Award on Reparation.

244 See Lauterpacht, *The Function of Law in the International Community*, 115.

245 *Trail Smelter* (1941) 3 RIAA 1905; Eritrea-Ethiopia Claims Commission, *Final Award – Ethiopia's Damages Claims* (2009) 26 RIAA 631, 633. See also the discussion in *Rainbow Warrior (New Zealand* v. *France)* (1990) 20 RIAA 215, 272–275. For non-adjudicatory compensation, see *Cosmos 954* (1979) 18 ILM 899.

246 Kévine Kindji and Michael Faure, 'Assessing Reparation of Environmental Damage by the ICJ: A Lost Opportunity?' (2019) 57 *Questions of International Law* 5–33.

arbitration and the Eritrea-Ethiopia Claims Commission, in particular, with regard to evidence on damage calculation and the causal nexus between the wrongful conduct and the damage. In *Armed Activities*, citing the Eritrea-Ethiopia Claims Commission, the ICJ determined that a state 'that is not in a position to provide direct proof of certain facts' should be allowed 'liberal recourse to inferences of fact and circumstantial evidence'.[247] In *Certain Activities*, citing *Trail Smelter*, the ICJ ruled that it could 'decide whether there is a sufficient causal nexus between the wrongful act and the injury suffered', and that for this purpose it could make 'just and reasonable inference' from the available evidence.[248] At the same time, in *Alleged Violations*, the ICJ rejected Nicaragua's claim for compensation, reasoning that compensation depends on the provision of 'evidence capable of demonstrating . . . financially assessable injury'.[249] The ECtHR, which has recently become an active forum for inter-state disputes, has issued compensation for injury, for instance, in *Cyprus* v. *Turkey* and *Georgia* v. *Russia* (I).[250]

The expansion of compensation onto the realm of collective and environmental damages has significant consequences in terms of amounts. It is one thing to be ordered to pay a few thousand dollars (as in *Diallo*)[251] or even a few million dollars (as in *M/V 'SAIGA'*)[252] for injuries caused to particular agents. However, the full compensation for violations consisting of series of acts within the context of a conflict, or of broader policies affecting thousands or millions, could quickly rise to levels that defy the capacity of many states to pay these awards.[253] The Eritrea-Ethiopia Claims Commission noted in this regard that awarding

[247] *Armed Activities on the Territory of the Congo (Democratic Republic of the Congo* v. *Uganda) (Reparations)*, [2022] ICJ Reports, p. 13, 132–133. p. 13, 52 – 54.

[248] *Certain Activities Carried Out by Nicaragua in the Border Area (Costa Rica* v. *Nicaragua)*, Compensation, Judgment, ILC Reports 2018, p. 15, 26–27.

[249] *Alleged Violations of Sovereign Rights and Maritime Spaces in the Caribbean Sea (Nicaragua* v. *Colombia)*, Judgment of 21 April 2022, para. 198 (quoting *Dispute regarding Navigational and Related Rights (Costa Rica* v. *Nicaragua)*, Judgment, [2009] ICJ Reports, p. 213, para. 149).

[250] *Cyprus* v. *Turkey (Merits)*, Application No. 25781/94, Judgment of 10 May 2001, para 189; *Georgia* v. *Russia (I) (Just Satisfaction)*, Application No. 13255/07, Judgment of 31 January 2019, paras. 19–28.

[251] *Ahmadou Sadio Diallo (Republic of Guinea* v. *Democratic Republic of the Congo)*, Compensation, Judgment, [2012] ICJ Reports, p. 324, 345.

[252] *M/V 'SAIGA' (No. 2) (Saint Vincent and the Grenadines* v. *Guinea*), Judgment, ITLOS Reports 1999, p. 10, para. 183(12).

[253] Martins Paparinskis, 'A Case against Crippling Compensation in International Law of State Responsibility' (2020) 83(6) *Modern Law Review* 1246–1286.

large amounts of compensation 'would impose crippling burdens upon the economies and populations of ... the paying country – and its citizens needing health care, education and other public services'.[254] The final amounts granted were modest in the context: Eritrea was ordered to pay US$174 million in compensation;[255] Ethiopia, US$163 million.[256]

This development may have been influenced by the multi-billion-dollar awards for damages issued by investment tribunals, in disputes that concerned injury to specific private interests.[257] In Investor-State Dispute Settlement (ISDS), pecuniary compensation is the standard remedy. States undertake to enforce ISDS arbitral awards within their territories as if they were final domestic judgments.[258] Some investment tribunals have nonetheless attempted to go beyond ordering compensation. In *Texaco* v. *Libya*, the ICSID Tribunal ordered Libya to return to compliance.[259] In *Goetz* v. *Burundi*, while not discarding the retrospective remedy to which claimants are entitled, the arbitral tribunal provided Burundi with the option of *restitutio in integrum* or voluntary compensation. It cautioned Burundi that, if it failed to adopt either option, 'the international responsibility of the Burundian state would be established'[260] and compensation would be due. In *Enron* v. *Argentina*, Argentina argued that an ICSID tribunal could not issue specific injunctions but 'could only establish whether there has been an expropriation, its legality or illegality and the corresponding compensation'. The tribunal disagreed. Invoking the authority of *Rainbow Warrior*, it concluded

[254] Eritrea-Ethiopia Claims Commission, *Final Award – Eritrea's Damages Claims* (2009) 26 RIAA 505, 523.

[255] Ibid., 768–769.

[256] Eritrea-Ethiopia Claims Commission, *Final Award – Ethiopia's Damages Claims* (2009) 26 RIAA 631, 629–630.

[257] See, most impressively, the *Yukos* awards, which, if taken together, added up to almost USD 50 billion: *Yukos Universal* v. *Russia*, PCA Case No. AA 227, Final Award, 18 July 2014; *Yukos* v. *Russia (Just Satisfaction)*, Application No. 14902/04, Judgment of 31 July 2014. See also *Tethyan Copper* v. *Pakistan*, ICSID Case No. ARB/12/1, Award, 12 July 2019 (USD 6 billion); *ConocoPhillips* v. *Venezuela*, ICSID Case No. ARB/07/30, Award of the Tribunal, 8 March 2019 (USD 8.7 billion).

[258] ICSID Convention, Article 54(1); New York Convention, Articles III and IV.

[259] *Texaco* v. *Government of the Libyan Arab Republic* (1977) 53 ILR 389; But see *BP Exploration Company (Libya) Ltd* v. *Government of Libyan Arab Republic* (1973) 53 ILR 297 and *LIAMCO* v. *Government of Libyan Arab Republic* (1982) 62 ILR 140.

[260] *Goetz and Others* v. *Burundi (I)*, ICSID Case No. ARB/95/3, Award, 10 February 1998, paras. 131–132.

that it had 'the power to order measures involving performance or injunction of certain acts'.[261]

Even in these cases, however, in international investment law substantive compliance is seen as merely one option of the parties. Ordinarily, the totality of the responsibility of states in this field may be discharged with the payment of damages.[262] Crawford remarked that '[t]he ultimate effect of the *Texaco* order was, it appears, a higher settlement'.[263] In *Goetz* v. *Burundi*, the Tribunal subsequently found that Burundi had failed to comply with some of the conditions of *restitutio in integrum* and awarded the claimants monetary compensation.[264] The *Enron* v. *Argentina* Tribunal, despite affirming its power to issue injunctions, decided to award damages.[265]

4.4.2 Remedial Value and Effects

Considered in the abstract, Consequential Duties have a twofold effect. First, they afford relief to those whose interests were affected by the breach. This is what Petros Mavroidis labels the '*ex post*' function of remedies: redressing unlawful injury.[266] Second, Consequential Duties aim to prevent the offender from securing a gain from the breach. Considered '*ex ante*' (and regardless of whether obtaining a gain is the motivation behind the violations), the prospect that a price will have to be paid for injury may dissuade from engaging in unlawful conduct potential wrongdoers who see a violation as a means of obtaining a material or political gain. As a result, Consequential Duties produce a second effect: preventing breaches, constituting in this sense a *deterrent*.

As a matter of law, Consequential Duties under international law do not have as their purpose to act as a deterrent. The purpose of

261 *Enron* v. *Argentina*, ICSID Case No. ARB/01/3, Award on Jurisdiction, 14 January 2004, para. 76.

262 *ADC Affiliate Limited and ADC & ADMC Management Limited* v. *Republic of Hungary*, ICSID Case No. ARB/03/16, Award (2 October 2006) para. 497. See David Khachvani, 'Compensation for Unlawful Expropriation: Targeting the Illegality' (2017) 32 *ICSID Review* 385–403.

263 James Crawford, *State Responsibility: The General Part* (Cambridge: Cambridge University Press, 2013), 469.

264 *Goetz and Others* v. *Burundi (II)*, ICSID Case No. ARB/01/2, Award, 21 June 2012.

265 *Enron* v. *Argentina*, ICSID Case No. ARB/01/3, Award on Jurisdiction, 14 January 2004, para. 245. The award was ultimately annulled. See *Enron* v. *Argentina*, ICSID Case No. ARB/01/3, Decision by the Annulment Committee, 30 July 2010.

266 Mavroidis, 'Remedies in the WTO Legal System', 763–764. Dinah Shelton privileges the punitive *ex post* function of remedies. Shelton, *Remedies in International Human Rights Law*, 13.

cessation, as the ILC put it in its Commentary to ARSIWA, is 'securing an end to continuing wrongful conduct'.[267] As regards reparations, the traditionally quoted statement is the note by the Umpire in the *Lusitania* case that '[t]he remedy should be commensurate with the loss, so that the injured party may be made whole'.[268] Even in the field of human rights, the IACtHR noted in *Velásquez-Rodríguez*, awards of compensation are not 'meant to deter or to serve as an example'; reparation in international law 'is compensatory and not punitive'.[269]

Examined closely, the situation is more complex. Consequential Duties can serve as a deterrent *ex ante* if they are perceived as a penalty once awarded (and if the likelihood of them being awarded is significant). Perception of compensation as a penalty depends less on the intention of the adjudicator than on the assessment by the wrongdoer that its wrongful conduct not only may not result in a gain but may, de facto, result in a loss relative to what the state considered to be its previous position.[270] In the absence of voluntary retaliation, some of this loss will come from the involuntary sanctions resulting from a Declaration of Breach. The additional penalty value of Consequential Duties depends on the perception that they will result in losses for the wrongdoer.

This raises the question of the effects of Consequential Duties in terms of international law's compliance motivators. In principle, all Consequential Duties amount to judicial specifications of obligations that a wrongdoer must fulfil in order to re-establish lawful relations with other actors. Under international law, these obligations arise regardless of adjudication – and even regardless of their invocation by another state. All that the adjudicator does is specify which duties arise in a particular case. As the ILC put it:

> Although State responsibility arises under international law independently of its invocation by another State, it is still necessary to specify what other States faced with a breach of an international obligation may do,

[267] ILC Ybk 2001, II.2, p. 88.

[268] *Lusitania* (1923) 7 RIAA 32, 39.

[269] *Velásquez-Rodríguez* v. *Honduras*, Reparations and Costs, Judgment, 21 July 1989, IACHR Ser. C No. 7, para. 38.

[270] Anne van Aaken and Betül Simsek, 'Rewarding in International Law' (2021) 115(2) *American Journal of International Law* 195–241 ('Rewards, as understood here, are improvements in a target's value position relative to a baseline of expectations. Rewards are transfers of positively valued material or immaterial goods, such as opportunities for and benefits of cooperation, money, technology, or social approval/good reputation. Penalties are deprivations relative to the same baseline' (footnote omitted)).

> what action they may take in order to secure the performance of the obligations of cessation and reparation on the part of the responsible State.[271]

Discussions regarding the specific consequences of breach may take place horizontally: through the invocation of responsibility by other states, through retorts from the state deemed responsible, through negotiations, and potentially through countermeasures (and other forms of reciprocal response) applied between the parties. A determination of Consequential Duties by an adjudicator provides an alternative, likely less confrontational and less costly, manner of settling this matter. In a sense, Consequential Duties complement Mere Adjudication, establishing a focal point, a baseline for future interactions between a wrongdoer and parties injured by the breach (and, potentially, third parties).

While Mere Adjudication establishes focal points regarding the generally applicable normative framework object of the dispute, Consequential Duties concern the new normative relations that emerge for the wrongdoer from its violation. Most Consequential Duties have low deterrent value, merely requiring a wrongdoer to return to its pre-breach position. This is clear for those prospective Consequential Duties that involve merely specifying conduct required for a return to lawful interaction: declaring the duty of cessation, determining certain conduct required for this purpose, and sometimes establishing (non-IACtHR) guarantees of non-repetition. But this also applies to purely prospective restitution, requiring materially the same conduct as that required for cessation. When employed as an alternative to Consequential Duties, satisfaction in fact relieves the wrongdoer from any further duty, allowing the parties to wipe the slate clean and move on in their mutual relations. Neither remedy, it would seem, produces for the wrongdoer a loss when compared to its pre-violation position.

More deterrent potential exists in judicially determined Consequential Duties that go beyond demanding a return to performance of primary obligations and require additional action to offset the injury caused. This is the case of restitution that goes beyond mere cessation, of IACtHR measures of satisfaction and guarantees of non-repetition, and of monetary compensation. In order to be perceived, *ex ante*, as deterrents, Consequential Duties must cause the wrongdoer (whether one sees this as the state as a whole or the specific individuals responsible for the

[271] ILC Ybk 2001, II.2, p. 116.

wrongful conduct) to perceive the outcome as a loss compared to the pre-violation situation – to perceive the Consequential Duties, one might say, as sanctions. These Consequential Duties would not be 'sanctions' in a Kelsenian sense of coercive actions imposed by others[272] but would be so in the sense that they impose on the wrongdoer a perceived cost, compared to its pre-adjudication baseline perception of its entitlements and liabilities.

This sanctioning effect is less noticeable for restitution. The clearest award of beyond-cessation restitution issued by the ICJ, in *Temple of Preah Vihear*, still merely required Thailand to restore to Cambodia any 'sculptures, stelae, fragments of monuments, sandstone model and ancient pottery which have been removed from the Temple by the Thai authorities since 1954'.[273] Restitution of objects can be perceived as a loss, if those within the state required to provide it consider that the state was previously entitled to the relevant objects, as opposed to being required to return temporarily arrested persons or seized property. This may be the case of the required return of disputed cultural objects,[274] as well as of the return of property that a state had considered as lawfully expropriated.[275]

In the practice of most ICs, awards of retrospective monetary compensation for injury constitute the most 'tangible' remedy available to international adjudicators. Monetary compensation is an important instrument for adjudicators to provide individuals with redress for injury. In the cases of specific violations of material and moral damages caused by violations, of human rights, of investors' rights, or of a shipowner's rights, monetary damages may provide the affected individuals with appropriate redress. In other cases, concerning 'general State interests',[276] the injury

272 See Section 5.2.

273 *Case concerning the Temple of Preah Vihear (Cambodia* v. *Thailand)*, Merits, Judgment of 15 June 1962: [1962] ICJ Reports, p. 6, 11.

274 See Ana Filipa Vrdoljak, *International Law, Museums and the Return of Cultural Objects* (Cambridge: Cambridge University Press, 2006); Francesco Francioni and James Gordley (eds.), *Enforcing International Cultural Heritage Law, Cultural Heritage Law and Policy* (Oxford: Oxford University Press, 2013).

275 *Appeal from a Judgment of the Hungaro-Czechoslovak Mixed Arbitral Tribunal* (*the Peter Pázmány University* v. *the State of Czechoslovakia*) (1933) PCIJ Ser. A/B No. 61. See more generally Burzu Sabahi, *Compensation and Restitution in Investor-State Arbitration: Principles and Practice* (Oxford: Oxford University Press, 2011), 65–67.

276 Lauterpacht, *The Function of Law in the International Community*, 3–4. These cases can include symbolic violations of sovereignty, destruction of cultural heritage, environmental degradation, or serious violations of basic human rights.

caused by the breach cannot be cured by compensation. In these cases, compensation does not address the injury caused by the breach and may even be perceived as a licence for such breaches. In fact, concentration on reparation may give the impression that there is no problem with violating the relevant rule, as long as the proper price is paid.[277]

Considering compensation as sufficient redress is a common position in the field of investment law, in which monetary concerns are preponderant. If, however, substantive compliance is the goal, mere monetary compensation may not be sufficient. While *ex post* this may be the sole available alternative – for someone unlawfully jailed, or for the family of the deceased – *ex ante* and while the breach lasts the mere prospect of future reparation appears insufficient.[278]

Some ICs sought to address this issue. In *Ilascu* v. *Moldova and Russia*, the ECtHR held that, while it can indicate monetary satisfaction, it can also stipulate 'appropriate, individual measures to be adopted in its domestic legal order to put an end to the violation'.[279] And, once more, it is the IACtHR that has provided the most creative jurisprudence on this issue. In requiring from human rights-violating states 'measures of satisfaction' such as naming of public places after human rights defenders or victims of violations,[280] adoption of educational programmes and scholarships for studying human rights,[281] or national commemoration of the dates of crucial events,[282] the IACtHR imposes a 'loss' not for the state as a whole but for those who, within a state, promote, advocate, and perpetrate the condemned human rights violations.

277 See Uri Gneezy and Aldo Rustichini, 'A Fine Is a Price' (2000) 29 *Journal of Legal Studies* 1–17.

278 See Veronika Fikfak, 'Compliance and Compensation: Money as a Currency of Human Rights', in Rachel Murray and Debra Long (eds.), *Research Handbook on Implementation of Human Rights in Practice* (Cheltenham: Elgar, 2022); Roach, *Remedies for Human Rights Violations*.

279 *Ilascu* v. *Moldova and Russia*, Application No. 48787/99, Judgment of 9 July 2004, para. 487.

280 *González and others* v. *Mexico*, Preliminary objections, merits, reparations and costs, Judgment, 16 September 2009, IACHR Ser. C No. 205 (a monument to commemorate victims); *Jose Miguel Gudiel Alvarez and others* v. *Guatemala*, Merits, Reparations and Costs, Judgment, 20 November 2012, IACHR Ser. C No. 253 (the creation of a park or plaza).

281 *Myrna Mack Chang* v. *Guatemala*, Merits, Reparations and Costs, Judgment, 25 November 2003, IACHR Ser. C No. 101 (a student scholarship in the victim's name).

282 *Case of the 19 Merchants* v. *Colombia*, Merits, Reparations and Costs, Judgment, 5 July 2004, IACtHR Ser. C No. 109 (a public acknowledgement of the State's responsibility in which the officials have to take part).

A duty to provide compensation may thus be thought of not only as a loss for the state but also, where it is a credible prospect in case of violation, as a deterrent.[283] Indeed, the notion that the obligation to compensate investors may have a 'chilling effect' on necessary governmental policy is widespread.[284] At the same time – and even setting aside the prospect that politicians might benefit politically from an outsider bringing an international claim against one of their policies[285] – the delay between the violation, the filing of a claim, and an adjudicator ruling on it may mean that those responsible for the violation can expect to have left power before an international adjudicator is in a position to impose costs on the state for the violation. Although this is not a reason to leave unlawful injuries unredressed, it shows the limits of applying to complex entities, such as states, concepts regarding the deterrent effect of judicial remedies developed for unitary actors whose interests are stable over time.

4.4.3 *Jurisdiction*

Consequential Duties are often considered the remedies 'par excellence' available to ICs. References to 'remedies' often seem to gloss over Mere Adjudication and Declaration of Breach, limiting the concept to the consequences a court may derive from these prior findings.[286] It is often taken for granted that international adjudicators tasked with interpreting and applying legal rules may go beyond adjudicating on the interpretative dispute and declaring violations and may determine Consequential Duties for violations of obligations that they are empowered to interpret and apply.

The possibility of judicial determination of consequences was affirmed strongly by the PCIJ in *Factory at Chorzów*. Poland had claimed that the arbitration clause granting jurisdiction to the Court concerned solely the

283 Mavroidis, 'Remedies in the WTO Legal System'.

284 Carolina Moehlecke, 'The Chilling Effect of International Investment Disputes: Limited Challenges to State Sovereignty' (2020) 64 *International Studies Quarterly* 1–12; Eckhard Janeba, 'Regulatory Chill and the Effect of Investor State Dispute Settlements' (2019) 27 *Review of International Economics* 1172–1198.

285 Matthew A. Baum, 'The Constituent Foundations of the Rally-Round-the-Flag Phenomenon' (2002) 46 *International Studies Quarterly* 263–298.

286 Mann, 'The Consequences of an International Wrong', 2; van Aaken and Simsek, 'Rewarding in International Law'.

'interpretation and application' of treaty provisions, and did not comprise jurisdiction to assess reparation for breach of these provisions. The Permanent Court disagreed, arguing that the 'more important jurisdiction' over determination of breach would also 'cover the less important disputes' concerning the nature and extent of reparation.[287] The PCIJ stated:

> An interpretation which would confine the Court simply to recording that the Convention had been incorrectly applied or that it had not been applied, without being able to lay down the conditions for the re-establishment of the treaty rights affected, would be contrary to what would, prima facie, be the natural object of the clause; for a jurisdiction of this kind, instead of settling a dispute once and for all, would leave open the possibility of further disputes.[288]

The ICJ followed essentially the same reasoning in *Corfu Channel* to affirm its jurisdiction to determine the amount of compensation. The Court reasoned that, were it to 'limit itself to saying that there is a duty to pay compensation without deciding what amount of compensation is due, the dispute would not be finally decided. An important part of it would remain unsettled. ... It would leave open the possibility of a further dispute'.[289] Other international tribunals have followed suit and found that making determinations with regard to reparation constitutes an integral part of their function.[290]

In *LaGrand*, the ICJ broadened this finding to encompass the whole field of Consequential Duties, which it identified with remedies. Confronted with the issue of whether its jurisdiction covered a request for guarantees of non-repetition, the Court concluded that, '[w]here jurisdiction exists over a dispute on a particular matter, no separate basis for jurisdiction is required by the Court to consider the remedies a party has requested for the breach of the obligation'.[291] In other words, the

287 *Factory at Chorzów*, Jurisdiction, (1927) PCIJ Ser. A No. 9, p. 23.

288 Ibid., p. 25.

289 *Corfu Channel case (United Kingdom* v. *Albania)*, Judgment of 9 April 1949: [1949] ICJ Reports 1949, p. 4, 26.

290 *Aloeboetoe* v. *Suriname*, Reparation and Costs, Judgment, 10 September 1993, IACHR Ser. C No. 11, para. 43; *Francovich* v. *Italy* [1991] Case No. C-6/90, ECR I-5357, para. 33–36; *Papamichalopoulos and Others* v. *Greece (Article 50)*, Application No. 14556/89, Judgment of 31 October 1995, para. 34; Eritrea-Ethiopia Claims Commission, *Final Award – Ethiopia's Damages Claims* (2009) 26 RIAA 631, 633.

291 *LaGrand (Germany* v. *United States of America)*, Judgment, [2001] ICJ Reports, p. 466, 485.

jurisdiction required for declaring a breach ordinarily allows the relevant adjudicator – subject to the *non ultra petita* rule – to assess which Consequential Duties flow from the breach declared. Similarly, the Arbitral Tribunal in *Rainbow Warrior* stated that 'the authority to issue an order for the cessation or discontinuance of a wrongful act or omission results from the inherent powers of a competent tribunal which is confronted with the continuous breach of an international obligation which is in force and continues to be in force'.[292]

Other courts have employed similar reasoning. In *SERAP* v. *Nigeria*, the ECOWAS Community Court of Justice (ECCJ) held that, in the context of its jurisdiction over human rights violations, 'its function in terms of protection does not stop at taking note . . . If it were to end in merely taking note of human rights violations, the exercise of such a function would be of no practical interest for the victims'.[293] As regards the type of appropriate Consequential Duty, this Court noted that, for 'human rights violations that affect indetermined number of victims or a very large population, as in the instant case, the compensation shall come not as an individual pecuniary advantage, but as a collective benefit adequate to repair, as completely as possible, the collective harm that a violation of a collective right causes'. The ECCJ accordingly issued an order, ordering Nigeria to: 'i. Take all effective measures, within the shortest possible time, to ensure restoration of the environment of the Niger Delta; ii. Take all measures that are necessary to prevent the occurrence of damage to the environment; iii. Take all measures to hold the perpetrators of the environmental damage accountable'.[294]

4.5 Conclusion

This chapter has offered a fourfold classification of judicial remedies available to international adjudicators and examined the three categories of judicial remedies usually associated with final decisions of ICs and tribunals. These are, first, Mere Adjudication, sometimes termed a 'declaratory remedy', by which adjudicators determine and interpret

292 *Rainbow Warrior (New Zealand* v. *France)* (1990) 20 RIAA 215, 217, 270.

293 ECCJ, Application No. ECW/CCJ/APP/08/09, *SERAP* v. *Nigeria*, Judgment, 14 December 2012 (ECW/CCJ/JUD/18/12), para. 118.

294 Ibid., 116, 121.

the applicable legal norms. Second, Declarations of Breach, by which an adjudicator establishes that a violation has been committed. Third, Consequential Duties, by which the adjudicator determines what consequences flow from a violation. Chapter 5 will be dedicated exclusively to the fourth category, which requires more elaboration: Permissible Responses.

5

Authorising Sanctions

Permissible Responses as a Judicial Remedy

5.1 Introduction

Most ICs and tribunals see their role as limited to providing the remedies explored in Chapter 4: adjudication of rights and obligations, declarations of breach, and consequential duties of cessation and reparation falling on the wrongdoer. At the same time, this delimitation of the scope of judicial remedies excludes from the purview of adjudication an entire set of legal consequences of internationally wrongful conduct: the measures that become permissible for other actors owing to a breach, or to non-compliance with the obligations that arise from the breach.

These measures can be termed 'sanctions', in the sense that they are responses available under international law to a failure to comply with obligations.[1] If their permissibility and permissible content cannot be established *ex ante* by an adjudicator, they must be determined and applied in a decentralised fashion. Responses to wrongful conduct must thus be adopted as 'unilateral remedies',[2] termed 'implementation by extra-judicial process',[3] 'self-help',[4] or 'mechanism of private justice'.[5] Even sanctions adopted by international organisations given specific authority to impose them can be challenged as ultra vires or excessive.[6]

[1] These are sanctions as defined in Section 5.2. As discussed in Chapter 4, many judicial determinations may produce sanctioning effects without being sanctions in the technical sense.

[2] Elisabeth Zoller, *Peacetime Unilateral Remedies: An Analysis of Countermeasures* (Dobbs Ferry, NY: Transnational Publishers, 1984).

[3] James Crawford, *State Responsibility: The General Part* (Cambridge: Cambridge University Press, 2013), 675.

[4] Lassa Oppenheim, *International Law: A Treatise* (New York: Longmans Green, 1905), 13.

[5] Dennis Alland, *Justice privée et ordre juridique international* (Paris: Pedone, 1994).

[6] See the discussion on sanctions adopted under the Montreal Protocol in Section 3.4.4.

Though these measures may be justiciable *ex post*, in the absence of *ex ante* judicial determination of their permissibility, adoption remains unilateral. Even where the violation to which they respond has been judicially established, the entitlement to adopt them may be disputed. The resulting legal uncertainty gives credence to the view that the implementation of judgments is a 'political' matter.[7] Considering the matter not too long ago, Nigel White and Ademola Abass noted that 'enforcement by means of non-forcible measures is one of the least developed areas of international law'.[8] Writing more recently, Devika Hovell termed unilateral sanctions an 'unfinished business of international law'.[9]

This chapter considers whether and how ICs can provide the remedies that appear in the fourth quadrant of the typology laid down in Chapter 1: Permissible Responses.[10] In awarding Permissible Responses as a remedy, an adjudicator establishes that a state's unlawful conduct permits other actors to adopt specific measures. As with the three other categories of remedies, Permissible Responses are communications regarding the interpretation and application of rules. Thus, they operate entirely on the legal plane and do not require or involve the deployment of material resources. Nor do Permissible Responses involve, as a matter of law, the creation of new rights and obligations. As with other remedies, in issuing Permissible Responses the adjudicator merely determines the content of parties' rights and obligations in light of its interpretation and application of a normative framework.

Following this introduction, Section 5.2 surveys the main instruments available under international law for decentralised permissible responses to violations and examines their adjudication by ICs. Sections 5.3 and 5.4 discuss the possibilities for *ex ante* judicial determinations of Permissible Responses, showing that, though limited by an adjudicator's jurisdiction

[7] *Northern Cameroons, Cameroon* v. *United Kingdom*, Preliminary Objections, [1963] ICJ Reports 15, p. 37 ('the use which the successful party makes of the judgment is a matter which lies on the political and not on the judicial plane'). See the discussion in Section 1.2.1.

[8] Nigel White and Ademola Abass, 'Countermeasures and Sanctions', in Malcolm Evans (ed.), *International Law*, 3rd edn (Oxford: Oxford University Press, 2010), 531.

[9] Devika Hovell, 'Unfinished Business of International Law: The Questionable Legality of Autonomous Sanctions' (2019) 113 *AJIL Unbound* 140–145.

[10] As previously in this book, capitalisation indicates a judicial remedy of Permissible Responses. Where not capitalised, references to 'permissible responses' include responses that are permissible under international law generally, regardless of judicial determination.

and applicable admissibility requirements, awarding remedies of this type is within the powers of most international adjudicators.

Section 5.5 takes this reasoning further, examining a specific type of permissible response: the application by states of measures of constraint against the property of a wrongdoing state, or against its representatives. Though ICs lack the power (*potestas*) to determine the application of coercive measures against the leaders and property of states, it is not beyond their reach to determine or authoritatively declare that these measures are permissible under the applicable international law. And, as international investment law and international criminal law demonstrate, specific legal mechanisms may permit – and even declare obligatory – the application of credible sanctions, in the sense of measures of constraint against state assets or their representatives, by the coercive apparatus of *other* states. Section 5.6 concludes.

5.2 Sanctions, Permissible Responses, and Adjudication: Five Types of Permissible Responses

The object of Permissible Responses, like that of Consequential Duties, are the legal consequences of a violation. Rather than a determination of the new obligations that emerge for a wrongdoer, Permissible Responses focus on the measures that become permissible – and, in some cases, obligatory – for other actors as a result of the violation. Measures adopted as permissible responses, whether or not authorised by an adjudicator, are applied (a) by actors other than the wrongdoer (b) to harm the wrongdoer's interests and (c) as a response to a violation of the normative order.

Permissible measures taken in response to unlawful conduct, grounded on the principle of reciprocity, are often considered international law's last resort: its 'back-up enforcement mechanism'[11] or 'what it does in response to breach'.[12] Most permissible responses involve non-performance by other states of agreed commitments, or general duties of non-interference and cooperation. The underlying assumption is that, as Judge Simma put it in his separate opinion in *Interim Accord*, 'reciprocal

[11] Joost Pauwelyn, *Optimal Protection of International Law: Navigating between European Absolutism and American Voluntarism* (New York: Cambridge University Press, 2008), 159.

[12] Joel P. Trachtman, 'The WTO Cathedral' (2007) 43 *Stanford Journal of International Law* 127, 146.

interest in the observance of rules . . . supplies one, if not the main reason for international law somehow managing to accomplish its tasks, despite the absence of most features considered indispensable by domestic lawyers'.[13] The Arbitral Tribunal in *Air Service Agreement*, considering the permissibility of reciprocal non-performance of a treaty, by a state that determines that another state has breached the treaty, noted that these countermeasures serve to 'restore in a negative way' the equality between the parties and 'encourage them to continue negotiations with mutual desire to reach an acceptable solution'.[14]

Labelling this remedy 'permissible responses' avoids the term 'sanctions', which Devika Hovell has noted is 'notoriously difficult to define' and 'does not itself appear in the key international instruments'.[15] This broad concept of permissible responses includes measures that would not be unlawful if adopted outside the context of a response to a violation (that is, retorsions), as well as measures that produce effects primarily on the normative rather than the material plane, such as depriving a state of certain treaty rights or suspending or terminating its participation in a legal regime.[16] Though avoiding the terminology, there is little doubt that measures adopted as permissible responses are often adopted with a sanctioning purpose.

Characterising this varied array of responses as international law's sanctions may seem unsatisfactory to those who take the view, often associated with John Austin and Hans Kelsen, that sanctions must be coercive acts. The underlying dissatisfaction, however, concerns not the characterisation of permissible responses as international law's sanctions but the lack, in the international society, of a centralised coercive apparatus capable of deploying overwhelming force against states.[17]

[13] *Application of the Interim Accord of 13 September 1995, Macedonia* v. *Greece*, Judgment, [2011] ICJ Reports 644, p. 699 (J. Bruno Simma).

[14] *Case concerning the Air Service Agreement of 27 March 1946, United States of America* v. *France*, (1978) 18 RIAA 417, 444–445.

[15] Devika Hovell, 'Unfinished Business of International Law: The Questionable Legality of Autonomous Sanctions' (2019) 113 *AJIL Unbound* 140.

[16] This concept however does not include the duty to provide reparation, which is an obligation falling upon the wrongdoer rather than an authorisation for other actors to take measures against the wrongdoer. See on this Hans Kelsen, *The Pure Theory of Law* (transl. Max Knight) (Clark, NJ: Lawbook Exchange, 2005), 123–124: 'The obligation to make reparation for the damage is not a sanction, but a substitute obligation. The sanction of civil execution takes place only when this obligation is not fulfilled'.

[17] On this, see Section 1.2.3. See also Frederick Schauer, 'Was Austin Right after All? On the Role of Sanctions in a Theory of Law' (2010) 23 *Ratio Juris* 1; Anthony Kronman, 'Hart,

Kelsen himself equivocates in this regard. Although stating that the characteristic sanctions of international law are 'reprisals and war', his definition of reprisals extends beyond forceful measures, encompassing any 'interference ... in the sphere of interest of a state ... without and against the will of the state concerned [that] is in this sense a coercive act, even if it is executed without physical force'.[18] As used in this chapter, 'sanctions' include all measures by actors other than the wrongdoer, targeting its interests, without or against its will, and taken as a response to a legal violation.

Permissible Responses are predicated on a normative determination that a breach has occurred. In case of dispute, and under the conditions discussed in this chapter, an adjudicator with jurisdiction to determine the occurrence of a breach may also be empowered to determine whether a measure is a permissible response to the breach. And, as an analysis of the jurisprudence will show, adjudicators with jurisdiction to consider an allegation of breach have often considered themselves equally empowered to examine, at least *ex post*, (i) whether a response to a breach was permissible, and (ii) whether an otherwise permissible response was, as adopted, excessive or disproportionate, or failed to comply with relevant procedural and substantive requirements.

The question of the lawfulness of permissible responses usually reaches adjudicators as a defence: a plea by the asserted wrongdoer that otherwise unlawful measures are justified as permissible responses to prior unlawful conduct.[19] In this scenario, ICs have often held that they have jurisdiction to assess the lawfulness of measures of response whenever they have jurisdiction to examine the principal claim.[20] More rarely, the matter has been brought by claimants whose actions were challenged by the respondent.[21] Besides being addressed in disputes, the entitlement (and obligation) to take permissible responses has also been debated within advisory opinions.

Austin, and the Concept of a Legal System: The Primacy of Sanctions' (1974–1975) 84 *Yale Law Journal* 607.

18 Kelsen, *The Pure Theory of Law*, 320–321.

19 In the case of termination or suspension of treaties, the argument is slightly distinct: it is that the alleged violation is no violation at all, because the treaty that it allegedly violates is no longer applicable or no longer prohibits that conduct. This subtlety can be lost on the parties and adjudicators. See, for example, *Interim Accord*, [2011] ICJ Reports 644, para. 170.

20 On the scope of this jurisdiction, see Section 5.4.3.

21 See Section 5.2.3.

Certain international legal regimes establish specific systems of permissible responses. These responses can be decided by an authoritative institution or adopted by states in a decentralised fashion. The most significant regime in which decentralised permissible responses are centrally authorised is the WTO, where an authoritative body (the Dispute Settlement Body) must authorise *ex ante* WTO Members to adopt permissible responses to violations of WTO law, and only does so following an adjudicative procedure.[22] A decentralised regime of permissible responses prevails in diplomatic law, governed by the Vienna Convention on Diplomatic Relations.[23] In *Tehran Hostages*, the ICJ noted that 'diplomatic law . . . provides the necessary means of defence against, and sanction for, illicit activities by members of diplomatic or consular missions' and noted Iran's right to unilaterally 'employ the remedies placed at its disposal by diplomatic law'.[24]

Additionally, general international law offers states various categories of decentralised permissible responses. These instruments, grounded in the principle of reciprocity, can be employed by states to respond directly to a breach, to induce the offender to cease the violation and comply with its substantive obligations, or to demand or secure reparation for injury. This section considers five categories of permissible responses: retorsions, countermeasures, the exception of non-performance, the suspension or termination of treaties in response to their breach, and self-defence – noting the challenge posed by armed reprisals.

5.2.1 *Retorsions*

Retorsions are lawful but unwelcome or unfriendly measures, adopted by a state to express dissatisfaction with what it views as another state's breach of its legal obligations. Examples traditionally given include withdrawal or removal of ambassadors and cancellation of cooperation projects or joint military exercises.[25] Being lawful, retorsions may in

[22] This system is thoroughly examined in Chapter 6.

[23] Vienna Convention on Diplomatic Relations, Vienna, 18 April 1961, in force 24 April 1964, 500 UNTS 95.

[24] *United States Diplomatic and Consular Staff in Tehran, United States of America* v. *Iran*, Judgment, [1980] ICJ Reports 3, p. 39, 41.

[25] Tom Ruys, 'Sanctions, Retortions and Countermeasures: Concepts and International Legal Framework', in Larissa van den Herik (ed.), *Research Handbook on UN Sanctions and International Law* (Cheltenham: Elgar, 2017), 19–51; Jean-Marc Thouvenin, 'Articulating UN Sanctions with Unilateral Restrictive Measures', in Charlotte

principle be taken freely by all states. The only distinction between retorsions and regular lawful conduct – such as suspension of cooperation due to dissatisfaction with another state's governmental policies, or removal of an ambassador due to a politically offensive remark – is that a retorsion is avowedly adopted in response to unlawful conduct.

Legal regulation of retorsions is scarce. The International Law Commission (ILC) Articles mention them expressly solely in the context of third-state responses to particularly grievous breaches. Article 54 provides that any state has a 'right . . . to take lawful measures' against a state responsible for a serious violation 'to ensure cessation of the breach and reparation in the interest of the injured State or of the beneficiaries of the obligation'.[26]

Due to their lawful character, retorsions have rarely been subject to adjudication. The key exception is where a treaty precludes specific responses to unlawful conduct or mandates a certain course of action. Most ostensibly, at the World Trade Organization (WTO), Article 23 of the Dispute Settlement Understanding (DSU) prohibits WTO Members from resorting to unilateral determinations and unilateral responses in order to 'seek the redress of a violation' of WTO law.[27] Though this provision was generally established to prohibit countermeasures (that is, unilateral trade retaliation following claims of violation), the Panel in *US – Section 301* interpreted this as meaning that WTO dispute settlement operates 'to the exclusion of any other system, in particular a system of unilateral enforcement of WTO rights and obligations'.[28] This was taken to its logical conclusion by the Panel in *EC – Vessels*. In this dispute, South Korea argued that an otherwise WTO-consistent regulation adopted by the European Communities was impermissible due to being a response to an alleged breach by South Korea of WTO

Beaucillon (ed.), *Research Handbook on Unilateral and Extraterritorial Sanctions* (Cheltenham: Elgar, 2021), 152.

26 International Law Commission, *Articles on Responsibility of States for Internationally Wrongful Acts*, UN Doc. A/56/49(Vol. I)/Corr.4., Article 54 ('ARSIWA').

27 DSU, Article 26(1) obliges Members to have recourse to procedures authorised by the DSU to 'seek the redress of a violation' of WTO law (including specific provisions, general objectives, and 'other nullification or impairment'). Under Article 23(2), Members are prohibited from (a) making unilateral determinations of breach, (b) unilaterally establishing a period of time for another Member to comply with WTO rulings, or (c) adopting unilateral measures in reaction to other Members' WTO law violations.

28 Panel Report, *US – Sections 301–310 of the Trade Act of 1974*, WT/DS152/R, adopted 27 January 2000, para. 7.43.

law. The Panel, having found that the European Union's (EU's) measure was a 'response to what [the European Communities] considered to be a violation by Korea of its obligations',[29] concluded that it was indeed a violation of DSU Article 23, which 'covers any act of a Member in response to what it considers to be a violation of a WTO obligation',[30] regardless of whether the measure in question would have been lawful if taken outside of the context of a response to unlawful conduct.

The WTO Agreements are a rare exception in their express prohibition of horizontal, unilaterally determined responses to unlawful conduct. Other ICs have, however, suggested that agreements that feature dedicated enforcement mechanisms leading to specified sanctions preclude resort by the parties to unilateral enforcement mechanisms that are the hallmark of horizontal legal orders. In 1964, the Court of Justice of the European Union (CJEU) stated in *Commission* v. *Luxemburg and Belgium* that 'the [EU] Treaty is not limited to creating reciprocal obligations ... but establishes a new legal order ... as well as the necessary procedures for taking cognizance of and penalizing any breach of it'. The CJEU concluded from this that, 'except where otherwise expressly provided, the basic concept of the treaty requires that the member states shall not take the law into their own hands'.[31] Similarly, the Mercosur *Ad Hoc* Arbitral Tribunal in *Award No. VIII (Cigarettes)* determined that there is 'no sense ... in having resort to measures of retorsion [when] there are dispute settlement mechanisms that allow, through law, the application of adequate sanctions'.[32]

This jurisprudence must be assessed having in mind that both cases concerned measures of response that were unlawful under the relevant agreements – qualifying as countermeasures rather than retorsions. However, the phrasing used by these ICs suggests that they envisaged a broader prohibition of unilateral enforcement within the respective legal regimes. Even the Arbitral Tribunal in *Air Service Agreement*, which

[29] Panel Report, *EC – Commercial Vessels*, WT/DS301/R, adopted 20 June 2005, at para. 7.207.

[30] Ibid., at para. 7.220.

[31] Joint Cases 90/63 and 91/63, *Commission* v. *Luxemburg and Belgium* [1964] ECR 625, 631.

[32] Award No. VIII, Mercosur *Ad Hoc* Tribunal, 21 May 2002, 213 ('No tiene sentido, en un proceso de integración, que se recurra a la retorsión. Por eso mismo, hay mecanismos de solución de disputas que permiten aplicación, por medio del derecho, de sanciones adecuadas').

affirmed a general entitlement to adopt countermeasures unilaterally, may be read as implying this view.[33] It would not be surprising to see adjudicators in similar contexts, where agreements feature compulsory adjudication combined with specific post-adjudication enforcement mechanisms, determining that self-judging horizontal sanctions become impermissible, even when carried out through otherwise lawful means, if and to the extent that adjudication-based enforcement is legally and practically available.

5.2.2 *Countermeasures*

Perhaps the most common form of horizontal sanctioning is through countermeasures: the reciprocal non-performance of obligations with the intention of both highlighting a violation and responding to it. Articles on State Responsibility (ARSIWA) Article 49 codifies the entitlement of injured states to apply countermeasures, defined as 'the non-performance for the time being of international obligations of the State taking the measures towards the responsible State'.[34] Countermeasures are therefore measures taken by a state against an offender, short of the use of force, that would be unlawful – that is, would violate the adopting state's international obligations towards the target state – *but for* the fact that they are applied following a breach by the target state.

There is no requirement that countermeasures be grounded on an adjudicatory ruling or collective determination. Their 'unilateral' or 'self-judging' character stems from the fact that they may be adopted based on a state's unilateral assessment that another state has violated its obligations, as well as on its unilateral determination that certain countermeasures are warranted and appropriate. As the *Air Service Agreement* arbitrator put it, '[i]f a situation arises which, in one State's view, results in the violation of an international obligation by another State, the first State is entitled, within the limits set by the general rules of international law pertaining to the use of armed force, to affirm its rights through

[33] *Air Service Agreement*, (1978) 18 RIAA 417, 445 (discussing countermeasures: 'If the proceedings form part of an institutional framework ensuring some degree of enforcement of obligations, the justification of counter-measures will undoubtedly disappear').

[34] ARSIWA, Article 49(2).

"counter-measures"'.[35] As a result, adjudication regarding countermeasures usually takes place *ex post facto*, following a claim by the target state that they were wholly unwarranted, that the measures applied were impermissible or excessive, or both.

Adjudication of non-performance in response to violations dates back to two arbitrations, *Cysne* and *Naulilaa*, concerning Germany's (forceful) reprisals against Portuguese nationals and their property during World War I, in which Portugal was a neutral state. *Cysne* concerned the destruction by Germany of a Portuguese ship that was taking cargo to a private company in England. Germany argued that the destruction constituted 'a lawful reprisal against the violation of Article 28 [of the Declaration of London] by England and its allies'.[36] The arbitrators defined reprisals as 'act[s] in principle contrary to the law of nations . . . justified as long as they are provoked by another act equally contrary to this law'.[37] Reprisals would have been lawful against the offender (England, or rather, the United Kingdom of Great Britain and Ireland), not against the assets or citizens of a neutral state (Portugal). In *Naulilaa*, Germany argued that its destruction of a Portuguese outpost in Naulilaa, Angola, was a response to an incident in the outpost in which two German officials were killed. The arbitrators considered that the attacks '[could] not be considered as lawful reprisals for the incident in Naulilaa or for subsequent acts of Portuguese authorities, due to a lack of a sufficient reason, of previous notification, and of an admissible proportion between the alleged offence and the reprisals exercised'.[38]

[35] *Air Service Agreement*, (1978) 18 RIAA 417, 443. But see the ARSIWA Commentary: 'A State which resorts to countermeasures based on its unilateral assessment of the situation does so at its own risk and may incur responsibility for its own wrongful conduct in the event of an incorrect assessment' (International Law Commission, Draft Articles on Responsibility of States for Internationally Wrongful Acts, with commentaries, A/56/10, 2001 ('ARSIWA Commentary'), p. 130).

[36] *Cysne Case, Portugal* v. *Germany*, (1930) 2 UNRIAA 1035, 1055 ('une représaille licite *contre la violation de l'article 28 commise par l'Angleterre et ses alliés*'). The Declaration of London is the Declaration concerning the Laws of Naval War, (1909) 208 Consol. T.S. 338.

[37] Ibid., at 1057: '*les représailles, consistant en un acte en principe contraire au droit des gens, ne peuvent se justifier qu'autant qu'elles ont été provoquées par un autre acte également contraire à ce droit.* Les représailles ne sont admissibles que contre l'État provocateur'.

[38] *Colonies Portugaises (Naulilaa), Portugal* v. *Germany*, (1928) 2 UNRIAA 1011, 1028 ('*ne peuvent être considérées comme représailles licites de l'incident de Naulilaa ou d'actes postérieurs des autorités portugaises, ce faute de motif suffisant, de sommation préalable et d'une proportion admissible entre l'offense alléguée et les représailles exercées*').

Cysne and *Naulilaa* thus produced a first outline of the regulation of permissible responses, in a setting in which armed action was not only lawful but was considered a regular component of interaction among states. This changed when, in 1945, Article 2(4) of the UN Charter established a prohibition in principle on the threat or use of force 'against the territorial integrity or political independence of any state'.[39] This was interpreted as precluding the adoption of forceful reprisals already in the International Court of Justice's (ICJ's) first judgment on the merits, in *Corfu Channel.* The Court rejected the argument that a minesweeping operation, conducted in Albanian waters and involving a British aircraft carrier, cruisers, and other war vessels, was admissible as a means of 'self-protection or self-help'.[40] In *Guyana* v. *Suriname*, a United Nations Convention on the Law of the Sea (UNCLOS) Tribunal rejected the argument that a 'threat that force might be used' could be a lawful countermeasure, stating that it is 'a well established principle of international law that countermeasures may not involve the use of force'.[41]

Countermeasures have been considered by the ICJ on a number of instances, in which the Court mostly found countermeasures to be unwarranted or disproportionate. In *Nicaragua*, while rejecting the argument that the forceful measures adopted by the United States could qualify as countermeasures, the ICJ stated that the breaches the United States asserted 'could only have justified proportionate counter-measures on the part of the State which had been the victim of these acts'.[42] In *Gabčíkovo-Nagymaros*, the ICJ condemned Czechoslovakia's otherwise valid countermeasure for not being proportional to the original breach.[43] In *Interim Accord*, the ICJ considered that Greece's measure

[39] Charter of the United Nations, San Francisco, 26 June 1945, in force 24 October 1945, XV UNCIO 335, amendments in 557 UNTS 143, 638 UNTS 308 and 892 UNTS 119 ('UN Charter'), Article 2(4): 'All Members shall refrain in their international relations from the threat or use of force against the territorial integrity or political independence of any state, or in any other manner inconsistent with the Purposes of the United Nations'.

[40] *Corfu Channel (Merits), United Kingdom of Great Britain and Northern Ireland* v. *Albania*, Judgment, [1949] ICJ Reports 4, p. 35. The ICJ condemned the British intervention as 'the manifestation of a policy of force, such as has, in the past, given rise to most serious abuses and such as cannot, whatever be the present defects in international organization, find a place in international law' (Ibid.).

[41] *Delimitation of the Maritime Boundary between Guyana and Suriname, Guyana* v. *Suriname*, (2008) PCA 47 ILM 166, 231.

[42] *Military and Paramilitary Activities in and against Nicaragua, Nicaragua* v. *United States of America (Merits)*, Judgment, [1986] ICJ Reports 14, p. 127.

[43] *Gabčíkovo-Nagymaros Project*, Hungary/Slovakia, Judgment, [1997] ICJ Reports 7, p. 56.

was not justified as a countermeasure because it had not been carried out with the purpose of achieving the cessation of a breach.[44]

Adjudicatory findings that certain measures are permissible due to their character as countermeasures are relatively rare. In *Tehran Hostages*, the ICJ noted that a number of US measures had been 'taken in response to what the United States believed to be grave and manifest violations of international law by Iran'.[45] Because Iran did not appear before the Court, the legality of the US measures was not challenged.[46] A clearer case was the ruling by the arbitral tribunal in *Air Service Agreement*. The tribunal examined measures taken by the United States to pressure France to permit a US carrier to fly to Paris via London, something the United States believed was provided for in the US–France Air Service Agreement. The US countermeasure was a requirement for French companies to provide specific information regarding their flights going through US territory, combined with a threat to prevent Air France from operating some of these flights.[47] The Arbitral Tribunal accepted the lawfulness of this countermeasure, on the basis that, besides not being 'clearly disproportionate when compared to those taken by France', it was 'accompanied by an offer for a procedure affording the possibility of accelerating the solution of the dispute'.[48]

In another instance, Mexico argued before three NAFTA Investment Tribunals that Mexican taxes and production requirements affecting high-fructose corn syrup (HFCS) were imposed as countermeasures against the United States, which according to Mexico had 'frustrated the operation' of the North American Free Trade Agreement (NAFTA) dispute settlement following Mexico's claim of violation of NAFTA market access commitments for sugar.[49] The Tribunal in *ADM v. Mexico* was the only one to assess the substance of Mexico's argument. It held that, though it had 'no jurisdiction to decide whether the United

[44] *Interim Accord*, [2011] ICJ Reports 644, p. 692.

[45] *United States Diplomatic and Consular Staff in Tehran*, Judgment, [1980] ICJ Reports 3, p. 27–28.

[46] Ibid., p. 43.

[47] *Air Service Agreement*, (1978) 18 RIAA 417, 420–421.

[48] Ibid., p. 444–445.

[49] *Corn Products International (CPI) v. Mexico*, [2008] ICSID Case No. ARB(AF)/04/01, Decision on Responsibility, 15 January 2008, paras. 39, 398. See also *Archer Daniels Midland Company and Tate & Lyle Ingredients Americas, Inc. v. Mexico*, [2007] ICSID Case No. ARB(AF)/04/05, Award, 21 November 2007, para. 110.

States committed an internationally wrongful act which justified a countermeasure', it did have 'jurisdiction to decide any defense ... including a countermeasures defense'.[50] Examining Mexico's defence on the merits, the Tribunal concluded that Mexico's sweetener tax 'was not a valid countermeasure because it was not adopted to induce US' compliance with the NAFTA; nor does the Tax meet the proportionality requirements under customary international law'.[51]

As codified in ARSIWA, countermeasures are subject to various procedural and substantive requirements. They may only be adopted following a call for the violator to fulfil its secondary obligations of cessation and reparation.[52] They must be reversible,[53] must be suspended once a tribunal is able to adjudicate on the dispute,[54] and must cease when the target state has complied with its secondary obligations.[55] When applied, countermeasures must be proportional to the gravity of the unlawful act and the injury suffered.[56] Additionally, countermeasures cannot affect some 'core' obligations of states. These comprise *jus cogens* obligations, obligations relating to the use of force, human rights and humanitarian law, as well as procedural obligations, including under dispute settlement procedures and the law of diplomatic relations (which guarantees communication between states).[57]

A final issue regarding the ARSIWA regulation of countermeasures is that, pursuant to Article 49, lawful adoption of countermeasures is limited to injured states. In case a violated obligation is owed to a state individually, this state is automatically entitled to adopt countermeasures as an injured state, regardless of whether the breach produced an 'injury' in the sense of material damage. In case of obligations owed to a group of states, ordinarily only states 'specially affected' by the breach may react through reciprocal non-performance. The exception, under ARSIWA Article 42(b)(ii), is where the breach 'is of such a character as radically change the position of all other States to which the obligation is owed

[50] *Archer Daniels Midland Company and Tate & Lyle Ingredients Americas, Inc. (ADM)* v. *Mexico*, [2007] ICSID Case No. ARB(AF)/04/05, paras. 131–132.
[51] Ibid., para. 180.
[52] ARSIWA, Article 52(1).
[53] Ibid., Article 49(3).
[54] Ibid., Article 52.3(b).
[55] Ibid., Article 53.
[56] Ibid., Article 51.
[57] Ibid., Article 50.

with respect to the further performance of the obligation'.[58] Even in this case, solely states to which the obligation is owed may respond.

Third-party countermeasures are a more complex issue. ARSIWA Article 54 safeguards for non-injured states solely the right 'to take lawful measures', that is, retorsions, 'to ensure cessation of the breach and reparation in the interest of the injured State or of the beneficiaries of the obligation breached'. If one considers ARSIWA as a comprehensive regulation of the matter, this would seem to foreclose the use of otherwise unlawful measures by third parties.[59] At the same time, in the Commentary to Article 54, the ILC asserts that a 'sparse' and 'embryonic' state practice exists in relation to third-party countermeasures, leaving 'the resolution of the matter to the further development of international law'.[60] This seems to leave the door open for further development that permits third-party countermeasures.[61]

5.2.3 *(Partial) Suspension or Termination of Treaties*

A further manifestation of the principle of reciprocity is the permissible suspension or termination of treaties as a response to their violation. While retorsions and countermeasures involve primarily conduct, the suspension or termination of treaties operates at the level of norms. Maria Xiouri notes that, contrary to countermeasures, 'the termination or suspension of a treaty, in whole or in part, deprives the treaty of its legal force, permanently or temporarily'.[62] Bhek Sinha mentions late eighteenth-century correspondence by James Madison and Thomas Jefferson declaring that a violation of a treaty by one party leaves the other party 'at liberty' to consider the treaty as partially or totally

[58] Mark Villiger notes that this paragraph 'has so-called integral treaties in mind, e.g., on disarmament, where a breach by one party tends to undermine the whole regime of the treaty as between all the parties' (Mark E. Villiger, *Commentary on the 1969 Vienna Convention on the Law of Treaties* (Boston, MA: Martinus Nijhoff, 2009), 745).

[59] ARSIWA, Article 22 (precluding solely the wrongfulness of measures that qualify as 'countermeasure[s] taken . . . in accordance with chapter II of part three').

[60] ARSIWA Commentary, p. 139.

[61] For assessments of this practice, see Martin Dawidowicz, *Third-Party Countermeasures in International Law* (Cambridge: Cambridge University Press, 2017), 111 ff. Christian J. Tams, *Enforcing Obligations Erga Omnes in International Law* (Cambridge: Cambridge University Press, 2005), 198 ff.

[62] Maria Xiouri, *The Breach of a Treaty: State Responses in International Law* (Leiden: Brill | Nijhoff, 2021), 29.

abrogated.[63] Marjorie Whiteman refers to a French declaration, made before the Council of the League of Nations, affirming the guarantees to the rights of Romania's Jewish minority contained in the Treaty of Versailles. In case of attacks on this minority, the statement read, the French and British governments would 'regard the entire treaty, including the portions which give Transylvania and Bessarabia to [Romania], annulled by the action of the Rumanian Government itself'.[64] More recently, the CJEU affirmed that, where no specific sanctioning mechanism is established, a 'rule of customary international law' permits a party to a bilateral treaty to respond to its breach by suspending other commitments under the treaty.[65]

An early adjudication of the termination or suspension of treaties as a remedy for their violation took place in 1925, in the *Tacna-Arica* arbitration between Peru and Chile, concerning the 1883 Treaty of Ancon. Its Article 3 established that a plebiscite would be organised to establish 'dominion and sovereignty' over two provinces, Tacna and Arica, occupied by Chile during the Pacific War.[66] Peru claimed that 'Chile by preventing the performance of Article 3 has discharged Peru from her obligations thereunder ... and that Chile should be regarded as a trespasser in the territory in question'.[67] The Arbitrator refused to issue this declaration, holding that it was 'unable to find in the expulsions which have taken place any such serious and deliberate violation of Peru's treaty rights as to justify Peru in repudiating the plebiscitary obligations'.[68] For this to be the case, 'it would be necessary to establish such serious conditions as the consequence of administrative wrongs as would operate to frustrate the purpose of the agreement'.[69]

63 Bhek P. Sinha, *Unilateral Denunciation of Treaty Because of Prior Violations of Obligations by Other Party* (The Hague: M. Nijhoff, 1966), 105–106.

64 Marjorie M. Whiteman (ed.), *Digest of International Law* (Washington: US Government Printing Office, 1970), 473.

65 *Opinion 2/15, The Free Trade Agreement with Singapore*, [2017] ECLI:EU:C:2017:376, para. 161: 'a breach of the [trade agreement] provisions concerning social protection of workers and environmental protection ... authorises the other Party – in accordance with the rule of customary international law codified in Article 60(1) of the Convention on the law of treaties ... to terminate or suspend the liberalisation, provided for in the other provisions of the envisaged agreement, of that trade'. The CJEU's description of this mechanism seems to merge countermeasures with the unilateral remedy for material breach under the law of treaties.

66 *Tacna-Arica Question, Chile/Peru*, (1925) 2 UNRIAA 921, 926.

67 Ibid., 929.

68 Ibid., 943.

69 Ibid., 944. On subsequent events in this dispute, see Section 5.4.1.

The legal standard established by the Arbitrator in *Tacna-Arica* was considered excessive by the fifth ILC Special Rapporteur on the law of treaties, Humphrey Waldock, who reasoned that the regulation of termination and suspension of treaties should be cognisant of their value 'as a sanction for securing the observance of treaties'.[70] Waldock established the term 'material breach'[71] as the legal standard that permits a state to adopt responses to unlawful conduct under the law of treaties. Vienna Convention on the Law of Treaties (VCLT) Article 60(3) defines a material breach as either '(a) a repudiation of the treaty not sanctioned by the present Convention; or (b) the violation of a provision essential to the accomplishment of the object or purpose of the treaty'.[72]

Suspending or terminating a treaty, in whole or in part, is a response that takes place at the level of the normative framework rather than that of conduct. There is no requirement that the conduct adopted as a consequence be reversible or that it be proportionate to the breach. As Special Rapporteur Gerald Fitzmaurice noted when considering states' entitlement to respond in this manner to violations, 'in the case of termination . . . the treaty ends altogether, while in [countermeasures]- . . . the non-performance is not only justified, but "looks towards" a resumption of performance so soon as the factors causing and justifying non-performance are no longer present, or have ceased to exist'.[73]

The VCLT does not impose a proportionality constraint on this remedy but provides other limitations. First, not every breach of a treaty allows other states to react under the law of treaties. A 'material breach', required to justify this response, must be a violation of an obligation essential for the accomplishment of the object and purpose of the treaty, or amount to an unlawful 'repudiation' of the treaty by the offending party. The limitation seeks to prevent legitimating what Shabtai Rosenne termed the 'Sportpalast Diplomatie' practised by the Nazi regime: the 'repeated, flagrant and at times violent instances of deliberate breaches of treaty' on the pretext of responding to a minor violation by another party.[74] The VCLT does not refer to a *serious* breach, suggesting that any breach of a particularly important provision could meet this

[70] Humphrey Waldock, 'Second Report on the Law of Treaties', II ILC Ybk 1963, p. 74.
[71] Ibid., p. 76.
[72] In *Gabčíkovo-Nagymaros*, the ICJ found that VCLT rules on suspension and termination of treaties are 'declaratory of customary law . . . in many respects' (*Gabčíkovo-Nagymaros Project*, [1997] ICJ Reports 7, p. 62).
[73] Gerald Fitzmaurice, 'Fourth Report on the Law of Treaties', II ILC Ybk 1959, 41.
[74] Shabtai Rosenne, *Breach of Treaty* (Cambridge: Grotius Publications, 1985), 11.

threshold.[75] This wording seemingly contradicts the intentions of the ILC, which 'was unanimous that the right to terminate or suspend must be limited to cases where the breach is of a serious character'.[76]

Second, in the case of breach of a multilateral treaty affecting a single other party, only the 'party specially affected' may adopt this response, and only in relation to the wrongdoer.[77] A procedure for collective decision-making is provided for violations of obligations in multilateral treaties that do not affect a state in particular, or in case parties other than the state directly injured wish to respond. Under VCLT Article 60 (2)(a), if all other parties unanimously agree, they may determine the suspension or termination of a treaty, or of some of its provisions, vis-à-vis the wrongdoer. In other words, acting unanimously, the other parties may expel the (material) offender from the treaty regime or suspend some of its rights under it.

The ICJ only ever asserted the lawfulness of a termination of a treaty in response to its breach once, in the *Namibia* Advisory Opinion. A UN General Assembly resolution had found that, by failing to secure the moral and material being of 'the indigenous inhabitants of South West Africa', South Africa had 'disavowed the Mandate' it had received from the League of Nations to govern Namibia. The resolution considered the mandate as 'therefore terminated'.[78] Before the ICJ, South Africa argued that only an agreement between the parties, or a judicial decision, could have led to the termination of the mandate. The ICJ stated that South Africa's policy of apartheid constituted 'a denial of fundamental rights' and 'a flagrant violation of the purposes and principles of the Charter'.[79] Having previously likened the mandate to a treaty, the Court concluded that the UN General Assembly had a 'right to terminate' the mandate in

[75] See Bruno Simma and Christian J. Tams, '1969 Vienna Convention: Article 60 – Termination or Suspension of the Operation of a Treaty as a Consequence of Its Breach', in Olivier Corten and Pierre Klein (eds.), *The Vienna Conventions on the Law of Treaties: A Commentary* (Oxford: Oxford University Press, 2011), pp. 1351–1378, 1359.

[76] ILC, 'Report of the International Law Commission', II ILC Ybk 1966, p. 255. See *Interim Accord*, [2011] ICJ Reports 644 at note 12 and accompanying text.

[77] Vienna Convention on the Law of Treaties, Vienna, 23 May 1969, in force 27 January 1980, 1155 UNTS 331, Article 60(2)(b) ('VCLT').

[78] General Assembly, Resolution 2145 (XXI), 27 October 1966. The International Court had previously asserted that the mandate, 'in fact and in law, is an international agreement having the character of a treaty or convention' (*South West Africa, Ethiopia* v. *South Africa*, Preliminary Objections, [1962] ICJ Reports 319, p. 330).

[79] *Legal Consequences for Continued Presence of South Africa in Namibia*, [1971] ICJ Reports 16, p. 47.

view of South Africa's 'deliberate and persistent violation of obligations which destroys the very object and purpose of that relationship'.[80]

The ICJ considered, and rejected, purported terminations or suspensions in *ICAO Council (India* v. *Pakistan)*, *Gabčíkovo-Nagymaros*, and *Interim Accord*. In *ICAO Council (India* v. *Pakistan)*, India argued that its entitlement to terminate or suspend the Treaties of the International Civil Aviation Organisation (ICAO) had its source in the general law of treaties, and thus outside the ICAO Treaties themselves.[81] India appealed a decision of the ICAO Council – the organ competent for the 'interpretation and application' of the ICAO Treaties – by which the Council accepted jurisdiction over a claim brought by Pakistan against India. India argued that, because it had terminated the treaty or suspended its operation between itself and Pakistan, the Council did not have jurisdiction over the claim: 'non-existent treaties cannot be interpreted or applied'.[82]

The ICJ disagreed, reasoning that a 'mere allegation, as yet unestablished, that a treaty was no longer operative' could not be used to defeat the jurisdictional clause in a treaty.[83] It would thus be up to the Council (and, on appeal, the ICJ) to determine whether the treaty had been validly suspended or terminated. The question of the existence of a material breach which would justify a termination or suspension of the treaty, the Court concluded, 'is inherently and by its very nature, one that must involve the examination of the Treaties'.[84] The ICAO Council thus had full jurisdiction over the dispute, including to determine the question of termination or suspension of the ICAO Treaties between the parties.[85]

[80] Ibid. See on this Herbert W. Briggs, 'Unilateral Denunciation of Treaties: The Vienna Convention and the International Court of Justice' (1974) 68 *AJIL* 51, 53–55 (arguing that the term 'right' is misleading).

[81] Chicago Convention on International Civil Aviation, Chicago, 7 December 1944, in force 4 April 1947, 15 UNTS 295; and Chicago International Air Services Transit Agreement, Chicago, 7 December 1944, in force 20 January 1945, 171 UNTS 387.

[82] *Appeal Relating to the Jurisdiction of the ICAO Council, India* v. *Pakistan*, Judgment, [1972] ICJ Reports 46, p. 65.

[83] Ibid., p. 54, 64.

[84] Ibid., p. 64–65.

[85] India claimed that, following hostilities between India and Pakistan starting in 1965, the ICAO Treaties had been terminated between them, after which neither party had revived the Treaties. In the alternative, India alleged that Pakistan's involvement in the hijacking of an Indian aircraft 'entitled [India] under general international law to terminate or suspend the Treaties as from January 1971, by reason of a material breach of them, for which Pakistan was responsible' (Ibid., p. 62).

In *Gabčíkovo-Nagymaros Project*, the ICJ acknowledged the entitlement to use this remedy, noting that 'Czechoslovakia repeatedly denounced Hungary's suspension and abandonment of works [on a joint dam project] as a fundamental breach of the 1977 Treaty and consequently could have invoked this breach as a ground for terminating the Treaty'.[86] By contrast, Hungary's subsequent decision to terminate the treaty in response to Czechoslovakia's beginning the implementation of an alternative plan, 'Variant C', was 'premature', in that '[n]o breach of the Treaty by Czechoslovakia had yet taken place'.[87] Subsequently, Hungary had 'prejudiced its right to terminate the Treaty' because Czechoslovakia's breach had been caused by 'Hungary's own prior wrongful conduct'.[88]

In *Interim Accord*, Greece argued that six alleged breaches by the Former Yugoslav Republic of Macedonia (FYROM) of the Interim Accord allowed it to terminate the treaty. The ICJ examined all the allegations and concluded that there was a sole breach for which Greece could present evidence. This breach was the use, by one regiment of FYROM's army and four years before Greece's alleged response, of a national symbol prohibited under the Accord. Referring to the breach as an 'incident', the Court noted that this was not a 'violation of a provision essential to the accomplishment of the object and purpose of the treaty'.[89] Though preventing the use by FYROM of words and symbols referring to Macedonia was an important reason for Greece to sign the Interim Accord, this ruling would seem to imply that a *serious* or *substantial* violation would have been required to constitute a material breach.

5.2.4 *Exception of Non-Performance*

A controversial permissible response to unlawful conduct is the so-called exception of non-performance, or *exceptio non adimpleti contractus*. The exception would prevent a state that has failed to perform its obligations under a treaty from demanding performance by its counterpart. As Maria Xiouri notes, the exception is not so much a legal instrument but, 'as the term *exceptio* denotes, a means of defence'.[90] Serena Forlati

[86] *Gabčíkovo-Nagymaros Project*, [1997] ICJ Reports 7, p. 53.
[87] Ibid., p. 56.
[88] Ibid., p. 7, 67.
[89] *Interim Accord*, [2011] ICJ Reports 644, p. 692.
[90] Maria Xiouri, *The Breach of a Treaty*, at 53.

described the exception 'as a form of countermeasure, which "operate[s] as a shield rather than a sword"' and 'would simply justify temporary non-performance of obligations that remain in force and, in principle, applicable between the parties'.[91] The very existence and content of this exception are debated. Malgosia Fitzmaurice finds that 'its existence appears to be elusive'.[92] James Crawford and Simon Olleson distinguish two different versions. Under the 'narrow version', a state is barred from demanding performance of an obligation if it has itself prevented this performance by a prior wrongful act. A 'wider form' of the exception would positively entitle a state to withhold performance of an obligation until the other party performs its counterpart obligations.[93]

The exception was articulated by the Permanent Court of International Justice (PCIJ) in *Chorzów Factory* in its narrow form: 'one Party cannot avail [it]self of the fact that the other has not fulfilled some obligation or has not had recourse to some means of redress, if the former Party has, by some illegal act, prevented the latter from fulfilling the obligation in question'.[94] In *Diversion of Waters from the Meuse*, the Permanent Court avoided dealing with the issue[95] and it fell upon individual judges to pronounce on the status of the exception.[96]

At the ILC, Special Rapporteurs Wilhelm Riphagen and Gaetano Arangio-Ruiz both treated *exceptio non adimpleti contractus* as a particular aspect of countermeasures.[97] Special Rapporteur James Crawford's proposal to incorporate the *exceptio* into ARSIWA as an independent circumstance precluding wrongfulness was met with criticisms, by both ILC members and states, and eventually withdrawn.[98] The Commentary to the ILC Articles describes it as 'a specific feature of

[91] Serena Forlati, 'Reactions to Non-Performance of Treaties in International Law' (2012) 25(3) *Leiden Journal of International Law* 759, 766 (quoting ARSIWA Commentary, p. 71. The ILC remark refers to all circumstances precluding wrongfulness.).

[92] Malgosia Fitzmaurice, 'Angst of the *Exceptio Inadimplenti Non Est Adimplendum* in International Law', in Lorand Bartels and Federica Paddeu (eds.), *Exceptions in International Law* (Oxford: Oxford University Press, 2020), 285–304, 304.

[93] James Crawford and Simon Olleson, 'The Exception of Non-Performance: Links between the Law of Treaties and the Law of State Responsibility' (2000) 21 *Australian Yearbook of International Law* 55, 62.

[94] *Factory at Chorzów (Jurisdiction), Germany* v. *Poland*, Judgment, (1927) PCIJ Ser. A No. 9, p. 31.

[95] *Diversion of Waters from the Meuse, Netherlands* v. *Belgium*, Judgment, (1937) PCIJ Ser. A/B No. 70, p. 8.

[96] Ibid., p. 39–40 (Judge Altamira), 50 (Judge Anzilotti, diss.), 77 (Judge Hudson).

[97] Crawford and Olleson, 'The Exception of Non-Performance', 61.

[98] Ibid., 62.

certain mutual or synallagmatic obligations and not a circumstance precluding wrongfulness'.[99]

The ICJ appears to have subsumed the concept under the remedy of suspension or termination of a treaty under the law of treaties. In *Gabčíkovo-Nagymaros Project*, the ICJ found that Hungary's non-performance was not justified as a response because 'Czechoslovakia [had] committed the internationally wrongful act of putting into operation Variant C as a result of Hungary's own prior wrongful conduct'.[100] In *Interim Accord*, Greece argued that the exception has 'conditions ... less rigid' than those of VCLT Article 60 or countermeasures, and that 'no procedural requirements' are attached to its invocation.[101] The ICJ found the exception inapplicable because Greece's alleged response was adopted long after its alleged cause, so that it was 'unnecessary ... to determine whether that doctrine forms part of contemporary international law'.[102]

The exception of non-performance is likely to be acceptable essentially in its narrow version, as described by the PCIJ in *Chorzów Factory* and the ICJ in *Gabčíkovo-Nagymaros Project*. As regards the broader version, it seems hazardous to retain a legal mechanism that, having content largely matching two codified possibilities for suspending performance, under the law of responsibility and the law of treaties, would relieve its user from any of the procedural and substantive safeguards that prevent abuse of these other legal instruments.

5.2.5 *Self-Defence and Reprisals*

A final form of response against unlawful conduct permitted under international law is self-defence. Article 51 of the UN Charter provides for 'the inherent right of individual or collective self-defense if an armed attack occurs against a Member of the United Nations'.[103] Among states, the entitlement to act in self-defence permits a state faced with a breach of the law by another state 'to suspend temporarily, in the relation between the two states, the observance of a particular rule of the Law of Nations'.[104] The rule, however, is one of the cardinal rules of

[99] ARSIWA Commentary, p. 72.
[100] *Gabčíkovo-Nagymaros Project*, [1997] ICJ Reports 7, p. 57.
[101] *Interim Accord*, [2011] ICJ Reports 644, p. 680–681.
[102] Ibid., para. 161.
[103] UN Charter, Article 51.
[104] *Colonies Portugaises (Naulilaa)*, (1928) 2 UNRIAA 1011, 1026 (referring to reprisals).

contemporary international law – the prohibition on the use of force in international relations under Article 2(4) of the Charter. The Charter does not specify a purpose for self-defence other than by stating that it is only available in response to an armed attack. And the entitlement to adopt measures in self-defence persists only 'until the Security Council has taken measures necessary to maintain international peace and security'.[105]

Lawful exercises of self-defence have been recognised by adjudicators. The Eritrea-Ethiopia Claims Commission, in its award on *Jus ad Bellum*, found that Eritrea held 'liability for the unlawful armed attack on the Western Front that began on May 12, 1998', leading Ethiopia to 'act in self-defense'.[106] In Nicaragua, the ICJ held – though reasoning hypothetically – that 'collective self-defence' is permissible if 'the State for whose benefit this right is used … declare[s] itself to be the victim of an armed attack'[107] And, in *Armed Activities* (*DRC* v. *Uganda)*, the ICJ restricted the lawfulness of recourse to force in self-defence to measures necessary to 'repeal' the attack – thus bringing an end to the breach – rather than more generally to 'respond' to it. The Court held that Uganda's military intervention in the territory of the Democratic Republic of the Congo constituted an 'illegal use of force by Uganda against the DRC … It follows that the DRC was entitled to use force in order to repel Uganda's attacks'.[108] This would seem to rule out the possibility of lawful reprisals, which are forceful measures taken to respond to a prior use of force, justified as 'appropriate punishment' with 'deterrent value'.[109]

On two occasions, the ICJ has found that self-defence did not excuse the use of force. In *Nicaragua*, the Court determined that self-defence

105 UN Charter, Article 51.

106 Eritrea-Ethiopia Claims Commission, *Partial Award – Jus Ad Bellum – Ethiopia's Claims 1–8*, (2005) 27 RIAA 457, 465.

107 *Military Activities in Nicaragua*, [1986] ICJ Reports 14, p. 94, 104.

108 *Armed Activities in the Territory of the Congo, Democratic Republic of the Congo* v. *Uganda*, Judgment, [2005] ICJ Reports 168, p. 269.

109 Michael A. Newton, 'Reconsidering Reprisals' (2010) 20 *Duke Journal of Comparative & International Law* 361, 361. The lawfulness of armed reprisals is the subject of heated debate, at whose heart is the question whether their utility as a deterrent to destructive behaviour is eclipsed by their own destructiveness. See Mary Ellen O'Connell, 'The Popular But Unlawful Armed Reprisal' (2018) 44 *Ohio Northern University Law Review* 325; Yishai Beer, 'Regulating Armed Reprisals: Revisiting the Scope of Lawful Self-Defense' (2020) 59 *Columbia Journal of Transnational Law* 117; Francesco Romani, *Belligerent Reprisals from Enforcement to Reciprocity: A New Theory of Retaliation in Conflict* (Cambridge: Cambridge University Press, 2024); Eliav Lieblich, 'The Death and Life of the Prohibition on Forcible Reprisals', (2025) 51 *Yale Journal of International Law* [forthcoming].

does not arise from 'use of force of a lesser degree of gravity' than an armed attack, and response must involve measures 'proportional to the armed attack and necessary to respond to it'.[110] The ICJ also condemned the US measures against Nicaragua for having occurred 'several months after the major offensive of the armed opposition against the Government of El Salvador had been completely repulsed'.[111] The Court made similar findings in *Oil Platforms*.[112] In *Armed Activities*, the ICJ highlighted that self-defence 'does not allow the use of force by a State to protect perceived security interests' beyond the parameters of Article 51.[113]

5.3 Determining Permissible Responses as an *Ex Ante* Judicial Remedy

As the jurisprudence in Section 5.2 demonstrates, ICs routinely pronounce upon measures allegedly adopted in response to violations of international law. Most of this jurisprudence concerns adjudication *ex post* of alleged permissible responses. This raises the question of the availability of Permissible Responses as an *ex ante* judicial remedy, by which an IC establishes that a certain measure is both warranted and permissible as a response to a violation.[114]

Setting aside procedural objections specific to each IC and the question (examined in Section 5.4) of the scope of measures that an IC may declare permissible, three related general objections may be raised to the possibility of issuing Permissible Responses as a remedy. The first concerns the very object of the remedy, contending that issuing declarations of lawfulness of

[110] *Military Activities in Nicaragua*, [1986] ICJ Reports 14, p. 94, 127.

[111] Ibid., p. 122–123.

[112] In *Oil Platforms*, the ICJ found that Iran's alleged conduct had not constituted an armed attack justifying measures of self-defence, that the US attacks on oil platforms had not been necessary to respond to the alleged attack, and that the force employed had not been proportionate to the injury suffered by the United States (*Oil Platforms (Merits), Iran* v. *United States*, [2003] ICJ Reports 161, p. 196–199). See Tom Ruys, *'Armed Attack' and Article 51 of the UN Charter: Evolutions in Customary Law and Practice* (Cambridge: Cambridge University Press, 2011), 139 ff, and Abdulqawi A. Yusuf, 'The Notion of 'Armed Attack' in the Nicaragua Judgment and Its Influence on Subsequent Case Law' (2012) 25 *Leiden Journal of International Law* 461–470.

[113] *Armed Activities in Congo*, [2005] ICJ Reports 168.

[114] Here, 'warranted' indicates the permissibility of a certain type of response, while 'permissible' indicates that a specific measure meets the procedural and substantive requirements to be adopted as a response to a particular breach.

conduct goes beyond the judicial function of ICs. The second concerns the concreteness of the dispute, reasoning that, even if issuing declarations of lawfulness is permissible for an IC, requesting them *ex ante* would require the IC to settle a hypothetical dispute. The third objection concerns the legal interest in, or practical consequence of, such a remedy. As this section will show, there are precedents admitting both requests for a declaration of lawfulness and requests concerning non-implemented and proposed courses of action. At the same time, the need for concreteness of the dispute and legal interest in its adjudication may limit the possibilities for awarding Permissible Responses as remedies.

5.3.1 *The Permissibility of Declarations of Compliance*

A remedy of Permissible Responses is a judicial declaration that (i) a certain violation warrants a response under international law, and (ii) a specific measure becomes permissible in light of the violation. Put otherwise, the IC is asked to declare that, should a state (or other actor) adopt a certain conduct, it will not be violating its international obligations.

The ICJ has received, and accepted, a few requests for declarations of lawfulness. In *U.S. Nationals in Morocco*, the ICJ accepted to determine, at the request of France, whether a French decree '[wa]s in conformity with the treaty provisions which are applicable to Morocco and binding on France and the United States'.[115] The Court concluded that the decree was not lawful under the treaty.[116] In *Lockerbie*, the ICJ found admissible Libya's request for a declaration that Libya had 'fully complied with all of its obligations under the Montreal Convention' and was thus 'justified in exercising the criminal jurisdiction provided for by that Convention'.[117] The dispute was settled before a ruling on the merits.

In *Allegations of Genocide*, Russia challenged the permissibility of Ukraine's request for a declaration of lawfulness of conduct. Ukraine requested from the ICJ what the Court described as 'a declaration that the Applicant did not breach its obligations under the [Genocide]

[115] *Rights of Nationals of the United States of America in Morocco, France* v. *United States*, Judgment, [1952] ICJ Reports 176, p. 182.

[116] Ibid., p. 185–186. The United States had not disputed the Court's entitlement to issue a judgment.

[117] *Questions of Interpretation and Application of the 1971 Montreal Convention Arising from the Aerial Incident at Lockerbie, Libya* v. *United States of America*, Preliminary Objections, [1998] ICJ Reports 115, para. 14.

Convention'.[118] Russia objected that the jurisdictional clause in the Genocide Convention 'was not intended for "reverse compliance requests"'.[119] The ICJ noted that the jurisdictional clause referred to disputes 'relating to the interpretation, application or fulfilment' of the Genocide Convention and specifically 'include[d] disputes "relating to the responsibility of *a* State for genocide" and provide[d] that "*any* of the parties to the dispute" may submit such a dispute to the Court'.[120] This wording, the Court concluded, did not limit its jurisdiction to claims regarding the conduct of another state.

Considering the admissibility of Ukraine's request, the ICJ found that the relevant question concerned the existence of legal interest in the declaration. The Court noted that, in *Lockerbie*, it had accepted Libya's request for a declaration that it had complied with its obligations under the Montreal Convention Faced with harsh measures taken in response to its alleged breach, Libya sought 'to assert its right to exercise criminal jurisdiction as provided for by the Convention'.[121] The ICJ noted the similar legal interest in the two cases:

> Ukraine made a request for a declaration that it did not breach its obligations under the Genocide Convention in the context of an armed conflict between the Parties. The Respondent took the allegedly unlawful measures in and against Ukraine with a stated purpose of preventing and punishing genocide allegedly committed in the Donbas region. In such a special context, the Court recognizes the legal interest that Ukraine has under the Genocide Convention to resolve the dispute . . . A judgment of the Court . . . will clarify the rights and obligations of the Parties under the Genocide Convention, in particular whether Ukraine acted in accordance with its obligations under Article I of the Convention.[122]

The ICJ determined that Ukraine's request was 'not inadmissible' in 'the particular circumstances' of the case.[123] Its reasoning suggests it was seeking to avoid opening the door to future requests for declarations of conformity in response to hypothetical or insufficiently crystallised controversies. It connected Ukraine's legal interest in the ruling to the fact

[118] *Allegations of Genocide under the Convention on the Prevention and Punishment of the Crime of Genocide, Ukraine* v. *Russian Federation: 32 States Intervening*, Preliminary Objections, [2024], para. 93. Ukraine termed this 'a declaration of conformity or compliance' by a state with its obligations (Ibid., para. 87).

[119] Ibid., para. 96.

[120] Ibid., para. 98. Convention on the Prevention and Punishment of the Crime of Genocide, Paris, 9 December 1948, in force 12 January 1951, 78 UNTS 276, Article IX.

[121] *Alleged Violations, Ukraine* v. *Russia*, [2024], para. 101.

[122] Ibid., para. 108.

[123] Ibid., para. 109.

that Russia had not only made allegations of genocide but had adopted harsh, forceful measures in response to the alleged genocide. Thus, the relevant legal questions regarding requests for declarations of lawfulness of conduct concerned not the nature of the requested declaration but the utility of the ruling, connected to the existence of a discernible legal interest. For purposes of the remedy of Permissible Responses, the relevant questions accordingly concern the utility of obtaining them and the connected legal interest in requesting them.

5.3.2 *The Admissibility of Requests concerning Proposed Measures*

A judicial remedy of Permissible Responses is more than a declaration of compliance in response to an allegation of breach. It is an *ex ante* declaration that a certain conduct is or will become permissible due to another state's unlawful conduct or failure to abide by the duties that emerge from this conduct. The remedy does not concern a state's future compliance with its regularly applicable obligations; it delineates the scope of lawful action available to that state as a response to another state's legal violation.

Setting aside the question of the potential content of this remedy (considered in Section 5.3.3), two objections may be raised to the admissibility of requests for Permissible Responses. The first is that a dispute would only emerge with the adoption of a measure, rendering inadmissible a request for a judicial statement on a merely proposed course of conduct. This objection may find support in the ICJ's statement in *Fisheries Jurisdiction* that 'the Court only pronounces on the case which is before it and not on any hypothetical situation which might arise in the future'.[124] The second is that, even if it is admissible, such a request should not be granted due to a lack of what the ICJ termed, in *Northern Cameroons*, 'continuing applicability' or 'forward reach'.[125]

To be admissible pursuant to the first requirement, a request for Permissible Responses must indicate a clearly defined proposed response to a clearly defined, and already ascertainable, breach. The key question in this regard is whether the proposed character of the measure of

[124] *Fisheries Jurisdiction, United Kingdom* v. *Iceland*, Judgment, [1974] ICJ Reports 3, p. 32. See also *Delimitation of the Continental Shelf beyond 200 Nautical Miles, Nicaragua* v. *Colombia*, Preliminary Objections, [2016] ICJ Reports 100, p. 138 ('it is not for the Court to determine the applicable law with regard to a hypothetical situation').

[125] *Northern Cameroons*, [1963] ICJ Reports 15, p. 37.

response means that the dispute falls short of the threshold for justiciability. There does not seem to be an absolute obstacle to the admissibility of preventive requests. Edwin Borchard argued, already in 1935, that states should be able to request declaratory judgments preventively, 'before either party has acted on [its] own assumption as to [its] rights and broken the *status quo*'.[126] Christine Gray agreed that declaratory judgments may be issued regarding a 'proposed course of conduct', even before a concrete violation takes place.[127]

The ICJ offered some insights on the matter in its Advisory Opinion in *PLO Headquarters*, where it found that disputes concerning measures enacted but not yet carried into effect are justiciable. The underlying issue was a US law de facto prohibiting the operation of the Mission of the Palestinian Liberation Organization (PLO) to the United Nations (UN) and its compatibility with United States' Headquarters Agreement with the UN.[128] Though enforcement of this law was pending before US courts, the law had already entered into force and had produced consequences for the PLO Mission, leading the UN Secretary-General to conclude that the measures 'would be incompatible with the Agreement if they were to be applied to that Mission'.[129] The question submitted to the Court was whether this context triggered the obligation under the Headquarters Agreement to submit a dispute to arbitration. The ICJ answered that, '[w]hile the existence of a dispute does presuppose a claim arising out of the behaviour of or a decision by one of the parties, it in no way requires that any contested decision must already have been carried into effect'.[130]

In judicial and arbitral practice, requests for declarations of lawfulness of proposed measures are rare, but not unheard of. In the (jointly requested) *Lac Lanoux* arbitration, France asked the arbitrators to establish that its planned works on Lake Lanoux, if carried out, would not violate Spain's rights under the Treaty of Bayonne governing their common interests in the waters of the Pyrenees. The arbitrators

[126] Edwin M. Borchard, 'Editorial Comment – Declaratory Judgments in International Law' (1935) 29 *AJIL* 488, 489.

[127] Christine D. Gray, *Judicial Remedies in International Law* (Oxford: Clarendon, 1987), 101.

[128] *Applicability of the Obligation to Arbitrate under Section 21 of the United Nations Headquarters Agreement of 26 June 1947*, Advisory Opinion, [1988] ICJ Reports 12, p. 22–23.

[129] Ibid, p. 31.

[130] Ibid., p. 30.

concluded that, in carrying out its proposed works, France would be 'simply exercising a right' and not violating Spain's rights.[131] In *Lockerbie*, Libya requested the ICJ to declare that it was not under an obligation to extradite two alleged terrorists to the United States and the United Kingdom, and instead 'Article 7 of the Montreal Convention gives it the right to submit them to its competent authorities for the purpose of prosecution in accordance with Libyan law'.[132] The ICJ found this request admissible, since in each case 'the Respondent dispute[d] that the Montreal Convention confers on Libya the rights it claims to enjoy'.[133]

More commonly, parties request adjudicators to declare the other party's planned or proposed conduct unlawful. In *Great Belt*, Finland asked the ICJ to declare that 'the construction of a fixed bridge over the Great Belt as currently planned by Denmark would be incompatible' with Finland's 'right of free passage through the Great Belt'.[134] In the *Indus Waters (Kishenganga) Arbitration*, Pakistan requested the PCA-administered Court of Arbitration to declare that 'India's proposed diversion of the river Kishenganga (Neelum) into another Tributary ... breaches India's legal obligations owed to Pakistan' and to establish whether India could lawfully 'deplete or bring the reservoir level of a run-of-river Plant below Dead Storage Level'.[135] The Court of Arbitration did not consider the request inordinate, and went on to establish the contours of permissible action for India under the treaty – all before any part of India's planned works was implemented.[136] In a follow-up dispute,

131 *Lac Lanoux, France* v. *Spain*, (1957) 12 RIAA 281, 316 ('ne fait qu'user d'un droit').

132 *Questions of Interpretation and Application of the 1971 Montreal Convention Arising from the Aerial Incident at Lockerbie, Libya* v. *United Kingdom*, Preliminary Objections, [1998] ICJ Reports 9, p. 124; *Lockerbie (Libya* v. *USA)*, [1998] ICJ Reports 115, p. 19.

133 *Lockerbie (Libya* v. *UK)*, p. 19; *Lockerbie (Libya* v. *USA)*, p. 124.

134 *Great Belt (Provisional Measures), Finland* v. *Denmark*, Judgment, [1991] ICJ Reports 12, p. 14. The parties subsequently settled the dispute.

135 *Award in the Arbitration regarding the Indus Waters Kishenganga between Pakistan and India, Pakistan* v. *India*, (2013) 31 RIAA 1, 12.

136 The Tribunal found that India was permitted to 'divert water from the Kishenganga/Neelum River for power generation'. India was however 'under an obligation to construct and operate the Kishenganga Hydro-Electric Plant in such a way as to maintain a minimum flow of water in the Kishenganga/Neelum River'. The Tribunal also held that 'the Treaty does not permit reduction below Dead Storage Level of the water level in the reservoirs of Run-of-River Plants on the Western Rivers' (Ibid., 244). In its Final Award, the Tribunal determined the daily minimum flow of water that India's power plant was required to release into the river going to Pakistan, a flow below which India would be obliged to release '100 percent of the daily average flow' (Ibid., 358).

Pakistan challenged the consistency with the Treaty of 'India's proposed design' for various hydro-electric plants in the area.[137]

Pursuant to this jurisprudence, the scope for justiciability extends beyond measures already producing unlawful effects and encompasses sufficiently crystallised measures at the planned or concretely proposed stage. If a 'decision' or 'behaviour' can be discerned,[138] conduct that is still at the stage of a plan or proposal, and thus has not yet produced effects or given rise to injury, may be justiciable. The key questions concern the existence of a discernible dispute regarding the lawfulness of the identified measures and, consequently, legal interest in, and concrete effects of, adjudication.

5.3.3 *Ex Ante Adjudication of Proposed Measures: Is There a Dispute?*

Once it is accepted that ICs may pronounce on proposed measures, a second challenge may be raised to the admissibility of requests for Permissible Responses. This challenge is that, unless the other party expressly objects to the permissibility of the proposed response, there is no dispute to be adjudicated upon. This objection finds its roots in the ICJ's finding, in *Northern Cameroons*, that its judicial function requires 'an actual controversy':

> The function of the Court is to state the law, but it may pronounce judgment only in connection with concrete cases where there exists at the time of the adjudication an actual controversy involving a conflict of legal interests between the parties. The Court's judgment must have some practical consequence in the sense that it can affect existing legal rights or obligations of the parties, thus removing uncertainty from their legal relations. No judgment on the merits in this case could satisfy these essentials of the judicial function.[139]

Citing this precedent, the ICJ stated in *Frontier Dispute* that merely recording agreements between the parties 'is not compatible with its

[137] *Indus Waters Treaty Arbitration, Pakistan* v. *India*, (2023) PCA Case No. 2023-01, Award on the Competence of the Court, paras 9, 318(H).

[138] *PLO Headquarters Advisory Opinion*, p. 30.

[139] *Northern Cameroons*, [1963] ICJ Reports 15, p. 33–34. See also Ibid., p. 33 ('If the Court were to proceed and were to hold that the Applicant's contentions were all sound on the merits, it would still be impossible for the Court to render a judgment capable of effective application').

judicial function'.[140] In *Use of the Waters of the Silala*, the ICJ found that the views of the parties converged on the legal issues they put before it. The Court refused to adjudicate, reasoning that 'the parties have come to agree in substance regarding a claim or a counter-claim'. In these instances, the ICJ concluded that 'such a claim or counterclaim has become without object', so that 'there is no call for a declaratory judgment'.[141]

Another relevant parallel may be found in the *Ecuador* v. *United States* inter-state arbitration under their Bilateral Investment Treaty (BIT). Faced with the United States' refusal to disavow the findings of the investor-state Arbitral Tribunal in *Chevron* v. *Ecuador*, Ecuador sought through state-to-state arbitration an authoritative interpretation of the BIT 'in order to protect itself from liability to US investors on the basis of what [Ecuador] claims to be an erroneous construction of that provision'.[142] The state-to-state Arbitral Tribunal held that it could not issue a ruling on Ecuador's interpretation unless 'the Respondent had put forward an opinion that differed from that of Ecuador on the proper interpretation', had 'expressed approval for the *Chevron* award's conclusions', or had 'taken issue with Ecuador's actual or proposed implementation of its obligations'.[143]

Absent any express opposition from the United States, the Arbitral Tribunal concluded that it could not see 'practical consequences for both parties in the resolution of the matter of interpretation placed before the tribunal'.[144] This contradicts earlier jurisprudence, such as the PCIJ's statement that it may issue 'interpretations unconnected with concrete cases of application'.[145] The requirement of 'practical consequences' is nonetheless in line with the ICJ's conditioning of admissibility on a

140 *Frontier Dispute, Burkina Faso/Niger*, Judgment, [2013] ICJ Reports 44, p. 72.

141 *Dispute over the Status and Use of the Waters of the Silala, Chile* v. *Bolivia*, Judgment, [2022] ICJ Reports 614, 636.

142 *Ecuador* v. *United States*, (2012) PCA Case No. 2012-05, Award, para. 199 (referring to *Chevron Corporation and Texaco Petroleum Company* v. *The Republic of Ecuador*, PCA Case No. 2009-23, Partial Award).

143 *Ecuador* v. *United States*, PCA Case No. 2012-05, para. 207.

144 Ibid., para. 203. See also Ibid., para. 196.

145 *Certain German Interests in Polish Upper Silesia (Merits), Germany* v. *Poland*, Judgment, (1926) PCIJ Ser. A No. 7, p. 18. See Ibid., p. 18–19: 'There seems to be no reason why States should not be able to ask the Court to give an abstract interpretation of a treaty; rather would it appear that this is one of the most important functions which it can fulfil'.

request's 'connection with concrete cases'.[146] The risk involved in requesting a determination of Permissible Responses is that the alleged wrongdoer might remain silent on the matter (as the United States did in *Ecuador* v. *United States*) and refuse to engage on the substance, stating that, since no dispute exists, the request is inadmissible.

In *South West Africa*, the ICJ stated that, to characterise a dispute, 'it must be shown that the claim of one party is positively opposed by the other'.[147] The Court has subsequently stated that positive opposition does not require express disagreement: 'the existence of a dispute may be inferred from the failure of a State to respond to a claim in circumstances where a response is called for'.[148] In *Cameroon* v. *Nigeria*, in the absence of an 'explicit challenge' by Nigeria to the boundary proposed by Cameroon, the ICJ inferred the existence of a dispute from Nigeria's conduct.[149] The Court noted:

> a disagreement on a point of law or fact, a conflict of legal views or interests, or the positive opposition of the claim of one party by the other need not necessarily be stated *expressis verbis*. In the determination of the existence of a dispute, as in other matters, the position or the attitude of a party can be established by inference, whatever the professed view of that party.[150]

This issue was also examined in the *PLO Headquarters* Advisory Opinion. The ICJ noted that 'the United States had not expressly contradicted the interpretation of the Headquarters Agreement expressed by the UN Secretary-General and endorsed by the General Assembly. At the same time, the Court stated, 'the United States has nevertheless taken measures against the PLO Mission to the United Nations'.[151] The ICJ reasoned:

[146] See note 134 and accompanying text. See also the jurisprudence cited by the ICJ in *Frontier Dispute* [2013] ICJ Reports 44, p. 72.

[147] *South West Africa, Liberia* v. *South Africa*, Preliminary Objections, [1962] ICJ Reports 319, p. 328.

[148] *Case concerning the Application of the International Convention on the Elimination of All Forms of Racial Discrimination, Georgia* v. *Russia*, Preliminary Objections, [2011] ICJ Reports 70, p. 84.

[149] *Land and Maritime Boundary between Cameroon and Nigeria, Nigeria* v. *Cameroon*, Preliminary Objections, [1998] ICJ Reports 275. The Court noted that 'incidents and incursions reported by Cameroon do not establish by themselves the existence of a dispute concerning all of the boundary between Cameroon and Nigeria' (Ibid., p. 315), but 'there can be no doubt about the existence of disputes with respect to [the] Darak [peninsula] and adjacent islands' (Ibid., p. 314).

[150] Ibid., p. 315.

[151] *The Obligation to Arbitrate under Section 21 of the United Nations Headquarters Agreement*, [1988] ICJ Reports 12, p. 28.

> where one party to a treaty protests against the behaviour or a decision of another party, and claims that such behaviour or decision constitutes a breach of the treaty, the mere fact that the party accused does not advance any argument to justify its conduct under international law does not prevent the opposing attitudes of the parties from giving rise to a dispute concerning the interpretation or application of the treaty.[152]

To ensure that a ruling will produce effects on the legal relations of the parties, a claimant requesting Permissible Responses must be able to establish that there is a dispute regarding the permissibility of the proposed measures. A dispute regarding Permissible Responses may be demonstrated if the respondent formally opposes the entitlement of the claimant to adopt specific measures. This may be facilitated if there is a prior notification of proposed measures, as is required for countermeasures[153] as well as for the termination or suspension of a treaty, or parts thereof, as a response to a breach.[154] Measures adopted in self-defence do not need to be notified previously (which might defeat their purpose), but, under the UN Charter, they 'shall be immediately reported to the Security Council'.[155]

Establishing a dispute may be an issue where a respondent does not verbally oppose an interpretation or entitlement asserted by the claimant. The Arbitral Tribunal in *Ecuador* v. *United States* stated that 'the inference of "positive opposition" is warranted only when all other reasonable interpretations of the respondent's conduct and surrounding facts can be excluded'.[156] If a state adopts or notifies the future adoption of measures that, in its view, constitute permissible responses, and the target state avowedly adopts measures of response of its own, a request for a Declaration of Breach is admissible. This request can then be combined with a request for a judicial declaration

[152] Ibid. The Court concluded: 'the United States has taken a number of measures against the PLO Observer Mission to the United Nations in New York. The Secretary-General regarded these as contrary to the Headquarters Agreement. Without expressly disputing that point, the United States stated that the measures in question were taken "irrespective of any obligations the United States may have under the Agreement". Such conduct cannot be reconciled with the position of the Secretary-General. There thus exists a dispute between the United Nations and the United States concerning the application of the Headquarters Agreement' (Ibid., p. 32).

[153] ARSIWA, Article 52(1)(b).

[154] VCLT, Articles 60, 65(1), 67(1).

[155] UN Charter, Article 51.

[156] *Ecuador* v. *United States*, PCA Case No. 2012-05, para. 223.

that the originally adopted measures are Permissible Responses to an original violation.[157]

A claimant's request for an *ex ante* judicial declaration of the permissibility of a certain response removes the element of legal uncertainty from its adoption. As Bruno Simma noted, a key difficulty with international law's horizontal sanctioning mechanisms is leaving the enforcement of international commitments 'to the mercy of individual auto-determination and self-enforcement'.[158] Under legal uncertainty, the most powerful states are able to adopt overwhelming measures of response, causing disproportionate harm to less powerful states, acting on the basis of their entitlement to interpret the applicable law and the factual situation. Conversely, a less powerful state's attempts to affirm its rights in response to unlawful conduct may be met with severe reaction, based on an asserted interpretative divergence and a challenge to the smaller state's entitlement to adopt measures of response.

Whether or not major power differentials are involved, a judicial statement that a claimant is entitled to adopt certain measures in response to a breach removes uncertainty regarding the lawfulness of a response. It assures the responding state, and the international community more broadly, of the lawfulness of its actions, and delegitimises a counter-response by the targeted state. Although, as in other cases, a judicial pronouncement does not eclipse the power-political context, these effects give the remedy of Permissible Responses effective applicability, as a statement 'capable of effective application'[159] with 'practical consequences for both parties'.[160]

5.3.4 Adjudication of Obligatory Responses

ICs have occasionally been asked to determine not that responses are permissible but that they are obligatory, sometimes for actors other than the requesting party. The ICJ has expressed views on the matter in the two advisory opinions relating to Israel and Palestine. In the *Wall*

[157] This remains subject to the adjudicator having jurisdiction to pronounce on the requested responses. See on this Section 5.3.5.

[158] Bruno Simma, 'From Bilateralism to Community Interests' (1994) 250 *Recueil des Cours* 217, 331.

[159] *Northern Cameroons*, [1963] ICJ Reports 15, p. 33.

[160] *Ecuador* v. *United States*, PCA Case No. 2012-05, para. 203.

Opinion, the ICJ found that, in certain cases, all states are obliged to respond to unlawful conduct. Having concluded that the construction of a wall in occupied Palestinian territory involved 'breaches by Israel of various of its obligations', the Court stated that owing to the Fourth Geneva Convention 'all States are under an obligation not to recognize the illegal situation resulting from the construction of the wall' and 'not to render aid or assistance in maintaining the situation created by such construction'.[161]

The ICJ reaffirmed substantially the same position in the *Occupied Palestinian Territory* Opinion.[162] Additionally, in this opinion the Court sought to mobilise Layer 4 and Layer [5] sanctions, finding that 'international organizations, including the United Nations, are under an obligation not to recognize as legal the situation arising from the unlawful presence of the State of Israel in the Occupied Palestinian Territory', while specifying that 'it is for the General Assembly and the Security Council to consider what further action is required to put an end to the illegal presence of Israel, taking into account the present Advisory Opinion'.[163]

The issue is more challenging in contentious cases. In *Bosnian Genocide* and *Genocide in the Gaza Strip*, applicants requested the ICJ to determine rights and obligations for third states. In *Bosnian Genocide*, Bosnia and Herzegovina asked for declarations that the 'all Contracting Parties to the Genocide Convention' were obliged to prevent the commission of specified acts of genocide and the 'partition and dismemberment' of Bosnia and Herzegovina, and were required to 'have the ability to provide military weapons, equipment, supplies and armed forces (soldiers, sailors, airpeople) to the Government of Bosnia and Herzegovina at its request'. It also requested a declaration that 'United Nations Peace-keeping Forces in Bosnia and Herzegovina (i.e., UNPROFOR) must do all in their power to ensure the flow of

161 *Legal Consequences of the Construction of a Wall in the Occupied Palestinian Territory*, Advisory Opinion, [2004] ICJ Reports 136, p. 194, 200. See also *Legal Consequences for States of the Continued Presence of South Africa in Namibia (South West Africa) notwithstanding Security Council Resolution 276 (1970)*, Advisory Opinion, [1971] ICJ Reports 16, p. 47; *Legality of the threat or Use of Nuclear Weapons*, Advisory Opinion, [1996] ICJ Reports 226, p. 263; Doing so in a contentious context may be more difficult.

162 *Legal Consequences Arising from the Policies and Practices of Israel in the Occupied Palestinian Territory, including East Jerusalem*, Advisory Opinion of 19 July 2024, para. 285(7)–(8).

163 Ibid., paras. 281, 285(8)–(9).

humanitarian relief supplies to the Bosnian People through the Bosnian city of Tuzla'.[164] The ICJ replied that the *inter partes* nature of its judgments prevented it from accepting these requests:

> the Court may ... indicate provisional measures to be taken by the parties, but not by third States or other entities who would not be bound by the eventual judgment to recognize and respect those rights [or] indicate by way of 'clarification' that those States or entities should take, or refrain from, specific action in relation to the acts of genocide which the Applicant alleges are being committed in Bosnia-Herzegovina[.][165]

The ICJ quoted this paragraph in *Genocide in the Gaza Strip*, in response to South Africa's request for a declaration that '[a]ll Parties to the Convention on the Prevention and Punishment of the Crime of Genocide must ... refrain from any action, and in particular any armed action or support thereof, which might prejudice the right of the Palestinians in Gaza to be protected from acts of genocide and related prohibited acts'.[166] The Court responded that it could not issue 'measures requested by South Africa addressed to States or entities not parties to the present proceedings'.[167]

The Economic Community of West African States (ECOWAS) Community Court of Justice (ECCJ) has refused to require the adoption of institutional sanctions as well as of authorised sanctions in response to non-compliance with its rulings. In *Karim Meissa Wade* v. *Senegal*, the ECCJ rejected a request that it order the '[s]uspension of Senegal from participation in all ECOWAS activities' due to Senegal's non-compliance with an earlier ruling.[168] In *Chude Mba* v. *Ghana*, the plaintiff brought a compliance dispute against all ECOWAS member states, as well as the President of the ECOWAS Commission and the Chair of the Authority of Heads of State and Government. Besides requesting compensation from

[164] *Application of the Convention on the Prevention and Punishment of the Crime of Genocide (Bosnia and Herzegovina* v. *Yugoslavia (Serbia and Montenegro))*, Provisional Measures, Order of 13 September 1993, [1993] ICJ Reports, p. 324, 332–333.

[165] Ibid., p. 344.

[166] See *Application of the Convention on the Prevention and Punishment of the Crime of Genocide in the Gaza Strip (South Africa* v. *Israel)*, Order of 28 March 2024 (Provisional Measures), para. 11(3).

[167] Ibid., para. 44.

[168] Application No. ECW/CCJ/APP/09/13, *Karim Meissa Wade* v. *Republic of Senegal*, Judgment, 19 July 2013 (ECW/CCJ/JUD/19/13), para. 54. The request was dismissed on grounds that individuals lack *locus standi* to bring before the ECCJ claims of non-compliance with ECCJ judgments.

Ghana, the plaintiff requested the ECCJ to declare an obligation for other ECOWAS member states 'to take all reasonable steps to compel [Ghana] to comply with the decision and orders of this Honourable Court made in favour of the Applicant' and 'to enforce the decision and orders of this Honourable Court made in his favour against any of [Ghana's] assets that may be found within any of their territories without any regard to [Ghana's] putative sovereign immunity'. The plaintiff requested 'an order mandating [the President and the Chair] to impose the sanctions prescribed in Article 77 of the ECOWAS Revised Treaty on [Ghana] if it continues in its refusal, failure and/or neglect to comply with the decision and orders of this Honourable Court made against it'.[169] The ECCJ noted that the ECOWAS Revised Treaty entrusted the Authority of Heads of State and Government (ECOWAS' highest decision-making body) with bringing non-compliance claims to the Court and applying sanctions against wrongdoing states, and concluded that the Court 'has no jurisdiction to enforce its own decisions as this action is seeking to do, hence this action will not be entertained by the court'.[170]

By contrast, the Andean Court of Justice (ACJ), which is empowered to authorise suspension of trade benefits in case of state non-compliance with rulings,[171] has gone beyond authorising tariff retaliation vis-à-vis non-complying members and has sought to ensure their application. In 2003, the ACJ ruled that, in light of Venezuela's non-compliance with a ruling, other member states were not merely *permitted* to retaliate; they were under an 'obligation to impose the sanctions authorised by this Court, for the correct and opportune application of the community norms'.[172] In 2018, following thirteen years of Colombia's non-compliance with one of its judgments, the ACJ decided to 'increase the authorised sanction with the aim of ensuring compliance with the Judgment'.[173] Besides authorising other Andean Community member

[169] ECCJ, Application No. ECW/CCJ/APP/22/16, *Chude Mba* v. *Republic of Ghana and Others*, Judgment, 12 March 2019 (ECW/CCJ/JUD/30/18), p. 5–6.

[170] Ibid., p. 18.

[171] Treaty Creating the Court of Justice of the Andean Community, 10 March 1996, Article 27.

[172] ACJ, *Case No. 13-AI-2002 (Non-compliance with Judgment) (Summary Procedure)*, Order, 26 February 2003, p. 1 ('obligación de imponer las sanciones autorizadas por este Tribunal, para la correcta y oportuna aplicación de la normativa comunitaria').

[173] ACJ, *Case No. 118-AI-2003 (Non-compliance with Judgment of 14 April 2005) (Second Summary Procedure)*, Order, 28 June 2018, p. 4 ('modificar la sanción autorizada con la finalidad de lograr el cumplimiento de la Sentencia').

states to impose additional tariffs of 10 per cent on Colombian goods, the ACJ instructed the members to inform the Court and the Andean Secretariat of the measures they would adopt 'so as to ensure application of the authorised sanctions'.[174] At least in the ACJ's view, therefore, ICs entrusted with safeguarding a certain legal framework may go beyond authorising measures of response. They may determine that, in certain cases, adopting such measures of response under that legal framework (inter-state and institutional) becomes obligatory for other actors.

5.4 The Scope of Permissible Responses: Intra-Regime and Cross-Regime Responses

Permissible Responses can be requested as an alternative remedy in case of non-compliance with Consequential Duties, or as an additional, self-standing remedy. Permissible Responses can also be requested following an earlier judicial Declaration of Breach, when the violation persists, or in case of avowed non-compliance with the obligations of cessation and reparation. In the simplest scenario, the proposed response affects obligations of the same type, or with the same source, affected by the breach.[175] Adjudication becomes more complex for requested Permissible Responses that involve different sources of obligation, in particular if the adjudicating IC lacks primary jurisdiction over either the response or the obligation violated.

5.4.1 Intra-Regime Permissible Responses

Prospective international judicial determinations that a response is authorised are rare. As regards self-defence, adjudicators have sometimes determined retrospectively that armed attacks warranted armed action in self-defence.[176] Perhaps understandably, none have ever prospectively

[174] Ibid., p. 6 ('para que las sanciones autorizadas se hagan efectivas por los países membros').

[175] See *Air Service Agreement of 27 March 1946*, (1978) 18 RIAA 417, para. 82 ('in the present case, both the alleged violation and the counter-measure directly affect the operation of air services provided for in the Agreement and the Exchange of Notes of 5 April 1960'). See Lorand Bartels, 'Jurisdiction and Applicable Law Clauses: Where Does a Tribunal Find the Principal Norms Applicable to the Case before It?', in Tomer Broude and Yuval Shany, *Multi-Sourced Equivalent Norms in International Law* (Oxford: Hart Publishing, 2011), 115, 117.

[176] *Armed Activities in Congo*, [2005] ICJ Reports 168, p. 269; Eritrea-Ethiopia Claims Commission, *Award – Jus Ad Bellum*, p. 467.

asserted that a future use of force would be permissible as a response to a specific act or conduct. At most, in *the Nuclear Weapons* Advisory Opinion, the ICJ stated that it '[could not] reach a definitive conclusion as to the legality or illegality of the use of nuclear weapons by a State in an extreme circumstance of self-defence, in which its very survival would be at stake'.[177]

Similarly, though the ICJ considered a number of claims by states that they had suspended or terminated a treaty in response to its breach, only once did it find a lawful instance of such termination, and in a non-contentious setting – the *Namibia* Advisory Opinion.[178] As regards contentious cases, in the *Tacna-Arica* arbitration, Peru requested the Arbitrator to declare that Chile's violations of their peace treaty 'discharged Peru from her obligations' under the treaty, which required the organisation of a plebiscite to determine sovereignty over Tacna and Arica.[179] The Arbitrator, though not awarding the requested remedy, foresaw the termination of this 'plebiscitary obligation' if Chile were to 'frustrate the purpose of the agreement'.[180] In 1926, the Commission established to organise the foreseen plebiscite wrote to the Arbitrator – US President Calvin Coolidge – stating that Chile 'ha[d] frustrated the efforts of the Commission' and that 'a free and fair plebiscite, as required by the Award, [wa]s impracticable of accomplishment'.[181] Rather than organising a plebiscite, Chile and Peru divided between them the disputed area.

Other adjudicators have recognised the right to adopt countermeasures in case of persistent or subsequent breach. In *Lac Lanoux*, the arbitrator signalled that, if France were to reduce the flow of river water to Spain to levels that would cause a breach of the Treaty of Bayonne, France would 'expose itself, throughout the border, to fearsome reprisals'.[182] In *Military and Paramilitary Activities*, the ICJ noted that Nicaragua's conduct, if 'established and imputable to that State, could only have justified proportionate counter-measures on the part of the

[177] *Legality of the Threat or Use of Nuclear Weapons*, Advisory Opinion, [1996] ICJ Reports 226, p. 263.

[178] See note 79 and accompanying text.

[179] *Tacna-Arica Question*, (1925) 2 UNRIAA 921, 929.

[180] Ibid., 935, 937.

[181] *Papers Relating to the Foreign Relations of the United States 1926*, (Washington: Government Printing Office, 1941), vol. I, p. 459.

[182] *Lac Lanoux*, (1957) 12 RIAA 281, 305 ('*elle s'exposerait, sur toute la frontière, à des redoutables représailles*').

State which had been the victim of these acts'.[183] Like the statement by the Arbitrator in *Tacna-Arica*, these statements were not worded as judicial remedies. They nonetheless provided the actors involved in implementing the ruling with an authoritative determination that, if the condition provided for were to take place, a specific response would become permissible.

5.4.2 *Cross-Regime Responses and Incidental Jurisdiction*

If a dispute can be established regarding the permissibility of responses and an adjudicator accepts the admissibility of a request for Permissible Responses, there is still the issue of which measures an adjudicator is empowered to consider permissible. The jurisdiction of an IC is usually limited both by the scope of the dispute brought to it and by the IC's jurisdiction *ratione materiae*.[184] At the same time, in order to reach conclusions regarding the legal norms over which it is given jurisdiction, an IC may be required to apply norms beyond the scope of this principal jurisdiction.

As the PCIJ before it, the ICJ's jurisdiction to assess violations is often limited, in each particular case, to a specific treaty, set of rules or legal regime, delimitated by a *compromis* or jurisdictional clause in a treaty. In *Genocide (Bosnia* v. *Serbia)*, the ICJ noted that '[t]he jurisdiction of the Court in this case is based solely on Article IX of the [Genocide] Convention ... It has no power to rule on alleged breaches of other obligations under international law, not amounting to genocide, particularly those protecting human rights in armed conflict'.[185] In other cases, a broad jurisdictional clause in a treaty or *compromis* may allow the Court 'to decide on the basis of the [specific treaty] and rules and principles of general international law, as well as such other treaties as the Court may find applicable'.[186]

183 *Military Activities in Nicaragua*, [1986] ICJ Reports 14, p. 127.

184 See the discussion in *Allegations of Genocide (Ukraine* v. *Russian Federation)*, [2024], paras. 131–148.

185 *Application of the Convention on the Prevention and Punishment of the Crime of Genocide, Bosnia and Herzegovina* v. *Serbia and Montenegro*, Judgment, [2007] ICJ Reports 43, 104.

186 *Gabčíkovo-Nagymaros Project*, [1997] ICJ Reports 7, p. 11 (referring to the *compromis*). Judgments based on broad jurisdictional clauses in treaties include *Jurisdictional Immunities of the State, Germany* v. *Italy: Greece intervening*, Judgment, [2012] ICJ Reports 99, p. 118; *Territorial and Maritime Dispute (Nicaragua* v. *Colombia)*, Preliminary Objections, [2007] ICJ Reports 832, p. 853.

Even when its jurisdiction is limited, the ICJ has often applied a variety of legal sources, relying on its mandate, under Article 38(1) of the Statute, to 'decide in accordance with international law such disputes as are submitted to it'.[187] The sources the Court applies include not only general international law but also other international agreements. In *Certain German Interests*, the PCIJ stated that 'the interpretation of other international agreements is indisputably within the competence of the Court if such interpretation must be regarded as incidental to a decision on a point in regard to which it has jurisdiction'.[188]

This statement reveals a broader point regarding international adjudication. As Lorand Bartels noted, in most disputes, ICs have limited 'principal jurisdiction', in that claims of violation are restricted to a specific treaty or legal regime; but, in their reasoning towards conclusions regarding these claims, ICs may be able to consider and apply, incidentally, norms besides those over which they have principal jurisdiction. Provided that an adjudicator is empowered to *apply* a certain norm, it may make incidental findings regarding these norms, to the extent 'necessary for it to be able to make principal determinations'.[189] As discussed in Section 5.4.3, an IC's applicable law can be broader than the law over which it has jurisdiction to make principal determinations.

The question of jurisdiction *ratione materiae* over requests for Permissible Responses emerges chiefly with respect to proposed countermeasures. The termination or suspension of a treaty as a response to its material breach almost by definition requires a ruling on a treaty over which the IC has jurisdiction; self-defence will usually be invoked in disputes in which the IC has already determined that it can assess violations of obligations regarding the use of force. By contrast, countermeasures have a broad scope *ratione materiae*. ARSIWA Article 40 provides that the entitlement to take countermeasures does not affect the prohibition on the use of force, the protection of fundamental rights, the

[187] Statute of the International Court of Justice, San Francisco, 24 October 1945, in force 18 April 1946, XV UNCIO 355 ('ICJ Statute'), Article 38(1). See Alain Pellet and Daniel Müller, 'Article 38', in Andreas Zimmermann, Christian J. Tams, Karin Oellers-Frahm, and Christian Tomuschat (eds.), *The Statute of the International Court of Justice: A Commentary*, 3rd edn (Oxford: Oxford University Press, 2019), 924. Parties may of course restrict the jurisdiction of the Court, but not prevent it from applying Article 38.

[188] *Certain German Interests*, (1926) PCIJ Ser. A No. 7, p. 18.

[189] Bartels, 'Jurisdiction and Applicable Law Clauses', 115, 117.

humanitarian prohibition of reprisals, and other *jus cogens* norms.[190] The ARSIWA Commentary states that '[c]ountermeasures are more likely to satisfy the requirements of necessity and proportionality if they are taken in relation to the same or a closely related obligation [to the one violated]' but finds 'no requirement that States taking countermeasures should be limited to suspension of performance of the same or a closely related obligation'.[191]

Different adjudicators are likely to be in different positions in this regard. The most restrictive approach is to determine that an IC is limited to establishing Permissible Responses within the treaty or legal regime over which it has principal jurisdiction. A more expansive approach allows the IC to determine Permissible Responses involving any norm over which it has jurisdiction, including incidental jurisdiction. The difference between these approaches may be major for the ICJ, whose principal jurisdiction is often restricted to interpreting and applying a specific treaty, while its constitutive instrument empowers it to apply a variety of legal norms and 'decide in accordance with international law'.[192]

In *Allegations of Genocide*, the ICJ seems to have favoured the restrictive approach. The Court accepted to assess Ukraine's request for a declaration that Ukraine had not violated the Genocide Convention but did not find that it was empowered to assess the lawfulness of Russia's measures allegedly motivated by the asserted genocide. The ICJ reasoned that, even if Russia had taken measures under the pretext that Ukraine had committed genocide, 'this would not in itself constitute a violation of obligations under … the Convention'.[193] The measures adopted by Russia in response to a false allegation of genocide might violate 'the

[190] ARSIWA, Article 40. See ICJ, *Application of the Convention on the Prevention and Punishment of the Crime of Genocide, Bosnia and Herzegovina* v. *Serbia and Montenegro*, Counter-Claims, [1997] ICJ Reports 243, 258 (due to 'the *erga omnes* character of the obligations flowing from the Genocide Convention … in no case could one breach of the Convention serve as an excuse for another').

[191] ARSIWA Commentary, p. 129 (commentary to Article 26).

[192] ICJ Statute, Article 38(1).

[193] *Allegations of Genocide (Ukraine* v. *Russian Federation)*, [2024] Preliminary Objections, para. 143. The Court also stated: 'It is certainly not consistent with the principle of good faith to invoke a treaty abusively, by claiming that there is a specific situation falling within its scope when it is clearly not the case, or by deliberately interpreting the treaty incorrectly for the sole purpose of justifying a given action. However, while such an abusive invocation will result in the dismissal of the arguments based thereon, it does not follow that, by itself, it constitutes a breach of the treaty' (Ibid.).

relevant rules of international law applicable to the recognition of States and the use of force', but '[t]hese matters are not governed by the Genocide Convention and the Court does not have jurisdiction to entertain them in the present case'.[194]

The same ICJ seems to have adopted a more expansive approach to jurisdiction over countermeasures in its Judgments on appeal in *ICAO Council (International Air Services Transit Agreement (IASTA)/Convention on International Civil Aviation (CICA)).*[195] The ICJ upheld the exercise, by the Council of the International Civil Aviation Organization (ICAO Council), of jurisdiction over the respondent's claims, under IASTA and CICA, even though the applicants asserted that their alleged breaches were countermeasures for violations of norms outside these treaties. The ICJ recalled the PCIJ's statement, in *Certain German Interests*, that its jurisdiction extends to the interpretation of norms 'if such interpretation must be regarded as incidental to a decision on a point in regard to which it has jurisdiction'.[196] Similarly, the ICJ concluded that the ICAO Council was empowered to 'consider issues falling outside the scope of [IASTA/CICA] solely in order to settle a disagreement relating to the interpretation or application of [IASTA/CICA]'. A request involving such an incidental determination 'would not render the application submitting that disagreement to it inadmissible'.[197]

Rather than an inconsistency, what this indicates is that the reasoning is unidirectional. What *ICAO Council (IASTA/CICA)* reaffirms is that an international adjudicator may acquire incidental jurisdiction to apply a certain rule, if applying such rule is necessary in order to adjudicate a principal claim. In *Allegations of Genocide*, Ukraine unsuccessfully sought to compound its principal claim (concerning the Genocide Convention) with an additional claim concerning Russia's forceful measures, allegedly adopted in response to Ukraine's alleged violation.

[194] Ibid., para. 146.

[195] *Appeal relating to the Jurisdiction of the ICAO Council under Article II, Section 2, of the 1944 International Air Services Transit Agreement (Bahrain, Egypt and United Arab Emirates* v. *Qatar),* Judgment, [2020] ICJ Reports 172, p. 184 ('ICAO Council IASTA'); *Appeal relating to the Jurisdiction of the ICAO Council under Article 84 of the Convention on International Civil Aviation (Bahrain, Egypt, Saudi Arabia and United Arab Emirates* v. *Qatar),* Judgment, [2020] ICJ Reports 81, p. 9 ('ICAO Council CICA').

[196] *Certain German Interests,* (1926) PCIJ Ser. A No 7, p. 18.

[197] ICAO Council IASTA, [2020] ICJ Reports 172, p. 196; ICAO Council CICA, [2020] ICJ Reports 81, p. 104–105.

Addressing the additional claim was not necessary for the ICJ to resolve the dispute concerning the Genocide Convention.

Applying this reasoning to Permissible Responses leads to significant limitations over the countermeasures that an IC may be empowered to determine are permissible. If a state claims that a measure breaches a treaty and an IC has jurisdiction over this treaty, this IC will have incidental jurisdiction to assess a respondent's allegation that its non-performance is a countermeasure, adopted in response to a violation affecting a different legal regime. By contrast, a state may not compound a claim of violation of one legal regime (over which an IC has jurisdiction) with a request for a judicial declaration that non-compliance with the rules of a different legal regime, which the IC may only apply incidentally, is a permissible response. The determination regarding the permissibility of this response will no longer be incidental but additional, involving an impermissible extension of jurisdiction.

The outcome may be more nuanced than one might expect. An IC that refuses to issue a remedy of Permissible Responses on grounds of a lack of incidental jurisdiction *ratione materiae* is not technically asserting that the underlying or proposed permissible responses are impermissible. Even if the IC cannot adjudicate on the permissibility of the specific responses proposed, a claimant faced with a continuing breach may be entitled to pursue its rights through measures of response. And, both in its Declaration of Breach and in its rejection of the remedy of Permissible Responses, it is possible for an IC to employ wording that suggests this permissibility without adjudicating on it.

5.4.3 *Jurisdiction over Cross-Regime Permissible Responses: Principal and Incidental Jurisdiction*

Arbitrators whose jurisdiction arises from agreements without an applicable law clause, such as those in *Cysne*, *Naulilaa*, *Tacna-Arica*, and *Air Service Agreement*, can generally rely on their entitlement to address legal relations between the parties broadly, at least insofar as these relations arise under general international law.[198] This empowers adjudicators

[198] See on this *Dispute concerning Access to Information under Article 9 of the OSPAR Convention, Ireland* v. *United Kingdom*, (2003) 23 RIAA 59, para. 84: 'An international tribunal, such as this Tribunal, will also apply customary international law and general principles unless and to the extent that the Parties have created a *lex specialis*'; *Norwegian Shipowners, Norway* v. *United States of America*, (1922) 1 RIAA 307, 331: 'If no special principles are prescribed to the arbitrator, he must doubtless decide in the

with broad applicable law to adjudicate on permissible responses, at least *ex post* and faced with a defence that an alleged violation is justifiable as a permissible response to a prior breach. As the ICJ explained in *Genocide Convention (Bosnia* v. *Serbia)*:

> In order to determine whether the Respondent breached its obligation under the Convention . . . and, if a breach was committed, to determine its legal consequences, the Court will have recourse not only to the [Genocide] Convention itself, but also to the rules of general international law on treaty interpretation and on responsibility of States for internationally wrongful acts.[199]

A more complex position is that of specialised adjudicators, empowered to interpret and apply a specific treaty or legal framework. In these cases, these adjudicators' constitutive instruments, as well as the instrument providing them with jurisdiction, may limit the law they are empowered to apply.

The limitations on the law an IC may apply may be different from its jurisdiction. UNCLOS, for example, establishes that courts or tribunals adjudicating under its dispute settlement chapter have 'jurisdiction over any dispute concerning the interpretation or application of this Convention'.[200] Its applicable law clause, Article 293(1), is broader than this, stating that adjudicators deriving their jurisdiction from UNCLOS may 'apply this Convention and other rules of international law not incompatible with this Convention'.[201]

On this basis, the International Tribunal for the Law of the Sea (ITLOS) and some Arbitral Tribunals have asserted a broad entitlement to rule on matters connected to the principal dispute. In *M/V 'Saiga' (No 2)*, ITLOS found that 'international law [was] applicable by virtue of article 293 of the Convention' and Guinea 'used excessive force contrary to international law'.[202] In *Guyana/Suriname*, the Arbitral Tribunal quoted this finding before ruling that Suriname had engaged in 'a threat

first place in accordance with international law to be applied from both sources of this science, not only from treaties, but also from customary law, and the practice of judges in other international courts'.

199 *Convention on the Prevention and Punishment of the Crime of Genocide*, [2007] ICJ Reports 43, p. 105.

200 United Nations Convention on the Law of the Sea, Montego Bay, 10 December 1982, in force 16 November 1994, 1833 UNTS 397, Article 288(1) ('UNCLOS').

201 UNCLOS, Article 293(1).

202 *M/V 'SAIGA' (No 2), Saint Vincent and the Grenadines* v. *Guinea*, ITLOS, (1998) 120 ILR 144, 197, 201.

of the use of force in contravention of the Convention, the UN Charter and general international law'.[203] In *'ARA Libertad'*, ITLOS found that the mere reference in UNCLOS Article 32 to the immunity of warships empowered it to issue provisional measures mandating Ghana to release a detained Argentinean warship.[204]

These statements have been criticised as extending beyond what is necessary to settle the UNCLOS claims.[205] Indeed, the approach of these UNCLOS adjudicators has been precisely the opposite of the cautious approach the ICJ adopted to the rules concerning the use of force in *Allegations of Genocide*. Given this jurisprudence, one may expect UNCLOS adjudicators to be more open than other adjudicators to ascertain the permissibility of measures taken to induce compliance with UNCLOS obligations or objectives, including measures not in principle governed by UNCLOS itself.

Even as regards UNCLOS, however, this view is not unanimous. The Arbitral Tribunal in *Mox Plant (UNCLOS)* found that the combination of the jurisdictional and applicable law clauses produces a 'cardinal distinction' between the rules it was empowered to enforce directly (those in UNCLOS) and those that it could apply incidentally (other rules of international law not incompatible with UNCLOS). As a result, to the extent that 'claims arise directly under legal instruments other than the Convention, such claims may be inadmissible'.[206] The *Eurotunnel* Arbitral Tribunal, quoting this statement, distinguished between 'the scope of the rights and obligations which an international tribunal has jurisdiction to enforce' and 'the law which it will have to apply in doing so',[207] meaning that a tribunal may be able to apply rules which it would not have jurisdiction to enforce.

[203] *Guyana* v. *Suriname*, Award, (2007) 30 RIAA 1, 126.

[204] *'ARA Libertad', Argentina* v. *Ghana*, Provisional Measures, ITLOS, (2012) ITLOS Case No. 20, 15, paras. 47, 66. Contrast this with the findings by the ICJ in *Immunities and Criminal Proceedings, Equatorial Guinea* v. *France*, Preliminary Objections, [2018] ICJ Reports 292, p. 321–323.

[205] Lorand Bartels, 'Jurisdiction and Applicable Law Clauses', 129 (finding that 'these tribunal decisions are wrong' because 'a tribunal is not able to apply, as principal norms for purposes of making a principal determination, norms not included among norms expressly set out in a jurisdiction clause').

[206] *MOX Plant (UNCLOS), Ireland* v. *United Kingdom*, (2003) PCA Order No. 3, Suspension of Proceedings on Jurisdiction and Merits and Request for Further Provisional Measures.

[207] Ibid. (quoting *Eurotunnel, France* v. *United Kingdom*, (2007) PCA, Partial Award, para. 152).

This same logic has been affirmed by the ICJ in relation to the ICAO Council, a political body tasked with the interpretation and application of, among other instruments, CICA and IASTA. These Conventions empower the ICAO Council to 'decide[]' on 'any disagreement between two or more contracting States relating to the interpretation or application of this Convention'.[208] The Council's decision can be appealed to the ICJ.[209] In the three instances in which an appeal was filed, the appellants argued that the Council lacked jurisdiction because the measures being challenged had been adopted as permissible responses to legal violations. They contended that, because the Council was entrusted solely with 'the interpretation or application' of the Convention, deciding on the lawfulness of these permissible responses was outside the jurisdiction of the Council.

In *ICAO Council (India* v. *Pakistan)*, the ICJ rejected India's claim that the ICAO Council lacked jurisdiction to examine a dispute submitted to it by Pakistan, due to India's asserted prior suspension or termination of the treaty between itself and Pakistan. India argued that 'the issue involved ... is one of the termination or suspension of the Treaties, not of their interpretation or application which alone the Council is competent to deal with under the relevant jurisdictional clauses'.[210] The ICJ noted that the argument was 'destructive of the whole object of adjudicability'.[211] The Court reasoned:

> India's allegation of a material breach of the Treaties by Pakistan, as justifying India in treating them as terminated or suspended, is inherently and by its very nature, one that must involve the examination of the Treaties in order to see whether, according to the definition of a material breach of treaty contained in Article 60 of the 1969 Vienna Convention on the Law of Treaties, there has been (paragraph 3 (b)) a violation by Pakistan of 'a provision essential to the accomplishment of the object or purpose of the Treaty'.[212]

The ICJ found that the ICAO Council was 'competent to entertain the Application, and Complaint laid before it by the Government of Pakistan'.[213] This included assessing India's claims that, owing to

208 Convention on International Civil Aviation, Article 84.
209 Ibid. (the text refers to the PCIJ).
210 *Appeal Relating to the Jurisdiction of the ICAO Council*, [1972] ICJ Reports 46, p. 62.
211 Ibid., p. 65.
212 Ibid., p. 67.
213 Ibid., p. 70.

Pakistan's prior breaches, India had lawfully adopted a permissible response and suspended or terminated the treaty between itself and Pakistan.

The ICJ subsequently applied the same reasoning to another category of alleged permissible responses: countermeasures. The appeals in *ICAO (CICA)* and *ICAO (IASTA)* were brought by various Arab states against Qatar, after the ICAO Council accepted to consider Qatar's challenges to the aviation restrictions the appellants imposed on Qatari companies.[214] These restrictions were imposed as part of the appellants' severing of diplomatic relations with Qatar. The appellants argued that 'the ICAO Council lacked jurisdiction . . . since the real issue in dispute between the Parties involved . . . whether the aviation restrictions could be characterized as lawful countermeasures under international law'.[215] Thus, they reasoned, 'to pronounce on the dispute would require the Council to rule on questions that fall outside its jurisdiction, specifically on the lawfulness of the countermeasures, including "certain airspace restrictions", adopted by the Appellants'.[216]

The ICJ stated that the ICAO Council did not cease to have jurisdiction over the dispute 'because the Appellants characterize their aviation restrictions imposed on Qatar-registered aircraft as lawful countermeasures'.[217] As previously in *ICAO Council (India* v. *Pakistan)*, the ICJ reasoned that the ICAO Council was entitled to consider the argument that the claim was inadmissible because the measure in question was a countermeasure. The Court stated:

> the integrity of the Council's dispute settlement function would not be affected if the Council examined issues outside matters of civil aviation for the exclusive purpose of deciding a dispute which falls within its jurisdiction under Article 84 of the Chicago Convention. Therefore, a possible need for the ICAO Council to consider issues falling outside the scope of the Chicago Convention solely in order to settle a disagreement relating to the interpretation or application of the Chicago Convention would not render the application submitting that disagreement to it inadmissible.[218]

214 ICAO Council IASTA, [2020] ICJ Reports 172, p. 184; ICAO Council CICA, [2020] ICJ Reports 81, p. 93.

215 ICAO Council IASTA, [2020] ICJ Reports 172, p. 185; ICAO Council CICA, [2020] ICJ Reports 81, p. 94.

216 ICAO Council IASTA, [2020] ICJ Reports 172, p. 189; ICAO Council CICA, [2020] ICJ Reports 81, p. 98.

217 ICAO Council IASTA, [2020] ICJ Reports 172, p. 192; ICAO Council CICA, [2020] ICJ Reports 81, p. 101.

218 ICAO Council IASTA, [2020] ICJ Reports 172, p. 196; ICAO Council CICA, [2020] ICJ Reports 81, p. 104–105.

In none of these cases was there a ruling on the merits. The ICAO Council first decided on the merits of a dispute in 2025, in the *MH17 Case (Netherlands and Australia* v. *Russia).*[219] These three ICJ Judgments on ICAO Council jurisdiction nonetheless affirm the same general principle developed by the arbitral tribunals in *Mox Plant* and *Eurotunnel*. Pursuant to this approach, an adjudicator with jurisdiction to interpret and apply a set of rules may only issue a Declaration of Breach of these rules. But it is empowered to assess, incidentally, defences and justifications under general international law invoked by the parties, including when they involve the assessment of a claim of violation of another rule of international law.

5.4.4 *Regime-Specific Adjudicators and Cross-Regime Responses*

Not all adjudicators have accepted this incidental/principal distinction. In four disputes concerning Mexican measures affecting US sugar producers, purportedly adopted as countermeasures for US violations of the NAFTA, only one adjudicator accepted its incidental jurisdiction to assess the substance of Mexico's argument that its measures were countermeasures: the NAFTA Investor-State Dispute Settlement (ISDS) Arbitral Tribunal in *ADM* v. *Mexico*. The WTO Appellate Body, as well as one other NAFTA ISDS Tribunal, refused to ascertain the lawfulness of Mexico's measures, whether under NAFTA or under public international law, reasoning that they did not have jurisdiction over the matter. A third NAFTA ISDS Tribunal found that investors derived rights from the NAFTA's Investment Chapter that could not be targeted by countermeasures against their state of nationality.

In all four cases, Mexico alleged that the violations in question, though incompatible with the commitments ordinarily applicable under those agreements, were justifiable because they had been adopted to enforce compliance by the United States with its obligation under NAFTA. Prior to adopting these measures, Mexico had requested a NAFTA panel on US restrictions on Mexican sugar. The United States objected to all proposals for a procedure to compose the panel.[220]

[219] ICAO, 'ICAO Council vote on Flight MH17 case', *Press Release* (12 May 2025); Russia has appealed from this decision to the ICJ. See Michael Milde, *International Air Law and ICAO*, 3rd edn (The Hague: Eleven, 2016), 204. See Cecily Rose, 'Appeal Relating to the Jurisdiction of the ICAO Council' (2021) 115 *AJIL* 301.

[220] See Joost Pauwelyn, 'Editorial Comment: Adding Sweeteners to Softwood Lumber: The WTO–NAFTA "Spaghetti Bowl" Is Cooking' (2006) 9 *Journal of International Economic Law* 197.

In the WTO dispute *Mexico – Soft Drinks*, Mexico presented its measures simultaneously as countermeasures under general international law and as measures justifiable under an intra-WTO general exception.[221] The Appellate Body ostensibly set aside the extra-WTO element in its legal assessment. It considered only whether the trade restrictions were justifiable under General Agreement on Tariffs and Trade (GATT) Article XX(d), as measures 'necessary to secure compliance with laws or regulations which are not inconsistent with the provisions of this Agreement', and rejected the reading according to which this provision would justify the adoption of countermeasures.[222]

Additionally, the Appellate Body suggested that it considered itself unable to assess, even incidentally, whether a WTO Member's measures are justifiable as permissible countermeasures. The Appellate Body invoked Article 3.7 of the DSU, which provides that WTO dispute settlement 'serves to preserve the rights and obligations of Members under the covered agreements, and to clarify the existing provisions of those agreements'. It reasoned:

> Mexico's interpretation would imply that, in order to resolve the case, WTO panels and the Appellate Body would have to assume that there is a violation of the relevant international agreement (such as the NAFTA) by the complaining party, or they would have to assess whether the relevant international agreement has been violated. WTO panels and the Appellate Body would thus become adjudicators of non-WTO disputes. As we noted earlier, this is not the function of panels and the Appellate Body as intended by the DSU.[223]

Danae Azaria has argued that this ruling is problematic.[224] It would imply that, because WTO adjudicators are not empowered to (or do not have 'the function of') adjudicate non-WTO disputes, responses that are permissible as a matter of general international law cannot affect WTO obligations. Even under the WTO Agreements, the Appellate Body could equally appropriately have considered that the DSU requires a WTO adjudicator to 'make an objective assessment of the matter before it'.[225] An objective assessment of the matter should

[221] Appellate Body Report, *Mexico – Soft Drinks*, WT/DS308/AB/R, adopted 24 March 2006, para. 14.
[222] Ibid., para. 75.
[223] Ibid., para. 78 (footnotes omitted).
[224] Danae Azaria, 'Trade Countermeasures for Breaches of International Law Outside the WTO' (2022) 71 *International and Comparative Law Quarterly* 389, 421.
[225] DSU, Article 11.

arguably include an assessment of whether a measure is a permissible response to another violation.[226]

As Gabrielle Marceau and Anastasios Tomazos noted, the WTO 'is not a world government and its dispute settlement system even less so'.[227] At the same time, accepting to engage in this incidental jurisdiction might turn WTO adjudicators into universal adjudicators, making trade sanctions into an instrument to trigger the adjudication, chiefly by trade diplomats and lawyers, of international obligations which are not directly justiciable by any IC, regarding the use of force, human rights, the law of the sea, or environmental law. The Appellate Body's rejection of jurisdiction over countermeasures was expressly designed to avoid this outcome.

The same measures examined in *Mexico – Soft Drinks* for violating WTO law were considered by three NAFTA ISDS tribunals, in *ADM* v. *Mexico*, *CPI* v. *Mexico*, and *Cargill* v. *Mexico*. Of these, the Tribunal in *Cargill* v. *Mexico* rejected Mexico's claim that its tax was justifiable as a countermeasure, on grounds that countermeasures may not lawfully affect the rights of investors. The Tribunal reasoned that the defence of countermeasures is opposable to the state but does not permit violations of 'specific obligations owed to *nationals* of the offending State'.[228] Noting that 'it is the investor that institutes the claim, that calls a tribunal into existence, and that is the named party in all respects to the resulting proceedings and award', the Tribunal concluded that investors are the 'holders' of rights set out in NAFTA's Investment Chapter.[229]

226 At the same time, the DSU also provides that 'Recommendations and rulings of the DSB cannot add to or diminish the rights and obligations provided in the covered agreements' (Article 3.2) and that, 'in their findings and recommendations, the panel and Appellate Body cannot add to or diminish the rights and obligations provided in the covered agreements' (Article 19.2). See Lorand Bartels, 'Applicable Law in WTO Dispute Settlement Proceedings' (2001) 35 *Journal of World Trade* 499 (arguing that these provisions are an indirect normative conflict clause requiring WTO adjudicators to give precedence to WTO law).

227 Gabrielle Marceau and Anastasios Tomazos, 'Comments on Joost Pauwelyn's Paper: "How to Win a WTO Dispute Based on Non-WTO Law?"' in Stefan Griller (ed.), *At the Crossroads: The World Trading System and the Doha Round* (Vienna: Springer, 2008), 55–81, 57. Human rights lawyers might also be suspicious of this move. Faced with arguments regarding a WTO-authorised enforcement of human rights, Philip Alston concluded that '[t]he human rights thus granted would be a mirage which would have little impact other than to reinforce the strength of trade norms and the role of the WTO while leaving the existing, significantly ineffectual, human rights legal regime intact' (Philip Alston, 'Resisting the Merger and Acquisition of Human Rights by Trade Law: A Reply to Petersmann' (2002) 13 *European Journal of International Law* 815–844, at 836).

228 *Cargill, Inc.* v. *Mexico*, [2009] ICSID Case No. ARB(AF)/05/2, para. 422.

229 Ibid., para. 426.

The Tribunal in *CPI* v. *Mexico* equally found that an investor 'has rights of its own under Chapter XI [Investment] of the NAFTA', so that 'a countermeasure taken ... against the State of nationality of the investor cannot deprive that investor of its rights'.[230] Going further than the Tribunal in *Cargill* v. *Mexico*, this Tribunal reasoned that it could not in any event entertain Mexico's claims, because 'the Tribunal lacks jurisdiction to determine whether or not the United States was in breach of the NAFTA'.[231] In this regard, the *CPI* v. *Mexico Tribunal* adopted a position similar to that of the WTO Appellate Body in *Mexico – Soft Drinks*.

The ISDS arbitral tribunal in *ADM* v. *Mexico* – chronologically, the first of the three to issue an award – was the only one to assess the substance of Mexico's argument. This Tribunal rejected the view that investment obligations were owed to investors.[232] As regards its ability to assess the argument that the measures were lawful countermeasures, it noted that its jurisdiction was to 'decide the issues in dispute in accordance with [the NAFTA] and applicable rules of international law',[233] and that in any case 'customary international law – as codified in the ILC Articles – ... operates in a residual way'.[234] This Tribunal applied the distinction between rules over which it has jurisdiction and rules that it may apply incidentally, affirmed by the UNCLOS Arbitral Tribunal in *Mox Plant* and by the ICJ in the *ICAO Council* cases. The *ADM* v. *Mexico* Tribunal stated that it had 'no jurisdiction to decide whether the United States committed an internationally wrongful act which justified a countermeasure', but that it did have 'jurisdiction to decide any defense ... including a countermeasures defense'.[235] Examining Mexico's defence on the merits, it then concluded that Mexico's sweetener 'Tax was not a valid countermeasure because it was not adopted to induce US' compliance with the NAFTA; nor d[id] the Tax meet the proportionality requirements under customary international law'.[236]

[230] *Corn Products International (CPI)* v. *Mexico*, [2008] ICSID Case No. ARB(AF)/04/01, Decision on Responsibility, para. 176.

[231] Ibid., para. 183.

[232] *ADM v. Mexico*, para. 179.

[233] Ibid., para. 119 (quoting Article 1131.1, of the North American Free Trade Agreement, Washington and Mexico City and Ottawa, 17 December 1992, in force 1 January 1994, 32 ILM 289).

[234] Ibid.

[235] Ibid., paras. 131–132.

[236] Ibid., para. 180.

These cases show that specialised ICs may have difficulty assessing the lawfulness of alleged permissible responses even *ex post*, if they find that their adjudicative powers are restricted to applying rules over which they have principal jurisdiction. This may be particularly problematic for adjudicators, such as WTO adjudicators, whose constitutive instruments heavily constrain them.[237]

On the other hand, the position asserted by a number of arbitral tribunals, and confirmed by the ICJ in the *ICAO Council (CICA/IASTA)* Judgments, provides most international adjudicators with a legal basis to assess arguments regarding permissible responses. Pursuant to this approach, adjudicators are empowered to examine, at least incidentally and *ex post*, a respondent's argument that the conduct that is the subject matter of a claim of violation is justified as a permissible response to a previous legal violation. If a claimant state can establish that a violation exists and it has a legal interest in a judicial determination on the lawfulness of a proposed response, an adjudicator with jurisdiction *ratione materiae* may be able to provide it with the remedy of Permissible Responses – or at least with an authoritative pronouncement finding that responses are warranted, and perhaps that its chosen response is permissible.

5.5 Coercive Measures as Permissible Responses: Enforceable Judicial Remedies

This section explores the limits of Permissible Responses as a remedy. As discussed in Chapter 1, a defining characteristic of ICs is their lack of *potestas*: they are not embedded within a centralised coercive apparatus capable of enforcing their rulings by mobilising political or economic resources against wrongdoing. To examine the boundaries of international judicial remedies is to reassess this foundational premise and consider how, if at all, certain remedies might link ICs to social apparatuses capable of coercive enforcement. In the absence of a supranational coercive apparatus, enforceable IC rulings must rely on the *domestic* enforcement mechanisms of individual states.[238]

[237] DSU, Article 19.2 provides that 'in their findings and recommendations, the panel and Appellate Body cannot add to or diminish the rights and obligations provided in the covered agreements'.

[238] To the extent that international organisations whose acts can be hierarchically determined by an IC are able to apply coercive measures, this IC will have a corresponding

Unlike earlier sections, which inferred legal possibilities from patterns of judicial practice or broadly applied norms, this section is fundamentally exploratory. It considers whether existing – albeit fragmented – legal concepts and mechanisms might be considered and combined to yield a transformative outcome: enforceable international judicial rulings. To that end, I examine elements of current adjudicative practice, often confined to a single international legal regime and, in some cases, underexplored, to assess their potential as blueprints for broader application across regimes. The focus, then, is not on how procedural rules are currently applied, nor on the lawfulness of particular interpretations of state obligations or judicial powers. Rather, in this section, I am interested in the potential of certain rules, asserted judicial powers, and interpretations of the relationship between international courts and state coercion that can pave the way for a system in which international judicial remedies are enforceable. In such a system, domestic authorities could, as a matter of obligation, implement responses that adjudicators declare to be permissible to enforce IC rulings – not against their own state (which would amount to voluntary compliance), but against other states.

The measures of response considered so far correspond to what Michael Reisman has labelled 'indirect enforcement' of obligations, through which other actors 'impose sanctions on the miscreant in order to persuade [it] to comply with community norms'.[239] Direct enforcement, by contrast, entails 'the physical transfer of an equivalent in value to the original object of the decision'.[240] In this section, I will consider the prospects for IC mobilisation of coercive enforcement, involving '[t]he principal weapons of enforcement used by domestic courts', that is, 'restraints on the person, or restraints upon assets or real property'.[241]

ability to mobilise this coercive apparatus. To the same extent, however, this adjudicator will cease to be in the position of ICs that is the focus of this book. On the sanctioning abilities of the EU and its relationship to the CJEU, see Stefano Montaldo, Francesco Costamagna and Alberto Miglio (eds.) *EU Law Enforcement: The Evolution of Sanctioning Powers* (London: Routlege, 2021).

239 W. Michael Reisman, 'The Enforcement of International Judgments' (1969) 63 *American Journal of International Law* 1, 6. The reference to 'community norms' does not mean that sanctions are only applied to violations of *erga omnes* obligations. The tenet *pacta sunt servanda* and the obligation to comply with judicial rulings are community norms.

240 Ibid. Following a criminal condemnation, fulfilment of the arrest warrant is a form of direct enforcement.

241 Robert Jennings, 'The Judicial Enforcement of International Obligations' (1987) 47 *ZaöRV* 3, 4.

Since ICs are not hierarchically connected to coercive apparatuses, they are often presumed to be unable to offer direct enforcement. 'For these measures, a territorial competence is obviously essential.'[242] However, while international adjudicators may be unable to *order* the application by a coercive apparatus of enforcement measures, this inability does not prevent them from *determining* that this application by other states is permissible in a particular case. The key obstacle in this regard is not any limitation to IC adjudicative powers but the rules of international law that prevent the application of measures of constraint against the property of states and their representatives. The law of state immunities traditionally precludes the application of measures of constraint by one state's coercive apparatus vis-à-vis the property and the representatives of other states. As this section demonstrates, this law is not the absolute obstacle to direct enforcement that it once was.

A non-absolute law of state immunity permits the development of a type of judicial remedy that remains underexplored: a determination of permissible direct enforcement, which may be termed a 'declaration of enforceability'. If the law of state immunity contains exceptions, an IC is empowered to determine that, as a matter of international law, these exceptions apply, permitting or even obliging other states to apply measures of constraint against a wrongdoer state's assets, or against its representatives.[243] Though at present no IC is permitted to declare specific rulings enforceable in this manner, some international adjudicators – ISDS tribunals and the International Criminal Court – are empowered to issue rulings leading to measures of constraint, applied by other states, against state assets and the persons of state representatives.

[242] Ibid.

[243] Representatives of states are usually subject to measures of constraint for their individual conduct rather than the conduct of their states. This section focuses on the enforcement of ICC arrest warrants against a state's highest officials, for war crimes, crimes against humanity, genocide, and aggression. In this context, there is a significant overlap between individual conduct and the conduct of states that violates international law. If one were to stretch this concept to apply to all officials, every international ruling concerning the application of a state's criminal law against foreign officials, for conduct that plausibly amounts to a violation of their state's international obligations, might be considered a ruling on Permissible Responses. See, for example, *S.S. Lotus, France* v. *Turkey*, Judgment, (1927) PCIJ Ser. A No. 10; *The 'Enrica Lexie' Incident, Italy* v. *India*, (2020) PCA Case No. 2015-28, Award, 21.

5.5.1 *Judicial Powers and Enforceability: Jurisdictio and Imperium*

The essential limitation on the enforceability of international judicial remedies is the inability of international adjudicators to determine the application of coercive measures against a wrongdoer, owing to their lack of connection to a social apparatus capable of applying coercion at these adjudicators' instructions. This limitation relates to the distinction, explored in Chapter 1, between the adjudicators' lack of *potestas* (authority within the context of a hierarchical system connected to a coercive social apparatus) and their potentially extensive *auctoritas* (authority outside such a hierarchy).[244] As regards the function and operation of judicial remedies, a related distinction, equally inspired in Roman law, is illuminating: that between *jurisdictio* and *imperium*.

Jurisdictio was described in Roman law as the '*ius dicentis officium*'[245] – the task of stating what the law provides in a particular case. *Imperium*, on the other hand, is described as the 'power of the sword' ('*gladii potestatem*').[246] *Imperium* was a specific form of *potestas* in Roman law, referring essentially to the power to command the Roman army.[247] Whereas an entity with *potestas* can hold both *jurisdictio* and *imperium*, an entity with mere *auctoritas* is unable to issue (at least with a meaningful degree of expected effectiveness) commands to those who are able to employ coercive force.

The literature on arbitration has explored the impact on remedies of this distinction between *jurisdictio* and *imperium* to establish the extent and limitations on the powers of arbitrators as compared to those of state judges. In Charles Jarrosson's definition, *imperium* 'comprises all that relates to the public force, the power to command and to coerce, which

[244] See Section 1.4.3.

[245] Johannes Blaeu and others, *Corpus Iuris Civilis* (Amsterdam: Blaeu and Elsevier, 1659), 87.

[246] Ibid., at 84, 87. *Imperium* appears in Roman authors as the power held by individuals to command armies on behalf of the Roman state. See William Smith (ed.), *Dictionary of Greek and Roman Antiquities* (Boston: Little, Brown, 1870), 628–630.

[247] Fred K. Drogula, '*Imperium*, *Potestas*, and the *Pomerium* in the Roman Republic' (2007) 56 *Historia: Zeitschrift für Alte Geschichte* 419, 423 ('*Potestas* was the word the Romans used to describe the specifically civil powers of a magistrate, whether or not that magistrate also possessed *imperium*'). As the author notes, there is academic debate regarding the precise contours of these concepts in Roman times.

flows from the State'.[248] An adjudicator's exercise of *imperium*, such as ordering a seizure of assets, requires a connection to the coercive apparatus of the state (*potestas*) to be effective. By contrast, the ability to state the law (*jurisdictio*) may coexist with, but is not dependent upon, access to means of coercion. *Jurisdictio* derives from the authority entrusted to adjudicators to interpret and apply certain (or all) legal rules in a manner that binds the parties under the relevant legal framework. Domestic laws often entrust (non-inter-state) arbitrators with *jurisdictio* without endowing them with *imperium*.

The distinction between *jurisdictio* and *imperium* affords a clearer view of the separation between adjudicatory functions and functions of *imperium*. Adjudicatory functions, comprising the settlement of disputes on the interpretation of the law and its application to facts, involve *jurisdictio* and can be entrusted to actors with mere *auctoritas*. *Imperium* functions, which involve the employment of coercion, require *potestas* and therefore remain the prerogative of actors embedded in the coercive apparatus of the state.

States set up international adjudicators to exercise *jurisdictio*: to interpret and apply legal rules. Despite the many differences in constitutive instruments, composition, and practice, the core function of all ICs is essentially the same: interpreting states' rights and obligations and determining whether obligations have been violated.[249] However, ICs may be empowered to determine the lawfulness under international law of the application, by the coercive apparatus in one state, of measures of constraint against the assets and representatives of another state. Additionally or alternatively, specific legal mechanisms may set aside state immunities with regard to particular international judicial rulings, making these rulings enforceable, as a matter of international and

[248] Charles Jarrosson, '*Réflexions sur l'*imperium', in *Etudes offertes à Pierre Bellet* (Paris: Litec, 1991), 245–279, 247 ('l'*imperium* regroupe tout ce qui concerne la force publique, le pouvoir de commandement et de contrainte et qui relève de l'Etat'). There is no reason to revise the end of this sentence with respect to international law. The power to mobilise concrete resources is as concentrated on states in international law as it is in domestic law. See also Pierre Mayer, '*Imperium* et mesures provisoires', in Jacques Haldy and Jean-Marie Rapp et Phidias Ferrari (eds.), *Mélanges de procédure et d'arbitrage en l'honneur de Jean-François Poudret* (Lausanne: Université de Lausanne, 1999), 437–452.

[249] International criminal courts ostensibly have a different primary mandate, judging individuals who are often already in custody. They nonetheless perform this mandate by interpreting treaties, and other legal documents and rules, under delegation from states. They are relevant for this book insofar as they also perform a secondary task: seeking to secure compliance by states, for example, with their arrest warrants.

domestic law, without the need for a specific international judicial remedy to be awarded.

In this manner, while ICs are unable to order enforcement of international law (that is, they cannot order with *potestas* the seizing of assets or the arresting of state representatives), they may be able to declare these measures permissible and even obligatory under international law. If this declaration is combined with a willingness, within another state, to enforce the ruling (whether grounded in an organ's discretionary decision or in a domestic court's understanding of its duties under domestic law), this combination de facto endows the IC with the ability to issue rulings with potential for enforceability.

5.5.2 Determining Enforceability: State Immunities, Express and Implicit Direct Enforcement in International Adjudication

In a determination or declaration of enforceability, an IC concludes that the nature and context of a violation empowers, or requires, a state or states to apply measures of constraint against the wrongdoing state's property or its representatives. A determination of enforceability falls into the category of Permissible Response insofar as its content is not that the wrongdoer is obliged to apply coercive measures against persons or property under its jurisdiction. Instead, the adjudicator determines that one or more elements of state immunity may or must be set aside *by other states* in the context of the case. These elements include immunity of state assets from adjudication, attachment, and execution, but also immunity of state representatives from arrest.[250]

State immunity is a cornerstone of international law. In *Jurisdictional Immunities of the State*, the ICJ reaffirmed the International Law Commission's finding that 'jurisdictional immunities of foreign States and their property' developed into 'a general rule of customary international law solidly rooted in the current practice of States'.[251] The law of state immunities is complex and multi-sourced, largely customary and grounded especially on national legislation and domestic judicial rulings. Hazel Fox and Philippa Webb termed immunity 'a doctrine of international law which is applied in accordance with national law in local

[250] An alternative proposition is that immunity applies but can be set aside as a countermeasure. This proposition is examined at the end of this section.

[251] International Law Commission, 'Jurisdictional Immunities of States and Their Property', II.2 ILC Ybk 1980, p. 147.

courts',[252] while Burkhard Hess, commenting on the ILC's draft for a convention on immunity from jurisdiction, noted that 'immunity . . . is at the point of intersection of international law and national procedural law'.[253] The ILC draft eventually led, in 2004, to the signing by some states of a United Nations Convention on Jurisdictional Immunities of the State. This UN Convention remains far from entering into force,[254] while the European version has few parties[255] and the Inter-American one remains unsigned.[256] These three documents were nonetheless cited by the ICJ in *Jurisdictional Immunities* when considering the customary international law of state immunities.[257]

Exceptions to state immunity are a highly sensitive matter. In *Jurisdictional Immunities*, the ICJ stated that 'the rule of State immunity ... derives from the principle of sovereign equality of States'.[258] The European Court of Human Rights (ECtHR) in *Al Adsani* v. *United Kingdom* made a similar finding, indicating that 'sovereign immunity is a concept of international law, developed out of the principle *par in parem non habet imperium*, by virtue of which one State shall not be subject to the jurisdiction of another State'.[259] The ICJ reiterated this point, with regard to the immunity of state officials and immunity of state property from execution, in *Immunities and Criminal Proceedings*.[260] In *Jurisdictional Immunities*, the ICJ inferred from this

[252] Hazel Fox and Philippa Webb, *The Law of State Immunity*, 3rd edn (Oxford: Oxford University Press, 2015), 1.

[253] Burkard Hess, 'The International Law Commission's Draft Convention on the Jurisdictional Immunities of States and Their Property' (1993) 4 *EJIL* 269, 271.

[254] United Nations Convention on Jurisdictional Immunities of States and Their Property, UNGA Res 59/38, 2 December 2004, UN Doc. A/59/508, Annex. Article 30 of this Convention requires thirty ratifications before the Convention enters into force. At the time of writing, the Convention has thirty-seven signatories, twenty-three of which have ratified it.

[255] European Convention on State Immunity, Basel, 16 May 1972, in force 11 June 1976, 11 ILM 470 (parties: Austria, Belgium, Cyprus, Germany, Luxembourg, Netherlands, Switzerland, United Kingdom).

[256] Inter-American Juridical Committee of the Organization of American States, Draft Inter-American Convention on Jurisdictional Immunity of the States, adopted 21 January 1983, 22 (2) ILM 292.

[257] *Jurisdictional Immunities*, [2012] ICJ Reports 99, p. 124–125, 138.

[258] Ibid., 123.

[259] Application No. 35763/97, *Al-Adsani* v. *the United Kingdom*, [2001] ECHR 761, para. 54.

[260] *Immunities and Criminal Proceedings, Equatorial Guinea* v. *France*, Preliminary Objections, [2018] ICJ Reports 292, p. 320–321.

that '[e]xceptions to the immunity of the State represent a departure from the principle of sovereign equality'.[261]

There are a few generally recognised exceptions to state immunity from enforcement, or, as the UN Convention puts it, 'post-judgment measures of constraint, such as attachment, arrest or execution, against property of a State'.[262] The Convention recognises exceptions of three kinds. First is the express waiver by a state of its immunity from enforcement, which may be provided through an agreement *ex ante*, but also by consent *ex post*.[263] Second is the specific allocation or earmarking by a state of its property for the satisfaction of the specific claim being adjudicated upon.[264] Third is the possibility of applying enforcement measures on assets 'specifically in use or intended for use by the State for other than governmental non-commercial purposes'.[265] While the two former exceptions require express state consent, the third one – the lack of immunity from execution of assets used for '*acta jure gestionis*', that is, for commercial purposes[266] – has a broader character. In *Jurisdictional Immunities*, the ICJ concluded that, under customary international law, 'measure[s] of constraint may be taken against property belonging to a foreign State' only under one of these three conditions:

> the property in question must be in use for an activity not pursuing government non-commercial purposes, or . . . the State which owns the property has expressly consented to the taking of a measure of constraint, or . . . that State has allocated the property in question for the satisfaction of a judicial claim.[267]

Scholars and some domestic courts have sought to establish a fourth exception, for *acta jure imperii* that amount to grave violations of particularly important international rules.[268] The *Jurisdictional*

261 *Jurisdictional Immunities*, [2012] ICJ Reports 99, p. 123.

262 UN Convention on Jurisdictional Immunities of States and their Property, Article 19.

263 Ibid., Article 19(a).

264 Ibid., Article 19(b).

265 Ibid., Article 19(c).

266 *Jurisdictional Immunities*, [2012] ICJ Reports 99, p. 124: 'many States . . . now distinguish between *acta jure gestionis*, in respect of which they have limited the immunity which they claim for themselves and which they accord to others, and *acta jure imperii*'.

267 Ibid., p. 148. See also Ibid., p. 147: 'A waiver by a state of its immunity from adjudication does not imply waiver of its immunity from enforcement'.

268 Andrea Bianchi, 'Human Rights and the Magic of *Jus Cogens*' (2008) 19 *EJIL* 491, 499–505; Lorna McGregor, 'State Immunity and Human Rights: Is There a Future after *Germany* v. *Italy*?' (2013) 11 *JICJ* 125, 128–130.

Immunities case arose after Greek and Italian courts held that state immunities from jurisdiction and execution could not shield Germany from providing reparation for World War II atrocities.[269] However, the ICJ rejected Italy's contention that Germany 'was not entitled to immunity [for] acts involv[ing] the most serious violations of rules of international law of a peremptory character for which no alternative means of redress was available'.[270] Italy sought to justify its courts' setting aside of German sovereign immunity on the basis of the gravity of the breach and the lack of reparations, as well as the 'tort exception', both of which had been applied by a number of domestic courts.[271] The ICJ held that '[t]he rules of State immunity are procedural in character and are confined to determining whether or not the courts of one State may exercise jurisdiction in respect of another State', so that 'there is no conflict between [peremptory] rules and the rules on State immunity'.[272]

Domestic courts have not necessarily accepted this finding. Even after the ICJ ruling in *Jurisdictional Immunities*, the Italian Constitutional Court found that Italian authorities could seize German assets.[273] In 2022, Italy attempted to seize other German assets in Rome, prompting Germany to initiate proceedings against Italy at the ICJ, referencing the findings from *Jurisdictional Immunities*.[274] Subsequently, Italy passed a law blocking the seizing of these properties,[275] potentially ending the saga.[276]

[269] See *Prefecture of Voiotia* v. *Federal Republic of Germany*, Areios Pagos (Hellenic Supreme Court), Case No. 11/2000, 4 May 2000; *Ferrini* v. *Federal Republic of Germany*, Corte di Cassazione (Sezioni Unite), Judgment No. 5044, 6 November 2003.

[270] *Jurisdictional Immunities*, [2012] ICJ Reports 99, p. 125.

[271] Ibid., p. 61. See also Eleni Methymaki and Antonios Tzanakopoulos, 'Freedom with Their Exception: Jurisdiction and Immunity as Rule and Exception', in Lorand Bartels and Federica Paddeu (eds.), *Exceptions in International Law* (Oxford: Oxford University Press, 2020).

[272] *Jurisdictional Immunities*, [2012] ICJ Reports 99, p. 140.

[273] See Marco Longobardo, 'The Italian Constitutional Court's Ruling against State Immunity When International Crimes Occur: Thoughts on Decision No 238 of 2014' (2015) 16(1) *Melbourne Journal of International Law* 255.

[274] Application Instituting Proceedings, *Questions of Jurisdictional Immunities of the State and Measures of Constraint against State-Owned Property, Germany* v. *Italy*, 29 April 2022.

[275] Decree Law No. 36 of 30 April 2022.

[276] Paolo Caroli, 'Compensation without Recognition: The German-Italian Dispute over War Crime Compensation and Transnational Justice' (Verfassungsblog, 6 June 2022), available at https://verfassungsblog.de/compensation-without-recognition.

In a similar vein, Iran has instituted ICJ proceedings against Canada, alleging that the 'terrorism-exception' in Canadian immunity legislation contradicts the customary international law rules identified by the ICJ in *Jurisdictional Immunities*.[277] Additionally, in 2022, the Ukrainian Supreme Court issued several judgments stating that Russia's immunity could be denied due to its aggression against Ukraine, allowing Ukrainian courts to entertain claims for damages against Russia without needing its consent.[278] Ernest Bankas has expressed concern with these developments, finding that 'the application of restrictive immunity remains patently problematic' and characterising it as a 'quest by some states to take measures of constraint or enforcement action against state property'.[279]

In *Jurisdictional Immunities*, the ICJ spelt out the consequence of putting substantive and procedural rules on different planes: for the ICJ, state immunity from jurisdiction 'cannot ... be made dependent upon the outcome of a balancing exercise of the specific circumstances of each case to be conducted by the national court before which immunity is claimed'.[280] The ECtHR reached a similar conclusion in *Al Adsani* v. *United Kingdom*, finding that there is no violation of the right to access (domestic) courts if a state adopts 'measures ... which reflect generally recognised rules of public international law on State immunity'.[281] Though the ECtHR contemplated a future change in this regard in view of 'the growing recognition of the overriding importance of the prohibition of torture', it did not 'find it established that there is yet acceptance in international law of the proposition that States are not entitled to immunity in respect of civil claims for damages for alleged torture committed outside the forum State'.[282]

Pursuant to the ICJ's understanding, the procedural/substantive distinction precludes domestic courts from (lawfully under international law) setting aside jurisdictional immunities in view of the gravity of the

[277] Application Instituting Proceedings, *Alleged Violations of State Immunities, Islamic Republic of Iran* v. *Canada*, 27 June 2023.

[278] Case No. 308/9708/19 of 14 April 2022 (Ukrainian Supreme Court); Case No. 428/11673/19 of 18 May 2022 (Ukrainian Supreme Court); Ielyzaveta Badanova, 'Jurisdictional Immunities v Grave Crimes: Reflections on New Developments from Ukraine' (8 September 2022 EJIL: Talk!), available at www.ejiltalk.org/jurisdictional-immunities-v-grave-crimes-reflections-on-new-developments-from-ukraine.

[279] Ernest K. Bankas, *The State Immunity Controversy in International Law: Private Suits against Sovereign States in Domestic Courts*, 2nd edn (Berlin: Springer, 2022), vii.

[280] Ibid., 145.

[281] *Al-Adsani* v. *the United Kingdom*, [2001] ECHR 761, para. 56.

[282] Ibid., para. 66.

wrongful conduct.[283] And, as long as international adjudicators uphold this distinction, they will be unable to award a determination authorising direct enforcement vis-à-vis one state's assets, or the application of coercion vis-à-vis a state representative endowed with immunity, as a function of the gravity of a breach. For an express determination of enforceability, as conceptualised here, the adjudicator must be able to determine that a particular violation, in its context, warrants the application of coercive measures against state assets or state representatives.

What this entails is that the lack of enforceability that we associate with international law is, at least partially, a function of the dominant understanding of the rules on state immunity. If, following some dissenting judges, these ICs had found that state immunity is subject to a balancing exercise between the value of the norm violated, the gravity of the breach, and the sovereign rights of the wrongdoing state, this would ultimately have empowered ICs to determine whether a specific context warrants setting aside state immunity. Though these dissenting judges all stated that it should be domestic courts conducting this balancing exercise,[284] it is difficult not to see as the logical outcome of this reasoning the formation of a new international legal framework. In case of a dispute, this legal framework would allow an international adjudicator with jurisdiction over the matter to grant, as a remedy, a declaration that a specific set of circumstances allows, and perhaps requires, a state's courts to disregard the immunity of another state from jurisdiction and enforcement. ICs would be empowered to award, as a judicial remedy in a dispute, a declaration of direct enforceability of rulings.

A similar issue lies at the heart of the parallel debate over whether lifting state immunity from adjudication (and possibly from execution) can serve as a form of 'judicial countermeasure' in international law.[285]

[283] See Bankas, *The State Immunity Controversy*, 659, 662–663.

[284] *Jurisdictional Immunities*, [2012] ICJ Reports 99, p. 179 (Judge Cançado Trindade), 290: 'There can be no prerogative or privilege of State immunity in cases of international crimes'; Ibid., p. 291 (Judge Yusuf), 307: 'in those exceptional circumstances where immunity may prevent the victims of international crimes from obtaining an effective remedy or where no other means of redress is available, such immunity should be granted or set aside by domestic courts'. *Al-Adsani* v. *the United Kingdom*, [2001] ECHR 761 (Dissenting Opinion of Judge Loucaides): 'The courts should be in a position to weigh the competing interests in favour of upholding an immunity or allowing a judicial determination of a civil right, after looking into the subject matter of the proceedings'.

[285] Patricia Tarre Moser, 'Non-Recognition of State Immunity as a Judicial Countermeasure to *Jus Cogens* Violations: The Human Rights Answer to the ICJ Decision on the *Ferrini* Case' (2012) 4(3) *Gottingen Journal of International Law* 809.

From this perspective, state immunity would generally apply to all violations, but domestic courts in other states could decide to set aside this immunity as a form of countermeasure. Marco Longobardo surveys relevant state practice and jurisprudence, noting that, for a judicially imposed countermeasure to function, a domestic judge would first need to determine whether the foreign state has violated international law – something state immunity itself would ordinarily preclude.[286] While this objection could arguably be raised to any exception to immunity, the assessment of whether a state has breached its international obligations, and what response is appropriate, is generally seen as falling within the remit of a state's political branches. Longobardo concludes that 'the denial of sovereign immunity as a countermeasure is unlawful without a prior determination of the government, and very impractical even if based on such a determination'.[287]

Discussions regarding immunity from execution have become equally serious due to the decision by various governments to freeze Russian assets, and the debates regarding seizing them, by legislative and administrative action. Philipp Janig concluded that seizure of assets in these circumstances poses serious difficulties under international law.[288] As in the case of 'judicial countermeasures', if such a practice takes hold, the questions of its permissibility is likely to reach adjudicators. Subjecting the matter to a ruling by an international adjudicator would offer an authoritative determination, removing the matter from the realm of unilateral action. Although all of these questions would arguably be best addressed through formal law-making processes, they are likely to appear before international adjudicators long before states can agree on a legal text.

5.5.3 *Coercion over State Property: Direct Enforceability of Investment Awards*

No IC has been expressly entrusted with the power to establish direct enforceability, setting aside state immunity in particular contexts. However, enforceability can also be a feature of an adjudicator's

[286] Marco Longobardo, 'State Immunity and Judicial Countermeasures' (2021) 32(2) *European Journal of International Law* 457–484, 472.

[287] Ibid., 484.

[288] Philipp Janig, 'State Immunity from Non-Judicial Measures of Constraint' (2025) 74(1) *International and Comparative Law Quarterly* 179–204.

rulings, not as a power expressly awarded but as a consequence implicit in the organisation of the adjudicator's powers and its connection to domestic law. Without the adjudicator being required to issue any specific determination in this regard, an IC's determinations may be considered enforceable under the domestic law of states other than the wrongdoer.

International investment law permits investors to bring disputes against states before arbitral tribunals. Besides binding the parties to the dispute and engendering an obligation to comply, ISDS awards can be enforced before the domestic courts of various states. ISDS enforcement relies either on the Convention on the Settlement of Investment Disputes, for arbitrations administered by the International Centre for Settlement of Investment Disputes (ICSID), or on the New York Convention, for other arbitrations. The ICSID Convention requires its 154 contracting parties to 'recognize an award rendered pursuant to this Convention as binding and enforce the pecuniary obligations imposed by that award within its territories as if it were a final judgment of a court in that State'.[289] Article III of the New York Convention requires its 172 states parties to 'recognize [covered] arbitral awards as binding and enforce them in accordance with the rules of procedure of the territory where the award is relied upon'.[290]

The ability of the state of enforcement to seize assets to enforce an ISDS award is limited by sovereign immunity. The ICSID Convention expressly safeguards 'the law in force in any Contracting State relating to immunity of that State or of any foreign State from execution'.[291] Similarly, an investor seeking to enforce an award under the New York Convention may be faced with the objection that seizing a foreign state's assets is contrary to the public policy of that state. Though the New York Convention does not govern state immunity specifically, it provides that recognition and enforcement may be refused where '[t]he

289 Convention on the Settlement of Investment Disputes between States and Nationals of other States, Washington, 18 March 1965, in force 14 October 1966, 575 UNTS 159 ('ICSID Convention'), Article 54(1).

290 United Nations Convention on the Recognition and Enforcement of Foreign Arbitral Awards, New York, 10 June 1958, in force 7 June 1959, 330 UNTS 3 ('New York Convention'), Article III. The New York Convention is not specific to investment law, applying to all 'arbitral awards not considered as domestic awards in the State where their recognition and enforcement are sought' (Ibid., Article I:1).

291 ICSID Convention, Article 55.

recognition or enforcement of the award would be contrary to the public policy of that country'.[292] In this way, domestic rules on state immunity from enforcement may mean that an ISDS award, though legally enforceable, may face obstacles regarding its execution vis-à-vis a foreign state.

At the same time, the fact that states own significant assets abroad, and that many of these assets are used for commercial or non-sovereign purposes, opens for claimants the possibility of requesting from other states' courts measures of constraint against a state's assets in case of non-compliance with arbitral awards. As regards investment awards, the mechanics of recognition and enforcement vary from jurisdiction to jurisdiction and depend on whether the arbitration is ICSID or non-ICSID. The ICSID Convention establishes a procedure, under Article 52, for parties to request annulment of awards to an international adjudicator, providing that awards 'shall not be subject to any appeal or to any other remedy except those provided for in this Convention'.[293] Conversely, domestic courts are in principle required to recognise a non-annulled ICSID award. A party to the ICSID Convention must 'enforce the pecuniary obligations imposed by [an ICSID] award within its territories as if it were a final judgment of a court in that State'.[294]

Investors have sometimes sought to enforce ICSID awards in states other than the respondent. These attempts were multiplied following rulings of the CJEU, in *Achmea*,[295] *Komstroy*,[296] and *PL Holdings*,[297] finding that investment arbitration based on investment obligations between EU Member States ('intra-EU') to be incompatible with EU law, and concluding that the underlying treaties had an 'invalid arbitration clause'.[298] This has led some courts within the EU to set aside intra-

[292] New York Convention, Article V.2(b).

[293] ICSID Convention, Article 53(1); See Kateryna Bondar, 'Annulment of ICSID and Non-ICSID Investment Awards: Differences in the Extent of Review' (2015) 32 *Journal of International Arbitration* 621; Emmanuel Gaillard and Yas Banifatemi (eds.), *Annulment of ICSID Awards* (New York: Juris, 2004).

[294] ICSID Convention, Article 54(1). See George A. Bermann, 'Understanding ICSID Article 54' (2020) 35 *ICSID Review – Foreign Investment Law Journal* 311.

[295] Case No. C-284/16, *Slovakia* v. *Achmea BV* [2018] ECLI:EU:C:2018:158; [2018] 2 CMLR 40.

[296] Case No. C-741/19, *Moldova* v. *Komstroy* [2021] ECLI:EU:C:2021:655.

[297] Case No. C-109/20, *PL Holdings* v. *Poland* [2021] ECLI:EU:C:2021:875.

[298] Ibid., para. 47.

EU ICSID awards, such as the Higher Regional Court of Cologne[299] and Luxembourg's Court of Cassation.[300]

On the other hand, courts outside the EU have been less willing to accept the view that EU law can invalidate an arbitration clause in a treaty. Australian courts requested to enforce the intra-EU ICSID awards in *Antin* v. *Spain*[301] and *Eiser* v. *Spain*[302] rejected the objection to enforcement grounded on EU law, understanding instead that Spain had waived its immunity to enforcement by consenting to arbitration and to the ICSID Convention. Similarly, the United Kingdom Supreme Court lifted the stay on the enforcement of the ICSID award in *Micula* v. *Romania*, determining that international and English law did not justify the stay and that UK obligations under the ICSID Convention were not overridden by EU law.[303] The US District Court of Columbia Circuit also upheld enforcement of the award in *Micula* v. *Romania*. Noting that there is an 'arbitration exception' in the US Foreign Sovereign Immunities Act (FSIA) and Romania had agreed to arbitration, this US Court found that the CJEU's rulings could not have 'retroactively rendered the arbitration agreement void when it joined the EU'.[304]

It is less clear that waiving immunity from enforcement can lead to execution of state assets. Katherine Reece Thomas argues that 'it is important for state assets to be protected and ... immunity remains a key international mechanism for stability'.[305] In Australia, the High Court found that the ICSID Convention 'amount[s] to a waiver of

299 Higher Regional Court of Cologne, *RWE AG and RWE Eemshaven Holding II BV* v. *Kingdom of the Netherlands* (Case No. OLG Köln, 19 U 63/21, 2022), Judgment, 1 September 2022; and Higher Regional Court of Cologne, *Uniper SE, Uniper Benelux Holding B.V. and Uniper Benelux N.V.* v. *Kingdom of the Netherlands* (Case No. 19 SchH 14/21), Judgment, 1 September 2022.

300 Luxembourg Court of Cassation, *Ioan Micula, Viorel Micula, S.C. European Food S.A., S.C. Starmill S.R.L. and S.C. Multipack S.R.L.* v. *Romania* (Case No. 6/2022, Cas-2021-00061), 14 July 2022.

301 High Court of Australia, *Kingdom of Spain* v. *Infrastructure Services Luxembourg S.à.r.l.* (Case No. NSD 602 of 2019), Judgment, 12 April 2023.

302 Federal Court of Australia, *Eiser Infrastructure Ltd.* v. *Kingdom of Spain* (Case No. NSD 601 of 2019 and NSD 602 of 2019), Judgment, 24 February 2020.

303 *Ioan Micula et al.* v. *Romania* [2018] EWCA Civ 1801.

304 District Court of Columbia Court of Appeals, *Ioan Micula et al.* v. *Government of Romania* (Case No. 23-7008), Judgment, 14 May 2024, p. 2.

305 See Katherine Reece Thomas, *The Commercial Activity Exception to State Immunity: An Introduction* (Cheltenham: Edward Elgar, 2024), 104.

foreign State immunity from the jurisdiction of the courts of Australia to recognise and enforce, but not to execute, the award [and] leaves unaffected any foreign State immunity enjoyed by Spain in relation to execution'.[306] This was cited approvingly by the England and Wales High Court in *Infrastructure Services Luxembourg Sarl* v. *Spain*, holding that 'a party with an ICSID award may seek recognition without enforcement' defining this cryptically as 'without at that stage execution'.[307] In *Border Timbers* v. *Zimbabwe*, a judge at the same High Court issued a ruling, similar in tone, which seemed to foreclose the possibility of execution. The High Court found that investors have 'an entitlement to register the award conferred by the ICSID Convention [but] Zimbabwe can in any event rely on state immunity in order to resist any attempt by the Claimants to proceed beyond mere registration towards execution'.[308]

In non-ICSID cases, the legal issues involved are somewhat distinct. The New York Convention entrusts domestic courts with assessing the conformity of arbitral awards, among others, with domestic public policy.[309] Domestic courts have found that investment disputes arise from commercial transactions, thus falling under the commercial exception to state immunity. In *Yukos Capital* v. *OAO Rosneft (Russian Federation)*, the Supreme Court of the Netherlands confirmed decisions by the District Court of Amsterdam and the Amsterdam Court of Appeals allowing enforcement of the arbitral awards. All three courts found that OAO Rosneft's actions were commercial in nature, negating state immunity.[310] More recently, in *Yukos Capital Limited* v. *Russian Federation*, a Dutch court dismissed Russia's immunity claims, emphasising that Russia waived its immunity from enforcement by signing the Energy Charter Treaty (ECT).[311] The US District Court of Columbia also rejected Russia's immunity claim, noting the FSIA's commercial activities exception, as well

[306] High Court of Australia, *Spain* v. *Infrastructure Services Luxembourg S.a.r.l.*, [2023] HCA 11, para. 8.

[307] *Infrastructure Services Luxembourg Sarl* v. *Spain* [2023] EWHC 1226 (Comm).

[308] *Border Timbers Ltd* v. *Republic of Zimbabwe* [2024] EWHC 58 (Comm), para. 118.

[309] New York Convention, Article V.2(b).

[310] Amsterdam Court of Appeals, *Yukos Capital s.a.r.l. (Luxembourg)* v. *OAO Rosneft (Russian Federation)* (Case No. 200.005.269/01), Decision, 28 April 2009.

[311] Amsterdam Court of Appeals, *Yukos Universal Limited and Hulley Enterprises Limited* v. *The Russian Federation* (Case No. C/09/477160 / HA ZA 15-1, C/09/477162 / HA ZA 15-2, C/09/481619 / HA ZA 15-112), Judgment, 20 February 2024.

as Russia's waiver of immunity through the New York Convention.[312] And, in *Franz Sedelmayer* v. *Russian Federation*, the Swedish Supreme Court differentiated between commercial and non-commercial state property, allowing enforcement measures against property used for commercial purposes, despite state immunity claims.[313]

The matter has been discussed further in the wake of the CJEU's rulings finding intra-EU investment arbitration to be invalid. Some EU Courts have accordingly set aside intra-EU non-ICSID awards, including the Swedish Supreme Court[314] and Court of Appeals[315] and the Paris Court of Appeal.[316] At the same time, courts within the EU have rejected requests to prevent the pursuit of enforcement of intra-EU awards outside the EU. The District Court of Amsterdam rejected Spain's request for anti-suit injunctions with respect to enforcement proceedings of ISDS awards initiated against Spain, under the New York Convention, in the United States.[317] This Dutch court emphasised that Spain's anti-enforcement actions were not permissible under the New York Convention, upholding the claimants' right to seek enforcement. Similarly, in *Poland* v. *LC Corp*,[318] the District Court of Amsterdam ruled that EU law did not apply to arbitration proceedings seated in the post-Brexit UK, rejecting Poland's arguments based on EU law. These rulings, while not addressing state immunities directly, demonstrate the potential for the enforcement apparatus of other states to be used to seek measures of constraint against the assets of a state found by an international adjudicator to be in breach of its commitments.

In conclusion, both the New York Convention and the ICSID Convention render ISDS awards enforceable. In case of non-

[312] US District Court of the District of Columbia, *Yukos Universal Limited and Hulley Enterprises Limited* v. *The Russian Federation* (Civil Action No. 14-1996), Memorandum Opinion, 17 November 2023.

[313] Swedish Supreme Court, *Franz Sedelmayer* v. *The Russian Federation* (Case No. Ö 170-10), Decision, 1 July 2011, para. 9.

[314] Swedish Supreme Court, *PL Holdings S.à.r.l.* v. *Republic of Poland* (Case No. T 1569-19), Judgment, 14 December 2022.

[315] Svea Court of Appeal, *Novenergia II – Energy & Environment (SCA)* v. *Kingdom of Spain* (Case No. T 4658-18, Judgment, 13 December 2022.

[316] Paris Court of Appeal, *Komstroy LLC* v. *Republic of Moldova* (Case No. 15/21703), Judgment, 10 January 2023.

[317] Amsterdam Court of Appeals, *The Kingdom of Spain* v. *AES Solar Energy Cooperative UA and Ampere Equity Fund BV* (Case No. C/13/730418 / KG ZA 23-164 EAM/MV), Judgment, 4 March 2023.

[318] Amsterdam Court of Appeals, *Republic of Poland* v. *LC Corp BV* (Case No. C/13/721410/HA ZA 22-614), Judgment, 8 March 2023.

compliance with a pecuniary award issued by an investment tribunal, the investor may seek enforcement before all other states parties to the relevant convention. Investors are not restricted to pursuing compliance before the domestic institutions of the state found in breach, combined with seeking bilateral or diffuse enforcement measures from their home state, other states, and international organisations. In other words, the investment tribunal's award no longer relies entirely on *auctoritas*; through the New York Convention or the ICSID Convention, domestic courts, endowed with *potestas*, are required to accord to ISDS awards the value of a ruling emanating from an entity embedded within the hierarchy of their state, and mobilise the coercive apparatus of the state accordingly.

5.5.4 *Coercion over State Leaders: Direct Enforceability of ICC Arrest Warrants*

Besides seizing property, the other form of coercion that is commonly found not to be available to international adjudicators is the ability to determine the application of measures of constraint against individuals. However, this inability is not inherent to international adjudicators. Indeed, the International Criminal Court (ICC) may issue arrest warrants against individuals when '[t]here are reasonable grounds to believe that [a] person has committed a crime within the jurisdiction of the Court'.[319]

ICC arrest warrants are issued separately from an assessment of states' violation of international obligations.[320] In three instances so far, the ICC has issued arrest warrants for sitting heads of state, in connection with conduct in principle amounting to a violation of that state's international

[319] Rome Statute of the International Criminal Court, Rome, 17 July 1998, in force July 1, 2002, 2187 UNTS 90 ('ICC Statute'), Article 58.1(a). This must be for one of the reasons set out in subparagraph (b).

[320] International criminal law covers a subset of the types of wrongful conduct that the first draft of ARSIWA qualified as 'international crimes of state'. See Joseph H.H. Weiler, Antonio Cassese and Marina Spinedi, *International Crimes of State: A Critical Analysis of the ILC's Draft Article 19 on State Responsibility* (Berlin: Walter de Gruyter, 1989). The proposal was ultimately rejected by the ILC and the additional consequences of serious breaches were limited to those in ARSIWA Articles 40 and 41. See ILC Ybk II.2 2001 p. 110 ff. Thus, 'international crimes' under the ICC Statute are not necessarily connected to the violation by states of their international obligations. At the same time, whenever high state representatives are involved, international crimes are almost by definition connected to a state's violation of international law.

obligations.[321] In one instance – that of Sudanese President Omar Al Bashir[322] – the ICC has actively sought enforcement of the arrest warrant in states other than the state led by the accused.[323]

Under the ICC Statute, the ICC may 'make requests to States Parties for cooperation'.[324] Requests are subject to the 'General obligation to cooperate' in Article 86 of the Statute, which requires states to cooperate with the Court 'in its investigation and prosecution of crimes'.[325] Specifically with regard to arrest warrants, Article 89 provides that the ICC may 'transmit a request for the arrest and surrender of a person to any State on the territory of which that person may be found and shall request the cooperation of that State in the arrest and surrender of such a person'. States parties to the ICC Statute are required to 'comply with requests for arrest and surrender'.[326]

The ICC Statute also provides for specific remedies in case of non-compliance by states with ICC requests. Under Article 87(7), the ICC

[321] ICC, *Prosecutor vs Al-Bashir*, Pre-Trial Chamber 1, Case No. ICC-02/05-01/09, *Decision of the Prosecution's Application for a Warrant of Arrest*, 4 March 2009 (ICC-02/05-01/09-3); Ibid., *Second Decision of the Prosecution's Application for a Warrant of Arrest*, 12 July 2010 (ICC-02/05-01/09-94); Paola Gaeta and Patryk I. Labuda, 'Trying Sitting Heads of State: The African Union versus the ICC in the Al Bashir and Kenyatta Cases', in Charles Chernor Jalloh and Ilias Bantekas (eds.), *The International Criminal Court and Africa* (Oxford: Oxford University Press, 2017). At the stage of revisions of this book, the ICC issued further arrest warrants for two sitting heads of state: ICC, *Warrant of Arrest for Vladimir Vladimirovich Putin*, ICC-01/22-18-SECRET; ICC, 'Situation in the State of Palestine: ICC Pre-Trial Chamber I rejects the State of Israel's challenges to jurisdiction and issues warrants of arrest for Benjamin Netanyahu and Yoav Gallant', *Press Release*, 21 November 2024.

[322] At the stage of revisions, the ICC had also issued a declaration of non-compliance vis-à-vis Mongolia for its failure to arrest President Putin (ICC, *Finding under article 87(7) of the Rome Statute on the non-compliance by Mongolia with the request by the Court to cooperate in the arrest and surrender of Vladimir Vladimirovich Putin and referral to the Assembly of States Parties*, 24 October 2024 (ICC-01/22)); and had initiated an investigation into Hungary's failure to arrest Prime Minister Netanyahu (ICC, *Transmission of Hungary's submission in response to Pre-Trial Chamber I's 'Invitation to Hungary to provide submissions for the purposes of proceedings under article 87(7) of the Rome Statute'*, 16 April 2025 (ICC-01/18-433)).

[323] The ICC may also determine the 'identification, tracing and freezing or seizure of proceeds, property and assets and instrumentalities of crimes for the purpose of eventual forfeiture' (ICC Statute, Article 93(k)).

[324] ICC Statute, Article 87.1(a)

[325] ICC Statute, Article 86.

[326] ICC Statute, Article 89(1). The provision ambiguously states that this requirement is to be fulfilled 'in accordance with the provisions of this Part and the procedure under their national law'. The provision does not clarify which prevails.

may 'make a finding' of non-compliance in case a state party 'fails to comply with a request to cooperate by the Court contrary to the provisions of [the ICC] Statute'.[327] In this case, the ICC may also 'refer the matter to the Assembly of States Parties or, where the Security Council referred the matter to the Court, to the Security Council'.[328]

The issuing of ICC arrest warrants against heads of state and other high state officials raises particular challenges regarding compliance. States parties may be wary of enforcing ICC arrest warrants issued for state representatives endowed with state or diplomatic immunity, in particular those that Hazel Fox and Philippa Webb refer to as 'the *troika* of Head of State, head of government and Foreign Minister'.[329] Article 27 of the ICC Statute, entitled 'Irrelevance of official capacity', provides: 'Immunities or special procedural rules which may attach to the official capacity of a person, whether under national or international law, shall not bar the Court from exercising its jurisdiction over such a person'.[330]

Article 27 refers to the jurisdiction of the ICC, but its title, text, and context may suggest that all states parties are obliged to surrender persons in their territory against whom an arrest warrant has been issued, regardless of '[i]mmunities or special procedural rules' existing not only under domestic law but also under international law. In other words, the '[i]rrelevance of official capacity' in Article 27 could apply not solely 'vertically', between the ICC and the authorities of each state party, but also horizontally, depriving each state's nationals of state and diplomatic immunities in the territories of states parties to the Statute.

A contextual element supporting this reading is Article 98(1), governing relations with non-parties, which acknowledges that a state party may have 'obligations under international law with respect to the State or diplomatic immunity of a person or property of a third State'. In this case, the ICC must 'first obtain the cooperation of that third State for the waiver of the immunity' before proceeding with a request for surrender or assistance from the state party. An *a contrario* reading of this provision implies that there is no such need for obtaining cooperation, where the state or diplomatic immunity in question protects the persons and property of other states parties to the ICC Statute.

327 ICC Statute, Article 87(7).
328 Ibid.
329 Fox and Webb, *The Law of State Immunity*, 619.
330 ICC Statute, Article 27(2).

The ICC and the Constitutional Court of South Africa have offered interpretations of these provisions. In 2009 and 2010, an ICC Pre-trial Chamber issued arrest warrants for Omar Al Bashir, sitting President of Sudan, for participation in war crimes, crimes against humanity, and genocide.[331] Sudan is not a party to the ICC Statute; the underlying situation was referred to the ICC by Resolution 1593 of the UN Security Council, issued under Chapter VII. In it, the Council decided that 'the Government of Sudan and all other parties to the conflict in Darfur shall cooperate fully with and provide any necessary assistance to the Court and the Prosecutor pursuant to this resolution'.[332] In 2015, in view of Sudan's non-cooperation and refusal to engage with the Court, an ICC Pre-trial Chamber held that 'the Court cannot but refer the matter to the [Security Council] for the Council to take appropriate measures'.[333]

The ICC did not limit its efforts to seeking compliance with the warrant by Sudan. It also sought enforcement of the arrest warrant in various states parties to its Statute. After the warrant was issued, Al Bashir visited a number of other states, principally in Africa, for bilateral meetings or summits of heads of state. Following notice of these visits, the ICC sought the cooperation of the relevant states. No state has proceeded to arrest Al Bashir, resulting in ICC decisions on non-compliance regarding Kenya, Djibouti, Malawi, Chad, the Democratic Republic of the Congo, Sudan, Uganda, Jordan, and South Africa.[334] Though this case illustrates the distance that may exist between enforceability of an IC ruling and its enforcement by the coercive apparatus of states, it also exemplifies the kind of mechanism that, under different circumstances, might lead to effective determinations of enforceability by international adjudicators.

331 ICC, Pre-trial Chamber I, *Warrant of Arrest for Omar Hassan Ahmad Al Bashir*, 4 March 2009 (ICC-02/05-01/09-1), p. 7–8 (war crimes and crimes against humanity). ICC, Pre-trial Chamber I, *Second Warrant of Arrest for Omar Hassan Ahmad Al Bashir*, 12 July 2010 (ICC-02/05-01/09-94), p. 8–9 (genocide).

332 UN Security Council, Resolution S/RES/1593 (2005), adopted 31 March 2005, p. 1.

333 ICC Pre-Trial Chamber II, *Decision on the Prosecutor's Request for a Finding of Non-Compliance against the Republic of the Sudan*, 9 March 2015 (ICC-02/05-01/09-227).

334 Jeremy Julian Sarkin, 'Will the International Criminal Court (ICC) Be Able to Secure the Arrest of Vladimir Putin When He Travels? Understanding State Cooperation through Other ICC Non-Arrest Cases against Malawi, Chad, Nigeria, the Democratic Republic of Congo, South Africa, Djibouti, Uganda, and Jordan' (2023) 12 *International Human Rights Law Review* 26–68.

Of the various states whose cooperation the ICC sought to enforce the arrest warrant against Al Bashir, two have challenged the Court's use of its powers: South Africa and Jordan. South Africa contacted the Court prior to Al Bashir's participation in an African Union Summit in Johannesburg in 2015. Noting that Sudan was not a party to the Statute, South Africa requested from the ICC clarification on the content of, and interaction between, its obligations under the ICC Statute, under the UN Charter, and pursuant to the law of jurisdictional immunities. Before the Court, South Africa claimed that it was not clear either that Security Council Resolution 1593 'constitute[d] a waiver of Omar Al-Bashir's immunity' or that 'the Security Council has the authority to waive immunities of Heads of State'.[335]

The ICC reasoned that there was no need to waive immunity. The Security Council's referral of the situation to the ICC, combined with its imposition on Sudan of an obligation to 'cooperate fully with' the Court, led the ICC Statute to apply, *in totum*, to the situation referred.[336] This meant that Article 27 not only applied to Sudan in a 'vertical' manner, depriving its representatives of immunity vis-à-vis the ICC, but also produced 'horizontal effect'. In the Court's reading, Article 27(2) means that 'a State Party to the Statute cannot refuse to arrest and surrender to the Court an individual on the ground that that individual enjoys immunities belonging to another State Party'.[337] Following the referral by the Security Council, 'all immunities based on official capacity which could bar the Court from exercising its jurisdiction have been made inapplicable'.[338] Article 27(2) of the Statute, the ICC concluded, thus 'applies equally with respect to Sudan, rendering inapplicable any immunity on the ground of official capacity belonging to Sudan that would otherwise exist under international law'.[339]

Importantly, the ICC was not alone in its interpretation. The Supreme Court of Appeal of South Africa (ZASCA) found that its

335 ICC Pre-Trial Chamber II, *Decision under Article 87(7) of the Rome Statute on the non-compliance by South Africa with the request by the Court for the arrest and surrender of Omar Al-Bashir*, 6 July 2017 (ICC-02/05-01/09-302), para. 31.

336 Ibid., para. 85: 'the effect of a Security Council resolution triggering the Court's jurisdiction under article 13(b) of the Statute is that the legal framework of the Statute applies, in its entirety, with respect to the situation referred'.

337 Ibid., para. 94.

338 Ibid., para. 96.

339 Ibid., para. 91.

government's failure to arrest Al Bashir in 2015 was unlawful and unconstitutional.[340] On 15 March 2016, the ZASCA acknowledged the conflict between South Africa's obligations under the customary international law of immunities (and as a member of the African Union, whose summit it was hosting) and as a party to the Rome Statute. In light of the domestic law implementing the ICC Statute, the ZASCA concluded that head of state immunity should not constitute a bar to South Africa's cooperation with the ICC, including 'by way of the arrest and surrender of persons ... where an arrest warrant had been issued and a request for cooperation made'.[341]

At the same time, the South African government's response has been to challenge this obligation. On 19 October 2016, South Africa issued a notification of its withdrawal from the ICC Statute, citing the 'unenviable position where it [South Africa] was faced with conflicting international law obligations which had to be interpreted within the realm of hard diplomatic realities and overlapping mandates'.[342] The withdrawal was revoked before it could take effect, on 7 March 2017, following a High Court decision that withdrawal required parliamentary approval.[343] The issue arose again in March 2023, when Russian President Vladimir Putin, subject to another arrest warrant issued by the ICC, was due to attend the BRICS conference hosted in South Africa. President Cyril Ramaphosa again announced that South Africa would 'leave' the ICC owing to the tension between international norms in respect of ICC arrest warrants for heads of state. The statement was retracted only a few hours later,[344] and South Africa subsequently

[340] ZASCA, *Southern Africa Litigation Centre* v. *Minister of Justice and Constitutional Development & others*, 2015 (5) SA 1 (GP).

[341] Ibid., para. 103. ZASCA found that the case was an example of the maxim *generalia specialibus non derogant* (general words and rules do not derogate from special ones) (Ibid., para. 102).

[342] Declaratory statement by the Republic of South Africa on the decision to withdraw from the Rome Statute of the International Criminal Court, 19 October 2016, C.N.786.2016., TREATIES XVIII.10 (Depositary Notification).

[343] UN, 'South Africa: Withdrawal of notification of withdrawal, 7 March 2017 (C.N.121.2017.TREATIES-XVIII.10 (Depositary Notification)); High Court of South Africa, *Democratic Alliance* v. *Minister of International Relations and Cooperation and Others (Council for the Advancement of the South African Constitution Intervening)* (83145/2016) [2017] ZAGPPHC 53.

[344] Julian Borger, 'South Africa's president and ANC sow confusion over leaving ICC' (25 April 2023 The Guardian), available at www.theguardian.com/world/2023/apr/25/south-africas-president-and-party-sow-confusion-over-leaving-icc.

announced that, by mutual agreement, Putin would not attend the conference.[345]

The ICC Appeals Chamber reaffirmed the horizontal application of the ICC Statute in 2019, in a ruling vis-à-vis Jordan for the arrest of Al Bashir. The Court stated that there was no 'rule of customary international law recognising Head of State immunity vis-à-vis international courts'.[346] The Security Council's decision requiring Sudan to 'cooperate fully' with the ICC implied 'cooperation on the basis of the regime established for States Parties to the Statute'.[347] In case of referrals by the Security Council, the ICC was 'a tool to maintain or restore international peace and security, thus obviating the need for the UN Security Council to create new *ad hoc* tribunals for this purpose'.[348] Just as a state party 'cannot invoke Head of State immunity if another State Party proceeds to arrest and surrender the former State's Head of State on the basis of a request for cooperation by the Court ... Sudan cannot invoke Head of State immunity if a State Party is requested to arrest and surrender Mr Al-Bashir'.[349]

In both the case of South Africa and that of Jordan, the ICC found that state engagement with the Court meant that their objective non-compliance did not warrant a referral to the Security Council. The Appeals Chamber ruled that the Pre-trial Chamber II had erred in exercising its discretion to refer Jordan to the Security Council under Article 87 of the Rome Statute,[350] reasoning that this measure should be reserved for circumstances where non-compliance is 'grave enough', preventing the ICC from exercising its functions and powers under the Statute.[351] The Court found that Jordan had sought to consult the Court with respect to the norm, which could not lead to a 'presumption of bad fait'.[352] In the case of South Africa, the government indicated hesitancy in complying with the Court's decision concerning immunities, twice

[345] Zoe Jay and Matt Killingsworth, 'To Arrest or Not Arrest? South Africa, the International Criminal Court, and New Frameworks for Assessing Noncompliance' (2024) 68(2) *Intl Studies Qtr* 10.
[346] ICC Appeals Chamber, *Judgment in the Jordan Referral re Al-Bashir Appeal*, 6 May 2019, (ICC-02/05-01/09 OA2), para. 114.
[347] Ibid., para. 141.
[348] Ibid., para. 135.
[349] Ibid., paras. 143, 149.
[350] Ibid., para. 207.
[351] Ibid., para. 8.
[352] Ibid., para. 205.

threatening withdrawal from the Statute. In relation to Putin, South Africa sought to avoid non-compliance while also avoiding executing the arrest warrant, by simply not hosting Putin.

These rulings contrast with the decisions issued by the ICC with regard to the states that, having equally failed to deliver Al Bashir to the Court, did not put forward legal arguments in this respect. As regards these non-engaging states, the ICC employed its ultimate power under the Statute: referring non-compliance to the UN Security Council and Assembly of States Parties.[353] These referrals, and the lack of action on the part of the Council, which has the power to deploy Layer [5] sanctions, reveal the ultimate limit of this enforcement strategy. ICs, no matter what pronouncements they make, are ultimately limited by their reliance on *auctoritas*. They may issue pronouncements declaring obligatory the deployment of *potestas* by domestic authorities, but these pronouncements depend for effectiveness on the IC's *auctoritas* – its ability to change state agents' perceptions, and influence their behaviour, without the prospect of IC-ordered coercive measures against them in case of non-fulfilment.

5.6 Conclusion: An Underexplored Category of Remedies

Determinations of permissible responses connect international adjudication to the measures often considered as the true sanctions of international law. The acts of enforcement that necessarily require a connection to the apparatus of the state are limited to those involving the concrete mobilisation of political and economic resources. In this strict sense, enforcement is unavailable to ICs. However, the scope of the restriction does not by necessity extend to the ability of ICs to make legal determinations in this respect. If new relations emerge from a violation, including the permissibility of responses to a legal breach, a judicial determination of the relevant legal situation remains an act of *jurisdictio*. By exercising jurisdiction, the IC is not invading the sphere of state

[353] See, for example, *Decision on the non-compliance by the Republic of Uganda with the request to arrest and surrender Omar Al-Bashir to the Court and referring the matter to the UNSC and ASP*, ICC-02/05-01/09-267-ENG (11 July 2016). See Lorraine Smith-van Lin, 'Non-Compliance and the Law and Politics of State Cooperation: Lessons from the Al Bashir and Kenyatta Cases', in Olympia Bekou and Daley Birkett (eds.), *Cooperation and the International Criminal Court: Perspectives from Theory and Practice* (Leiden: Brill/Nijhoff, 2016), 114–151.

action but making a legal determination regarding the applicable rights and obligations.

Combined with the fourfold typology of legal remedies, these considerations open the door for an assessment of the full range of remedies that ICs may potentially deploy through mere *jurisdictio*. Their lack of *potestas* prevents them from deploying remedies that involve the exercise of *imperium*. At the same time, this does not limit international adjudicators' powers to settle legal and factual disputes that arise in the application of the horizontal normative framework of international law, regardless of where these disputes fall in the process that leads from interpretation of norms and identification of conduct to the adoption – by other states, by international organisations, possibly by private actors – of measures that are permissible in response to a violation. The possibility of findings of Permissible Response, determining that certain otherwise impermissible conducts become permissible in light of a breach, makes judicial pronouncements on the exercise of *imperium* a concrete possibility for international adjudicators.

At the same time, one may question the wisdom, for an adjudicator incapable of ordering the exercise of acts of *imperium*, of making pronouncements concerning these acts. As the ICC's attempts to mobilise domestic judiciaries against heads of state show, ultimately ICs rely on implementation by actors with *potestas*. For this reason, ICs may seek alternatives that are more productive than threatening to adopt measures whose application they cannot ensure.

As Part III of this book will now show, the more helpful strategy ICs have found is not to threaten to authorise or require measures whose application the court cannot ensure but to deploy their remedies, especially the more typical ones – Mere Adjudication, Declaration of Breach, and Consequential Duties – so as maximise their effectiveness. A manner of doing so is to provide resolution of key elements of the dispute while withholding the more constraining remedies available to them. In so doing, ICs offer states room to comply or to settle, while retaining the prospect of subsequent adjudication and remedy escalation in case of non-compliance.

PART III

Remedies and Compliance in International Judicial Practice

6

From Mere Adjudication to Permissible Responses

The WTO System of Remedy Repetition and Remedy Escalation

6.1 Introduction

This chapter inaugurates the third part of this book. Parts I and II were dedicated to considering the range of judicial remedies that are available to international adjudicators. They also ascertained how international judicial remedies may be instrumental in furthering compliance with, and enforcing, international law, in spite of the inability of international courts (IC) to determine the mobilisation of economic and political resources against recalcitrant states. International judicial remedies operate by mobilising, sharpening, and providing a focal point for, the forces that ordinarily lead states to adjust their conduct as a result of international law. Part III examines how international judicial practice reflects, and is affected by, these conclusions.

To recall, a traditional view of the role of ICs and their judicial remedies assumes a separation between the judicial role, limited to issuing a ruling on the interpretation and application of the law, and the 'political' tasks of demanding compliance with violations, and enforcing the law through sanctions. This view appears in the International Court of Justice's (ICJ's) statement, in *Haya de la Torre*, that it is 'not part of the Court's judicial function' to pronounce on questions of implementation of judgments, which depend 'only on considerations of practicability or political expediency'.[1] In a similar vein, the European Court of Human Rights (ECtHR) stated, in *Lyons* v. *United Kingdom*, that judgment implementation is a matter for a dialogue 'between the Committee of Ministers [of the Council of Europe] and the respondent Government'

[1] *Haya de la Torre (Peru* v. *Colombia)*, [1951] ICJ Reports 71, p. 79.

and 'the Court cannot assume any role in this dialogue'.[2] Though both courts affirmed the existence of an obligation to comply with their rulings,[3] these statements reinforce the view of adjudication as a task dissociated from implementation and compliance.

As Part III shows, this view is contradicted by the practice of a number of international adjudicators. Based on treaty text or their own understanding of their inherent powers (including power over their procedure), ICs have often employed their judicial authority to seek compliance with, and occasionally determine the means for lawful enforcement of, international law as established by their rulings. This practice challenges the rigid separation between the 'judicial plane' of adjudication and the 'political plane' in which compliance and implementation are pursued. Through this practice, ICs do not replace states and political bodies, which are the ones capable of mobilising resources and adopting sanctioning measures. ICs nonetheless employ the remedies available to them in pursuit of the ultimate objectives of a normative order disturbed by a violation: ensuring that compliance is restored, wrongs get reversed or compensated, and wrongdoers suffer consequences.[4]

This chapter focuses on the World Trade Organization (WTO) system of remedies, often termed 'prospective' or 'forward-looking', in that it does not offer retrospective Consequential Duties.[5] Instead, WTO remedies focus, at a first stage, on providing what in Chapter 1 is defined as Mere Adjudication and Declarations of Breach. In case of non-compliance, a further adjudication procedure leads to an additional Declaration of Breach, now declaring non-compliance with the previous ruling. And, in case of persistent non-compliance, a WTO body is

[2] ECtHR, Application No. 15227/03, *Lyons and Others* v. *United Kingdom*, [2003] Fourth Decision on Admissibility, p. 9.

[3] The ECtHR noted that implementation must be 'compatible with the conclusions set out in the Court's judgment' (Ibid.). The ICJ stated that the Judgment 'entails for [the parties] the obligation of compliance therewith' (*Haya de la Torre*, p. 79).

[4] See, for example, Grotius: 'Injuries done might be considered in a twofold Respect, either as they may be repaired or punished' (Hugo Grotius, *The Rights of War and Peace: Including the Law of Nature and of Nations* (Indianapolis: Liberty Fund, 2005), Bk. 2, Ch. 20, para. 1(1)). Anzilotti considered that 'the legal system . . . as an order of rules and sanctions relating to real relationships, demands to be effectively translated into action, and, consequently, that lesions to the rights of others be repaired by those who caused them' (Dionisio Anzilotti, *Teoria generale della responsabilità dello stato nel diritto internazionale* (Florence: Lumachi, 1902), 25 (author's translation)).

[5] See Geraldo Vidigal, 'Re-Assessing WTO Remedies: The Prospective and the Retrospective' (2013) 16(3) *Journal of International Economic Law* 505–534, and the literature cited therein.

empowered to award Permissible Responses, or 'authorize suspension of concessions and other obligations under the [WTO] agreements'.[6]

This authorisation to suspend concessions or other obligations, often termed 'WTO retaliation', provides a model instance of internationally authorised Permissible Responses. The authorisation is formally issued by a political body, the WTO Dispute Settlement Body (DSB). It is only available, however, as a 'last resort'[7] or '*ultima ratio*'.[8] It is awarded in case of non-compliance with prior WTO rulings, issued by an adjudicatory body after an assessment of the parties' WTO rights and obligations. Additionally, the authorisation to retaliate is subject to binding arbitration, to determine whether a claimant's proposed response is warranted and permissible. Finally, the authorisation is withdrawn once compliance is re-established, a matter that can also be determined through adjudication.

The WTO system of prospective remedies is now codified in the Dispute Settlement Understanding, an agreement that governs in detail the remedies available to WTO adjudicators and the conditions for adjudication of Permissible Responses.[9] As Section 6.2 shows, however, this system developed gradually, and largely based on practice, during the pre-WTO era of the 1947 General Agreement on Tariffs and Trade (GATT). This chapter sets the stage for considering the emerging practice of other ICs in this field, not against a fixed concept of the judicial function but in light of the potential for adjudicators to engage with issues of implementation within the limits of their jurisdiction and in light of the objective constraints that the lack of a connection to a coercive apparatus imposes.

Next, Section 6.3 considers the structure of the WTO system of remedies, in which an 'original' adjudication stage is followed by an

[6] Understanding on Rules and Procedures Governing the Settlement of Disputes, Marrakesh, 15 April 1994, 1869 UNTS 401 ('DSU'), Article 2.1.

[7] DSU, Article 3.7.

[8] Petros C. Mavroidis, 'Remedies in the WTO Legal System: Between a Rock and a Hard Place' (2000) 11 *European Journal of International Law* 763, 806.

[9] Throughout this chapter, I am interested primarily in the system of remedies leading to Mere Adjudication, Declarations of Breach, and authorised Permissible Responses. I thus examine WTO dispute settlement as it was designed to operate under the DSU, and as it operated between 1995 and 2020, leading to a number of such authorisations. The Appellate Body was dismantled at the end of 2020, meaning that a degree of party agreement is now necessary for WTO dispute settlement to operate conclusively. See Geraldo Vidigal, 'Living without the Appellate Body: Multilateral, Bilateral and Plurilateral Solutions to the WTO Dispute Settlement Crisis' (2019) 20 *Journal of World Investment & Trade* 862–890.

'implementation' or 'compliance' stage. In the former, only Mere Adjudication and Declarations of Breach are awarded. The latter includes both remedy repetition, in the form of compliance adjudication, and the possibility of remedy escalation, if the aggrieved party requests an authorisation to retaliate. Section 6.4 argues that, since the WTO authorisation to retaliate is a Permissible Response, analogies with the remedy of monetary compensation or 'damages', a Consequential Duty, can confuse more than they clarify. Section 6.5 examines the practice of WTO Permissible Responses, arguing that the prospect of remedy escalation is more valuable to members than the deployment of retaliation. Section 6.6 concludes, arguing that the WTO's remedial logic – which makes available remedy repetition and offers remedy escalation as a credible threat – provides a helpful framework for considering the use of remedy repetition, remedy escalation and remedy withholding by other international adjudicators.

6.2 From Suspension of Concessions to Retaliation in the GATT

The current system of WTO remedies originates from the compliance control procedure under the 1947 GATT. Its single provision on dispute settlement, Article XXIII, provided that, following unsuccessful consultations between parties, disputes could be referred to the 'Contracting Parties'.[10] The Contracting Parties – an organ composed of representatives of all the parties to the GATT acting collectively – were empowered under Article XXIII:2 to 'investigate any matter . . . referred to them', make 'appropriate recommendations', and 'give a ruling, as appropriate'. In case of 'serious enough' circumstances, they could 'authorize a contracting party or parties to suspend the application' of

[10] The GATT uses uppercase to refer to the Contracting Parties as an organ, acting collectively. General Agreement on Tariffs and Trade 1947, Geneva, 30 November 1947, in force 1 January 1948, 55 UNTS 194 ('GATT'), Article XXIII:2. Disputes 'may be referred to the CONTRACTING PARTIES. The CONTRACTING PARTIES shall promptly investigate any matter so referred to them and shall make appropriate recommendations to the contracting parties which they consider to be concerned, or give a ruling on the matter, as appropriate. . . . If the CONTRACTING PARTIES consider that the circumstances are serious enough to justify such action, they may authorize a contracting party or parties to suspend the application to any other contracting party or parties of such concessions or other obligations under this Agreement as they determine to be appropriate in the circumstances'.

GATT concessions and obligations towards the offender.[11] The authorisation to suspend concessions was therefore associated not with the failure to comply with previous decisions but rather with particularly grievous circumstances.

While the GATT is silent regarding the purpose of suspensions of concessions, it is likely that this was not initially intended as a means of exerting pressure on the wrongdoer. Writing in 1949, Clair Wilcox, who chaired the negotiations leading to the GATT, noted that authorising the reciprocal suspension of concessions was regarded by negotiators 'as a method of restoring a balance of benefits and obligations' between the parties. At the same time, he predicted already that this instrument would 'operate in fact as a sanction and a penalty'.[12]

6.2.1 The Early Years: Retaliation in GATT Practice

The Contracting Parties authorised suspension of concessions under Article XXIII:2 only once in the history of the GATT 1947. In 1951, a dispute settlement report found that US restrictions on dairy imports were impairing GATT benefits of the Netherlands and Denmark. This report stated that the circumstances of the violation were serious enough to justify suspension of concessions.[13] Rather than authorising this response, however, the Working Party that drafted it counselled the two claimants 'to afford to the United States Government a reasonable period of time . . . to rectify the situation'.[14] In deferring retaliation, the Working Party treated reciprocal suspension of concessions not as a sufficient remedy in and of itself (i.e. as a means of reparation) but as a subsidiary possibility, available in case the offender failed to 'rectify' its conduct: a Permissible Response.

In 1952, claiming US non-compliance with the 1951 report, the Netherlands requested authorisation to retaliate, restricting its imports of wheat flour from the United States in the following year to 57,000 tons, in response to the United States' failure to comply with the report in *US – Dairy Products.* A follow-up Working Party was constituted to address the appropriateness of the request. The terms of reference, drafted by the

[11] GATT, Article XXIII:2.
[12] Clair Wilcox, *A Charter for World Trade* (New York: MacMillan, 1949), 159.
[13] GATT, *United States Import Restrictions on Dairy Products – Resolution (US – Dairy Products)*, GATT/CP/130 – BISDII/16, 26 October 1951.
[14] Ibid., para. 1.

Contracting Parties, indicated that this Working Party should assess the 'equivalence of the measure proposed to the impairment' caused by the violation.[15] The 1952 Working Party found that the response proposed by the Netherlands was not unreasonable. Conducting an 'independent review'[16] of the matter, it authorised the Netherlands to limit its imports of wheat flour from the United States in 1953 to 60,000 tons.[17]

Despite its success from a legal perspective, this early instance of GATT-authorised suspension of concessions did not lead to actual retaliation. In subsequent cases, the Contracting Parties never authorised retaliation again, instead emphasising the need for compliance.[18] A 1955 Secretariat report stated that the primary objective of the GATT, following a finding of inconsistency, should be 'to secure the withdrawal of the measures', offering as an alternative the possibility of temporary compensation for the damage suffered.[19] Even panels that identified clear breaches of GATT provisions recommended negotiation and withdrawal of GATT-inconsistent measures.[20] In *France – Import Restrictions*, the Panel recommended to the United States, the claimant, 'that it refrain, for a reasonable period, from exercising its right . . . to propose suspension of the application of equivalent obligations or concessions'.[21]

Thus, the experience of the GATT 1947 suggests a preference of parties and adjudicators for Mere Adjudication and specification of (prospective) Consequential Duties over Permissible Responses. This

15 GATT, *Summary Record of the Tenth Meeting*, SR.7/10, 31 October 1952, 9.

16 GATT Working Party Report, *Netherlands Action under Article XXIII:2*, L/61, 7 November 1952, 6.

17 Ibid., at 7. The report was adopted by the Contracting Parties with both parties to the dispute abstaining while declaring that they considered the report to be satisfactory. Other contracting parties (New Zealand and Czechoslovakia) questioned whether the working group should have second-guessed a proposal that it considered not to be unreasonable (GATT, *Summary Record of the Sixteenth Meeting*, SR.7/16, 11 November 1952, 4.

18 The European Communities and Canada attempted – unsuccessfully – to reproduce this experience in the *US – Superfund* dispute. See Communication from the European Communities, *United States – Taxes on Petroleum and Certain Imported Substances: Follow-Up on the Panel Report*, C/W/540, 14 March 1988; GATT Council of Representatives, *Minutes of Meeting*, C/M/236, 11 October 1989, 20.

19 Working Party IV on Organization and Functional Questions, *Report of Review*, L/327/Reb.1, 4 April 1955, 64.

20 GATT Panel Report, *Italian Discrimination against Imported Agricultural Machinery*, L/833 – 7S/60, adopted 23 October 1958, 25; GATT Panel Report, *French Assistance to Exports of Wheat and Wheat Flour*, L/924, 7S/46, adopted 21 November 1958, 12.

21 GATT Panel Report, *French Import Restrictions*, L/1921 – 11S/94, adopted 14 November 1962, 7.

became clear in the 1962 dispute *Uruguayan Recourse to Article XXIII*. This panel, after finding a number of violations, established what it termed a 'two-stage procedure'. It recommended the removal of the GATT-inconsistent measures, followed by 'the possibility of further action, in case of non-fulfilment'. Failing compliance within a reasonable period of time (RPT), Uruguay would 'be entitled immediately to ask for the authorization of suspension of concessions or obligations'.[22]

In follow-up proceedings, Uruguay did not request Permissible Responses, focusing instead on findings of non-compliance with the previous rulings and recommendations for substantive performance. A 1963 report, identifying persistent violations of GATT rules, recommended their withdrawal by the wrongdoers, highlighting that Uruguay was entitled to request suspension of concessions.[23] A subsequent report restated this view, specifying that 'the relevant recommendations [for performance] would *ipso facto* have become inoperative with the disappearance of the restrictive measures'.[24]

In short, GATT Article XXIII:2 enabled adjudicators to follow recommendations with an immediate determination of Permissible Responses under GATT. However, adjudicators and parties mostly favoured requests for substantive performance. The panels in *US – Dairy Products* and *France – Import Restrictions* deferred Permissible Responses, instead awarding the offender a 'reasonable period' to comply with its rulings. Permissible Responses were therefore not seen, by parties or panels, as means to achieve 'reparation' or re-establish a 'balance of concessions', but as potential instruments to enforce rulings and obtain substantive performance – as Permissible Responses. In *Uruguayan Recourse to Article XXIII*, the claimant itself preferred a new Declaration of Breach in respect of the challenged measures over an authorisation for Permissible Responses.

The standard of suspending 'substantially equivalent concessions'[25] appears in a number of GATT provisions as a means of 'rebalancing'

[22] GATT Panel Report, *Uruguayan Recourse to Article XXIII (1962)*, L/1923 – 11S/95, adopted 16 November 1962, 19–21.

[23] GATT Panel Report, *Uruguayan Recourse to Article XXIII (1963)*, L/2074 – 13S/35, adopted 3 March 1965, 6.

[24] GATT Panel Report, *Uruguayan Recourse to Article XXIII (1964)*, L/2278 – 13S/45, adopted 3 March 1965, 6.

[25] GATT, Article XXVIII:3, XXVIII:4(d). See also GATT, Article XVIII:7(b), Article XVIII:21, XIX:3(a).

the agreement, allowing a wronged party to 'take back' concessions it made in negotiations.[26] In practice, however, neither adjudicators nor parties treated retaliation as an acceptable substitute for performance. Reciprocal suspension of concessions was used as a means of retaliating against, or sanctioning, the non-complying party, and pressuring it to comply with its commitments.

The two decades following *Uruguayan Recourse to Article XXIII* saw the rise of an 'antilegalistic' sentiment at the GATT.[27] The volume of GATT adjudication decreased substantially.[28] In spite of this, the idea that GATT retaliation had significant potential, and utility as a threat, had taken roots. In 1970, Kenneth Dam noted that suspension of concessions was 'the heart of the GATT enforcement system'.[29]

6.2.2 *Legalised Dispute Settlement and Unilateral Retaliation*

In 1965, a Note from the GATT Secretariat reaffirmed the two-phase structure set out by the panel in *Uruguayan Recourse to Article XXIII*, one phase for adjudication and the other for determination of Permissible Responses.[30] This structure was then consolidated by the Contracting Parties, in the 1979 Tokyo Round Understanding on Dispute Settlement (TRUDS). TRUDS and its Annex, the 'Agreed Description of the Customary Practice of the GATT in the Field of Dispute Settlement', codified and gave legal status to adjudicatory panels (which are not mentioned in the GATT) as well as to the performance-oriented two-phase approach to remedies. Prior to TRUDS, therefore,

[26] Under GATT Article XXVIII, a state may respond to a withdrawal of concessions with a reciprocal withdrawal of 'substantially equivalent concessions'.

[27] Kenneth W. Dam, *The GATT: Law and International Economic Organization* (Chicago: University of Chicago Press, 1970), 356.

[28] One important trade dispute at the time, the so-called *Chicken War* between the United States and the EEC, was resolved through recourse to an '*ad hoc* panel' outside the framework of the GATT. Panel on Poultry, *Report of the Panel*, L/2088, 21 November 1965. See Herman Walker, 'The Chicken War' (1964) 58 *AJIL* 671, 683 (praising this 'improvisation'). See also Robert E. Hudec, *Enforcing International Trade Law: The Evolution of the Modern GATT Legal System* (Salem, NH: Butterworth, 1991), 13 ('GATT adjudication simply vanished').

[29] Dam, *The GATT*, p. 364.

[30] Committee on Trade and Development, *Note by the Secretariat: Compensation to Less-Developed Contracting Parties for Loss of Trading Opportunities Resulting from the Application of Residual Restrictions*, COM.TD/5, 2 March 1965, 8–10.

this entire construction was based on the embryonic practice of the 1950s and early 1960s, codified by the GATT Secretariat.[31]

TRUDS required GATT dispute settlement panels to make 'an objective assessment of the facts of the case and their conformity with the General Agreement' and issue 'findings in a written form'.[32] If the panel found a violation, the party found in breach should resume performance of its commitments. A negotiated arrangement, or an authorisation to retaliate, could be available 'as a temporary measure' if 'immediate withdrawal of the [violating] measure is impracticable'.[33] The 'last resort' in this system of remedies was to authorise a Permissible Response, in the form of Article XXIII:2 suspension of concessions or other obligations 'on a discriminatory basis vis-à-vis the [wrongdoer]'.[34]

This system was further consolidated in response to the practice by the United States, especially in the 1980s, of responding unilaterally to measures it believed harmed US trade interests, which Jadish Bhagwati labelled 'aggressive unilateralism'.[35] This unilateral enforcement of perceived trade harms, Robert Hudec recalls, was the 'precipitating event' of the Uruguay Round negotiations that established the WTO.[36] Andrew Stoler, the main negotiator for the United States, concurs that a major

[31] See, for example, Ibid., 8; WTO, *Decision of 5 April 1966 on Procedures under Article XXIII*, BISD 14S/18, paras. 9–10.

[32] Understanding Regarding Notification, Consultation, Dispute Settlement and Surveillance, L/4907, adopted 28 November 1979 ('TRUDS'), Articles 16–17. John Jackson notes that many panels had responded to the antilegalistic sentiment of the 1960s and 1970s by 'tr[ying] to play the role of conciliators . . . assisting the negotiation in reference to the power positions of the disputing parties and not with reference to the interpretation or application of an agreed-upon rule' (John H. Jackson, 'The Birth of the GATT-MTN System: A Constitutional Appraisal' (1980) 12 *Law & Policy in International Business* 21, 42). In one case involving Jamaican preferences, the panel effectively recommended the adoption of a waiver to accommodate temporary non-compliance (GATT Panel Report, *Jamaica – Margins of Preference*, L/3485 – 18S/183, adopted 2 February 1971, 15–17).

[33] This adjustment, labelled 'compensation', should not be confused with the homonymous remedy under general international law.

[34] TRUDS Annex, Paragraph 4. This provision originated from Article 3.7 of the DSU.

[35] See Jagdish N. Bhagwati and Hugh T. Patrick (eds.), *Aggressive Unilateralism: America's 301 Trade Policy and the World Trading System* (Ann Arbor: University of Michigan Press, 1990). But see Alan O. Sykes, 'Constructive Unilateral Threats in International Commercial Relations: The Limited Case for Section 301' (1992) 23 *Law and Policy in International Business* 263.

[36] Robert E. Hudec, 'Broadening the Scope of Remedies in WTO Dispute Settlement', in Friedl Weiss and Jochem Wiers (eds.), *Improving WTO Dispute Settlement Procedures* (London: Cameron May, 2000), 345–376, 373–374.

objective of all other contracting parties at the Uruguay Round was to prevent US unilateralism.[37]

The resulting trade-off resulted in a highly legalised WTO Dispute Settlement Understanding. The Dispute Settlement Understanding (DSU), on the one hand, ensures that WTO Members may resort to adjudication, ultimately leading to authorised Permissible Responses in case of non-compliance. On the other hand, it legally prohibits resort by WTO Members to unilaterally determined trade retaliation.

6.3 The Structure of WTO Remedies

The WTO dispute settlement procedure codified in the DSU – as designed and before the Appellate Body became non-operational – may be divided into two phases. The 'original' adjudication stage focuses on the settlement of the interpretative disputes between the parties and establishment of violations.[38] Panels (and, on appeal, the Appellate Body) assess the facts of the dispute, determine the applicable WTO obligations, and verify the conformity of the alleged wrongdoer's conduct with WTO obligations. If this assessment results in a finding of inconsistency with WTO law, an implementation stage follows. The key issues of interpretation of applicable WTO rules and identification of the character of violations having been settled, the system's 'first objective' becomes to 'secure' the elimination of WTO-inconsistent conduct.[39]

6.3.1 WTO Remedies at the 'Original' Adjudication Stage: Mere Adjudication and Declaration of Breach

At the original adjudication stage, a WTO panel is established at the request of a WTO member to examine 'measures taken by another Member' that the complainant alleges are 'affecting the operation' of WTO Agreements, nullifying or impairing benefits it derives from WTO law.[40] A WTO panel has the same two distinctive tasks – rule

[37] Andrew L. Stoler, 'The WTO Dispute Settlement Process: Did the Negotiators Get What They Wanted?' (2004) 3 *World Trade Review* 99, 103.

[38] The term 'original' is found in DSU Articles 10.4, 21.5, 22.6, and 22.7 (note 16).

[39] DSU, Article 3.7.

[40] DSU, Articles 3.3, 3.5, 4.2. Absent exceptional circumstances, this nullification or impairment derives from a violation of WTO law: 'where there is an infringement of the obligations assumed under a covered agreement, the action is considered *prima facie* to constitute a case of nullification or impairment' (DSU, Article 3.8).

interpretation and rule application – as any adjudicator competent to interpret and apply an international agreement. First, a panel must 'clarify the existing provisions of [WTO] agreements in accordance with customary rules of interpretation of public international'.[41] Second, it must examine the 'conformity with the relevant [WTO] agreements' of the conduct identified by the complainant as a potential violation of WTO rules.[42]

A panel's determinations are not final. The panel submits to the WTO DSB the panel report, containing its assessment of the facts, legal reasoning, findings, and conclusions. Any party to the dispute dissatisfied with the panel's interpretation and application of WTO rules may appeal 'issues of law covered in the panel report and legal interpretations developed by the panel'[43] to the Appellate Body. The WTO Appellate Body – a standing adjudicative body composed of seven 'persons of recognized authority' in the field – may 'uphold, modify or reverse the legal findings and conclusions of the panel'.[44] Its report is then submitted to the DSB, which adopts it – together with the panel report – unless all WTO members (including the complainant) consensually decide not to adopt it.[45]

6.3.2 *The Original Adjudication Stage*

Conclusions and findings are declaratory judicial remedies.[46] In the typology established in Chapter 1, they amount to Mere Adjudication and Declarations of Breach. Through their findings, WTO adjudicators establish interpretations of provisions of WTO law and, as the case may be, declare that there has or there has not been a breach of these provisions. Once adopted by the DSB, 'conclusions and findings' of panels and the Appellate Body become 'rulings' of the Dispute Settlement Body and are binding under WTO law. Like declaratory judgments, rulings of the DSB may be said to ensure definitive

[41] DSU, Article 3.2.
[42] DSU, Article 11.
[43] DSU, Article 17.6.
[44] DSU, Articles 17.3, 17.13.
[45] DSU, Article 17.14. In case there is no appeal, the DSB adopts the panel report directly (DSU, Article 16.4).
[46] Christine Gray, 'Types of Remedies in ICJ Cases: Lessons for the WTO', in Friedl Weiss and Jochem Wiers (eds.), *Improving WTO Dispute Settlement Procedures* (London: Cameron May, 2000), 401–415, 405–406.

recognition of a situation at law.[47] Besides findings, WTO adjudicators award two further legal remedies at the original adjudication stage. First are recommendations 'that the Member concerned bring the measure into conformity with that agreement'. Second are suggestions of 'ways in which the Member concerned could implement the recommendations'.[48]

Recommendations envisage an end which is ultimately 'negative': eliminating the WTO-inconsistency. Suggestions concern the 'positive' means to attain this end – the courses of action by which the adjudicator believes the member may eliminate the WTO-inconsistency. Recommendations are compulsory: adjudicators 'shall' make them whenever they find the existence of a breach, generating 'prospective implementation obligations'.[49]

Suggestions are optional for adjudicators and do not bind members. The adjudicator merely points to possible manners in which compliance could be achieved. Thus, members may choose alternative paths to eliminate the WTO-inconsistency.[50] Conversely, choosing the suggested

[47] *Interpretation of Judgments Nos 7 and 8 (Factory at Chorzow), Germany* v. *Poland*, Judgment, (1927) PCIJ Ser A No 13, p. 20. See Section 2.1. In fact, in *US – Stainless Steel from Mexico*, the Appellate Body opined that the relevance of DSB rulings, especially those deriving from Appellate Body reports, applies beyond this: 'While the application of a provision may be regarded as confined to the context in which it takes place, the relevance of clarification contained in adopted Appellate Body reports is not limited to the application of a particular provision in a specific case' (Appellate Body Report, *US – Stainless Steel from Mexico*, WT/DS344/AB/R, adopted 20 May 2008, para. 161).

[48] DSU Article 19.1.

[49] Appellate Body Report, *US – Cotton (21.5)*, WT/DS267/AB/RW, adopted 20 June 2008, fn. 494. As declaratory judicial pronouncements, findings (and rulings) may address the WTO-legality of expired measures; WTO adjudicators may declare that the measures at issue were adopted inconsistently with WTO rules, regardless of their current status. See Appellate Body Report, *US – Certain EC Products*, WT/DS165/AB/R, adopted 10 January 2001, paras. 128(e), 129; Appellate Body Report, *US – Clove Cigarettes*, WT/DS406/AB/R, adopted 24 April 2012, para. 297. With regard to expired measures, a declaratory remedy is all that WTO adjudicators can provide. As the Appellate Body clarified in *China – Raw Materials*, the exception lies in measures that while apparently time-bound, actually constitute a single continuing breach. In this dispute, the panel issued a recommendation for China 'to bring its measures into conformity with its WTO obligations such that the "series of measures" does not operate to bring about a WTO-inconsistent result'. (Panel Report, *China – Raw Materials*, WT/DS394/R, WT/DS395/R, WT/DS398/R, adopted 22 February 2012, at 8.8, 8.15, 8.22, para. 264 (footnotes omitted)). See also Appellate Body Report, *Chile – Price Band System*, WT/DS207/AB/R, adopted 22 October 2002, para. 144.

[50] Appellate Body Report, *EC – Bananas (21.5 II – Ecuador; 21.5 – US)*, WT/DS27/AB/RW2/ECU, adopted 11 December 2008, WT/DS27/AB/RW/USA, adopted 22 December 2008, para. 324; Appellate Body Report, *US – OCTG Sunset (21.5)*, WT/DS268/AB/RW, adopted 17 December 2004, para. 173.

path does not, without elimination of the WTO-inconsistent conduct, lead to compliance with the recommendations.

In the few cases in which panels have used this remedy, suggestions simply highlighted ways in which the wrongdoer 'could implement' the recommendation,[51] or the means by which 'compliance can best be achieved'.[52] But suggestions may be more strongly worded. In *Argentina – Poultry*, the panel found that it 'd[id] not perceive how Argentina could properly implement our recommendation without revoking the anti-dumping measure at issue in this dispute'.[53] In *US – Byrd Amendment*, the panel held that, 'although there could potentially be a number of ways in which the United States could bring the [unlawful measure] into conformity', it 'f[ou]nd it difficult to conceive of any method which would be more appropriate and/or effective than the repeal of the ... measure'.[54]

6.3.3 WTO Adjudication at the Implementation Stage: Remedy Repetition and Remedy Escalation

The DSU does not provide for reparation of injury caused by the breach. As the International Law Commission (ILC) has noted, a feature of DSU remedies is that they 'lack ... reparation'; the focus of WTO dispute settlement 'is on cessation rather than reparation'.[55] Though some scholars have suggested that WTO adjudicators should be able to award damages, none has ever done that.[56]

Rather than reparation, the implementation stage is focused on seeking the cessation of the unlawful conduct identified at the original stage. For this purpose, the WTO system offers three remedies. First is

[51] Panel Reports, *EC – Trademarks and Geographical Indications*, WT/DS174/R, adopted 20 April 2005, para. 8.5.

[52] Panel Report, *US – Underwear*, WT/DS24/R, adopted 25 February 1997, para. 8.3.

[53] Panel Report, *Argentina – Poultry Anti-Dumping Duties*, WT/DS241/R, adopted 19 May 2003, para. 8.7.

[54] Panel Report, *US – Byrd Amendment*, WT/DS217/R, WT/DS234/R, adopted 27 January 2003, para. 8.6.

[55] ILC, Draft Articles on Responsibility of States for Internationally Wrongful Acts, with commentaries, A/56/10, 2001 ('ARSIWA Commentary'), p. 89, fn. 431.

[56] See Vidigal, 'Re-assessing WTO Remedies'. See, on this debate, Marco Bronckers and Freya Baetens, 'Reconsidering Financial Remedies in WTO Dispute Settlement' (2013) 16 (2) *Journal of International Economic Law* 281; Bryan Mercurio, 'Why Compensation Cannot Replace Trade Retaliation in the WTO Dispute Settlement Understanding' (2009) 8(2) *World Trade Review* 315–338.

compliance adjudication, by panels and the Appellate Body. Second is a bilateral remedy to be agreed between the wrongdoer and the complainant: an agreement for compensation. Third is an authorisation for aggrieved members to retaliate, suspending concessions or other obligations under the WTO Agreements.

6.3.3.1 Compliance Adjudication: Remedy Repetition, Discursive Escalation

Pursuant to DSU Article 19.1, a finding that a measure adopted by a WTO member violates WTO obligations must be combined with a recommendation for the member to 'bring the measure into conformity' with these obligations within an RPT.[57] Once the RPT expires, DSU Article 21.5 permits a new recourse to WTO dispute settlement to solve any 'disagreement as to the existence or consistency with a covered agreement of measures taken to comply with the recommendations and rulings' of the DSB.[58]

Like original panels, an Article 21.5 panel may be established by unilateral request.[59] A party may request a compliance panel at any point in time after the end of the original RPT, as long as the original dispute has not been terminated and the parties disagree over compliance.[60] The ensuing compliance panel, also termed 'Article 21.5 panel' or 'implementation panel', is established to decide not on the interpretation of WTO rules – although this may be required for it to reach its findings – but on the consistency with WTO law of the measures taken by the violator to comply with the recommendations and rulings of the original report.

Article 21.5 therefore does not permit adjudication *ex novo*. It requires WTO adjudicators to determine whether compliance was achieved, in

[57] DSU, Article 19.1. The DSU demands from members, if practicable, 'prompt compliance' with recommendations and rulings adopted by the DSB. If this is 'impracticable', it should afford the wrongdoing member a reasonable period of time (RPT) to comply (DSU, Articles 21.1, 21.3).

[58] DSU, Article 21.5.

[59] Both the original complainant and the original respondent may request the establishment of an Article 21.5 panel. See Appellate Body Report, *US – Continued Suspension*, WT/DS320/AB/R, adopted 14 November 2008, para. 347. ('the text of Article 21.5 does not preclude an original respondent from initiating proceedings under that provision to obtain confirmation of the consistency with the WTO agreements of its implementing measure').

[60] Ibid., paras. 374, 354. For a mutually agreed solution that did terminate the dispute, see, Notification of a Mutually Agreed Solution, *US – Cotton*, WT/DS267/46, 23 October 2014, p. 1 ('no further action shall be taken under DSU Article 21.5').

light of the recommendations and rulings issued at the original adjudication stage.[61] The examination of 'measures taken to comply' may encompass not only whether the legislation or acts judged WTO-inconsistent have been abrogated but also whether any new legislation or new acts have produced (or impeded) substantive compliance with WTO law. As the Appellate Body explained in *EC – Bananas (21.5 – II)*, *substantive compliance* is essential. The obligation that ensues is not of means – abrogating the legislation found incompatible with WTO law or taking any specific measures regarding affected parties – but of result: bringing the measure into conformity. Thus, 'what matters in Article 21.5 proceedings is whether the result of implementation – whatever means are chosen – brings about substantive compliance with the DSB recommendations and rulings'.[62]

The requirement that implementation measures must produce substantive compliance limits the relevance of suggestions. Even if a panel or the Appellate Body suggest means of compliance with their general recommendation, a member's adoption of these suggestions is not dispositive of its compliance with the recommendations to achieve conformity. In *EC – Bananas (21.5 – II)*, the Appellate Body rejected the view that 'the measure implementing such a suggestion can be presumed to be WTO-consistent'.[63] Even the adoption of a mutually agreed solution between the parties does not preclude the original complainant from

[61] Appellate Body Report, *EC – Bed Linen (21.5)*, WT/DS141/AB/RW, adopted 24 April 2003, para. 78 ('If a claim challenges a measure which is not a "measure taken to comply", that claim cannot properly be raised in Article 21.5 proceedings').

[62] *EC – Bananas III (21.5 – Ecuador II)*, para. 322. See also *US – Continued Suspension*, para. 374; Appellate Body Report, *US – Softwood Lumber IV (21.5)*, WT/DS257/AB/RW, adopted 20 December 2005, para. 77; *EC – Bed Linen (21.5)*, para. 78; Appellate Body Report, *Canada – Aircraft (21.5)*, WT/DS70/AB/RW, adopted 4 August 2000, para. 36; Appellate Body Report, *US – FSC (21.5 II)*, WT/DS108/AB/RW2, adopted 14 March 2006, para. 93. The same standard is applied to subsidies, even if recommendations are worded differently under the Agreement on Subsidies and Countervailing Measures, 15 April 1994, in force 1 January 1995, 1869 UNTS 14 ('SCM Agreement'). For prohibited subsidies, see *US – FSC (21.5 II)*, para. 83 ('full withdrawal of a prohibited subsidy within the meaning of Article 4.7 of the SCM Agreement cannot be achieved by a "measure taken to comply" that replaces the original subsidy with yet another subsidy found to be prohibited'). For actionable subsidies, see Appellate Body Report, *US – Cotton (21.5)*, para. 238 ('a Member would not comply with the obligation in Article 7.8 to withdraw the subsidy if it leaves an actionable subsidy in place, either entirely or partially, or replaces that subsidy with another actionable subsidy').

[63] *EC – Bananas (21.5 – Ecuador II)*, para. 324.

subsequently having recourse to Article 21.5, absent 'a clear indication ... of a relinquishment of [this] right'.[64]

In terms of the categories of remedies outlined in Chapter 1, what a complainant can obtain from a compliance panel is remedy repetition: a new exercise of Mere Adjudication, addressing disagreements on what compliance requires, and an application of the norms to conduct possibly leading to a new Declaration of Breach. An Article 21.5 panel's remedies do not (yet) amount to remedy escalation, as these new pronouncements are remedies of the same category as those issued at the end of original adjudication.

There is nonetheless a discursive escalation involved in a finding of non-compliance. At the original adjudication stage, a WTO member's actions may be found to be inconsistent with its WTO obligations, but the enjoinment to change conduct is prospective only. Although from a legal standpoint the member may have been found in breach, the dispute settlement system operates as if the interpretative dispute is genuine up to the point at which a multilateral ruling on it is issued. At the end of the RPT, the member's behaviour can be assessed against a legal framework that is no longer in doubt. A compliance panel does not merely assert a breach but determines that the member has 'failed to comply with the recommendations and rulings of the DSB in the original dispute'.[65] The condemnation by an Article 21.5 panel thus symbolically sanctions a wrongdoer that, even after being informed of its precise obligations and being afforded an RPT to comply, fails to change its conduct so as to re-establish lawful relations with the aggrieved party (and, arguably, all other WTO members).

A parallel may be drawn between the finding of WTO-inconsistency at the original stage and the decision by ICs not to engage the responsibility of the wrongdoer under some circumstances, or not to issue a declaration of breach when they believe Mere Adjudication provides a sufficient remedy.[66] Though original WTO adjudication already involves a finding of breach, the finding of non-compliance implies a discursive escalation in the same way a Declarations of Breach involves a discursive escalation

[64] Ibid., para. 212.

[65] Appellate Body Report, *US – Zeroing (21.5)*, WT/DS294/AB/RW, adopted 11 June 2009, para. 9.1(b)(i). An alternative formulation is that the member 'has not implemented the recommendations and rulings of the DSB' (Appellate Body Report, *Chile – Price Band System (21.5)*, WT/DS207/AB/RW, adopted 22 May 2007, para. 254(b)(ii)).

[66] See Section 4.2.1.

when compared to Mere Adjudication.[67] A key difference is that WTO remedies are not exhausted by the determination of non-compliance: a finding of non-compliance opens the door for remedy escalation.

6.3.3.2 WTO Compensation: A Voluntary Transactional Remedy

The first possibility of remedy escalation is compensation. WTO compensation is not awarded by an adjudicator as a Consequential Duty but is a voluntary transactional remedy. In case of persistent non-compliance by a respondent after the RPT, DSU Article 22(1) foresees, as alternative 'temporary measures', WTO compensation and WTO retaliation. Pursuant to this provision, '[c]ompensation is voluntary': it is a transactional remedy (rather than a judicial one), by which the wrongdoer provides advantages to the aggrieved member in order to prevent the adoption of permissible measures of response against it.

WTO compensation is thus different from the Consequential Duty of compensation under general international law. As explained by the ILC, compensation under international law 'generally consists of a monetary payment . . . intended to offset, as far as may be, the damage suffered by the injured State as a result of the breach'.[68] By contrast, WTO compensation may consist in any form of benefit voluntarily offered by the wrongdoer to the aggrieved party for the latter to temporarily accept non-compliance and refrain from adopting Permissible Responses under WTO law.

Being voluntary, WTO compensation may take a variety of forms. It may involve commercial advantages, as agreed in *Japan – Alcoholic Beverages*[69] or *Turkey – Textiles*.[70] If it takes a monetary form, compensation may be provided as a 'lump sum' payment, but also as continued provisions of money corresponding to the damage caused periodically by the persistent non-compliance. The latter occurred in *US – Copyright*, where, after an initial agreement to a 'lump sum',[71] the United States apparently (but without notification) paid periodic sums to

[67] See, for example, *United States Diplomatic and Consular Staff in Tehran*, *United States of America* v. *Iran*, Judgment, [1980] ICJ Reports 3, p. 41.

[68] ARSIWA Commentary, p. 99.

[69] DSB, *Minutes of DSB Meeting*, WT/DSB/M/41, 22 January 1998, 2.

[70] *Notification of Mutually Acceptable Solution*, WT/DS34/14, 19 July 2001.

[71] *Notification of a Mutually Satisfactory Temporary Arrangement*, WT/DS160/23, 26 June 2003.

the European Union (EU).[72] In *US – Cotton*, the initial agreement included both periodic pecuniary payment and trade benefits.[73] A subsequent agreement declared the dispute 'terminated', with the United States paying 'the amount of US$300 million' in a lump sum transfer to the Brazilian Cotton Institute.[74]

The DSU provides that compensation must be 'voluntary and, if granted, shall be consistent with the covered agreements'.[75] This means, first, that no WTO law procedure exists to determine an *obligation* to grant compensation. Additionally, compensation for a violation must not include any measures in breach of WTO rules. A key consequence of the latter limitation is the requirement that any 'advantage, favour, privilege or immunity' granted to products and services of the injured Member, as part of the WTO compensation agreement, must be extended 'immediately and unconditionally' to all other members of the organisation.[76] Thus, any trade advantages granted to the aggrieved party as compensation must be granted to the entire WTO membership.[77]

6.3.3.3 WTO Retaliation: Authorised and Justiciable Permissible Responses

Failing compliance and voluntary compensation, the DSU offers as a 'last resort' to aggrieved members an authorisation to adopt Permissible Responses – that is, WTO retaliation – against the wrongdoer.[78] The

[72] *Status Report by the United States*, WT/DS160/24/Add.235, 13 May 2025. See Bernard O'Connor and Margareta Djordjevic, 'Practical Aspects of Monetary Compensation: The US – Copyright Case' (2005) 8 *Journal of International Economic Law* 127.

[73] Joint Communication from Brazil and the United States, *US – Cotton*, WT/DS267/45, 31 August 2010. In this case and in *US – Copyright*, the relevant agreements were not labelled 'compensation'; in *US – Cotton*, even the label 'mutually satisfactory solution' was avoided.

[74] Notification of a Mutually Agreed Solution, *US – Cotton*, WT/DS267/46, 23 October 2014, p. 1, 2.

[75] DSU, Article 22.1.

[76] GATT, Article I:1; General Agreement on Trade in Services, Uruguay, 15 April 1994, in force 1 January 1995, 1869 UNTS 183 ('GATS'), Article II:1.

[77] This also means that WTO compensation may not include restrictions on the exports from the violator to the aggrieved member – as this would fall under 'voluntary export restrictions', which are prohibited by Agreement on Safeguards in the Marrakesh Agreement, 15 April 1994, in force 1 January 1995, 1869 UNTS 154, Article 11.1(b). The fact that the WTO structure does not include a third-party law enforcer capable of challenging a voluntary export restriction in the absence of initiative from affected members does not mean that such arrangements are legal. Members may not use WTO compensation to unlawfully renegotiate WTO law as between themselves (see DSU, Article 3.5).

[78] DSU, Article 3.7.

DSU refers to WTO retaliation as 'suspension of concessions or other obligations'.[79] DSU Article 22.2 permits members that brought proceedings against a non-complying wrongdoer to 'request authorization from the DSB to suspend the application to the [wrongdoer] of concessions or other obligations under the covered agreements'.[80] Article 22.8 provides that this retaliation 'shall be temporary and shall only be applied until' compliance is achieved.[81]

The authorisation to retaliate may be granted without adjudication. Claimants may request authorisation to retaliate twenty days after the end of the RPT. The DSB must grant it failing a negative consensus.[82] The member requesting the authorisation must specify in its request (a) the level of retaliation it wishes to apply and (b) the agreements in which it wishes to suspend concessions and other obligations towards the persistent violator. It falls upon the violator to request arbitration, under Article 22.6, in case it believes that the retaliation requested is unwarranted or excessive.

The DSU limits retaliation in two ways. First, Article 22.4 imposes a *quantitative* limitation: '[t]he level of suspension of concessions or other obligations authorized by the DSB shall be equivalent to the level of the nullification or impairment' caused by the breach. Second, DSU Article 22.3 *qualitatively* restricts permissible responses to specific WTO obligations. In the DSU, both limitations are worded as self-judging, meaning that the retaliating member must itself conform to these limitations when determining its proposed level of retaliation. In case of challenge, an 'Article 22.6 arbitrator' is tasked with examining whether the proposed retaliation is within the parameters set by the DSU.

Regarding the quantitative limitation, 'equivalence' must be measured against the 'nullification or impairment' caused by the breach. In *EC – Hormones*, the arbitrator described its task as a determination of the 'annual prospective US exports of hormone-treated beef and beef products to' the European Communities (EC) if the breach had ended by the end of the RPT.[83] Subsequent arbitrators likewise examined the impact of

[79] DSU, Article 22.1.

[80] DSU, Article 22.2.

[81] DSU, Article 22.8.

[82] DSU Articles 22.2 and 22.6. 'Negative consensus' means a consensus at the DSB not to grant the authorisation. If a proposal is put forward for the DSB *not* to grant the authorisation, the member that requested the authorisation may block consensus on the adoption of the proposal and thus ensure the DSB's authorisation.

[83] Decision of the Arbitrator, *EC – Hormones (22.6)*, WT/DS26/ARB, 12 July 1999, para. 38.

the breach on the market of the complaining parties.[84] In *US – 1916 Act*, the EC requested not to raise tariffs but to adopt 'mirror legislation' to the US' WTO-inconsistent measure. The arbitrator found this response permissible, provided that the level of retaliation did not exceed that of the nullification or impairment caused to EC companies by the violation.[85]

In each case, the arbitrators inferred from the temporary nature of the 'suspension of concessions and other obligations' that the purpose of this suspension is to induce compliance with WTO law.[86] The sole partial exception is *US – Byrd Amendment*, in which the Article 22.6 arbitrator did not agree that the purpose of suspension of concessions and other obligations would be 'exclusively to induce compliance'. The arbitrator found that inducing compliance is 'at most … one of a number of purposes in authorizing the suspension of concessions or other obligations'.[87] However, it also noted that the authorisation to retaliate is limited by the parameters set out in the DSU, and in particular by the requirement that retaliation be authorised at a level equivalent to that of the nullification or impairment caused by the violation.[88]

The Agreement on Subsidies and Countervailing Measures (SCM Agreement) provides specific parameters for retaliation in disputes involving subsidies. It uses the terms 'countermeasures' and provides that they must be 'appropriate', 'not disproportional', or 'commensurate',

[84] *EC – Bananas (22.6 – US)*, 9 April 1999, para. 6.16; Decisions of the Arbitrator, *EC – Bananas III (22.6 – ECU)*, WT/DS27/ARB/ECU, 24 March 2000, para. 169; *US – Byrd Amendment (22.6)*, para. 3.79; Decision of the Arbitrator, *US – Gambling (22.6)*, WT/DS285/ARB, 21 December 2007, para. 3.187; Decision of the Arbitrator, *US – Cotton (22.6, 4.11)*, WT/DS267/ARB/1, 31 August 2009, para. 4.87.

[85] Decision of the Arbitrator, *US – 1916 Act (22.6)*, WT/DS136/ARB, 24 August 2004, paras. 7.7–7.8.

[86] Decision of the Arbitrator, *Canada – Aircraft II (22.6)*, WT/DS222/ARB, 17 February 2003, para. 3.122. See also *EC – Bananas (22.6 – US)*, para. 6.3; Decision of the Arbitrator, *Brazil – Aircraft (22.6)*, WT/DS46/ARB, 28 August 2000, para. 3.58; Decision of the Arbitrator, *US – 1916 Act (22.6)*, para. 5.3; Decision of the Arbitrator, *US – Gambling (22.6)*, para. 2.7; Decision of the Arbitrator, *US – Cotton (22.6, 4.11)*, para 4.112; Decision of the Arbitrator, *US – Cotton (22.6, 7.10)*, WT/DS267/ARB/2, 31 August 2009, para. 4.59.

[87] Decision of the Arbitrator, *US – Byrd Amendment (22.6)*, para. 3.74.

[88] Decision of the Arbitrator, *EC – Bananas III (22.6 – US)*, para. 6.3; Decision of the Arbitrator, *EC – Hormones (22.6)*, para. 21; Decision of the Arbitrator, *EC – Bananas (22.6 – ECU)*, para. 72; Decision of the Arbitrator, *US – 1916 Act (22.6)*, paras. 5.8; Decision of the Arbitrator, *US – Byrd Amendment (22.6)*, para. 3.74, 6.3; Decision of the Arbitrator, *US – Gambling (22.6)*, para. 1.5.

instead of the usual 'equivalent to the level of nullification or impairment'. Arbitrators have tended to consider this as implying that more-than-equivalent retaliation is warranted under this agreement and developed various formulas to determine the relevant amount, sometimes adjusting the final result on grounds that retaliation must perform the function of inducing compliance.

In *Brazil – Aircraft*, the Article 22.6 arbitrator expressly stated that requiring equivalence when the SCM Agreement establishes a different standard 'would be contrary to the principle of effectiveness by significantly limiting the efficacy of countermeasures in the case of prohibited subsidies'.[89] In *US – FSC*, the arbitrator labelled the obligation not to provide prohibited subsidies 'an *erga omnes* obligation' and calculated retaliation based on the full impact caused worldwide by the US subsidy, rather than simply the impact on the EC's economy.[90] In *Canada – Aircraft II*, the arbitrators, having calculated the amount of subsidy granted by Canada, raised that amount by 20 per cent 'to take into account the fact that Canada, until now, has stated that it does not intend to withdraw the subsidy at issue and the need to reach a level of countermeasures which can reasonably contribute to induce compliance'.[91] Where they have allowed more-than-equivalent retaliation, arbitrators have pointed out that even the more lax terminology used by the SCM Agreement still acts as a limitation on the level of retaliation that members may be authorised to impose.[92]

In addition to the quantitative limitation, Article 22.3(a) establishes a *qualitative* limitation on retaliation, setting out 'the general principle . . . that the complaining party should first seek to suspend concessions or other obligations with respect to the same sector(s) as that in which the panel or Appellate Body has found a violation or other nullification or impairment'. 'Sectors' are subdivisions of the General Agreement on Trade in Services (GATS) and of the Agreement on Trade-Related Aspects of Intellectual Property Rights (TRIPS). The GATT and all other agreements on goods (contained in Annex 1A) constitute a single sector. Thus, if the violation affects trade in goods, the complaining party may

89 Decision of the Arbitrator, *Brazil – Aircraft (22.6)*, para. 3.58.

90 Decision of the Arbitrator, *US – FSC (22.6)*, WT/DS108/ARB, 30 August 2002, para. 6.10 (footnotes omitted).

91 Decision of the Arbitrator, *Canada – Export Credits and Loan Guarantees for Regional Aircraft (22.6, 4.11)*, WT/DS222/ARB, 17 February 2003, para. 3.119.

92 Ibid., para. 3.48.

only affect the wrongdoer's trade in goods (usually done by raising tariffs); if the breach affected a sector in services or a certain type of intellectual property (IP) right, the aggrieved party may suspend equivalent rights of nationals of the wrongdoer solely in these sectors.

Only if retaliation in the same sector is 'not practicable or effective' does the DSU allow the aggrieved member to retaliate in a different sector of the same agreement.[93] 'Cross-retaliation', the suspension of rights of the violator under an agreement (goods, services, or IP rights) other than the one violated, is available solely when, in addition to the retaliation being 'not practicable or effective', 'the circumstances are serious enough'.[94] The DSU itself provides guidance on how to interpret these criteria of practicability, effectiveness and seriousness. The relevant factors are (i) the importance of the trade in the violated sector or agreement to the party damaged by the violation and (ii) the 'broader economic elements' related to the trade lost by that party and 'the broader economic consequences' of applied retaliation.[95]

6.4 WTO Permissible Responses as Sanction and Deterrent

WTO retaliation is sometimes described or discussed as a form of compensation, capable of providing aggrieved parties with a 'remedy' in the same sense that compensation under international law provides, or at least of allowing it to 'rebalance' the WTO bargain in its favour.[96] David Palmeter and Stanimir Alexandrov, for example, state that the WTO system 'offers a choice: compliance or payment of damages or compensation for the injury suffered'.[97]

It is possible for a WTO member to obtain a monetary payment by threatening retaliation, as Brazil did in *US – Cotton*. However, applying

[93] DSU, Article 22.3(b).

[94] DSU, Article 22.3(c).

[95] DSU, Article 22.3(d). See Decision of the Arbitrator, *EC – Bananas (22.6 – ECU)*, paras. 72–81; Decision of the Arbitrator, *US – Gambling (22.6)*, paras. 4.91–4.114; Decision of the Arbitrator, *US – Cotton (22.6, 4.11)*, paras. 5.140–5.221; Decision of the Arbitrator, *US – Cotton (22.6, 7.10)*, paras. 5.140–5.221.

[96] Rachel Brewster, 'The Remedy Gap: Institutional Design, Retaliation, and Trade Law Enforcement' (2011) 80 *George Washington Law Review* 102, 104; Warren F. Schwartz and Alan O. Sykes, 'The Economic Structure of Renegotiation and Dispute Resolution in the World Trade Organization' (2002) 31 *The Journal of Legal Studies* S179.

[97] David Palmeter and Stanimir A. Alexandrov, '"Inducing Compliance" in WTO Dispute Settlement', in Daniel L.M. Kennedy and James D. Southwick (eds.), *The Political Economy of International Trade – Essays in Honour of Robert E. Hudec* (Cambridge: Cambridge University Press, 2002), 646–666.

retaliation in itself, no matter how high the amount or how expedited the authorisation, can never 'make whole' the aggrieved party. It is equivalent to 'shooting oneself in the foot' with the aim of hurting the other party more than one's own industry.[98] Authorised WTO retaliation is a Permissible Response, not a Consequential Duty. It acts as an instrument of indirect enforcement, harming the interests of a persistent violator, creating a disincentive for it to persist further in its breach, and thereby acting, *ex ante*, as a deterrent against potential wrongdoing.

In this regard, the DSU regulation of retaliation has two effects that may appear contradictory. On the one hand, it ensures that retaliation will be authorised if a breach continues and the aggrieved party so requests. On the other hand, it imposes on the aggrieved party a duty to go through a number of steps, preventing it from immediately adopting retaliatory measures. Especially at the WTO, the system appears almost designed to delay the time at which retaliation is authorised.[99]

This apparent contradiction is explained, first, by the history of the DSU. The current design of WTO remedies was introduced not to empower states to respond to breaches but to limit their response – in particular, US resort to unilateral retaliation under the 1947 GATT.[100] The entitlement to adopt permissible responses, which under general international law arises immediately following the breach, under WTO rules is subject to a number of procedural and substantive limitations. If heavier and swift retaliations were the strongest incentives to compliance, the DSU would hamper rather than strengthen enforcement. This leads to the second, and central, reason for the seemingly overly long proceedings: the real utility of WTO retaliation, at least for the vast majority of members if not for all of them, is not that of a sanction but that of a *threat*.

6.4.1 *The Remedial Value of Permissible Responses: Remedy Escalation as Threat*

As discussed previously, the common basis for all measures of response in international law, including WTO retaliation, is the general principle

98 Mavroidis, 'Remedies in the WTO Legal System', 763, 807.

99 As discussed in Section 7.3, regional trade agreements often permit earlier retaliation.

100 Stoler, 'The WTO Dispute Settlement Process'.

of reciprocity.[101] In the absence of a centralised authority capable of enforcing rules, states ensure compliance with international law by making their own respect for legal rules contingent on similar respect by other states. In and of itself, reciprocity is a 'basic principle of international relations'[102] or even a 'basic phenomenon of social interaction'[103] whereby the conduct of two agents towards each other is 'determined mutually'.[104]

Inter-state reciprocity, especially 'negative reciprocity',[105] which consists in reacting to a state's non-cooperative behaviour with equivalent behaviour, offers what international institutions have difficulty providing: concrete adverse consequences for unlawful conduct. International relations scholars have long identified the 'tit-for-tat' strategy as the basic approach through which states enforce agreements in the absence of adjudication. States do so by complying with their obligations towards those states that adopt similarly complying conduct, while reacting to instances of non-compliance with an equivalent act of non-compliance towards the offender.[106] It is in this sense that Hans Kelsen observes that 'international law is characterised by the principle of self-help'.[107]

The measures of response unilaterally adopted by the United States during the GATT years were not unlawful per se. Unilateral responses are the means, alternative to adjudication, that states generally employ to induce other states' compliance with their international obligations.[108] Unless a rule exists prohibiting unilateral recourse to decentralised responses (in the WTO, this rule is conveyed by Article 23 of the DSU), states may employ countermeasures 'to induce the wrongdoing State to comply with its obligations under international law'.[109]

[101] See Sections 3.2, 3.3, and 5.2.

[102] Elisabeth Zoller, *Peacetime Unilateral Remedies: An Analysis of Countermeasures* (New York: Transnational, 1984), 48.

[103] Bruno Simma, 'Reciprocity', (2008) Max Planck Encyclopedia of International Law, para. 1.

[104] Francesco Parisi and Nita Ghei, 'The Role of Reciprocity in International Law' (2004) 36 *Cornell Journal of International Law* 93, 95.

[105] Simma, Reciprocity, para. 16. See also *Case concerning the Air Service Agreement of 27 March 1946, United States of America* v. *France*, (1978) 18 RIAA 417, 445 ('the United States counter-measures restore in a negative way the symmetry of the initial positions').

[106] Robert Axelrod, *The Evolution of Cooperation* (New York: Basic Books, 1984).

[107] Hans Kelsen, *The Law of the United Nations* (London: Stevens & Sons, 1951), 707.

[108] See Section 1.2.2.

[109] *Gabčíkovo-Nagymaros Project*, Hungary/Slovakia, Judgment, [1997] ICJ Reports 7, p. 65. See Section 5.2.

Although retaliation is sometimes regarded as responsible for making the WTO a 'GATT with teeth',[110] the DSB only authorises WTO members to adopt measures that they would have been able to adopt unilaterally under general international law. In fact, the effect of the DSU is to substantially *limit* members' ability to resort to reciprocal responses as means of enforcing obligations.

WTO law imposes quantitative and qualitative limitations on retaliation, as well as the requirement of prior DSB authorisation. Authorisations for retaliation are only granted after a lengthy procedure, involving multiple stages of adjudication and many opportunities for the parties to delay enforcement. The Appellate Body underscored in *US – Continued Suspension* the relevant steps of this 'multi-stage dispute settlement process'.[111] The process involves consultations, panel proceedings, appellate review, adoption of the panel and Appellate Body reports, arbitration to determine an RPT for implementation, compliance panel proceedings, compliance appellate review, and arbitration to determine the level of suspension of concessions.

In exchange for imposing quantitative, qualitative and temporal limitations on retaliating members, the DSB's authorisation provides *legal certainty* and *collective and judicial legitimacy*. This means that reciprocity is no longer an inter-state matter but based on an authorisation given by the membership, and its application takes place under the watch of all WTO members. Equally importantly, the permissibility of retaliation is justiciable: an adjudicator can be called upon to assess whether the proposed retaliation is warranted and permissible. These safeguards cannot guarantee that a politically powerful wrongdoer will refrain from responding to lawful retaliation with measures directed at hurting the retaliating party. However, a member that takes this route creates further harm both to its reputation and to the legitimacy of the system as one based on rules rather than political and economic power. Small economies may face difficulties finding a way in which 'shooting themselves in the foot' hurts a large economy more than

[110] Miguel Montana i Mora, 'A GATT with Teeth: Law Wins over Politics in the Resolution of International Trade Disputes' (1993) 31 *Columbia Journal of Transnational Law* 131; Steve Charnovitz, 'Should the Teeth Be Pulled? An Analysis of WTO Sanctions', in Daniel L.M. Kennedy and James D. Southwick (eds.), *The Political Economy of International Trade – Essays in Honour of Robert E. Hudec* (Cambridge: Cambridge University Press, 2002), 602–635.

[111] *US – Continued Suspension*, para. 317.

their own.[112] But it has never been claimed that a WTO member was responding to authorised WTO retaliation with unlawful counter-retaliatory measures.

In terms of its ability to induce compliance, there are two ways to interpret the WTO process that ultimately leads to authorisations to retaliate. First, one may consider that the process is a necessary evil to ensure the legitimacy of retaliation. From this perspective, any procedural 'inefficiencies' – the sometimes overly long RPT, the possibility for defendants of delaying panel reports, and the bifurcation of remedies at the implementation stage between Article 21.5 panels (compliance adjudication) and Article 22.6 arbitration (adjudication of permissible retaliation) – should be eliminated in order to allow quicker 'redress' to be granted to the aggrieved party.

This assessment is sometimes linked to the misinterpretation of retaliation as a Consequential Duty. It may also be associated with demands for stronger incentives for compliance. Thus, Gary Horlick labels the compliance proceedings 'a cost-free opportunity to delay compliance for several months'.[113] William Davey finds that 'the prospective nature of WTO remedies currently gives countries no incentive to comply promptly, and may even encourage foot dragging'.[114] Likewise, Rajesh Babu sees in the RPT 'a tool for buying several months of additional time to evade implementation', and in recourse to compliance proceedings a 'delaying tactic employed by Members'.[115] Rachel Brewster identifies the whole WTO compliance process with an overly long 'remedy gap', producing a de facto escape clause for the duration of the legal proceedings.[116]

A different view is that the process itself, with its remedy repetition and remedy escalation, is the compliance-inducing mechanism. While formally directed at the authorisation of Permissible Responses, the

[112] See Joost Pauwelyn, 'Enforcement and Countermeasures in the WTO: Rules Are Rules – Toward a More Collective Approach' (2000) 94 *American Journal of International Law* 335–347.

[113] Gary N. Horlick, 'Problems with the Compliance Structure of the WTO Dispute Resolution Process', in Daniel L. M. Kennedy and James D. Southwick (eds.), *The Political Economy of International Trade Law* (Cambridge: Cambridge University Press, 2002), 636–645, 637.

[114] William J. Davey, 'Compliance Problems in WTO Dispute Settlement' (2009) 42 *Cornell International Law Journal* 120, 126.

[115] Rajesh Babu, *Remedies under the WTO Legal System* (Leiden: Martinus Nijhoff, 2012), 214.

[116] Brewster, 'The Remedy Gap', 104.

multi-stage compliance process has intrinsic value. On the one hand, it imposes reputational costs and magnifies the ability of claimants to seek compliance through persuasion; on the other, it reinforces the role of retaliation as a credible threat.

6.4.2 Declarations of Breach and Declarations of Non-Compliance: The Value of Remedy Repetition

The authorisation to retaliate is often considered to be the 'real' remedy offered by WTO dispute settlement. However, members employ authorisations for retaliation as a source of what Joost Pauwelyn labels 'community costs', affecting the reputation of the violator.[117] Hudec noted that community pressure is 'the ultimate "remedy" which made the GATT dispute settlement procedure as successful as it was'.[118]

In this regard, as long as condemnatory decisions are not so frequent as to become banal, their existence offers opportunities for the aggrieved member to seek voluntary compliance by drawing attention to the breach. Although asserting simply that the Declaration of Breach draws to the wrongdoer 'the odium of having violated the law' may sound naïve,[119] as discussed in Chapters 2 and 3, the declaration by an authoritative body that a state is in breach of its obligations may mobilise forces for compliance both internal and external to the offending state. This may lead to compliance even where the wrongdoer would suffer no concrete adverse consequences from persistent non-compliance.

The existence of an RPT for compliance establishes an endpoint to the organisation's tolerance of non-compliance; the alternative being no tolerance, but also no benchmark to determine when non-compliance becomes intolerable. Rather than entrusting enforcement solely to the aggrieved member, the system empowers this member to produce reputational costs for the wrongdoer. Due to the compliance procedure, these costs do not end with the first Declaration of Breach. A subsequent

[117] Joost Pauwelyn, *Optimal Protection of International Law: Navigating between European Absolutism and American Voluntarism* (New York: Cambridge University Press, 2008), 128.

[118] Hudec, 'Broadening the Scope of Remedies', 400. Mavroidis, however, questions the extent to which Hudec's analysis may be influenced by selection bias – since established panels were those which defendants allowed to be established in the first place. Mavroidis, 'Remedies in the WTO Legal System', 810.

[119] Hersch Lauterpacht, *The Function of Law in the International Community* (Oxford: Oxford University Press, 2011/1933), 427–428.

process can lead to a new condemnation (both judicial and collective), highlighting not only the initial breach but also the member's subsequent failure to comply with a collective ruling.

In this regard, the seemingly vestigial step of adoption of panel and Appellate Body reports by the DSB augments the pressure of pro-compliance forces: on the one hand, it allows other WTO members to individually join the aggrieved party in stating that prompt compliance is required; on the other, it puts the weight of the entire WTO membership behind the decision. This is the sense of Jason Kearns' and Steve Charnovitz's observation that Article 21.5 'incorporates the best elements of bilateral dispute settlement into a multilateral compliance management system'.[120] Giovanni Maggi concludes that the experience of the WTOs shows 'an effective – if subtle – role of multilateral enforcement pressures in improving compliance with international trade agreements'.[121]

In the typology developed in Chapter 2, the pressure generated by a Declaration of Breach operates primarily under Layer 4, that is, as an institutional discursive sanction applied by the organisation itself. Collective adoption, the debate that surrounds it, and the automatic addition of unresolved cases to the agenda of the DSB for 'surveillance',[122] means that WTO rulings also permit diffuse pressure from other members under Layer 3. The seeming remedy repetition that emerges with a ruling of non-compliance, then, imposes all the costs that can be expected to be imposed without mobilisation of more concrete political and economic resources. Importantly, this declaration of non-compliance also opens the door for the adoption of a Layer [5] sanction: an authorisation for bilateral retaliation.

In this regard, the limitations to retaliation provided for in the DSU may seem to limit states' ability to apply retaliation. This is true if one considers that WTO retaliation is equivalent to inter-state retaliation, and thus operates under Layer 2. However, the adjudication process and institutional authorisation change the nature of the measure, from Layer 2 bilateral sanctioning to Layer [5] authorised sanctioning. Once this shift is accounted for, the real benefit of the WTO procedure emerges.

[120] Jason E. Kearns and Steve Charnovitz, 'Adjudicating Compliance in the WTO: A Review of DSU Article 21.5' (2002) 5 *Journal of International Economic Law* 331, 335.

[121] Giovanni Maggi, 'The Role of Multilateral Institutions in International Trade Cooperation' (1999) 89 The American Economic Review 190, 192.

[122] DSU, Article 21.6.

A retaliating WTO member is not applying a measure of response within the context of a dispute characterised by legal uncertainty; it is applying an authorised sanction, acting as a rule enforcer for the membership as a whole.

Framing DSU limitations as nothing more than limits to retaliation can also be misleading. While members are accordingly limited in their ability to apply retaliation, their ability to *threaten* it is in fact *amplified*. Hudec states this in relation to the GATT 1947, noting that '[a]lthough their direct coercive power is limited, the GATT's retaliation provisions play a significant role in deploying the GATT's normative pressures'.[123] The fact that retaliation is only forthcoming following a definitive, and often distant, authorisation by the DSB, allows members time to issue threats, raising the awareness of actors within the wrongdoer that may be affected, without either themselves or the offending government needing to deal with concrete economic and political consequences of imposing retaliatory measures.

At the end of the RPT, members may not only verbally threaten retaliation but formally request it. Aggrieved parties may calculate the level of retaliation using figures that, once an arbitrator intervenes, prove greatly inflated.[124] They may draw up comprehensive lists of products that will be subject to this retaliation, further inducing the formation within the offender of coalitions against continuation of the breach.[125] They may also not draw up any lists of products but mention specific industries that they intend to target, generating apprehension and uncertainty which may be sufficient for these industries to press their government for compliance.

By contrast, in a situation in which countermeasures can be applied freely, they are only credible as threats if accompanied by concrete

[123] Robert E. Hudec, *Adjudication of International Trade Disputes*, Thames Essay No. 16 (London: Trade Policy Research Center, 1978), 83.

[124] In *US – Gambling*, Antigua requested to retaliate the United States in the amount of US$3.443 billion US Dollars. The arbitrator reduced this amount to US$21 million (*US – Gambling (22.6)*, para. 1.5, 3.188). In *US – Cotton*, Brazil's requested authorisation for retaliation for different subsidies, adding up to US$2.681 billion US Dollars for the first year. The arbitrator authorised retaliation in an amount determined according to a mathematical formula. This yielded US$294.7 million annually using the data for Fiscal Year 2006 (*US – Cotton (22.6, 4.11)*, para. 2.6, 5.101; *US – Cotton (22.6, 7.10)*, paras. 4.1, 5.101). Recalculating it two years later using the data for Fiscal Year 2008, Brazil arrived at the amount of US$829.3 million – still one-third of the amount originally requested.

[125] Hudec notes that this already occurred at the time of the GATT (Hudec, 'Broadening the Scope of Remedies', 388, fn. 34).

measures. In the *Air Service Agreement* arbitration, for example, the United States had initiated a domestic procedure to apply a concrete countermeasure: prohibiting Air France flights from flying from Paris to Los Angeles via Montreal.[126] Once these concrete measures are revealed, however, affected parties may simply incorporate the corresponding 'price' into their calculations. This price may be found to be negligible; or the concrete measures may prove more damaging to the state 'shooting itself in the foot' than to the target state. As evidenced by the practice of the WTO, small states have difficulty even conceiving of retaliatory measures capable of tangibly harming larger offenders without hurting themselves far more seriously.

Thus, the burdensome procedure to obtain retaliation pursuant to the DSU may in fact increase WTO members' capacity to apply a *threat strategy* rather than a *retaliation strategy*. The difference between these, Hudec remarked, is that while retaliations are 'a punishment for a violation, the threat is a forceful move in a continuing bargaining process'.[127] In this scenario, '[t]he actual retaliation is almost an anti-climax, and sometimes seems less important for its direct political impact than for its function in giving credibility to the earlier, broader threats in cases to come'.[128] By making retaliation impermissible for the duration of the compliance proceedings, the DSU in practice enhances its value as a threat.

This aligns with Daniel Drezner's findings regarding sanctions more generally. The game-theoretical model of sanctions accounts for the fact (not unique to the WTO) that sanctions both harm the sanctioned party and are costly to the party imposing them. In the case of trade sanctions, this takes the form of disrupted economic exchange and loss of welfare for the retaliating state.[129] A WTO member threatening retaliation indicates to the offender its intention to impose sanctions, but also its willingness to bear the relevant costs. The targeted member may then

126 *Air Service Agreement*, (1978) 18 RIAA 417, 443–444.

127 Hudec, *Adjudication of International Trade Disputes*, 94.

128 Hudec, 'Broadening the Scope of Remedies', 369, 388, fn. 34.

129 But see Kyle Bagwell, 'Remedies in the WTO: An Economic Perspective', in Merit E. Janow, Victoria J. Donaldson, and Alan Yanovitch (eds.), *The WTO Governance, Dispute Settlement and Developing Countries* (New York: Juris, 2008), 733–770, 737–738, and Henning Grosse Ruse-Kahn, 'A Pirate of the Caribbean? The Attraction of Suspending TRIPS Obligations' (2008) 11 *Journal of International Economic Law* 313, 335–339, both arguing that there is potential (so far unrealised) for forms of wealth-enhancing retaliation.

choose whether to comply (or settle) or to suffer the cost of sanctions. A choice to suffer the costs of retaliation incorporates into the calculation of costs and benefits, *ex ante*, the harm caused by the retaliation.

WTO retaliation thus intervenes in a scenario in which the wrongdoer has already factored in its costs. The result is that retaliation does not add to these costs: 'successful instances of economic coercion are much more likely to end at the threat stage than the imposition stage ... when sanctions are actually imposed, the outcome is a sustained deadlock between adversaries'.[130] By prolonging the threat stage, WTO rules aim to prevent such a deadlock. By ensuring the continued availability of adjudication even after authorising retaliation, they also ensure that there is a readily available alternative to purely bilateral negotiations for parties to exit the deadlock.

6.4.3 *WTO Permissible Responses and Efficient Breach*

Two elements contribute to the widespread opinion that WTO Permissible Responses amount to a form of reparation, whereby members injured by breaches of WTO rules can be 'made whole' alternatively by compliance, by WTO compensation, or by WTO retaliation. These are a certain textual ambiguity regarding the obligation to comply with (i.e. to substantively perform) WTO obligations, on the one hand; and the notion that, whatever the WTO Agreements ostensibly provide, the mechanism they set up is one in which a member can choose to comply or to 'pay' damages by suffering retaliation.

First, as John Jackson acknowledged when making the case for the binding character of adopted panel and Appellate Body reports, the DSU 'does not solidly "nail down" the issue' of the existence of an obligation of performance.[131] Under DSU Article 3.7, 'a solution mutually acceptable to the parties to a dispute and consistent with the covered agreements is clearly to be preferred'. Only absent such a solution does it speak of eliminating violations – and even then not as a requirement but as the system's 'first objective', implying that there may be other acceptable, if less desirable, outcomes. DSU Article 21.1 states not that compliance

[130] Daniel Drezner, 'The Hidden Hand of Economic Coercion' (2003) 57 *International Organization* 643, 645, 647.

[131] John H. Jackson, 'The WTO Dispute Settlement Understanding – Misunderstandings on the Nature of Legal Obligation' (1997) 91 *AJIL* 60, 62.

with rulings is obligatory but that it is 'essential in order to ensure effective resolution of disputes to the benefit of all Members', and provides that compliance is merely 'preferred' to compensation and retaliation. Finally, Article 3.3 states that the 'prompt settlement' of disputes is 'essential' not to ensure the cessation of breaches but 'to the effective functioning of the WTO and the maintenance of a proper balance between the rights and obligations of Members'. This could imply that conduct that contravenes WTO provisions is acceptable as long as this 'balance' is maintained.

Second, the quantitative limitation placed upon WTO retaliation requires that the maximum amount of suspension of concessions authorised by the DSB be 'equivalent to the level of nullification or impairment' caused. The standard applicable to the level of WTO retaliation is therefore similar to that applied to the provision of pecuniary compensation, or 'damages', under the rules of general international law. Regarding the latter, one may recall Umpire Parker's statement in the *Lusitania* arbitration that:

> ...the words exemplary, vindictive, or punitive as applied to damages are misnomers. The fundamental concept of 'damages' is satisfaction, reparation for a *loss* suffered; a judicially ascertained *compensation* for wrong. The remedy should be commensurate with the loss, so that the injured party may be made whole.[132]

WTO arbitrators have sometimes transposed this reasoning to WTO retaliation, stating that the requirement of equivalence means that WTO retaliation should not be 'punitive'.[133] Although this requirement does not change the nature of WTO remedies – which are Permissible Responses, not Consequential Duties – the coincidence of standards for assessment of the proper level of the remedy leads to confusion. Many have compared WTO retaliation to 'damages' in reparatory remedy systems, concluding from this that WTO members may discharge themselves of their WTO obligations by accepting that a corresponding

[132] *Lusitania (Germany* v. *United States of America)*, (1923) 7 RIAA 32, 39.

[133] Decision of the Arbitrator, *EC – Bananas III (22.6 – US)*, para. 6.3; Decision of the Arbitrator, *US – FSC (22.6)*, para. 5.62; Decision of the Arbitrator, *US – 1916 Act (22.6)*, para. 5.8; Decision of the Arbitrator, *US – Gambling (22.6)*, para. 3.24. This is noticed by Schwarz and Sykes, 'The Economic Structure of Renegotiation and Dispute Resolution', S179, S189 ('By refusing to permit the imposition of "punitive" sanctions, the arbitrators impliedly acknowledged that the sanction is more in the nature of compensation than punishment').

'payment' be exacted from them by other members, in the form of suspension of concessions and other obligations.

Judith Bello first suggested this in the organisation's infancy. She famously argued that, because '[t]he WTO has no jailhouse, no bail bondsmen, no blue helmets, no truncheons or tear gas', WTO rules are 'not "binding" in the traditional sense'.[134] Members 'may choose' not to comply with WTO rulings; the maximum penalty for this is for the wrongdoer to 'suffer … retaliation against its exports authorized by the WTO for the purpose of restoring the balance of negotiated concessions'.[135]

Jackson subsequently rebutted Bello's stance and argued convincingly, based on an analysis of the DSU, that WTO obligations certainly 'are binding in the traditional *international law* sense'.[136] As a matter of law, there is little doubt that WTO rules are binding, and decisions of adjudicators that 'clarify' the meaning of these rules are equally binding.[137] Article 2.2 of the Agreement Establishing the WTO provides that all WTO Agreements 'are binding on all Members'. This applies equally, as a matter of legal logic, to adopted panel and Appellate Body reports, so that, within the WTO system, these reports 'lead to a binding decision'.[138]

The essence of Bello's objection, however, concerns not the conceptual status of WTO commitments but the consequences of breaching these commitments. Joel Trachtman argues that 'a legal realist and a legal economist would ask not what the formal law specifies, but what it does in response to breach … as a matter of fact and practice, if not as a matter of legal doctrine, the WTO legal system is best characterized as employing a liability rule'.[139]

This view has found echo in much of the literature, with the argument that, even if there is a *preference* for compliance, breaches can be equally

[134] Judith H. Bello, 'The WTO Dispute Settlement Understanding: Less is More' (1996) 90 *AJIL* 416, 416–417.
[135] Ibid., 417.
[136] Jackson, 'The WTO Dispute Settlement Understanding', 60, 63.
[137] See John H. Jackson, 'International Law Status of WTO Dispute Settlement Reports: Obligation to Comply or Option to "Buy Out"?' (2004) 98 *AJIL* 109; Jide Nzelibe, 'The Credibility Imperative: The Political Dynamics of Retaliation in the World Trade Organization's Dispute Resolution Mechanism' (2005) 6 *Theoretical Inquiries in Law* 215, 250–253; Ibid.; Jide Nzelibe, 'The Case against Reforming the WTO Enforcement Mechanism' (2008) 1 *University of Illinois Law Review* 319.
[138] Appellate Body Report, *US – Continued Suspension*, para. 340.
[139] Joel Trachtman, 'The WTO Cathedral' (2007) 43 *Stanford Journal of International Law* 127, 146.

addressed by retaliation – often inadequately labelled 'damages'.[140] Brewster finds that WTO 'sanctions are the functional equivalent of compensatory damages' and proposes that, in order to reinforce the binding character of WTO law, the DSB should be empowered to 'authorize the award of unconditional and retrospective damages – the approach taken by domestic contract law'.[141] Mavroidis, while acknowledging the distinction between retaliation and reparation, also merges the two on occasion: 'the term "equivalent" makes it plain that there is no room for punitive damages in the WTO context'.[142]

Employing the concept of 'efficient breach' developed in contract theory, some of this literature goes as far as claiming the WTO 'contract' in fact *encourages* 'efficient' breaches. Warren Schwartz and Alan Sykes conclude from an economic analysis that the WTO system 'acknowledges that the joint interests of the parties may be better served by compensation or retaliation that restores the benefits of the bargain to aggrieved parties while allowing officials in the violator nation to continue doing what must be done out of political necessity'.[143] Sykes grounds this view on the notion that state officials may prefer protectionism even if economically inefficient, and 'employ trade sanctions to protect import-competing firms that value such protection, and that will directly reward their officials for protecting it'.[144]

These views lead to two types of assessment. On the one hand, some conclude that WTO remedies require strengthening, through higher levels of retaliation, to ensure 'full reparation'. Others claim that WTO rules are well tailored to allow for 'efficient breach', with the aggrieved parties being 'made whole' through the permission to retaliate. In the first

140 Ibid., 140, 146; Alan O. Sykes, 'The Remedy for Breach of Obligations under the WTO Dispute Settlement Understanding: Damages or Specific Performance?', in Marco Bronckers and Reinhard Quick (eds.), *New Directions in International Economic Law: Essays in Honour of John H. Jackson* (The Hague: Kluwer, 2000), 347–351.

141 Brewster, 'The Remedy Gap', 146.

142 Mavroidis, 'Remedies in the WTO Legal System', 800. Ibid., 812: 'the appropriate remedy in the case of illegal subsidies is that which will persuade violators to abandon their illegal practices and not that which will simply *remove the damage suffered by injured parties*' (emphasis added).

143 Schwarz and Sykes, 'The Economic Structure of Renegotiation and Dispute Resolution', S189.

144 Alan O. Sykes, 'Optimal Sanctions in the WTO: The Case for Decoupling (and the Uneasy Case for the Status Quo)', in Chad P. Bown and Joost Pauwelyn (eds.), *The Law, Economics and Politics of Retaliation in WTO Dispute Settlement* (Cambridge: Cambridge University Press, 2010), 339–354, 348.

group, Trachtman proposes to increase retaliation levels by accounting for injury caused by the breach in the past. He argues that 'in order to equate retaliation with a welfare-based calculation of damage, it would be necessary to calculate damage on both a retrospective and prospective basis'.[145] Babu follows the same line, equating compensation with retaliation and claiming that 'retroactivity' would enable Members to benefit fully from the Uruguay Round's concessions and rights.[146] Brewster proposes 'retrospective and unconditional retaliation', the latter meaning retaliation that could be applied even after the offender came into compliance within the RPT; this would 'alter the WTO's remedy rules to more closely resemble domestic contract law'.[147]

Those on the other side reject proposals for increasing the amount of retaliation, though often equally relying on the conflation of the entitlement to retaliate with compensatory contract damages. Palmeter and Alexandrov argue that the balance struck in the WTO Agreements should not be altered by arbitrators simply in light of the objective of inducing compliance.[148] While this is a proper characterisation of the duty of Article 22.6 arbitrators, they assume that retaliation is equal to 'payment of damages'. Schwarz and Sykes embrace a similar assessment to conclude that two valid alternatives to compliance are 'compensation or retaliation that restores the benefits of the bargain to aggrieved parties'.[149]

The analogy between WTO retaliation and compensatory damages, however, is faulty, because WTO retaliation is a Permissible Response. Retaliation serves two main purposes. First, it affirms the value of the agreed rules and ensures that breaches do not go without consequences.[150] This corresponds to Mavroidis' '*ex ante*' function of all remedies creating harm to wrongdoers: to prevent breaches by 'act[ing] as a "credible threat" against potential violators'.[151]

However, the second, *ex post*, purpose of retaliation, is not to compensate the aggrieved member but to induce compliance. Hudec describes this as 'to assemble enough additional forces within the target government

[145] Trachtman, 'The WTO Cathedral', 140.

[146] *Babu, Remedies under the WTO Legal System*, 467.

[147] Brewster, 'The Remedy Gap', 143.

[148] Palmeter and Alexandrov, "Inducing Compliance" in WTO Dispute Settlement, 663.

[149] Schwarz and Sykes, 'The Economic Structure of Renegotiation and Dispute Resolution', 191.

[150] Andrew T. Guzman, 'A Compliance-Based Theory of International Law' (2002) 90 *California Law Review* 1823, 1868.

[151] Mavroidis, 'Remedies in the WTO Legal System', 764.

to precipitate a decision to remove the offending measure'[152] This is achieved by targeting, with retaliation, particularly influential domestic interests, capable of persuading the government to change its policies.

From the viewpoint of a wrongdoer, being forced to pay continuous amounts in damages and being subjected to continuous retaliation measures may be similarly harmful and deter violations. At the same time, the WTO is not capable of forcing payments, nor does it seek to do so to any extent. WTO retaliation is an economic sanction and, as international relations scholars have long warned, 'impose[s] costs on both the target and sender relative to the status quo by disrupting economic exchange'.[153] Applying trade retaliation does not make the retaliating party better off but amounts to hurting its economy, aiming to create a disincentive for continued breach.[154]

To overcome this problem, certain 'welfare-enhancing' retaliation possibilities have been considered, including retaliation in IP rights. Steve Charnovitz notes that, unlike lower tariffs on trade in goods and services, higher protection of IP rights is not considered economically beneficial for a state's aggregate welfare.[155] Henning Grosse Ruse-Kahn argues that IP retaliation could allow developing country members to obtain otherwise expensive software, media, or pharmaceuticals; or it could allow access to industrial technology that would otherwise be prohibitively costly.[156] Suspending IP rights would thus be less akin to 'shooting oneself in the foot'; it could, in fact, *enhance* the retaliating member's economic welfare.

Practice, however, has yet to confirm this. In the three cases in which developing countries requested authorisation to apply retaliation on IP rights, arbitrators authorised it, considering that retaliation affecting trade in goods and services was not 'practicable or effective' for these countries and that, partly for this reason, the circumstances were 'serious enough' to warrant cross-retaliation.[157] But, as Section 6.5 explains, in

152 Hudec, 'Broadening the Scope of Remedies', 388. A third objective Hudec points is to placate the domestic audience of the retaliating government, assuring it that its government has punished the wrongdoer by imposing retaliation.

153 Drezner, 'The Hidden Hand of Economic Coercion', 643, 645.

154 Mavroidis, 'Remedies in the WTO Legal System', 806; Steve Charnovitz, 'The WTO's Problematic "Last Resort" against Noncompliance' (2002) 57 *Aussenwirtschaft* 409.

155 Charnovitz, 'Should the Teeth Be Pulled?'.

156 Ruse-Kahn, 'A Pirate of the Caribbean?'.

157 Decision of the Arbitrator, *EC – Bananas III (22.6 – ECU)*, para. 173; *US – Gambling (22.6)*, 4.91–4.94, 4.114, 5.6; *US – Cotton (22.6)*, paras. 5.201, 5.220–5.221.

none of these cases did members proceed to suspending IP rights belonging to the wrongdoer's companies.

Kyle Bagwell examined retaliation in goods from an economic perspective and using terms-of-trade theory, which contends that states may improve their terms of trade by adopting high tariffs. He concluded that a member could employ retaliation to its own advantage where it is a 'large' importer, that is, in areas where its imports represent a significant amount of the global market for the product in question. In this case, the higher tariffs may lower the product's world price, improving the retaliating country's terms of trade.[158]

However, to achieve this, retaliation would have to be set (and applied) at a more-than-equivalent level, so as to produce a benefit.[159] In the sole instance in which more-than-equivalent retaliation has been authorised – prohibited subsidies – Bagwell found that trade-of-terms theory discouraged disproportionate retaliation.[160] While this could be a normative argument for higher authorised retaliation, the practice of WTO retaliation casts doubt on whether members even attempt to apply it in a way that will make them 'better off'. To the extent that retaliating member states target industries for which locally produced substitutes exist, they do so to reduce the harm imposed on their economy. Most often, their attitude has been the opposite: to raise, to prohibitive levels, tariffs on luxury goods that cannot be obtained from local suppliers, and thus to harm the wrongdoer's industry without providing easily identifiable benefits to any domestic competitors.

6.5 The Practice of WTO Remedies: Threatening Permissible Responses, Requesting Compliance Adjudication

The uses members make of WTO retaliation are key in determining whether they are perceived, and should be treated, as an instrument to extract a form of reparation from wrongdoers or as a self-harming sanctioning instrument, costly in itself but potentially useful to induce a change in behaviour. A 'law-in-action'[161] approach cannot be adopted halfway and requires examining the concrete practice of WTO members with regard to retaliation. Conceivably, tariffs may be designed with a

158 Bagwell, 'Remedies in the WTO', 733–770, 737–738.
159 Ibid., 748.
160 Ibid., 769.
161 Trachtman, 'The WTO Cathedral', 146.

reparatory objective, that is, aiming to maximise their economic benefits to domestic producers, or with a retaliatory purpose, seeking to maximise their harmful political effect. Vattel recognised early on these two alternative uses for measures of reaction, seeing the possibility of resort to self-help as a method of *indirect enforcement*, but also as a potential mechanism for obtaining *direct redress*.[162]

If WTO retaliation, regardless of its level, were used as a means of obtaining direct redress, the practice of WTO members should provide evidence of members attempting to extract benefits from retaliation. Members would (i) employ all means available to obtain the authorisation for retaliation as quickly as possible; (ii) apply retaliation as soon as they obtained the right to do so, and as intensely as permitted by the DSB authorisation; and (iii) continue to apply retaliation even after compliance is achieved, insisting that the offender must have recourse to Article 21.5 to obtain a declaration of compliance. This would allow aggrieved members to enjoy precious extra months of retaliation – perhaps compensating for the absence of 'retrospective damages' in the DSU.

If, on the other hand, retaliation is merely a costly instrument to induce compliance, this should also show in the practice of WTO members. Members should, in the first place, accept deferrals of the authorisation to retaliate, in the hope of inducing compliance through the continued, and low-cost, threat. Members should apply the authorised retaliation reluctantly, targeting influential industries within the wrongdoer and inducing them to mobilise political resources for compliance. Finally, members should not be content with receiving the entitlement to retaliate, continuing to press for compliance by other means. They should in fact relax retaliation measures when offered credible promises of compliance, to be able to threaten to employ these measures again if these promises do not materialise.

An analysis of all the cases in which WTO retaliation was authorised shows that the latter hypothesis is correct.

6.5.1 *Accepting Deferrals of the Process: Sequencing Agreements*

The very fact that members have recourse to Article 21.5 panel proceedings before requesting retaliation provides evidence that delays in the process leading to retaliation are accepted even when aggrieved members

[162] Emer de Vattel, *Le droit des gens, ou Principes de la loi naturelle, appliqués à la conduite et aux affaires des Nations et des Souverains* (London, 1758), Bk. 2, Ch. 18, para. 342.

consider that the wrongful measure subsists.[163] This is relevant because, due to the 'sequencing problem' between Articles 21 and 22 of the DSU, in practice members acting aggressively may request (and obtain) the authorisation to retaliate without previously having a dedicated Article 21.5 panel determine compliance.[164]

Twenty days after the end of the RPT and absent an agreement for compensation, DSU Article 22.2 allows an aggrieved WTO member to request an authorisation for retaliation '[i]f the [wrongdoer] fails to bring the measure found to be inconsistent with a covered agreement into compliance'. In such a case, Article 22.6 provides that the DSB 'shall grant authorization to suspend concessions or other obligations within 30 days of the expiry of the reasonable period of time'. This leaves open the question of how to determine the persistence of the breach.

Ordinarily, such a determination would fall under the purview of Article 21.5 panels. However, under Article 22.6 of the DSU, authorisation for retaliation, when requested, *must* be granted within thirty days of the end of the RPT 'unless the DSB decides by consensus to reject the request'. The only way for the offender to prevent this authorisation is to object, under Article 22.6, to the level or type of retaliation proposed. In this case, the matter is referred to arbitration, which the DSU provides 'shall be completed within 60 days after the date of expiry of the reasonable period of time'.[165]

DSU Article 21.5 provides that Members 'shall' have recourse to new panel proceedings in case of 'disagreement as to the existence or consistency with a covered agreement of measures taken to comply'. In *US – Continued Suspension*, the Appellate Body interpreted this as meaning that 'Article 21.5 dictates that panel proceedings pursuant to this

[163] It is often the case that parties to disputes accept deferrals of the process because of ongoing negotiations. These are difficult to quantify, and may be due to the aggrieved party effectively considering that the wrongdoer has changed its measures and complied with rulings, or to an offer of compensation. Anecdotal evidence nonetheless abounds. See Gregory Shaffer and Daniel Ganin, 'Extrapolating Purpose from Practice: Rebalancing or Inducing Compliance', in Chad P. Bown and Joost Pauwelyn (eds.), *The Law, Economics and Politics of Retaliation in WTO Dispute Settlement* (Cambridge: Cambridge University Press, 2010), 73–85, 80–81.

[164] See Cherise M. Valles and Brendan McGivern, 'The Right to Retaliate under the WTO Agreement: The "Sequencing Problem"' (2000) 34 *Journal of World Trade* 63.

[165] DSU, Article 22.6. Article 22.7 then provides: 'The DSB shall be informed promptly of the decision of the arbitrator and shall upon request, grant authorization to suspend concessions or other obligations where the request is consistent with the decision of the arbitrator, unless the DSB decides by consensus to reject the request'.

provision are the procedures that must be followed for adjudicating the cause of action as framed in its opening clause'.[166] This apparently implies an obligation to have recourse to Article 21.5 compliance proceedings.

However, in *US – Certain EC Products* the Appellate Body also stated, specifically with respect to the sequencing problem, that amending or interpreting the DSU is 'not the task of either panels or the Appellate Body [but] clearly the responsibility solely of the Members of the WTO'.[167] Thus, the member requesting retaliation may ultimately push for an authorisation to retaliate if it so wishes. The Article 22.6 arbitrator is then required to make an assessment of whether and at what level nullification or impairment subsist, which obliges it to determine (even if indirectly) whether consistency has been achieved.

In *EC – Bananas III*, the United States took, and the arbitrators accepted, the approach of pushing for earlier retaliation. The EC objected that direct recourse to Article 22, when a dispute existed regarding compliance, would amount to empowering the Article 22.6 arbitrators to 'consider the WTO consistency of its banana regime [and] deprive Article 21.5 of its *raison d'être*'.[168] The arbitrators disagreed and found that conditioning their decision to an Article 21.5 report 'would in fact read the time-limit foreseen in Article 22.6 out of the DSU'.[169] If the United States could not convince them that nullification or impairment subsisted, they would simply 'set the level of suspension of concessions at zero'.[170]

Indonesia in *US – Cloves* adopted the same approach, requesting authorisation to retaliate without going through a compliance panel, despite a declaration by the offender that it had complied. Though the United States protested and enjoined Indonesia to 'first obtain a DSB ruling on the issue of compliance before engaging in and completing an Article 22.6' arbitration, the United States nonetheless objected to the level and type of retaliation proposed at the DSB meeting, thereby referring the matter to arbitration. The Chair of the DSB then confirmed that the dispute was to be 'referred to arbitration, as required by Article 22.6 of the DSU'.[171]

166 Appellate Body Report, *US – Continued Suspension*, para. 336.
167 Appellate Body Report, *US – Certain EC Products*, para. 92.
168 Decision of the Arbitrator, *EC – Bananas (22.6 – US)*, WT/DS27/ARB, 9 April 1999, para. 4.11.
169 Ibid.
170 Ibid, para 4.13.
171 DSB, *Minutes of Meeting*, WT/DSB/M/335, 23 August 2013, 3–4.

These two cases show that members *may* adopt an aggressive approach to retaliation. In the vast majority of disputes, however, whenever a dispute existed regarding compliance, aggrieved members have first requested an authorisation to retaliate (to safeguard their right to a DSB decision by negative consensus), then entered into a 'sequencing agreement' with the offender.[172] Through these agreements (often signed after the aggrieved party has requested retaliation under Article 22.2 and the wrongdoer has objected to the amount), rather than moving forward with the Article 22.6 arbitration, the aggrieved member consents to suspension of the arbitration until 'compliance adjudication under Article 21.5', continuing only if this adjudication 'results in a finding that compliance was not achieved'.[173]

The issue of sequencing provoked much debate when it first arose in 1999, in *EC – Bananas*. The United States requested retaliation right at the end of the RPT, while Ecuador preferred to first request an Article 21.5 panel.[174] This remained the sole such case until Indonesia's insistence on its request for retaliation in 2013, in *US – Cloves*. All other disputes in which an offender claimed to have complied were referred to a compliance panel under Article 21.5, with the parties undertaking to follow this panel with an Article 22.6 arbitration. Other than in cases in which wrongdoers admitted to not having taken *any* measures to comply, parties otherwise entered into sequencing agreements in all disputes that ultimately led to an authorisation for retaliation.[175]

Thus, although members may technically proceed straight to requesting retaliation, they voluntarily choose to go through the process of compliance adjudication. On the rare occasions in which they considered this helpful, aggrieved members have proceeded directly to requesting authorisation to retaliate. In the vast majority of cases, members have

[172] Sylvia A. Rhodes, 'The Article 21.5/22 Problem: Clarification through Bilateral Agreements?' (2000) 3 *Journal of International Economic Law* 553.

[173] See, for example, Understanding between China and the United States Regarding Procedures under Articles 21 and 22 of the DSU, WT/DS413/10, 21 August 2013.

[174] DSB, *Minutes of Meeting* (*EC – Bananas*), WT/DSB/M/54, 20 April 1999.

[175] See Communication to DSB (Brazil – Aircraft), WT/DS46/13, 23 November 1999; Understanding between the European Communities and the United States Regarding Procedures under Articles 21 and 22 of the DSU and Article 4 of the SCM Agreement (*US – FSC*), WT/DS108/12, 5 October 2000; Agreement between Antigua and Barbuda and the United States Regarding Procedures under Articles 21 and 22 of the DSU (*US – Gambling*), WT/285/16, 26 May 2006; Understanding between Brazil and the United States Regarding Procedures under Articles 21 and 22 of the DSU and Article 4 of the SCM Agreement (*US – Cotton*), WT/267/22, 8 July 2007.

preferred an additional and time-consuming procedure for compliance adjudication over demanding retaliation straight away.

This provides a first indicator that retaliation is not perceived as a form of reparation. If it were, members, already aggrieved by the unremedied breach, would certainly do all within their power to obtain their reparation as soon as possible. Instead, they allow the compliance dispute to take place before requesting the authorisation to retaliate.

6.5.2 Adoption of Limited or No Retaliation Subsequent to DSB Authorisation

If retaliation served a 'rebalancing' function, or if WTO members believed they could employ it to obtain reparation, in addition to attempting to obtain authorisations quickly, they would always retaliate when so authorised, and would do this immediately, at as high a level as feasible for them and permitted by the decision of the DSB.

In practice, however, most DSB authorisations for retaliation are never employed. Where they are, members often retaliate at a lower level than that authorised. And, whether or not they ultimately retaliate, members afford wrongdoers time to comply rather than applying retaliation immediately. Even after it is authorised, then, retaliation is employed as a deterrent to continued breach, and, if necessary, as a sanction (application of which is costly), rather than as a tool to obtain benefits. Finally, in the cases in which it is authorised, the practice of retaliation evidences a purpose not of exacting compensation but of harming politically influent interests.

6.5.2.1 Cases of Non-Application of Retaliation

Threats of retaliation never materialised in five cases out of the nine in which it was authorised. In *EC – Bananas (Ecuador)*, *Brazil – Aircraft*, *Canada – Aircraft II*, *US – Gambling*, and *US – Cotton*, threatened retaliation was never applied.

In *EC – Bananas (Ecuador)*, the arbitrator calculated the nullification or impairment caused to Ecuador at US$201.6 million, emphasising that, 'given the fact that Ecuador, as a small developing country, only accounts for a negligible proportion of the EC's exports', authorised retaliation could be impossible to apply, and if applied could harm Ecuador more than the EC.[176] While the arbitrators authorised

[176] Decision of the Arbitrator, *EC – Bananas (22.6 – ECU)*, para. 95.

Ecuador to suspend TRIPS obligations in a fairly liberal manner (in relation to phonograms, geographical indications, and industrial designs),[177] Ecuador later confirmed that it had found it impossible to apply this suspension as well.[178]

In *Brazil – Aircraft* and *Canada – Aircraft II*, a situation in which the two members were of roughly equal economic strength and the disputes were factually linked, involving subsidies to competitors Embraer and Bombardier, neither party applied retaliation. The result of the arbitrations, which authorised similar levels of retaliation for the two breaches, was a mutually agreed solution.[179] Indeed, the arbitrator of *Canada – Aircraft II* foresaw this outcome, holding that 'a mutually satisfactory agreement between the parties' would be the preferred option 'given the particular circumstances of th[e] case'.[180]

In *US – 1916 Act*, in which a US law was found to violate WTO commitments if ever fully applied, the EC and Japan received authorisation to retaliate, but only if final decisions were made under the WTO-inconsistent legislation against companies based in the EC or Japan. The act was repealed before any EC companies could have been affected. Only one Japanese company was affected, and no notice was given of actual application.[181]

In *US – Gambling*, Antigua never retaliated despite its many threats, in particular to apply retaliation in IP rights.[182] The outcome was that the United States used the intra-contractual flexibility of GATS Article XXI to renegotiate concessions. According to the United States, this deprived

177 Ibid., para. 173.

178 Contribution of Ecuador to the Improvement of the DSU, WT/DS/W/9, 28 June 2002, p. 2.

179 Hunter Nottage, 'Evaluating the Criticism That WTO Retaliation Rules Undermine the Utility of WTO Dispute Settlement for Developing Countries', in Chad P. Bown and Joost Pauwelyn (eds.), *The Law, Economics and Politics of Retaliation in WTO Dispute Settlement* (Cambridge: Cambridge University Press, 2010), 319, 334.

180 Decision of the Arbitrator, *Canada – Aircraft Credits and Guarantees* (Article 22.6), WT/DS222/ARB, 17 February 2003, para. 4.4.

181 Lothar Ehring, 'The European Community's Experience and Practice in Suspending WTO Obligations', in Chad P. Bown and Joost Pauwelyn (eds.), *The Law, Economics and Politics of Retaliation in WTO Dispute Settlement* (Cambridge: Cambridge University Press, 2010), 244–266, 252.

182 Mark E. Mendel, 'Retaliation in the WTO: The Experience of Antigua and Barbuda in US – Gambling', in Chad P. Bown and Joost Pauwelyn (eds.), *The Law, Economics and Politics of Retaliation in WTO Dispute Settlement* (Cambridge: Cambridge University Press, 2010), 310–316, 313.

Antigua of its entitlement to retaliate.[183] Antigua has not so far accepted this result, but neither has it retaliated. It decided instead to negotiate with the United States 'in the hope of reaching some kind of agreed accommodation'.[184]

Finally, in *US – Cotton*, Brazil threatened to retaliate against the United States in the amount of US$829.3 million – including US$283 million in IP rights.[185] Over the months following the decision of the Article 22.6 arbitrators, Brazil drafted a list of products that would be subject to retaliation and passed legislation that would allow it to retaliate by suspending IP rights of US companies.[186] One day before the scheduled application of Brazil's tariff retaliation, the two parties signed a framework agreement, followed by a Memorandum of Understanding on the matter. In addition to a number of trade benefits, the United States undertook to pay US$147.3 million in assistance to Brazilian cotton producers.[187] The case was settled in 2014 with a lump sum agreement, with the US paying to the Brazilian Cotton Institute over 1 billion dollars over the years.[188]

6.5.2.2 Retaliation Applied Below the Authorised Level

In *US – FSC*, the arbitrator calculated the amount of permissible retaliation at the highest level so far: US$4.043 billion annually, 'in the form of the imposition of a 100 per cent ad valorem charge on imports of certain goods from the United States'.[189] The EC adopted retaliation in the form of additional ad valorem customs duties applicable to a number of US products. The design of the retaliation measures, however, evidences the purpose of maximising its value as an irritant and a deterrent rather than of attempting to 'rebalance' the bargain by imposing revenue-maximising or industry-protecting tariffs.

The EC set up a system whereby retaliatory tariffs would increase over time. Initially, duties on various US products were set at 5 per cent ad

[183] USTR Press Release, Statement on Internet Gambling, (21 December 2007 Office of the United States Trade Representative), available at https://ustr.gov/archive/Document_Library/Press_Releases/2007/December/Statement_on_Internet_Gambling.html.

[184] Mendel, 'Retaliation in the WTO'. See Minutes of DSB Meeting, WT/DSB/M/486, 18 December 2023, p. 7–8.

[185] *Communication from Brazil*, WT/DS267/43, 12 March 2010.

[186] Brazil Law No. 12270 of 24 June 2010.

[187] *Joint Communication from Brazil and the United States*, WT/DS267/44, 5 May 2010.

[188] See Section 6.3.3.2.

[189] *US – FSC (22.6)*, 30 August 2002, para. 8.1.

valorem, starting three months after the regulation was enacted – a delay in itself incompatible with seeking reparation. Moreover, using the wide margin that the high value of authorised retaliation afforded, the EC set the value of the retaliation to increase by an additional 1 per cent every month in the subsequent months, until it reached 17 per cent.[190] As Gregory Shaffer and Daniel Ganin observed, even if some have argued that this retaliation was welfare-enhancing for the EC,[191] this gradual escalation only makes sense if the EC was not seeking this objective but 'relying on the threat that it would increase countermeasures over time'.[192] Eight months after the initial tariffs were imposed, and six months before they were set to reach their maximum level, the United States passed legislation intended to implement the ruling, to which the EC responded – even if it did not agree that this achieved compliance – by suspending the additional tariffs.

6.5.2.3 Retaliation Effectively Applied at Maximum Levels

The United States is the key exception to the rule that members defer retaliation, and apply it at a level lower than authorised. The United States has twice applied retaliation measures at the maximum authorised level against the EC. However, the way in which it did so indicates an attempt to sanction and induce compliance rather than obtain benefits from protectionism. In *EC – Bananas*, the United States imposed additional customs tariffs of 100 per cent ad valorem on a number of EC products. Instead of focusing on protecting inefficient domestic industries from competition, the United States targeted industries within 'the two leading banana supporters'[193] in the EC: France and the United Kingdom.

The outcome was the EU–US Understanding on Bananas, signed relatively quickly in 2001, leading to the suspension of US retaliation. The process of bringing the EC's banana regime into compliance with

190 Council Regulation (EC) No 2193/2003 establishing additional customs duties on imports of certain products originating in the United States of America, Article 2.

191 Fritz Breuss, 'WTO Dispute Settlement: An Economic Analysis of Four EU–US Mini Trade Wars – A Survey' (2004) 4 *Journal of Industry, Competition and Trade* 275.

192 Shaffer and Ganin, 'Extrapolating Purpose from Practice', p. 83.

193 Scott D. Andersen and Justine Blanchet, 'The United States' Experience and Practice in Suspending WTO Obligations', in Chad P. Bown and Joost Pauwelyn (eds.), *The Law, Economics and Politics of Retaliation in WTO Dispute Settlement* (Cambridge: Cambridge University Press, 2010), 172, 235, 238.

WTO rules, however, was far slower. Only in 2012 was an official mutually agreed solution achieved.[194]

In *EC – Hormones*, the United States adopted the same approach: targeted retaliation, focusing on beef and pork imports from the EC member states it saw as supporting the hormones ban the most. The United States also threatened to adopt (but never adopted) a 'carousel approach', whereby the list of products would change periodically, thus threatening a larger number of industries and increasing economic uncertainty.[195] Following years of retaliation, in September 2009 the parties reached an understanding that did not involve performance but a form of compensation. The EU committed to progressively allow the importation of 'High Quality Meat' from the United States, which in turn progressively reduced the amount of retaliation applied.[196]

Thus, US retaliation successfully induced negotiations, bringing it some important benefits. In this sense, even if it did not produce substantive performance, retaliation performed a key role of Permissible Responses: empowering the aggrieved party in post-judgment negotiations. Even the US' 'maximalist' approach to applying retaliation rights, however, was not adopted with a view to using retaliation as a form of reparation. Given the size of the US economy, it might conceivably attempt to 'recover' concessions or 'rebalance' the bargain by applying higher, but not prohibitive, tariffs on a variety of EC products, with emphasis on those for which the US industry demanded protection.

Instead, as Shaffer and Ganin note, it imposed almost prohibitive tariffs on 'a small number of politically significant products'.[197] In *EC – Bananas*, the targets included Louis Vuitton bags, Italian handbags and pecorino cheese, and British cashmere sweaters. In *EC – Hormones*, the affected products included 'select, high-end agricultural products ... including Roquefort cheese, Dijon mustard, and Danish ham'.[198] These retaliatory tariffs clearly aimed to create as much political harm as possible and to avoid creating economic harm domestically, rather than directly to produce advantages for US producers (by imposing tariffs on

[194] Notification of a Mutually Agreed Solution, WT/DS105/11, 12 November 2012.

[195] Andersen and Blanchet, 'The United States' Experience and Practice', 239.

[196] See Joint Communication from the European Union and the United States, WT/DS26/29, 17 April 2014.

[197] Shaffer and Ganin, 'Extrapolating Purpose from Practice', 80–81.

[198] Ibid.

import-competing sectors) or for the US government (by imposing low tariffs on a broad range of products).

The same may be said of the 'collective' retaliation applied against the United States in *US – Byrd Amendment*.[199] In this dispute, eleven complainants obtained authorisation to apply retaliation. Four of them – the EC, Japan, Canada, and Mexico – imposed retaliatory tariffs on US products, aiming at the highest permissible level.[200] The level of retaliation applied varied according to the disbursement made by the United States. However, this level remained relatively low (27.81 million for the EC, 52.1 million for Japan, 11.6 million for Canada).[201] A lawyer at the European Commission Directorate General for Trade summarised the retaliating members' goal when selecting target products: 'minimising economic harm in the EC and . . . strengthening the political leverage on the US side'.[202] Applying retaliation was seen as a necessary evil to induce compliance rather than a means to obtain an advantage.

6.5.3 *Requests for Adjudication after Authorised Retaliation*

Perhaps the clearest evidence of the perception and use of WTO retaliation as a compliance-inducing instrument is the decision by aggrieved members to engage in a second procedure for compliance adjudication *after* receiving an authorisation to apply retaliation. This is sometimes coupled with a suspension of retaliatory measures while new panel proceedings take place.

A second compliance panel was first requested in *Brazil – Aircraft*.[203] A first Article 21.5 panel report, upheld by the Appellate Body, found that Brazil had failed to implement the original panel's recommendation. Following the decision of an Article 22.6 arbitrator, the DSB authorised Canada to apply retaliation on Brazilian goods in the amount of C$344.2 million annually. Canada never applied the authorised retaliation; when

199 The 'Byrd Amendment' obliged the US government to transfer to the industries having made a successful complaint of dumping the value of anti-dumping duties collected.

200 Jorge A. Huerta-Goldman, 'Is Retaliation Useful? Observations and Analysis of Mexico's Experience', in Chad P. Bown and Joost Pauwelyn (eds.), *The Law, Economics and Politics of Retaliation in WTO Dispute Settlement* (Cambridge: Cambridge University Press, 2010), 281, 284.

201 Ehring, 'The European Community's Experience and Practice in Suspending WTO Obligations', 252 (no information is provided regarding Mexico).

202 Ibid.

203 Panel Report, *Brazil – Aircraft (21.5 II)*, WT/DS46/RW/2, adopted 23 August 2001, paras. 1.6–1.8.

Brazil changed its policies and declared that it had thereby complied with the ruling, Canada requested a second Article 21.5 panel to examine the matter. This second panel found that Brazil's new measure had eliminated inconsistencies found in the previous Article 21.5 report and, while its application could lead to WTO-inconsistencies, Canada had not provided evidence of these.[204]

Another instance of a second recourse to Article 21.5 occurred in *US – FSC*. Following a condemnation of the US measure by both the panel and the Appellate Body under Article 21.5, the EC was authorised to retaliate and started applying retaliation. In October 2004, the United States enacted new legislation to implement the recommendations. The EC then suspended its retaliation[205] and requested new Article 21.5 proceedings.[206]

Both the panel and, in March 2006, the Appellate Body found that the United States 'continue[d] to fail to implement fully the operative DSB recommendations and rulings to withdraw the prohibited subsidies and to bring its measures into conformity with its obligations'.[207] The EU then reinstated its threatened countermeasures, announcing that from 16 May 2006 the relevant products would incur an additional 14 per cent ad valorem duty.[208]

Five days before that, on 11 May 2006, the US Congress repealed the WTO-inconsistent provisions.[209] On 15 May, the Commission suspended the retaliatory tariffs, conditioning their definitive termination upon the US President signing the new legislation into law.[210] Once this occurred, the regulation was fully repealed.[211]

A third time a member filed a second request for compliance adjudication, after being authorised to retaliate, was in *EC – Bananas*

[204] Ibid., 6.12–6.2.

[205] Council Regulation (EC) No 171/2005 of 31 January 2005 amending and suspending the application of Regulation (EC) No 2193/2003 establishing additional customs duties on imports of certain products originating in the United States of America, Council Regulation (EC) No 171/2005.

[206] DSB, *Minutes of Meeting*, WT/DSB/M/183, 17 February 2005, 8.

[207] Appellate Body Report, *US – FSC (21.5 II)*, para. 100(b).

[208] Notice (2006/C 104/08), OJEU 3.5.2006 C 104/18.

[209] DSB, *Minutes of Meeting*, WT/DSB/M/212, 20 June 2006, 18.

[210] Council Regulation (EC) No 728/2006 of 15 May 2006 suspending and conditionally repealing Regulation (EC) No 2193/2003 establishing additional customs duties on imports of certain products originating in the United States of America – Article 1, Council Regulation (EC) No 728/2006.

[211] Notice (2006/C 126/07), OJEU 30.5.2006 C 126/7.

II. Ecuador and the United States had been authorised to retaliate against the EC for its unlawful regime for importation of bananas. While the United States had indeed applied its authorised retaliation of US$191.4 million per year since 1999, Ecuador, authorised to retaliate in an amount of US$201.6 million per year since 2000, had not implemented retaliatory measures.[212] Following the signature of understandings between the EC and each of the complainants, the United States ceased its retaliation. A waiver was adopted to allow the EC to keep its regime in force until 31 December 2007. Two ad hoc arbitrations took place in 2005 under the Understandings on Bananas, both of which found that an EC proposal for market access remained WTO-inconsistent.[213]

Shortly before the expiry of the waiver, Ecuador and the United States requested a new compliance panel. Its conclusion, upheld by the Appellate Body, was that the EC's tariff quotas remained inconsistent with WTO commitments despite the elimination of some inconsistencies at the end of 2007.[214] A new settlement occurred in 2010. On 8 November 2012, the parties notified a mutually agreed solution to the DSB.[215]

In all of these cases, the members' response to purported implementation measures that they considered unsatisfactory was not to apply (or re-apply) retaliation. When faced with measures of implementation, aggrieved members generally stopped retaliation and requested a new compliance panel.[216]

One exception to this pattern was *US/Canada – Continued Suspension*, concerning the conduct of the United States and Canada in the aftermath of the *EC – Hormones* dispute. In the latter dispute, after the United

[212] *EC – Bananas (21.5 II – Ecuador, 21.5 – US)*, adopted 11 December 2008 and 22 December 2008, para. 7.

[213] ACP-EC Partnership Arbitration, WT/L/616, 1 August 2015; Second ACP-EC Partnership Arbitration, WT/L/625, 27 October 2005.

[214] *EC – Bananas (21.5 II)*, adopted 11 December 2008 and 22 December 2008, paras. 478–479. Because the United States had opted for requesting authorisation straight away in 1999, its request was the first under Article 21.5. The 1999 Article 22.6 arbitrators had nonetheless determined the continuing inconsistency of the EC regime for bananas with WTO law.

[215] *Notification of a Mutually Agreed Solution*, WT/DS27/98, 8 November 2012.

[216] A fourth case, although atypical, took place in *US – Tuna II*, where Mexico and the United States continued to argue over compliance, before a panel and then the Appellate Body, after Mexico was authorised to retaliate in 2017. In 2019, the Appellate Body report concluded that the United States' revised measure was WTO-consistent. Appellate Body Report, *US – Tuna II (21.5 II)*, WT/DS381/AB/RW/USA, WT/DS381/AB/RW2, adopted 11 January 2019, fn. 53 and para. 7.16. Mexico never applied the authorised retaliation.

States and Canada had been authorised to retaliate, the EC declared itself in compliance. The complainants rejected this declaration, and maintained their retaliatory tariffs. They argued that the EC's purported implementation essentially kept in place the full ban on hormone-treated beef that had been considered WTO-inconsistent, and failed to provide a scientific assessment.[217] The EC then initiated independent WTO proceedings against both members.

The EC claimed that, given its declaration of compliance, the aggrieved members were under an obligation to suspend the retaliatory tariffs and request a new Article 21.5 panel. The Appellate Body disagreed. In US/Canada – Continued Suspension, it held instead that (i) members are not obliged to suspend or cease authorised retaliation in response to a mere declaration of compliance; (ii) all the parties to the dispute are able to request new compliance proceedings; and (iii) 'once substantive compliance has been confirmed through WTO dispute settlement procedures, the authorization to suspend concessions lapses by operation of law (*ipso jure*)'.[218] In January 2009, the EC requested a new Article 21.5 panel,[219] which never delivered a report. A mutually agreed solution followed the request months later.[220]

The *US/Canada – Continued Suspension* ruling ensures an important balance, guaranteeing that mere self-declared compliance is insufficient to reverse years of dispute settlement decisions. Additionally, it reaffirms the entitlement of members to have continuous recourse to Article 21.5 for multilateral determinations of both compliance and non-compliance. This means that, even after the WTO has deployed its 'last resort', disputes remain within the purview of WTO adjudication and may be dealt with under the general regime for compliance adjudication.

6.6 Conclusions: Remedy Repetition and Remedy Escalation as Adjudicatory Strategies

The DSU system of remedies features a multi-stage procedure culminating in an authorisation to apply retaliatory measures, often issued as an upper limit on the volume of trade that may be affected. This structure of

[217] *US/Canada – Continued Suspension*, paras. 10–15.
[218] Ibid., para. 310.
[219] Request for Consultations, *EC – Hormones*, WT/DS26/23, 8 January 2009.
[220] See Joint Communication from the European Union and the United States, WT/DS26/28, 30 September 2009.

remedies has led to the misapprehension of WTO retaliation as a form of 'damages'. However, pursuant to the classification introduced in Chapter 1, the WTO authorisation to retaliate is a form Permissible Responses rather than Consequential Duties.

WTO dispute settlement, at least as it operated between 1995 and 2020, shows that an adjudication system may offer aggrieved members multiple sequential remedies: first, an impartial Declaration of Breach, then a declaration of non-compliance. These are adopted by the DSB, giving the aggrieved member the opportunity to rally the support of other WTO members. It is not the authorisation to retaliate but the broader dispute settlement process that lends the WTO its real 'teeth'. DSU remedies induce compliance with adjudicatory decisions and promote the performance of WTO obligations, not by facilitating swift retaliation but by empowering aggrieved members to repeatedly seek impartial adjudication and strategically defer retaliation.

Under WTO law, these steps were integrated into the regular dispute settlement procedure. Members could credibly threaten retaliation without applying it – not because they lacked the capacity to retaliate but because authorisation was deliberately withheld. By withholding immediate authorisation of Permissible Responses, the system enabled members to rely on the threat of retaliation without incurring the corresponding costs.

It remains unlikely that international adjudicators will be equipped with authority to order the application of coercion (*potestas*). The WTO's gradualist approach to remedies, and ability to determine Permissible Responses, enshrined a means of offering an alternative for protecting performance entitlements. By combining remedy repetition with remedy escalation, the WTO system reserved the most significant consequences it could produce for persistent wrongdoers. It strengthened an aggrieved party's ability to mobilise the various layers of compliance control that exist under international law. Chapters 7, 8 and 9 explore the extent to which this approach has been, and can be, adopted by other international adjudicators.

7

Between Remedy Repetition and Remedy Escalation

Post-Judgment Procedures in International Law

7.1 Introduction

Post-judgment procedures[1] permitting compliance adjudication with international court (IC) rulings are more common than assertions that compliance is 'political' would suggest.[2] A few treaties establishing open-ended adjudication regimes, including the UN Convention on the Law of the Sea (UNCLOS), the 1907 Hague Convention on the Pacific Settlement of Disputes, and most regional trade agreements (RTAs), expressly provide for post-judgment adjudication on matters of compliance with, or implementation or execution of, judgments or awards. Additionally, some treaties establishing ad hoc jurisdiction for a single dispute contemplate the possibility that implementation of judicial decisions may be problematic and provide international courts with post-judgment jurisdiction over implementation. Some international courts (ICs) have established their own post-judgment procedures for compliance adjudication. Finally, post-judgment procedures not aimed at compliance adjudication – in particular, procedures permitting judicial interpretation of prior rulings – may be triggered by parties seeking determinations that reduce the scope for disputes regarding compliance, and in some cases requesting, directly or indirectly, remedies for non-compliance.

This chapter analyses and examines the operation of procedures expressly permitting post-judgment adjudication, allowing it to take place under the same jurisdictional basis that justified the original

[1] Throughout this chapter, 'post-judgment' refers to procedures available after an international court, tribunal, or other adjudicator has issued its final ruling on a matter, and is in principle *functus officio*.

[2] See Section 1.2.1.

exercise of adjudication. Section 7.2 analyses the general functioning of these provisions. Sections 7.3, 7.4, and 7.5 examine three sources of compliance adjudication: the dedicated compliance procedures established in RTAs; the provision in treaties and *compromis* for adjudication on 'implementation' or 'execution' of rulings; and the mechanisms for compliance adjudication set up by ICs themselves. Section 7.6 discusses the extent of the review of state conduct permitted at this stage, as well as the remedies available to adjudicators. Section 7.7 considers how requests for interpretation have been used to seek adjudication on compliance. Section 7.8 concludes.

7.2 Post-Judgment Remedies in General International Law: From the 1899 Hague Convention to the ICJ Statute

International adjudication requires the consent of the states whose rights and obligations are being adjudicated. Every exercise of jurisdiction requires, as the International Court of Justice (ICJ) stated in response to the Democratic Republic of the Congo's (DRC's) second request in *Armed Activities in the Territory of the Congo*, 'an unequivocal indication of voluntary and undisputable acceptance of the Court's jurisdiction'.[3] In principle, once an international adjudicator has fulfilled its task, it is *functus officio* and can no longer issue rulings in the same dispute.[4] Treaties that set up adjudication procedures usually provide limited possibilities for post-judgment rulings allowing solely requests for interpretation.[5]

[3] *Armed Activities in the Territory of the Congo (New Application: 2002), Democratic Republic of Congo* v. *Rwanda*, Judgment, [2006] ICJ Reports 6, p. 6–7.

[4] But see Muqtar Al-Qahtani, 'The Role of the International Court of Justice in the Enforcement of Its Judicial Decisions' (2002) 15 *Leiden Journal of International Law* 781, 783; William Michael Reisman, *Systems of Control in International Adjudication and Arbitration: Breakdown and Repair* (Durham: Duke University Press, 1992), 48.

[5] Statute of the International Court of Justice, San Francisco, 24 October 1945, in force 18 April 1946, XV UNCIO 355 ('ICJ Statute'), Article 38(1): 'The judgment is final and without appeal. In the event of dispute as to the meaning or scope of the judgment, the Court shall construe it upon the request of any party'; American Convention on Human Rights, San Jose, 22 November 1969, in force 18 July 1978, 1144 UNTS 123, Article 67 ('ACHR'): 'The judgment of the Court shall be final and not subject to appeal. In case of disagreement as to the meaning or scope of the judgment, the Court shall interpret it at the request of any of the parties, provided the request is made within ninety days from the date of notification of the judgment'; Convention on the Settlement of Investment Disputes between States and Nationals of other States, Washington, 18 March 1965, in force 14 October 1966, 575 UNTS 159 ('ICSID Convention'), Article 50 (1): 'If any dispute

As regards compliance, Edward Fry, British delegate at the 1907 Hague Peace Conference tasked with revising the Convention for the Pacific Settlement of International Disputes, initially refused to include a provision permitting adjudication of disputes arising 'as to the interpretation and execution of the judgment' by the same tribunal that pronounced the original decision.[6] He argued that this exercise of jurisdiction would be a 'new arbitration', requiring a new *compromis*.[7] Fry subsequently accepted the proposal of the Austrian delegate, Heinrich Lammasch, to include the proposed provision, adding that the *compromis* could provide otherwise.[8] As a result, the final text of Article 22 of the 1907 Hague Convention reads:

> Any dispute arising between the parties as to the interpretation and execution of the Award shall, in the absence of an Agreement to the contrary, be submitted to the Tribunal which pronounced it.[9]

Arbitral tribunals acting under the 1907 Hague Convention may thus pronounce both on the *interpretation* and on the *execution* of their awards. Though there seems to be no practice under this provision,[10] a number of legal questions might arise regarding the requirements for re-seising the adjudicator for a pronouncement on the execution of its decisions, the scope of judicial review that may be conducted at this stage, and the remedies that the adjudicator may determine.

This formulation, which ensures significant post-judgment jurisdiction for adjudicators, might have prevailed in subsequent treaties establishing

shall arise between the parties as to the meaning or scope of an award, either party may request interpretation of the award by an application in writing addressed to the Secretary-General'. Article 46(3) of the European Convention for the Protection of Human Rights and Fundamental Freedoms, as amended by Protocols Nos. 11 and 14, ETS 5, 4 November 1950, only allows requests for interpretation from the Committee of Ministers: '3. If the Committee of Ministers considers that the supervision of the execution of a final judgment is hindered by a problem of interpretation of the judgment, it may refer the matter to the Court for a ruling on the question of interpretation'.

6 The Convention for the Pacific Settlement of International Disputes, Hague, 29 July 1899, in force 04 September 1900, 1 AJIL 103, did not regulate the matter ('1899 Convention').

7 James Brown Scott (ed.), *The Proceedings of the Hague Peace Conferences: The Conference of 1907: Translation of the Official Texts* (Hague: Carnegie Endowment for International Peace, 1921), vol. II, p. 727.

8 Ibid.

9 The Convention for the Pacific Settlement of International Disputes, Hague, 18 October 1907, UKTS 6 (1971) Cmnd 4575, Article 82 ('1907 Convention').

10 Rosenne does not list any instance in which parties had recourse to this article. Shabtai Rosenne, *Interpretation, Revision and Other Recourse from International Judgments and Awards* (Leiden: Martinus Nijhoff, 2007), 112–128.

international courts and tribunals. For the most part, however, subsequent treaties followed the path established in the same year of 1907 for the Central American Court of Justice (CACJ). Article XXIV of the CACJ Statute provided that the Court's judgments, once 'notified', could 'not be altered on any account'. At the request of any parties, the Court could 'declare the interpretation to be given to its judgments'.[11] Pursuant to Article XXV, parties to the Statute engaged themselves to submit to the judgments of the CACJ, as well as 'to lend all moral support that may be necessary in order that they may properly be fulfilled', as a 'real and positive guarantee of respect' for the Court.[12]

The Permanent Court of International Justice (PCIJ) Statute followed the latter approach. A section of the Draft of the Five Neutral Powers, which provided the basis for the Statute, was dedicated to the 'execution of the sentences of the Court'.[13] Article 52(1) foresaw a degree of oversight, requiring states to 'inform the registry of the Court of the manner in which the sentence has been carried out'. Article 52(2) empowered the PCIJ to interpret its decisions '[i]n doubtful cases', and Article 53(1) provided that the 'performance of the terms of all sentences [wa]s placed under the guarantee of the League of Nations'.[14] The Draft thus enshrined a separation of tasks between the interpretation of judgments, entrusted to the adjudicator, and their execution, reserved for states and intergovernmental bodies.

The matter was not raised again in subsequent debates. The final text of this provision, which remains in Article 60 of the current ICJ Statute, reproduces that adopted without discussion by the Advisory Committee of Jurists in 1920.[15] It provides that, '[i]n the event of dispute as to the meaning or scope of the judgment, the Court shall construe it upon the request of any

[11] 'Convention for the Establishment of a Central American Court of Justice', (1908) 2(1) Special Suppl. AJIL 231, 240–241.

[12] Ibid., 241. Curiously, Article XIX also empowered the CACJ to 'address itself to the Governments or tribunals of justice of the contracting States ... in order to have the measures that it may dictate within the scope of its jurisdiction carried out' (Ibid., 239).

[13] Advisory Committee of Jurists, 'Draft for the establishment of the Permanent Court of International Justice provided for in Article 14 of the Covenant of the League of Nations (Plan of the five neutral powers)'; *Documents Presented to the Committee Relating to Existing Plans for the Establishment of a Permanent Court of International Justice* (League of Nations, 1920), pp. 301, 323. The five Neutral Powers were Denmark, the Netherlands, Norway, Sweden, and Switzerland.

[14] Advisory Committee of Jurists, *Procès-Verbaux of the Advisory Committee of Jurists, June 16–July 24, 1920 with Annexes* (The Hague: Van Langenhuysen, 1920), 642.

[15] Ibid.

party'.[16] Even the requirement for states parties to inform the PCIJ registry of measures taken in implementation was removed from the final text.

A deliberate decision to entrust the execution of rulings to political bodies was made in 1945, when a Committee of Jurists met in Washington with the task of drafting the ICJ Statute. While the PCIJ Statute was used as a basis for, and essentially became, the ICJ Statute, the Committee of Jurists discussed a number of changes to the text. A member of the Committee raised the issue of whether the Statute should include 'a provision concerning the proper means for assuring' the 'exact execution of the decisions of the Court'.[17] Another member answered that 'it was not the business of the Court to ensure the execution of its decisions' and that, just as the execution of the decisions of the PCIJ was entrusted to the Council of the League of Nations, in the new organisation 'the matter concern[ed] rather the Security Council'.[18] The Committee decided to leave to the UN Charter the task of determining what follow-up to give to ICJ judgments.

In addition to requests for interpretation, the sole other post-judgment remedy provided for in the ICJ Statute is the remedy of revision, which aims at a modification of judgments in light of newly discovered facts.[19] The only reference to 'compliance' in the ICJ Statute appears in Article 61 (3), which provides that '[t]he Court may require previous compliance with the terms of the judgment before it admits proceedings in revision'. Mutlaq Al-Qahtani described this as an 'enforcement power' of the ICJ.[20] However, it is the party requesting the revision that must have complied with its obligations under the judgment before filing its claim – it would make little sense for the Court to dismiss an application for revision on grounds that the *respondent* in the application has not complied with the original judgment.[21] This provision therefore cannot serve as a means for a party to request indirectly a determination of non-compliance.

16 ICJ Statute, Article 60.

17 'Documents of the United Nations Conference on International Organization', (1945) 14 UNCIO 853.

18 Ibid.

19 Rosenne, *Interpretation, Revision and Other Recourse*; Kaiyan Homi Kaikobad, *Interpretation and Revision of International Boundary Decisions* (New York: Cambridge University Press, 2012).

20 Al-Qahtani, 'The Role of the International Court of Justice', 783.

21 See in this regard *Land, Island and Maritime Frontier Dispute (El Salvador* v. *Honduras)*, Judgment [2003] ICJ Reports 329, p. 399, in which the Chamber held that it had 'the possibility at any time to require previous compliance with the terms of the judgment whose revision is sought, before it admits proceedings in revision'.

Under the ICJ Statute, the sole possibilities for a judgment following the judgment on the merits (besides determinations of the amount of compensation, examined in Section 9.4) are requests for interpretation and revision, considered in Section 7.7. At the same time, nothing prevents states from establishing in their agreements to adjudication that other post-judgment remedies are available.

Some treaties empower international courts and tribunals to adjudicate on matters of compliance with, implementation of, or execution of decisions. In these cases, courts and tribunals are not entrusted with the mere interpretation of the judgment or award but may be called upon to intervene in other situations. Since much depends on the wording of the relevant provisions, these treaties must be examined before any conclusions may be drawn from them regarding the extent of judicial powers in post-judgment procedures.

7.3 Remedies for Non-Compliance in International Trade Agreements

Post-judgment procedures are generally available under RTAs. RTA procedural rules tend to feature a system of remedies similar to that established in the Dispute Settlement Understanding (DSU) and examined in Chapter 6, including adjudication on Permissible Responses, with one procedural difference: there is no need for a collective authorisation for their application. In case of non-compliance with the ruling, RTAs usually provide that a successful complainant may propose Permissible Responses (under different labels)[22] and, if the proposal is not challenged, apply them unilaterally. If the respondent challenges their permissibility, an adjudicator is called upon to determine whether the proposed measures are warranted and lawful in light of the original breach and ongoing conduct of the wrongdoer.

Intergovernmental trade agreements providing for compliance adjudication largely follow the model of the DSU. These RTAs initially included the North American Free Trade Agreement (NAFTA), now replaced with the United States–Mexico–Canada Agreement (USMCA),[23] and

[22] See, for example, notes 35, 47, 57.

[23] North American Free Trade Agreement, Washington and Mexico City and Ottawa, 17 December 1992, in force 1 January 1994, 32 ILM 289 (signed before the WTO Agreements but based on the dispute settlement procedure of the GATT); United States of America – Mexico – Canada Agreement, Mexico City, 30 November 2018, in force 1 July 2020, 134 Stat.11.

the Common Market of the South (Mercosur).[24] Today, although dozens of RTAs follow virtually the same structure of remedies and relationship between adjudication and the adoption of Permissible Responses,[25] practice remains embryonic. Among institutionalised adjudicators, the Andean Court of Justice (ACJ) has a significant practice in awarding 'sanctions' in the form of authorised Permissible Responses.[26] Among inter-state mechanisms, only in Mercosur has adjudication on compliance and Permissible Responses between states taken place.[27] Under NAFTA, two less typical instances of formal resort to RTA countermeasures took place. The remainder of this section examines this practice, as well as the two models of RTA remedies that prevail in contemporary treaty-making.

7.3.1 Remedies for Non-Compliance in Mercosur

Like the DSU, the 2002 Mercosur Olivos Protocol on dispute settlement provides for compulsory adjudication by ad hoc adjudicators (the '*Ad Hoc* Arbitral Tribunals'),[28] with the possibility of appeal of 'legal issues' and 'legal interpretations' to a permanent body (the 'Mercosur Court').[29] In case of appeal, the Mercosur Court may 'confirm, modify or revoke the juridical basis and the decisions of the *Ad Hoc* Arbitral Tribunals'.[30] Unlike World Trade Organization (WTO) adjudicators, Mercosur *Ad Hoc* Tribunals may issue provisional measures. If confirmed in their final award, these measures may be reversed in preliminary proceedings before the Mercosur Court.[31]

[24] Olivos Protocol for the Solution of Controversies in the Mercosur, Olivos, 18 February 2002, 2251 UNTS 244 ('Olivos Protocol').

[25] See Geraldo Vidigal, 'Remedies and Compliance', in Daniel Bethlehem et al. (eds.), *The Oxford Handbook of International Trade Law* (Oxford: Oxford University Press, 2012).

[26] See, most recently, ACJ, *Case No. 118-AI-2003 (Non-compliance with Judgment of 14 April 2005) (Second Summary Procedure)*, Order, 10 October 2023, 3.1.32. See also ACJ, *Case No. 118-AI-2003 (Non-compliance with Judgment of 14 April 2005) (Second Summary Procedure)*, Request for Interpretation, 24 October 2023.

[27] See, however, the jurisprudence of the Central American Integration System (SICA), in particular Case MSC-01-16, *Guatemala – Importation of Juices in Panama*, Award of the Arbitral Tribunal, 16 February 2017 ('*Guatemala – Procedimientos de la Autoridad Panameña de Seguridad Alimentaria para la deshabilitación de los registros necesarios para la importación de néctares, Laudo del Tribunal Arbitral*'), paras. 657–668.

[28] Olivos Protocol, Articles 9–16 ('Tribunal Arbitral *Ad Hoc*').

[29] Ibid., Articles 17–24 ('Tribunal Permanente de Revisión').

[30] Ibid., Article 22.

[31] Ibid., Article 15.

The Olivos Protocol contains no provision regarding remedies at the original adjudication stage, except for the specification that awards are binding, final, and 'shall be enforced in the way and with the scope determined therein'.[32] Article 28 establishes a procedure permitting requests for 'clarification of the award' or regarding 'the way in which the award has to be enforced' within fifteen days of the delivery of a decision.[33]

A party with a duty of implementation must inform the other party and a collective body (the Common Market Group) of the measures it will take to implement the award.[34] Under Article 30, if the 'State benefitting from the award' is not satisfied that the measures taken by an offender have led to compliance, it may have recourse to the adjudicator that issued the award (*Ad Hoc* Arbitral Tribunal or Mercosur Court), which then has thirty days to determine whether 'the measures taken do not comply with the award'. Mercosur courts may therefore adjudicate on compliance with their prior awards.[35]

In case of total or partial non-compliance, the party benefitting from the award may, within the following year, adopt 'temporary compensatory measures, such as the interruption of concessions or other similar obligations, with the aim of inducing compliance with the award'.[36] These measures must in principle affect the same sector as the violation; if the state taking the measures considers that this is 'impracticable or ineffective', it shall explain its reasons for adopting measures affecting other sectors. Despite the label 'compensatory measures' ('*medidas compensatorias temporarias*'), the form of the permitted measures, their temporary character, and the stated objective of inducing compliance, all correspond not to awards of compensation, a Consequential Duty, but to determinations of Permissible Responses.

Pursuant to Article 31(3), the member adopting these Permissible Responses must inform the offender of their content fifteen days prior to applying the measures. Article 32 then allows the wrongdoer to challenge proposed measures on two different grounds. Before measures

[32] Ibid., Articles 26–27.

[33] Argentina unsuccessfully attempted to employ this procedure to reverse the decision of the Tribunal in *Uruguay* v. *Argentina*, (2006) Tribunal Permanente de Revisión del Mercosur No 1/2006.

[34] Olivos Protocol, Article 29(3).

[35] This appears to be a power different from that of WTO adjudicators, which are empowered to verify compliance *with the agreement* violated. On this, see Section 6.3.

[36] Olivos Protocol, Article 31(1).

are applied, the offender may only challenge them arguing that it has complied with the award.[37] Once the aggrieved state applies retaliation, the wrongdoer may also argue that the measures are not proportional to the breach or have been wrongfully applied in a sector different from that affected by the breach.[38]

In Mercosur, therefore, adjudication of the permissibility or proportionality of compensatory measures occurs *ex post*, after the measures themselves are applied, and not *ex ante* as would be the case in the WTO. Contrasting with the WTO requirement of Dispute Settlement Body (DSB) authorisation, the entitlement to retaliate in Mercosur does not depend on an authorisation from an institutional organ. Mercosur courts may nonetheless be called upon to establish, *ex ante*, the permissibility of proposed responses, and, *ex post*, the proportionality of Permissible Responses adopted unilaterally. The judicial remedy available against these responses may be assimilated to the general possibility of requesting, from any adjudicator with jurisdiction over a set of norms, an *ex post* assessment of the lawfulness of responses adopted unilaterally by states.[39] On the other hand, the prior procedure and the specific regulation of these measures, as well as their justiciability *ex ante*, makes them similar to judicially reviewable – though not subject to prior authorisation – Permissible Responses.

The only Mercosur dispute to have reached the retaliation stage was *Remoulded Tyres*. At the original adjudication stage, the Mercosur Court, acting on appeal, found that Argentina's ban on the importation of remoulded tyres from Uruguay violated Mercosur rules. The Court rejected Argentina's argument that the goal of environmental protection permitted the adoption of restrictions on intra-Mercosur trade. It provided Argentina with 120 days to enact implementing legislation.[40]

After this period, Uruguay asserted that Argentina had not implemented the ruling and responded by adopting an additional 16 per cent tariff on tyres from Argentina. Argentina requested the Mercosur Court to rule that this response was disproportionate to its own breach. It argued that Uruguay could only adopt measures blocking Argentinean trade equivalent to that nullified by Argentina's ban.[41]

[37] Ibid., Article 32(1).
[38] Ibid., Article 32(2).
[39] See Section 5.2.
[40] *Award No 1/2005*, Mercosur Court, 20 December 2005, pp. 8–9.
[41] *Award No 1/2007*, Mercosur Court, 8 June 2007, p. 4.

Without having been given specific data regarding the effects of Uruguay's measures on trade, the Mercosur Court found that Uruguay's response was not disproportionate in the circumstances, given the trade imbalance in this field: Argentina received 43 per cent of Uruguay's exports of tyres, while Uruguay received a mere 2 per cent of Argentina's.[42] The Court also stated that even measures harming Argentina more than the original breach harmed Uruguay should be permissible, given the 'institutional damage' caused by 'non-compliance with the first award delivered by the Mercosur Court'.[43] The Court concluded that Uruguay's measures were 'proportionate and not excessive in relation to the consequences of non-compliance with Award No 1/2005', and were thus lawful Permissible Responses to Argentina's breach.[44]

The following year, Argentina replaced the prohibition on importation of remoulded tyres with a number of restrictive measures, leading to the same effects on Uruguayan exports. Without withdrawing its retaliatory measures, Uruguay initiated a compliance dispute before the Mercosur Court. Argentina restated the environmental arguments it had advanced in 2005. The Mercosur Court rejected these arguments, holding that 'Argentina cannot modify its law, justifying the new legal text based on arguments that have already been dismissed by the Court'.[45] The Mercosur Court declared Argentina was 'not in compliance with Award No 1/2005', and that, in light of this non-compliance, Uruguay 'ha[d] the right to maintain the compensatory measures until compliance with the referred award is achieved'.[46]

7.3.2 Remedies for Non-Compliance Under NAFTA

In NAFTA, the general provisions for inter-state adjudication were found in its Chapter 20. If political settlement by the NAFTA Free Trade Commission was unsuccessful, a party could request the Commission to establish an arbitral panel under Article 2008. The remedies that NAFTA panels could issue were determined in Article 2016, and included (a) findings of fact, including the possibility for the panel of

42 Ibid., p. 10.
43 Ibid.
44 Ibid, p. 11.
45 *Award No 1/2008*, Mercosur Court, 25 April 2008, p. 14.
46 Ibid, p. 15–16.

determining 'the degree of adverse trade effects on a party of any measure found not to conform with the obligations of the Agreement or to have caused nullification or impairment'; (b) 'determinations as to whether the measure at issue is or would be inconsistent with [NAFTA] or cause nullification or impairment'; and (c) 'recommendations, if any, for the resolution of the dispute'.

In original reports, NAFTA panels interpreted rules and applied them to the facts of the dispute, issuing Declarations of Breach and possibly indicating potential means for compliance. Article 2018 governed implementation of decisions. Pursuant to Article 2018(1), the outcome of negotiations should 'normally . . . conform with the determinations and recommendations of the panel'. Thus, NAFTA expressly permitted solutions deviating from NAFTA rules. Article 2018(2) guided this negotiation, specifying that the preferred remedy was 'the non-implementation or removal of a measure not conforming with this Agreement or causing nullification or impairment', and that only 'failing such a resolution' should parties resort to (WTO-like) compensation.

Finally, Article 2019 dealt with non-implementation after thirty days from the reception of the final panel report by the parties. If the report included a determination of the adverse trade effects caused by the wrongful measure,[47] Article 2019(1) entitled the complaining party to suspend application to the offender 'of benefits of equivalent effect'. The preference was for suspension of benefits to occur in the sector affected by the breach, unless this was not practicable or effective. Under Article 2019(3), any party – and not just the wrongdoer – could request a panel to 'determine whether the level of benefits suspended by a Party pursuant to Paragraph 1 is manifestly excessive'.

NAFTA inter-state dispute settlement saw limited use because panellists had to be selected from a roster of names presented by the parties. Under Article 2011(3), parties could 'exercise a peremptory challenge against any individual not on the roster . . . proposed as a panelist'. Since the United States never presented a roster, NAFTA Chapter 20 adjudication became de facto non-compulsory.[48] Only three disputes were adjudicated by Chapter 20 panels, all between 1995 and 1998.

[47] Under Article 2016, original NAFTA panels could already determine the adverse trade effects of NAFTA-inconsistent measures.

[48] See Joost Pauwelyn, 'Adding Sweeteners to Softwood Lumber: The WTO-NAFTA "Spaghetti Bowl" Is Cooking' (2006) 9 *Journal of International Economic Law* 1.

Of these, in one dispute the panel found no violation.[49] The other two were disputes brought by Mexico against the United States. In *Broom Safeguards*, the panel found that US safeguards on brooms had been imposed on brooms from Mexico in breach of NAFTA procedural requirements.[50] Mexico preceded this request with what the panel describes as 'retaliatory tariffs against certain imports from the United States, which Mexico asserted had substantially equivalent effect to the U.S. safeguard action ... approximately $1.4 million in the first year'.[51] This special unilateral response was permissible under NAFTA Article 801(4), under which a party adopting safeguards was required to offer compensation to the affected NAFTA party. Failing agreed compensation, the affected party was permitted to 'take tariff action having trade effects substantially equivalent to the action taken',[52] which Mexico did prior to initiating that dispute.[53]

The third dispute followed more closely the ordinary procedure leading to NAFTA retaliation. The 2001 panel in *Cross-Border Trucking Services* found that the United States was breaching NAFTA by refusing to consider applications by Mexican-owned carrier companies for authorisation to provide cross-border trucking services.[54] After a period in which the United States used various schemes to achieve an acceptable degree of openness to Mexican carriers, in 2009 the last of these schemes was cancelled. Mexico invoked NAFTA Article 2019 and imposed retaliatory tariffs, from 10 to 45 per cent, on 90 products imported from the United States, worth $2.4 billion.[55]

None of these disputes reached the stage of post-ruling adjudication. While NAFTA lacked a dedicated compliance panel, panels on suspension

[49] NAFTA Panel Report, *Tariffs Applied by Canada to Certain U.S.-Origin Agricultural Products*, (1996) CDA-USA-1995-2008-01, para. 209.

[50] NAFTA Panel Report, *U.S. Safeguard Action Taken on Broom Corn Brooms from Mexico*, (1997) USA-MEX-1997-2008-01, paras. 72, 77.

[51] Ibid., para. 16.

[52] NAFTA, Article 801(4).

[53] David A. Gantz, 'Dispute Settlement Under the NAFTA and the WTO: Choice of Forum Opportunities and Risks for the NAFTA Parties' (1999) 14 *American University International Law Review* 1025, 1068–1069.

[54] NAFTA Panel Report, *Cross-Border Trucking Services*, (1998) USA-MEX-1998-2008-01, para. 95.

[55] Presidential Decree, *Diario Oficial de la Federación*, 18 March 2009. See Klint W. Alexander and Bryan J. Soukup, 'Obama's First Trade War: The US-Mexico Cross-Border Trucking Dispute and the Implications of Strategic Cross-Sector Retaliation on U.S. Compliance under NAFTA' (2010) 28 *Berkeley Journal of International Law* 313, 321–324.

of benefits could presumably conclude that no adverse trade effects persisted. The entitlement to suspend 'benefits of equivalent effect' to the breach would then be set at a level of suspension of zero. This would amount in practice to making a determination that compliance has been re-established.[56] Alternatively, a party that believed it had complied with a panel's determinations could request a new NAFTA panel to examine, under Article 2004, whether the continued application of retaliation was consistent with the retaliating party's NAFTA obligations.

7.3.3 Remedies for Non-Compliance within Regional Trade Agreements: Institutionalised Communities and Intergovernmental

Regional economic agreements establishing highly institutionalised communities, with specific rule-making processes and complex systems of adjudication, often rely wholly on voluntary compliance for implementation. Many institutionalised economic agreements do not feature specific procedures for compliance adjudication, leading claimants faced with non-compliance to bring fresh disputes – a situation examined in Chapter 8. An exception is the constitutive treaty of the ACJ, amended in 1999 to provide the ACJ with jurisdiction over compliance and empower it to establish sanctions for non-compliance. In case of non-compliance, the ACJ is required to 'determine the limits within which the complainant, or any other member state, may restrict or suspend, wholly or partially, the benefits under the Cartagena Agreement that benefit the recalcitrant member state'.[57] The ACJ has been prolific in issuing authorisations, and sometimes recommendations, for the adoption of Permissible Responses against persistent wrongdoers, often enjoining not only the injured party but all Andean Community member states to adopt retaliatory tariffs.[58] In 2023, the ACJ went a step further and determined that it could respond to persistent non-compliance by

[56] See, Decision of the Arbitrator, *EC – Bananas (22.6 – US)*, WT/DS27/ARB, 9 April 1999, para. 4.13.

[57] Treaty Establishing the Court of Justice of the Cartagena Agreement, as amended, in force 29 August 1999 (Official Gazette of the Cartagena Agreement No 483, 17 September 1999), Article 27, para. 2: 'determinará los límites dentro de los cuales el país reclamante o cualquier otro País Miembro podrá restringir o suspender, total o parcialmente, las ventajas del Acuerdo de Cartagena que beneficien al País Miembro remiso'.

[58] Some of this jurisprudence is examined in Sections 5.3.4 and 8.4.2.2. For a broader view of the ACJ, see Karen J. Alter and Laurence R. Helfer, *Transplanting International Courts – The Law and Politics of the Andean Tribunal of Justice* (Oxford: Oxford University Press, 2017).

imposing on recalcitrant member states pecuniary fines, relying on its power under the Cartagena Agreement to determine 'other measures if the restriction or suspension of benefits under the Cartagena Agreement aggravates the situation or is not effective'.[59]

More intergovernmental RTAs – other than those that establish highly institutionalised economic communities[60] – adopt a system of prospective remedies similar to Mercosur and NAFTA. In this system, original adjudication is followed by an allotted period for implementation and, in case of non-compliance, permissible retaliation. Compared to their equivalents in the DSU, provisions on remedies in these agreements put less emphasis on compliance adjudication and more on adjudication of the entitlement to adopt Permissible Responses. Dispute settlement practice under RTAs has recently re-emerged after a decade of dormancy, though no compliance adjudication or adjudication on Permissible Responses has yet been requested.[61]

Despite RTAs being extremely diverse, they follow essentially the same approach to remedies, with slight differences between the models championed by the United States and the European Union.[62] In US

[59] Treaty Establishing the Court of Justice of the Cartagena Agreement, Article 27, para. 3: 'En todo caso, el Tribunal podrá ordenar la adopción de otras medidas si la restricción o suspensión de las ventajas del Acuerdo de Cartagena agravare la situación que se busca solucionar o no fuere eficaz en tal sentido'. See ACJ, *Case No. 118-AI-2003 (Non-compliance with Judgment of 14 April 2005) (Second Summary Procedure)*, Request for Interpretation, 24 October 2023.

[60] For the 'infringement proceedings' mechanism within the European Union, see Carlos Closa and Gisela Hernández, 'Defining and Operationalising Defiant Non-Compliance in the EU: The Rule of Law Case' (2025) 63 *Journal of Common Market Studies* 964–986; Luca Prete, 'The Systemic Criterion in the Use of Infringement Proceedings' (2023) 24 *German Law Journal* 1011; Camilla Burelli, 'The Deterrent Effect of Financial Sanctions Pursuant to Article 260(2) TFEU in the Context of Violations of Environmental Obligations' (2023) 3 *Italian Review of International and Comparative Law* 367. For challenges of non-compliance and backlash against regional economic community adjudicators in Africa, see Karen J. Alter, James T. Gathii, and Lawrence R. Helfer, 'Backlash against International Courts in West, East and Southern Africa: Causes and Consequences' (2016) 27 *European Journal of International Law* 293; Nicole De Silva and Misha Ariana Plagis, 'NGOs, International Courts, and State Backlash against Human Rights Accountability: Evidence from NGO Mobilization against Tanzania at the African Court on Human and Peoples' Rights' (2023) 57 *Law & Society Review* 36.

[61] See Geraldo Vidigal, 'Regional Trade Adjudication and the Rise of Sustainability Disputes: Korea – Labor Commitments and Ukraine – Wood Export Bans' (2022) 116 *American Journal of International Law* 567.

[62] Remedies can be different for 'non-trade' chapters. Marco Bronckers and Giovanni Gruni have identified, especially with regard to so-called 'trade and sustainable development' chapters, a US 'sanctions-based' approach and a 'promotional' approach. See Marco

RTAs,[63] condemnatory panels' reports are followed by a period for implementation by the party found in breach. In this period, parties are under an obligation to 'agree on the resolution of the dispute, which normally shall conform with the determinations and recommendations, if any, of the panel', including 'whenever possible' cessation of the RTA-inconsistent conduct.[64] Like NAFTA, then, US RTAs acknowledge the possibility that arrangements will deviate from the rules set out in the text of the agreements.

In case it finds that the breach persists after a period of time, usually forty-five days, and absent an agreement on monetary compensation, the aggrieved party may retaliate (suspend concessions and benefits under the relevant agreement) against the wrongdoer. It must notify the wrongdoer of its decision in writing, describing the level of retaliation proposed. The wrongdoer may challenge this level before the panel on grounds of lack of proportionality, but it may also claim that retaliation is unwarranted because it 'has eliminated the non-conformity or the nullification or impairment that the panel has found'.[65] In the latter case, the panel tasked with examining the amount of retaliation also holds jurisdiction to assess whether compliance was achieved. If it finds that the wrongdoer has eliminated the non-conformity or the nullification or impairment, no retaliation is warranted.[66]

Bronckers and Giovanni Gruni, 'Retooling the Sustainability Standards in EU Free Trade Agreements' (2021) 24 *Journal of International Economic Law* 25.

[63] United States-Australia Free Trade Agreement, 18 May 2004 (US – Australia); United States-Bahrain Free Trade Agreement, 14 September 2014 (US – Bahrain); Dominican Republic-Central America-United States Free Trade Agreement, 5 August 2004 (US – CAFTA – DR); United States-Chile Free Trade Agreement, 6 June 2003 (US – Chile); United States-Korea Free Trade Agreement, 30 June 2007 (US – Korea); United States and Morocco Free Trade Agreement, 15 June 2004 (US – Morocco); United States-Oman Free Trade Agreement, 19 January 2006 (US – Oman); United States-Panama Trade Promotion Agreement, 28 June 2007 (US – Panama); United States-Peru Trade Promotion Agreement, 12 April 2006 (US – Peru); United States-Singapore Free Trade Agreement, 6 May 2003 (US – Singapore), all available at www.ustr.gov/trade-agreements/.

[64] US – Australia, Article 21.10; US – Bahrain, Article 19.10; US – CAFTA – DR, Article 20.15; US – Chile, Article 21.14; US – Korea, Article 21.12; US – Morocco, Article 20.10; US – Oman, Article 20.10; US – Panama, Article 20.14; US – Peru, Article 21.15; US – Singapore, Article 20.5.

[65] US – Australia, Article 21.11(3)(b); US – Bahrain, Article 19.11(3)(b); US – CAFTA – DR, Article 20.16(3)(b); US – Chile, Article 21.15(3)(b); US – Korea, Article 21.13(3)(b); US – Morocco, Article 20.11(3)(b); US – Oman, Article 20.11(3)(b); US – Panama, Article 20.15(3)(b); US – Peru, Article 21.16(3)(b); US – Singapore, Article 20.6(3)(b).

[66] US – Australia, Article 21.11(4); US – Bahrain, Article 19.11(4); US – CAFTA – DR, Article 20.16(4); US – Chile, Article 21.15(4); US – Korea, Article 21.13(4); US –

In addition to this, a stand-alone 'compliance review' procedure is available to the wrongdoer at any time. The task of a compliance review panel is to assess whether the wrongdoer 'has eliminated the non-conformity or the nullification or impairment that the panel has found'.[67] A finding that compliance was achieved obliges the formerly aggrieved party to reinstate all benefits to the former wrongdoer; any monetary compensation being paid may be stopped.

One interesting option that exists in US RTAs is for retaliation rights to be converted into duties to pay monetary compensation, which a wrongdoer may prefer over suffering retaliation. The amount of this compensation is in principle negotiated by the parties. However, if the parties cannot agree on an amount, the RTAs establish *ex ante* that payment of '50 percent of the level that the complaining party has proposed to suspend'[68] precludes recourse to retaliation measures. US RTAs therefore de jure allow a party to continue to deviate from its obligations by paying a price that, even if based on an estimation of injury by the complainant, is established in the RTAs themselves.

With some more variation, RTAs signed by the European Union also specifically provide for compliance adjudication. In the EU's traditional approach, found in EU – Colombia/Peru,[69] EU – Korea,[70] and EU – Serbia,[71] for example, a party that views another party's measures as inconsistent with the agreement may request the establishment of an 'arbitration panel' to hear its complaint. If this panel finds an RTA-inconsistent

Morocco, Article 20.11(4); US – Oman, Article 20.11(4); US – Panama, Article 20.15(4); US – Peru, Article 21.16(4); US – Singapore, Article 20.6(4).

[67] US – Australia, Article 21.13; US – Bahrain, Article 19.13; US – CAFTA – DR, Article 20.16; US – Chile, Article 21.17; US – Korea, Article 21.14; US – Morocco, Article 20.13; US– Oman, Article 20.13; US – Panama, Article 20.16; US – Peru, Article 21.17; US – Singapore, Article 20.8.

[68] US – Australia, Article 21.11(5); US – Bahrain, Article 19.11(5); US – CAFTA – DR, Article 20.16(6); US – Chile, Article 21.15(5); US – Korea, Article 21.13(5); US – Morocco, Article 20.11(5); US – Oman, Article 20.11(5); US – Panama, Article 20.15 (6); US – Peru, Article 21.16(5); US – Singapore, Article 20.6(5).

[69] Trade Agreement between the European Union and its Member States, of the one part, and Colombia and Peru, of the other part, 26 June 2012, OJ L 354, 21 December 2012 (EU – Colombia/Peru).

[70] Free trade Agreement between the European Union and its Member States, of the one part, and the Republic of Korea, of the other part, 6 October 2010, OJ L 127, 14 May 2011 (EU – Korea).

[71] Interim Agreement on trade and trade-related matters between the European Community, of the one part, and the Republic of Serbia, of the other part, 24 April 2008, OJ L 28, 30 January 2010 (EU – Serbia).

measure, a reasonable period of time (which may be agreed upon or judicially determined) is given for the wrongdoer to comply.

In EU RTAs, compliance adjudication is available at two stages. During the reasonable period of time for compliance, a party found in breach must notify the other party (as well as a committee of representatives of the parties) of any measure it takes to comply. If the complainant believes that this measure fails to achieve compliance with the relevant agreement, it may request the arbitration panel to be reconvened to rule on the matter. In case this panel finds that the implementing measures have successfully eliminated the breach, no retaliation is warranted.[72]

A different form of compliance adjudication applies, after retaliation measures have been adopted, if the offender declares to have 'compl[ied] with the ruling of the arbitration panel'.[73] In this case, it would seem that an unchallenged assertion requires the complainant to cease applying retaliation, although this is only specified in EU – Colombia/Peru.[74] In EU – Korea and EU – Serbia, the agreement tasks the complainant (i.e. the party applying retaliation) with requesting compliance adjudication,[75] without specifying its legal interest in doing so. In EU – Serbia, the post-retaliation compliance panel has the option of determining that retaliation may continue 'at a different level'[76] – presumably because the level of adverse economic effect caused by the violation has changed.

In the decade between 2005 and 2018, dispute settlement mechanisms under preferential trade agreements saw hardly any use. This is possibly due to these agreements being enforced through direct resort to unilateral remedies.[77] Without the collective pressure that is exercised at the WTO, adjudication may prove to be less effective than direct threat of, and recourse to, self-help measures. If a party can prevail simply by

[72] EU – Colombia/Peru, Article 309; EU – Korea, Article 14(9); EU – Serbia, Protocol 6, Article 8(1).

[73] EU – Colombia/Peru, Article 311(1); EU – Korea, Article 14(12)(1); EU – Serbia, Protocol 6, Article 10(1).

[74] EU – Colombia/Peru, Article 311(1); the period for cessation is thirty days.

[75] Under EU – Korea Article 14.12(2), this is an obligation ('shall'), and compliance adjudication is exercised by the original arbitration panel. Under EU – Serbia, Protocol 6, Article 10(2), this is a faculty ('may'), and compliance adjudication is exercised solely by the chairperson of the original panel.

[76] EU – Serbia Article 10(2).

[77] Geraldo Vidigal, 'Why Is There So Little Litigation under Free Trade Agreements? Retaliation and Adjudication in International Dispute Settlement' (2017) 20 *Journal of International Economic Law* 927; Vidigal, 'Regional Trade Adjudication and the Rise of Sustainability Disputes'.

persuasion and (threats of) self-help, it may prefer to take this route even where a formal dispute settlement mechanism is available. This may also explain the low levels of Mercosur litigation, which is compulsory.

Conversely, in a bilateral setting, if a party cannot prevail through self-help and resorts to adjudication, providing it with a right to retaliate at the end of the adjudication process changes little in its relative position. Especially in cases of great imbalances of power, the possibility of a remedy of last resort may be more important in that it provides an object for continued litigation, and ensures the imposition of reputational costs through successive decisions, than as a basis for adopting Permissible Responses.

7.4 Jurisdictional Clauses Providing for Compliance Adjudication

Provisions dedicated to adjudication of compliance with rulings are rarer outside the field of trade. The jurisdictional provisions of some multilateral treaties – most meaningfully, UNCLOS – endow ICs with jurisdiction to adjudicate on the 'execution' or 'manner of implementation' of their rulings. Additionally, agreements to adjudicate specific disputes occasionally establish proceedings allowing subsequent recourse to the same IC for an assessment of implementation of final rulings.

7.4.1 Implementation Adjudication in Multilateral Treaties

Two prominent multilateral treaties outside the field of trade feature specific provisions permitting adjudication on implementation of judicial rulings. The first is the 1907 Hague Convention on the Pacific Settlement of International Disputes. The 1899 Hague Convention did not regulate implementation beyond a provision stating that the signature of a *compromis* 'implies the undertaking of the parties to submit loyally to the Award'.[78] By contrast, Article 82 of the 1907 Convention provides that '[a]ny dispute arising between the parties as to the interpretation *and execution* of the Award shall, in the absence of an Agreement to the contrary, be submitted to the Tribunal which pronounced it'.[79]

[78] 1899 Convention, Article 31. Articles 55 and 56 of the 1899 Convention provide for procedures for revision and interpretation of the award by the arbitral tribunal.

[79] 1907 Convention, Article 82 (emphasis added). Rosenne, *Interpretation, Revision and Other Recourse*, 112–128, does not list any instance on which parties had recourse to this article.

Thus, in cases in which the 1907 Hague Convention regulates the procedure, a party is able to bring a dispute concerning the execution of an arbitral award before the original arbitral tribunal for adjudication. This is particularly relevant because the procedural rules of the 1907 Hague Convention apply by default to claims filed under the jurisdictional clauses of a number of other treaties, including the two General Acts for the Pacific Settlement of International Disputes,[80] as well as to arbitration under the European Convention for the Peaceful Settlement of Disputes.[81]

Adherence to the 1949 General Act is limited[82] and the legal status of the 1928 General Act is unclear.[83] As regards the European Convention, only an arbitration initiated under its Chapter III triggers the application of the procedural rules of the 1907 Hague Convention.[84] However, the formulation of the jurisdictional clause ensures that the ICJ will have jurisdiction in the virtual totality of disputes between the parties, with arbitration being compulsory only for disputes 'other than' those entrusted to the ICJ.[85] The European Convention was successfully

[80] General Act for the Pacific Settlement of International Disputes, Geneva, entered into force on 26 September 1928, 93 LNTS 344, Article 18; Revised General Act for the Pacific Settlement of International Disputes entered into force 28 April 1949, 71 UNTS 101, Article 18.

[81] European Convention for the Peaceful Settlement of Disputes, Strasbourg, 29 April 1957, entered into force on 30 April 1958, 320 UNTS 243, Article 24 ('Convention for Settlement of Disputes 1957').

[82] Parties are currently (and since 1971) Belgium, Burkina Faso, Denmark, Estonia, Luxembourg, the Netherlands, Norway, and Sweden.

[83] See *Aerial Incident of 10 August 1999, Pakistan* v. *India*, Judgment, [2000] ICJ Reports 12, p. 23–24, and the jurisprudence referred therein. Current parties are Belgium, Canada, Australia, New Zealand, Ireland, Denmark, Ethiopia, Finland, Greece, Italy, Luxembourg, Norway, Peru, Switzerland, and Türkiye. The Netherlands and Sweden are parties to the act insofar as it concerns conciliation and judicial settlement.

[84] Convention for the Peaceful Settlement of Disputes 1957, Article 24. Current parties are Germany, Liechtenstein, the Netherlands, Norway, Slovakia, and Sweden.

[85] Ibid., Article 19: 'The High Contracting Parties shall submit to arbitration all disputes which may arise between them other than those mentioned in Article 1'. Ibid., Article 1: 'The High Contracting Parties shall submit to the judgement of the International Court of Justice all international legal disputes which may arise between them including, in particular, those concerning:

a. the interpretation of a treaty;

b. any question of international law;

c. the existence of any fact which, if established, would constitute a breach of an international obligation;

d. the nature or extent of the reparation to be made for the breach of an international obligation.'

invoked as a basis for ICJ jurisdiction in *Jurisdictional Immunities of the State*.[86] In *Certain Property*, the ICJ recognised that it had jurisdiction *ratione materiae* and *ratione personae*, though the claim was dismissed on grounds that the Court lacked jurisdiction *ratione temporis* – a limitation that would also have restricted arbitration.[87]

A further possibility is adjudication under the 1948 Pact of Bogotá, whereby fourteen states of the Americas agree *ex ante* to submit their disputes with 'any other American State' to the jurisdiction of the ICJ.[88] As regards the arbitration procedure, Article 67 of the Pact provides that 'differences that arise in regard to the interpretation or execution of the award shall be submitted to the decision of the Arbitral Tribunal that rendered the award'. Contrary to the European Convention, under the Pact of Bogotá the arbitral procedure may be compulsory in some cases. Pursuant to its Article 35, parties must resort to arbitration if the ICJ 'declares itself to be without jurisdiction to hear and adjudge the controversy' for reasons other than (i) that the claim concerns a matter that is within the domestic jurisdiction of a state; (ii) that the matter has already been settled by agreement, by arbitration or by judicial settlement; or (iii) that the matter relates to diplomatic protection.[89]

More relevantly, in view of the significant use of arbitration under the UN Convention on the Law of the Sea, UNCLOS Annex VII arbitration includes the possibility of compliance adjudication. Pursuant to UNCLOS Article 287(3), unless the two parties to a dispute have agreed to another form of dispute settlement, Annex VII arbitration is compulsory regarding matters of 'interpretation and application' of the Convention for its 168 states parties.[90] Article 12(1) of Annex VII provides:

> Any controversy which may arise between the parties to the dispute as regards the interpretation *or manner of implementation* of the award may be submitted by either party for decision to the arbitral tribunal which made the award.[91]

[86] *Jurisdictional Immunities of the State (Italy* v. *Germany)*, [2012] ICJ Reports, p. 99, 105.

[87] *Certain Property, Liechtenstein* v. *Germany*, Judgment, [2005] ICJ Reports 6, p. 10.

[88] American Treaty on Pacific Settlement 'Pact of Bogotá', Bogota, 30 April 1948, 30 UNTS 55, 82, Article 31. The current parties to the Pact are Bolivia, Brazil, Chile, Costa Rica, the Dominican Republic, Ecuador, Haiti, Honduras, Mexico, Nicaragua, Panama, Paraguay, Peru, and Uruguay. Colombia and El Salvador have denounced the Pact following adverse ICJ decisions.

[89] Ibid., Articles 35, 5–7.

[90] United Nations Convention on the Law of the Sea, Montego Bay, 10 December 1982, in force 16 November 1994, 1833 UNTS 39, Article 287 (3) ('UNCLOS').

[91] Ibid., Article 12(1).

This empowers UNCLOS arbitral tribunals to examine, in a derivative procedure, disputes as to how implementation must take place.

The scholarship has generally paid little attention to this provision. John Merrills, noting that 'apparently' this clause entails the compulsory jurisdiction of the tribunal over matters of implementation, labels this provision 'surprising'.[92] Myron Nordquist's commentary to UNCLOS notes briefly that 'it would appear' that an Article VII arbitral tribunal would have 'some competence to verify the conformity of the implementation of its award should the need arise' but fails to see any difference between this and a request for interpretation, arguing that a dispute over the manner of implementation 'is easily concretized' as a dispute over the interpretation of the award.[93]

The latter point is interesting for the question, examined below, of whether requests for interpretation may be employed to request judicial determinations regarding implementation.[94] However, a clause permitting subsequent disputes regarding the 'manner of implementation' of an award clearly provides courts with a broader jurisdiction than a clause solely allowing requests for interpretation of its earlier decisions.

Most relevant for present purposes, the UNCLOS provision permitting adjudication on the 'manner of implementation' of a decision allows for judicial pronouncements regarding acts subsequent to the final judgment or award. These pronouncements include, on the one hand, determinations that the 'manner' a wrongdoer has chosen to implement an award (including provisions for reparation contained therein) is inconsistent with the award. It would also seem to permit declarations that the manner by which a *prevailing* party has chosen to implement an award is in contradiction with the rules of UNCLOS or of general international law. Thus, an arbitral tribunal could be called upon to assess both a claim of failure by a party found in breach to implement the award and, for example, a claim that the prevailing party applied unwarranted or disproportional coercion in its conduct in implementation of the award.

Given that this provision applies to cases in which UNCLOS arbitration is compulsory, the same claims could arguably be brought in

[92] J.G. Merrills, *International Dispute Settlement*, 5th edn (Cambridge: Cambridge University Press, 2011), 178.

[93] Myron H. Nordquist (ed.), *United Nations Convention on the Law of the Sea 1982 – A Commentary* (Netherlands: Martinus Nijhoff, 1989), vol. 5, p. 436–437.

[94] See Section 7.7.

independent proceedings. In this regard, recourse to adjudication on implementation has two main advantages. On the one hand, it allows the same tribunal to reconvene for the purpose of examining the matter of implementation. This ensures a quicker response, as well as familiarity of the members of the tribunal with the case. Additionally, Article 12(1) would seem to prevent wrongdoers from avoiding compliance adjudication by denouncing UNCLOS.

Article 12(1) may prove particularly significant in view of the decision by some states not to appear before Annex VII tribunals.[95] Given the inevitable political undertones of post-judgment negotiations in these cases, the availability of adjudication on implementation may provide the weakest party with a neutral institution to which it may have recourse to reaffirm the rights determined in the award, and perhaps provide it with further remedies.

7.4.2 Compromis Permitting Adjudication on Implementation: Gabčíkovo-Nagymaros

Besides multilateral treaties, states may permit adjudication on implementation in ad hoc agreements to adjudicate a dispute. Such adjudication has been ongoing for decades in the *Gabčíkovo-Nagymaros* dispute between Hungary and Slovakia. In the underlying *compromis*, Article 5(2) provides for the 'final and binding' character of an ICJ judgment. In addition to this, in case the parties cannot agree on how to implement the judgment, Article 5(3) empowers each party to request from the ICJ 'an additional Judgment to determine the modalities for executing its Judgment'.[96] This provision may be invoked if the parties are 'unable to reach agreement within six months' of the decision, with no time limitation for the exercise of this right.

In 1997, the ICJ issued a judgment on the merits, requiring Hungary and Slovakia to 'negotiate in good faith . . . to ensure the achievement of

[95] *Arctic Sunrise, Netherlands* v. *Russia*, Provisional Measures, ITLOS, (2013) ITLOS Case No 22, para. 9; Stefan A.G. Talmon, 'The South China Sea Arbitration: Is There a Case to Answer?', in Stefan Talmon and Bing Bing Jia (eds.), *The South China Sea Arbitration: A Chinese Perspective* (Oxford: Hart, 2014), 15–79 (noting China's statement that it 'will not have any part' in the arbitration instituted by the Philippines against it).

[96] *Gabčíkovo-Nagymaros Project*, Hungary/Slovakia, Judgment, [1997] ICJ Reports 7, 12 ('If they are unable to reach agreement within six months, either Party may request the Court to render an additional Judgment to determine the modalities for executing its Judgment').

the objectives of the Treaty of 16 September 1977'.[97] Almost one year later, Slovakia invoked Article 5(3) to request a new judgment. It asked the ICJ, inter alia, to declare that 'Hungary bears responsibility for the failure of the Parties to agree on the modalities for executing the Judgment'.[98] Slovakia also requested the Court to declare that Hungary must comply with a number of obligations in order to give effect to the judgment, including appointing a plenipotentiary to fulfil the objectives of their 1977 treaty, as well as set out time-frames for the parties to agree on how to implement the judgment.

Almost three decades later, the *Gabčíkovo-Nagymaros* case on implementation remains pending before the ICJ. After Slovakia re-seised the Court in 1998, Hungary rejoined implementation negotiations it had abandoned. The parties subsequently concluded a number of agreements and established working groups to decide on specific matters related to the dispute. In 2017, Slovakia discontinued the procedure for a new judgment, but in the process of accepting this, 'both Parties reserved their respective right ... to request the Court to render an additional judgment to determine the modalities for executing its Judgment of 25 September 1997'.[99] Even if both parties appear to prefer a negotiated solution to another judicial determination, the *compromis* ensures that negotiations remain based on the 1997 Judgment, giving each party the right to request adjudication on its implementation.[100]

The *Gabčíkovo-Nagymaros* special agreement is not unique. Article 7(3) of the *Benin/Niger* and *Burkina Faso/Niger* special agreements also contain specific authorisation for 'either Party' to seise the Court after the final judgment 'in case of difficulty in the implementation of the Judgment'.[101] Interestingly, these provisions allow parties to re-seise the Court 'pursuant to Article 60 of its statute', implying that the Court

97 Ibid., p. 83.

98 ICJ, Press Release 1998/28, 3 September 1998.

99 *Gabčíkovo-Nagymaros Project (Hungary/Slovakia)*, 'The Court places on record the discontinuance by Slovakia of the procedure begun by means of its Request for an additional judgment', *ICJ Press Release No. 2017/31* (21 July 2017), p. 2. .

100 In this regard, a Hungarian negotiator argues that the parties have irreconcilable interests and therefore 'will have to return to the International Court of Justice (or another third party) to seek a more detailed and concrete guidance' (Marcel Szabó, 'The Implementation of the Judgment of the ICJ in the Gabcíkovo-Nagymaros Dispute' (2009) 39 *Environmental Policy and Law* 97, 98).

101 *Frontier Dispute, Benin/Niger*, Judgment, [2005] ICJ Reports 90, p. 96; *Frontier Dispute, Burkina Faso/Niger*, Judgment, [2013] ICJ Reports 44, p. 52.

would be able to adjudicate on implementation under this provision.[102] In *Burkina Faso/Niger*, the special agreement also empowered the ICJ to appoint three experts to assist the parties in the demarcation process, providing the Court with a further role in implementation – one which it exercised in 2013.[103]

It remains to be seen whether including provisions of this kind in special agreements will become standard practice.[104] What is clear from the experiences in *Gabčíkovo-Nagymaros* and *Burkina Faso/Niger* is that there is value in establishing a role for the ICJ – or any other IC seised by common agreement – in the implementation of judgments. Expressly setting out such a role not only preserves the possibility of adjudication but also permits the IC to award specific remedies, without inviting the objection that the adjudicator is not empowered to consider matters relating to the implementation of its judgments.

7.4.3 Agreement to Arbitrate Permitting Adjudication on Implementation: The Argentina–Chile Border Disputes

Prior to the establishment of the WTO, possibly the single most frequently used clause for post-ruling adjudication on implementation was that of the 1902 Treaty of Arbitration between Argentina and Chile ('1902 Treaty'). Under Article XII of the 1902 Treaty, the two parties agreed to settle all their disputes by arbitration, nominating as arbitrator 'His Britannic Majesty's Government'.[105] The arbitrator was competent

[102] Articles 7(2) and 7(3) read: '2. From the day on which the judgment is rendered, the Parties shall have eighteen (18) months in which to commence the works of demarcation of the boundary. 3. In case of difficulty in the implementation of the judgment, either Party may seise the Court pursuant to Article 60 of its Statute' (Ibid.).

[103] The ICJ appointed the experts in *Frontier Dispute, Burkina Faso/Niger*, Appointment of Experts, 12 July 2013.

[104] No similar provision was included in the special agreements in *Pedra Branca/Pulau Batu Puteh, Middle Rocks and South Ledge, Malaysia/Singapore*, Judgment, [2008] ICJ Reports 12, p. 19 or *Pulau Litigan and Pulau Sipadan, Indonesia/Malaysia*, Judgment, [2002] ICJ Reports 625, p. 631. The special agreement in *Kasikili/Sedudu Island, Botswana/Namibia*, Judgment, [1999] ICJ Reports 1045, p. 105, provides simply that 'the parties shall take steps necessary to carry out the judgment'. *The Agreement to Arbitration in Boundary dispute between Argentina and Chile concerning the frontier line between Boundary Post 62 and Mount Fitzroy, Chile* v. *Argentina* (1995) 113 ILR 1, 23 ('Laguna del Desierto') provides that the award is 'binding on the Parties, final and not subject to appeal, and compliance with it shall be entrusted to the honour of both Nations'.

[105] Treaty of Arbitration concluded between Argentina and Chile, signed 28 May 1902, (1907) 1(3) Special Suppl. AJIL 290, 292 (Article III).

not only to settle the substantive disputes between the parties but also to settle 'difficulties' in agreeing to a procedure and form of arbitration, as well as those regarding the powers of the arbitrator.[106] Finally, the arbitrator should in its awards fix a period of time within which these were to be executed. Following the delivery of an award, the arbitrator remained 'competent to settle any questions which may arise with respect to its execution'.[107]

The same year, King Edward VII delivered an arbitral award pursuant to the 1902 Treaty, establishing the border between Argentina and Chile along the Cordillera of the Andes.[108] Perhaps unsurprisingly, this very short award, setting out in broad strokes the contours of one of the longest borders on the planet, subsequently generated significant uncertainty as to how it was to be interpreted and implemented at various points of the border.

The *Frontier Dispute* arose between the parties concerning a section of the boundary determined by the award. Chile submitted the dispute to Queen Elizabeth II for consideration. In 1965, the Queen 'determined' the terms of the new arbitral agreement ('*compromiso*') between the parties to settle this dispute, specifying that the new award would be delivered 'in pursuance of Article V of the Treaty of Arbitration'.[109] Article IX of the *compromiso* empowered the 'Court of Arbitration' appointed by the Queen to establish, in its award, 'by whom, in what manner and the time within which it shall be executed'. The same clause provided that this Court of Arbitration would 'not be *functus officio* until it . . . ha[d] notified Her Majesty's Government that in the opinion of the Court of Arbitration the Award has been executed'.[110]

Following the 1966 arbitral award, the Queen accordingly established the procedure for its implementation and nominated a demarcation authority.[111] Robert Jennings attributes the success of this 'execution by a tribunal of its own decision' to the fact that an executive authority (Her Majesty's Director of Military Survey) was responsible for the

[106] Ibid., 293 (Articles IV–V).

[107] Ibid. (Article XII): 'The Arbitrator shall fix in the Award the time within which it shall be executed, and be competent to settle any questions which may arise with respect to its execution'.

[108] *Cordillera of the Andes Boundary, Argentina/Chile*, (1902) 20 RIAA 37.

[109] *Argentine-Chile Frontier Case, Argentina/Chile*, (1966) 16 RIAA 109, 112 (she also noted that the parties had agreed to the terms of the new adjudication).

[110] Ibid., 120.

[111] Ibid., 113.

demarcation.[112] Although certainly an adjudicator without an executive arm would have been unable to *carry out* the demarcation, the question should not be confused with that of whether it would be able to make the relevant *legal determination.*[113]

A similar solution was found in the 1971 *compromiso* between the same parties to settle the *Beagle Channel* dispute, concerning a boundary not delimitated by the 1902 Award.[114] The arbitration agreement was again 'determined' by Queen Elizabeth, and included an Article XV, providing that the Court of Arbitration would only become *functus officio* after informing the British government that 'the Award ha[d] been materially and fully executed'.[115]

A Court of Arbitration was convened and, in 1977, delivered a new award confirming that the disputed islands belonged to Chile.[116] The Court determined a period of execution of nine months, and 'direct[ed] the Parties' to inform the registrar of all measures they 'deem[ed] necessary to be taken by either or both of them, in order to execute the . . . Decision', as well as of 'the steps actually taken . . . for the execution of the Decision'.[117] Finally, the Court of Arbitration 'declare[d]' its continuing jurisdiction over the case, stating that it:

> (i) continues in being for the purposes specified in paragraph 3 of this Dispositif, until it has notified Her Britannic Majesty's Government that, in the opinion of the Court, the Award specified in Article XIII (1) of the Compromiso has been materially and fully executed;
> (ii) remains at the disposal of the Parties for the purpose of giving them such guidance or instructions as they may require in order duly to implement the Award.[118]

Subsequently, Queen Elizabeth – as designated arbitrator under the 1902 Treaty – issued a declaration to 'ratify the Decision of the Court of

112 Robert Jennings, 'The Judicial Enforcement of International Obligations' (1987) 47 *ZaöRV* 3, 7.

113 See footnote no. 96 concerning the role of the ICJ in *Frontier Dispute, Burkina Faso/Niger*, [2013] ICGJ 491.

114 *Dispute between Argentina and Chile concerning the Beagle Channel, Argentina/Chile*, (2006) 21 RIAA 53.

115 Argentina/Chile Beagle Channel Arbitration Agreement, 22 July 1971, (2006) 21 RIAA 53, 70.

116 *Beagle Channel Arbitration*, (2006) 21 RIAA 190.

117 Ibid.

118 Ibid.

Arbitration and declare that the said Decision constitutes the Award in accordance with the Treaty'.[119] Noting that Argentina had denounced the 1902 Treaty, the Queen's 1977 declaration observed that Argentina's denunciation did not affect the *Beagle Channel* Arbitration.

Argentina responded with a 'Declaration of Nullity', in which it stated, vaguely, that the Court of Arbitration had failed to take into account principles of general international law, making the award 'null and void'.[120] Chile rejected the declaration. This was followed by a period of tense negotiations between the parties, leading to the 1979 'Act of Montevideo', by which the two parties requested the mediation of Pope John Paul II.[121] Following papal mediation, Argentina and Chile signed in 1984 a Treaty of Peace and Friendship (1984 Treaty) which, without mentioning the *Beagle Channel* award, recognised the border as settled in 1977 by the Court of Arbitration.[122]

The 1984 Treaty introduced a new provision on compulsory arbitration.[123] While the implementation of arbitral awards was 'entrusted to the honour of the nations signing the Treaty',[124] the adjudicator retained a role. Article 37 of the Dispute Settlement Annex empowered Arbitral Tribunals to set out the time period within which decisions were to be executed. Article 38 provided that a Tribunal 'shall not terminate its functions until it has declared that, in its opinion, the decision has been carried out materially and completely'.[125] Article 39 provided express grounds for post-judgment jurisdiction:

> Unless the Parties have agreed otherwise, the disagreements which may arise between the Parties about the interpretation or the manner of execution of the arbitral decision may be brought by any Party before the Tribunal which rendered the decision. For this purpose, any vacancy occurring in the Tribunal shall be filled in the manner established [for original Tribunals].[126]

119 *Beagle Channel Arbitration*, Declaration of Her Majesty of 18 April 1977, (2006) 21 RIAA 224, 225.

120 *Beagle Channel Arbitration*, Declaration of Nullity, (2006) 21 RIAA 227, 228.

121 *Beagle Channel Arbitration*, Act of Montevideo of 8 January 1979, (2006) 21 RIAA 240.

122 *Beagle Channel Arbitration*, Treaty of Peace and Friendship of 29 November 1984, (2006) 21 RIAA 250.

123 Ibid., 252 (Article 6).

124 Ibid., 261 (Annex I, Article 36).

125 Ibid.

126 Ibid.

Argentina and Chile therefore confirmed their intention to allow continued adjudication not only on the interpretation but also on the *execution* of awards. As the treaty includes a procedure for filling vacancies in the Arbitral Tribunal, adjudication would not require continued availability of the individuals involved in the original award.

The stance unequivocally taken by the parties in the 1984 Treaty, favouring continued access to adjudication, contrasts with the 1978 decision taken by the Court of Arbitration in *Beagle Channel*. This Court of Arbitration did not wait for the final resolution of the dispute. In early 1978, it requested information on execution of the decision from the parties.[127] When it received Argentina's 'declaration of nullity' of the earlier award, the Court responded with a new communication, asserting that Argentina's declaration was unwarranted under the *compromiso* and that 'any pronouncements in that sense must themselves be regarded as nullities, devoid of all legal force and effect'.[128]

In its new communication, the Court of Arbitration informed Argentina that the deadline for requesting revision of the original award had expired, meaning the award was definitive and, under Article XIII of the 1902 Treaty of Arbitration, 'intrusted to the honour' of the parties.[129] It once more called upon the government of Argentina to provide information on the steps it was taking to fulfil the award.

In July 1978, the President of the Court of Arbitration addressed a Note to the United Kingdom, stating these facts and arguing that there was not 'anything of substance that remains to be done in order to enable the Award to stand implemented'. Any unilateral attempt to reverse, alter, or modify the situation generated by the award 'would constitute a breach of it', and would be 'inadmissible and invalid'.[130] Faced with a situation labelled 'highly anomalous and virtually without precedent', the President held that it was 'not admissible that ... the Court should be compelled to remain indefinitely in existence in a state of suspended

[127] *Beagle Channel Arbitration*, Communication of the Court of Arbitration to the Parties, (1978) 17 ILM 1203.

[128] *Beagle Channel Arbitration*, Further Communication to the Parties in View of Article XV of the Compromiso and Paragraphs 3 and 4 of the Dispositif of the Award, (1978) 17 ILM 1204, 1205.

[129] Ibid.

[130] *Beagle Channel Arbitration*, Note of the President of the Court of Arbitration to the United Kingdom with regard to the Execution of the Award, (1978) 17 ILM 1198, 1201–1202.

animation'. He considered that its award 'st[ood] fully and materially executed – and, accordingly, deem[ed] itself to be *functus officio*'.[131]

This appears to have been an unwarranted exercise of judicial power, contravening as it does the letter of the agreement instituting the Court of Arbitration. Just as an adjudicator that considers itself as not *functus officio* when this should clearly be the effect of its final judgment,[132] an adjudicator that declares itself *functus officio* before the conditions for this are met fails to fulfil its mandate. The importance of post-judgment jurisdiction becomes clear in cases in which questions regarding the scope of a judgment (as in *Temple of Preah Vihear*)[133] or award (as the 1965 *Frontier Case* itself) appear decades after the original judicial decision. The concept of *functus officio* cannot serve to deny to a party the right to resort to an adjudicator under a consensually agreed provision.

A final chapter of the Argentina–Chile border dispute was the *Laguna del Desierto* arbitration under the 1984 Treaty. The Arbitral Tribunal's task was framed as determining sovereignty over the area around the Laguna del Desierto 'by interpreting and applying the Award of 1902, in accordance with international law'.[134] In a 1994 'Judgment', the Tribunal not only determined *what* the proper interpretation of a passage of the 1902 Award ought to be but also established *how* the border was to be demarcated, appointing an Expert Geographer to 'indicate the places where the boundary posts are to be erected' and to 'take the necessary measures for the demarcation'.[135]

Chile subsequently filed a claim requesting both a declaration on the 'interpretation and manner of execution' of the 1994 Judgment and a revision of this judgment. With respect to the latter request, the Tribunal dismissed Chile's claim, finding that its request amounted to an attempt to appeal from the 1994 Judgment.[136] The Tribunal rejected Chile's contention that its interpretation of the 1902 Award was tainted by a geographical change between the two dates. The Tribunal held that its 1994 judgment had interpreted the terms of the 1902 Award and that this interpretation was not dependent on the relevant geographical points having remained the same:

[131] Ibid.
[132] See Section 7.5.
[133] *Temple of Preah Vihear (Interpretation), Cambodia* v. *Thailand*, Judgment, [2013] ICJ Reports 28, para. 12.
[134] *Laguna del Desierto*, (1991) 113 ILR 1, 4.
[135] *Laguna del Desierto*, (1994) 113 ILR 1, 80.
[136] *Laguna del Desierto*, (1995) 113 ILR 194, 201.

> The 1994 Judgment determined the course of that line and ruled that, given that its decision was both interpretative and declaratory in nature, its effect in law was retrospective to the date of the 1902 Award. This means that, from the legal point of view, the line as now defined is to be regarded *as if it had existed* ever since that date.[137]

The Tribunal found that Chile's request for a decision as to the manner of implementation of the judgment did not raise any significant issues affecting the work of the Expert Geographer. It held that the Geographer 'had duly carried out' the instructions provided for in the 1994 Judgment.[138] On the same day as it delivered its second judgment, the Tribunal issued a Resolution, approving the conformity of the report and map submitted by the Expert Geographer and giving instructions for the erection of boundary posts.[139] Chile, while expressing disagreement with the Tribunal's reasoning and decision, agreed to respect the boundary line established in the judgment.[140]

This history shows that Argentina and Chile developed an impressive legal machinery to adjudicate their boundary disputes. Almost a century of litigation occurred, concerning various points of the border. While on occasion the parties were dangerously close to armed conflict over allegedly mistaken awards, the availability of an impartial third party to assess implementation of the 1902 award was instrumental in ultimately avoiding any recourse to force.

This case also shows that the most effective impartial third party was not always an adjudicator. Actual recourse to force was very close to taking place before papal intervention following the *Frontier Dispute* award, after the Tribunal (acting against the letter of the 1902 Treaty and the 1965 Agreement to Arbitration) prematurely decided to consider itself *functus officio*. Argentina's agent recalls that it was the intervention of the Pope that 'rescued' the two countries from 'the brink of war'.[141] A commentator argues that the 'unique religious authority' of the Pope was perceived as higher than the legal authority of a tribunal.[142]

137 Ibid., 214. This point is in consonance with the PCIJ's decision in *Monastery of Saint Naoum*, Advisory Opinion, (1924) PCIJ Ser B No 9, p. 7, 21–22.

138 Ibid., 232.

139 *Laguna del Desierto*, Resolution of 13 October 1995, (1995) 113 ILR 257.

140 *Laguna del Desierto*, Statement of the Government of Chile, (1995) 113 ILR 259, 260.

141 Julio Barboza, 'The Beagle Channel Dispute: Reflections of the Agent of Argentina' (2014) 13 *Chinese Journal of International Law* 147, 152.

142 See M.C. Miron, 'International Law and Religion in Latin America: The Beagle Channel Dispute' (2005) 28 *Suffolk Transnational Law Review* 1, 16.

7.5 Judicially Established Jurisdiction over the Implementation Phase

Adjudication over implementation should be grounded on consent to jurisdiction, which provides the basis for all international adjudication. As Kaiyan Kaikobad observes with regard to judicial interpretation of judgments, 'where states agree to resolve their dispute by way of an international tribunal, that agreement will not in principle extend to allowing that tribunal to give judicial clarification'.[143] This follows the PCIJ's statement, in the *Jaworzina Frontier* Advisory Opinion, that, '[i]n the absence of an express agreement between the parties, the Arbitrator is not competent to interpret, still less to modify his award by revising it'.[144] The same logic should in principle apply to adjudication on implementation.

However, some international adjudicators have concluded otherwise, determining that their adjudicatory powers included the ability to assess whether their rulings have been properly implemented. A particularly striking, if peculiar, case is that of the *Brčko* arbitration. A more consequential case of self-established entitlement to adjudicate on compliance is the Inter-American Court of Human Rights (IACtHR) practice of exercising continued, open-ended surveillance over compliance with its judgments. This practice has been replicated more recently by the African Court of Human and People's Rights (AfCHPR) and, in one case, by the Caribbean Court of Justice (CCJ).

7.5.1 Subsequent Adjudication as a Remedy for Non-Compliance: The Brčko Arbitration

The *Brčko* arbitration is a limit case of textually ultra vires adjudicatory rulings becoming effective due to subsequent practice. Following the partition of Yugoslavia, the region of Brčko in Bosnia and Herzegovina was claimed by the two political entities that compose the state of Bosnia and Herzegovina. One of them, the Republika Srpska, consists of two swathes of land connected only by the Brčko area. The other, the

143 Kaikobad, *Interpretation and Revision of International Boundary Decisions*, 102.

144 *Question of Jaworzina*, Advisory Opinion, (1923) PCIJ Ser B No 8, p. 38 (assimilating the duties of a Conference of Ambassadors to those of an Arbitrator). Chester Brown argues that international courts and tribunals may hold an 'inherent power' to interpret and revise their judgments. The case law he adduces is less than uniform, though, and favourable statements appear essentially in the form of *obiter dicta* (Chester Brown, *A Common Law of International Adjudication* (New York: Oxford University Press, 2007), 165–171).

Federation of Bosnia and Herzegovina, has in Brčko its sole connection to its canton of Posavina. In the 1995 Dayton Agreement that put an end to the Bosnian War, the two political entities were unable to reach agreement on the issue of which of them should have control over Brčko; not having a continuous territory appeared unacceptable to both parties. The Dayton Agreement therefore left 'the disputed portion of the Inter-Entity Boundary Line' (IEBL) to be determined by arbitration, to be conducted in accordance with United Nations Commission on International Trade Law (UNCITRAL) rules.[145]

In the First Arbitral Award, issued in February 1997, the Arbitral Tribunal, rather than establishing a boundary line and attributing the Brčko area to either of the parties, concluded that at that time 'it would be inappropriate to make a final choice as to which of the competing political entities should be given control of the town'.[146] Invoking 'broad international interest and concern', the Tribunal instead established a system for international supervision of the area, to be conducted by a Supervisor appointed by the Office of the High Representative for Bosnia and Herzegovina, an entity established by the Dayton Accords. This was in itself a decision of doubtful legality, possibly both extra petita and ultra vires.[147] More importantly for present purposes, the Tribunal decided that it would not become *functus officio* upon issuing its award. It stated that:

> after the interim international supervision has had a chance to operate, either party may approach the Tribunal to request further action with respect to Brčko . . . any response by the Tribunal shall form a part of the Award.[148]

The Tribunal grounded its power to remain seised of the dispute in Article 15 of the 1976 UNCITRAL rules, which empowers a Tribunal to 'conduct the arbitration in such manner as it considers appropriate, provided that the parties are treated with equality'.[149] The First Award

[145] General Framework Agreement for Peace in Bosnia and Herzegovina with Annexes, Paris, 14 December 1995, (1996) 35 ILM 75, 113 ('Dayton Accords').

[146] *Control over the Brčko Corridor, Republika Srpska* v. *the Federation of Bosnia and Herzegovina*, (1997) 36 ILM 396, 432.

[147] The Presiding Arbitrator in fact is the only person to have signed the award, something the parties had agreed to *ex ante*. See Christoph Schreuer, 'The Brcko Award of 14 February 1997' (1998) 11 *Leiden Journal of International Law* 71, 75.

[148] *Control over the Brčko Corridor* (1997) 36 ILM 396, 443.

[149] General Assembly, UNCITRAL Arbitration Rules – Resolution 31/98, (1976) UN Doc A/RES/31/98, 15 December 1976. The same is provided for by Article 17(1) of the 2010 Rules.

thus established (i) that between 1 December 1997 and 15 January 1998 the parties could submit 'requests for further action affecting the Award with respect to the allocation of political responsibilities in the area'; and (ii) that it would 'render any further decision by 15 March 1998'.[150]

The Federation of Bosnia and Herzegovina submitted a request for further action, leading to the delivery of a 'Supplemental Award' on 15 March 1998.[151] The Supplemental Award found a number of actions taken by the Republika Srpska 'in flagrant violation of the Dayton Accords and the [First] Award', and a less than perfect 'record of compliance' by the Federation.[152] In response to the requests of the parties that it finally establish the IEBL as required by the Dayton Accords, the Tribunal observed that there was a chance that the new leadership in Republika Srpska would change its attitude and comply with the Accords. The Supplemental Award deferred the final ruling to 1999, established a number of conditions for Republika Srpska not to lose the Brčko area to the Federation,[153] and gave the parties the following 'notice':

> 1. that any further Tribunal action is likely to be significantly affected by the degree to which the respective parties have acted in good faith to comply with the Dayton Accords and the Tribunal's orders, and
> 2. that among the alternative solutions that will be seriously considered by the Tribunal, upon proper request, will be
>   a. the location or relocation of the IEBL in such a way as to place Brčko and its surroundings within the territory of one party or the other, and
>   b. the conversion of the pre-war Brčko Opstina into a 'neutral district' beyond the exclusive control of either Entity.[154]

[150] *Control over the Brčko Corridor* (1997) 36 ILM 396, 443.

[151] *Arbitration for the Brcko Area (Supplemental Award), Republika Srpska* v. *the Federation of Bosnia and Herzegovina* (1998) UN Doc. S/1998/248.

[152] Ibid., paras. 4–8.

[153] Ibid., para. 21: 'the Tribunal's final IEBL decision in late 1998 or early 1999 will surely diminish the RS's position in the Brcko area unless the RS by that time has carried the burden of demonstrating very clearly that it has truly reversed course and committed itself to an apparently permanent program of full Dayton compliance and revitalization of the area. To carry that burden the RS will need to be in a position to show significant new achievements in terms of returns of former Brcko residents, unfettered freedom of movement, strong support for the multi-ethnic governmental institutions including the multi-ethnic police force, and full cooperation with the Supervisor and the authorities responsible for conducting fair and democratic elections in September 1998'.

[154] Ibid., para. 27.

On 5 March 1999, the Tribunal delivered what it labelled a 'Final Award'.[155] The Award found a problematic record of wilful non-compliance by the authorities of Republika Srpska, but, pointing to a 'less than satisfactory' performance of its duties by the Federation of Bosnia and Herzegovina, decided it would not attribute the Brčko area to the Federation either.[156] In view of these findings, the Tribunal decided to make permanent the provisional situation produced by its first award, and established in this Final Award a 'multi-ethnic democratic District government under international supervision'.[157] An Annex attached to the Final Award set out the fundamental political structure of the 'new Brčko District'.[158]

This Final Award was still not final in the sense of rendering the Arbitral Tribunal *functus officio*. It did not provide the remedy the Tribunal was expressly tasked with awarding: a final and binding delimitation of the boundary between the parties. Instead, the Tribunal in the Final Award, on the one hand, urged the parties 'to engage in inter-party negotiations as to the final terms of the Annex, rather than leaving the final formulation to the Tribunal'.[159] On the other hand, the Tribunal decided to 'retain jurisdiction over [the] dispute until such time' as the Brčko Supervisor, whom the Tribunal had itself appointed in the First Award, had notified the Tribunal that both parties had complied with the Final Award and that the institutions created for the administration of the Brčko District were functioning 'effectively and apparently permanently'.[160]

Until it received this notification, the Tribunal determined, it would remain in existence '[t]o provide the Supervisor with an alternative remedy'. The alternative remedy included 'penalties in the form of additional relief', as well as the 'authority to modify [the] Final Award as necessary in the event of serious non-compliance', including the possibility of sanctioning the non-complying entity by placing the District within the exclusive control of the other party.[161]

[155] *Dispute over Inter-Entity Boundary in Brčko (Final Award), Federation of Bosnia and Herzegovina* v. *Republika Srpska*, (1999) 38 ILM 534.

[156] Ibid., 539–542, 545.

[157] Ibid., 545.

[158] Ibid., 547.

[159] Ibid., 546.

[160] Ibid., 547.

[161] Ibid.

The degree of procedural and substantive creativity employed by the Arbitral Tribunal in *Brčko*, and the repetition of these features over three potentially final but formally open-ended awards, makes any doctrinal criticism of its decisions appear of little avail. Christoph Schreuer put it mildly by stating that the arbitration included 'several unusual features'.[162] It would be a remarkable development for tribunals with such a defined mandate to start employing their judicial authority in this manner, and to use their power over the procedure to prolong their own jurisdiction indefinitely.

The *Brčko* Tribunal thus employed its authority in a very different manner than is commonly considered acceptable and even lawful for international arbitrators. In a situation in which any boundary line might have been unacceptable, it simply did not fulfil its mandate of drawing a boundary line. Instead, the three awards provided detailed guidance for the parties to negotiate a settlement. Additionally, the authority of the tribunal to ultimately fulfil its mandate, potentially by attributing the Brčko region to either party, was constantly used as a threat to provide incentives for negotiation and cooperation. Rather than permitting parties to adopt Permissible Responses, the *Brčko* Tribunal determined that it was itself empowered to respond to non-compliance, modifying the parties' rights and obligations so as to prejudice the non-complying party's interests.

It may be highlighted that the parties repeatedly rejected 'political' solutions to the question of Brčko, and accepted (if perhaps grudgingly) the adjudication-based solution. Additionally, the Tribunal's First Award, establishing the supervision regime, was immediately supported by a Security Council Resolution.[163] The solution determined by the arbitrator, consisting in establishing the District of Brčko (which remains in existence and under the authority of a Supervisor),[164] appears appropriate for an expressly political organ such as the UN Security Council (UNSC). The political and material support provided by the Council was decisive for the 'separate District' solution ultimately to function. On the

[162] Schreuer, 'The Brcko Award of 14 February 1997', 575, 579.

[163] UN Security Council, Resolution S/RES/1103, adopted 31 March 1997 ('Reminding all parties to Annex 2 to the Peace Agreement of their obligation, in accordance with Article V of that Annex, to be bound by the decision of the arbitral tribunal and to implement it without delay').

[164] See Office of the High Representative, 'Brčko District is a testament to the power of reconciliation and coexistence, authorities must use the opportunities ahead', *Speech by Brčko Supervisor Jonathan Mennuti*, 8 March 2024.

other hand, it might have been considered illegitimate for the Council to outright dictate this solution to the parties. Thus, the solution of an ostensibly ultra vires adjudicatory ruling, supported by the material means of UN Members acting through the Council, appears as an attempt to combine the political authority and control over resources of the Council with the adjudicatory authority of the Arbitral Tribunal. The sequence of arbitral awards legitimised the Council's building on these rulings to slowly consolidate the regime which ultimately led to a (fragile) peace in the region.

In this context, it is difficult to assess the precedential value of this Tribunal's awards. They may be seen as evidence of the value of adjudication in the settlement of a 'political' dispute, as well as of the inadequacy of traditional responsibility-attributing, single-decision adjudication for ICs dealing with intensely political issues. While the tribunal repeatedly reminded the parties of its authority to attribute responsibility for breach and determine consequences for the wrongdoer, neither a Declaration of Breach nor Consequential Duties were ultimately deployed as remedies to sanction the non-complying party and provide a gain to the aggrieved party. Rather, in each award the power of attributing responsibility and harming a wrongdoer were used as deterrents against persistent breach and non-compliance with the Tribunal's decisions.

Additionally, assigning the disputed area to a party would ultimately lead that party, likely backed by larger states, to deploy resources to assert sovereign control over the area, depriving the wrongdoer of its connections to the area. In this regard, the practice of the *Brčko* Tribunal may be conceived of as a threat to engage in remedy escalation. In case of non-compliance, the Tribunal might not only proceed to remedy repetition, and condemn the violations, but also adopt Layer [5] sanctions, and harm the wrongdoer permanently by authorising other actors to deploy resources and take control of the disputed territory.

7.5.2 Court-Established Mechanism for Monitoring Compliance

Another adjudicator, the IACtHR, has established since the late 1980s a consistent practice of examining legal issues at the implementation phase. And, while the *Brčko* arbitration dealt with a single issue under very specific circumstances, the adoption of this practice by permanent courts with open-ended, compulsory jurisdiction represents a qualitative change. Coupled with the very specific remedies that human rights courts award, this extension implies a high degree of judicial intervention at the implementation stage. The practice of monitoring compliance, initially developed by the IACtHR, seems to have been followed more recently by the AfCHPR and CCJ.

The IACtHR's practice is grounded on Article 65 of the American Convention on Human Rights (ACHR). This article provides that, in its annual reports to the Organization of American States (OAS) General Assembly, the IACtHR must 'specify, in particular, the cases in which a state has not complied with its judgments, making any pertinent recommendations'.[165] Article 65 thus creates for the IACtHR the duty to express a view on whether states have complied with its judgments. On the other hand, Article 65 arguably does not meet the threshold of an 'unequivocal indication of voluntary and undisputable acceptance of the Court's jurisdiction'.[166] Jurisdiction being normally the result of specific consent, this provision seems to provide a thin basis for the exercise of continued jurisdiction.

Yet, as with respect to the remedies it employs in adjudication, the IACtHR has adopted with regard to its jurisdiction at the implementation stage a liberal and rather activist approach. Over the past two decades, the Court has established a regular practice of compliance adjudication going far beyond that which would be necessary to inform annual reports to the OAS General Assembly.

7.5.2.1 The IACtHR Practice of Monitoring Compliance

The practice of compliance adjudication by the IACtHR started with its 1989 judgment in *Velásquez Rodríguez*. In the absence of agreement on reparation, the Inter-American Commission re-seised the Court to complete its decision. The IACtHR not only held that the state had not fully implemented its 1988 judgment on the merits, and determined the indemnity for the violations,[167] but also established its jurisdiction to assess compliance with this determination:

[165] ACHR, Article 65: 'To each regular session of the General Assembly of the Organization of American States the Court shall submit, for the Assembly's consideration, a report on its work during the previous year. It shall specify, in particular, the cases in which a state has not complied with its judgments, making any pertinent recommendations.'

[166] *Armed Activities in the Territory of the Congo (New Application: 2002)*, [2006] ICJ Reports 6, p. 7. See also Ibid., p. 18–19.

[167] *Velásquez Rodríguez* v. *Honduras (Reparation and Costs)*, IACtHR, (1989) Ser C No. 7, paras. 22, 35, 49, 52. The indemnity corresponded to the injury suffered originally, not to non-compliance.

> The whole process of compliance with the compensatory indemnification will be under the surveillance of the Court. The process will be concluded once the Government has complied entirely with the current judgment.[168]

In 1990, the Inter-American Commission on Human Rights filed before the Court a request for interpretation of this judgment. The Commission requested not solely an interpretation but also an 'amplification' of the judgment.[169] Arguing that high inflation had substantially reduced the value of the indemnity determined in 1989, the Commission requested a declaration that the Honduran government had delayed the payment of compensation and should pay interest and adjust for inflation the amount determined by the Court.

The IACtHR observed that the request did not concern the 'meaning or scope' of its previous decision but indeed required a declaration of 'non-performance of clearly stated terms of the judgment'.[170] This request could not be examined within a ruling on interpretation. Rather than rejecting the request, the Court held that, since it had reserved a supervisory function over compliance with the prior judgment, it not only 'retain[ed] jurisdiction' over the case but was also 'empowered to decide on the consequences of the Government's delay in paying the assessed damages'.[171] The IACtHR proceeded to grant the Commission's requests and order Honduras to 'compensate the injured parties for the delays in the payment of damages and in setting up the trust as ordered'.[172]

The subsequent step in the formation of the Court's compliance-monitoring mechanism occurred in cases involving Peru during its two-year absence from the Court: *Castillo Pérez*, *Loaza Tamayo*, *Castillo Petruzzi et al.*, *Ivcher Bronstein*, and *Constitutional Court*. In July 1999, Peru withdrew its consent to jurisdiction of the IACtHR.[173] The IACtHR held this withdrawal to be unlawful in view

168 Ibid., para. 59.

169 *Velásquez-Rodríguez* v. *Honduras (Interpretation of the Judgment on Reparations and Costs)*, IACtHR, (1990) Ser C No. 9, para. 6 ('*ampliación*').

170 Ibid., para. 36.

171 Ibid., para. 37. Similar decisions were made in *Godinez Cruz* v. *Honduras (Merits)*, IACtHR, (1989) Ser C No. 5, para. 201. *Godínez Cruz* v. *Honduras (Reparation and Costs)*, IACtHR, (1989) Ser C No. 8, para. 55(5); *Godínez Cruz* v. *Honduras (Interpretation)*, IACtHR, (1990) Ser C No. 10, para. 37.

172 Ibid., para. 44(4).

173 *Ivcher Bronstein* v. *Peru (Competence)*, IACtHR, (1999) Ser C No. 54, para. 23.

of the specific character of the ACHR.[174] It continued to regularly condemn Peru for violations of the Convention, determining positive obligations of performance and awarding reparation for injury (including compensation and restitution). It also continued its practice of 'oversee [ing] compliance with the orders given'.[175]

In order to continue to exert pressure on Peru, the Court issued 'Orders' (in Spanish: '*Resolución*') on 'Compliance with Judgments', in which it recalled that Peru had a 'duty to promptly comply' with its judgments on reparation.[176] In 2001, after a regime change in Peru, the IACtHR issued a general Order on Compliance for the five cases. This order reaffirmed the binding character of the judgments the Court had issued during Peru's purported absence, took note of Peru's acceptance of the Court's decisions in this regard, and acknowledged Peru's progress in pursuing compliance with its earlier rulings.[177] Peru accepted the Court's orders.

This outcome may have prompted the Court to broaden the scope of the mechanism. The following year, the IACtHR issued eleven new Orders on Compliance, each dealing with an individual judgment. Without making formal findings of non-compliance, these orders examined implementation, reaffirmed previous orders for specific measures of reparation, established amounts of pecuniary compensation, and enjoined states to cease practices found to violate the ACHR. Besides specifying conduct required for compliance, the IACtHR also ordered

[174] ACHR, Article 29(a) prohibits states from 'suppress[ing] the enjoyment or exercise of the rights and freedoms recognized in [the] Convention'. The Court interpreted this prohibition as encompassing not only substantive provisions of human rights treaties but also procedural provisions. The IACtHR determined that permitting the withdrawal of recognition of the Court's jurisdiction would 'deprive all the Convention's beneficiaries of the additional guarantee of protection of their human rights that the Convention's jurisdictional body affords' (Ibid., 36–41). The IACtHR thus concluded that, contrary to the practice with regard to the optional clause for compulsory jurisdiction of the International Court of Justice, consent to its jurisdiction cannot be withdrawn. Only by denouncing the entire ACHR, and only after the year it takes for denunciation to take effect, may a state free itself from the jurisdiction of the Court. In late 2012, Venezuela denounced the ACHR.

[175] *Castillo Petruzzi et al.* v. *Peru (Merits, Reparation and Costs)*, IACtHR, (1999) Ser C No. 52, para. 226(16).

[176] *Loayza Tamayo* v. *Peru (Compliance with Judgment)*, IACtHR, (1999) Ser C No. 60, operative part; *Castillo Petruzzi et al.* v. *Peru (Compliance with Judgment)*, IACtHR, (1999) Ser C No. 59, operative part.

[177] *Castillo Pérez, Loaza Tamayo, Castillo Petruzzi et al., Ivcher Bronstein and Constitutional Court (Monitoring Compliance with Judgment)*, IACtHR, Order, 1 June 2001.

states to submit information regarding steps taken to comply with its orders. Decades later, the Court has issued almost 800 orders on monitoring compliance with judgments.[178]

7.5.2.2 Challenge to and Consolidation of the Procedure for Monitoring Compliance

The IACtHR's practice of compliance adjudication did not go unchallenged. Among the orders on compliance the IACtHR issued in 2002, two were issued in the case *Baena Ricardo* v. *Panama*. The first order, issued in June 2002, mandated payment of compensation to 270 workers for violations of their human rights.[179] In the second order, issued in November 2002, the Court held that Panama's offer to the victims, of an indemnity lower than that established by the Court, was not sufficient for compliance.[180]

Following the latter order, Panama challenged the jurisdiction of the IACtHR to issue orders on compliance. Panama claimed that the Court did not have jurisdiction to monitor compliance with its judgments, a task which was of 'political rather than judicial nature': 'The stage of monitoring compliance with judgment is a "post-judgment" stage ... that does not fall within the judicial sphere of the Court, but strictly within the political sphere, which, in this case [, is] exclusive to the General Assembly of the Organization of American States'.[181] The Court's obligation under ACHR Article 65 to report cases of non-compliance to the General Assembly, Panama argued, did not entitle it to examine compliance, much less to investigate *motu proprio* cases of non-compliance. In doing so, the IACtHR was acting in *excès de pouvoirs*.

As a response, in *Baena Ricardo* v. *Panama (Competence)*, the Inter-American Court asserted its jurisdiction to engage in compliance adjudication. The Court grounded this jurisdiction, inter alia, in ACHR Articles 67 (providing that judgments are 'final and not subject to appeal') and 68 (establishing the obligation to comply). The IACtHR

[178] The 818 orders issued so far are available at www.corteidh.or.cr/supervision_de_cumplimiento.cfm?lang=en (accessed 22 November 2024).

[179] *Baena Ricardo et al.* v. *Panama (Monitoring Compliance with Judgment)*, IACtHR, 21 June 2002.

[180] *Baena Ricardo et al.* v. *Panama (Monitoring Compliance with Judgment)*, IACtHR, 22 November 2002.

[181] *Baena Ricardo et al.* v. *Panama (Monitoring Compliance with Judgment)*, IACtHR, 28 November 2003, para. 54(a).

noted that '[w]hen the Court has ruled on the merits and reparation and costs submitted to its consideration, the State must observe the norms of the Convention that refer to compliance with that judgment or those judgments'.[182] The Court added that the obligation to give effect to the ACHR 'is applicable not only with regard to the substantive norms of the human rights treaties . . . but also with regard to procedural norms, such as those referring to compliance with the decisions of the Court'.[183]

Regarding Panama's contention that surveillance of judgments did not 'fall within the judicial sphere', the Court contrasted its powers with those of the European Court of Human Rights (ECtHR). European Convention on Human Rights (ECHR) Article 46 provides that a 'final judgment of the Court shall be transmitted to the Committee of Ministers, which will monitor its execution'.[184] In contrast with the political compliance control mechanism established by the European Convention, the IACtHR argued, the American Convention 'does not establish a specific body responsible for monitoring compliance with the judgments delivered by the Court'.[185]

Having recourse to the *travaux préparatoires* of ACHR Article 65, the IACtHR found that, despite its procedure being generally based on that of the ECtHR, a deliberate decision had been made to provide the IACtHR with 'broad competence' and empower it to 'indicate the cases in which a State ha[d] not complied with its judgments'.[186] The Court also argued that the object and purpose of the ACHR was precisely to ensure the protection of human rights by entrusting the assessment of violations to a judicial body, capable of ordering reparations. Judicial assessment of compliance with these orders was, the IACtHR concluded, essential to attain this object and purpose.

The Court reasoned that its practice of highlighting non-compliance had been initiated over a decade earlier (in *Velásquez Rodríguez* v. *Honduras*), that states had acquiesced to it, and that it had therefore become a customary practice within the Inter-American human rights system. The OAS General Assembly, which Panama claimed was the organ responsible for compliance monitoring, had supported, rather than protested, the compliance-monitoring activities of the Court. Thus, the

182 Ibid., para. 60.
183 Ibid., para 66.
184 Ibid., paras. 54(a), 86. The ECHR was subsequently amended. See Section 8.3.1.2.
185 Ibid., para. 88.
186 Ibid., para. 89.

IACtHR concluded, its jurisdiction to monitor compliance was 'grounded on the constant and standard practice of the Court and in the resulting *opinio juris communis* of the States Parties to the Convention'.[187]

Additionally, Panama itself had not expressed discontent or requested an interpretation of the June 2002 judgment in *Baena Ricardo* v. *Panama*, in which the IACtHR had 'reserve[d] the power to supervise the overall compliance with th[e] judgment'.[188] The Court found that, by its conduct in previous phases of the judgment as well as by providing the IACtHR with information on compliance, Panama had acquiesced to the jurisdiction of the Court to monitor compliance.

Perhaps most importantly, the IACtHR found that the consent to jurisdiction granted under ACHR Article 62(1), concerning 'all matters relating to the interpretation and application' of the Convention, encompasses consent to jurisdiction over implementation of judgments. Although perhaps going too far in saying that this is an 'obvious' interpretation, the Court pointed out that the objective of preventing suppression or restriction of human rights supported its determination:

> An interpretation of the American Convention that did not allow any body to monitor compliance with judgments by the responsible States would run counter to the goal and purpose of this treaty, which is the effective protection of human rights, and would deprive all the beneficiaries of the Convention of the guarantee of protection of those rights by the actions of its jurisdictional body, and the consequent execution of the latter's decisions. Allowing States to comply with the reparations ordered in the judgments without adequate monitoring would be equal to leaving the execution of the Court's decisions to their free will.[189]

As Laurence Bourgogue-Larsen argues, in *Baena Ricardo (Judgment on Compliance)*, the Court employed 'all available interpretation techniques' with a view to 'clos[ing], once and for all, not only the debate triggered by Panama but also all discussion as to its competence on the matter'.[190]

The 2009 Rules of Procedure of the Inter-American Court codified the Court's practice. Article 69 regulates the 'procedure for monitoring

[187] Ibid., para. 102.
[188] Ibid., para. 125.
[189] Ibid., para. 95 (footnote omitted).
[190] Laurence Burgorgue-Larsen, 'The Powers of the Court to Monitor Compliance with Its Judgments', in Laurence Burgorgue-Larsen and Amaya Ubeda de Torres (eds.), *The Inter-American Court of Human Rights – Case Law and Commentary* (Oxford: Oxford University Press, 2011), 171–192, 179.

compliance with the judgments and other decisions of the Court'. This procedure involves submission of reports by states found in breach and an opportunity for victims' representatives and the Inter-American Commission to present observations.[191] The IACtHR may convene the parties at a hearing, if it deems it appropriate.[192] Following these steps, the Court is to 'determine the state of compliance with its decisions and issue the relevant orders'[193] – a phrasing that highlights the possibility of new orders at this stage.

7.5.2.3 Remedies for Non-Compliance without Enforcement Power: The Search for Remedy Escalation

Compliance does not necessarily ensue from the IACtHR's activity of monitoring compliance. Not every case reaches the stage of full compliance. David Baluarte found rates of compliance of 60 per cent for monetary damages,[194] 64 per cent for symbolic measures of satisfaction,[195] 19 per cent for orders for legislative changes,[196] and under 2 per cent for measures ordering the investigation, prosecution, and punishment of the individuals who committed the identified human rights violations.[197] These numbers may partially be attributed to the particularly high performance demands the IACtHR puts on states, demanding the adoption of specific measures and policies as measures of satisfaction and guarantees of non-repetition.[198] They nonetheless show that litigation on compliance does not always lead to compliance itself.

Given this record, it is unsurprising that the Court must often point in its decisions to the non-compliance by states found in breach with the very obligation to report on compliance.[199] In most cases, it is true, the

[191] Rules of Procedure of the Inter-American Court of Human Rights, approved 28 November 2009, Article 69(1).
[192] Ibid., Article 69(3).
[193] Ibid., Article 69(4).
[194] David C. Baluarte, 'Strategizing for Compliance: The Evolution of a Compliance Phase of Inter-American Court Litigation and the Strategic Imperative for Victims' Representatives' (2012) 27 *American University International Law Review* 263, 290 (payment ensued in 126 out of 208 cases in which the Court ordered damages).
[195] Ibid., 292 (84 out of 131 sets of measures were fully complied with).
[196] Ibid., 295 (finding full implementation of 15 out of 77 legislative and administrative measures ordered).
[197] Ibid., 298 (out of 57 orders, only one was fully complied with).
[198] See Section 4.4.1.
[199] *Constitutional Court (Aguirre Roca, Rey Ferry and Revoredo Marsano)* v. *Peru (Compliance with Judgment)*, IACtHR, 5 August 2008, para. 8.

Court concludes that states have made various good faith efforts to comply, and acknowledges partial compliance[200] until finally closing the case if it deems full compliance to have been achieved.[201]

With its compliance surveillance procedure, the IACtHR goes much further than informing the OAS General Assembly of the compliance status of cases. Its practice involves constant remedy repetition, with the aim to mobilise the pro-compliance forces within states. While not going as far as to threaten remedy escalation and further harm to the respondent's interests in case of non-compliance (as the *Brčko* Tribunal did), the Court seeks to substitute other states in what would in principle be their task: mobilising resources to persuade the wrongdoer ultimately to comply. With its rulings on compliance, it imposes Layer 4 institutional sanctions in the hope of triggering other internal and external pro-compliance forces.

But repeated institutional sanctions, especially the discursive ones that ICs are able to employ autonomously, have decreasing effects. Contrary to WTO adjudicators and to the *Brčko* arbitrator, the IACtHR's findings of non-compliance cannot foreshadow a concrete (i.e. non-reputational) harm to a recalcitrant wrongdoer's interests by authorising Layer [5] sanctions. Over time, especially since the IACtHR's procedure does not depend on provocation but is initiated *motu proprio*, the growing backlog of cases of non-compliance, without any prospect of remedy escalation, tends to put increasing stress on the Court's scarce resources. Given the limits of the audience's attention and of the ability of even willing enforcers to deploy resources, including discursive ones, against many wrongdoers across dozens of issues, the constant repetition of IC declarations of non-compliance may, in fact, decrease the sanctioning value of each new such declaration. Remedy repetition, especially for remedies of this type, is only meaningful if declarations are not issued so frequently that they become banal.

The IACtHR thus developed its own instrument for remedy escalation. In a 2005 Order on the *Applicability of Article 65 of the American Convention on Human Rights*, the IACtHR established that, in case of persistent non-compliance, the 'last resort' available to the Court is to definitively report non-compliance to the OAS General Assembly under

[200] *Gutiérrez-Soler* v. *Colombia (Compliance with Judgment)*, IACtHR, 30 June 2009, Declarations, para. 1.

[201] *Claude Reyes et al.* v. *Chile (Compliance with Judgment)*, IACtHR, 24 November 2008, Declarations, paras. 1–2, Decisions, para. 1.

Article 65.[202] Once it decides to definitively report a case of non-compliance to the political body, the Court no longer requests reports on compliance and instead considers the state as being in non-compliance until the state itself provides evidence that it has fulfilled the obligations determined in the original judgment.

The ultimate sanction developed by the IACtHR, when remedy repetition fails to induce compliance, is a form of remedy escalation: a formal declaration of failure to comply, coupled with a reference of the case to the highest political body in the Inter-American system. The Court first employed this mechanism in *Apitz Barbera et al.* v. *Venezuela (Compliance)*. The IACtHR had condemned Venezuela for removing from office three judges who had issued a decision that contradicted the views of government officials, and had ordered the reinstatement of the removed judges.[203] The Supreme Court of Venezuela declared the Inter-American Court's judgment non-enforceable, on grounds that the IACtHR did not enjoy 'supra-constitutional' status.[204] The Supreme Court of Venezuela added that:

> it is clear that the Inter-American Court of Human Rights, by failing to restrict itself to ordering compensation for the supposed violation of rights, used the judgment analyzed to interfere unacceptably in the regulation and administration of the judicial sector which corresponds exclusively to the Supreme Court of Justice.[205]

In its Order on Compliance, the IACtHR identified the Supreme Court decision as 'manifest non-compliance' with its judgment on the merits, and 'an attempt to make it ineffective'.[206] The IACtHR considered that Venezuela had 'rejected, and refused and failed to comply with the measures ordered', warranting not only a declaration of non-compliance but a reporting of this non-compliance to the General Assembly under ACHR Article 65:

[202] *Applicability of Article 65 of the American Convention on Human Rights (Order)*, IACtHR, 29 June 2005.

[203] *Apitz Barbera et al.* v. *Venezuela (Preliminary Objection, Merits, Reparations and Costs)*, IACtHR, (2008) Series C No. 182, paras. 224, 267.

[204] *Apitz Barbera et al.* v. *Venezuela (Compliance with Judgment)*, IACtHR, 23 November 2012, para. 13(ii).

[205] *Apitz Barbera et al.* v. *Venezuela (Compliance with Judgment)*, IACtHR, 23 November 2012, para. 13(v).

[206] Ibid., Declaration, para 1; Decision, para. 1.39.

> [T]he Court will incorporate this Order into its 2012 Annual Report so that it may be submitted to the consideration of the General Assembly of the Organization of American States. This course of action is necessary in cases such as this, where the State's highest court has issued a ruling indicating the frank intention of not meeting the obligation to comply with a judgment of the Court. In this situation, the American States have established a system of collective enforcement where all the States Parties must make every effort to ensure that there is no evident failure to comply with the Court's judgments.[207]

The IACtHR has since employed variations of this remedy in other rulings. In *Yvon Neptune* v. *Haiti (Compliance)*, Haiti responded to the Court's request for information on compliance by terming the underlying Judgment 'unjust' and 'inappropriate'. The IACtHR termed this response an 'evident disregard for the obligatory character of Judgment of this Court'.[208] Besides recording its decision to refer the case to the OAS General Assembly, the IACtHR found that the OAS Charter included 'a system of collective guarantee', holding that 'all States Parties must make every effort so that there is no obvious abandonment by the States of their obligation to comply with and abide by the Court's Judgments'.[209] The Court has reiterated these statements in another case involving Haiti,[210] and in various cases involving Venezuela (which denounced the Inter-American Convention in 2012).[211]

These attempts at remedy escalation implicitly acknowledge the Court's limited ability to influence conduct through institutional sanctions. In case of open defiance, an IC cannot itself press for compliance by mobilising resources. Though the IACtHR did not specify which permissible responses it had in mind, the suggestion that OAS states proceed to 'collective' action indicates a demand for at least state-to-state discursive sanctions and perhaps for an institutional sanction (Layer 4), coming not from the Court but from the OAS' political bodies.

The IACtHR thus sought to deploy against defiant non-compliance a form of Layer [5] sanction, declaring the obligation of other OAS

207 Ibid., para. 45.

208 *Yvon Neptune* v. *Haiti (Compliance with Judgment)*, IACtHR, 20 November 2015, para. 7.

209 Ibid., para. 9.

210 *Fleury et al.* v. *Haiti (Compliance with Judgment)*, IACtHR, 22 November 2019, para. 11.

211 See Lucas Lixinski, 'Mechanisms of Systemic Change in Regional Human Rights Courts: Swinging the Pendulum between Legitimacy and Impact' (2019) 8 *Cambridge International Law Journal* 60, 74.

member states to deploy 'collective enforcement'. The absence of a specific authorised sanctioning instrument makes this classification imprecise. It is clear, however, that the Court's intention was to mobilise, through its adjudicatory rulings, sanctions to be applied not only by the OAS institutions, at the symbolic level, but also by individual member states, deploying their individual political and economic resources against the wrongdoer.

7.5.2.4 The Adoption of Compliance Monitoring by Other Courts

Other ICs have sought to develop mechanisms similar to the IACtHR compliance monitoring, and faced a similar dilemma. In 2020, the AfCHPR added to its Rules of Court a 'Procedure for Monitoring Compliance with Decisions', grounded on its duty to report on non-compliance to the African Union Assembly.[212] The new Article 81 requires states to submit reports on compliance and allows the Court to 'make a finding' or 'issue an order to ensure compliance'.[213] The Court may subsequently 'report the non-compliance to the Assembly' and 'make available . . . all relevant information it may deem useful for the purpose of execution'.[214]

This is a novel procedure, by which the AfCHPR develops a 'role . . . largely based on judicial activism at that level, following the path charted by the Inter-American Court'.[215] The first hearing under it took place in late 2024, in the *Ogiek of the Mau Forest* case, to assess compliance with the orders for 'the restitution of the Ogiek ancestral lands, the recognition of the Ogiek as an indigenous people, and the establishment of mechanisms/frameworks for consultation and dialogue with the Ogiek on all matters affecting them'.[216] While the original Judgment set a twelve-month deadline for compliance,[217] the post-hearing decision allowed a

[212] Protocol to the African Charter on Human and Peoples' Rights on the Establishment of an African Court on Human and Peoples' Rights, signed 10 June 1998, entered into force 25 January 2004, Article 31(2).

[213] AfCHPR, Rules of Court (1 September 2020), Article 81(3).

[214] Ibid., Article 81(4)–(5).

[215] See Tarisai Mutangi, 'Enforcing Compliance with the Judgments of the African Court on Human and Peoples' Rights: Prospects and Challenges', in Adeola Aderomola (ed.), *Compliance with International Human Rights Law in Africa: Essays in Honour of Frans Viljoen* (Oxford: Oxford University Press, 2022).

[216] AfCHPR, Application 006/2012 (The *African Commission on Human and Peoples' Rights vs Republic of Kenya)*, Judgment (Reparations), 23 June 2022, para. 150.

[217] Ibid., para. 160(xv–xvi)

further 'three-month deadline for the Republic of Kenya to file a report on the measures it has taken to comply with its judgments in Application No. 006/2012'.[218] This, together with controversy over the AfCHR's ability to impose pecuniary compensation in case of non-compliance (examined in Section 8.3.1.2), demonstrates the challenges faced by ICs when seeking to adjudicate on, and provide remedies for, non-compliance with their rulings.

The Caribbean Court of Justice established a similar, if ad hoc, mechanism for compliance adjudication in *Rudisa* v. *Guyana*, after issuing an order for Guyana to cease collection of a discriminatory tax, long considered unlawful by Caribbean Community (CARICOM) member states, and reimburse the applicant. The Court reasoned that, since 'compliance with and implementation of the Court's orders are essential ... [t]he Court therefore has a responsibility to monitor compliance with its orders'.[219] The CCJ set a time for Guyana to report on its compliance, after which, 'the parties [would] have liberty to apply [to the Court] in respect of any matter contained in the said report'.[220] The same procedure was subsequently applied, in *Jaleel* v. *Guyana*, in respect of the same tax.[221]

7.6 Adjudicating Non-Compliance: Scope of Review and Remedies

Post-judgment adjudication on compliance is sometimes based on provisions, such as those in trade agreements, that specify the remedies available at this stage. In these cases, it would seem that *lex specialis* applies. The adjudicator is permitted, and perhaps required, to award specific remedies, but is precluded from making determinations beyond

[218] AfCHPR, 'African Court Sets Deadline for Kenya to Comply with the Ogiek Judgment', Press Release, 12 November 2024.

[219] CCJ, *Rudisa Beverages & Juices N.V. and Caribbean International Distributors Inc.* v. *The Co-Operative Republic of Guyana*, App. No. OA 003 of 2013 (Original Jurisdiction), Judgment, 8 May 2014, para. 38.

[220] Ibid., para. 40. On these CCJ cases, see Section 8.4.2.2. See also Salvatore Caserta and Mikael Rask Madsen, 'Between Community Law and Common Law: The Rise of the Caribbean Court of Justice at the Intersection of Regional Integration and Post-Colonial Legacies' (2016) 79 *Law and Contemporary Problems* 89.

[221] CCJ, *SM Jaleel & Co Ltd & Guyana Beverages Inc Claimants and The Co-Operative Republic of Guyana*, CCJ Application No. TTOJ2016/001 (Original Jurisdiction), Judgment, 9 May 2017, para. 62.

those permissible under each treaty.[222] In other cases, provisions establishing jurisdiction over the 'execution' or 'manner of implementation' of rulings provide no specification regarding remedies available at this stage.

The question then arises of what remedies are permissible within compliance adjudication. Contrary to interpretations of the earlier ruling (examined in Section 7.7), these remedies may comprise not only declaratory rulings but also Declarations of Breach, targeting non-compliance with the earlier judgment, and the determination by the adjudicator of Consequential Duties. Consequential Duties may in turn include determinations of positive obligations for the parties, as well as the establishment of duties of reparation.

7.6.1 Conduct Examined and Scope of Review at the Implementation Stage

Post-judgment compliance adjudication extends beyond an interpretation of the prior judgment; it enables the adjudicator to evaluate whether its rulings have been complied with, implemented, or executed. Unlike requests for interpretation – examined below – which are limited to clarifying the meaning or scope of a prior decision, compliance adjudication is not bound by such restrictions. While the adjudicator's assessment must remain consistent with the original judgment's terms, the focus of the review and the remedies awarded is the parties' subsequent actions rather than the text of the judgment itself.

The Mercosur Court examined the issue when acting under Article 30 of the Mercosur Olivos Protocol, which empowers it to examine allegations that 'the measures taken do not comply with the award'. In *Remoulded Tyres (Compliance)*, the Court described its task as 'limited to deciding whether or not Law No 26.239 achieves compliance with Award No 1/2005'.[223] The Court reasoned that:

[222] See International Law Commission, Articles on Responsibility of States for Internationally Wrongful Acts, UN Doc. A/56/49(Vol. I)/Corr.4., Article 55, and accompanying Commentary – International Law Commission, Draft Articles on Responsibility of States for Internationally Wrongful Acts, with commentaries, A/56/10, 2001 (noting that in some cases the rules on responsibility are set aside and 'only the consequences specified are to flow').

[223] *Award No 1/2008*, Mercosur Court, 25 April 2008, p. 11 ('debe limitarse a decidir acerca de si la Ley N° 26.239 supone o no el cumplimiento del Laudo N° 1/2005').

> Argentina cannot modify its law, justifying the new legal text based on arguments already dismissed by the Court; otherwise it could comply with the Award by the mere formal expedient of modifying its laws, while maintaining substantively the same position.[224]

The obligation created by the Court's earlier Award was therefore not simply to remove the Mercosur-inconsistent measure; any subsequent modification had to eliminate the inconsistency between the Argentinean measure and Mercosur law as interpreted in the Award. The Tribunal therefore determined that Argentina was obliged 'to derogate or modify [its laws] to the extent required by Award No 1/2005'.[225]

The same reasoning was used by the Appellate Body to reject contentions by WTO members that recommendations and rulings of the DSB, when they require the 'withdrawal' of a subsidy, apply solely to the subsidy existing at the moment the adjudicators make the recommendations. In *Canada – Aircraft (21.5)*, Canada claimed (and the panel accepted) that one of its measures, adopted following the original panel report, should not be examined because it had not been the object of a recommendation for withdrawal. The Appellate Body disagreed.

> That recommendation to 'withdraw' the prohibited export subsidy did not, of course, cover the new measure – because the new measure did not exist when the DSB made its recommendation. . . . Article 21.5 proceedings involve, in principle, not the original measure, but rather a new and different measure which was not before the original panel.[226]

Regarding *which conduct* may be examined, then, compliance adjudication under WTO law has the same scope as Mercosur adjudication on compliance with arbitral awards. These ICs are empowered not only to verify that the original wrongful conduct has ceased but also that it has not been replaced with new wrongful conduct to the same effect. The same reasoning should apply to adjudication of disputes on implementation or execution of judicial decisions. Clearly, the conduct to be examined cannot be that which gave rise to the original judgment but must be the conduct adopted in execution or implementation of the judgment.

224 Ibid., p. 14 ('Argentina no puede modificar la ley, justificando el nuevo texto legal en base a supuestos que ya fueron descartados por el Tribunal, de lo contrario se podría dar cumplimiento al Laudo por el simple expediente formal de la modificación de la ley, aunque substancialmente se mantenga la misma postura').

225 Ibid., p. 15 ('con el alcance expuesto en el Laudo 1/2005').

226 Appellate Body Report, *Canada – Aircraft (21.5)*, WT/DS70/AB/RW, adopted 4 August 2000, paras 40–41.

On the other hand, it may be that procedural rules differ regarding the *scope of the review* of the relevant conduct. The obligation established by the recommendations of WTO adjudicators is expressly formulated as to 'bring the [WTO-inconsistent] measure into conformity' with the WTO Agreement violated. This has been interpreted as permitting an overall assessment of the lawfulness of the conduct of the party found in breach, instead of a simple assessment of whether the original decision was complied with.

In *EC – Bed Linen (21.5)*, the Appellate Body clarified that the requirement of substantive compliance empowers complainants to 'raise *new* claims, arguments, and factual circumstances different from those raised in the original proceedings'.[227] This element of the decision still relates to *which* measures are subject to review. The Appellate Body's reasoning went further, though, and established as the applicable legal standard full substantive compliance with the agreements violated, rather than mere compliance with the specific terms of the ruling:

> [T]he mandate of Article 21.5 panels is to examine either the 'existence' of 'measures taken to comply' or, more frequently, the '*consistency with a covered agreement*' of implementing measures ... a 'measure taken to comply' may be *inconsistent* with WTO obligations in ways different from the original measure ... an Article 21.5 panel could not properly carry out its mandate to assess whether a 'measure taken to comply' is *fully consistent* with WTO obligations if it were precluded from examining claims additional to, and different from, the claims raised in the original proceedings.[228]

Most international agreements do not specify that adjudication on compliance, implementation or execution comprises an overall assessment of the legality of the party's conduct in light of its substantive obligations. This may mean that subsequent conduct may be assessed solely in light of the remedies expressly provided in the prior decision. In this case, any subsequent conduct that contradicts the wrongdoer's international obligations more broadly would not be subject to scrutiny at this stage.

On deeper analysis, this difference between scopes of review will most of the times be merely apparent. A duty of cessation, which arises

[227] Appellate Body Report, *EC – Bed Linen (21.5)*, WT/DS141/AB/RW, adopted 24 April 2003, para. 79.

[228] Ibid.

automatically from the declaration that a breach has occurred,[229] means that a breach must cease wholly. It does not suffice for the wrongdoer to cease the conduct specifically referred to in the original ruling, while continuing to produce substantively the same impairment of the claimant's rights, causing the same injury to its interests through other means.

Adjudication on implementation may be particularly helpful in cases of simulated implementation that does not in fact eliminate the breach, or of insincere implementation of the judgment followed by subsequent conduct producing substantively the same effect as the original breach. The utility of adjudication on implementation would be seriously curtailed if courts were able to verify at this stage solely whether the precise determinations made by the court in its original judgment have been followed to the letter, and were unable to assess whether, through simultaneous or subsequent conduct, the wrongdoer has undermined the utility of the judgment for the aggrieved party.

7.6.2 The Terminological Issue: 'Execution' and 'Implementation' as 'Application'

It may be asked whether jurisdiction over 'execution' or 'implementation' of a ruling involves an operation distinct from 'application' of a treaty. In principle, these terms are similar in meaning: all refer not to adjudication itself but to the conduct expected of states – executing, implementing, or applying the treaty. The role of the adjudicator is to determine whether the execution, implementation, or application of the underlying obligations was duly carried out. With regard to disputes relating to 'application' of a treaty, the PCIJ stated in *Chorzów Factory* that this includes jurisdiction over claims of non-application, that is, of breach:

> [D]ifferences relating to the application of [a treaty] include not only those relating to the question whether the application of a particular clause has or has not been correct, but also those bearing upon the applicability of these articles, that is to say, upon any act or omission creating a situation contrary to the said articles.[230]

229 *Navigational and Related Rights, Costa Rica* v. *Nicaragua*, Judgment, [2009] ICJ Reports 21, p. 267.

230 *Factory at Chorzów (Jurisdiction), Germany* v. *Poland*, Judgment, (1927) PCIJ Ser A No. 9, p. 20–21.

The same logic would seem to apply to jurisdiction over 'implementation' or 'execution' of rulings, when there is a dispute on whether a party has fulfilled its primary obligation of performance. Dispute settlement clauses sometimes refer not to the 'interpretation and application' of treaties but to their 'interpretation or execution'. In *Peace Treaties*, the ICJ interpreted a jurisdictional clause providing for adjudication in case of disputes concerning the 'interpretation or execution' of treaties as 'relat[ing] to the question of the performance or non-performance of the obligations provided in the articles' of the relevant treaties. The Court concluded that disputes on whether Bulgaria, Hungary, and Romania had or had not performed their obligations under the 1947 Peace Treaties 'are clearly disputes concerning the interpretation or execution of the Peace Treaties'.[231]

Other clauses refer to 'interpretation or implementation'. One such clause is Article 21(2) of the Interim Accord between Greece and Former Yugoslav Republic of Macedonia (FYROM), examined by the ICJ in *Interim Accord.* This Article allowed either party to submit to the ICJ '[a]ny difference or dispute ... concerning the interpretation or implementation of this Interim Accord'.[232] In its judgment, the ICJ stated that the question raised by FYROM, of whether Greece's 'conduct is a breach ... of the Interim Accord, is a legal question pertaining to the interpretation and implementation of a provision of that Accord'.[233]

A similar provision is found in Article 16 of the Convention for the Conservation of Southern Bluefin Tuna,[234] examined in the *Southern Bluefin Tuna* arbitration under UNCLOS. The Arbitral Tribunal employed two expressions – 'interpretation and application' and 'interpretation and implementation' – as equivalents.[235] In his dissenting

[231] *Interpretation of Peace Treaties with Bulgaria, Hungary and Romania*, Advisory Opinion (First Phase), [1950] ICJ Reports 65, p. 75.

[232] *Application of the Interim Accord of 13 September 1995, Macedonia* v. *Greece*, Judgment, [2011] ICJ Reports 644, p. 655.

[233] Ibid., p. 663.

[234] Convention for the Conservation of Southern Bluefin Tuna, Canberra, 10 May 1993, 1819 UNTS 359, Article 16: 'If any dispute arises between two or more of the Parties concerning the interpretation or implementation of this Convention, those Parties shall consult among themselves with a view to having the dispute resolved by negotiation, inquiry, mediation, conciliation, arbitration, judicial settlement or other peaceful means of their own choice.'

[235] *Southern Bluefin Tuna, New Zealand – Japan, Australia – Japan*, ITLOS, (2000) 119 ILR 508, 530 ('The dispute necessarily is one concerning the interpretation and

opinion, Judge Keith found that 'implementation' was 'perhaps a wider word than application'.[236]

There is little reason for a different standard to apply when a court is dealing with the 'execution' or 'implementation' of previous judicial decisions rather than treaties. In this regard, a parallel may be drawn with the award in the *Argentina-Chile Frontier Case*. A 1965 Agreement for Arbitration empowered the Court of Arbitration to decide on a 'controversy' between Chile and Argentina regarding the 'interpretation and fulfilment' ('*interpretación y cumplimiento*') of King Edward VII's 1902 Award.[237] The tribunal interpreted this term as 'the equivalent of "interpretation and application" which appears in many compromissory clauses'.[238] Despite the difference in terminology, the Court held, the phrase indicated:

> the desire of the Parties to get disputes finally settled, which might not otherwise be the case if the tribunal authorised to decide the dispute were empowered to interpret only. [. . .] [T]he whole purpose of the *Compromiso* is that the Parties, having failed to interpret and fulfil the Award themselves, have now through the bringing into operation of the General Treaty of Arbitration of 1902 turned the task over to the Court.[239]

The Court of Arbitration therefore regarded itself as competent not only to determine the proper interpretation to be given to the 1902 award but also to examine the subsequent actions of the parties taken in 'fulfilment' of the award, making adjustments where the conduct required by the award seemed not to be congruous with the reality on the ground.[240] The Court went on to settle the dispute and determine the course of the boundary between Chile and Argentina.

The same should apply when a provision entrusts an adjudicator with settling disputes regarding not only the interpretation but also the 'execution' or 'implementation' of the judgment or award. The express permission for parties to have new recourse to an adjudicator occurs precisely because parties anticipate that they may fail to ensure the proper execution or implementation of the rulings. If this occurs, the

implementation of the CCSBT and not a dispute concerning the interpretation or application of UNCLOS').

236 Ibid., 561 (Keith, diss).

237 *Argentine-Chile Frontier Case, Argentina/Chile*, (1966) 16 RIAA 109, 118.

238 Ibid.

239 Ibid., p. 175.

240 Ibid., p. 177–178.

adjudicator should logically be able to intervene, at the request of either party, to fulfil the task the parties themselves have established for it and determine the appropriate means for execution or implementation of the relevant judgment or award. Rather than constituting judicial activism, these pronouncements give effect to the decision of the parties to entrust an adjudicator with settling questions of implementation or execution when the parties themselves are unable to do this.

7.6.3 Remedies at the Implementation Stage

In the *Argentina-Chile Frontier Case*, the jurisdiction of the arbitral tribunal to proceed to the 'fulfilment' of the earlier award did not empower it to carry out itself any acts of *imperium*, which remain the exclusive prerogative of states. It did, however, allow the tribunal to employ its *jurisdictio* to examine the actions undertaken by the parties to carry out the original award, to determine whether these actions were consistent with the award, and to state with legal authority the ensuing rights and obligations of the parties. This corresponds to the functions ordinarily performed by courts and tribunals tasked with determining borders based on treaty provisions and customary rules.

A court or tribunal adjudicating on a dispute concerning the execution or implementation of an earlier ruling should, absent a provision to the contrary, perform adjudicative operations similar to those that the same court or tribunal would have performed in case the dispute involved a treaty or customary rules. These operations, which can be termed 'remedies' in the broad sense used in this book, include determining the rights and obligations of the parties. They also include establishing a duty of cessation in case of ongoing unlawful conduct. This duty, the ICJ has stated, 'derives by operation of law from the very fact that the [adjudicator] establishes the existence of a violation of a continuing character'.[241] In case there is a limited number of ways in which cessation may reasonably be achieved, available adjudicative operations also include a judicial determination of Consequential Duties in the form of specific performance required for full cessation of the breach.

A court or tribunal with jurisdiction over the implementation or execution of a ruling should be able to determine negative and positive implementation obligations even if the original judgment does not spell

[241] *Navigational and Related Rights*, [2009] ICJ Reports 21, p. 267.

out performance obligations but merely determines the rights and obligations of the parties. Thus, tribunals examining possible disputes regarding the 'manner of implementation' of the boundary delimitations by UNCLOS Article VII Tribunals (for example, in *Guyana* v. *Suriname*[242] and *Barbados/Trinidad and Tobago*)[243] must logically be able to establish, in case the parties have been unable to do so, not only that implementation was not achieved but also the 'manner' in which lawful implementation is to occur.

A more difficult issue is whether the rulings at this stage may include a determination of the reparation owed in case of non-implementation or non-execution. The question is twofold. First, a party may request from the adjudicator a determination of the form and quantum of reparation due for a breach already identified in the original ruling. A second question is whether the party may at this stage request the determination of new Consequential Duties for breach of the implementation obligation.

The first question must be answered in the affirmative. Especially where responsibility has already been determined in the original judgment, a judgment on its 'execution' or 'manner of implementation' may establish judicially what the IC initially left for determination by the parties. In *Gabčíkovo-Nagymaros*, Article 5(3) of the special agreement allowed the ICJ to determine, in its 'additional Judgment', solely the 'modalities for executing its Judgment'.[244] However, the fact that the original judgment itself included an order for compensation[245] means that both the amount of this compensation and the manner of its provision could arguably be determined by the Court as part of a decision on the 'modalities for executing' its prior rulings.

In its subsequent request, Slovakia did not ask the ICJ to determine the extent of Hungary's responsibility for the original damage. Instead, it asked the Court to establish that Hungary was 'responsible for' the failure

[242] *Delimitation of the Maritime Boundary between Guyana and Suriname*, *Guyana* v. *Suriname*, (2008) PCA 47 ILM 166, 231, 236.

[243] *Delimitation of the Exclusive Economic Zone and the Continental Shelf between Barbados and Trinidad and Tobago*, *Barbados* v. *Trinidad and Tobago*, (2006) PCA 45 ILM 839.

[244] *Gabčíkovo-Nagymaros*, [1997] ICJ Reports 7, 12 ('If they are unable to reach agreement within six months, either Party may request the Court to render an additional Judgment to determine the modalities for executing its Judgment').

[245] In fact, the two parties were considered as responsible for breaches and as owing compensation to each other (*Gabčíkovo-Nagymaros*, [1997] ICJ Reports 7, p. 81, 83).

of the parties to reach agreement on implementation.[246] If by 'responsible' it is meant not only that Hungary is bound by the obligation to cooperate in negotiations[247] but also that it incurs international responsibility for not cooperating, the question arises whether the Court should be able not only to establish responsibility but also to determine legal consequences for it.

The ICJ has never made a determination in this regard. An answer in the affirmative was implied in the repeated warnings, issued by the Arbitral Tribunal in the *Brčko* arbitration, that breaches of the regime established by the Tribunal could lead to the Brčko area being attributed to the non-breaching party as a consequence.[248] In *Velásquez Rodriguez*, the IACtHR stated that it could both establish non-compliance and 'decide on the consequences' of non-compliance.[249] This is not an obvious position, however. In *Noudehouenou* v. *Benin*, the AfCHPR identified Benin's 'failure to comply' with an earlier judgment but rejected the possibility of deriving additional legal consequences from this non-compliance.[250]

One may also draw attention to the language employed by the Court of Arbitration in the *Frontier Case*. The Court established that it would be empowered to determine with finality the boundary between the parties because the agreement clearly evidenced 'the desire of the Parties to get disputes finally settled'.[251] This language is similar to that employed by the PCIJ in *Chorzów Factory* to justify an award of reparation for non-performance as part of its task of 'interpretation and application' of a treaty. If it could not determine reparation, the PCIJ stated, its interventions would not fulfil the function of 'settling a dispute once and for all'; the judgment 'would leave open the possibility of further disputes'.[252]

Arguably, an adjudicator specifically empowered by the parties to settle *any* disputes regarding the execution or implementation of a judgment is also empowered to determine whether non-execution, or

[246] ICJ, Press Release 1998/28.

[247] This would correspond to what Triepel termed responsibility 'in the broad sense, which means merely the fact of being bound towards other subjects of the law' (Heinrich Triepel, *Droit international et droit interne* (Paris: Pédone, 1920/1899), 319).

[248] See Section 7.5.1.

[249] *Velásquez Rodriguez* v. *Honduras (Reparation and Costs)*, IACtHR, 37.

[250] AfCHPR, Application 028/2020 *(Houngue Eric Noudehouenou vs Republic of Benin)*, Judgment, 1 December 2022, paras. 162, 169–168. See Section 8.4.1.2.

[251] *Argentine-Chile Frontier Case, Argentina/Chile*, (1966) 16 RIAA 109, 175.

[252] *Factory at Chorzów (Jurisdiction)*, (1927) PCIJ Ser A No 9, p. 25.

non-implementation, constitutes a legal breach entailing a duty of reparation. A judicial ruling that condemned non-implementation or non-execution and attributed responsibility for this, without determining the extent of the consequences of this responsibility, might give rise to further tensions between the parties rather than alleviating the existing ones. Given that an important function of law-based dispute settlement is to convert diffuse tensions into specific disputes that can be settled, the ability to establish responsibility without the capacity to determine its content would seem to go against the very object and purpose of a provision allowing for adjudication on execution or implementation.

The question of the determination of new Consequential Duties could arise in particular under the scope of proceedings concerning implementation of arbitral awards delivered under UNCLOS. Many actions taken as part of a state's non-compliance, such as attacking ships and oil platforms in territory found to form part of another state, may cause serious injury. A dispute regarding the reparation owed for this injury – assuming it was caused by conduct directly connected to the non-execution or non-implementation of the judgment – is a dispute regarding the 'execution' or 'manner of implementation' of the award. In these cases, a tribunal exercising jurisdiction over a dispute regarding the manner of implementation of the award could deem it appropriate to 'lay down the conditions for the re-establishment of the ... rights affected'.[253]

7.7 Compliance Adjudication through Requests for Interpretation

In many cases, there is no specific provision permitting ICs to adjudicate on compliance with judgments or final awards. In these cases, complaints that substantively concern compliance with rulings may still be framed as wholly new disputes, as discussed in Chapter 8, or as disputes regarding the interpretation of the original judgment.

The key advantage of adjudication on interpretation is that far more treaties establishing international adjudication procedures expressly set up a procedure for interpretation of judgments than provide for post-judgment adjudication on compliance, implementation, or execution.[254]

[253] Ibid.

[254] See *Armed Activities in the Territory of the Congo (New Application: 2002)*, [2006] ICJ Reports 6, as well as footnote no. 224 to 229.

These treaties include the ICJ Statute, whose Article 60 requires the Court, '[i]n the event of dispute as to the meaning or scope of the judgment [to] construe it upon the request of any party'. And, as the ICJ observed in *Tunisia/Libya (Revision and Interpretation)*, even if this provision can be derogated from, a renunciation to the right to request an interpretation 'is not lightly to be presumed'.[255] The relevant questions concern, on the one hand, the extent to which this procedure can be used for compliance adjudication and, on the other hand, what kind of remedy an IC is able to issue within these proceedings.

7.7.1 *The Potential for Requests for Interpretation as Remedies for Non-Compliance*

Addressing non-compliance is not, in principle, the purpose of the legal instrument of request for interpretation. As the PCIJ stated in *Interpretation of Judgments No 7 and 8*, in these proceedings an adjudicator should 'confine[] itself to explaining, by an interpretation, that upon which it has already passed judgment'.[256] On the other hand, an interpretation by the adjudicator of its own prior decision may provide clarifications which de-legitimise non-compliance based on ambiguity or misinterpretations of a previous ruling. Thus, a request for interpretation may be brought against a respondent that, for example, formally changes its conduct and claims to have complied while failing to address the substance of the violation.

Rosenne objects to the possibility of using requests for interpretation to address issues of compliance, invoking the 1928 award in *Morgenstern et al.* v. *Germany*.[257] This award was issued by the German–Polish Mixed Arbitral Tribunal, set up to judge claims for pecuniary reparation following World War I. After the German government declared that it would not pay the compensation determined by the Tribunal, the claimants requested from the tribunal a declaration that non-compliance was unlawful and a determination of the consequences arising for Germany from its failure to comply with the award.

[255] *Continental Shelf, Tunisia/Libya*, Revision and Interpretation, [1985] ICJ Reports 192, p. 216 (the ICJ was careful not to affirm that this provision can be derogated from).

[256] *Interpretation of Judgments Nos 7 and 8 (Chorzów Factory), Germany* v. *Poland*, Judgment, (1927) PCIJ Ser A No. 13, p. 11–12.

[257] Shabtai Rosenne, *The Law and Practice of the International Court 1920–2005*, 4th edn (Leiden: Brill, 2006), 198.

The Tribunal's answer was that the procedural avenue of requests for interpretation (in that case, the only means available to re-seise that Tribunal following the delivery of the award) was not suitable for obtaining a decision on implementation:

> [T]he operative provision of the judgment ... does not demand any interpretation ... the disagreement concerns neither the scope of the judgement nor its final and enforceable character but solely the question of *how* it is to be implemented ... the Tribunal is unable to, in guise of interpretation, intervene in the enforcement procedure, or pronounce in advance on the consequences of a possible non-compliance...[258]

Although the *Morgenstern* Tribunal referred to the scope ('*portée*') of its judgment, the provision invoked by the litigants arguably did not entitle it to provide much in the way of relief. Article 75 of the Mixed Arbitral Tribunal's Rules of Procedure did not providc for a fully fledged interpretation but allowed for the 'modification' of awards, empowering the tribunal solely to 'rectify an obscure, incomplete, or contradictory award, or one that contains a clerical or calculation error'.[259]

By contrast, major standing international courts are empowered more broadly to determine, at the request of the parties, the *meaning* or *scope* of their judgments.[260] Under Article 60 of the ICJ Statute, parties may request the IC to settle, after delivering a final judgment, any 'dispute[s] as to the meaning or scope of the judgment'.[261] Analogous provisions, referring to 'meaning or scope', are found in the Statute of ITLOS,[262] in

[258] *Morgenstern et al.* v. *Germany*, (1928) 7 *Recueil des Décisions des Tribunaux Arbitraux Mixtes* 725, 727 ('...le dispositif de la sentence ... ne nécessite aucune interprétation ... le dissentiment existe non sur la portée de cette sentence ou sur son caractère définitif et exécutoire ... mais uniquement sur le point de savoir comment elle doit être exécutée ... le Tribunal ne saurait, sous couleur d'interprétation, s'immiscer sur la procédure d'exécution, ni se prononcer par avance sur les conséquences d'une inexécution éventuelle').

[259] *Règlement de Procédure*, Tribunal Arbitral Mixte Germano-Polonais, (1922) 1 Tribunaux Arbitraux Mixtes 687, Article 75 ('Le tribunal peut ... rectifier une sentence obscure, incomplète, ou contradictoire, ou qui contient une erreur d'écriture ou de calcul').

[260] Additionally, the refusal by the tribunal to 'pronounce in advance on the consequences of a possible non-implementation' foreshadows the possibility of it pronouncing on it *ex post*. See the decision of the Iran – US Claims Tribunal in *Iran* v. *US*, IUCT, (1987) Case No A21, Decision No 62-A21-FT.

[261] ICJ Statute, Article 60 ('In the event of dispute as to the meaning or scope of the judgment, the Court shall construe it upon the request of any party').

[262] UNCLOS, ITLOS Statute, 1833 UNTS 3, Annex VI, Article 33(3) ('In the event of dispute as to the meaning or scope of the decision, the Tribunal shall construe it upon the request of any party').

the ACHR,[263] and in the ICSID Convention.[264] The ECtHR Rules of Court allow parties to request authoritative interpretations of judgments within a year of their delivery.[265]

The notion that a request for interpretation may allow the adjudicator to determine not only the *meaning* of the judgment but also its *scope* is relevant in that it allows adjudication not only regarding the text of the judgment but also concerning the applicability of the rulings it contains to specific facts. Thus, a divergence with regard to the *meaning* of a judgment may be limited to the examination of the provisions of the judgment itself – the clarification of an ambiguity or of a seeming contradiction. A divergence concerning the *scope* of the judgment, on the other hand, may provide an opportunity for the adjudicator to clarify the *range of conducts* covered by its operative provisions.

A proper interpretation of a clause allowing requests for interpretation should give the word 'scope' *effet utile*. The inclusion of this word must add something to the situation in which, like in *Morgenstern et al.* v. *Germany*, the rules only allow disputes concerning a decision that is 'obscure, incomplete, or contradictory'.[266] Properly interpreted, a permission to request a court to determine the 'meaning or scope' of its judgment should therefore allow the adjudicator not only to solve matters left obscure or ambiguous in the text of the judgment itself but also to assess the extent of the obligations it establishes for the parties, including its applicability to specific acts or facts.

[263] ACHR, Article 67 ('In case of disagreement as to the meaning or scope of the judgment, the Court shall interpret it at the request of any of the parties, provided the request is made within ninety days from the date of notification of the judgment').

[264] ICSID Convention, Article 50: '(1) If any dispute shall arise between the parties as to the meaning or scope of an award, either party may request interpretation of the award by an application in writing addressed to the Secretary-General. (2) The request shall, if possible, be submitted to the Tribunal which rendered the award. If this shall not be possible, a new Tribunal shall be constituted in accordance with Section 2 of this chapter. The Tribunal may, if it considers that the circumstances so require, stay enforcement of the award pending its decision.'

[265] European Court of Human Rights, Rules of Court, 1 January 2014 (available on www.echr.coe.int/, visited 28 March 2024), Article 79: 'A party may request the interpretation of a judgment within a period of one year following the delivery of that judgment'. The ECHR itself is more restrictive: only the Committee of Ministers (the political organ responsible for supervising the execution of judgments) may request a new ruling from the ECtHR, in case it finds that 'the execution of a final judgment is hindered by a problem of interpretation of the judgment' (ECHR, Article 46(3)).

[266] Tribunal Arbitral Mixte Germano-Polonais, *Règlement de Procédure*, Article 75.

This was the understanding expounded by the PCIJ in *Interpretation of Judgments No 7 and 8*, in which the Court analysed a request made by Germany for the interpretation of its judgments in *Certain German Interests in Polish Upper Silesia*. The Permanent Court distinguished between 'the meaning to be attributed to the passage' that generated doubts and the determination of 'the scope of the Judgment':[267]

> [T]he second sentence of Article 60 was inserted in order, if necessary, to enable the Court to make quite clear the points which had been settled with binding force in a judgment. ... A difference of opinion as to whether a particular point has or has not been decided with binding force also constitutes a case which comes within the terms of the provision in question[.][268]

As regards the utility of requests for interpretation as instruments for adjudication on compliance, one issue may be that the assessment of the scope of the judgment does not allow courts to pronounce with authority on matters which have occurred *after* the judgment was issued. In *Interpretation of Judgments No 7 and 8*, the PCIJ dismissed Germany's request for a declaration that the transfer of ownership of the Chorzów factory by Poland, subsequent to the Court's judgment, was 'null and void':[269]

> [T]he Court, when giving an interpretation, refrains from any examination of facts other than those which it has considered in the judgment under interpretation, and consequently all facts subsequent to that judgment.[270]

On the other hand, an adjudicator is empowered at this stage to determine, without specific reference to the subsequent acts of the parties, the precise scope of its prior decision. This determination may not involve a Declaration of Breach, but the request for interpretation may concern the question whether an interpretation given by the IC (or a specific injunction for the termination of a wrongful conduct) required a wrongdoer to modify conduct that was already underway at the time of the original judgment.

Thus, the restriction on the assessment of subsequent conduct would not bar the adjudicator from examining whether the relevant conduct is

[267] *Interpretation of Judgments Nos 7 and 8*, (1927) PCIJ Series A No. 13, p. 20.
[268] Ibid., p. 11–12.
[269] Ibid., p. 8.
[270] Ibid., p. 21.

among those that the respondent was, already under the original judgment, obliged to cease. As the ICJ noted in *Temple of Preah Vihear (Interpretation)*, 'a dispute can, in itself, certainly arise from facts subsequent to the delivery of that judgment'.[271] A dispute regarding interpretation can indeed arise only after the judgment to be interpreted has been issued. While a formal Declaration of Breach regarding subsequent conduct may not be permissible, the wording of the request for interpretation may require the adjudicator to indirectly assess whether conduct that concretely occurred was permissible or prohibited under its prior judgment. As a matter of the typology of remedies established in Chapter 1, the interpretation may be restricted to Mere Adjudication. Coupled with a recording of events as described by the parties, however, such adjudication may produce some of the effects of a Declaration of Breach.

This explains the apparent contradiction in the judgment of the ICJ in *Avena (Interpretation)*. Ostensibly, the Court dismissed Mexico's request for a Declaration of Breach, stating that a request for interpretation did 'not allow it to consider possible violations of the Judgment which it is called upon to interpret'.[272] However, the ICJ did find that 'Mr. Medellín was executed without being afforded the review and reconsideration provided for by paragraphs 138 to 141 of the Avena Judgment'.[273] What was 'missing', as Judge Sepúlveda-Amor remarked, was a 'determination of the legal consequences which flow from the serious failure by the United States to comply with the Order and the *Avena* Judgment'.[274]

While ICs may be unable to address the issue of legal consequences arising from subsequent breach within a ruling on interpretation, they may provide a degree of relief for non-compliance simply by interpreting their earlier rulings and outlining the applicability of this interpretation to certain acts or facts. In *Temple of Preah Vihear (Interpretation)*, Cambodia asked the ICJ to declare that Thailand's obligations under the Court's 1962 judgment,[275] in which the Court attributed the temple

[271] *Temple of Preah Vihear (Interpretation)*, [2013] ICJ Reports 28, para. 12.

[272] *Request for Interpretation of the Judgment of 31 March 2004 in the Case concerning Avena and Other Mexican Nationals, Mexico* v. *United States of America*, Judgment, [2009] ICJ Reports 3, p. 20.

[273] Ibid., p. 23.

[274] Ibid., p. 33 (Sepúlveda-Amor (diss)). The Court had also issued an order reaffirming its 2004 judgment. *Avena (Interpretation) (Provisional Measures)*, [2008] ICJ Reports 311, p. 331.

[275] *Temple of Preah Vihear, Cambodia* v. *Thailand*, Judgment, [1962] ICJ Reports 6, p. 37.

to Cambodia, included not only the express duty to withdraw military and police forces stationed in the vicinity of the temple but also an implicit duty 'not to send those forces – or similar forces – back to the Temple or to nearby sites'.[276] Thailand on the other hand argued that it had 'discharged its obligation' under the 1962 judgment when it withdrew its personnel from the territory that, in its view, the 1962 judgment attributed to Cambodia.[277]

The ICJ noted that there was a dispute regarding 'the nature of Thailand's obligation to withdraw' imposed by the 1962 judgment. However, it did not accede to Cambodia's request for a specific declaration in this regard. The Court found that, as it had concluded that the 1962 judgment did attribute to Cambodia the territory surrounding the temple, such a declaration was unnecessary. The ICJ thus took the approach, adopted in *Nuclear Tests*,[278] of recording in its judgment a commitment as previously voiced by a party, rather than establishing itself the relevant obligation as a judicial remedy. Holding that Thailand had 'accepted that it has a general and continuing obligation to respect the integrity of Cambodian territory', the ICJ concluded that, once the dispute regarding entitlement had been settled 'and the uncertainty removed, each party must fulfil in good faith' its obligation to respect the other party's territorial integrity.[279]

7.7.2 The Requirements of a Request for Interpretation

In spite of having the potential to assist a party in obtaining redress at the post-judgment stage, requests for interpretation are limited by two requirements. The first is that there must exist a dispute between the parties with regard to the 'meaning or scope' of the decision. The second is that the exercise of interpretation must refer solely to the decision and may not require more than an interpretation of what has already been decided.

There are, however, two divergent positions regarding the application of these requirements. One of them, favoured by the PCIJ in *Interpretation of Judgments No 7 and 8* and which has apparently guided the ICJ for the most part, interprets these requirements in an *objective*

[276] *Temple of Preah Vihear (Interpretation)*, [2013] ICJ Reports 28, para. 12.
[277] Ibid., para. 51.
[278] See Section 9.5.2.
[279] *Temple of Preah Vihear (Interpretation)*, [2013] ICJ Reports 28, para. 105.

manner. In assessing the admissibility of a request for interpretation, adjudicators must examine whether a dispute – a 'conflict of legal views or interests' – exists objectively between the parties, and whether the ICJ's interpretation may clarify the meaning or scope of the decision. Likewise, the limitation on the remedies the court may provide is also objective: the judgment on interpretation may not go beyond a clarification of the terms of the prior decision.

In *Interpretation of Judgments No 7 and 8*, the PCIJ stated with regard to the requirement of a dispute that 'the manifestation of the existence of the dispute in a specific manner, as for instance by diplomatic negotiations, is not required'. Though states should in principle certify themselves that a dispute exists, it would be 'sufficient if the two Governments have in fact shown themselves as holding opposite views in regard to the meaning or scope of a judgment of the Court'.[280] This accords with the general interpretation of the requirement of a dispute for any exercise of adjudication.[281]

Under this view, the limits to an IC's decision on interpretation are similarly objective. Although the PCIJ refused to consider Poland's subsequent actions 'null and void' as Germany had requested, this did not prevent the Court from pronouncing on those aspects of the dispute that could be addressed in a request for interpretation. Rather than dismissing the application, the Permanent Court merely stated that it would 'confine[] itself to explaining, by an interpretation, that upon which it ha[d] already passed judgment'.[282]

A different view transpires from the ICJ judgment in *Asylum (Interpretation)*. The Court recalled the two requirements for requests for interpretation: first, obtaining clarification regarding the terms of the judgment must be the 'real purpose of the request';[283] second, there must be 'a dispute as to the meaning and scope of the judgment'.[284] But, contrary to the PCIJ, the ICJ employed a subjective rather than an objective standard to evaluate the fulfilment of these requirements. With regard to the first requirement, the Court held that the 'real

280 *Interpretation of Judgments Nos 7 and 8*, (1927) PCIJ Series A No. 13, p. 11–12.

281 See Section 8.4.2. In *Laguna del Desierto*, Argentina also claimed that Chile's request for interpretation was not the result of a real dispute but was filed 'with a view to the provocation of subsequent disagreement'. *Laguna del Desierto*, (1994) 113 ILR 1, 231.

282 *Interpretation of Judgments Nos 7 and 8*, (1927) PCIJ Series A No. 13, p. 21.

283 *Request for Interpretation of the Judgment of 20 November 1950 in the Asylum Case, Colombia* v. *Peru*, Judgment, [1950] ICJ Reports 395, p. 402.

284 Ibid.

purpose' of Colombia's request (despite the fact that Colombia clearly referred to a number of points left vague in the original judgment) was to 'obtain, by the indirect means of interpretation, a decision on questions which the Court [had] not [been] called upon by the Parties to answer' in the original judgment.[285]

Second, the ICJ found that a mere statement by one party that the judgment was obscure was insufficient to characterise a 'dispute'; this required 'a divergence of views between the parties on definite points'.[286] The ICJ concluded, based on the fact that Colombia had filed its request for interpretation on 'the very date' on which the original judgment was issued, that there had been no time for a concrete dispute to emerge between the parties.[287] It therefore dismissed Colombia's application in its entirety.

It may be that, in *Asylum*, the ICJ in fact sought to prevent the use by Colombia of the request for interpretation with a view to delaying compliance with the judgment. As the Court clarified in *Cameroon* v. *Nigeria (Interpretation)*, this remedy should not be employed as 'a device for gaining time'.[288] If this was the case, the Court should have explicitly noted this. The establishment of a standard of evaluation that gives primacy to the perceived subjective intentions of the parties rather than to their objective conduct produced a problematic precedent.

Subsequent judgments, despite recalling the criteria established in the *Asylum* decision, appear to have reverted to the objective (and preferable) standard. In *Tunisia/Libya (Revision and Interpretation)*, the ICJ rejected Libya's claim that interpretation was not 'the essence' of Tunisia's application, and found that there was effectively 'a dispute as to what in the 1982 judgment ha[d] been decided with binding force'.[289] Finding that Tunisia's request included matters not decided in the original judgment, the Court affirmed that, 'within the limits defined by Article 60 of the Statute, it [wa]s admissible'.[290] It then proceeded to interpret its original judgment.

[285] Ibid, p. 403.
[286] Ibid.
[287] Ibid.
[288] *Request for Interpretation of the Judgment of 11 June 1998 in the Case concerning the Land and Maritime Boundary between Cameroon and Nigeria, Cameroon* v. *Nigeria*, Preliminary Objections, [1999] ICJ Reports 31, p. 43.
[289] *Continental Shelf, Tunisia/Libya*, Revision and Interpretation, [1985] ICJ Reports 192, p. 217, 222.
[290] Ibid., p. 223. See also *Temple of Preah Vihear (Interpretation)*, [2013] ICJ Reports 28, para. 55.

The same objective approach to the limitations on its decision on interpretation was confirmed by the ICJ in *Temple of Preah Vihear (Interpretation)*. The Court stated that:

> its role under Article 60 of the Statute is to clarify the meaning and scope of what the Court decided in the judgment which it is requested to interpret. ... Accordingly, the Court must keep strictly within the limits of the original judgment and cannot question matters that were settled therein with binding force, nor can it provide answers to questions the Court did not decide in the original judgment.[291]

The adoption of an objective standard for the evaluation of the existence of a 'dispute' and of the 'real purpose' of the request increases the utility of requests for interpretation in cases of non-compliance. This was confirmed in *Avena (Interpretation)*. If no divergence exists and the non-compliance is acknowledged, interpretation cannot be used simply to put pressure on the wrongdoer. At most, an adjudicator can record this agreement and reaffirm 'the continuing binding character of the obligations' established in the original judgment.[292] However, in case a divergence does exist, evidenced not only by the declarations of the parties but also by their conduct, a request for interpretation may be used to determine which of the two competing interpretations should prevail. This was the strategy successfully employed by Cambodia in *Temple of Preah Vihear (Interpretation)*.

7.8 Conclusion

This chapter has explored the procedural provisions established by states or developed by adjudicators that allow ICs to assess compliance following a final ruling on a dispute. Among these, requests for interpretation represent the most limited mechanism, as their admissibility depends on a genuine dispute over the interpretation of a prior ruling, beyond mere factual non-compliance.

Courts with jurisdiction to directly assess non-compliance can adopt two primary approaches to remedial powers at this stage: remedy repetition and remedy escalation. In remedy repetition, the adjudicator reinforces earlier rulings by restating and refining its determinations

291 *Temple of Preah Vihear (Interpretation)*, [2013] ICJ Reports 28, para. 25.

292 *Avena (Interpretation) (Provisional Measures)*, [2008] ICJ Reports 311, p. 21. This dispute is examined in Section 9.6.2 owing to the provisional measures granted in this case.

about the applicable law, reiterating a Declaration of Breach – possibly extending it to new conduct that perpetuates the violation – and reaffirming the Consequential Duties outlined in the initial judgment.

Remedy escalation, on the other hand, involves the adjudicator adopting more constraining measures – within the limits of its jurisdiction – when prior remedies have proven insufficient to halt the breach or result in redress. Strategies of remedy escalation include issuing a Declaration of Breach where none was awarded before, determining Consequential Duties previously withheld, or shifting from prospective to retrospective Consequential Duties. In certain cases, adjudicators may also award Permissible Responses – though trade agreements remain the sole treaties where measures of response to wrongful conduct are expressly justiciable. Though remedy escalation does not always require a formal finding of non-compliance, it is most fitting when existing remedies fail to prompt the wrongdoer to comply adequately.

Compliance itself ultimately depends on states. As discussed in Chapter 3, international adjudication is not a panacea for ensuring compliance. It offers a neutral forum for articulating disputes, where arguments are assessed by an adjudicator applying agreed-upon rules. Adjudication complements direct negotiations rather than replacing them.

At the same time, ICs should be wary of overextending their reach. The IACtHR provides an example of how overreliance on the ability of remedies to influence conduct can backfire. As David Baluarte observes, the IACtHR's compliance monitoring is a 'fairly reliable procedure' that allows litigants to 'use the Court to apply pressure on the state after a decision has [been] issued'.[293] However, the Court's insistent remedy repetition can make its successive rulings decreasingly influential. Where repeated Declarations of Breach fail to yield results, the Court has sought to engage in remedy escalation, requesting OAS member states to mobilise political and economic resources against the violator. Given the IACtHR's lack of *potestas*, though, employing this strategy effectively would require genuine buy-in from key American states.

The territorial dispute between Argentina and Chile, spanning nearly a century, offers a valuable counter-example. The constant availability of a neutral third party to hear complaints and propose solutions has prevented disputes from escalating. The possibility of compliance

[293] Baluarte, 'Strategizing for Compliance', 279.

adjudication preserved a forum for disputes as an alternative to conflict, which sometimes enabled both states to achieve their core objectives. Chile secured its territorial claims, while Argentina upheld the 'Atlantic-Pacific principle', preserving its key strategic interest. While the availability of compliance adjudication alone does not eliminate the threat of coercive unilateral action in high-stakes disputes, it offers a structured alternative, providing the aggrieved party with a lawful means to seek redress, while giving the accused party an opportunity to challenge the claim of non-compliance without resorting to harmful countermeasures that could escalate the conflict.

8

Compliance Disputes before International Courts

Procedure and Remedies

8.1 Introduction

The two previous chapters have examined compliance adjudication under dedicated proceedings, established by treaty or by international courts (ICs), allowing ICs to adjudicate at the post-merits stage of a dispute and provide remedies for non-compliance. This chapter discusses means for judicial intervention, and possible judicial remedies, available to an IC after it has delivered a final ruling on a dispute and, in principle, fulfilled its jurisdictional task with regard to that dispute. As the substantial jurisprudence on the matter shows, it is not uncommon for ICs with continuing jurisdiction to be seised by parties claiming non-compliance with previous rulings. This raises questions concerning jurisdiction and admissibility at this stage, including the supposed inadequacy of adjudication at the 'political' implementation phase, and the possible concrete effects of new judicial interventions in the context of an already-adjudicated dispute.[1]

This chapter examines questions of jurisdiction, admissibility, and remedies available to ICs seised with claims that, expressly or implicitly, require them to adjudicate on compliance with previous rulings. As will become clear, there is significant variation in the approaches taken by the various international adjudicators requested to intervene after a final ruling to adjudicate on compliance with this ruling (whether or not the claim is framed as concerning 'non-compliance' or 'enforcement'). These variations notwithstanding, it is possible to assess the distinctive legal issues that arise at this stage, as well as to consider how the approaches adopted by different ICs, in light of sometimes similar constitutive and procedural texts, show different understandings of their roles at this stage.

[1] See the scholarly arguments in this regard in Section 1.2.1.

Section 8.2 discusses the issue of jurisdiction, arguing that the power to adjudicate at this stage of disputes can be determined in a similar manner to its assessment at the original adjudication stage. Section 8.3 considers objections to the admissibility of claims concerning compliance before ICs, showing that different ICs have adopted different approaches, grounded on their underlying legal texts but also on their perception of their role. Section 8.4 examines the techniques ICs have developed to ensure the legal utility and concrete effects of their rulings at this stage, ranging from procedural techniques that distinguish compliance adjudication from the original adjudication to instruments permitting remedy escalation. Section 8.5 concludes.

8.2 Jurisdiction over Compliance Disputes: Outline and Potential Obstacles

Adjudication on compliance involves a new recourse to an IC, usually by the claimant in the original judgment, seeking a judicial determination that a state has failed to perform the obligations clarified or established in the judgment, or derived from it. Rather than responding to non-compliance by adopting unilateral measures or by seising a political body, the claimant seeks a new judicial pronouncement on the matter, claiming non-compliance with the previously awarded remedies and/or requesting new remedies. As in the previous chapters, the terms 'compliance', 'implementation', and 'execution' are employed interchangeably in legal instruments addressing this issue and can be used interchangeably for present purposes.

For compliance adjudication to be possible, the IC in question must have jurisdiction over the dispute. Jurisdiction in international law is based on consent. It concerns the very authority to adjudicate, or 'power to rule',[2] which can only derive from the agreement of the parties. As discussed in Chapter 3, jurisdiction is 'the power, conferred by the consent of States, to hear and determine with binding force a dispute between those States'.[3] The International Court of Justice (ICJ) has

[2] Hugh Thirlway, 'The Law and Procedure of the International Court of Justice 1960–1989' (2011) 81(1) *BYIL* 76. Yuval Shany agrees that 'questions of jurisdiction . . . appertain to questions of power' (Yuval Shany, 'Jurisdiction and Admissibility', in Cesare P.R. Romano, Karen J. Alter, and Yuval Shany (eds.), *The Oxford Handbook of International Adjudication* (Oxford: Oxford University Press, 2014), 779–805, 787).

[3] Thirlway, 'The Law and Procedure', 90. See Section 3.1.

defined this consent as the 'unequivocal indication of voluntary and undisputable acceptance of the Court's jurisdiction'.[4] The question is thus whether the consent for an IC to adjudicate on a matter includes consent for this adjudicator to hear a subsequent dispute on compliance with its original rulings.

This question does not have a univocal answer. In some cases, such as those examined in Chapters 6 and 7, consent to adjudication on compliance, implementation, or execution is expressed in the instrument that endows the IC with jurisdiction. Conversely, a court or tribunal seised ad hoc, based on a *compromis*, may be limited to delivering a judgment or award pronouncing with authority on the issues the parties have empowered it to adjudicate upon. Any new exercise of adjudication requires 'unequivocal indication' of consent, on which the new recourse to the court can be based.[5]

Both the Permanent Court of International Justice (PCIJ) and the ICJ have passed on opportunities to affirm a specific legal framework for jurisdiction over compliance with prior rulings. In *Mavrommatis (Readaptation)*, Greece initially contended before the PCIJ that Britain 'ha[d] not complied with' the obligations laid down in the PCIJ judgment in *Mavrommatis Jerusalem Concessions*. Britain retorted that there was 'no provision giving the Court jurisdiction to decide whether one of its judgments has or has not been complied with'.[6] Greece then changed the basis of its claim, requesting the Court to declare that, by its conduct after that judgment, Britain should pay reparation for 'ha[ving] violated its international obligations within the meaning of Article II of the [British] Mandate [over Palestine], as this article has been construed by the Court'.[7] Besides noting that Greece had ultimately not based its claim on alleged non-compliance, the PCIJ observed:

> No special conclusion appears to have been drawn by the Greek government from the alleged non-fulfilment of the terms of Judgment [in *Mavrommatis Jerusalem Concessions*]. ... In these circumstances, the Court does not find it necessary to consider the question whether, in

[4] *Armed Activities in the Territory of the Congo (New Application: 2002), Democratic Republic of Congo* v. *Rwanda*, Judgment, [2006] ICJ Reports 6, p. 7. See also Ibid., p. 18–19.

[5] See, however, the jurisprudence examined in Section 7.5.

[6] *Mavrommatis Jerusalem Concessions (Readaptation), Greece* v. *Great Britain*, (1927) PCIJ Ser A No. 11, p. 12.

[7] Ibid., p. 5.

> certain cases, it might have jurisdiction to decide disputes concerning the non-compliance with the terms of one of its judgments.[8]

Greece's choice may have been influenced by the fact that the jurisdictional clause it invoked referred to the interpretation and application of the 'provisions of the Mandate'. It was thus able to choose between the two bases for its claim, non-compliance and subsisting violation. This illustrates a broader point: as long as an adjudicator has continued jurisdiction over disputes concerning the relevant subject matter, a claim concerning non-compliance with a prior ruling can be framed simply as a claim concerning the continued or repeated breach of a party's obligations.[9] Bringing a new claim in these circumstances may trigger issues of admissibility, examined in Section 8.3. But the mere fact that non-compliance is raised cannot, in and of itself, deprive a court of its jurisdiction.

Although other disputes have involved compliance indirectly,[10] the issue of jurisdiction over compliance disputes was put directly before the ICJ in *Violations of Sovereign Rights*, a case Nicaragua brought against Colombia in 2013. The ICJ had, in its 2012 Judgment in *Territorial and Maritime Dispute*, determined that certain areas where Colombia had been enforcing its laws were in Nicaragua's Exclusive Economic Zone (EEZ), while rejecting Nicaragua's request for a declaration that Colombia was 'not acting in accordance with its obligations under international law'.[11] In refusing to award a Declaration of Breach in this dispute, the ICJ reasoned that the proceedings concerned 'a maritime boundary which had not been settled prior to the decision of the Court' and that '[t]he consequence of the Court's Judgment is that the maritime boundary between Nicaragua and Colombia throughout the relevant area has now been delimited as between the Parties'.[12]

Following the 2012 Judgment, Colombia enacted a law establishing an 'integral contiguous zone', overlapping with Nicaragua's ICJ-declared EEZ, and withdrew from the treaty grounding the ICJ's jurisdiction, the

[8] Ibid., p. 13–14. The PCIJ dismissed the case on grounds that the conduct Greece challenged, even if its allegations were true, did not amount to a breach and that this would be a question for the merits stage (Ibid., p. 45 (Altamira, diss)).

[9] See the discussion in Section 8.4.

[10] See Section 8.4.1.1.

[11] *Territorial and Maritime Dispute, Nicaragua* v. *Colombia*, Judgment, [2012] ICJ Reports 624, p. 720.

[12] Ibid., p. 718.

'Pact of Bogotá'.[13] A day before this withdrawal took effect, Nicaragua filed another set of claims before the ICJ. Besides claiming that Colombia's post-judgment conduct violated Nicaragua's substantive rights, Nicaragua requested a declaration that 'Colombia is bound to comply with the Judgment of 19 November 2012, wipe out the legal and material consequences of its internationally wrongful acts, and make full reparation for the harm caused by those acts'.[14] In addition to grounding its request on Colombia's still-valid consent to ICJ jurisdiction under the Pact of Bogotá, Nicaragua claimed that the ICJ had an 'inherent power to pronounce on the actions required by its Judgments' and 'an inherent jurisdiction to entertain disputes regarding non-compliance with its judgments'.[15]

Regarding the claim that it had 'inherent' power or jurisdiction over compliance disputes, the ICJ, like the PCIJ before it, chose to set aside the issue. Colombia reasoned that accepting Nicaragua's argument 'would strike at the foundation of consensual jurisdiction' and 'ignore[] any conditions which States may have attached to their consent to jurisdiction'.[16] The ICJ, having concluded that the Pact of Bogotá remained a valid ground for its jurisdiction, found that there was 'no need to deal with Nicaragua's claim of "inherent jurisdiction"' over compliance matters and chose 'not [to] take any position on it'.[17]

Indeed, under the principle of consensual jurisdiction, any new exercise of adjudication requires a specific jurisdictional link on which the new recourse to the court can be based. The jurisdictional requirements that apply to a post-judgment compliance dispute, whether or not the claimant frames it as such, are the same as those applicable to any exercise of adjudication. While courts may have continued jurisdiction over a subject matter – in which case, the key issue are the obstacles to admissibility discussed in Section 8.3 – consent provided ad hoc for a court or tribunal to decide on a dispute does not automatically extend to disputes concerning the existence or manner of compliance with the rulings issued.[18]

[13] This is the American Treaty on Pacific Settlement ('Pact of Bogotá'), Bogota, 30 April 1948, 30 UNTS 55 ('ATPS').

[14] *Alleged Violations of Sovereign Rights and Maritime Spaces in the Caribbean Sea, Nicaragua* v. *Colombia*, Preliminary Objections, [2016] ICJ Reports 3, p. 11.

[15] Ibid., p. 9, 13.

[16] Ibid., p. 40.

[17] Ibid., p. 39.

[18] See *Question of Jaworzina*, Advisory Opinion, (1923) PCIJ Ser B No 8, p. 38 ('in the absence of an express agreement between the parties, the Arbitrator is not competent to interpret, still less modify his award by revising it').

A number of regional courts with compulsory jurisdiction have been seised with compliance disputes. When seised with fresh claims regarding non-compliance with previous rulings, the Southern African Development Community (SADC) Tribunal and the East African Court of Justice (EACJ) simply proceeded to examine the legal claims raised. The SADC Tribunal in *Campbell* v. *Zimbabwe* declared a 'failure on the part of the respondent and its agents to comply with the decision of the Tribunal'.[19] The EACJ in *Sitenda Sebalu* v. *Secretary General* declared a 'failure by the Partner States to implement the Court's orders' and found that it could hold EAC organs in contempt of court.[20] The Caribbean Court of Justice (CCJ) in *TCL* v. *Guyana* issued a Declaration of Breach of the treaty obligation to comply with that court's rulings,[21] while reserving judgment on whether it had jurisdiction to declare a party in contempt of court.[22]

By contrast, the Economic Community of West African States (ECOWAS) Community Court of Justice (ECCJ) and the Central American Court of Justice (CACJ) have rejected compliance jurisdiction. The ECCJ based this rejection on a specific ECOWAS instrument establishing a procedure for political sanctions for non-compliance with rulings.[23] In *Sambo Dasuki* v. *Nigeria*, for example, the ECCJ found that, unless seised by ECOWAS organs, it lacks jurisdiction to 'adjudicate on claims bordering on the enforcement of its own judgments'.[24] The CACJ, in *Sánchez Herrera* v. *Guatemala*, concluded that it could not rule on compliance with its rulings and referred the case to domestic courts and Central American political bodies.[25]

[19] SADC Tribunal, *Campbell* v. *Zimbabwe, Ruling*, Case No. SADCT: 03/2009 (18 July–June 2009), para. 4.

[20] EACJ, *Sitenda Sebalu* v. *EAC Secretary General*, Reference No. 8 of 2012, Judgment, 22 November 2013, para. 84(a)–(c).

[21] CCJ, *Trinidad Cement Limited and TCL Guyana Incorporated* v. *Guyana (Non-compliance/Contempt)*, CCJ Application No 2 of 2009 (Original Jurisdiction), Judgment, 29 March 2010, para. 25.

[22] Ibid., paras. 30–44.

[23] ECOWAS, *Supplementary Act A/SP.13/02/12 on Sanctions against Member States That Fail to Honour Their Obligations to ECOWAS* (Act 2-SP13 of 2012) (17 February 2012).

[24] Application No. ECW/CCJIAPP/20/21, *Sambo Dasuki* v. *Federal Republic of Nigeria*, Judgment, 6 June 2024 (ECW/CCJ/JUD/19/24), para. 29. See also the jurisprudence cited therein. The effects of 'political' enforcement mechanisms over IC jurisdiction over compliance are discussed in Section 8.3.1.

[25] CACJ, *Case No. 2-23-3-2018 (Gilmar Othmar Sánchez Herrera* v. *Guatemala) (Contempt of Court and Non-compliance)*, Judgment, 17 July 2019, p. 2: 'Póngase en conocimiento de las Cortes Supremas de Justicia de los Estados del Sistema de la Integración

The African Court of Human and People's Rights (AfCHPR) adopted an intermediate stance. In *Noudehouenou* v. *Benin*, it declared 'the Respondent's failure to comply with the Court's decisions' and mentioned this failure to comply when assessing moral damages. But the AfCHPR also held that, since it was not 'an enforcement judge of its own decisions', it could not award compensation for non-compliance itself, which it characterised as impermissible 'coercive measures compelling the Respondent State to enforce the decisions'.[26]

In itself, consent to an IC's jurisdiction over a 'compliance' dispute is not particular. This is not to say that all consent to jurisdiction includes implicit consent to compliance adjudication – merely that the latter can be ascertained using the same logic and principles as the former. Forms of expressing consent include (1) consent by special agreement, whereby parties agree to endow an adjudicator with jurisdiction over one particular dispute; (2) jurisdiction provided by treaty, *ex ante*, for a category of disputes; and (3) for some standing courts, consent granted *ex post*, through so-called *forum prorogatum*, whereby the respondent accepts the jurisdiction of an adjudicator after receiving notice of the claim.[27]

8.2.1 Consent to Compliance Adjudication through a New Agreement

Following a final judgment or award, parties may agree to submit to the same adjudicator (or to another one) a new dispute regarding compliance with the prior ruling. It may seem unusual for a party resisting compliance with a ruling to agree to a new adjudication on the matter. However, a party allegedly in breach may consent to adjudication on compliance the same way it may consent to adjudication after any dispute arises. The same reasons that lead any state to consent to adjudication after a dispute has emerged may lead it to agree to a new exercise of jurisdiction.

It is not unheard of for states to have recourse to adjudication to settle issues related to those determined in a prior judicial decision. In *Laguna del Desierto*, Chile and Argentina agreed in 1991 to request an arbitral tribunal to settle a question of delimitation 'by interpreting and applying

Centroamericana (SICA), a la Corte Constitucional de la República de Guatemala y al Secretario General del Sistema de la Integración Centroamericana (SICA)'.

26 AfCHPR, *Application 028/2020 (Houngue Eric Noudehouenou v, Republic of Benin)*, Judgment, 1 December 2022, paras. 162, 168, 175.

27 See Chittharanjan Felix Amerasinghe, *Jurisdiction of Specific International Tribunals* (Leiden: Martinus Nijhoff, 2009), 94 ff.

[an] Award of 1902, in accordance with international law'.[28] In the 1937 PCIJ case *Lighthouses in Crete and Samos*, France and Greece signed a new special agreement requesting the Permanent Court to determine whether its 1934 *Lighthouses* judgment applied to the Greek islands of Crete and Samos. Since this contentious issue had been expressly left out of the *Lighthouses* case, *Lighthouses in Crete and Samos* concerned not the interpretation of the previous decision but the question of 'the applicability in a particular case of the [*Lighthouses*] Judgment already rendered by the Court'.[29]

The terms of the new agreement may allow for limited review, requiring the IC to decide between two propositions of law. This was the case in the 1902 arbitration in *Pious Funds of the Californias*. In 1876, an arbitral award had determined that Mexico, which held in treasury the property of an ancient fund, was under the obligation 'to remit to the Bishop of California and his successors the interest on the proceeds of the property belonging to the Pious Funds'.[30] The operative part of the 1876 award only mentioned the duty to provide reparation for amounts unpaid up until the date of that award, and was silent on future obligations of Mexico.[31] Mexico paid the amount established in the award and asserted that this payment extinguished the Bishop's claim. The United States applied diplomatic pressure and Mexico agreed to submit a new dispute to arbitration. In the new special agreement, the parties asked the Arbitral Tribunal (i) to determine whether a statement made in the original award, but not followed by a determination in its operative part, had the force of *res judicata*, and (ii) 'to render such judgment or award as may be meet and proper under all the circumstances of the case'.[32]

The Arbitral Tribunal concluded that the question of Mexico's continued obligation to pay interest had been decided with the force of *res judicata* as regards the merits but not the form of payment. It ordered

[28] *The Agreement to Arbitration in Boundary dispute between Argentina and Chile concerning the frontier line between Boundary Post 62 and Mount Fitzroy, Chile* v. *Argentina*, (1995) 113 ILR 1, 20.

[29] *Lighthouses in Crete and Samos, France* v. *Greece*, Judgment, (1937) PCIJ Ser A/B No 71, p. 100. See *Lighthouses in Crete and Samos, France* v. *Greece*, Judgment, (1934) PCIJ Ser A/B No 62, p. 29.

[30] 'The Pious Fund Case', Award of Sir Edward Thornton, 11 November 1875, amended by him on 24 October 1876, in James Brown Scott, *The Hague Court Reports* (Hague: Carnegie Endowment for International Peace, 1916), 48–54, 51.

[31] Ibid., 53–54.

[32] *Pious Fund of the Californias, United States of America* v. *United Mexican States*, (1902) 9 RIAA 1, 8.

Mexico both to pay reparation for the payments unlawfully retained and to pay, 'in perpetuity', an annual amount to the US government.[33] Although the 1902 Tribunal made no direct determination on compliance, the implication of its decision is that Mexico failed to 'consciously execute' the 1876 award.[34] As remedies, the second *Pious Funds* Tribunal both ordered Mexico to retrospectively pay to the United States the equivalent of the injury suffered and established with finality a prospective obligation of payment.

8.2.2 Compliance Adjudication Based on Continuing Jurisdiction

A court or tribunal that has ruled on a dispute may have continuous jurisdiction allowing it to adjudicate on a new dispute between the parties. This may be because the IC was granted jurisdiction to settle all or certain categories of disputes between two parties, or is generally empowered to interpret and apply a set of rules, including between these parties. In either case, as long as the parties to the original dispute remain bound by the relevant rules and their consent to jurisdiction persists, the jurisdictional link permits the IC to continue adjudicating on new disputes. The mere fact that a ruling has been issued on a related dispute does not impinge on an IC's jurisdiction to examine a new legal dispute between the parties.[35]

Continued jurisdiction may exist in various forms. A convention may require all parties to consent to an IC's jurisdiction. The United Nations Convention on the Law of the Sea (UNCLOS) and the World Trade Organization (WTO) Agreements, as well as many regional human rights conventions, regional economic treaties, and international investment agreements, require consent to compulsory adjudication of disputes, whether by a permanent IC or by ad hoc adjudicators. Jurisdiction in these cases persists as long as the substantive rules of the relevant treaty continue to govern the relations between the parties. In the case of the American Convention on Human Rights (ACHR), the Inter-American Court of Human Rights (IACtHR) determined in *Ivcher-Bronstein* v. *Peru* that, even though acceptance of its jurisdiction is optional under

[33] Ibid., 14.

[34] Ibid., 13 (stating that Mexico 'consciously executed' the retrospective portion of the award).

[35] The IC's rulings on a dispute may create *res judicata* affecting the admissibility of certain claims. This issue is examined in Section 8.3.3.

ACHR Article 26, seeking to withdraw this acceptance is impermissible under Article 29(a), which provides that the Convention cannot be interpreted to allow parties to 'suppress the enjoyment or exercise of the rights and freedoms recognized in this Convention or to restrict them to a greater extent than is provided for herein'.[36] The IACtHR determined that '[a] State Party may only release itself from the Court's jurisdiction by renouncing the treaty as a whole'.[37]

Other conventions permit states to consent to compulsory jurisdiction while allowing them to later withdraw this consent without denouncing the entire treaty. This is the case of the ICJ Statute, whose Article 36(2) contains an 'optional clause' by which parties can consent to ICJ jurisdiction over any categories of disputes. It is also the case of compulsory jurisdiction clauses such as the Optional Protocol to the Vienna Convention on Consular Relations Concerning the Compulsory Settlement of Disputes. Certain treaties have as their main object and purpose reciprocal consent to adjudication for all disputes between the parties; jurisdiction can therefore be unlimited *ratione materiae* and restricted *ratione personae*. This is the case of instruments that empower adjudicators, often the ICJ, to adjudicate on 'all legal disputes' between a state and other states, based on geography,[38] reciprocity,[39] or both.[40] Where consent to jurisdiction has a continuing character, the adjudicator remains empowered to adjudicate on subsequent disputes between the parties, unless and until a denunciation of the relevant treaty takes effect or consent to jurisdiction is validly withdrawn.[41]

Given the potential for requests for adjudication on compliance, it is surprising that these requests have not been filed more often before ICs with continuing jurisdiction over specific sets of rules. This may be attributed to the lingering perception that political measures and

[36] American Convention on Human Rights, San Jose, 22 November 1969, in force 18 July 1978, 1144 UNTS 123, Article 29(a) ('ACHR'); *Ivcher-Bronstein* v. *Peru (Competence)*, IACtHR, (1999) Ser C No. 54, para. 41.

[37] Ibid., para. 46.

[38] ATPS, Article 31.

[39] General Act for the Pacific Settlement of International Disputes, Geneva, in force 26 September 1928, 93 LNTS 344, Article 18; Revised General Act for the Pacific Settlement of International Disputes, in force 28 April 1949, 71 UNTS 101, Article 18.

[40] European Convention for the Peaceful Settlement of Disputes, Strasbourg, 29 April 1957, in force 30 April 1958, 320 UNTS 243, Article 24.

[41] In part due to the potential for further adjudication, states have sometimes responded to judicial rulings condemning their conduct under a treaty by withdrawing consent to IC jurisdiction over the treaty, or by denouncing the relevant treaty.

negotiation are more adequate avenues for addressing compliance issues than resorting to adjudication anew.[42] In *Alleged Violations*, it is possible that Nicaragua only filed its request for a ruling on Colombia's compliance with a previous judgment in order to secure judicial scrutiny, in a situation where Colombia's denunciation of the Pact of Bogotá was scheduled to take effect, depriving Nicaragua of future chances to resort to adjudication on this issue. In new applications concerning compliance before regional courts, applicants commonly request additional judicial pronouncements after exhausting the possibilities for pressure through political mechanisms, and sometimes after resorting to domestic courts.[43]

Among compliance cases brought to an adjudicator with continuing jurisdiction is the PCIJ case *Chorzów Factory*, concerning the consequences arising from non-compliance with the earlier *Certain German Interests in Polish Silesia* judgment. In this judgment, the PCIJ declared that the expropriation of a factory owned by a German company in Poland was 'not in conformity with' the Germano-Polish Convention concerning Upper Silesia.[44] Following this judgment, Germany demanded from Poland that it restore the factory to its German owner, specifying that, in case Poland ignored its demand for compliance, 'the question should be settled by the institution of new procedures before the Court'. Poland retorted that it was 'unable to comply by reasons of fact and of law'.[45]

Germany filed a new claim before the PCIJ, based on the same treaty provision that had grounded its original claim in *Certain German Interests*, requesting reparation for Poland's failure to satisfactorily implement the judgment.[46] Poland challenged the jurisdiction of the PCIJ to award reparations, since the relevant treaty only referred to 'differences of opinion, resulting from the interpretation and application' of its provisions.[47] The PCIJ rejected this objection, reasoning that

[42] See Section 1.2.1.

[43] See Section 8.4.

[44] *Certain German Interests in Polish Upper Silesia (Merits), Germany* v. *Poland*, Judgment, (1926) PCIJ Ser A No. 7, p. 81.

[45] *Factory at Chorzów (Jurisdiction), Germany* v. *Poland*, Judgment, (1927) PCIJ Ser A No. 9, p. 16.

[46] Ibid., p. 19.

[47] Ibid., p. 20. The PCIJ was seised pursuant to Article 23 of the 1922 Germano-Polish Convention concerning Upper Silesia, which provided the PCIJ with jurisdiction over 'differences of opinion respecting the construction and application of Articles 6 to 22' of the Geneva Convention (*Certain German Interests in Polish Upper Silesia (Jurisdiction), Germany* v. *Poland*, Preliminary Objections, (1925) PCIJ Ser A No. 5, p. 13).

'[d]ifferences relating to reparations, which may be due by reason of failure to apply a convention [are] differences relating to its application'.[48] The Court went on to establish Poland's obligation to pay monetary compensation for the breach.[49]

Another early instance in which adjudication on compliance was exercised post-judgment, on the same jurisdictional basis as the original decision, was the *Junghans* case. In 1939, an Arbitral Tribunal, acting under the 1928 Berlin Convention between Germany and Romania, concluded that Romania was bound to restore to a German national the title to property over a forest expropriated by Romania, or pay an indemnity corresponding to the property value, within two months. This award did not specify that the Tribunal would have jurisdiction to determine the amount of the indemnity.[50]

Three months later, the Romanian government informed Germany that it would be unable to provide restitution of property and proposed to pay an amount as compensation. Germany did not accept the amount offered and 'seised the Arbitral Tribunal once more'.[51] In 1940, a new Arbitral Tribunal, established under the same provision of the 1928 Berlin Convention, observed that it considered itself to be 'another judge' rather than the same as the Tribunal that issued the 1939 award, but found that the dispute it was called upon to adjudicate was 'only the sequel of that which ended with the first award'.[52] Romania did not raise any objections to jurisdiction or admissibility. The 1940 Tribunal established the amount Romania should pay to the German government for the definitive resolution of the dispute.[53]

8.2.3 Forum prorogatum

A final case is that of *forum prorogatum*. As the ICJ explained in *Djibouti* v. *France*, this form of consent to jurisdiction applies when the

[48] Ibid, p. 20–21.

[49] *Factory at Chorzów (Merits), Germany* v. *Poland,* Judgment, (1928) PCIJ Ser A No. 17, p. 63–64. The parties subsequently settled the dispute (*Factory at Chorzów, Germany* v. *Poland,* Order of 25 May 1929 (1929) PCIJ Ser A No. 19, p. 12).

[50] *Affaire Junghans (Première Partie), Allemagne contre Roumanie,* (1939) 3 RIAA 1845, 1856.

[51] *Affaire Junghans (Deuxième Partie), Allemagne contre Roumanie,* (1940) 3 RIAA 1883, 1887 ('saisit à nouveau le Tribunal arbitral').

[52] Ibid., 1889 ('un autre juge'; 'Le litige actuel n'est que la suite de celui qui a abouti à la prémière sentence').

[53] Ibid., 1891.

'respondent State has, through its conduct before the Court or in relation to the applicant party, acted in such a way as to have consented to the jurisdiction of the Court'.[54] *Forum prorogatum* is codified in Article 38(5) of the ICJ Rules of Court and Article 54(5) of the International Tribunal for the Law of the Sea (ITLOS) Rules of the Tribunal, which provide that applicants may file claims without showing prior consent to jurisdiction by the respondent. In this case, the respective Registrars are to transmit the claim to the respondent and wait for consent before proceeding with the case.

To the extent that courts and tribunals are capable of acting upon *forum prorogatum*, parties may seise them with a post-judgment dispute even in the case of ad hoc agreements to adjudication, when no general *ex ante* agreement to jurisdiction exists, and in the absence of a provision for post-judgment remedies.

This occurred in *Haya de la Torre*. Following the dismissal of its request for interpretation of the ICJ's 1950 judgment in *Asylum* (a dispute over which jurisdiction was established by special agreement),[55] Colombia unilaterally filed an application requesting the International Court 'to adjudge and declare that Colombia is not bound, in execution of the said Judgment of November 20th, 1950, to deliver M. Victor Raul Haya de la Torre to the Peruvian authorities'.[56] Peru responded by arguing on the merits and did not challenge the jurisdiction of the Court. The ICJ concluded that the 'conduct of the Parties [wa]s sufficient to confer jurisdiction on the Court'.[57] The Court delivered a new judgment (*Haya de la Torre*), refusing to offer specific guidance but recalling that its earlier judgment in *Asylum* entailed for the parties 'the obligation of compliance'.[58]

It is less clear that arbitrators may acquire jurisdiction via *forum prorogatum*. The International Centre for Settlement of Investment Disputes (ICSID) Tribunal in *Klöckner* v. *Cameroon* accepted *forum prorogatum* with regard to the scope of its jurisdiction, stating, that once it had been validly seised, 'consent as to the "*ratione materiae*" extent of the Tribunal's jurisdiction may be expressed at any time, even in written

[54] *Mutual Assistance in Criminal Matters, Djibouti* v. *France*, Judgment, [2008] ICJ Reports 177, p. 204.

[55] *Asylum Case, Colombia* v. *Peru*, [1950] ICJ Reports 266, p. 267–278.

[56] *Haya de la Torre, Peru* v. *Colombia*, [1951] ICJ Reports 71, p. 75.

[57] Ibid., p. 78.

[58] Ibid., p. 79.

submissions to the Tribunal ("*forum prorogatum*")'.[59] This statement, which the Annulment Committee termed 'superfluous',[60] is described by Schreuer as 'probably based on a misunderstanding'.[61]

Other Tribunals have been assertive regarding the impossibility of *forum prorogatum*. In the *Young Loan Arbitration*, the Arbitral Tribunal stated that '[n]ot even an explicit agreement by the parties could confer on the Tribunal, a jurisdiction that is not contemplated by the [London Debt Agreement]'.[62] In *Burton Marks and Harry Umann*, the Iran–US Claims Tribunal affirmed that the 'jurisdictional boundaries' established in the Claims Settlement Declaration providing the tribunal with jurisdiction 'are absolute and cannot be waived or modified unilaterally by an arbitrating party or parties' – even to expand the scope of their own consent.[63] Amerasinghe states that, in international arbitration, it is 'unequivocally accepted' that *forum prorogatum* is not admitted.[64]

Schreuer takes a more nuanced position. At least in the ICSID context, he finds that the mere failure to object to jurisdiction does not create *forum prorogatum*. A tribunal should examine the question of its jurisdiction *proprio motu*, but defective consent can be 'cure[d]' by 'agreement between the parties before the [conciliation] commission or tribunal'.[65] His view appears to be based on a form of estoppel, by which a party which has 'indicated its consent during the proceedings' would be 'precluded' from objecting to jurisdiction later on.[66] One may debate, however, whether an agreement between host state and investor may expand a jurisdiction that is grounded on a treaty, one of the parties to which – the home state of the investor – is not a party to the arbitration and has not given its consent to such an expansion.

Standing courts have adopted different stances regarding the ability of state consent to permit resort to compliance jurisdiction – though this

[59] *Klöckner* v. *Cameroon*, [1983] ICSID Case No ARB/81/2, Award, 21 October 1983.
[60] *Klöckner* v. *Cameroon (Annulment)*, [1985] ICSID Case No ARB/81/2, Decision on Annulment, 3 May 1985, para. 9.
[61] Christoph Schreuer, *The ICSID Convention: A Commentary*, 2nd edn (Cambridge: Cambridge University Press, 2009), 223.
[62] *Young Loan Arbitration, Belgium and Ors.* v. *Germany*, (1980) 59 ILR 494, 524.
[63] *Burton Marks and Harry Umann* v. *Republic of Iran*, IUCT, (1985) 8 Iran-US CTR 290, 297.
[64] Chittharanjan Felix Amerasinghe, *International Arbitral Jurisdiction* (Leiden: Martinus Nijhoff, 2009), 51–53, 72–74.
[65] Schreuer, *The ICSID Convention*, 225.
[66] Ibid.

question may be more appropriately classified as one of admissibility. In *Baena Ricardo* v. *Panama (Monitoring Compliance with Judgment)*, the IACtHR invoked, among other reasons for the lawfulness of its compliance monitoring procedure, Panama's acquiescence to the Court's prior actions in this dispute.[67] The ECCJ, by contrast, has found its interventions at the implementation stage to be circumscribed to those specifically permitted under its statute. In *Sambo Dasuki* v. *Nigeria*, this Court justified not accepting claims of non-compliance by recalling that 'Courts are creatures of Statutes, and their jurisdiction is confined, limited, and circumscribed by the Statutes which created them'.[68]

8.3 Admissibility of Compliance Disputes: Political Bodies and *res judicata*

While objections to jurisdiction concern the power of the adjudicator to exercise jurisdiction over a dispute, objections to admissibility involve a bar to the exercise of jurisdiction in relation to specific claims. As Gerald Fitzmaurice explained, an objection to jurisdiction is 'a plea that the tribunal itself is incompetent to give any ruling at all' on the dispute, whereas an objection to admissibility 'is a plea that the tribunal should rule the claim to be inadmissible on some ground other than its ultimate merits'.[69] This was expressed by arbitrator Keith Highet in his dissenting opinion in *Waste Management*:

> Jurisdiction is the power of the tribunal to hear the case; admissibility is whether the case itself is defective – whether it is appropriate for the tribunal to hear it. If there is no title of jurisdiction, then the tribunal cannot act.[70]

[67] *Baena Ricardo et al.* v. *Panama (Monitoring Compliance with Judgment)*, IACtHR, 21 June 2002, paras. 126–127.

[68] Application No. ECW/CCJIAPP/20/21, *Sambo Dasuki* v. *Federal Republic of Nigeria*, Judgment, 6 June 2024 (ECW/CCJ/JUD/19/24), para. 22. See also Application No. ECW/CCJ/APP/12/15, *Aziagbede and Others* v. *Republic of Togo*, Judgment, 6 December 2016 (ECW/CCJ/JUD/29/16), para. 18.

[69] Gerald Fitzmaurice, 'The Law and Procedure of International Court of Justice, 1951–4: Questions of Jurisdiction, Competence and Procedure' (1958) 34 *BYIL* 1, 12–13. Jan Paulsson finds that, while an objection to jurisdiction involves the plea that there is 'a limitation on the tribunal, an objection to admissibility aims at the *claim*' (Jan Paulsson, 'Jurisdiction and Admissibility', in *Global Reflections on International Law: Commerce and Dispute Resolution: Liber Amicorum in Honour of Robert Briner* (Paris: ICC Publishing, 2005), 601–617, 616).

[70] *Waste Management, Inc.* v. *Mexico*, [2000] ICSID Case No ARB(AF)/98/2, Award, 2 June 2000, Keith Highet, diss, para. 58.

An objection to admissibility is therefore a request that a court or tribunal refrain from exercising existing jurisdictional powers with regard to specific issues submitted to adjudication. Objections to the admissibility involve the argument that the claim, although in principle subject to the jurisdiction of the tribunal *ratione personae*, *ratione materiae*, and *ratione temporis*, is defective as presented by the claimant and should not be adjudicated upon. Zachary Douglas characterises the issue of admissibility as pertaining to 'the *suitability* of the claim for adjudication on the merits'.[71]

8.3.1 *Enforcement Procedures, Political Bodies, and the Role of Adjudication*

It is sometimes claimed that the existence of a dedicated procedure for addressing claims of non-compliance – and, in particular, procedures conducted by political bodies – precludes bringing these claims before adjudicators. This claim may at first sight appear credible. Upon deeper examination, however, it seems grounded in two dubious assumptions: on the one hand, that entrusting a specific organ, especially a political organ, with an issue bars adjudicators from pronouncing on the same issue; and, on the other hand, that judicial remedies have little to add at the implementation stage. This section considers the first assumption.

8.3.1.1 Enforcement by the Security Council and ICJ Adjudication on Compliance

The most well-known procedure for 'political' enforcement of IC rulings is the one in Article 94(2) of the UN Charter. Article 94(2) empowers states parties to an ICJ judgment to call upon the UN Security Council to take 'measures' when 'any party to a case fails to perform the obligations incumbent upon it under a judgment of the [ICJ]'. It provides:

> If any party to a case fails to perform the obligations incumbent upon it under a judgment rendered by the Court, the other party may have recourse to the Security Council, which may, if it deems necessary, make recommendations or decide upon measures to be taken to give effect to the judgment.

[71] Zachary Douglas, *The International Law of Investment Claims* (Cambridge: Cambridge University Press, 2009), 148.

Karin Oellers-Frahm argues that Article 94(2) 'provides for institutional means for compliance with judgments of the ICJ which would otherwise not be provided'.[72] This is correct to the extent that it means that neither the Charter nor the ICJ Statute set up a dedicated procedure for bringing post-judgment claims of non-compliance before the ICJ, or provide specific judicial remedies for non-compliance. It also coincides with the view, expressed by the Washington Committee of Jurists, that it is 'not the business of the Court itself to ensure the execution of its decisions'.[73] However, neither the existence of a procedure for seising the UN Security Council (UNSC) with compliance issues nor the absence of specific judicial procedures for this purpose, in themselves, preclude the ICJ from examining compliance matters in subsequent disputes over which it has jurisdiction.

With regard to Article 94(2), the first point to note is that it is twice cast in permissive language ('may'). Both the seising of the Security Council by a party to the judgment and the taking of measures by the Council are optional. The language of Article 94(2) is, in this respect, not different from that of Article 35(1) of the Charter, which allows UN members to refer 'any dispute, or any situation' to the Council or the General Assembly – and does not thereby prevent members from referring disputes to the ICJ or other adjudicators. Additionally, Article 94(2) stresses the discretionary character of the Council's actions in case of non-compliance. Contrary to the Council of the League of Nations, which was under an obligation ('shall') to propose 'steps to be taken to give effect' to PCIJ judgments,[74] the UN Security Council has full discretion to decide on the measures, if any, that 'it deems necessary' to give effect to an ICJ judgment.

It may be argued that the Council is the designated enforcement agent for ICJ judgments. The term 'decide upon measures' is the same as that employed in Article 39 of the UN Charter, arguably allowing the Council to respond to non-compliance with Chapter VII-like sanctions even in the absence of a threat to the peace, breach of the peace or aggression. But no such enforcement has ever taken place. Nicaragua's attempt to

[72] See Karin Oellers-Frahm, 'Article 94 UN Charter', in Andreas Zimmerman *et al.* (eds.), *The Statute of the International Court of Justice: A Commentary* (Oxford: Oxford University Press, 2012), 159–175, 174.

[73] 'Documents of the United Nations Conference on International Organization', (1945) 14 UNCIO 853.

[74] Covenant of the League of Nations, Paris, 28 April 1919, in force 10 January 1920, (1919) UKTS 4 (Cmd. 153), Article 13(4).

employ Article 94(2) in this way against the United States, following US non-compliance with the ICJ judgment in *Nicaragua*, was met with the American veto and was predictably doomed from the outset.[75] After the ICJ Judgment in *Land, Island and Maritime Frontier*, Honduras unsuccessfully requested the Security Council, to 'intervene and assist in securing the execution of and faithful compliance with the judgment'.[76] The Council has not otherwise been requested to act as an 'enforcement agent' for ICJ judgments in the sense of employing sanctions to press for implementation. Even if this prerogative had ever been employed, this would not change the discretionary character of the Council's actions.

As a result, to recover the language of the Washington Committee of Jurists, 'to ensure the execution' of ICJ judgments is, in institutional practice, no more the 'business' of the Security Council than that of the ICJ. While referring a judgment to the Council is certainly a possibility that states have resorted to,[77] in other cases, including some where a Permanent Member of the UNSC was the complainant, Article 94(2) was simply not employed.[78] Rather than an enforcer, the function of the Council following ICJ judgments is at present that of a forum, where parties may voice their concerns with non-compliance and negotiate, within an institutional setting, a path to implement a judgment.

Additionally, the choice of a state faced with non-implementation is not solely between recourse to the Council and purely bilateral pressure for compliance. Other international institutions may be involved in implementation efforts without offence to Article 94(2). To discuss how to implement the ICJ judgment in *Asylum* after *Haya de la Torre*, Colombia resorted not to the Security Council but to the Inter-American Peace Commission.[79] The same Commission was seised by Nicaragua following the ICJ judgment in *Award of the King of Spain*.[80] In *Gabčíkovo-Nagymaros*, the ICJ itself stated that in future bilateral

[75] Constanze Schulte, *Compliance with Decisions of the International Court of Justice* (Oxford: Oxford University Press, 2004), 199–203.

[76] Letter dated 22 January 2002 from the Chargé d'affaires a.i. of the Permanent Mission of Honduras to the United Nations addressed to the President of the Security Council, UN Doc. S/2002/108 (23 January 2002). The Judgment is *Land, Island and Maritime Frontier Dispute (El Salvador/Honduras: Nicaragua intervening)*, Judgment, [1992] ICJ Reports 351.

[77] Schulte, *Compliance with Decisions*, at 121 (*Right of Passage*), 152 (*Fisheries Jurisdiction*), 199 (*Nicaragua*), 218 (*Land, Island and Maritime Frontier Dispute*).

[78] Ibid., 95 (*Corfu Channel*), 169–170 (*Hostages*).

[79] Ibid., 107–109.

[80] Ibid., 129.

negotiations the parties could 'profit from the assistance and expertise of a third party', hinting that this should be the European Commission.[81] Procedures such as good offices and mediation remain widely available.

Interpreting Article 94(2) as excluding the jurisdiction of the ICJ – or of other adjudicators – to deal with cases in which disputes arise following a judgment is thus unsustainable, unless one maintains that the character of the dispute changes with the issuing of a final judgment, so that it acquires a 'political' nature and does not admit of future adjudication. This however must be argued independently, without recourse to Article 94(2). In other disputes, the ICJ has been clear that the political elements of a dispute do not impinge on the Court's jurisdiction to consider its legal aspects. As the ICJ stated in *Nicaragua (Contras)*, '[t]he Council has functions of a political nature assigned to it, whereas the Court exercises purely judicial functions. Both organs can therefore perform their separate but complementary functions with respect to the same events'.[82]

The claim that the existence of Article 94(2) fundamentally alters the partition of roles between the ICJ and the Security Council misinterprets the *permission* for states to have recourse to the Council as a *prohibition* of recourse to adjudication. Given the widespread practice of resorting to third parties for guidance after judgments, this would imply that the *only* means of peaceful dispute settlement under Article 33 of the UN Charter that UN members are precluded from resorting to, following a final ICJ judgment, is judicial dispute settlement. Besides being conceptually flawed, this view is contradicted by the very jurisprudence of the PCIJ and ICJ discussed in this chapter that addresses various legal aspects of compliance disputes: *Mavrommatis (Readaptation)*, *Chorzów Factory*, *Lighthouses in Crete and Samos*, *Haya de la Torre*, and *Alleged Violations*.

8.3.1.2 Regional Courts and Political Bodies: Between Effectiveness of Law and Separation of Powers

Regional ICs have faced similar objections to their jurisdiction over compliance matters, grounded in the relevant political bodies' stated

[81] *Gabčíkovo-Nagymaros Project*, ICJ Reports 1997, p. 7, 79 ('both Parties have called upon the assistance of the Commission of the European Communities . . . after the present Judgment is given . . . both Parties can profit from the assistance and expertise of a third party'). See Schulte, *Compliance with Decisions*, at 246.

[82] *Military and Paramilitary Activities in and against Nicaragua (Jurisdiction)*, *Nicaragua* v. *United States of America*, [1984] ICJ Reports 392, p. 435. See also *United States Diplomatic and Consular Staff in Tehran*, *United States of America* v. *Iran*, Judgment, [1980] ICJ Reports 3, p. 22.

competence to oversee implementation. As regards the ECtHR, under Article 46(2), final ECtHR judgments are to be 'transmitted to the Committee of Ministers, which *shall* supervise its execution'. Thus, contrary to Article 94(2) of the UN Charter, the European Convention on Human Rights (ECHR) Article 46 is cast in obligatory language. With the addition of Protocol No 14 in 2010, ECHR Article 46(4) now empowers the Committee of Ministers of the Council of Europe (CoM), in cases in which a state 'refuses to abide by a final judgment', to notify that state and, by a two-thirds majority, 'refer to the Court the question whether that Party has failed to fulfil its obligation' to comply with judgments. Pursuant to Article 46(5), a positive answer from the ECtHR means that the case is sent back to the CoM 'for consideration of the measures to be taken'. A negative answer obliges the Committee to 'close its examination of the case'.

In the pre-Protocol No 14 case *Lyons* v. *United Kingdom*, the applicants claimed that the method of compliance chosen by the UK failed to grant them a fair trial and an effective remedy for breach, as required by the ECHR. The ECtHR found that the CoM was the sole entity competent to supervise compliance:

> subject to monitoring by the Committee of Ministers, the respondent State remains free to choose the means by which it will discharge its legal obligation under Article 46 of the Convention, provided that such means are compatible with the conclusions set out in the Court's judgment. . . . For its part, *the Court cannot assume any role in this dialogue.*[83]

This jurisprudence changed in the 2009 Judgment in *Verein Gegen Tierfabriken Schweiz (VgT)* v. *Switzerland (No 2)* issued before Protocol No 14 came into force in 2010. This case was brought to the ECtHR after an initial judgment in 2001 had found a breach by Switzerland of its ECHR obligations.[84] Switzerland objected to the second application, arguing that a new involvement of the Court, after the ECHR's final judgment on the matter in 2001 and a resolution of the CoM in 2003, would 'impinge[] on the basic principle of the separation of powers between the Court and the Committee of Ministers'.[85] The ECtHR Grand Chamber disagreed.

[83] *Lyons and Others* v. *United Kingdom*, [2003] Fourth Decision on Admissibility (emphasis added).

[84] *Verein gegen Tierfabriken Schweiz (VgT)* v. *Switzerland (Merits)*, [2001] ECHR 412, para. 79.

[85] *Verein gegen Tierfabriken Schweiz (VgT)* v. *Switzerland (No 2) (Merits)*, [2009] IHRL 3673, para. 49.

It reasoned that it was being tasked with assessing not the already-adjudicated facts but 'relevant new information in the context of a fresh application'. Additionally, the Committee had 'ended its supervision of the execution of the Court's judgment of 28 June 2001'.[86] Rejecting (by majority) the argument that the existence of the earlier judgment deprived it from jurisdiction *ratione materiae*, the Court noted that the CoM had not considered relevant factual developments taking place after its earlier judgment.

As regards Protocol No. 14, Switzerland also claimed in *Verein Gegen Tierfabriken Schweiz (VgT)* v. *Switzerland (No 2)* that, once it entered into force, the Court would be obliged to consider inadmissible further applications concerning the matter dealt with in its judgments, as only the Committee of Ministers would be able to institute 'infringement proceedings', and only 'in cases where a State persistently refused to abide by a final judgment'.[87] In a judgment subsequent to this protocol entering into force, however, the Court did not consider that the new provisions had this effect.

In *Ivanţoc* v. *Moldova and Russia*, the applicants claimed that the conditions of their detention had not changed after the Court had, in *Ilaşcu* v. *Moldova and Russia*, ordered the parties to 'take every measure to put an end to the arbitrary detention of the applicants'.[88] Pointing to the *Lyons* v. *United Kingdom* jurisprudence, the defendants requested that the Court declare the application inadmissible, on grounds that the Committee of Ministers was the competent organ to deal with implementation.[89] In response, the ECtHR stated that the role of the CoM in implementation did not exclude the possibility of the Court dealing with a *new application* on the matter. A continuing violation could give rise to new violations and further responsibility of the offenders:

> [T]he powers assigned to the Committee ... will not be encroached on where the Court has to deal with relevant new information in the context of a fresh application. ... in the specific context of a continuing violation ... it is not unusual for the Court to examine a second application concerning a violation of [the same] right in the subsequent period.[90]

One particularity of *Ivanţoc* v. *Moldova and Russia* was that the Committee of Ministers, after issuing recommendations concerning

[86] Ibid., paras. 67–68.
[87] Ibid., para. 50.
[88] *Ilaşcu* v. *Moldova and Russia*, [2004] ECHR 318, para. 490.
[89] *Ivanţoc* v. *Moldova and Russia*, [2012] ECHR, paras. 69–72.
[90] Ibid., paras. 84–87.

implementation of *Ilaşcu* v. *Moldova and Russia*, had itself decided to 'suspend its examination of this case and to resume it after the final determination of the new application' by the Court.[91] Although not exercising its power to request a decision on compliance under Article 46(4), the CoM had deferred to the Court on the matter, recognising that an authoritative judicial decision could contribute to the solution of the dispute.

This jurisprudence may be contrasted with that of regional adjudicators that reject the prospect of engaging in 'enforcement', pointing to the separation between their adjudicatory powers and the enforcement or rulings by political bodies or through inter-state mechanisms. The CACJ, in *Sánchez Herrera* v. *Guatemala*, summarily found that it could not adjudicate on compliance, but did not provide a reasoning; it simply referred the matter to domestic courts and Central American political bodies.[92] The ECCJ inferred from the lack of specific jurisdiction over compliance, combined with the potential for the ECOWAS Authority of Heads of State to sanction member states and the enforceability of rulings before domestic courts, that plaintiffs were barred from requesting adjudication on compliance with prior rulings. In *Chude Mba* v. *Ghana*, the ECCJ held that the ability granted to the Authority 'to take action to enforce' ECCJ rulings – even if the decision granting the Authority this ability does not touch upon ECCJ powers[93] – precluded the plaintiff from seeking to 'compel[] through the hands of this court' other ECOWAS member states and political bodies 'to perform their assigned treaty obligations of applying sanctions' against the non-complying state.[94]

The question was considered to be one of *locus standi*. Individuals may only bring to the ECCJ claims against an ECOWAS member state for

[91] CoE Committee of Ministers, Interim Resolution CM/ResDH(2007)106, 12 July 2007.

[92] CACJ, *Case No. 2-23-3-2018 (Gilmar Othmar Sánchez Herrera* v. *Guatemala) (Contempt of Court and Non-compliance)*, Judgment, 17 July 2019, p. 2: 'Póngase en conocimiento de las Cortes Supremas de Justicia de los Estados del Sistema de la Integración Centroamericana (SICA), a la Corte Constitucional de la República de Guatemala y al Secretario General del Sistema de la Integración Centroamericana (SICA)'.

[93] ECOWAS, *Supplementary Act A/SP.13/02/12 on Sanctions against Member States that Fail to Honour their Obligations to ECOWAS* (Act 2-SP13 of 2012) (17 February 2012).

[94] ECCJ, Application No. ECW/CCJ/APP/22/16, *Chude Mba* v. *Republic of Ghana and Others*, Judgment, 12 March 2019 (ECW/CCJ/JUD/30/18), p. 17–18. See also Application No. ECW/CCJ/APP/12/15, *Aziagbede and Others* v. *Republic of Togo*, Judgment, 6 December 2016 (ECW/CCJ/JUD/29/16); Application No. ECW/CCJIAPP/20/21; *Sambo Dasuki* v. *Federal Republic of Nigeria*, Judgment, 6 June 2024 (ECW/CCJ/JUD/19/24), paras. 25–31.

violations of their human rights. Within the ensuing proceedings, individuals may obtain Declarations of Breach and Consequential Duties, which must be enforceable before the domestic courts of the member state.[95] Under ECCJ jurisprudence, however, unless non-compliance involves an additional violation of human rights, individuals may not bring claims for non-compliance with ECCJ judgments.[96] As the ECtHR jurisprudence examined above shows, however, it is not clear that specific procedures empowering certain organs to act specifically to address non-compliance deprive others from seising the adjudicator through regular procedures, with claims that relate to the facts and violation addressed in a previous judgment.

The issue remains contested at the AfCHPR, which enshrined in its 2020 Rules of Court a procedure to address non-compliance.[97] In *Noudehouenou* v. *Benin*, the AfCHPR declared Benin's 'failure to comply with the Court's decisions'[98] but rejected the applicant's request for monetary compensation from Benin, reasoning that the Council of Ministers was tasked with monitoring the execution of judgment and it could not issue 'coercive measures compelling the Respondent State to enforce the decisions'.[99]

Individual AfCHPR Judges expressed divergent views on the matters. Judge Adjei stated that the Court should have rejected the claim entirely. Non-compliance, he argued, is not a violation of human or people's rights but a procedural violation, and does not 'entitle[] the Court to award reparations against the State for failing to comply with the judgment'. Instead, he argued, the 'procedure prescribed by [the AfCHRP] Protocol is to request the Council of Ministers to monitor the execution'[100] Judge Chafika expressed the opposite view, reasoning that '[t]he jurisdiction of the Court on the enforcement of its decisions is clearly enshrined and affirmed' in the 2020 Rules of Court, making it the 'enforcement judge of its decisions', and one that 'cannot decide *infra*

[95] ECOWAS, Protocol A/P.l/7/91 of 6 July 1991on the Community Court of Justice, as amended by Supplementary Protocol A/P.1/01/05 of 19 January 2005, Articles 10, 24.

[96] ECCJ, Application No. ECW/CCJ/APP/09/13, *Karim Meissa Wade* v. *Republic of Senegal*, Judgment, 19 July 2013 (ECW/CCJ/JUD/19/13), para. 83.

[97] See Section 7.5.2.3.

[98] AfCHPR, *Application 028/2020 (Houngue Eric Noudehouenou* v. *Republic of Benin)*, Judgment, 1 December 2022, para. 168.

[99] Ibid., para. 167.

[100] Ibid. (Judge Adjei, diss.), p. 3.

petita when it is requested to decide on the non-enforcement of its decisions'.[101]

8.3.1.3 *Judicial Compliance Proceedings and New Claims:* US/Canada – Continued Suspension

Not all dedicated enforcement procedures are 'political' in the sense that they are conducted without the involvement of adjudicators. At the WTO, the compliance control and enforcement procedure involves WTO panels, arbitrators, and the Dispute Settlement Body (DSB).[102] Even there, a debate arose regarding whether the specific Dispute Settlement Understanding (DSU) procedure for compliance adjudication precludes bringing before a new panel a dispute regarding compliance with prior DSB rulings. Employing a similar reasoning to that used for compliance surveillance by political bodies, it might be argued that a dedicated procedure for disputes on compliance is exclusive, preventing a claimant from filing a fresh claim with the same purpose. The fact that an adjudicator rather than a political body is competent to examine compliance matters means that the argument that these bodies 'perform separate but complementary functions'[103] does not apply.

However, a WTO panel and the Appellate Body rejected this interpretation in *US/Canada – Continued Suspension*, brought by the European Communities (EC). The EC claimed that its asserted compliance with the DSB report in *EC – Hormones* required the complainants in that dispute (the United States and Canada) to cease applying the Permissible Response of WTO retaliation, authorised by the WTO DSB following EC non-compliance with the original rulings. Rather than initiating a dispute on compliance, the EC argued that the presumption of good faith operated in its favour. In its view, the United States and Canada should cease applying retaliation and request a compliance panel under DSU Article 21.5. To demand performance of these alleged obligations, the EC started fresh WTO proceedings, before new panels.

These new WTO panels, in *US/Canada – Continued Suspension*, found that the procedure under Article 21.5 is 'the option naturally coming to mind when it comes to reviewing compliance', but that 'a practicable

[101] Ibid. (Judge Chafika, diss.), p. 4.

[102] See the analysis of this system in Chapter 6.

[103] *Military and Paramilitary Activities in and against Nicaragua (Jurisdiction), Nicaragua* v. *United States of America*, [1984] ICJ Reports 392, p. 435.

alternative' was to bring fresh proceedings.[104] The two panels concluded that, even if making new findings with regard to the EC measures was beyond their terms of reference, they 'should be entitled to determine whether the European Communities ha[d] removed the measure found to be inconsistent with a covered agreement in order to establish whether Article 22.8 has been breached' by the respondents.[105]

On appeal, the Appellate Body confirmed this view. It noted that Article 21.5 establishes 'specific procedures for adjudicating a disagreement as to the consistency with the covered agreements of measures taken by a Member to implement the DSB's recommendations and rulings'.[106] Article 21.5, 'cast in obligatory language', is a 'procedure [that] must be followed' when the parties to a dispute cannot consensually agree to an alternative. The Appellate Body, while acknowledging that Article 21.5, requiring the assessment of the matter by panellists already familiar with the dispute, was 'more efficient', noted that '[a]nother possibility' was recourse to new panel proceedings.[107]

While not expressly endorsing adjudication on compliance within the framework of new proceedings, the Appellate Body upheld the panels' finding that they had jurisdiction to 'consider the compatibility of the . . . implementing measure' with the WTO Agreement initially violated.[108] Because it found the panels' assessment of facts to be faulty, the Appellate Body could not complete the analysis and determine whether substantive compliance had been achieved. In these circumstances, it concluded, the recommendations and rulings adopted by the DSB in *EC – Hormones* 'remain[ed] operative'.[109] Conversely, if its assessment had resulted in a determination that compliance had occurred, this would have caused the authorisation for retaliation to lapse: 'Once substantive compliance has been confirmed through WTO dispute settlement procedures, the authorization to suspend concessions lapses by operation of law (*ipso jure*), because it has been determined that one of the resolutive conditions pursuant to Article 22.8 is fulfilled'.[110]

[104] Panel Reports, *US/Canada – Continued Suspension*, WT/DS320/R, WT/DS321/R, adopted 14 November 2008, para. 7.351-51/7.349-50.

[105] Ibid., para. 7.372/7.369.

[106] Appellate Body Report, *US/Canada – Continued Suspension*, WT/DS320/AB/R, WT/DS321/AB/R, adopted 14 November 2008, paras. 338, 341.

[107] Ibid., paras. 341–344.

[108] Ibid., para. 332.

[109] Ibid., para. 737.

[110] Ibid., para. 310.

In sum, WTO members seeking a ruling on compliance should have recourse to DSU Article 21.5, as the procedure specifically designated for 'disagreement[s] as to the existence or consistency with a covered agreement of measures taken to comply with the recommendations and rulings' of the DSB.[111] If a party requests a new panel for an illegitimate reason (e.g., because it is dissatisfied with the individuals selected for the original panel), perhaps the claim can be rejected in view of the obligation to engage in dispute settlement procedures in good faith.[112] However, there may be legitimate reasons for a party to request a new panel rather than resort to Article 21.5. As in the case of 'political' enforcement mechanisms, the mere existence of a procedure for assessing compliance is not sufficient to preclude a new panel from considering a dispute regarding compliance.

8.3.2 Res judicata and 'Disputes' in Compliance Adjudication

A potential objection to the admissibility of a claim regarding compliance is that this adjudication is precluded by the existence of a prior judicial ruling. This objection can be based on the view that bringing a new claim, or issuing a new ruling, would affect *res judicata*. It can also be grounded in the understanding that, if the wrongdoer simply does not change its conduct following a final ruling, or if it admits to non-compliance, there is no 'dispute' to adjudicate on. This section considers these objections.

8.3.2.1 Res judicata as an Obstacle to Compliance Adjudication

The doctrine of *res judicata* prevents re-litigation of issues determined with finality in prior adjudicatory decisions, acting as an obstacle to the admissibility of repeated claims. *Res judicata* has long been acknowledged by international legal scholars as a general principle of law.[113] Within the Advisory Committee of Jurists that drafted the PCIJ Statute, Lord Phillimore described the 'general principles of law', a source of law to applied by the future Court under Article 38(1)(c) of its Statute, as comprising those principles 'which were accepted by all nations in *foro*

[111] DSU, Article 21.5.

[112] Within WTO dispute settlement, this obligation is codified in DSU Article 3.10 ('if a dispute arises, all Members will engage in these procedures in good faith in an effort to resolve the dispute').

[113] Bin Cheng, *General Principles of Law as Applied by International Courts and Tribunals* (London: Stevens, 1953), 336; Hersch Lauterpacht, *The Development of International Law by the International Court* (London: Steven, 1958), 19, 325–326.

domestico, such as certain principles of procedure, the principle of good faith, and the principle of *res judicata*'.[114]

An early application of *res judicata* in a dispute regarding the implementation of a ruling occurred in 1902, when the Arbitral Tribunal in *Pious Funds* confirmed that an earlier tribunal's award constituted *res judicata*.[115] In *United Nations Administrative Tribunal*, the ICJ termed *res judicata* 'a well-established and generally recognised principle of law'.[116] The Arbitral Tribunal in *Trail Smelter* described it alternatively as 'an essential and settled rule of international law' and 'a principle of international law',[117] while the ICSID Tribunal in *Waste Management* v. *Mexico (No 2)* classified *res judicata* as 'a principle of international law, and even a general principle of law within the meaning of Article 38 (1) (c) of the Statute of the International Court of Justice'.[118]

A decision with the force of *res judicata* produces a twofold effect. First, the judgment or award to which *res judicata* attaches is conclusive, meaning that the judgment or award is final and binding on the parties. The legal interpretations developed in the award are definitive for the parties and the decisions of the adjudicator must be complied with in good faith.[119] In *Socobel*, the PCIJ observed that '[r]ecognition of an award as *res judicata* means nothing else than the recognition of the fact that the terms of that award are definitive and obligatory'.[120]

Second, a decision with the force of *res judicata* is preclusive, in that it precludes adjudication of matters to which *res judicata* attaches, so that 'the subject matter of the judgment or award cannot be re-litigated a

[114] Advisory Committee of Jurists, *Procès-Verbaux of the Advisory Committee of Jurists, June 16–July 24, 1920 with Annexes* (The Hague: Van Langenhuysen, 1920), 642.

[115] *Pious Fund of the* Californias, (1902) 9 RIAA 1, 6.

[116] *Effect of Awards of Compensation Made by the UN Administrative Tribunal*, Advisory Opinion, [1954] ICJ Reports 47, p. 53. See further ICJ jurisprudence on the matter in Iain Scobbie, 'Res Judicata, Precedent, and the International Court: A Preliminary Sketch' (1999) 20 *Australian Journal of International Law* 299, 300–301; August Reinisch, 'The Use and Limits of Res Judicata and Lis Pendens as Procedural Tools to Avoid Conflicting Dispute Settlement Outcomes' (2004) 3 *Law and Practice of International Courts and Tribunals* 37, 45–46.

[117] *Trail Smelter, United States of America* v. *Canada*, (1941) 3 RIAA 1905, 1950.

[118] See *Waste Management, Inc.* v. *Mexico ('Number 2')*, [2002] ICSID Case No. ARB(AF)/00/3), Mexico's Preliminary Objection concerning the Previous Proceedings, 26 June 2002, para. 39.

[119] *Interpretation of Judgments Nos 7 and 8 (Chorzów Factory), Germany* v. *Poland*, Judgment, (1927) PCIJ Ser A No. 13, p. 20.

[120] *Société Commerciale de Belgique, Belgium* v. *Greece*, Judgment, (1939) PCIJ Ser A/B No 78, p. 175.

second time'.[121] This preclusive effect of judgments attaches to international adjudicatory decisions in general.[122] This was highlighted by the Arbitral Tribunal in *Orinoco Steamship Company*:

> The general principle announced in numerous cases is that a right, question or fact *distinctly put in issue and directly determined* by a court of competent jurisdiction as a ground of recovery cannot be disputed.[123]

The extent to which matters have been 'put in issue' or 'determined' in any given decision, and the extent to which reasons given by the adjudicator are part of *res judicata*, can be disputed.[124] Whether a specific point in a decision constitutes *res judicata* is relevant for the purpose of determining whether it may be subject to interpretation proceedings and whether it generates an obligation of compliance.[125] This element also affects the preclusive effect of the final decision.

[121] International Law Association, International Commercial Arbitration, *Interim Report: 'Res Judicata' and Arbitration* (ILA, 2004), p. 2.

[122] Ibid., p. 18. See also International Law Association, Committee on International Commercial Arbitration, *Resolution No 1/2006, Annex 2* ('Recommendations on *res judicata* and Arbitration'); Cheng, *General Principles of Law*, 336.

[123] *Company General of the Orinoco, United States of America* v. *Venezuela*, (1905) 10 RIAA 184, 276 (citing the US Supreme Court).

[124] *Interpretation of Judgments Nos 7 and 8*, (1927) PCIJ Ser A No. 13, p. 23 (Anzilotti, diss.). Anzilotti noted that *res judicata* would attach solely to the 'binding portion of the judgment'. In some cases, international courts and tribunals have limited scope of *res judicata* to that which has been decided in the operative parts. See *Polish Postal Service in Danzig*, Advisory Opinion, (1925) PCIJ Ser B No 11, p. 28–29 ('it by no means follows that every reason given in a decision constitutes a decision'); *Channel Arbitration (Interpretation), United Kingdom* v. *France*, (1978) 54 ILR 139, 170 ('interpretation must genuinely be directed to the question of what it is that has been settled with binding force in the decision, that is in the *dispositif*'). It coexists, however, with a 'broader notion' under which *res judicata* includes not only the operative part of a judgment but also those decisions made by the adjudicator that can be deemed essential for it to have reached its conclusions. *Pious Fund of the Californias*, Award, (1908) 2 AJIL 893, 900 ('all the parts of a judgment or a decree concerning the points debated in the dispute enlighten and mutually supplement each other . . . they all serve to render precise the meaning and the bearing of the *dispositif*'); *Application of the Convention on the Prevention and Punishment of the Crime of Genocide, Bosnia and Herzegovina* v. *Serbia and Montenegro*, Judgment, [2007] ICJ Reports 43, p. 100 ('the 1996 Judgment contained a finding . . . which was necessary as a matter of logical construction . . . The force of *res judicata* attaching to that judgment therefore extends to that particular finding'). But see *Affaire Junghans (Deuxième Partie)*, (1940) 3 RIAA 1883, 1889 ('L'opinion que le juge exprime incidemment, sans la traduire par un dispositif, ne crée toutefois pas, en principe, chose jugée').

[125] See on this Andreas Kulick, 'Article 60 ICJ Statute, Interpretation Proceedings, and the Competing Concepts of Res Judicata' (2015) 28(1) *Leiden Journal of International Law* 73.

It could be argued that a request for compliance adjudication violates the rule *ne bis in idem*, which postulates that, 'as a matter of private justice, no one should be proceeded against twice for the same cause'.[126] In particular, in the broadest version of *res judicata*, the final judgment or award may be understood as the *final* resolution of the dispute, precluding not only new disputes regarding matters decided upon by the tribunal but also new claims relating to the same breach that the claimant *could have* put before the adjudicator but failed to, or chose not to. Under this view, claimants are precluded not only from raising before an adjudicator matters that have already been settled with binding force but also from raising new claims regarding injuries that have already been adjudicated upon.

This broad version of *res judicata* has been applied in international law mostly by claims commissions and administrative tribunals.[127] The Spanish–US Claims Commission adopted this understanding in *Machado*,[128] *Danford Knowlton & Co*,[129] *and Delgado*.[130] In *Delgado*, the Umpire considered that a claim involving a request for new remedies, based on an injury already adjudicated upon (the seizure of the claimant's land), was unwarranted '[e]ven if the claimant did not at the time of the former case ask indemnity . . . he can not have relief by a new claim before a new umpire'.[131] In *Machado*, the Umpire held that:

> the test is whether both claims are founded on the same injury. . . . In consequence claim No 129, as being part of an old claim, can not be presented as a new claim under a new number.[132]

A similar understanding was adopted by the Administrative Tribunal of the International Labour Organization (ILOAT) in *Chen (No 2)*, in which an employee attempted to seise the ILOAT a second time after a first claim had been rejected because the claimant 'had failed to exhaust the internal means of redress'.[133] The Organization of American States

126 William S. Dodge, '*Res Judicata*', Max Planck Encyclopedia of Public International Law, para. 2.

127 For a complete assessment, see Chittharanjan Félix Amerasinghe, *Jurisdiction of International Tribunals* (Leiden: Martinus Nijhoff, 2003), 426–438.

128 *Machado*, (1881) Spanish–United States Claims Commission, in John B. Moore, 3 *International Arbitrations* (1989) 2193, 2194.

129 Ibid., 2194, *Danford Knowlton & Co* (1881).

130 Ibid., 2196, 2199, *Delgado* (1881).

131 Ibid.

132 Ibid., 2194, *Machado* (1881).

133 *Chen (No 2)*, ILO Administrative Tribunal, (1983) Judgment No. 547 (the claim, however, was defective in a number of ways).

(OAS) Administrative Tribunal (OASAT) in *Hernández de Agüero* also agreed to hold a request for a new employment contract, put forward by Mr Hernández de Agüero, 'inadmissible, as *res judicata*', because it 'consider[ed] the matter … to have been settled in Judgment No. 24, of November 16, 1976'.[134]

On the surface, this version of *res judicata* may seem to preclude new claims concerning an already-adjudicated set of facts. However, in the administrative cases above, the claim considered inadmissible in fact involved an attempt by a claimant to reverse a prior decision made by the adjudicator. The preclusive effect of *res judicata* prevents the raising of a claim that aims to frustrate the conclusive effect of the original exercise of adjudication. In the case of requests for compliance adjudication, on the other hand, a claim that relates to the prior decision does not attempt to reverse this decision. Rather, the claimant requests the adjudicator to reaffirm a prior judicial decision determining rights and obligations for the parties. The objective of the claim is not to challenge or modify *res judicata* but to affirm it.

There is some support for the notion that *res judicata* might prevent a compliance claim. Seised with a claim of non-compliance with a prior judgment, the CACJ replied that there was 'no ground for the present claim, as this Court has already ruled on it in the Judgment issued on 31 October'.[135]

However, a request for adjudication on compliance will usually differ from the original request in its constitutive elements. For *res judicata* to apply, three elements must be the same in the two claims: the parties to the new dispute, the object of the request, and the cause of action of the request.[136] These elements were famously laid down by PCIJ Judge Anzilotti in his dissenting opinion in *Interpretation of Judgments No 7 and 8*: parties ('*persona*'), claim or request ('*petitum*'), and cause of action ('*causa petendi*').[137] The same elements were referred to by the Arbitral

[134] *Hernández de Agüero* v. *Secretary General of the Organization of American States*, OASAT, (1980) Judgment No. 51.

[135] CACJ, *Case No. 2-23-3-2018 (Gilmar Othmar Sánchez Herrera* v. *Guatemala) (Contempt of Court and Non-compliance)*, Judgment, 17 July 2019, p. 2: 'No ha lugar a la presente demanda por haberse pronunciado este Tribunal en Sentencia dictada el treinta y uno de octubre de dos mil diecisiete (Expediente No. 7-26-09-2017)'.

[136] See Iain Scobbie, 'Res Judicata, Precedent, and the International Court', 299, 304; Reinisch, 'The Use and Limits of Res Judicata and Lis Pendens', 46.

[137] *Interpretation of Judgments Nos 7 and 8*, (1927) PCIJ Ser A No. 13, p. 23 (Anzilotti, diss.).

Tribunal in *Trail Smelter*, as the 'three traditional elements for identification' of *res judicata*: 'parties, object and cause'.[138]

With regard to the first element, in *Border and Transborder Activities* Honduras objected to the admissibility of Nicaragua's requests, arguing that some of these requests had already been adjudicated upon in *Nicaragua (Contras)*. The ICJ retorted:

> Nor can it be accepted that once the Court has given judgment in a case involving certain allegations of fact, and made findings in that respect, no new procedure can be commenced in which those, as well as other, facts might have to be considered. In any event, it is for the Parties to establish the facts in the present case taking account of the usual rules of evidence, without it being possible to rely on considerations of *res judicata* in another case not involving the same parties[.][139]

An adjudicator may be able to issue a ruling on new facts that emerge between two parties to a dispute adjudicated upon. Similarly, a claim falls outside the scope of *res judicata* when the request for a new judicial decision has an *object* different from that which the previous decision ruled upon, or when the *cause of action* underlying the request is different from that which motivated the prior decision. The relevant jurisprudence will be examined after a related objection is considered: that, unless there is an expressed interpretative dispute regarding the earlier ruling, there is no justiciable 'dispute' at the implementation stage.

8.3.2.2 The Existence of a 'Dispute': Conflicts of Views and of Interests

The question may arise whether, at the post-judgment stage, an acknowledgement by the wrongdoer that the breach persists – for example, because it has been unable to comply with the judgment due to domestic law or politics – or simply their non-objection to the claim of non-compliance precludes further adjudication on the matter. It is common for ICs to refrain from pronouncing on specific issues within a dispute when the parties are in agreement regarding the interpretation of a rule or the character of a fact.[140] On occasion, courts have been confronted with the issue of whether the entire situation submitted to adjudication effectively constituted a 'dispute' upon which a court or tribunal is empowered

[138] *Trail Smelter*, (1941) 3 RIAA 1952.

[139] *Border and Transborder Armed Actions, Nicaragua* v. *Honduras*, Jurisdiction and Admissibility, [1988] ICJ Reports 69, p. 91–92.

[140] See, for example, *Société Commerciale de Belgique*, (1939) PCIJ Ser A/B No 78, p. 174.

to adjudicate. Thus, in *Peace Treaties*,[141] *South West Africa*,[142] *PLO Headquarters*,[143] *Cameroon* v. *Nigeria*,[144] *Liechtenstein* v. *Germany*,[145] and *Georgia* v. *Russia*,[146] the ICJ found the existence of a dispute despite contentions to the contrary by the states allegedly in breach of their obligations. The Arbitral Tribunal in *Air Service Agreement*,[147] ITLOS in *Southern Bluefin Tuna (Provisional Measures)*[148] and the ICSID Tribunal in *AGIP* v. *Congo*[149] reached the same conclusion.

On the other hand, adjudicators have refused to adjudicate in cases in which they found that no meaningful dispute existed between the parties. A judicial ruling must not only address a legal question in the abstract but must have what the ICJ labelled in *Northern Cameroons* 'applicability' or 'forward reach'.[150] In *Nuclear Tests*, the Court held that it cannot adjudicate where 'the objective of the Applicant has in effect been accomplished' and where the dispute has ceased 'to exist at the time when the Court makes its decision'.[151] The Arbitral Tribunal in *Ecuador* v. *United States* found that adjudication can only be exercised where 'the claim on the merits has some implications or consequences for the relations between Parties'.[152]

[141] *Interpretation of Peace Treaties with Bulgaria, Hungary and Romania*, Advisory Opinion (First Phase), [1950] ICJ Reports 65, p. 74.

[142] *South West Africa, Ethiopia* v. *South Africa*, Preliminary Objections, [1962] ICJ Reports 319, p. 329.

[143] *Applicability of the Obligation to Arbitrate under Section 21 of the United Nations Headquarters Agreement of 26 June 1947*, Advisory Opinion, [1988] ICJ Reports 12, p. 27–30.

[144] *Land and Maritime Boundary between Cameroon and Nigeria, Nigeria* v. *Cameroon*, Preliminary Objections, [1998] ICJ Reports 275, p. 316.

[145] *Certain Property, Liechtenstein* v. *Germany*, Preliminary Objections, [2005] ICJ Reports 6, p. 19.

[146] *Case concerning the Application of the International Convention on the Elimination of All Forms of Racial Discrimination, Georgia* v. *Russia*, Preliminary Objections, [2011] ICJ Reports 70, p. 120.

[147] *Air Service Agreement, United States of America* v. *France*, (1978) 18 RIAA 417, 426, 433 (the Tribunal, however, drew attention to the formal character of its decision: 'advisory report').

[148] *Southern Bluefin Tuna, New Zealand – Japan, Australia – Japan (Provisional Measures)*, ITLOS, (1999) 38 ILM 1624, 1632.

[149] *AGIP S.p.A.* v. *People's Republic of the Congo*, [1982] ICSID Case No. ARB/77/1) / (1982) 21 ILM 726, 730.

[150] *Northern Cameroons*, [1963] ICJ Reports 15, p. 37.

[151] *Nuclear Tests, Australia* v. *France*, [1974] ICJ Reports 253, 270; *Nuclear Tests, New Zealand* v. *France*, [1974] ICJ Reports 457, 476.

[152] *Ecuador* v. *United States*, (2012) PCA Case No 2012-05, para. 189.

Charges that, at the implementation stage, there is no meaningful dispute left to adjudicate seem intrinsically connected to the view that judicial remedies have no added value at this stage and what is required is political action. The issue of remedies available at this stage, including a declaration of non-compliance, is considered in Section 8.4. This section considers whether a 'dispute' can exist in the absence of express opposition by a wrongdoer to the prevailing claimant's view that the wrongdoer has failed to address its unlawful conduct. Shabtai Rosenne acknowledged that there is 'no reason in principle' why a dispute concerning the execution of an ICJ judgment could not, 'in the appropriate circumstances, constitute a "legal question"', but considered only the possibility that the Security Council or General Assembly might request an advisory opinion.[153] However, if a legal question exists and an IC has jurisdiction over it, there is little sense in institutional organs being entitled to request the IC to pronounce on the issue while the original claimant is precluded from bringing the same question to the court.

A parallel may be drawn with the argument of the United States in *Avena (Request for Interpretation)*.[154] After the ICJ's judgment in *Avena*, the US Supreme Court recognised that the ICJ judgment imposed international obligations on the United States but also held that it was not directly applicable under US law due to the Federal distribution of competences. This prevented the US president from giving effect to the judgment through a Presidential Memorandum, and the Supreme Court itself from affording a remedy to inmates in Texas.[155] The United States claimed that it agreed with Mexico's interpretation of the *Avena* judgment – that the judgment imposed 'an obligation of result' on the United States – and that therefore no dispute regarding the interpretation of the judgment existed.[156] The ICJ formulated the relevant legal question in terms of whether, in spite of the statements of the United States and of its courts, there was a 'difference of perception' between the parties regarding the interpretation of the judgment, and concluded that

[153] Shabtai Rosenne, *The Law and Practice of the International Court 1920 – 2005*, 4th edn (Leiden: Martinus Nijhoff, 2006), 211.

[154] One may consider this in relation to *Chorzów Factory*, too, although Poland never claimed that its acknowledgement impinged on the jurisdiction of the Court.

[155] Jesse Townsend, 'Medellín Stands Alone: Common Law Nations Do Not Show a Shared Postratification Understanding of the ICJ', (2009) 34 *Yale Journal of International Law* 463–497.

[156] *Request for Interpretation of the Judgment of 31 March 2004 in the Case concerning Avena and Other Mexican Nationals, Mexico* v. *United States of America*, Judgment, [2009] ICJ Reports 3, p. 9.

Mexico's claims did not concern the interpretation of the judgment itself but its effects in the US legal order.[157]

The existence of a 'difference of perception' between the parties may be a key issue in requests for interpretation. In these cases, the absence of a stated disagreement between the parties as regards the interpretation of the judgment may mean that courts should not exercise jurisdiction. With regard to other disputes, however, 'differences of perception' constitute solely one out of two possibilities for disputes that states may take to ICs and tribunals.

The definition of dispute established by the PCIJ in *Mavrommatis*, and cited as authoritative on a number of occasions by the ICJ[158] and arbitrators,[159] is that a dispute is 'a disagreement on a point of law or fact, a conflict of legal views or interests between two persons'.[160] This definition allows for two distinct types of disputes to be adjudicated. First are disagreements between the parties, whereby a respondent contradicts the allegations of the claimant concerning the interpretation of the law or facts in question. Second are disputes concerning conflicts *of legal interests*: cases in which, despite the representatives of the parties not asserting opposite legal positions, the conduct of one of them allegedly contradicts its obligations under the applicable law.

Even as regards the first category, the existence of a dispute is not determined by each individual party any more than the interpretation of its conduct is. In case the parties disagree as to the existence of a dispute, the question may be submitted to adjudication for 'objective determination',[161] grounded in the circumstances of the case. In *Cameroon* v. *Nigeria*, the ICJ explained that:

> a disagreement on a point of law or fact, a conflict of legal views or interests, or the positive opposition of the claim of one party by the other need not necessarily be stated *expressis verbis*. In the determination of the existence of a dispute, as in other matters, the position or the attitude of a party can be established by inference, whatever the professed view of that party.[162]

157 Ibid., p. 20.

158 See *Case concerning the Application of the International Convention – Georgia* v. *Russia*, Preliminary Objections, [2011] ICJ Reports 70, p. 84.

159 See *Ecuador* v. *United States*, Award, (2012) PCA Case No 2012-05, Award, para. 189.

160 *Mavrommatis Palestine Concessions, Greece* v. *Great Britain*, Preliminary Objections, (1924) PCIJ Ser A No 2, p. 11.

161 *Interpretation of Peace Treaties with Bulgaria, Hungary and Romania*, [1950] ICJ Reports 65, p. 74.

162 *Land and Maritime Boundary between Cameroon and Nigeria*, [1998] ICJ Reports 275, p. 315.

Thus, the existence of a dispute depends on the conduct of the responding party as much as on the views it expresses. In *Georgia* v. *Russia*, the ICJ held that the existence of a dispute 'may be inferred from the failure of a State to respond to a claim in circumstances where a response is called for'.[163] Similarly, the Arbitral Tribunal in *Ecuador* v. *United States* found that 'positive opposition' may be inferred 'when a State remains silent when faced a serious allegation of breach of its international obligations or when the situation presents mutually exclusive binary alternatives, one of which may be discarded as unreasonable'.[164]

Contrary to requests for authoritative interpretation of previous rulings, compliance disputes involve an alleged breach. In this case, the admissibility of a claim of non-compliance does not depend on the alleged wrongdoer openly contesting this allegation. It is its conduct rather than its words that is determinative. In *Peace Treaties*, the ICJ noted that a dispute may concern not only a difference between stated views but also the 'question of the performance or non-performance of certain treaty obligations'.[165] To establish the existence of a dispute, it should be sufficient for a claimant to state before the adjudicator the specific duty that, in its view, falls on the respondent, and to point to the conduct that would constitute 'non-performance' of this obligation. It then falls upon the adjudicator to ascertain whether a violation has taken place, consider any defences, and accordingly issue a Declaration of Breach and derive from this finding the applicable Consequential Duties or Permissible Responses.

8.4 Adjudicating and Remedying Non-Compliance

Compliance adjudication must produce concrete legal effects between the parties. As the ICJ stated in *Northern Cameroons*, adjudication must entail 'some practical consequence in the sense that it can affect existing legal rights or obligations of the parties, thus removing uncertainty from

163 *Case concerning the Application of the International Convention – Georgia* v. *Russia*, Preliminary Objections, [2011] ICJ Reports 70, p. 84.

164 *Ecuador* v. *United States*, (2012) PCA Case No 2012-05, para. 223. The Arbitral Tribunal cautioned that, in the absence of an alleged breach, inference of 'positive opposition' amounting to a dispute 'is warranted only when all other reasonable interpretations of the respondent's conduct and surrounding facts can be excluded' (Ibid.).

165 *Interpretation of Peace Treaties with Bulgaria, Hungary and Romania*, [1950] ICJ Reports 65, p. 74.

their legal relations'.[166] This means that seising an IC a second time to adjudicate on compliance should not result in a redundant ruling. If the IC is asked merely to restate legal points that have already been settled at the original adjudication, the charge that compliance adjudication lacks practical consequences, that it intervenes in a settled dispute, and even that it impinges upon *res judicata*, may become credible.

This section considers techniques and procedures developed, by complainants and ICs, to avoid these charges. These include dissociation of the dispute regarding compliance (or 'subsequent breach') from the original dispute regarding breach, as well as requests for, and determinations of, judicial remedies that target specifically, or respond to, non-compliance following the original rulings.

8.4.1 *Declarations of Non-Compliance as Distinctive Claims*

At the implementation stage, a claim of non-compliance focuses not on the original breach but on the respondent's alleged failure to comply with the original ruling. While the claim may involve a similar request – for instance, asserting that certain conduct constitutes a breach of international obligations – the request can be based on a different cause of action. Approaches adopted by ICs with this effect include (1) ascertaining the respondent's failure to fulfil the obligation to comply with the earlier judgment, which is distinct from the original substantive obligation, and (2) adjudicating upon the subsequent breach, that is, upon the portion of the violation that occurred after the original judgment, and thus was not originally adjudicated upon.

8.4.1.1 Claims with Different Causes of Action: The Obligation to Comply

Most treaties establishing adjudicatory bodies or setting up frameworks for ad hoc adjudication expressly provide for an obligation to comply with adjudicatory decisions.[167] Clauses providing for the 'final and binding' status of judgments are possibly redundant for the purpose of making judicial decisions obligatory.[168] The binding character of these

[166] *Northern Cameroons*, [1963] ICJ Reports 15, 34.
[167] See Section 2.2.1.
[168] See ICJ, *Navigational and Related Rights, Costa Rica* v. *Nicaragua*, [2009] ICJ Reports 213, 267: 'when the Court has found that the conduct of a State is of a wrongful nature, and in the event that this conduct persists on the date of the judgment, the State

decisions is a function of the very concept of judicial dispute settlement, grounded on the tenet *pact sunt servanda*. E. K. Nantwi noted that 'refusal to comply with the judgment of an international tribunal is *ipso facto* a breach of an international obligation'.[169] On the other hand, these provisions expressly make compliance with judgments an independent treaty obligation to which states have subscribed and by which they must abide. As the CCJ put it in *TCL* v. *Guyana*, 'acts of disobedience constitute a breach of the Court's Order and consequently a breach of [the] obligation to obey the Court's Order promptly'.[170] In *Noudehouenou* v. *Benin*, the AfCHPR found 'a violation of Article 30 of the Protocol [requiring compliance with judgments] by virtue of the Respondent's failure to comply with the Court's decisions'.[171]

Both the PCIJ and the ICJ have acknowledged compliance issues, while avoiding the language of 'non-compliance'. The PCIJ stated that the object of *Chorzów Factory* was to ascertain the Consequential Duties arising from non-compliance with its ruling in *Certain German Interests*, where it had found '[t]he nonconformity of Poland's attitude in respect of the two Companies with Article 6 and the following articles of the Geneva Convention'.[172] Germany described its new claim as an 'appeal to the Court in regard to the execution of that judgment',[173] brought to the PCIJ after Poland declared that it was 'unable to comply for reasons of fact and of law' with the PCIJ's ruling.[174] Regarding the possible overlap between this case and *Certain German Interests*, the PCIJ noted that in *Chorzów Factory* it was asked to examine the dispute 'from a point of view which the Court ha[d] not hitherto had to concern itself, namely, that of the nature – and, if necessary, the amount and method of payment – of the reparation which may be due by Poland' as a result

concerned is obliged to cease it immediately. This obligation to cease wrongful conduct derives both from the general obligation of each State to conduct itself in accordance with international law and from the specific obligation upon States parties to disputes before the Court to comply with its judgments'.

169 E. K. Nantwi, *The Enforcement of International Judicial Decisions and Arbitral Awards in Public International Law* (Leiden: Sijthoff, 1966), 123.

170 CCJ, *Trinidad Cement Limited and TCL Guyana Incorporated* v. *Guyana (Non-compliance/Contempt)*, CCJ Application No 2 of 2009 (Original Jurisdiction), Judgment, 29 March 2010, para. 24.

171 AfCHPR, *Application 028/2020 (Houngue Eric Noudehouenou* v. *Republic of Benin)*, Judgment, 1 December 2022, para. 162.

172 *Factory at Chorzów (Jurisdiction), Germany* v. *Poland*, (1927) PCIJ Ser A No 9, p. 27.

173 Ibid., p. 16–17.

174 Ibid., p. 16.

of its breach.[175] The difference in the remedies requested was therefore sufficient to set the two cases apart.

In *Haya de la Torre*, the ICJ stated that its earlier judgment in *Asylum* entailed for the parties 'the obligation of compliance', while refusing to clarify what this obligation entailed or assessing compliance.[176] In *Alleged Violations*, the ICJ avoided declaring expressly Colombia's non-compliance with its 2012 judgment in *Territorial and Maritime Dispute*. At the same time, the Court agreed with Nicaragua that Colombia had, on a number of instances, 'breached its international obligation to respect Nicaragua's maritime zones as delimited by the Court in its 2012 Judgment', and called upon Colombia to 'bring [its laws] into conformity' with international law as declared in the 2012 judgment.[177] The ICJ thus seems more comfortable declaring the premise – that complying with its judgment is obligatory – than stating the logical consequence: that non-compliance constitutes a legal breach.

The PCIJ and the ICJ have adopted a similar approach to disputes involving prior arbitral awards. In *Socobel*, Belgium requested the PCIJ to adjudge and declare that Greece '[wa]s bound in law to execute' two arbitral awards issued in favour of *Société commerciale de Belgique*, a Belgian company. Greece acknowledged the binding character of the awards but requested from the PCIJ a declaration that it was 'materially impossible' for it to execute them.[178] With regard to Belgium's request that the Court establish Greece's obligation to execute the award, the Court noted that this obligation:

> follows logically from the definitive and obligatory character of the arbitral awards. If the awards are definitive and obligatory, it is certain that the Greek Government is bound to execute them and to do so as they stand.[179]

The ICJ has issued decisions to the same effect in cases concerning other adjudicators. In *Award of the King of Spain*, Honduras requested the ICJ to confirm the binding character of the arbitral award made by the King of Spain. It also asked the Court to declare that the 'failure by the Government of Nicaragua to give effect to the Arbitral Award ...

[175] *Factory at Chorzów (Merits), Germany* v. *Poland*, (1928) PCIJ Ser A No. 17, p. 18.
[176] Ibid., p. 79.
[177] *Alleged Violations of Sovereign Rights and Maritime Spaces in the Caribbean Sea, Nicaragua* v. *Colombia*, Judgment, [2022] ICJ Reports 226, p. 295. See Ibid., p. 314, 323, 340.
[178] *Société Commerciale de Belgique*, (1939) PCIJ Ser A/B No 78, p. 164.
[179] Ibid., p. 176.

constitute[d] a breach of an international obligation', and that 'non-execution involve[d] a consequent obligation to make reparation'.[180] Again the Court did not issue a Declaration of Breach or established any Consequential Duty, but limited itself to declaring that the award was 'valid and binding and that Nicaragua [wa]s under an obligation to give effect to it'.[181]

In *Award of 31 July 1989*, Guinea-Bissau seised the ICJ with the aim of obtaining a declaration that an arbitral award between itself and Senegal was null and void. In its counter-memorial, Senegal requested the Court not only to reject Guinea-Bissau's request but also to declare the binding character of the award and the obligation of the parties to apply it. The ICJ found that Guinea-Bissau was under 'the obligation to apply' the Award and that Senegal was 'justified in seeking to require the Government of Guinea-Bissau to apply' it.[182]

As regards remedies, the ICJ has sought to provide guidance while hesitating to engage in remedy escalation. In *Haya de la Torre*, the ICJ refused to provide instructions regarding the manner of implementation of its *Asylum* judgment, while asserting that, since parties are obliged to comply with its judgments, the asylum granted to Mr Haya de la Torre 'ought to have ceased after the delivery of the Judgment' in which the ICJ found that the asylum was unlawful 'and should terminate'.[183] In this case, as in other cases, the Court's decision did not include a Declaration of Breach or a determination of Consequential Duties for the non-complying party, even where, as in *Award of the King of Spain*, this was requested. The ICJ awarded solely Mere Adjudication, providing the parties with authoritative determinations of their rights and obligations and confirming the final and binding character of the previous rulings.

8.4.1.2 Claims with Different Causes of Action: Subsequent Breach

An indirect means of performing de facto compliance adjudication is to assess not a violation of the obligation to comply but the existence of a breach subsequent to the original judgment – including a 'new breach'

180 *Arbitral Award of the King of Spain, Honduras* v. *Nicaragua*, Judgment, [1960] ICJ Reports 192, p. 196.
181 Ibid., p. 217.
182 *Arbitral Award of 31 July 1989, Guinea-Bissau* v. *Senegal*, Judgment, [1991] ICJ Reports 53, p. 75–76 (Senegal did not request other remedies).
183 *Haya de la Torre*, [1951] ICJ Reports 71, p. 83.

that consists entirely in the continuation of the same violation. This approach, employed chiefly by the European Court of Human Rights (ECtHR), avoids conflict with the procedure for political compliance control and 'execution' conducted by the Committee of Ministers of the Council of Europe, established by ECHR Article 46.

ECHR Article 46(2) provides for final ECtHR judgments to be 'transmitted to the Committee of Ministers, which shall supervise [their] execution'. In *Lyons* v. *United Kingdom*, the ECtHR observed that the obligation created by an earlier judgment for the UK was 'to choose, subject to the supervision of the Committee of Ministers, the general and/or, if appropriate, individual measures to be adopted in their domestic legal order to put an end to the violation found by the Court and to redress so far as possible [its] effects'.[184] The applicants had claimed that the UK's chosen method of compliance (a re-trial of the accused resulting in a new condemnation) failed to grant them an effective remedy as required by the ECHR. The ECtHR, however, noted that the UK's breach in *Lyons* was not in condemning the applicants but in the manner in which the trial was conducted. This violation could thus be cured by a new, procedurally appropriate, trial. The Court added that this was 'not to say that the measures taken by a respondent State in the post-adjudication phase … fall outside the jurisdiction of the Court'. The ECtHR safeguarded in this regard both proceedings for just satisfaction[185] and 'a complaint that [the measure taken] by way of implementation of one of its judgments gives rise to a new breach of the Convention'.[186]

Admissibility is particular in the ECtHR because ECHR Article 35(2)(b) precludes adjudication on applications that are 'substantially the same as a matter that has already been examined by the Court', unless there is 'relevant new information'.[187] The failure to implement a ruling, assuming it does not aggravate the situation, may in principle be

[184] Application No. 15227/03, *Lyons and Others* v. *United Kingdom*, [2003] ECHR Fourth Decision on Admissibility. The earlier judgment was Application Nos. 29522/95, 30056/96, and 30574/96, *IJL, GMR and AKP* v. *the United Kingdom*, [2000] Judgment.

[185] See in this regard Application No. 2614/65, *Ringeisen* v. *Austria (Article 50)*, [1972] IHRL 8 (ECHR 1971).

[186] *Lyons and Others* v. *United Kingdom*, [2003] Fourth Decision on Admissibility.

[187] ECHR Art. 35 provides: '2. The Court shall not deal with any application submitted under Article 34 that … (b) is substantially the same as a matter that has already been examined by the Court or has already been submitted to another procedure of international investigation or settlement and contains no relevant new information.'

considered as part of a continuing breach. The underlying logic seems to be that there is little sense in the ECtHR engaging in remedy repetition, and simply adjudicating again on the same breach it already held to be unlawful.

Under the 'new breach' jurisprudence, the ECtHR considers that there are portions of a continuing breach. A condemnatory judgment declares as unlawful, and provides Consequential Duties for, the portion of the breach that occurred prior to this judgment. A continuation of the same breach after the judgment, on the other hand, is not covered by the prior judgment. This allows the Court to de facto exercise jurisdiction over the implementation of a judgment even if, under the rules codified in Articles on Responsibility of States for Internationally Wrongful Acts (ARSIWA), the breach is in fact a continuing one.[188]

This jurisprudence, considering that new ECtHR remedies may be awarded to account for post-judgment violations, generated a condemnation for non-compliance in *Verein Gegen Tierfabriken Schweiz (VgT)* v. *Switzerland (No 2)*. In this case, a specific subsequent development crystallised the 'new breach'. In the original *Verein gegen Tierfabriken Schweiz (VgT)* v. *Switzerland* judgment, the ECtHR had determined that Switzerland's prohibition of 'political advertisement', which prevented the broadcasting of a television commercial promoting vegetarianism, violated the applicant's freedom of expression.[189] Notwithstanding the ECtHR judgment, the prohibition was subsequently upheld by the Swiss Federal Court (i.e., Switzerland's supreme court).

Following a second application, the ECtHR held in *Verein Gegen Tierfabriken Schweiz (VgT)* v. *Switzerland (No 2)* that the refusal by the Swiss Federal Court to reverse the earlier judgment, after it had been condemned as a breach of the ECHR by the ECtHR, constituted 'relevant new information' in the sense of ECHR Article 35(2).[190] While it fell

[188] ARSIWA Article 14(2) provides that a breach 'having a continuing character extends over the entire period during which the act continues and remains not in conformity with the international obligation'. Under Article 14(3), a breach of an obligation 'to prevent a given event occurs when the event occurs and extends over the entire period during which the event continues and remains not in conformity with that obligation'. See *Rainbow Warrior Arbitration, New Zealand* v. *France*, Judgment, (1990) 20 RIAA 215, 263–264.

[189] Application No. 24699/94, *Verein gegen Tierfabriken Schweiz (VgT)* v. *Switzerland (Merits)*, [2001] ECHR 412, para. 79.

[190] Application No. 32772/02, *Verein Gegen Tierfabriken Schweiz (VgT)* v. *Switzerland (No 2) (Merits)*, [2009] IHRL 3673 (ECHR 2009), para. 67.

short of declaring non-compliance with its earlier ruling, the ECtHR held that the ECHR prohibition on limitations to freedom of expression generated 'positive obligations' for the states parties, and concluded that 'the Swiss authorities [had] failed to comply with their positive obligation under Article 10 of the Convention'.[191]

In *Ivanţoc* v. *Moldova and Russia*, the jurisprudence regarding new breaches led to an express finding of non-compliance with a prior judgment, in a case in which the state had not adopted any subsequent intervening measure but simply failed to comply. This case arose following the failure of the defendants to comply with the ECtHR's earlier determination (in *Ilaşcu* v. *Moldova and Russia*) that these states were required, in order to address the violation, to 'put an end to the arbitrary detention of the applicants still detained and to secure their immediate release'.[192] In *Ivanţoc* v. *Moldova and Russia*, Russia requested the rejection of the new application under ECHR Article 35 (2)(b). It argued that the object of the application – the conditions of arrest of the applicants – '[wa]s substantially the same as a matter that ha[d] already been examined by the Court' and that the request 'contain[ed] no relevant new information'.[193]

The ECtHR held that it had 'in principle no jurisdiction to review the general and/or individual measures, if any, adopted by the respondent States to secure the rights of the applicants which the Court found to be violated' in its prior judgment. However, the Court also found that it could 'take account of subsequent factual developments ... which are likely to have a bearing on its findings with regard to, inter alia, the potential responsibility of the respondent Governments in respect of alleged violations' that had occurred after the original judgment.

On these grounds, the ECtHR held that it was competent to examine both claims of continuation of the breach, which 'ha[d] not been previously examined by the Court', and 'the new complaint about the absence of an effective remedy against [the breach] during this period'.[194] It stated that it could:

191 Ibid., para. 98.

192 Application No. 48787/99, *Ilaşcu* v. *Moldova and Russia*, [2004] ECHR 318, para. 490. See Philip Leach, 'Beyond the Bug River – A New Dawn for Redress before the European Court of Human Rights?' (2005) 10 *European Human Rights Law Review* 148.

193 Application No. 23687/05, *Ivanţoc* v. *Moldova and Russia*, [2012] ECHR, para. 85.

194 Ibid., paras. 91–93.

> in the specific context of a continuing violation of a Convention right following adoption of a judgment in which the Court has found a violation of that right during a certain period of time ... examine a second application concerning a violation of that right in the subsequent period'.[195]

Thus, while the ECtHR may not exercise compliance adjudication based on the obligation to comply itself, it may exercise jurisdiction based on continuing violations of the ECHR, with substantively equivalent effects. In *Ivanţoc* v. *Moldova and Russia*, the Court offered an additional reason for its ruling. It noted in this regard that, were it to find itself without jurisdiction over the issue due to its prior judgment, 'not only would this matter escape all scrutiny under the Convention, but the applicants would be deprived, in case of a finding of a violation, of the just satisfaction' for the period of their detention that followed the first judgment awarding this form of reparation.[196]

This reasoning would seem to apply more broadly. If non-compliance consists in the original breach persisting after the final judgment, this means that a set of facts that constitutes a breach has not been pronounced unlawful – has not been the object of a Declaration of Breach – and the corresponding Consequential Duties have not been established. As a consequence, even where non-compliance derives not from a positive act but from the mere absence of implementing conduct, a party may file a new claim concerning the portion of the breach that took place after the original judgment.

8.4.2 *Concrete Effects of Post-Judgment Remedies: The Search for Remedy Escalation*

Drawing distinctions between the Declaration of Breach and a declaration of non-compliance is useful from a procedural perspective, allowing ICs to avoid charges of *bis in idem* or offence to *res judicata*. ICs may declare 'an aggravated violation', 'aggravated non-compliance' or 'contempt of court'.[197] This distinction can also serve to provide a

[195] Ibid., para. 87.

[196] Ibid., para. 96.

[197] ECtHR, *Ivanţoc* v. *Moldova and Russia*, [2012] ECHR, para. 144 ('an aggravated violation'); ACJ, *Case No. 118-AI-2003 (Non-compliance with Judgment of 14 April 2005) (Second Summary Procedure)*, Order, 28 November 2022, p. 6 ('desacato agravado'); EACJ, *Sitenda Sebalu* v. *EAC Secretary General*, Reference No. 8 of 2012, Judgment, 22 November 2013, paras. 84(a), (c) (contempt of court).

purely declaratory remedy with 'concrete effects', including in the sense of mobilising additional pro-compliance forces within the wrongdoer, as discussed in Section 4.3. At the same time, repetition of declaratory remedies yields diminishing returns in terms of its ability to mobilise pro-compliance forces; and, especially in the case of wilful non-compliance, an IC repeatedly awarding declarations of non-compliance is likely to seem decreasingly authoritative.[198]

It is thus understandable that claimants requesting compliance, as well as courts consenting to adjudicate on the matter, consider possible instruments allowing remedy escalation in case of non-compliance. Besides refining Mere Adjudication and awarding a Declaration of Breach – whether for the first time or in the form of a declaration of non-compliance – there are, within the typology of remedies introduced in Chapter 1, two possibilities. First, an IC may issue specific Consequential Duties to account for non-compliance. Second, the IC may determine Permissible Responses, authorising, and sometimes enjoining, other states, or international institutions, to adopt Layer 4 or Layer [5] sanctions against the wrongdoer. As this section demonstrates, a number of ICs have engaged in remedy escalation as a response to non-compliance – or have at least affirmed their entitlement to do so.

8.4.2.1 The 'New Breach' Jurisprudence: Challenges of Remedy Escalation

The ECtHR jurisprudence approaching non-compliance as a 'new breach' features a contradiction. The Court invokes a distinction between non-compliance and subsequent breach to counter objections to the admissibility of the fresh claim, in light of the competence of the Committee of Ministers to ensure the execution of ECtHR judgments. The distinctive character of non-compliance may, however, re-emerge in the ECtHR's determination of remedies. There, the Court has expressly taken into account the fact that the violation is a continuing one, and that the wrongdoer has failed to comply with the original judgment, in the determination of Consequential Duties.

One case which straddled the line between a request concerning subsequent breach and an award of specific remedies for non-compliance was *Wasserman* v. *Russia (No 2)*. In the original *Wasserman* v. *Russia* Judgment, the ECtHR found that Russia had not honoured a debt,

[198] See the rulings in *Apitz Barbera et al.* v. *Venezuela (Compliance with Judgment)*, IACtHR, 23 November 2012. See Section 7.5.2.3.

confirmed by a domestic judgment, that it owed to the applicant. Rather than providing compensation, the Court declared that Russia was under the 'obligation to enforce the judgment at issue' and directed the applicant to have recourse to 'domestic enforcement proceedings'.[199] In view of subsequent delays, the applicant returned to the ECtHR demanding a new finding of breach.

In *Wasserman* v. *Russia (No 2)*, Russia contended that, because the case concerned the execution of an earlier judgment, it was to be dealt with by the Committee of Ministers and fell outside the jurisdiction of the Court.[200] The ECtHR agreed that it did not have jurisdiction 'to verify whether a Contracting Party has complied with the obligations imposed on it by one of the Court's judgments'. However, it then applied its 'new breach' jurisprudence, finding that it had jurisdiction to examine 'a subsequent application raising a new issue undecided by the original judgment', including, in the context of a continuing violation, an application relating to the portion of the breach that occurred after the original judgment.[201]

Concluding that Russia had persisted in its violation and had failed to pay the entirety of its debt to the applicant, the ECtHR did not merely issue another order for performance. Instead, it awarded damages. The outstanding part of the debt was only €23 (increased to €350 due to interest); the court added to this €4,000 to account for non-pecuniary damage, mentioning not only the applicant's distress and frustration but also 'the fact that this [wa]s the second application concerning non-enforcement of the same [domestic] judgment'.[202] This additional damage was thus expressly linked to non-compliance.

The ECtHR went further than this in *Ivanţoc* v. *Moldova and Russia*, which arose following non-compliance with the judgment in *Ilaşcu* v. *Moldova and Russia*. Although issuing a judgment on subsequent breach, the Court expressly took into account the conduct of each of the states found in breach after the original judgment. In other words, the ECtHR did not examine the conduct of the respondents simply in light of their substantive ECHR obligations, as interpreted in the prior judgment. Instead, it examined whether the respondents had taken the measures

[199] Application No. 15012/02, *Wasserman* v. *Russia*, [2004] ECHR, para. 49.
[200] Application No. 21071/05, *Wasserman* v. *Russia (No 2)*, [2008] ECHR, para. 29.
[201] Ibid., paras. 31–33.
[202] Ibid., para. 72.

within their power to comply with the judgment – and calibrated its remedies accordingly.

To justify this approach, the ECtHR recalled its finding in *Ilaşcu* v. *Moldova and Russia* that Moldova was under 'a positive obligation . . . to take diplomatic, economic, judicial or other measures' to end the breach. The Court considered that Moldova had taken the measures within its reach to achieve implementation, and had therefore 'discharged its positive obligations', resulting in its responsibility not being engaged.[203]

With regard to Russia, by contrast, the ECtHR found that it had provided 'political, financial and economic support to the separatist regime [in Transnistria]' that carried out the violations, and had done nothing either to put an end to or to prevent the continuation of the violations.[204] In addition to awarding damages as just satisfaction – to be paid solely by Russia – the Court recalled its prior judgment and made an additional finding. In view of 'the disregard by the Russian Federation of the Court's firm injunction' in the previous case, the ECtHR concluded that there had been 'an aggravated violation' of the ECHR, and referred to 'the extreme seriousness of the violations' when determining the amount of just satisfaction.[205]

Thus, the ECtHR in *Wasserman* v. *Russia (No 2)* and *Ivanţoc* v. *Moldova and Russia* claimed not to be engaging in compliance adjudication. At the same time, when awarding remedies for the 'new breach', the Court both issued more grievous remedies (symbolically or materially) than the ones previously awarded and expressly linked this remedy escalation to non-compliance with its prior judgments.

The ECtHR's position appears to rely on wilful blindness by the Court to the character of the 'new breach' brought by the claimant. Other ICs, having identified the new application as an attempt to enforce a previous ruling, have found the request inadmissible. In *Noudehouenou* v. *Benin*, the AfCHPR established Benin's 'failure to comply with the Court's decisions' in prior judgments and ordered Benin to 'take all measures to comply' with the earlier judgment.[206] As regards Consequential Duties, the AfCHPR rejected the applicant's request for monetary compensation from Benin 'for not complying of the judgment of

[203] *Ivanţoc* v. *Moldova and Russia*, [2012] ECHR, paras. 105–111.
[204] Ibid., para 101.
[205] Ibid., paras. 118–120, 144, 150.
[206] AfCHPR, *Application 028/2020 (Houngue Eric Noudehouenou* v. *Republic of Benin)*, Judgment, 1 December 2022, paras. 162, 189.

4 December 2020 as well as the Rulings of provisional measures of 05 May and 25 September 2020'.[207] The AfCHPR's noted:

> [S]uch requests are tantamount to requests for coercive measures compelling the Respondent State to enforce the decisions, which would make it an enforcement judge of its own decisions . . . the Respondent State must comply with the Court's decisions without the need for further coercive measures.[208]

Despite this statement of principle, the AfCHPR also took into account the issue of non-compliance when awarding remedies. While declaring to be refusing to issue remedies for non-compliance, the Court awarded moral damages taking into account 'the violation of [the claimant's] rights . . . as well as the failure by the Respondent State to comply with the Court's decisions concerning him'.[209]

Other ICs have been wary of adjudicating on compliance, suggesting a concern that further remedies would be fruitless or harmful. Like the AfCHPR, these courts have sometimes identified claims for new Consequential Duties with requests for 'coercive' and 'enforcement' measures, concluding that such measures should be taken by their organisations' political bodies. The CACJ's summary dismissal of the claim of non-compliance in *Sánchez Herrera* v. *Guatemala (Compliance)* was accompanied by an instruction to the parties to '[a]dhere to what has been decided in' its previous ruling[210] and a notification of the case to Central American institutions and Guaremala's domestic authorities.[211] In *Chude Mba* v. *Ghana*, although the plaintiff framed his claims as requests for declaratory rulings, the ECCJ concluded: 'The court has no jurisdiction to enforce its own decisions as this action is seeking to do, hence this action will not be entertained by the court'.[212] Despite noting that the plaintiff 'claim[ed] his action is seeking declaratory reliefs' – a declaration of

207 Ibid., para. 167. These rulings were issued in AfCHPR, *Application 003/2020 (Houngue Eric Noudehouenou* v. *Republic of Benin)*, Judgment, 4 December 2020.

208 Ibid., paras. 168–169. Labelling a determination of consequential duties 'coercive' is technically incorrect.

209 Ibid., para. 175.

210 CACJ, *Case No. 2-23-3-2018 (Gilmar Othmar Sánchez Herrera* v. *Guatemala) (Contempt of Court and Non-compliance)*, Judgment, 17 July 2019, p. 2 ('Estese a lo resuelto en la misma').

211 Ibid. See note 91.

212 ECCJ, Application No. ECW/CCJ/APP/22/16, *Chude Mba* v. *Republic of Ghana and Others*, Judgment, 12 March 2019 (ECW/CCJ/JUD/30/18), p. 13.

non-compliance – the Court ruled that he was in effect 'seeking enforcement of the judgment of this Court'.[213]

The reasoning adopted by these courts may be legally sound within their adjudicatory systems. But it is difficult to ignore that they may equally have in mind their fragile position as international institutions adjudicating upon state conduct. As the CCJ put it in *TCL* v. *Guyana*, 'states are the defendants and cannot be imprisoned . . . regional international courts, such as this Court, have no tipstaff or gaols except where treaties so provide'.[214] More than that, the response to perceived excesses by ICs may be to seek to disband the IC entirely, as Zimbabwe managed to achieve with respect to the SADC Tribunal, and the United States with respect to the WTO Appellate Body.[215] At the same time, other adjudicators have identified potential instruments for remedy escalation. These are examined in Section 8.4.2.2.

8.4.2.2 Express Consequences of Non-Compliance: Remedy Repetition and Remedy Escalation

Adjudicators may respond to non-compliance with rulings by seeking to apply, within the limits of their remedial authority, more grievous remedies than those offered for the original violation. An IC that has initially avoided a Declaration of Breach (as the ICJ did in *Territorial and Maritime Dispute*) may decide that this declaration is warranted in the face of persistent breach – as the ICJ did in *Alleged Violations*.[216] A court that has already declared a breach may establish that non-compliance amounts to an aggravated violation (as the ECtHR did in *Ivanţoc* v. *Moldova and Russia*). A court that has refrained from deriving consequences from its Declaration of Breach, in particular by refraining from awarding monetary compensation, may consider that this remedy is warranted in the face of non-compliance (as it did in *Wasserman* v. *Russia (No 2)*).

[213] Ibid., p. 8.

[214] CCJ, *Trinidad Cement Limited and TCL Guyana Incorporated* v. *Guyana (Non-compliance/Contempt)*, CCJ Application No 2 of 2009 (Original Jurisdiction), Judgment, 29 March 2010, para. 40.

[215] See Karen J. Alter, James T. Gathii, and Lawrence R. Helfer, 'Backlash against International Courts in West, East and Southern Africa: Causes and Consequences' (2016) 27 *European Journal of International Law* 293; Geraldo Vidigal, 'Living without the Appellate Body: Multilateral, Bilateral and Plurilateral Solutions to the WTO Dispute Settlement Crisis' (2019) 20 *Journal of World Investment & Trade* 862–890.

[216] *Alleged Violations of Sovereign Rights and Maritime Spaces in the Caribbean Sea, Nicaragua* v. *Colombia*, Judgment, [2022] ICJ Reports 226, p. 366.

This was the approach the PCIJ adopted in *Chorzów Factory*. The Court noted that the indemnity afforded for a factory unlawfully expropriated could not be 'tantamount to rendering lawful liquidation and unlawful dispossession indistinguishable'.[217] In the operative part of its judgment, in which it established Poland's responsibility and the obligation to pay compensation, the Court also highlighted that this obligation arose:

> by reason of the attitude adopted by the Polish Government in respect of the [factory], which attitude has been declared by the Court not to have been in conformity with the provisions of . . . the Geneva Convention[.][218]

The PCIJ itself therefore linked the remedies it awarded not only to the particular character of the breach but also to the existence of a prior judicial ruling finding the conduct unlawful. Though the Court's reasoning regarding reparations has now become a touchstone of international adjudication, the key controversy raised by Poland was whether the PCIJ could employ its jurisdiction to engage in remedy escalation. The Court answered in the affirmative: in light of Poland's non-compliance with the performance obligations derived from the PCIJ's judgment in *Certain German Interests*, the Court declared Poland's responsibility engaged and established, as a Consequential Duty, its obligation to pay compensation to Germany.[219]

Some ICs have sought to engage in symbolic or rhetorical remedy escalation, framing their rulings as declarations of non-compliance or contempt of court. In *Sitenda Sebalu* v. *Secretary General*, the EACJ found that the East African Community institutions had not implemented an earlier ruling. It found three EACJ organs – the Council of Ministers, the Sectoral Committee on Legal Judicial Affairs and the Secretary General – to be in infringement of the EAC Treaty and in contempt of Court for 'failure . . . to implement the Judgment of the Court'.[220] In *TCL* v. *Guyana* , the CCJ concluded that Guyana was 'in breach of the obligation . . . to comply with the Court's judgment promptly'.[221]

[217] *Factory at Chorzów (Merits)*, (1928) PCIJ Ser A No. 17, p. 47.
[218] Ibid., p. 63.
[219] *Factory at Chorzów (Merits)*, (1928) PCIJ Ser A No. 17, p. 63–64.
[220] EACJ, *Sitenda Sebalu* v. *EAC Secretary General*, Reference No. 8 of 2012, Judgment, 22 November 2013, paras. 84(a), (c).
[221] CCJ, *Trinidad Cement Limited and TCL Guyana Incorporated* v. *Guyana (Non-compliance/Contempt)*, CCJ Application No 2 of 2009 (Original Jurisdiction), Judgment, 29 March 2010, para. 21. The condemnation is in para. 54.

Other regional courts have resorted to reporting non-compliance to the corresponding political body. Like the IACtHR,[222] the SADC Tribunal found that it was empowered to consider claims of non-compliance as part of its duty to report on non-compliance to the SADC Summit of Heads of State and Government. In *Gongo* v. *Zimbabwe*, the SADC Tribunal ordered Zimbabwe to pay the applicants compensation for expropriation, as awarded by its domestic courts. The Tribunal treated its power to refer matters to the Summit as a *ultima ratio*, adding that, '[i]n the event of non-compliance with the order made above ... the Applicants may revert to this Tribunal ... for further relief regarding enforcement'.[223] At the same time, the most grievous 'enforcement' instrument available under the Tribunal's procedural rules was to 'report its finding [of non-compliance] to the Summit for the latter to take appropriate action'.[224] The SADC Tribunal employed this last-resort remedy twice, both times against Zimbabwe, before becoming non-operational in 2010.[225]

The ACJ developed a particular form of remedy escalation in the context of long-standing non-compliance by Colombia. One year after the 2005 Judgment in *General Secretariat* v. *Colombia* declared Colombia's trade barriers to Andean countries' rice inconsistent with Andean law,[226] the ACJ issued the remedies it is expressly empowered to award: Permissible Responses in the form of authorised trade retaliation, at a level of 5 per cent additional tariffs on selected Colombian products, by all Andean Community members.[227] Six years later, it increased the level of the authorised retaliatory tariffs to 10 per cent.[228] Faced with continued non-

[222] See Section 7.5.2.3.

[223] *Gongo* v. *Zimbabwe*, Judgment, Case No. SADCT: 05/2008 (SADC, 9 December 2010), para. 46.

[224] SADC, Protocol on the Tribunal in the Southern African Development Community and Rules thereof (in force 7 August 2001, as amended up until 17 August 2008), Article 32 – Enforcement and execution: '4. Any failure by a Member State to comply with a decision of the Tribunal may be referred to the Tribunal by any party concerned. 5. If the Tribunal establishes the existence of such failure, it shall report its finding to the Summit for the latter to take appropriate action.'

[225] *Campbell* v. *Zimbabwe*, Ruling, Case No. SADCT: 11/18 (SADC, 18 July 2008), para. 6; *Fick* v. *Zimbabwe*, Ruling, Case No. SADCT: 01/2010 (SADC, 16 July 2010), para. 8.

[226] ACJ, *Case No. 118-AI-2003 (Secretary-General of the Andean Community* v. *Colombia)*, Judgment, 14 April 2005.

[227] ACJ, *Case No. 118-AI-2003 (Non-compliance with Judgment of 14 April 2005) (Summary Procedure)*, Order, 26 October 2006.

[228] ACJ, *Case No. 118-AI-2003 (Non-compliance with Judgment of 14 April 2005) (Second Summary Procedure)*, Order, 18 July 2012.

compliance, the ACJ expanded the list of products,[229] then requested the Andean Secretariat to explore in writing whether a 30 per cent additional tariff would be appropriate, as well as whether the ACJ was empowered to impose on recalcitrant states a pecuniary fine.[230] This latter remedy escalation, the ACJ reasoned, could be permissible in light of its power to order 'other measures if the restriction or suspension of benefits under the Cartagena Agreement aggravates the situation or is not effective'.[231]

In a subsequent phase of the dispute, Colombia was able to demonstrate compliance with the Andean rules on rice. This did not stop the ACJ from declaring itself 'competent to impose pecuniary fines as sanctions to member states that repeatedly fail to comply with infringement judgments'. The fine was expressly framed as an escalation: 'the fine will be applied subsidiarily, only if the suspension of benefits under the Cartagena Agreement aggravates the situation or is ineffective'.[232]

The CCJ adopted a similar approach in the face of Guyana's longstanding discriminatory environmental tax, even if the discriminatory effect had been declared by Caribbean Community (CARICOM) states rather than previously established by the court.[233] In *Rudisa* v. *Guyana*, the CCJ went beyond establishing Guyana's positive obligation to implement its ruling (in the same judgment) declaring a tax inconsistent with CARICOM commitments. The Court backed this order for performance with the threat of increased pecuniary awards. The CCJ stated that it had a 'responsibility to act as the guardian of the [CARICOM Treaty] and to ensure that States comply with their treaty obligations', reasoning that 'competence to review the legality of acts adopted by Community

[229] ACJ, *Case No. 118-AI-2003 (Non-compliance with Judgment of 14 April 2005) (Second Summary Procedure)*, Order, 28 June 2018.

[230] ACJ, *Case No. 118-AI-2003 (Non-compliance with Judgment of 14 April 2005) (Second Summary Procedure)*, Order, 28 November 2022.

[231] Treaty Creating the Court of Justice of the Andean Community, Article 27, para. 3: 'En todo caso, el Tribunal podrá ordenar la adopción de otras medidas si la restricción o suspensión de las ventajas del Acuerdo de Cartagena agravare la situación que se busca solucionar o no fuere eficaz en tal sentido'. See ACJ, *Case No. 118-AI-2003 (Non-compliance with Judgment of 14 April 2005) (Second Summary Procedure)*, Request for Interpretation, 24 October 2023.

[232] ACJ, *Case No. 118-AI-2003 (Non-compliance with Judgment of 14 April 2005) (Second Summary Procedure)*, Order, 10 October 2023. This was confirmed in ACJ, *Case No. 118-AI-2003 (Non-compliance with Judgment of 14 April 2005) (Second Summary Procedure)*, Request for Interpretation, 24 October 2023.

[233] CCJ, *Rudisa Beverages & Juices N.V. and Caribbean International Distributors Inc.* v. *The Co-operative Republic of Guyana*, Application No. OA 003 of 2013 (Original Jurisdiction), Judgment, 8 May 2014, para. 27.

institutions must perforce include competence to award appropriate relief to private entities that have suffered and established loss as a result of an illegal act or omission on the part of the Community'.[234] The Court concluded that, given a judgment declaring Guyana's policies unlawful and the long history of opportunities to comply, 'Guyana's failure to do so will continue to engage its liability for damage caused'.[235]

In *Jaleel* v. *Guyana*, a case subsequently brought by a different applicant against the same tax, the CCJ issued de facto pecuniary remedies for non-compliance with the *Rudisa* judgment. Identifying the subsistence of the tax, the Court immediately awarded monetary compensation, rather than issuing a declaratory remedy coupled with the threat of financial liability. The CCJ grounded this approach in Guyana's long-standing awareness of its obligations and its persistent breach following the Court's earlier judgment.[236]

8.5 Conclusion

In conclusion, there is in principle no bar to an IC or tribunal assessing a dispute simply because it is a 'compliance' dispute. There is no political question doctrine that would prevent an IC from considering the legal aspects of a dispute that has strong political components. And, as regards admissibility issues related to *res judicata*, *bis in idem*, or political compliance control mechanisms, an IC seised with a compliance dispute may affirm its entitlement to adjudicate on two grounds. First, the obligation to comply with an adjudicatory ruling differs from the substantive obligation whose violation may have been established in the original ruling, making the declaration of non-compliance legally distinct from the original Declaration of Breach. Alternatively, facts taking place subsequent to the issuing of the original ruling may not be covered by this ruling's remedies; they may warrant remedies that were not available, or were not issued, at the time of the original ruling.

[234] Ibid., paras. 26–27 (quoting CCJ, *Trinidad Cement Limited* v. *the Caribbean Community*, CCJ Application No 3 of 2008 (Original Jurisdiction), Judgment, 5 February 2009, para. 43).

[235] CCJ, *Rudisa Beverages & Juices N.V. and Caribbean International Distributors Inc.* v. *The Co-operative Republic of Guyana*, Application No. OA 003 of 2013 (Original Jurisdiction), Judgment, 8 May 2014, para. 38.

[236] CCJ, *SM Jaleel & Co Ltd & Guyana Beverages Inc Claimants and The Co-operative Republic of Guyana*, CCJ Application No. TTOJ2016/001 (Original Jurisdiction), Judgment, 9 May 2017, para. 12.

Even if a judgment nominally relates solely to the subsequent breach – and avoids assessing the breach of the obligation to comply – the challenge to the judicial authority that non-compliance represents is often reflected in the remedies awarded. IC seem to understand, concordantly if not always expressly, that non-compliance demands sterner condemnation, as well as more grievous Consequential Duties than those issued when the unlawful conduct could be excused (no matter how fictitiously) by the absence of legal certainty regarding its character as a breach of international obligations.

Some ICs have been wary of considering compliance matters, equating compliance adjudication with enforcement. However, as a matter of legal logic, there is no enforcement or coercion involved in a judicial declaration that the obligation to comply is being violated, or that action subsequent to the breach constitutes a violation warranting judicial remedies. Such determinations fall squarely within the adjudicatory powers of an IC with jurisdiction over the relevant rules. Finally, a judicial determination that certain legal consequences arise from a continued breach is no more an 'enforcement' ruling than a judicial determination that consequences arise from an original breach. An IC empowered to award certain remedies within regular adjudication is, a fortiori, able to award these remedies after the applicable law has been authoritatively interpreted, and a violation formally established.

9

Partial Adjudication and Remedy Foreshadowing

Final Rulings as Remedies for Non-Compliance

9.1 Introduction

This chapter discusses the use by international courts (ICs) of final rulings as deterrents to continued breach. This occurs when adjudicators establish (even if provisionally) duties of performance prior to issuing a final ruling on a dispute. In this case, the prospect of a final ruling, especially if accompanied by a judicial determination of Consequential Duties for breach, may serve a similar function to the prospect of Permissible Responses: inducing a wrongdoer to perform its obligations, or to settle the matter with the aggrieved party.

A judicial ruling that creates or increases the prospect of future remedies may operate as a deterrent, even without any explicit pronouncement to that effect. An adjudicator can achieve this by determining, for instance, that it has jurisdiction to issue a final ruling, that objections to admissibility are unfounded, or that provisional measures are warranted. To reinforce the deterrent effect, adjudicators may also *foreshadow* future remedies in partial or pre-final rulings, that is, decisions that do not exhaust the IC's jurisdiction over the dispute. An IC may expressly withhold a specific finding or refer to a potential remedy, thereby signalling the possibility of awarding that remedy at a later stage.

Especially for adjudicators that are unable or hesitate to assess compliance with final rulings, the prospect of further judicial pronouncements may be as valuable to a complainant, and sometimes more valuable, than a final ruling requiring implementation by an unwilling respondent, while depriving the complainant from the opportunity of further resort to adjudication. First, by preserving their jurisdiction, adjudicators ensure that post-(partial) ruling negotiations do not occur in an environment where the claimant is left only with the 'political' alternatives of persuasion and self-help. Second, if the partial ruling foreshadows specific remedies, a respondent has a specific additional incentive to settle: avoiding the incidence of these remedies. Third, through a partial ruling, rather than imposing an outcome, the IC allows the parties to negotiate it; obligations assumed within a settlement should have a higher chance of being performed voluntarily when compared to those determined by a court against a state's will.

A fourth effect may also be considered where the adjudicator makes partial determinations that require certain conduct: the adjustment of final remedies to the respondent's conduct. An adjudicator that provides all applicable remedies at once may be tempted to temper the remedies awarded so as to permit reconciliation between the parties and avoid imposing too heavy a burden on the wrongdoer.[1] On the other hand, a party that fails to comply with judicial determinations made in a partial ruling not only draws consequences in terms of its reputation but also risks seeing the adjudicator adopt more grievous remedies in its final ruling. Rather than merely being found in breach, the wrongdoer will then have failed to comply with a judicial determination.[2]

The use of final rulings and judicial remedies as deterrents raises a variety of legal issues. After discussing the legal permissibility of this manner of employing judicial remedies (Section 9.2), this chapter examines three forms of judicial decisions that may be termed partial rulings. Section 9.3 delves into the practice of deferring determinations on compensation, exploring its impact on compliance and its potential for inducing settlements. Section 9.4 focuses on the withholding of remedies at the merits stage, analysing cases where adjudicators issue findings on rights and obligations but stop short of declaring breaches or prescribing Consequential Duties. Section 9.5 discusses the role of declaratory judgments that provide authoritative guidance on parties' obligations while leaving room for further judicial involvement in the event of non-compliance. Section 9.6 evaluates the foreshadowing of substantive rulings during incidental proceedings, such as rulings on jurisdiction or

[1] See Andrea Gattini, 'Breach of the Obligation to Prevent and Reparation Thereof in the ICJ's Genocide Judgment' (2007) 18 *EJIL* 695.

[2] See *Chevron Corporation and Texaco Petroleum Corporation* v. *The Republic of Ecuador*, (2013) PCA Case No 2009-23, Fourth Interim Award on Interim Measures, Part IV, paras. 77–85 (finding the respondent 'in violation of the Tribunal's First and Second Interim Awards' and foreshadowing the determination of an obligation to 'compensate the First Claimant for any harm caused by the Respondent's violations of the First and Second Interim Awards').

provisional measures, which can foreshadow outcomes and shape party behaviour. Section 9.7 concludes.

9.2 Compensation and Declarations of Breach as Deterrents

In the structure of remedies formulated by the Permanent Court of International Justice (PCIJ) in *Chorzów Factory*, adopted (at least nominally) by most ICs, and codified in Articles on Responsibility of States for Internationally Wrongful Acts (ARSIWA), reparation is owed whenever injury is caused by a wrongful conduct.[3] In *Chorzów Factory*, the PCIJ established that reparation is the 'indispensable complement' of a breach. Reparation takes the form of '[r]estitution in kind, or, if this is not possible, payment of a sum corresponding to the value which a restitution in kind would bear'.[4] This hierarchy of remedies, between 'primary' restitution and 'secondary' compensation, has been codified in ARSIWA.[5] Article 35 establishes as the fundamental obligation of states to offer *restitutio in integrum*, and 're-establish the situation which existed before the wrongful act was committed'. Under Article 36, compensation is to be provided only to cover 'financially assessable damage' and only 'insofar as such damage is not made good by restitution'. Article 37 conveys the obligation of a wrongdoer to give satisfaction, applicable to 'injury caused by [the wrongful] act insofar as it cannot be made good by restitution or compensation'.

Though satisfaction tends to be awarded as redress for intangible damage, restitution and compensation often cover the same type of material injury, being applied sequentially as 'primary and 'secondary' remedies. The question, then, is whether this hierarchy of remedies is to be applied simply logically or whether it may also be applied chronologically. A logical hierarchy makes restitution the preferable remedy once the breach is found and if restitution has not been provided by the offender. Compensation is then awarded if restitution is impossible[6]

3 See Section 4.4.1.2.

4 *Factory at Chorzów (Merits), Germany* v. *Poland*, Judgment, (1928) PCIJ Ser A No. 17, p. 47.

5 See Anne van Aaken, 'Primary and Secondary Remedies in International Investment Law and National State Liability: A Functional and Comparative View', in Stephan W. Schill (ed.), *International Investment Law and Comparative Public Law* (Oxford: Oxford University Press, 2010), 721–754.

6 *Factory at Chorzów (Merits), Germany v. Poland*, Judgment, (1928) PCIJ Ser A No. 17, 47–48; *Velásquez Rodríguez* v. *Honduras (Merits)*, IACtHR, (1988) Ser C No. 4, para. 198; Eritrea-Ethiopia Claims Commission, *Final Award – Ethiopia's Damages Claims*, (2009) 26 RIAA 631, 712; *Libyan American Oil Company, LIAMCO* v. *Libya*, (1977) 62 ILR 140, 187.

or impracticable.[7] Satisfaction is reserved for cases in which restitution is impracticable and no financially assessable (or financially assessed) damage exists.[8]

If a chronological arrangement is possible, the determination that conduct constitutes a breach (a Declaration of Breach) may be made before any determination of consequences for this breach. An order for restitution may come next, without the IC establishing at this point whether restitution is possible or impossible. Both of these remedies would allow the wrongdoer an opportunity to amend its conduct or negotiate an acceptable arrangement with claimants. Only after this would the subsidiary remedies of compensation or, as the case may be, satisfaction intervene.

Of course, neither paying compensation nor providing satisfaction excuses states from performing their international obligations. In addition to the duty of reparation, a breach produces for the wrongdoer the obligation to cease its wrongful conduct.[9] As the International Court of Justice (ICJ) explained in *Navigational and Related Rights*, the duty of cessation applies immediately following a judgment that determines the existence of a legal violation.[10] Additionally, as ARSIWA Article 29 clarifies, the duty of states to perform their obligations subsists after the breach, regardless of the specific consequences that may arise from a particular violation.

However, a final judicial ruling may also mean the end of possibilities of resort to adjudication. A ruling that triggers specific enforcement mechanisms may improve the situation of the aggrieved party. But where no such mechanisms exist – as is usual for ICs – the aggrieved party may be left with the same remedies that would have been available to it in the absence of adjudication: recourse to political negotiations, bilateral or

[7] *Walter Fletcher Smith, Cuba/United States of America*, (1929) 2 UNRIAA 913, 918; *Forests of Central Rhodope (Merits), Greece* v. *Bulgaria*, (1933) 3 RIAA 1405, 1432.

[8] See *Oil Platforms (Merits), Iran* v. *United States*, Judgment, [2003] ICJ Reports 161, p. 207; *Fisheries Jurisdiction, United Kingdom* v. *Iceland*, Judgment, [1974] ICJ Reports 3, p. 34–35; *Fisheries Jurisdiction, Germany* v. *Iceland*, Judgment, [1974] ICJ Reports 175, p. 203; *Delimitation of the Maritime Boundary between Guyana and Suriname, Guyana* v. *Suriname*, (2008) PCA 47 ILM 166, 231, 236; *Navigational and Related Rights, Costa Rica* v. *Nicaragua*, [2009] ICJ Reports 21, p. 267.

[9] International Law Commission, Articles on Responsibility of States for Internationally Wrongful Acts, UN Doc. A/56/49(Vol. I)/Corr.4., Article 30.

[10] *Navigational and Related Rights*, [2009] ICJ Reports 21, p. 267.

through institutions, and recourse (by itself or by other states) to self-help measures to affirm the existence of obligations and demand compliance with the ruling.

By pronouncing on some matters under adjudication while leaving other matters for subsequent determination, ICs secure to aggrieved parties an alternative to persuasion and enforcement: recourse to adjudication. Thus, the establishment of consequences for breach, which otherwise serves merely to determine the obligations of the wrongdoer *ex post*, when foreseeable *ex ante* and imminent in case of non-compliance becomes (de jure or de facto) a Layer 4 sanction that applies in case a wrongdoer refuses to provide redress to the aggrieved party. Despite the different nature of the final remedies (Consequential Duties or Permissible Responses), the complainant's ability to request these further rulings may fulfil the same function fulfilled by the authorisation for trade retaliation in World Trade Organization (WTO) law: that of a *deterrent*, a credible threat that the injured party may use in negotiations with the wrongdoer, in order to demand performance or negotiate a favourable agreement.

9.3 Partial Exercises of Jurisdiction and Withholding of Remedies

In a partial exercise of jurisdiction, or 'partial ruling', an adjudicator delivers a decision in which it makes determinations on some but not all questions submitted to it, not exhausting its jurisdiction but remaining competent to examine issues not decided in the partial ruling. This contrasts with situations in which the adjudicator delivers a final ruling stating, for example, that it 'will not seek to ascertain' the applicability of consequences.[11] While, in the latter case, it may be possible for a party to re-seise the adjudicator requesting it to determine further remedies (an issue examined in Chapter 8), this would involve another exercise of jurisdiction – including, sometimes crucially, the need to establish a new jurisdictional link.

The judicial instruments used for exercising jurisdiction partially vary in name, and names may or may not indicate their partial character. Depending on the court or tribunal issuing them, partial rulings may be

[11] *Land and Maritime Boundary between Cameroon and Nigeria, Nigeria* v. *Cameroon*, [2002] ICJ Reports 303, p. 452; *Guyana* v. *Suriname*, (2008) 47 ILM 166, 232.

termed judgments,[12] partial awards,[13] or simply decisions.[14] These rulings all carry judicial authority – and produce *res judicata*[15] – without constituting final judgments or awards. As a result, these instruments do not exhaust the jurisdiction of the court or tribunal issuing them; they thus permit, and usually expressly foreshadow, a subsequent stage of adjudication by the same court or tribunal regarding the same dispute.

9.3.1 *Exercising Jurisdiction Partially*

Some adjudicators are expressly empowered to issue partial rulings, in constitutive treaties, rules of procedure, or documents endowing them with jurisdiction. In other cases, constitutive and jurisdiction-creating documents are silent on the issue, or even appear to curtail the capacity of ICs to issue partial rulings. Many ICs have interpreted their inherent powers as permitting them to divide the procedure into different phases – something known in arbitration as 'bifurcation' or 'trifurcation'[16] – and to pronounce with finality on specific points of law and fact while 'reserving' jurisdiction to make further determinations in subsequent rulings. Partial rulings are often issued for reasons of judicial economy or administration of the procedure. Whatever the adjudicator's intention, a partial ruling that affirms the possibility of a judicial remedy, or

[12] *Factory at Chorzów (Jurisdiction), Germany* v. *Poland*, Judgment, (1927) PCIJ Ser A No. 9; *Factory at Chorzów (Merits)*, (1928) PCIJ Ser A No. 17; *Velásquez Rodríguez (Merits)*, 29 July 1988, Ser C No 4, paras. 166, 181; Application No. 14556/89, *Papamichalopoulos and others* v. *Greece (Article 50)*, [1995] ECLI:CE:ECHR:1995:1031JUD001455689, para. 34.

[13] *Saluka Investments BV* v. *Czech Republic*, (2006) PCA IIC 210, Partial Award; Eritrea-Ethiopia Claims Commission, *Partial Award – Jus Ad Bellum – Ethiopia's Claims 1–8*, (2005) 27 RIAA 457, 465.

[14] *SGS* v. *Philippines*, [2004] ICSID Case No ARB/02/6, Decision on Jurisdiction, 29 January 2004; *BIVAC* v. *Paraguay*, [2012] ICSID Case No. ARB/07/9, Further Decision on Objections to Jurisdiction, 9 October 2012; *LG&E* v. *Argentina*, [2006] ICSID Case No ARB/02/1, Decision on Liability, 3 October 2006.

[15] *Corfu Channel (Compensation), United Kingdom* v. *Albania*, Judgment, [1949] ICJ Reports 244, p. 248. See, with regard to ICSID Arbitration, the majority decision in *ConocoPhillips Petrozuata B.V., ConocoPhillips Hamaca B.V. and ConocoPhillips Gulf of Paria B.V.* v. *Venezuela*, [2014] ICSID Case No ARB/07/30, Decision on Respondent's Request for Reconsideration, 10 March 2014, paras. 21, 24 (holding that decisions made before the Award 'that resolve points in dispute between the Parties have *res judicata* effect' and that 'the Tribunal . . . does not have the power to reconsider' them). But see the dissenting opinion of Georges Abi-Saab, Ibid.

[16] Lucy Greenwood, 'Does Bifurcation Really Promote Efficiency?' (2011) 28 *Journal of International Arbitration* 105.

expressly or implicitly foreshadows it, influences subsequent negotiations between the parties.

The ICJ, for example, has an established practice of issuing separate decisions on jurisdiction and on the merits. This practice was established early on by the ICJ's predecessor. In *Mavrommatis Palestine Concessions*, the PCIJ decided (with the consent of the parties) to make a determination regarding Britain's objection to jurisdiction before hearing the arguments of the parties on the merits; finding that it did have jurisdiction, the PCIJ 'reserve[d] the suit for judgment on the merits'.[17] The same procedure was adopted, without any reference to an agreement between the parties, in *Certain German Interests*[18] and in subsequent cases.[19] This preceded the inclusion, in 1940, of a formal provision in the Rules of the Court stating that, in case of a preliminary objection, the PCIJ could 'give its decision on the objection or ... join the objection to the merits'.[20] This provision survives in Article 79(1) of the ICJ Rules of the Court.[21]

Besides this pre-merits procedure, the PCIJ established in *Chorzów Factory* a post-merits procedure for determining the quantum of pecuniary reparation,[22] a practice the ICJ has subsequently adopted.[23] This procedure has been generally accepted as lawful. Elihu Lauterpacht understood it as legitimate when the Court lacks information to decide on the *quantum* of

[17] *Mavrommatis Palestine Concessions, Greece* v. *Great Britain*, Preliminary Objections, (1924) PCIJ Ser A No 2, p. 9.

[18] *Certain German Interests in Polish Upper Silesia, Germany* v. *Poland*, Preliminary Objections, (1925) PCIJ Series A No. 6, p. 27.

[19] For example, *Factory at Chorzów (Jurisdiction)*, (1927) PCIJ Ser A No. 9, p. 32; *Electricity Company of Sofia, Belgium* v. *Bulgaria*, Preliminary Objections, (1939) PCIJ Ser A/B No 77, p. 84.

[20] Statute and Rules of the Court, PCIJ Ser D No 1, p. 53, 4th edn., April 1940, Article 62(5).

[21] Rules of the Court, 1 July 1978, as amended from 21 October 2019, Article 79(1): 'Following the submission of the application and after the President has met and consulted with the parties, the Court may decide, if the circumstances so warrant, that questions concerning its jurisdiction or the admissibility of the application shall be determined separately'.

[22] *Factory at Chorzów (Merits)*, (1928) PCIJ Ser A No. 17, p. 64.

[23] *Corfu Channel (Merits), United Kingdom of Great Britain and Northern Ireland* v. *Albania*, Judgment, [1949] ICJ Reports 4, p. 36; *United States Diplomatic and Consular Staff in Tehran, United States of America* v. *Iran*, Judgment, [1980] ICJ Reports 3, p. 39, 45; *Military and Paramilitary Activities in and against Nicaragua, Nicaragua* v. *United States of America (Merits)*, Judgment, [1986] ICJ Reports 14, p. 149; *Gabčíkovo-Nagymaros Project*, Hungary/Slovakia, Judgment, [1997] ICJ Reports 7, p. 83; *Armed Activities in the Territory of the Congo, Democratic Republic of the Congo* v. *Uganda*, Judgment, [2005] ICJ Reports 168, p. 281–282.

reparation.[24] Shabtai Rosenne proposed that these proceedings are legitimate because they are 'necessary' in view of the lack of evidence, or of litigation, at the moment of the decision on the merits.[25]

However, a lack of evidence does not per se allow a tribunal to defer a portion of adjudication to a subsequent stage of proceedings; it may equally result in the remedy requested not being granted. In *Fisheries Jurisdiction*, the ICJ rejected Germany's request for a determination regarding compensation precisely in view of the absence of 'specific information and evidence concerning ... each incident and each head of damage'.[26] The United Nations Convention on the Law of the Sea (UNCLOS) Article VII Arbitral Tribunal in *Guyana* v. *Suriname* and the ICJ in *Navigational and Related Rights* rejected claims for compensation under the argument that the parties did not provide evidence of financially assessable injury.[27]

Rosenne simply assumed the legitimacy of the post-merits decision on reparation. While generally considering that 'in the present conception of international litigation' the ICJ becomes *functus officio* following a judgment on the merits, he carved out exceptions for 'certain derivative matters'.[28] This included the two post-judgment remedies provided for in the statute – interpretation and revision of judgments[29] – but also the subsequent 'special derivative procedure for the assessment of damages'.[30] In these cases, he argued, '[t]he parties' consent to the principal case automatically extends to this kind of derivative case'.[31]

These responses to the procedure for a post-merits decision on reparation may be contrasted with those that emerged in the two instances in which the ICJ issued partial decisions which reversed the usual order of analysis – *Nuclear Tests* and *Qatar* v. *Bahrain*. These judgments have

24 Hersch Lauterpacht, *The Function of Law in the International Community* (Oxford: Oxford University Press, 2011), 478–479.

25 Shabtai Rosenne, *The Law and Practice of the International Court 1920–2005*, 4th edn (Leiden: Martinus Nijhoff, 2006), 1204.

26 *Fisheries Jurisdiction*, [1974] ICJ Reports 175, p. 205.

27 *Guyana* v. *Suriname*, (2008) 47 ILM 166, 699; *Navigational and Related Rights*, [2009] ICJ Reports 213, p. 267.

28 Rosenne, *The Law and Practice of the International Court 1920–2005*, 199.

29 Statute of the International Court of Justice, San Francisco, 24 October 1945, in force 18 April 1946, XV UNCIO 355 ('ICJ Statute'), Articles 60–61.

30 Rosenne, *The Law and Practice of the International Court 1920–2005*, 525.

31 Shabtai Rosenne, 'International Courts and Tribunals, Jurisdiction and Admissibility of Inter-State Applications', (2006) Max Planck Encyclopedia of Public International Law, para. 20.

been criticised by scholars.[32] The basis for these deferrals seems to be the same as that for the deferral of the ruling on responsibility and compensation: a general power of the Court to defer rulings, irrespective of what elements of the dispute are deferred for subsequent adjudication.

Elihu Lauterpacht argued, with respect to the *Qatar* v. *Bahrain* partial judgment, that the ICJ regards its 'inherent jurisdiction as empowering it even to give a partial judgment, that is, one that does not dispose of the whole issues presented to it by the parties'.[33] He noted that the Court had not discussed the source, character or limits of this power, and argued that its source must be found in the doctrine of 'implied powers' which the ICJ established as regards the General Assembly in the *Reparation for Injuries* opinion.[34] This accords with the view, expressed by Judge Kooijmans, that the Court is 'master of its own procedure',[35] and may adopt innovative procedural solutions that it considers necessary in the circumstances.[36]

The European and Inter-American Courts of Human Rights have also, and without much discussion, asserted their power to divide their proceedings into phases of jurisdiction, merits, and determination of reparation (in the case of the European Court of Human Rights (ECtHR), 'just satisfaction').[37] The exception among standing courts, at least so far, is the International Tribunal for the Law of the Sea (ITLOS), which issues single judgments dealing with objections to jurisdiction and

[32] Regarding the *Nuclear Tests* decision, Hugh Thirlway stated that it 'promised to be a *unicum*, never to be repeated' (Hugh Thirlway, *The Law and Procedure of the International Court of Justice* (Oxford: Oxford University Press, 2013), 1023). Sir Elihu Lauterpacht found that in *Qatar* v. *Bahrain* 'the Court departed in a striking way from the general pattern of its previous jurisprudence' regarding decisions on jurisdiction and merits (Elihu Lauterpacht, 'Partial Judgments and the Inherent Jurisdiction of the International Court of Justice', in Vaughan Lowe and Malgosia Fitzmaurice (eds.), *Fifty Years of the International Court of Justice – Essays in Honour of Sir Robert Jennings* (Cambridge: Cambridge University Press, 1996), 465–486, 466.

[33] Elihu Lauterpacht, 'Partial Judgments and the Inherent Jurisdiction of the International Court of Justice', 478.

[34] Ibid., 477–478. See *Reparation for injuries suffered in the service of the Nations,* Advisory Opinion, [1949] ICJ Reports 174, p. 182 ('Under international law, the [UN] Organization must be deemed to have those powers which, though not expressly provided in the Charter, are conferred upon it by necessary implication as being essential to the performance of its duties').

[35] *Legality of Use of Force, Serbia and Montenegro* v. *United Kingdom*, [2004] ICJ Reports 1307, p. 1372 (J. Kooijmans).

[36] On this power, see Juliette McIntyre, 'Rules Are Rules: Reconceiving Monetary Gold as a Rule of Procedure, (2021) 115 *AJIL Unbound* 144–148.

[37] See Section 9.4.2.

admissibility, deciding on the merits, finding legal breaches and determining the amount of compensation owed by the wrongdoing state. The main instruments used by ITLOS to issue rulings prior to the final judgment are provisional measures of protection (examined in Section 9.6.2), which it is expressly empowered to award under UNCLOS Articles 290(1) and 290(5).

The practice of investment tribunals evidences a similar assumption of 'inherent powers' by these tribunals.[38] Under United Nations Commission on International Trade Law (UNCITRAL) Rules, it is unnecessary to have recourse to these powers: arbitral tribunals are expressly empowered to 'make separate awards on different issues at different times', and parties engage to 'carry out all awards without delay'.[39] This freedom has allowed a practice of partial awards of various kinds: on jurisdiction,[40] jurisdiction and admissibility,[41] jurisdiction and liability,[42] and liability.[43] Under UNCITRAL, tribunals appear to be essentially free to determine the extent to which it is in the best interest of the procedure to issue a partial award, as well as the precise scope of each award.

By contrast, Article 48(3) of the International Centre for Settlement of Investment Disputes (ICSID) Convention provides that 'the award shall deal with every question submitted to the Tribunal'. International Centre for Settlement of Investment Disputes tribunals have circumvented this provision by issuing 'decisions' instead of awards. Bifurcation between the pre-merits and the merits stage, with 'decisions on jurisdiction' like those issued by the ICJ, has long become commonplace,[44] and is justified under Article 41(2) of the ICSID Convention.[45] Subsequently, tribunals

[38] See Section 9.4.3.

[39] UNCITRAL Arbitration Rules (with new article 1, para. 4, as adopted in 2013), Article 34. This is also the case of many other rules of arbitration. See Emmanuel Gaillard and John Savage, *Fouchard, Gaillars, Goldman on International Commercial Arbitration* (The Hague: Kluwer, 1999), 740 ff.

[40] *Saar Papier Vertriebs GmbH* v. *Poland*, (1994) UNCITRAL, Interim Award (Jurisdiction).

[41] *Achmea B.V.* v. *Slovakia*, (2014) PCA Case No 2013-12, Award on Jurisdiction and Admissibility.

[42] See, for example, *Sergei Paushok et al.* v. *Mongolia*, (2011) UNCITRAL, Award on Jurisdiction and Liability.

[43] *Chevron Corporation (USA) and Texaco Petroleum Company (USA)* v. *Ecuador*, (2010) PCA Case No. 34877, Partial Award on the Merits.

[44] *SGS* v. *Philippines*, [2004] ICSID Case No ARB/02/6, Decision on Jurisdiction; *BIVAC* v. *Paraguay*, [2012] ICSID Case No. ARB/07/9, Further Decision on Objections to Jurisdiction.

[45] 'Any objection by a party to the dispute that that dispute is not within the jurisdiction of the Centre, or for other reasons is not within the competence of the Tribunal, shall be

started bifurcating the merits stage, issuing 'decisions on liability' and leaving for the final phase of litigation solely the question of the quantum of damages. While in most cases tribunals have not provided a justification for these decisions,[46] the *Suez* Tribunal justified this on the ground of judicial economy, basing its decision on the procedural powers of tribunals under the ICSID Convention:

> The Tribunal is aware that a bifurcation of the merits phase of an ICSID case into determination of liability and a determination of damages is not common. On the other hand, the ICSID Rules do not preclude such an approach. Indeed, Article 44 of the ICSID Convention ... specifically states: 'If any question of procedure which is not covered by this Section or the Arbitration Rules or any rules agreed upon by the parties, the Tribunal shall decide the question.' The Tribunal relies on Article 44 in deciding on bifurcating the merits phase of this case for the reasons outlined above.[47]

In short, ICs and arbitral tribunals have interpreted their inherent powers as allowing them to opt for issuing partial rulings. This accords with Chester Brown's observation that 'international tribunals have held that they are masters of their procedure'.[48] Under the prevailing view, it would seem, arbitral tribunals are empowered to issue partial decisions even when, as in the case of ICSID, the treaty providing them with jurisdiction clearly appears to favour a single decision.[49]

9.3.2 Demanding Performance and Withholding Remedies

The partial exercise of jurisdiction does not necessarily aim at inducing performance. In most cases, partial judgments, awards, or decisions are

considered by the Tribunal which shall determine whether to deal with it as a preliminary question or to join it to the merits of the dispute.'

46 *LG&E* v. *Argentina*, [2006] ICSID Case No ARB/02/1, Decision on Liability; *Total S.A.* v. *Argentina*, [2010] ICSID Case No ARB/04/1, Decision on Liability, 27 December 2010; *Burlington Resources Inc.* v. *Ecuador*, [2012] ICSID Case No ARB/08/5, Decision on Liability, 14 December 2012.

47 *Suez, Sociedad General de Aguas de Barcelona S.A. and Vivendi Universal S.A.* v. *Argentina*, [2010] ICSID Case No ARB/03/19, Decision on Liability, 30 July 2010, para. 273.

48 Chester Brown, 'The Inherent Powers of International Courts and Tribunals' (2005) 76 *BYIL* 195, 217.

49 See in this regard the discussion regarding whether the pre-Award decisions are final in *ConocoPhillips Petrozuata B.V.* v. *Venezuela*, [2014] ICSID Case No ARB/07/30 (holding that they are), and the dissent of Georges Abi-Saab, paras. 43–44 (arguing that these decisions only acquire finality once incorporated in the award, until which point the Tribunal remains free to change its mind).

issued with a view to determining a legal question that is severable from, and preliminary to, the final judgment. Regardless of the underlying intentions, partial decisions always give parties additional time to settle a matter – whether by performance or through a negotiated solution.

Procedural acts that do not constitute partial judgments (the 'interim report' issued by WTO panels being a clear example)[50] may also provide strong indication of the likely outcome of the proceedings. In the broadest sense, even the attitude of adjudicators towards the arguments of the parties at the hearings may indicate a leaning and therefore lead to a settlement. However, partial decisions are particular in that they are public. They therefore publicly announce an authoritative interpretation of the rights and obligations of parties. Even where no *res judicata* attaches to these decisions, this publicity generates the expectation of a negative outcome for the wrongdoer.[51] With a partial ruling, the adjudicator, without issuing the totality of the remedies at its disposal, sets out parameters for the remainder of the procedure, affirming the prospect of remedies and possibly providing the parties with guidance regarding the foreseeable outcome.

A partial ruling may go as far as including a Declaration of Breach, establishing the responsibility of the wrongdoer, and affirming as the Consequential Duty monetary compensation, leaving the IC no discretion regarding these matters. The matter withheld for subsequent ruling is then simply the determination of a quantum of compensation. If compensation is to cover solely past damage, the separation between a ruling that compensation is due and one determining its amount is merely procedural. Alternatively, the amount of compensation may depend on the ongoing conduct of the parties; the prospect of a larger indemnity to be paid if a violation continues can then act as a deterrent. Even where the amount of compensation refers entirely to injury that took place before the procedure, courts have often specifically directed the parties to try and reach a negotiated settlement, avoiding the judicial determination of the amount of compensation.[52]

[50] Understanding on Rules and Procedures Governing the Settlement of Disputes, Marrakesh, 15 April 1994, 1869 UNTS 401 ('DSU'), Article 15.

[51] There may of course be positive outcomes for the respondent, such as findings that parts of the claim are beyond the jurisdiction of the adjudicator, not admissible, or unwarranted. If there is no counterclaim and no negative outcome for the respondent may ensue, the decision providing for this is usually a final decision.

[52] See *North Sea Continental Shelf, Federal Republic of Germany/Netherlands*, [1969] ICJ Reports 3, p. 47–48; *Territorial and Maritime Dispute in the Caribbean Sea, Nicaragua* v. *Honduras*, [2007] ICJ Reports 659, p. 763.

Another possibility is for the IC not to rule, in its partial ruling, on the issue of responsibility.[53] The IC makes determinations regarding the rights and obligations of the parties but stops short of establishing Consequential Duties, or even issuing a Declaration of Breach. Partial rulings of this type may vary substantially; their common element is that the subsequent phase of the proceedings may be avoided in case of a mutually agreed solution. Further judicial intervention is conditioned upon the injured party asserting, some time after the partial ruling, that the offender has not complied with its obligations and has not provided a satisfactory alternative. Although a settlement is always available to the parties, these partial rulings offer an authoritative assessment of the applicable legal framework that was previously in dispute. The parties may then update their beliefs regarding their legal situation, providing an opportunity for wrongdoers to change their conduct or for the parties to reach a negotiated solution.[54]

This function can also be fulfilled by atypical legal instruments. A WTO panel report, featuring Mere Adjudication and Declarations of Breach, is the third document issued by the panel. It is first required to issue, solely to the disputing parties, a 'descriptive (factual and argument) sections of its draft report', then an 'interim report to the parties, including both the descriptive sections and the panel's findings and conclusions'.[55] Besides giving the parties the opportunity to comment on these drafts and make final arguments, these stages can (and often do) lead to settlements. For this, at least one of the parties must conclude that a bilateral settlement is sufficiently preferable to the issuing of the report as to require it to make an acceptable offer to the other party.[56]

[53] A variation of this type of remedy is a decision providing for reparation in the form of *restitutio in integrum* while expressly allowing for compensation as a subsidiary remedy in case the wrongdoer fails to provide restitution. Depending on the substantive rule violated and on the circumstances of the breach, the IC may find that there is a duty to provide reparation and failure to do so constitutes a new breach which requires compensation; or the wrongdoer may be given a choice between the two. In both cases, the partial ruling allows the IC to insist on performance rather than infer, from the continuing breach, that future performance is 'impossible', and the appropriate judicial response is therefore to award damages. See Section 9.5.3.

[54] See *Gabčíkovo-Nagymaros Project*, [1997] ICJ Reports 7, p. 83; *Texaco Overseas Petroleum Co* v. *Government of the Libyan Arab Republic*, (1979) 53 ILR 389, 507–508, 511; *Affaire Junghans (Première Partie), Allemagne contre Roumanie*, (1939) 3 RIAA 1845, 1855.

[55] DSU, Articles 15(1), 15(2).

[56] These developments are rarely expressly documented. But see the notes in, for example, Communication from the Chairman of the Panel, *Japan – Quotas on Laver*, WT/DS323/

9.3.3 *Partial Rulings and res judicata*

The question may arise whether and to what extent a partial ruling makes *res judicata*, binding not only the parties but also the adjudicator in its subsequent rulings. In *Bosnian Genocide*, the ICJ distinguished between 'issues which have been decided with the force of *res judicata*, or which are necessarily entailed in the decision of those issues', on the one hand, and 'peripheral or subsidiary matters, or *obiter dicta*', on the other.[57] The Court concluded that an issue determined in its judgment on preliminary objections was 'necessary as a matter of logical construction' for the outcome of the judgment, and therefore had been pronounced on with the force of *res judicata*. As a consequence, the decision was 'definitive both for the parties to the case, in respect of the case . . . and for the Court itself in the context of that case'.[58]

Pursuant to this finding, parties and the adjudicator alike are bound by determinations made with binding force in a judicial decision, whether partial or final, as well as by those statements that provide the fundamental reasoning underlying these determinations.[59] On the other hand, they are not bound by statements that are not necessary for attaining such determinations. This acquires particular relevance because partial decisions may include statements regarding matters to be ruled on at the subsequent stage. On these matters, although partial decisions may include guidance regarding the future direction of a case, their binding portion is restricted to that which is essential to the determination(s) made in the operative part of the partial decision.

This became significant in the ICJ's statements in *Corfu Channel (Compensation)* and *South West Africa (Merits)*. In *Corfu Channel (Compensation)*, Albania challenged the jurisdiction of the ICJ to

4, 8 December 2005; Notification of Mutually Agreed Solution, WT/DS323/5, 27 January 2006. See also the chronology of notes in Communication from the Panel, *China – Canola Seed (Canada)*, WT/DS589/7, 15 June 2022; Communication from the Panel, WT/DS589/8, 1 September 2022; and Note by the Secretariat, WT/DS589/9, 1 September 2023.

[57] *Application of the Convention on the Prevention and Punishment of the Crime of Genocide, Bosnia and Herzegovina* v. *Serbia and Montenegro*, Judgment, [2007] ICJ Reports 43, p. 95. A third category is that of 'matters which have not been ruled upon at all' (Ibid.).

[58] Ibid., p. 100–101.

[59] On the different versions, see, Andreas Kulick, 'Article 60 ICJ Statute, Interpretation Proceedings, and the Competing Concepts of Res Judicata' (2015) 28 *Leiden Journal of International Law* 73–89.

determine reparation after the Court's judgment on the merits. The ICJ answered that, although the judgment on the merits had not brought the case to an end, the ruling that Albania disputed was *res judicata* and could no longer be challenged.[60] In *South West Africa*, on the other hand, the ICJ found that statements included in a decision on preliminary objections 'can never be preclusive of a matter appertaining to the merits' and a decision on preliminary objections that addresses the merits does so 'in a provisional way'.[61]

In practice, this means that decisions on preliminary objections have only relative impact upon questions of interpretation of substantive obligations. Their main effect in this regard is to determine which matters may and may not be decided by the adjudicator at the merits stage. This precludes the court or tribunal from subsequently making findings regarding matters beyond their jurisdiction. Conversely, interpretations of substantive obligations and findings of breach made at the merits stage are binding on the parties and on the adjudicator in post-merits proceedings. These partial rulings set the parameters for subsequent judgments concerning forms of reparation. Rosenne notes in this regard:

> The essential feature of all instances of derivative jurisdiction is that the parameters of the Court's jurisdiction in these cases [are] strictly limited by the judgment out of which the proceedings derive, and (except where a request for revision of a judgment is admitted) they cannot affect the existence of the *res iudicata*.[62]

Thus, interpretations by a court or tribunal and declarations of breach issued at the merits stage bind the adjudicators as well as the parties at the reparations stage. However, they only oblige the adjudicator to provide any particular form or quantum of reparation if this is specifically determined in the judgment on the merits.

9.4 Deferral of Determinations concerning the Quantum of Compensation

A number of ICs have adopted the practice of separating their ruling on the merits from the determination of the quantum of compensation,

[60] *Corfu Channel (Compensation)*, [1949] ICJ Reports 244, p. 248.

[61] *South West Africa (Second Phase), Ethiopia* v. *South Africa*, Judgment, [1966] ICJ Reports 6, p. 37.

[62] Rosenne, 'International Courts and Tribunals, Jurisdiction and Admissibility of Inter-State Applications', para. 20.

sometimes expressly enjoining the parties to reach an agreement on the matter and avoid the post-merits proceedings. In fact, it has become common procedure for courts and tribunals to determine the incidence of responsibility (or 'liability') at the merits stage and only subsequently to decide on its extent.

It is difficult to establish with certainty the extent to which leaving the quantification of injury for a later stage induces parties to comply or negotiate. As this section shows, in various cases, and before different ICs, parties have reached negotiated solutions after an IC determined the existence of a duty to pay compensation and while the procedure for establishing the relevant amount was pending.

9.4.1 Permanent Court and International Court

The practice of deferring compensation to a subsequent stage of proceedings follows the approach adopted by the PCIJ in *Chorzów Factory*. At the merits stage, the Permanent Court held that Poland was under an obligation to pay compensation to Germany but refrained from exercising jurisdiction to the full extent requested by Germany. The parties reached a settlement, and no decision was ever issued on the amount of compensation.

The ICJ has deferred determination of the amount of compensation in a number of cases. Of these, the question remains pending since 1998 in *Gabčíkovo-Nagymaros*; in *DRC* v. *Uganda*, the issue remained pending for seventeen years while the parties pursued negotiations.[63] In both cases, the ICJ declared breaches and found that compensation was due but deferred the ruling of the quantum of reparation to subsequent proceedings, 'failing agreement between the parties'.[64] As there was no time limitation for this, the parties could seise the Court for this purpose at any time. By contrast, in *Certain Activities* and *Certain Iranian Assets*, after finding that a party was under an obligation to provide compensation to the other for material injury, the ICJ determined minimum time periods, of twelve and twenty-four months, respectively, for the parties to agree on compensation.[65]

[63] *Armed Activities on the Territory of the Congo (Reparations), Democratic Republic of the Congo* v. *Uganda*, [2022] ICJ Reports 13, p. 26–28.

[64] *Armed Activities in the Territory of the Congo*, [2005] ICJ Reports 168, p. 282; *Gabčíkovo-Nagymaros Project*, [1997] ICJ Reports 7, p. 83.

[65] *Certain Activities Carried Out by Nicaragua in the Border Area and Construction of a Road in Costa Rica along the San Juan River (Merits), Costa Rica* v. *Nicaragua and*

This practice has produced mixed results in terms of inducing compliance, or at least channelling negotiations. In *Hostages* and *Nicaragua*, the parties agreed to a settlement without having to return to the Court (although time and political circumstances, more than the ICJ itself, may have been responsible). In *Corfu Channel*, *Diallo*, and *Certain Activities*, the parties could not agree to a settlement and the Court had to determine the *quantum* of compensation.

a Deferrals Leading to Agreement

The first deferral of a ruling on *quantum* to lead to agreement occurred in *Chorzów Factory*. The PCIJ ruled that Poland owed Germany compensation for breach, which should be paid in a lump sum, but 'reserve[d] the fixing of the amount of this compensation', together with the conditions and methods for payment, 'for a future judgment'.[66] The Court thus left open the proceedings for a future stage, in which the issue of the amount of compensation could be litigated by the parties, after an expert assessment of the issue.[67] Immediately upon issuing its judgment, the PCIJ initiated a procedure to constitute the Committee of Experts that would assess the amount of compensation due.[68] This was followed by an order composing this Committee and establishing its mandate.[69] The Committee held five meetings and decided to conduct an inspection on the premises of the factory. After the president of the Court fixed a date for the presentation of the experts' report, the parties reached an agreement regarding compensation.[70]

In *Hostages*, the ICJ found that Iran had committed 'successive and continuing breaches' of its obligations towards the United States under a number of treaties. The Court thus engaged Iran's international responsibility. Regarding the consequences of this determination, the ICJ stated that the breach:

> clearly entails an obligation on the part of the Iranian State to make reparation for the injury thereby caused to the United States. Since however Iran's breaches of its obligations are still continuing, the form and amount of such reparation cannot be determined at the present date.[71]

Nicaragua v. *Costa Rica*, [2015] ICJ Reports 665, p. 741; *Certain Iranian Assets, Islamic Republic of Iran* v. *United States of America (Merits)*, [2013] ICJ Reports 51, p. 129.

66 *Factory at Chorzów (Merits)*, (1928) PCIJ Ser A No. 17, p. 64.

67 Ibid.

68 *Factory at Chorzów (Order of 13 September 1928)*, (1928) PCIJ Ser A No 17, p. 100.

69 *Factory at Chorzów (Order of 16 October 1928)*, (1928–1929) PCIJ Ser E, p. 196.

70 *Factory at Chorzów (Order of 25 May 1929)*, (1929) PCIJ Ser A No 19, p. 13.

71 *United States Diplomatic and Consular Staff in Tehran*, [1980] ICJ Reports 3, p. 41–42.

The Court reserved the matter of 'the form and amount of such reparation' to a subsequent procedure. In setting out the parameters for compensation, the ICJ implied that Iran's conduct subsequent to the judgment on the merits would have an impact upon the quantum of compensation eventually determined by the Court. Iran would thus be able to mitigate the consequences of its actions by terminating the violation promptly.

After troubled negotiations, Iran and the United States entered into undertakings consolidated in a set of Declarations made by Algeria in 1981 (the 'Algiers Declarations').[72] Pursuant to these Declarations, the United States would withdraw its claim for reparation, and the Iran–US Claims Tribunal (IUCT) would be established to examine claims by each state's nationals regarding breaches committed by the other state. Iranian funds frozen in US banks would be used to award compensation to US nationals. The United States subsequently requested that the ICJ case be discontinued.[73]

Needless to say, US coercive power played a large role in this outcome. It is possible that, given the freezing of Iranian assets in US banks (which Robert Jennings considered as a measure taken 'by way of reprisals'),[74] the United States would have been able to resort to self-help and withhold these assets to pay compensation to its own citizens, regardless of the prospect of an ICJ ruling. But it would have been difficult to obtain the agreement of Iran – and, according to Jennings, that of British courts[75] – regarding the legality of a unilateral seizing of assets. These measures could in fact have made it more difficult to ensure compliance by Iran with its substantive obligations regarding the US hostages. As Thomas Franck noted, the ICJ judgment:

> help[ed] to generate the diplomatic climate in which Iran felt impelled to release the hostages and, incidentally, to submit the rival monetary claims of the United States and Iran to another system of international adjudication. The unilateral use of US power had failed to achieve that desired result.[76]

[72] Declaration of the Government of the Democratic and Popular Republic of Algeria Concerning the Settlement of Claims by the Government of the United States of America and the Government of the Islamic Republic of Iran, (1981) 20 ILM 230.

[73] Constanze Schulte, *Compliance with Decisions of the International Court of Justice* (Oxford: Oxford University Press, 2004), 169–171.

[74] Robert Jennings, 'The Judicial Enforcement of International Obligations' (1987) 47 *ZaöRV* 3, 13.

[75] Ibid., 14.

[76] Thomas Franck, 'Icy Day at the ICJ' (1985) 79 *AJIL* 379, 384.

In *Nicaragua*, the ICJ found that the United States was obliged to make reparation to Nicaragua for breaches of customary international law and of a bilateral Friendship, Commerce and Navigation Treaty. The judgment on the merits provided that 'the form and amount of such reparation, failing agreement between the parties, [would] be settled by the Court'. The ICJ 'reserve[d] for this purpose the subsequent procedure in the case',[77] specifically stating that this would give Nicaragua the possibility to revise its claims for damages to fit the breaches established by the Court.[78]

In 1988, Nicaragua filed its memorial regarding compensation, to which the United States responded with a letter restating its view that the ICJ was without jurisdiction. Following a change in government in Nicaragua, the oral proceedings were adjourned in 1990. The entire claim was dropped in September 1991, within a comprehensive settlement that included a $500 million US aid package, support to Nicaragua through international financial institutions, and opportunities for trade and investment.[79] Though political circumstances cannot be ignored, Nicaragua's judicially declared entitlement to compensation, and ability to obtain an ICJ ruling on the matter, provided a baseline for a settlement and legitimised the significant financial disbursement by the United States.

b Rulings Foreshadowing Compensation

In *Corfu Channel*, *Diallo*, and *Certain Activities*, the decision to defer the issue of the quantum of compensation did not lead to a settlement between the parties, and the ICJ was then re-seised to determine this amount. In *Corfu Channel*, the ICJ determined at the merits stage that Albania was responsible for loss of life and property in two British ships caused by the explosion of mines in Albanian waters, thus owing

[77] *Military and Paramilitary Activities in and against Nicaragua*, [1986] ICJ Reports 14, p. 149.

[78] Nicaragua also requested from the International Court an interim assessment of 'minimum (and in that sense provisional) valuation of direct damages'. The ICJ held that it found 'no provision in the Statute of the Court either specifically empowering the Court to make an interim award of this kind, or indeed debarring it from doing so'. The ICJ found that it was not appropriate to issue such an award in the circumstances of the case but that this could occur 'in exceptional circumstances, and where the entitlement of the State making the claim was already established with certainty and precision' (Ibid., p. 142–143).

[79] Schulte, *Compliance with Decisions of the International Court of Justice*, 206.

financial compensation to the United Kingdom for the corresponding losses.[80] The Court stated, however, that it could not, at the merits stage, establish the amount of compensation. It found that 'further proceedings on this [we]re necessary' and 'reserve[d] for future consideration the assessment of the amount of compensation'.[81] Rejecting Albania's subsequent objection to the Court's jurisdiction to determine compensation, the ICJ went on to award damages to the United Kingdom in the amount of 843,947 British pounds.[82]

Only in 1992 (after the People's Socialist Republic of Albania had come to an end) was an indemnity paid to the United Kingdom, and at a level that was nominally the same as that determined in 1949 – and therefore in effect far lower.[83] This testifies to the difficulty of obtaining compliance with an international judgment, even one for compensation. On the other hand, the payment of the indemnity and its amount show that a judicial determination that compensation is due remains a significant element, which may guide an inter-state transaction to re-establish relations, over four decades after the ruling.

In *Diallo* and *Certain Activities*, the ICJ also followed a procedure in two stages. In *Diallo*, the Court found that the arrest and expulsion from the Democratic Republic of the Congo of Mr Diallo, a Guinean citizen, violated the DRC's treaty obligations.[84] The ICJ held that among the 'consequences flow[ing] from these internationally wrongful acts giving rise to the DRC's international responsibility'[85] was the duty to pay compensation, and enjoined the parties to find a negotiated solution. If they could not arrive at a mutually agreeable amount within six months, the matter would 'be settled by the Court in a subsequent phase of the proceedings'.[86] The same approach was adopted in *Certain Activities*, giving parties twelve months to agree on an amount.[87]

[80] *Corfu Channel (Merits)*, [1949] ICJ Reports 4, p. 22–23.
[81] Ibid., p. 26, 36.
[82] *Corfu Channel (Compensation)*, [1949] ICJ Reports 244, p. 248, 250.
[83] Pierre d'Argent, 'Reparations and Compliance', in Karine Bannelier, Theodore Christakis and Sarah Heathcote (eds.), *The ICJ and the Evolution of International Law – The Enduring Impact of the Corfu Channel Case* (London: Routledge, 2012), p. 335–356, 353–356.
[84] *Ahmadou Sadio Diallo (Merits), Republic of Guinea* v. *Democratic Republic of the Congo*, [2010] ICJ Reports 639, p. 667, 669, 673.
[85] Ibid., p. 691.
[86] Ibid., p. 691–692.
[87] *Certain Activities Carried Out by Nicaragua in the Border Area*, [2015] ICJ Reports 665, para. 229.5(b).

In both cases, the parties failed to agree on an amount within the allotted time and the *quantum* was established by the ICJ.

The failure of the parties to agree on compensation becomes more understandable in the circumstances of these disputes. Guinea's claim was for over 11 million US dollars,[88] while the amount awarded by the ICJ was 95 thousand dollars, or less than 1 per cent of the amount requested. The ICJ awarded compensation corresponding solely to Mr. Diallo's wrongful imprisonment and loss of personal property, rejecting Guinea's request for relief for the injury he indirectly suffered as a shareholder of two companies the DRC had allegedly expropriated.[89] In *Certain Activities*, a significant portion of the compensation awarded was granted for environmental damages – a category of injury for which the ICJ had never awarded compensation before.[90]

9.4.2 Human Rights Courts

In the European Convention on Human Rights (ECHR), Article 41 (formerly Article 50) allows the ECtHR to 'afford just satisfaction to the injured party' in case of a violation for which 'the internal law of the Party concerned allows only partial reparation'. This formulation implies that, despite using the term 'satisfaction', Article 41 refers to Consequential Duties, including all forms of reparation, rather than to judicial satisfaction as a heightened form of the Declaration of Breach.

The ECHR does not mention the possibility of a judgment in two parts. Since the so-called *Vagrancy* cases, however, the ECtHR has adopted the practice of establishing violations in its decisions on the merits and '[r]eserv[ing] for the applicants the right, should the occasion arise, to apply for just satisfaction' under Article 41.[91] This is now

[88] This included over 6 million dollars for loss of earnings, over 4 million for loss of potential earnings, half a million for material damages and half a million for legal expenses. See *Ahmadou Sadio Diallo (Compensation), Republic of Guinea* v. *Democratic Republic of the Congo*, [2012] 324, p. 345.

[89] Ibid., 343. Annemarieke Vermeer-Künzli, 'Diallo: Between Diplomatic Protection and Human Rights' (2013) 4 *JIDS* 487.

[90] *Certain Activities Carried Out by Nicaragua in the Border Area (Compensation), Costa Rica* v. *Nicaragua*, [2018] ICJ Reports 15, p. 28.

[91] Application Nos. 2832/66, 2835/66, 2899/66, *Cases of De Wilde, Ooms and Versyp (Merits)* [1971] ECHR 1. See Dinah Shelton, *Remedies in International Human Rights Law*, 2nd edn (Oxford: Oxford University Press, 2005), 194–196. The *Vagrancy* cases were the first ones in which applicants concretely sought just satisfaction.

codified in the Rules of Court, which allow it to 'give in the same judgment a ruling on the application of Article 41 [just satisfaction] if . . . the question is ready for decision; if the question is not ready for decision, the Chamber or the Committee shall reserve it in whole or in part and shall fix the further procedure'.[92]

This technique was employed on a number of occasions, including in cases in which the Court subsequently ordered restitution of property[93] and in those in which it left to the state the choice between restitution and compensation.[94] In *Loizidou* v. *Turkey*, the Court withheld application of Article 41 with express reference to 'the possibility of agreement being reached between the Turkish Government and the applicant'.[95] In the inter-state case *Cyprus* v. *Turkey*, the ECHR withheld any determination on Article 41 in its 2001 judgment on the merits.[96] Only in 2010 did Cyprus apply for just satisfaction. It justified this in the following terms:

> [A]fter the delivery of the principal judgment, Cyprus had hoped *bona fide* that it would be properly enforced through the usual mechanism of the Committee of Ministers of the Council of Europe. Only several years later, when it had become obvious that Turkey was unwilling to solve the issue by political means (i.e. through the adoption of general and specific measures), the Cypriot Government had realised that it had no other option than turning to the Court again, in order to ensure a proper execution of the judgment by means of awarding just satisfaction.[97]

The ECtHR accepted Cyprus' request and calculated the injury suffered by victims of human rights violations in the Turkish-sponsored state of Northern Cyprus as 90 million euros. In a note that hints at the limits of the capacity of judicial bodies to ensure implementation, however, the Court highlighted that its judgment on just satisfaction 'conclude[d] the consideration of the matter'.[98]

As usual, the Inter-American Court of Human Rights (IACtHR) has been more assertive regarding its role in implementation. Under Article

[92] European Court of Human Rights Rules of Court 28 March 2024, Rule 75(1).
[93] Application No. 28342/95, *Brumarescu* v. *Romania (Merits)*, [1999] ECHR 105, para. 84.
[94] Application No. 25701/94, *Former King of Greece* v. *Greece (Merits)*, [2000] ECHR 640, para. 107.
[95] Application No. 15318/89, *Loizidou* v. *Turkey (Merits)*, [1996] ECHR 70, para. 69.
[96] Application No. 25781/94, *Cyprus* v. *Turkey (Merits)*, [2001] ECHR 331, operative part, VIII.
[97] Application No. 25781/94, *Cyprus* v. *Turkey (Just Satisfaction)*, [2014] ECHR, para. 13.
[98] Ibid., para. 30.

63(1) of the American Convention on Human Rights, the IACtHR is empowered to follow findings of breach with rulings 'that fair compensation be paid to the injured party'. Starting from its 1988 judgments condemning Honduras in *Velásquez Rodríguez* and *Godínez Cruz,* the Inter-American Court has often reserved the quantification of compensation for a separate phase of proceedings.

Following its condemnatory judgment in *Velásquez Rodríguez* v. *Honduras*, the IACtHR offered the parties an opportunity to settle the case, 'believ[ing] that the parties could agree on the damages',[99] . At the same time, the Court 'reserve[d] the right to homologate the agreement and the power to establish the amount and form [of reparation], if there is none'.[100] In 1989, in the absence of agreement on reparation, the Inter-American Commission re-seised the Court to complete its ruling. The IACtHR then determined that the parties had not complied with its 1988 decision and established an amount of compensation.[101]

The Inter-American Court issued similar rulings in *Godinez Cruz* v. *Honduras.*[102] In *Durand and Ugarte* v. *Peru*, an agreement to provide reparation was merely homologated by the IACtHR.[103] In *Barrios Altos* v. *Peru*, the reparation negotiated included measures to ensure education and health care to the survivors of a massacre committed by members of the Peruvian armed forces, as well as symbolic measures of satisfaction. The Court not only 'confirmed' the agreement but restated its terms in the judgment on reparations, 'reserv[ing] authority to monitor integral compliance'.[104]

99 *Velásquez Rodríguez* v. *Honduras (Merits)*, (1988) Ser C No. 4, para. 191.

100 Ibid., paras. 194(6), 194(7).

101 *Velásquez Rodriguez* v. *Honduras* (*Reparation and Costs*), IACtHR, (1989) Ser. C No 7, paras. 22, 49, 52. See also *Velásquez Rodriguez* v. *Honduras* (*Interpretation of Reparation and Costs*), IACtHR, (1990) Ser. C No. 9, para. 36 (where the Court stated that it was 'empowered to decide on the consequences of the Government's delay in paying the assessed damages').

102 *Godínez Cruz* v. *Honduras (Merits)*, IACtHR, (1989) Ser. C No. 5, para. 201; *Godínez Cruz* v. *Honduras (Reparation and Costs)*, IACtHR, (1989) Ser. C No. 8, para. 55(5); *Godínez Cruz* v. *Honduras (Interpretation)*, IACtHR, (1990) Ser. C No. 10, para. 37.

103 See, for example, IACtHR, *Durand and Ugarte* v. *Peru (Reparations)*, IACtHR, (2001) Ser. C No. 89, Section VIII.

104 *Barrios Altos* v. *Peru (Reparation and Costs)*, IACtHR, (2001) Ser. C No. 87, at VIII. For the IACtHR's compliance monitoring procedure, see Section 7.5.2.3.

9.4.3 Investment Tribunals

In recent practice, investment tribunals usually operate either under the ICSID Convention[105] or under the Arbitration Rules of UNCITRAL.[106] Investment Tribunals acting under UNCITRAL rules are empowered under Article 34(1) to 'make separate awards on different issues at different times'. The same language is found in Article 34(1) of the Permanent Court of Arbitration (PCA) Arbitration Rules 2012.[107] The PCA Optional Rules for arbitrating disputes involving states are more specific, providing that, '[i]n addition to making a final award, the arbitral tribunal shall be entitled to make interim, interlocutory, or partial awards'.[108]

With regard to these rules, Emmanuel Gaillard and John Savage state that, absent party agreement on the matter, 'the arbitrators are responsible for deciding whether it is appropriate to decide by way of partial awards'.[109] Arbitrators may therefore consider the opportunity of issuing partial awards to determine jurisdiction, applicable law, liability, and quantum of damages. Although these partial awards are often issued with the agreement of the parties and are not issued with the express aim of fostering negotiations, this has sometimes been their practical effect. As the authors note, 'a partial award on liability may encourage a settlement'.[110]

This occurred in an investment arbitration under UNCITRAL rules in *Saluka* v. *Czech Republic.* In a partial award, the PCA Arbitral Tribunal found that the Czech Republic's conduct did not amount to unlawful expropriation but that its actions breached the standard of fair and equitable treatment of investment.[111] Shortly after the partial award, the parties – which had been in negotiations for years – were able to

105 Convention on the Settlement of Investment Disputes between States and Nationals of other States, Washington, 18 March 1965, in force 14 October 1966, 575 UNTS 159 ('ICSID Convention').

106 UNCITRAL Arbitration Rules, 2021.

107 PCA, Arbitration Rules 2012, Article 34(1).

108 PCA, Optional Rules for Arbitrating Disputes between Two States 1992, Article 32(1); PCA, Optional Rules for Arbitrating Disputes between Two Parties of which Only One is a State 1993; PCA, Optional Rules for Arbitrating Disputes Involving International Organizations and States 1996, Article 32(1).

109 Gaillard and Savage, *Fouchard, Gaillars, Goldman on International Commercial Arbitration*, 740–744.

110 Ibid.

111 *Saluka Investments BV (Partial Award)*, (2006) PCA IIC 210, paras. 265, 281.

reach first a partial agreement, then a full settlement. Saluka subsequently withdrew its claim.[112]

Given the prohibition on partial awards imposed by the ICSID Convention, the solution encountered by a number of ICSID tribunals has been to issue 'decisions' on specific issues. It is now a regular practice for ICSID tribunals to issue 'decisions on jurisdiction' prior to determining liability and reparation. Although these decisions do not generally impinge on questions of merits, touching upon them may be unavoidable: an entire case may hinge on whether the claimant has made an 'investment' that is protected under treaty rules and whether it is thus entitled to file a claim. In making determinations in this regard, a decision on jurisdiction may serve as a catalyst for negotiations.

There are concrete examples of this effect. In *Telefónica* v. *Argentina*, shortly after the ICSID Tribunal rejected Argentina's objections to jurisdiction,[113] Argentina restored tariff levels that had been frozen for four years. At the request of the parties, the proceedings were subsequently suspended and, three years later, discontinued.[114] In *Trans-Global* v. *Jordan*, after the Tribunal defined that some of the claimant's requests were 'manifestly without legal merit',[115] the parties reached a settlement and requested that the Tribunal record the agreement in the form of an award (as permitted by ICSID Arbitration Rule 43(2)).[116]

More recently, and probably based on the practice of UNCITRAL Tribunals, some ICSID Tribunals have started issuing independent 'decisions on liability', leaving the final stage of the procedure to deal solely with the calculation of damages. Thus, in *LG&E* v. *Argentina*, the Tribunal decided to consider Argentina's claim of necessity in a separate decision prior to the award. In its decision, 'partially granting LG&E's claims', the Tribunal found that Argentina had 'breached the standard of fair and

[112] George Stephanov Georgiev, 'The Award in Saluka Investments v Czech Republic', in W. Michael Reisman (ed.), *The Reasons Requirement in International Investment Arbitration* (Leiden: Martinus Nijhoff, 2008), 149–190, 188.

[113] *Telefónica S. A.* v. *Argentina*, [2006] ICSID Case No ARB/03/20, Decision on Objections to Jurisdiction, 25 May 2006.

[114] Ignacio Torterola and Diego Brian Gosis, 'Argentina', in Jonathan C. Hamilton, Omar E. Garía-Bolívar, and Hernando Otero (eds.), *Latin American Arbitration and Investment Protection* (Brill, 2012), 5–52, 32.

[115] *Trans-Global Petroleum, Inc.* v. *Jordan*, [2008] ICSID Case No ARB/07/25, Decision on the Respondent's Objection under Rule 41(5) of the ICSID Arbitration Rules, 12 May 2008, para. 124(2).

[116] *Trans-Global Petroleum, Inc.* v. *Jordan*, [2009] ICSID Case No ARB/07/25, Consent Award, 8 April 2009.

equitable treatment', was liable for damages, and owed compensation for the losses suffered by the claimant. The question of the amount of compensation was left to 'be determined in a next phase of the arbitration and in respect of which the Tribunal retain[ed] jurisdiction'.[117]

This procedure was repeated by the Tribunal in *Suez* v. *Argentina*, which felt compelled to justify its decision on grounds of the powers accorded to the tribunal by the ICSID Convention.[118] Adding to this jurisprudence, the Tribunal in *Total* v. *Argentina* held that 'Argentina breached its obligations under Article 3 of the BIT ... causing damage to Total', asserting that Total needed to be 'compensated'. It left the assessment of damages to 'be determined in a separate quantum phase of the[] arbitration proceedings ... in respect of which the Tribunal retains jurisdiction'.[119] This formula was repeated by the Tribunal in *Burlington* v. *Ecuador*, which '[d]eclare[d] that Ecuador breached Article III of the Treaty by unlawfully expropriating Burlington's investment'.[120]

9.4.4 *Bifurcation, Trifurcation, and Reverse Bifurcation*

Splitting the procedure into different phases ('bifurcation' or 'trifurcation') may not always be the best decision for purposes of producing speedy reparation. Lucy Greenwood finds that bifurcation may not save time or costs and may be explored by a wrongdoer as a delaying tactic.[121] In *Apotex* v. *US* the ICSID Tribunal, 'weighing for both sides the benefits of procedural fairness and efficiency against the risks of delay, wasted expense and prejudice', decided not to bifurcate the proceedings.[122]

If on the other hand the tribunal aims to produce incentives for settlement (including, in case of continuing breaches, a return to voluntary performance), issuing a public decision assessing liability ensures that the respondent receives an official determination

[117] *LG&E* v. *Argentina*, [2006] ICSID Case No ARB/02/1, Decision on Liability, para. 267(e).

[118] *Suez, Sociedad General de Aguas de Barcelona S.A.* v. *Argentina*, [2010] ICSID Case No ARB/03/19, Decision on Liability, para. 273.

[119] *Total S.A.* v. *Argentina*, [2010] ICSID Case No ARB/04/1, Decision on Liability, para. 485(a), (d).

[120] *Burlington Resources Inc.* v. *Ecuador*, [2012] ICSID Case No ARB/08/5, Decision on Liability, para. 546(C)(1), (D)(1).

[121] Greenwood, 'Does Bifurcation Really Promote Efficiency?', 105.

[122] *Apotex Holdings Inc. and Apotex Inc.* v. *United States of America*, [2013] ICSID ARB (AF)/12/1, Procedural Order deciding Bifurcation, 25 January 2013, para. 10.

highlighting the impending condemnation. This decision may foster a re-establishment of relations or a settlement before the claim leads to an award of damages.

A final possibility, which has not been explored in international law, is so-called reverse bifurcation, in which a partial decision regarding the quantification of the alleged damages precedes the decision on liability.[123] Reverse bifurcation may be useful when a respondent denies that a breach has produced any significant injury. As Thomas Tallerico and Adam Behrendt note, this may 'assist the parties in trying to shape settlement negotiations'.[124] A decision regarding the amount of damage clarifies the stakes involved. At the same time, reverse bifurcation may leave the tribunal with a binary choice at the subsequent stage: declaring the respondent liable for the entirety of the injury caused, or not liable at all.

9.5 Deferral of Remedies at the Merits Stage

Another possibility for ICs issuing partial rulings is to limit the judgment on the merits to Mere Adjudication, withholding not only the determination of the amount of reparation but the very Declaration of Breach and engagement of responsibility, or at least the determination of which Consequential Duties arise. An adjudicator adopting this approach limits its judicial intervention to interpreting the relevant rules and affirming applicable performance obligations. This provides parties with a definition of their obligations without ascribing responsibility for violations. The IC may also foreshadow the incidence of further remedies, including a Declaration of Breach, to be ascertained at a subsequent stage.

Although a judicial Declaration of Breach is arguably a less persuasive deterrent than an award of damages, the underlying logic is the same. Rather than issuing the Declaration of Breach immediately and using it as a form of reparation or sanction, which might exhaust the possibilities for judicial remedies, an IC authoritatively determines the relevant rights

123 Drury D. Stevenson, 'Reverse Bifurcation' (2008) 75 *University of Cincinnati Law Review* 213 (finding that early assessment of damages in asbestos litigation fostered settlements, among other effects).

124 Thomas J. Tallerico and J. Adam Behrendt, 'The Use of Bifurcation and Direct Testimony Witness Statements in International Commercial Arbitration Proceedings' (2003) 3 *Journal of International Arbitration* 20.

and obligations but withholds any ruling on the conformity of state conduct with duties. This provides the complainant with the possibility to negotiate directly with the respondent, and, if this is not fruitful, to resort to adjudication once more, requesting a formal Declaration of Breach and the establishment of Consequential Duties. At the subsequent phase, the IC can then consider the matter taking into account the totality of the behaviour of the parties.

ICs often issue decisions that merely establish legal entitlements, withholding an assessment of responsibility or even a Declaration of Breach. If an IC issues a single final decision, its choices are either to determine fully the consequences of internationally wrongful conduct (and to risk providing unsatisfactory remedies)[125] or to consider that the declaration regarding entitlement sufficiently addresses the requests of the claimant.[126]

Courts seeking to favour performance may offer a third response: clarifying the obligations of the parties and establishing that a party's conduct may be (or, more controversially, that it may soon become) inconsistent with its obligations while withholding a ruling on the matter. Rather than fully discharging its duties by issuing a final ruling that might make it *functus officio*, the adjudicator issues a (de jure or de facto) partial ruling and directs the parties to find a solution through negotiation.

By withholding its ruling on one or more of these issues, the IC thus preserves its ability to engage in remedy escalation. The court or tribunal retains jurisdiction to hear subsequent claims, if the complainant argues that the defendant has failed to provide it with satisfactory relief or that the conduct it objects to persists. International courts have occasionally adopted the approach taken early on by General Agreement on Tariffs and Trade (GATT) adjudicators (now codified in the WTO DSU) and established a *reasonable period of time* within which parties must reach a settlement without further judicial intervention.[127] After this time, each party is again empowered to have resort to the adjudicator to pronounce with finality on the existence of breach and ensuing Consequential Duties.

[125] See Gattini, 'Breach of the Obligation to Prevent and Reparation Thereof in the ICJ's Genocide Judgment', 695.

[126] *Land and Maritime Boundary between Cameroon and Nigeria*, [2002] ICJ Reports 303, p. 451; *Territorial and Maritime Dispute, Nicaragua* v. *Colombia*, [2012] ICJ Reports 624, p. 718.

[127] See Section 6.3.

9.5.1 Declaratory Judgments and Withholding of Remedies

When entering into special agreements, parties may request that the court or tribunal deliver decisions in more than one phase, withholding judicial remedies and allowing the parties time to agree on a path forward based on a judicial determination of their rights and obligations. In *Free Zones of Upper Savoy and the District of Gex*, the special agreement between France and Switzerland required the PCIJ to settle the dispute in two phases. In the first phase, the Court would only determine whether the 1919 Treaty of Versailles had abrogated a regime operating between the parties under the 1815 Treaty of Paris. The PCIJ should, 'before rendering any judgment, ... accord to the two Parties a reasonable time to settle between themselves the new régime to be applied in those districts'.[128] If the parties could agree on this regime, the Court would not be required to issue a final ruling.

In the 1929 Order that concluded the first phase, the PCIJ found it 'impossible to conclude' that the Treaty of Versailles had abrogated the prior regime. It accorded the parties nine months to settle the dispute between themselves.[129] When Switzerland subsequently filed an application requesting a decision from the Court, rather than issuing the 'single judgment' on the matter (as required by the special agreement), the PCIJ found that some outstanding legal disputes prevented the parties from reaching 'a settlement covering the whole problem'.[130] The PCIJ then issued a second order, making judicial pronouncements on the legal relations between the parties.

In its operative part, the second Order in *Free Zones* merely provided the parties with eight more months to settle their dispute. The Court expressed its intention 'to offer the parties ... a further opportunity for achieving [a settlement]'.[131] Only when the parties could not reach agreement did the PCIJ finally issue a judgment. Regretting that the parties had not achieved a settlement and highlighting the limitations inherent to its judicial function, the Court issued a judgment 'limited to questions of law'.[132]

[128] *Free Zones of Upper Savoy and the District of Gex (First Phase) (Order), France* v. *Switzerland*, Judgment, (1929) PCIJ Ser A No 22, p. 7.

[129] Ibid., p. 21.

[130] *Free Zones of Upper Savoy and the District of Gex (Second Phase) (Order), France* v. *Switzerland*, Judgment, (1930) PCIJ Ser A No 24, p. 15.

[131] Ibid.

[132] *Free Zones of Upper Savoy and the District of Gex, France* v. *Switzerland*, Judgment, (1932) PCIJ Ser A/B No 46, p. 162.

The main question raised in *Free Zones* concerned the extent to which the PCIJ could intervene beyond 'the sphere in which a Court of Justice, concerned with the application of rules of law, can help in the solution of disputes between two States'.[133] The parties convened a group of 'experts-arbitrators' to rule on the remainder of the dispute, establishing a customs regime for the free zones 'more in accordance with the current economic conditions'.[134]

On a number of other occasions, ICs have taken approaches similar to that adopted by the PCIJ in *Free Zones*. In particular, adjudicators have often rejected requests to follow interpretations of rights and obligations, that is, Mere Adjudication, with determinations of Consequential Duties or even Declarations of Breach. Especially in inter-state disputes, ICs – whether or not limited by their constitutive instrument or the agreement of the parties – often declare the rights and obligations of parties without seeking to establish a breach or determine consequences for it.

This has been the dominant approach to adjudication in border disputes. In *Nigeria* v. *Cameroon*, the ICJ affirmed that the judgment determining the respective territories of the parties 'sufficiently addressed' the injury suffered by Cameroon and stated that it would not 'seek to ascertain' Nigeria's responsibility for the occupation of Cameroonian territory.[135] Likewise, the UNCLOS Article VII Tribunal in *Guyana* v. *Suriname* declared that there had been a breach involving the threat of the use of force;[136] however, in response to Guyana's request that Suriname's responsibility be engaged, it stated that 'Guyana now has undisputed title to the area where the incident occurred – the injury done to Guyana has thus been "sufficiently addressed"'.[137] In *Territorial and Maritime Dispute*, the ICJ rejected Nicaragua's request for a declaration that Colombia was acting inconsistently with its obligation. Its grounds were, first, that the judgment delimited a border which was previously in dispute; and, second, that it attributed to Colombia some of the area which Nicaragua was claiming. This, the Court explained, made a Declaration of Breach unwarranted even if, in retrospect, its judgment meant that Colombia had effectively been arresting Nicaraguan ships in

133 Ibid.

134 *Free Zones of Upper Savoy and the District of Gex, France* v. *Switzerland*, Award, (1933) 3 RIAA 1455, 1457.

135 *Land and Maritime Boundary between Cameroon and Nigeria, Cameroon* v. *Nigeria: Equatorial Guinea Intervening*, Judgment, [2002] ICJ Reports 303, p. 317–321, 452.

136 *Guyana* v. *Suriname*, (2008) 47 ILM 166, 231.

137 Ibid., 232.

the Nicaraguan Exclusive Economic Zone.[138] The ICJ would only issue a formal Declaration of Breach in a subsequent dispute, *Alleged Violations*, in which Nicaragua showed that Colombia had not respected its rights as determined in *Territorial and Maritime Dispute*.[139] In *Ghana/Côte d'Ivoire*, the ITLOS Special Chamber summarised this practice thus:

> [M]aritime activities undertaken by a State in an area of the continental shelf which has been attributed to another State by an international judgment cannot be considered to be in violation of the sovereign rights of the latter if those activities were carried out before the judgment was delivered and if the area concerned was the subject of claims made in good faith by both States.[140]

Formal Declarations of Breach have also been avoided by the ICJ in non-border disputes, where the Court concluded that Mere Adjudication constituted sufficient remedy. In *Asylum*, the ICJ found that Colombia's grant of asylum to Mr Haya de la Torre 'was not made in conformity with' Colombia's international obligations towards Peru, without determining any consequences for this assessment.[141] In *Award of the King of Spain*, Honduras requested the ICJ to find that the 'non-execution' of the award by Nicaragua involved 'a consequent obligation to make reparation'.[142] The Court did not examine the matter. It determined simply that the award was 'valid and binding and that Nicaragua [wa]s under an obligation to give effect to it'.[143]

An adjudicator may of course dismiss or reject the request for determination of consequences, exhausting its jurisdiction over the dispute. In this case, any new claims must be based on new grounds of jurisdiction. By contrast, a court aiming to create an incentive for performance may withhold the Declaration of Breach and the establishment of Consequential Duties, reserving these remedies for cases in which the determinations made are insufficient to lead to the resolution of the dispute. Indeed, the adjudicator sometimes specifically authorises

138 *Territorial and Maritime Dispute*, [2012] ICJ Reports 624, p. 718.

139 *Alleged Violations of Sovereign Rights and Maritime Spaces in the Caribbean Sea (Merits), Nicaragua* v. *Colombia*, [2022] ICJ Reports 266, p. 366.

140 *Delimitation of the Maritime Boundary in the Atlantic Ocean (Ghana/Côte d'Ivoire)*, Judgment, ITLOS Reports 2017, p. 4, 159.

141 *Asylum Case*, [1950] ICJ Reports 266, p. 288.

142 *Case concerning the Arbitral Award made by the King of Spain on 23 December 1906, Honduras* v. *Nicaragua*, [1960] ICJ Reports 192, p. 196.

143 Ibid., p. 217.

the claimant to seise it again if the respondent subsequently fails to comply with the obligations defined in its ruling.

9.5.2 *Withholding Declarations of Breach: Nuclear Tests, Case A/21 and Goetz* v. *Burundi*

In three distinct contexts of adjudication, the ICJ in *Nuclear Tests*, the IUCT in *Case A/21*, and the ICSID Tribunal in *Goetz* v. *Burundi* have withheld declarations of breach. Using their judicial authority in an unorthodox manner, in their partial decisions these adjudicators stated – but claimed not to be determining – the legal obligations of the asserted wrongdoers.

The ICJ took this approach in *Nuclear Tests* – two cases brought by Australia and New Zealand concerning the legality of atmospheric nuclear tests carried out by France in the Pacific region. Rather than pronouncing on jurisdiction, the ICJ decided first to inquire on the 'pre-preliminary' issue[144] of the existence of a dispute. The Court then interpreted public, out-of-court statements by French authorities that France would no longer carry out further atmospheric tests as entailing for France a voluntary legal commitment to refrain from carrying out such tests.

With this commitment established and interpreted as a legal obligation, the Court reasoned, 'the objective of the Applicant[s] has in effect been accomplished',[145] making any further pronouncement by the Court 'devoid of purpose'.[146] The ICJ thus refrained from making any determinations with respect to the legality of France's conduct, even when this was specifically requested (by New Zealand), or to determine, as France requested, its lack of jurisdiction. Instead, the Court merely established the existence of a self-imposed obligation by France to cease all atmospheric tests and considered that this provided the applicants with the remedy they demanded.

The ICJ followed this purported non-decision with a provision that, 'if the basis of [the *Nuclear Tests*] Judgment were to be affected' (i.e. in case of non-compliance by France with its (allegedly) self-imposed obligation), the applicants would be entitled to a new recourse to the Court:

144 The term was used by Judge Fitzmaurice in *Northern Cameroons, Cameroon* v. *United Kingdom*, Preliminary Objections, [1963] ICJ Reports 15, p. 103 (Fitzmaurice).

145 *Nuclear Tests, New Zealand* v. *France*, [1974] ICJ Reports 457, p. 474.

146 Ibid., p. 476.

> [If]f the basis of this Judgment were to be affected, the Applicant could request an examination of the situation in accordance with the provisions of the Statute; the denunciation by France, by letter dated 2 January 1974, of the General Act for the Pacific Settlement of International Disputes, which is relied on as a basis of jurisdiction in the present case, cannot constitute by itself an obstacle to the presentation of such a request.[147]

There is no provision in the ICJ Statute admitting an earlier judgment as a ground of jurisdiction. Nevertheless, the judgment in *Nuclear Tests* empowered the claimants to file a fresh application before the Court, at any point in time, requesting a judgment on France's compliance with the ICJ-determined version of France's self-imposed commitments. The *Nuclear Tests* judgment thus established an ad hoc basis for ICJ jurisdiction – granting it jurisdiction over compliance with one of its rulings.

Two decades later, when France once more conducted nuclear tests in the same region, this time underground, New Zealand invoked this ad hoc non-compliance procedure. The claim was unsuccessful, as the ICJ concluded that its initial judgment 'dealt exclusively with atmospheric nuclear tests'.[148] While this could be read as too literal an interpretation of the original judgment, in their original requests both applicants had referred solely to atmospheric tests.

Additionally, the existence of a general rule of customary international law prohibiting nuclear tests – the sole source of substantive obligations invoked by the parties – was reasonably in doubt with regard to atmospheric testing. A judicial determination establishing a prohibition on underground tests would have not only exceeded the scope of the requests underlying the 1974 judgment but also rested on a seriously tenuous legal foundation.

The unorthodox procedure the ICJ employed in *Nuclear Tests* was largely a function of the very particular features of this case. Hugh Thirlway criticised the Court for keeping alive jurisdiction when France had denounced the treaty providing for it. He nonetheless highlighted the implications of the decision:

> [T]he Court has recognized that it can provide in advance for something that might be called a reopening of a case concluded with a judgment [even if] by doing so it cannot preserve a jurisdiction that has in the

147 Ibid., p. 477.

148 *Request for an Examination of the Situation (Nuclear Tests), New Zealand* v. *France*, [1995] ICJ Reports 288, p. 306.

> meantime been terminated by the State so as to extend to acts and events subsequent to that termination; at most, [jurisdiction] may still be exercised . . . in respect of elements of the original claim. Reopenings of this kind must in any event remain highly exceptional, and there would be no need to provide for them in the Statute and Rules of the Court, which – it appears – are in this respect not exhaustive.[149]

Its uniqueness notwithstanding, the *Nuclear Tests* case shows that, conceivably, an IC ruling setting out obligations for the parties may establish judicial review over subsequent conduct of the parties in violation of the adjudicated obligations. The prospect of a Declaration of Breach, and potentially Consequential Duties, then becomes a deterrent to non-compliance with the obligations set out in the initial decision.

The *Nuclear Tests* judgment may offer the impression of being less intrusive than a condemnatory judgment, as it does not formally declare a legal breach or award any reparation. However, by allowing the aggrieved party access to a judicial remedy for non-compliance, this ruling gave Australia and New Zealand a legal instrument to address non-compliance. Whatever one thinks of its persuasiveness, such instrument would have been unavailable if the Court had declared the unlawful character of the tests, leaving the question of compliance to be addressed entirely through non-adjudicative, political processes.

The IUCT adopted a similar approach in *Case A/21*, foreshadowing a Declaration of Breach without formally issuing it. Iran claimed that the United States was responsible under the Algiers Declarations for the non-payment of five IUCT awards issued against American private parties. According to Iran, the United States had a duty to give effect to IUCT awards and was therefore under the obligation to pay the amounts not paid by its nationals.

The IUCT held that, while the Algiers Declarations did not create for the United States an obligation to pay the awards that its nationals failed to pay, as a matter of international law both the United States and Iran had an obligation to implement the Declarations in good faith. While '[t]he good faith obligation leaves a considerable latitude' to the parties regarding the means of enforcement, it was 'incumbent on each State Party to provide some procedure or mechanism whereby enforcement may be obtained within its national jurisdiction'.[150] Because Iran had not made any attempts to enforce the awards in US courts, the Tribunal

[149] Thirlway, *The Law and Procedure of the International Court of Justice*, 1026.
[150] *Case No A/21*, IUCT, (1987) Decision No 62-A21-FT, para. 15.

concluded, the United States had not failed to implement the Algiers Accords. In elliptic language, the IUCT then stated:

> Only if systems existing in the United States had not resulted in the enforcement of awards of this Tribunal against United States nationals would the question arise as to what further measures, if any, the United States might be required to take in order to ensure the 'effectiveness' of the Algiers Declarations.[151]

As a standing tribunal with continuing jurisdiction, the IUCT did not have to provide specifically for its own jurisdiction to examine US compliance. This point was noted by Judge Paraviz Ansari in his separate opinion.[152]

A decade later, Iran returned to the IUCT claiming that US courts had refused to enforce two awards issued by the Tribunal. The IUCT first reaffirmed that it had 'no authority under the Algiers Declarations to prescribe the means by which each of the States provides for . . . enforcement'. However, the Tribunal held, the 'procedures and mechanisms among which a State Party . . . may chose must also be adequate to achieve the objective envisaged by the Declarations, i.e., the enforceability of Tribunal decisions and awards as final and binding'.[153]

Keeping in line with its previous ruling, the IUCT refused to issue a determination, requested by Iran, that the United States was under a duty to establish a more suitable procedure for the enforcement of future awards of the Tribunal. However, faced with non-compliance, the IUCT issued a Declaration of Breach and determined Consequential Duties. It found that, in the specific cases presented by Iran, the United States had 'not fulfilled its obligations under the Algiers Declarations' and awarded Iran compensation, to be paid by the United States, equivalent to the losses suffered by Iranian companies as a result of non-enforcement by US courts of awards of the Tribunal.[154]

A similar remedial strategy was employed by the ICSID Arbitral Tribunal in *Goetz* v. *Burundi*. In its award, the Tribunal held that

[151] Ibid., para. 16.

[152] Ibid. (Parviz Ansari), para. 3.

[153] *Case No A27*, IUCT, (1995) Award No 586-A27-FT, para. 59.

[154] Ibid., paras. 74–75. The IUCT specified that its ruling related to non-enforcement of specific awards by US courts. 'Only after Iran has made timely attempts to enforce those . . . awards in United States courts, and only if Iran establishes that those courts have wrongfully refused to implement the awards', could similar requests succeed (Ibid., para. 81).

Burundi's conduct (the withdrawal of certificates that provided for special 'free zone' treatment to a company owned by the claimants) constituted a 'measure with similar effect' to expropriation.[155] Instead of proceeding to declare a breach and order compensation, the tribunal found, without offering much in the way of reasoning, that at the time of this ruling 'the question of the international legality of the Decision of the 29 May 1995 remain[ed] open'.[156] Burundi could still avoid a Declaration of Breach by acting in one of two ways. It could award the claimants an 'adequate and effective indemnity',[157] or it could provide it with *restitutio in integrum*, restoring to the affected company its free zone certificate, without having to indemnify it for past injury.[158] If Burundi failed both to restore the claimants' company's status as a duty-free enterprise and to pay adequate and effective indemnity, the arbitral tribunal foreshadowed further remedies: 'the international responsibility of the Burundian state would be established'.[159]

Investment law is particular in that offering compensation, even if delayed, may make an expropriation lawful. However, no equivalent effect attaches to restitution. The Tribunal nonetheless established a period of time of four months for Burundi to proceed to either restitution or compensation. After this, the claimants would be allowed to return to the tribunal requesting a Declaration of Breach and seeking Consequential Duties, that is, monetary compensation.[160] The award therefore afforded Burundi the opportunity to resume the performance of its obligations and avoid all international responsibility for the injury caused.

The *Goetz* v. *Burundi* ruling was initially successful in inducing the parties to agree on a path towards performance. Three months after it

[155] *Goetz and Others* v. *Burundi*, [1998] ICSID Case No ARB/95/3, Judgment (First Part), 2 September 1998, para. 130.

[156] Ibid., para. 131.

[157] Ibid.

[158] Ibid., para. 132 ('En pareil cas, la licéité internationale de l'action de la République du Burundi ne ferait plus problème. Le rétablissement de l'agrément d'AFFIMET en qualité d'entreprise franche n'aurait certes d'effet que pour l'avenir, et la question d'une réparation pour les dommages causés entre la date de la révocation de l'agrément et celle de son rétablissement pourrait se poser. Le Tribunal estime toutefois que, la révocation de l'agrément ayant été légale au regard du droit national burundais et n'ayant engendré aucune responsabilité de l'Etat burundais dans le cadre de son droit interne, il n'y aurait pas lieu à une indemnisation de tels dommages, à supposer même qu'ils puissent être établis.')

[159] Ibid., para. 131.

[160] Ibid., para. 137.

was issued, the parties reached an agreement whereby Burundi would reimburse the claimants' company for taxes unlawfully collected. The agreement also established a convention for the operation of the company, to be 'ratified' by ICSID (*'ratifiée par le CIRDI'*). A 'second part' of the award, delivered by the same Tribunal, incorporated the agreement of the parties and provided that performance of its obligations would be subject to the jurisdiction of ICSID arbitral tribunals.[161]

Two years later, the investors initiated a new dispute before ICSID, arguing that Burundi had not respected some provisions of the tribunal-approved agreement. The new procedure was riddled with difficulties as a new Arbitral Tribunal had to be composed. It took a decade for this Tribunal to issue a new decision. In its decision, the Tribunal rejected the claimants' contention that Burundi's post-1999 measures constituted a new indirect expropriation; but it awarded the claimants indemnities, with interest, for the original indirect expropriation and for a number of subsequent unlawful acts for which it found Burundi responsible.[162]

As in *Nuclear Tests* and *Case A/21*, in *Goetz* v. *Burundi* the adjudicator could conceivably have issued a Declaration of Breach, coupled with Consequential Duties, as requested by the claimant. It could also have dismissed the claims as premature. Instead, these adjudicators provided judicial guidance on the applicable law – Mere Adjudication – while withholding formal Declarations of Breach and establishing Consequential Duties. The adjudicators nonetheless foreshadowed these remedies, setting up a judicial procedure to which the claimants could resort in case the respondents failed to comply with their obligations as established in the partial decision.

9.5.3 Employing Compensation as a Subsidiary Remedy

A further possibility exists for IC to enjoin performance and foreshadow the issuing of a remedy in case of non-compliance. The IC may award as a remedy *restitutio in integrum* while establishing monetary compensation as a subsidiary remedy in case this restitution is not provided. This combines a preference for the remedy which has primacy under international law (restitution) with the prospect that, since restitution cannot usually be imposed on the offending state, any injury that

[161] *Goetz and Others* v. *Burundi*, [1999] ICSID Case No ARB/95/3, Judgment (Second Part), 29 January 1999.

[162] *Goetz and Others* v. *Burundi*, [2012] ICSID Case No. ARB/01/2, Judgment, 21 June 2012.

remains unaddressed will be subject to judicially determined compensation. Outside the context of expropriation, the Andean Court of Justice (ACJ) has adopted a similar stance, using the prospect of pecuniary damages to demand from Colombia compliance with trade commitments.

The degree to which restitution is preferred over compensation varies according to the primary rules breached and the circumstances of the breach. Expropriation, for example, may violate investment obligations as well as human rights obligations. In the case of permitted expropriations that violate obligations due to the lack of compensation, an adjudicator may offer the state a choice between compensation and restitution. In other cases, restitution may be the primary remedy awarded, while an award for compensation is expressly foreshadowed in case restitution is not provided. The investment tribunals in *Texaco* v. *Libya*, *Arif* v. *Moldova* and *Siemens* v. *Argentina* favoured restitution while foreshadowing compensation as a deterrent in case of non-compliance.

The cases may be distinguished based on the obligation involved. In *Texaco* v. *Libya*, the Tribunal established, at the request of the claimant, a duty of restitution; in case Libya did not restore its investment in five months, Texaco could request a determination of damages from the tribunal.[163] In *Arif* v. *Moldova*, at the request of the host state (and against the preference expressed by the claimant), the ICSID Tribunal offered to the state the possibility of providing restitution rather than issuing an order for compensation. While framed as an alternative for the state, restitution in *Arif* v. *Moldova* was made subject to the state's offered restitution being *acceptable to the investor*. Moldova, the Tribunal noted, had not shown evidence that it would be able to provide the restitution it offered.

[163] *Texaco Overseas Petroleum Co* v. *Government of the Libyan Arab Republic*, (1979) 53 ILR 389, 507–511. In some cases, tribunals have considered that damages for uncompensated expropriation should in fact be awarded at a higher level than the compensation that would be owed in cases in which expropriation is permitted. This distinction was made by the PCIJ in *Factory at Chorzów (Merits)*, (1928) PCIJ Ser A No. 17, p. 47 (arguing that using the same criteria would be 'tantamount to rendering lawful liquidation and unlawful dispossession indistinguishable'). On this, see International Law Commission, Draft Articles on Responsibility of States for Internationally Wrongful Acts, with commentaries, A/56/10, 2001, p. 102. See also *ADC Affiliated Limited and ADC & ADMC Management Limited* v. *Hungary*, [2006] ICSID Case No ARB/03/16, 2 October 2006, para. 481. *Texaco Overseas Petroleum Co* v. *Government of the Libyan Arab Republic*, (1979) 53 ILR 389, 507–511.

The Tribunal thus suspended the remedy of compensation for ninety days; if restitution were not possible, or if the claimant found Moldova's proposal for restitution unsatisfactory, compensation would become due.[164] To avoid another stage of proceedings, the Tribunal included in the ruling in which it afforded Moldova the possibility of restitution a calculation of the compensation that would be owed if Moldova could not provide the investor with acceptable restitution.

The *Siemens* v. *Argentina* award combined the two approaches. As the obligation to be performed (the return of a performance bond in the amount of 20 million US dollars) had a clear monetary content, the Tribunal could simply determine that the primary remedy was the restitution of the bond Argentina owed to Siemens. If the bond were not returned in thirty days, an equivalent amount would be owed as compensation.[165]

The European Court of Human Rights has sometimes adopted in relation to expropriation a solution similar to that adopted by these investment tribunals. In *Papamichalopolous* v. *Greece*, the ECtHR held that the continued occupation of the applicants' land by the Greek military constituted a breach of the applicants' right to property. In its decision on reparation, rather than simply ordering compensation, the Court offered Greece the choice between 'return[ing] to the applicants, within six months, the land in issue', or 'failing such restitution' to pay an amount of compensation already determined in the decision.[166]

In *Brumarescu* v. *Romania*, the ECtHR adopted a different position, closer to *Texaco* v. *Libya* than to *Arif* v. *Moldova*. At the merits stage, the Court held that the taking of the applicant's house without justification unlawfully deprived him of his right to property, constituting a breach of the ECHR. The applicant requested restitution of the house, or, failing this, payment or equivalent compensation. Finding that a mutually agreeable solution remained attainable, the ECtHR stated that 'the question of the application of Article 41 [wa]s not ready for decision' and reserved the matter for further proceedings.[167] The Court invited the parties to submit written observations on the outcome of the dispute

[164] *Arif* v. *Moldova*, [2013] ICSID Case No ARB/11/23, Award, 8 April 2013, para. 570–572.

[165] *Siemens A.G.* v. *Argentina*, [2007] ICSID CASE No. ARB/02/8, Award, 6 February 2007, para. 403(9).

[166] Application No. 14556/89, *Papamichalopoulos (Article 50)*, [1995] ECLI:CE:ECHR:1995:1031JUD001455689, paras. 2–3.

[167] Application No. 28342/95, *Brumarescu (Merits)*, [1999] ECHR 105, paras. 79–84.

within three months. At this stage, this was still a partial exercise of jurisdiction with deferral of consequences.

The parties not having reached a settlement, in 2001 the ECtHR determined under ECHR Article 41 not that compensation was due but that Romania was under an obligation to return to the applicant, within six months, his house and the land on which it was. Failing restitution, Romania would be obliged to pay compensation for the lost property.[168] Romania subsequently restored to Mr Brumarescu 'some of the contested property', paying material damages for the remainder of the property and moral damages and legal costs determined by the ECtHR. The Committee of Ministers considered the reparation satisfactory and closed the case.[169]

In *Former King of Greece* v. *Greece*, the ECtHR adopted a third approach. In this case, the taking of the applicants' property (Greece's former royal estates) was considered to have been lawful and in the public interest as required by the ECHR. However, the absence of any compensation made the expropriation a breach of the applicants' right to property.[170] The Court allowed six months for agreement between the parties. In its Article 41 judgment, rather than ordering restitution as requested by the applicants, the ECtHR took into account the relevance of the property for the Greek state and simply awarded to the claimants compensation.[171] Greece then paid the compensation due.[172]

In a different context, the ACJ adopted a similar procedure. Faced with Colombia's failure to comply with a 2005 judgment, the ACJ – which had until then issued declaratory rulings establishing non-compliance with prior judgments, as well as declarations of Permissible Responses – took the step of inquiring whether the Court could determine monetary compensation as a sanction for 'aggravated non-compliance'.[173] Rather than establishing compensation outright, the ACJ requested the opinion

[168] Application No. 28342/95, *Brumarescu (Article 41)*, [2001] ECHR paras. 22–23.
[169] Committee of Ministers (CoE), *Execution of Brumarescu and 30 Other Cases against Romania*, 20 July 2007, CM/ResDH, 90.
[170] Application No. 25701/94, *Former King of Greece* v. *Greece (Judgment)*, [2000] ECHR 640, paras. 87, 99.
[171] Application No. 25701/94, *Former King of Greece* v. *Greece (Article 41)*, [2002] ECHR, para. 77.
[172] Committee of Ministers (CoE), *Execution of Former King of Greece and Others against Greece*, 22 February 2006, CM/ResDH, 5.
[173] ACJ, *Case No. 118-AI-2003 (Non-compliance with Judgment of 14 April 2005) (Second Summary Procedure)*, Judgment, 12 July 2023, para. 4.1.26.

of the Andean Community Secretariat on the permissibility and opportunity of awarding compensation as a sanction, affording Colombia time to consider a change of conduct.[174] The next year, Colombia appeared before the Court and demonstrated its objective compliance with the ruling (though Peru and Ecuador argued that this was 'opportunistic compliance').[175]

9.6 Anticipation of Rulings in Incidental Proceedings: Decisions on Jurisdiction and Provisional Measures

Just as it may provide for judicial determinations without following them with specific remedies at the merits stage, a court or tribunal may make provisions for substantive rights and obligations of the parties within one of the incidental proceedings that may arise prior to judgments on the merits, such as rulings on jurisdiction and provisional measures. This has two advantages over similar determinations made at the merits stage: first, the adjudicator may provide judicial guidance more quickly than if it reserves the matter in its entirety to a ruling on the merits; second, there is no need to withhold remedies, as these remedies could in any case only be provided at the merits stage.

This section examines two techniques ICs have used to foreshadow rulings on the merits and judicial remedies within pre-merits decisions. First is the inclusion, in rulings on jurisdiction, of pronouncements on the legal standard that will be applied at the merits stage. Besides indicating to the parties the IC's inclination, these pronouncements offer defendants a chance to avoid a ruling on the merits by offering transactional remedies. Second is the granting of provisional measures that, if complied with, do not solely safeguard the utility of the final ruling but de facto provide the claimant with the object of its claim.

9.6.1 Anticipating Legal Standards at the Jurisdictional Stage: SGS v. *Philippines and BIVAC* v. *Paraguay*

At the jurisdictional stage of a dispute, an adjudicator in principle limits itself to finding whether or not it has jurisdiction over the dispute, and

[174] Ibid., para. 4.2.6.

[175] ACJ, *Case No. 118-AI-2003 (Non-compliance with Judgment of 14 April 2005) (Second Summary Procedure)*, 10 October 2023, Order, para. 3.1.32. See also ACJ, Case No. 118-AI-2003 (Non-compliance with Judgment of 14 April 2005) (Second Summary Procedure), Request for Interpretation, 24 October 2023.

whether or not claims are admissible.[176] Decisions by which an IC accepts jurisdiction and/or determines the scope of the justiciable claim may cause the parties to update their beliefs about the prospects for gains and losses, thereby facilitating negotiations and a settlement. Though guiding negotiations in this manner may be a useful incidental effect of rulings made at this stage, its technical purpose is simply to establish the scope of the dispute, or that of its justiciable elements.

Despite this primary function, some ICSID Arbitral Tribunals have anticipated at this stage the legal standard they would apply to the challenged conduct at the merits stage.[177] The relevant cases, *SGS* v. *Pakistan* and *SGS* v. *Philippines*, concerned a particular substantive question: whether the failure of a state to abide by the terms of a *contract* with the investor may constitute a breach of an international investment *treaty*. The relevant contracts provided for the exclusive jurisdiction of local courts to settle disputes concerning them. At the same time, the investment treaties these tribunals were empowered to apply contained 'umbrella clauses', by which host states agreed to observe commitments and obligations assumed towards covered investors.[178] Performance of contracts was therefore guaranteed by the international agreement, making it an international obligation.

The prior jurisprudence of ICSID Tribunals had not been uniform regarding the existence of jurisdiction of investment tribunals in these cases. In the previous case *SGS* v. *Pakistan*, the Tribunal had determined that it had no jurisdiction over the matter, because a breach of contract is not, 'by itself, a violation of international law'.[179] In *CMS* v. *Argentina*, by contrast, the Tribunal had stated that a treaty claim may arise out of a breach of contract, if there is 'significant interference by governments or public agencies with the rights of the investor'.[180]

[176] The 'jurisdictional' stage of international disputes often concerns primarily, and sometimes solely, the admissibility of claims. On these two concepts, see Sections 8.2 and 8.3.

[177] This was perhaps also the case in *Nuclear Tests*, though the ICJ then issued a final judgment rather than merely a decision on jurisdiction. See Section 9.5.2.

[178] See Tarcisio Gazzini and Attila Tanzi, 'Handle with Care: Umbrella Clauses and MFN Treatment in Investment Arbitration' (2013) 14 *Journal of World Investment & Trade* 978.

[179] *SGS* v. *Pakistan*, [2003] ICSID Case No ARB/01/13, Decision of the Tribunal on Objections to Jurisdiction, para. 167.

[180] *CMS Gas Transmission Co* v. *Argentine Republic*, [2005] ICSID No ARB/01/8, Award, para. 299.

The *SGS* v. *Philippines* Tribunal's ruling was described as treading a 'middle ground'.[181] It held that the failure of the Philippines to abide by the contract could constitute a breach of the obligation of fair and equitable treatment, allowing SGS to submit a claim under the investment treaty. However, SGS had not yet attempted to obtain the contractual amounts it claimed through judicial proceedings before local courts. A breach of treaty would only occur if domestic courts failed to provide SGS with the appropriate redress for the violation of the contract. For this reason, this Tribunal found, SGS's claim had been filed prematurely; it was 'within jurisdiction but inadmissible'.[182]

Rather than dismissing the claim, the Arbitral Tribunal in *SGS* v. *Philippines* decided to stay proceedings pending 'determination of the amount payable, either by agreement between the parties or by the Philippine courts'.[183] The Tribunal thus essentially granted the Philippines an opportunity to perform its treaty obligations, including through a domestic court ruling securing respect for the contract. In this case, the Philippines would not breach its treaty obligations, and no international claim would arise. The ICSID Tribunal went beyond this statement and instituted a genuine mechanism for compliance control, establishing for the parties a duty to report to the Tribunal on compliance every six months.[184] Four years later, the Tribunal rendered an award embodying the parties' settlement agreement.[185]

BIVAC v. *Paraguay* also involved a claim of breach of the standard of fair and equitable treatment. The claimant argued that Paraguay had failed to respect a contract, though the contract was subject to the exclusive jurisdiction of the Courts of Asunción. As in the previous case, this ICSID Arbitral Tribunal held that the treaty claim would be inadmissible if, through proceedings before Paraguay's domestic courts, BIVAC were able to vindicate its rights.[186] The Tribunal stayed its proceedings

[181] Matthew Wendtlandt, 'SGS v Philippines and the Role of ICSID Tribunals in Investor-State Contract Disputes' (2008) 43 *Texas International Law Journal* 523, 555.

[182] *SGS* v. *Philippines*, [2004] ICSID Case No ARB/02/6, Order on Objections to Jurisdiction, para. 171.

[183] Ibid., para. 175.

[184] Ibid., para. 176 ('The parties are directed to report briefly to the Tribunal, either jointly or separately, at six-month intervals commencing 1 July 2004, on the steps being taken for the resolution of the present claim').

[185] ICSID Secretariat, 25(1) *News from ICSID* (2008) 7.

[186] *BIVAC* v. *Paraguay*, [2012] ICSID Case No. ARB/07/9, Further Decision on Objections to Jurisdiction, 9 October 2012, para. 282.

and provided BIVAC with three months to pursue a claim before the local courts.

The *BIVAC* v. *Paraguay* Tribunal went further than the previous one. This Tribunal expressly established conditions, applicable both to the Paraguayan government and to the Paraguayan courts, for a finding that Paraguay had 'deal[t] fairly with the claims' of BIVAC:

> [T]he Tribunal expects that Paraguay will not introduce any new factual elements in defending its claim or invoke the statute of limitation which it assures has not lapsed. The Tribunal further expects that Paraguay will not avail itself of any procedures that are aimed at introducing any inappropriate delays or other obstacles to the timely and efficient exercise of jurisdiction by the tribunals of the City of Asunción in dealing fairly with the claims for outstanding payments under the Contract. In the event that Paraguay or any of its organs, including the courts, fail to address any such claim in accordance with the requirements of Article 3(1) of the Treaty, the Claimant will be free to make an application to this Tribunal.[187]

Following the approach taken in *SGS* v. *Philippines*, the *BIVAC* v. *Paraguay* Tribunal accepted to exercise a 'supervisory function'[188] over implementation. It 'directed' the parties to 'report to the Tribunal, separately or jointly, on the status of those proceedings at intervals of six months'.[189] In 2014, the Tribunal issued a procedural order taking note of the discontinuance of the proceedings by agreements between the parties.[190]

Commenting on these cases, Katia Yannaca-Small notes that, in adopting this approach, an ICSID Arbitral Tribunal seeks to address relevant concerns by the respondents regarding the primacy of their courts under the applicable contracts. At the same time, in both cases the Tribunal chose a path that 'leaves the door open for a full application of the [treaty obligations] down the road and closely monitors the application of the local remedies'.[191]

Thus, while not formally performing Mere Adjudication that creates *res judicata*, these arbitral tribunals offered, at the jurisdictional stage, an

187 Ibid., para. 285.
188 Ibid., para. 288.
189 Ibid., para. 284.
190 *BIVAC* v. *Paraguay*, [2014] ICSID Case No. ARB/07/9, Procedural Order taking note of the discontinuance of the proceeding pursuant to ICSID Arbitration Rule 43(1), 7 August 2014.
191 Katia Yannaca-Small, 'Case Comment – BIVAC v Paraguay versus SGS v Paraguay – The Umbrella Clause Still in Search of One Identity' (2013) 28 *ICSID Review* 307, 313.

interpretation of the parties' rights and obligations. In doing so at this stage, they established for host states a path to avoid having their international responsibility engaged. By the same token, however, the *SGS* v. *Philippines* and *BIVAC* v. *Paraguay* Tribunals issued rulings that operated as a deterrent to prospective breaches. While not formally awarding remedies, their partial rulings set out the applicable legal standard (engaging, in this sense, in Mere Adjudication) and foreshadowed consequences of non-compliance therewith: remedy escalation, in the form of a Declaration of Breach and Consequential Duties. Though not formally featuring a judicial condemnation or monetary awards, these partial rulings empowered the claimants to credibly threaten to bring the dispute to adjudication, in case the host states – including their domestic courts – failed to abide by the legal standards set out in the arbitral Tribunals' rulings.

9.6.2 *Anticipating Decisions in Indications of Provisional Measures*

It is currently recognised that most ICs may order provisional measures – orders for performance or non-performance, issued during the course of proceedings, ordinarily aimed at preserving the rights and obligations of the parties pending the final judgment.[192] Whether or not there is an 'inherent power' of adjudicators to provide this remedy,[193] many key treaties grounding adjudication regimes (with the notable exception of the WTO's DSU and other adjudication regimes in trade agreements) expressly provide for provisional measures.[194] The ECtHR and the IUCT, though not expressly empowered to do so by their constitutive treaties, have established their own powers to award 'interim measures' binding on the parties.[195] The ICJ was, until 2001, elusive regarding the binding

[192] Chester Brown, *A Common Law of International Adjudication* (New York: Oxford University Press, 2007), 121; Shabtai Rosenne, *Provisional Measures in International Law: The International Court of Justice and the International Tribunal for the Law of the Sea* (Oxford: Oxford University Press, 2005).

[193] See Brown, *A Common Law of International Adjudication*, 127–132 (arguing that 'such a power is necessary for the performance of their functions).

[194] ICJ Statute, Article 41; United Nations Convention on the Law of the Sea, Montego Bay, 10 December 1982, in force 16 November 1994, 1833 UNTS 39, Article 290(1), 290(5); ICSID Convention, Article 47; American Convention on Human Rights, San Jose, 22 November 1969, in force 18 July 1978, 1144 UNTS 123, Article 63(2).

[195] European Court of Human Rights Rules of Court, Rule 39; Iran–US Claims Tribunal Rules of Procedure, 1 Ir-USCTR 57, Article 26.

character of the measures Article 41 of the ICJ Statute empowers it to 'indicate'.[196] Then, in *LaGrand*, the Court affirmed the view – which it has since affirmed consistently – that ICJ provisional measures are binding and entail an obligation to comply.[197]

The ICJ derived its finding in *LaGrand* from the object and purpose of provisional measures: 'the power in question is based on the necessity, when the circumstances call for it, to safeguard, and to avoid prejudice to, the rights of the parties as determined by the final judgment of the Court'.[198] Similarly, Article 47 of the ICSID Convention permits provisional measures with the purpose of 'preserv[ing] the respective rights of either party'. This implies an essentially procedural function for provisional measures, which accounts for the rationales Hugh Thirlway identifies for provisional measures: preservation of rights, prevention of irreparable prejudice, non-escalation of the dispute, and preservation of evidence.[199]

In other adjudicatory systems, the function of provisional measures is not exclusively procedural. They may alternatively, or additionally, aim at preserving particularly important substantive interests. Under UNCLOS Article 290(1), provisional measures serve 'to preserve the respective rights of the parties to the dispute or to prevent serious harm to the marine environment, pending the final decision'. American Convention on Human Rights (ACHR) Article 63(2) allows the IACtHR to adopt measures 'it deems pertinent' in 'cases of extreme gravity and urgency, and when necessary to avoid irreparable damage to persons'. Similarly, Rule 39(2) of the ECtHR Rules of Court allows 'interim measures . . . in the interests of the parties or of the proper conduct of the proceedings'.

To the extent that they aim at protecting the procedure rather than ensuring protection for particularly important substantive interest, provisional measures are subject to the requirement that Thirlway labels

[196] Article 41 reads: '1. The Court shall have the power to indicate, if it considers that circumstances so require, any provisional measures which ought to be taken to preserve the respective rights of either party. 2. Pending the final decision, notice of the measures suggested shall forthwith be given to the parties and to the Security Council'.

[197] *LaGrand, Germany* v. *United States of America*, Judgment, [2001] ICJ Reports 466, p. 501–506. See, more recently, *Allegations of Genocide, Ukraine* v. *Russian Federation*, Provisional Measures, [2022] ICJ Reports 211, p. 230.

[198] *LaGrand*, [2001] ICJ Reports 466.

[199] Hugh Thirlway, 'The Indication of Provisional Measures by the International Court of Justice', in Rudolf Bernhardt (ed.), *Interim Measures Indicated by International Courts* (New York: Springer-Verlag, 1994), 1, 5–16.

'non-anticipation of the Court's decision'.[200] While making judicial pronouncements relevant to the substantive dispute may be inevitable,[201] the purpose of procedural provisional measures is to preclude the respondent from preventing the final enjoyment by the claimant of rights that it plausibly holds. As the ICJ noted in *Chorzów Factory (Indemnities) (Provisional Measures)*, the measures indicated should be 'provisional measures of protection'; they cannot be used by applicants 'to obtain an interim judgment in favour of a part of the claim'.[202] In particular, provisional measures should not shift from the respondent to the claimant the ability to deprive the final ruling of meaningful effects.

Just as decisions on jurisdiction, indications of provisional measures may also serve as a catalyst for negotiations. In *Great Belt*, the ICJ's rejection of Finland's request for provisional measures permitted a settlement between Finland and Denmark, considered to be 'based on the Court's order'.[203] The ICJ determined that Finland had not provided evidence of damage to its shipping industry from Denmark's construction of a fixed traffic connection across the strait of the Great Belt. At the same time, the Court found that it could ultimately order the dismantling of the works if they were deemed unlawful.[204] Per Magid argued that this determination worked as 'mediation in disguise . . . an indication which can pave the way for a political solution'.[205]

[200] Ibid., 11.
[201] Ibid.
[202] *Factory at Chorzów (Indemnities), Germany* v. *Poland*, Provisional Measures, (1927) PCIJ Ser A No 12, p. 10. See also *Allegations of Genocide*, [2022] ICJ Reports 211, p. 227:

> 'The Court is not called upon, for the purposes of its decision on the request for the indication of provisional measures, to establish the existence of breaches of obligations under the Genocide Convention, but to determine whether the circumstances require the indication of provisional measures for the protection of the right found to be plausible. It cannot at this stage make definitive findings of fact, and the right of each Party to submit arguments in respect of the merits remains unaffected by the Court's decision on the request for the indication of provisional measures'.

[203] Martti Koskenniemi, 'Case Concerning Passage through the Great Belt' (1996) 27 *Ocean Development & International Law* 255, 274.
[204] *Case concerning Passage through the Great Belt, Finland* v. *Denmark*, Provisional Measures, [1991] ICJ Reports 12, p. 18–19.
[205] Per Magid, 'The Post-Adjudicative Phase', in Connie Peck and Roy S Lee (eds.), *Increasing the Effectiveness of the International Court of Justice – Proceedings of the ICJ/UNITAR Colloquium to Celebrate the 50th Anniversary of the Court* (The Hague: Martinus Nijhoff, 1997), 324–369, 365.

In *Great Belt*, the Court was careful to note that its decision 'in no way prejudge[d] any question relating to the merits of the case'.[206] In other cases, however, adjudicators have been less careful regarding the prospects of the parties' arguments. Provisional measures sometimes give the parties a clear indication of the IC's inclinations regarding the rights in dispute. Occasionally, their content is such that compliance by the respondent engenders a possible *fait accompli*, permitting the claimant to deprive any final rejection of its claims of meaningful effect. This section examines provisional measures granted by the ICJ and ITLOS that had this effect.

The ICJ has awarded provisional measures with these characteristics in *Hostages* and in *Avena (Interpretation)*. In *Hostages*, the Court stated that the inviolability of embassies and diplomatic envoys, which the United States accused Iran of breaching, was a 'fundamental prerequisite for the conduct of relations between States'.[207] On this basis, the Court found that Iran was under an obligation to ensure (i) the return to US control of the premises of the United States embassy in Tehran; (ii) the immediate release of the embassy personnel held hostage by Islamist militants; and (iii) the restoration to diplomatic and consular personnel of all their rights, including the right to leave Iranian territory.[208]

Iran did not comply with the measures and, at the merits stage, the ICJ awarded the same three rulings, framing them as obligations of specific performance.[209] If Iran had complied and the personnel in question had left its territory, there would be little effect to the Court deciding that Iran was not, in fact, responsible for the actions of the militants and was thus not under any corresponding obligation. The decision on interim measures therefore anticipated the final ruling rather than being a means to preserve its applicability.

A similar logic seems to have guided the ICJ in its order on provisional measures and remedies in the (otherwise very different) *Avena (Interpretation)* case. Following the ICJ's 2004 *Avena* judgment, Mexico filed a request for interpretation, requesting provisional measures whose content, in essence, amounted to demanding US

206 *Great Belt (Provisional Measures)*, [1991] ICJ Reports 12, p. 20.

207 *United States Diplomatic and Consular Staff in Tehran, Iran* v. *United States of America*, Provisional Measures, [1979] ICJ Reports 7, p. 19.

208 Ibid., p. 21.

209 *United States Diplomatic and Consular Staff in Tehran*, [1980] ICJ Reports 3, p. 44. These rulings were presented as Mere Adjudication. As regards the foreshadowing of Consequential Duties to induce compliance, see Section 9.4.1.

compliance with the 2004 judgment. While the ICJ ultimately dismissed the request for interpretation as relating to a matter not discussed in its 2004 judgment,[210] the Court awarded provisional measures by seven votes to five. It determined that the United States should 'take all measures necessary' to 'ensure' that Mexican citizens were not executed pending its final decision on Mexico's request for interpretation, stating that this measure was applicable 'unless and until these five Mexican nationals receive review and reconsideration consistent with paragraphs 138 to 141 of the Court's Judgment delivered on 31 March 2004'.[211] The ICJ's 2008 Order on Provisional Measures in *Avena (Interpretation)* in fact merely reaffirmed the rulings and remedies in the *Avena* judgment.[212]

In its 2009 judgment on the merits in *Avena (Interpretation)*, the ICJ adopted contradictory rulings. On the one hand, the Court found that Mexico's request did not concern the interpretation of the 2004 Judgment and that therefore the Court did not have jurisdiction to entertain Mexico's request. On the other hand, the ICJ not only 'reaffirme[d] the continuing binding character of the obligations of the United States of America' established in the 2004 *Avena* judgment but also unanimously condemned the United States for having 'breached the obligation incumbent upon it under the Order indicating provisional measures of 16 July 2008, in the case of Mr. José Ernesto Medellín Rojas'.[213]

Thus, even though the ICJ ultimately ruled that no difference in interpretation existed requiring a judgment,[214] the Court nonetheless employed remedy repetition to put additional pressure on the United States for performance. First, it granted provisional measures that solely reaffirmed

210 *Request for Interpretation of the Judgment of 31 March 2004 in the Case concerning Avena and Other Mexican Nationals, Mexico* v. *United States of America*, Judgment, [2009] ICJ Reports 3, p. 20.

211 *Request for Interpretation of the Judgment of 31 March 2004 in the Case concerning Avena and Other Mexican Nationals, Mexico* v. *United States of America*, Provisional Measures, [2008] ICJ Reports 311, p. 331.

212 *Avena and Other Mexican Nationals, Mexico* v. *United States of America*, Judgment, [2004] ICJ Reports 12, p. 72 ('to provide, by means of its own choosing, review and reconsideration of the convictions and sentences of the Mexican nationals').

213 *Avena (Interpretation)*, [2009] ICJ Reports 3, p. 21.

214 In his Declaration, Judge Koroma notes that the Court was unclear on whether this meant that the request was inadmissible (Ibid., p. 23). The views that the request was inadmissible and admissible were articulated respectively by Judges Abraham (Ibid., p. 27) and Sepúlveda-Amor (Ibid., p. 30).

the United States' obligations established in the previous judgment. Second, awarding these provisional measures allowed the ICJ to subsequently condemn, at the merits stage, the United States' lack of compliance with its provisional measures, which, given the decision at the merits stage, the Court arguably did not have jurisdiction to award in the first place.

The Court's stance seems motivated by two desires. On the one hand, to produce a similar effect to that expected from compliance adjudication: engaging in remedy repetition, so as to impose on the United States reputational costs for its non-compliance with the 2004 judgment, additional to those created by the original Declaration of Breach.[215] On the other hand, to avoid being faced with a barrage of requests for interpretation de facto seeking compliance adjudication, which, without the prospect of remedy escalation, would result in innumerable judgments featuring mere remedy repetition, to diminishing levels of added effect.

Another adjudicator that often employs provisional measures that impinge on the merits stage is ITLOS. Pursuant to UNCLOS Article 290(5), until an Annex VII Tribunal is composed to act on the matter, ITLOS is empowered to award provisional measures. In *Southern Bluefin Tuna*, the Tribunal responsible for judging the merits of the case ultimately concluded that the dispute was not within its jurisdiction.[216] At the provisional measures stage, however, ITLOS had not only instructed the parties to refrain from taking action that might aggravate the dispute but also established a maximum number of annual catches of tuna that each party was permitted to take.[217]

One may question whether the scope of these provisional measures is consistent with the goal of safeguarding the ultimate decision; given that the UNCLOS Arbitral Tribunal issued its decision the following year, the urgency of establishing these maximum catch quotas before the Tribunal's award was debatable. Rather, the measures ordered appear guided by the objective, mentioned in UNCLOS Article 290(1) as a legitimate purpose of ITLOS provisional measures, to 'prevent serious harm to the marine environment'. As Barbara Kwiatkowska noted, the impression is that 'the standard of preventing such harm

[215] For the relevance of this effect, see Chapter 4.

[216] *Southern Bluefin Tuna, New Zealand – Japan, Australia – Japan*, ITLOS, (2000) 119 ILR 508.

[217] *Southern Bluefin Tuna, New Zealand – Japan, Australia – Japan (Provisional Measures)*, ITLOS, (1999) 38 ILM 1624, 1632.

served as the Tribunal's overriding objective, to which its treatment of prima facie jurisdiction, urgency, and other procedural issues was subordinated'.[218]

This same standard, however, was subsequently applied in cases in which no question of harm to the maritime environment was present. In *Straits of Johor (Provisional Measures)*, in response to Malaysia's request that Singapore suspend all activities in the disputed area, ITLOS ordered the parties jointly to 'establish promptly a group of independent experts' to examine Singapore's claim and propose a solution.[219] This group of experts was indeed constituted; the two parties then 'accepted its recommendations' and submitted them to the UNCLOS Arbitral Tribunal for adoption 'in the form of an agreed Award which is final and binding on the Parties'.[220] By guiding parties towards a negotiated solution, ITLOS's provisional measures thus made the exercise of adjudication by the Arbitral Tribunal unnecessary.

In *ARA Libertad (Provisional Measures)* and *Arctic Sunrise (Provisional Measures)*, ITLOS issued provisional measures which arguably, once complied with, pre-empted the Arbitral Tribunal's decision on the merits. In *ARA Libertad (Provisional Measures)*, Ghanaian courts had seized an Argentinean warship at the request of a private party that held unpaid Argentinean bonds. Argentina requested the release of the vessel. ITLOS considered that UNCLOS Article 32, which establishes that 'nothing in this Convention affects the immunities of warships', rather than constituting a carve-out from Convention obligations (a 'saver clause' as Ghana termed it), in fact prima facie provided UNCLOS adjudicators with jurisdiction over violations of the immunity of warships.[221] Finding that the 'ARA Libertad' enjoyed immunity 'in accordance with general international law', that Ghana's conduct affected the enjoyment by this warship of its immunity, and that this could constitute a source of conflict and endanger the relations between the two states, ITLOS concluded that:

[218] Barbara Kwiatkowska, 'Southern Bluefin Tuna (New Zealand v. Japan; Australia v. Japan), Order on Provisional Measures (ITLOS Cases Nos. 3 and 4)' (2000) 94 *AJIL* 150, 155.

[219] *Land Reclamation by Singapore in and around the Straits of Johor, Malaysia* v. *Singapore (Provisional Measures)*, ITLOS, (2003) 126 ILR 487, 505–506.

[220] *Land Reclamation by Singapore in and around the Straits of Johor, Malaysia* v. *Singapore*, (2005) PCA XXVII RIAA 133, Award on Agreed Terms, Annex, 2, 7.

[221] *'ARA Libertad', Argentina* v. *Ghana*, Provisional Measures, ITLOS, (2012) ITLOS Case No 20, 15, paras. 47, 66.

> the urgency of the situation requires the prescription by the Tribunal of provisional measures that will ensure full compliance with the applicable rules of international law, thus preserving the respective rights of the Parties;[222]

While purportedly not prejudging the questions of either jurisdiction or merits, ITLOS determined that Ghana was under an obligation to release the 'ARA Libertad', allowing the warship, its commander, and its crew to leave Ghana.[223]

The 'ARA Libertad' left Ghana four days after the ITLOS decision. Six months later, the Ghanaian Supreme Court examined the matter of jurisdictional immunities and concluded that states hold immunity from enforcement for state property 'used or intended to be used in connection with a military activity'.[224] The two parties entered into an agreement to terminate the arbitral procedure, which incorporated the Supreme Court judgment. Argentina declared that this judgment and 'its dissemination at the international level ... constitute[d] sufficient satisfaction to discharge any injury occasioned by the injunction measure over the Argentine warship'.[225] Had the Annex VII Arbitral Tribunal decided in favour of Ghana (or, perhaps more likely, had it decided that it did not have jurisdiction on the matter), it is difficult to see how else Ghana could have enforced the rights of the creditor that requested the seizure of the ship.[226] Arguably, ITLOS's provisional measure did not safeguard the applicability of the decision on the merits but in fact undermined the applicability of a future decision in favour of the respondent.[227]

222 Ibid., paras. 95–100.

223 Ibid., para. 108(1).

224 Supreme Court of Ghana, *The Republic* v. *High Court (Comm Div) Accra*, Judgment No. J5/10/2013.

225 Agreement between Argentina and Ghana (27 September 2013), available at https://pcacases.com/web/sendAttach/429.

226 Compare with *M/V 'Saiga' (Prompt Release)*, in which ITLOS ordered the release of the ship against the posting of a bond of security as determined by UNCLOS Article 292. *M/V 'Saiga' (Prompt Release), Saint Vincent and the Grenadines* v. *Guinea*, (1997) ITLOS Case No 1, paras. 83(3)–83(5).

227 ITLOS issued a similar order for provisional measures in a similar case in *Case concerning the detention of three Ukrainian naval vessels, Ukraine* v. *Russian Federation*, Provisional Measures, ITLOS, (2019) ITLOS Case No. 26, paras. 110–123. The PCA avoided the issue in its award in *Detention of Ukrainian Naval Vessels and Servicemen Ukraine* v. *Russia, Award on Preliminary Objections* (2022) PCA Case No. 2019-28, paras. 152–155.

A similar situation occurred in *'Arctic Sunshine' (Provisional Measures)*, a case initiated by the Netherlands against Russia. A Greenpeace ship, bearing the Dutch flag, was detained by Russia after its crew attempted to board a Gazprom oil platform in Russia's Exclusive Economic Zone.[228] The Netherlands requested that ITLOS, and subsequently a UNCLOS Annex VII Tribunal, order the release of the 'Arctic Sunrise' and its crew. Russia did not participate in the proceedings, stating that it was exercising 'its jurisdiction, including criminal jurisdiction', as a coastal state under the terms of UNCLOS.[229]

The Netherlands argued that an order from ITLOS for the 'immediate release' of the vessel was a provisional measure 'appropriate to preserve the rights of the Netherlands'. Without basing its decision on any substantive right of the Netherlands, or inquiring into the situation of the vessel or its crew, ITLOS simply held that 'the urgency of the situation require[d] the prescription by the Tribunal of provisional measures'.[230] ITLOS not only ordered the release of the vessel and of the individuals detained but also determined that this release be effected upon the posting by the Netherlands of a bond (or other financial security) of 3.6 million euros.[231] The Netherlands posted the bond shortly after the decision, and the Russian Duma approved an amnesty law that allowed for the subsequent release of the 'Arctic Sunrise' and its crew.[232]

ITLOS stated that its decision would not prejudge 'the question of the jurisdiction of the Annex VII arbitral tribunal to deal with the merits of the case, or any questions relating to the merits themselves'.[233] Clearly, however, this decision did not serve the purpose of safeguarding the rights of the Netherlands to an applicable decision on the merits. The 'provisional' measures in fact provided it, in anticipation, with the full object of its claim (the Netherlands itself had offered to post a bond).

In awarding provisional measures in this manner, ITLOS (in *'Arctic Sunrise'* as well as in *'ARA Libertad'*) and the ICJ (in *Hostages*, and in a different way in *Avena (Interpretation)*) in fact issued what the PCIJ

[228] Douglas Guilfoyle and Cameron Miles, 'Provisional Measures and the MV Arctic Sunrise' (2014) 108 *AJIL* 271.

[229] *'Arctic Sunrise'*, *Netherlands* v. *Russia*, Provisional Measures, ITLOS, (2013) ITLOS Case No 22, para. 65.

[230] Ibid., paras. 86, 89.

[231] Ibid., paras. 95–96.

[232] Steven Lee Myers, 'Russia Releases Greenpeace Ship', New York Times, 6 June 2014.

[233] Ibid., para. 100.

considered impermissible in *Chorzów Factory*: an interim judgment, not safeguarding the utility of the final judgment but in fact providing the claimant with the object of its request. As Douglas Guilfoyle and Cameron Miles observed, these decisions were not limited to 'provisional' or 'interim' aspects, but 'amounted to a final judgment – if not de jure, then certainly de facto'.[234]

In this regard, there is a fundamental difference between issuing these orders for provisional measures and awarding the same injunctions as final judicial remedies. When awarded at the provisional stage, these orders do not exhaust the jurisdiction of the relevant adjudicator. Rather, the case remains under review by the court or tribunal and may be subject to further judicial remedies. This allows claimants to continue to exercise pressure, not only through political channels and self-help but also by threatening to continue to pursue the case. Additionally, in case of non-compliance, there is a credible prospect of remedy escalation. Faced with non-compliance with provisional measures, an IC may issue a Declaration of Breach and establish Consequential Duties when, in the absence of prior provisional measures, it might cautiously deem Mere Adjudication to be a sufficient remedy in the dispute.

9.7 Conclusion: Judicial Discretion, Procedure, and Purpose

In conclusion, international courts and tribunals across adjudicatory regimes have utilised their procedural powers, and a variety of legal instruments, to combine partial rulings with the prospect of subsequent or final decisions, sometimes foreshadowing their likely content. By doing so, they enhance their ability to employ remedy repetition and escalation in cases of non-compliance, offering creative solutions to the challenges of enforceability in international adjudication. Partial rulings may help international adjudication fulfil its role by affirming a claimant's entitlements while creating structured opportunities for compliance, rather than purporting to impose solutions that the IC cannot enforce. By foreshadowing the possibility of more severe remedies in the event of non-compliance, ICs provide injured parties with leverage in negotiations. This approach to partial rulings allows ICs to act as *ex ante* facilitators of performance rather than *ex post* determiners of compensation.

[234] Guilfoyle and Miles, 'Provisional Measures and the MV *Arctic Sunrise*', 284. They also noted that this may have been an 'abuse of judicial discretion' (Ibid., 276).

In the absence of robust enforcement mechanisms for non-compliance in general international law, courts have developed innovative methods – sometimes stretching or reinterpreting their mandates – to simultaneously establish duties of performance and maintain judicial oversight. By using partial rulings for this purpose, adjudicators avoid becoming *functus officio*, retaining jurisdiction to address future non-compliance while strengthening claimants' positions during negotiations. Another technique involves setting time limits after which claimants may automatically access judicial remedies if transactional remedies, such as restitution, are not delivered.

These practices also reflect ICs' recognition of the value of flexibility in dispute resolution. Withholding remedies and encouraging negotiated solutions provide less intrusive alternatives to immediate judicial establishment of a duty to provide pecuniary remedies. This approach is particularly effective where the claimant seeks substantive performance, as implementation of voluntary undertakings may be more practicable than that of duties determined against a state's will. Even in cases involving pecuniary obligations, settlements negotiated within the framework of partial rulings have a higher likelihood of voluntary, timely compliance than amounts established by adjudicators.

The practice analysed in this chapter also highlights ICs' ability to strategically foreshadow outcomes within incidental rulings on jurisdiction or provisional measures. While these pronouncements can serve to guide negotiations, their use to pre-empt final rulings risks blurring procedural boundaries. This creative use of incidental rulings thus raises questions about judicial propriety and risks undermining the reputation of the adjudicator issuing them. In systems where decisions are reviewable, such practices may lead to reversals or annulments.

Of course, most ICs operate without formal mechanisms for annulment or review. While this lack of accountability may limit immediate recourse for states and actors that value judicial propriety, the lack of review does not inherently render a ruling lawful. Judicial creativity which takes an IC outside the boundaries of its ostensible role and powers may threaten the long-term legitimacy of adjudication.

10

Conclusion

A Judicialised Order in the Anarchical Society

It is not so long ago that the prospect of a meaningful role for adjudication in international relations seemed like a distant ideal. At the 1899 Hague Peace Conference, in which states first sought to establish a permanent system for inter-state arbitration, Frederic de Martens, the Russian delegate and rapporteur charged with proposing an outline for the prospective arbitration system, reasoned that disputes concerning whether a state 'shall or shall not exercise certain given attributes of the sovereign Power' were not appropriate for arbitration.[1] Requiring states to modify their conduct, he reasoned, could easily interfere with 'the national honor or vital interests' of states. The ensuing non-compliance would in turn 'discredit arbitration in the eyes of Governments and peoples'.[2]

Judged by this standard, the evolution of international adjudication over the past century can be called revolutionary. Building on the institutional framework of eighteenth- and nineteenth-century adjudication, which depended on specific, *ex post* state consent, states have over the twentieth-century built adjudicators that play a central role in determining, enforcing, and (inevitably) developing international law. *Ex ante* consent to jurisdiction, though still scattered and domain-specific, is no longer exceptional. Instruments establishing a so-called second generation of international adjudicators go beyond extending judicialisation to new areas and 'thicken' the role of adjudication, endowing international courts (ICs) with compulsory jurisdiction and sometimes an integral role in the enforcement process.[3]

1 James Brown Scott (dir.), *The Proceedings of the Hague Peace Conferences – The Conference of 1899* (New York: Oxford University Press, 1920), 175.

2 Ibid., 175–176.

3 See Celso Lafer, 'The Dispute Settlement System in the World Trade Organization', Gilberto Amado Memorial Lecture, 18 June 1996; Gary Born goes as far as saying these adjudicators have 'render enforceable decisions' (Gary Born, 'A New Generation of International Adjudication' (2012) 61 *Duke Law Journal* 775).

At the same time, this judicialisation did not alter the core structure of the international society. Control over means of coercion remains concentrated in the hands of the various independent hierarchical social apparatuses known as states. The resulting duality, in which interpretative authority is dissociated from sanctioning ability, is commonly considered the irremediable defect at the heart of the edifice of international law. Raymon Aron placed the lack of 'indisputable interpretation' side by side with 'effective sanction' as an element making international law structurally flawed, only to note that the 'essential point' is that international law is unable, in itself, to mobilise 'the only effective sanction against the state that has committed the illicit act . . . the use of force'.[4] While the former issue has been somewhat remedied by judicialisation, the latter has not.

Judicialisation has produced significant changes to the manner in which states and other actors deploy the claims and criticisms, expressions of expectations, and sanctions that constitute international law.[5] It is decreasingly accurate to reproduce without qualifications H.L.A. Hart's view that international law lacks enforceability because, 'in contrast with municipal courts, no state can be brought before these international tribunals without its prior consent'.[6] On the other hand, it remains true that 'the law enforcement provisions of the [UN] Charter, admirable on paper, have been paralysed by the veto and the ideological divisions and alliances of the great powers'.[7] In the most serious cases – those in which legal disputes risk escalating into armed conflagrations – 'there can be no standing assurance that the combined strength of those on the side of international order is likely to preponderate over the powers tempted to aggression'.[8] The movement towards judicialization, and even the placing of some sanctioning decisions formally in the hands of international organisations, have not changed the basic infrastructure of power and authority that defines the international society. For the foreseeable future, control over the political and economic resources that provide instruments of coercion will remain decentralised, in the hands of polities organised as states. Ultimate control over the means of

[4] Raymond Aron, *Peace and War: A Theory of International Relations* (New Jersey: Transaction, 2003), 110.

[5] Karen Alter, *The New Terrain of International Law: Courts, Politics, Rights* (Princeton: Princeton University Press, 2014), 32.

[6] H.L.A. Hart, *The Concept of Law* (Oxford: Clarendon Press, 1961), 232.

[7] Ibid., 233.

[8] Ibid., 219.

organised coercion, which may be what we call sovereignty, implies the ultimate ability of each polity to renege on international commitments and follow its own path.

The obverse of this decentralised control is the structural limitation to the powers of international courts and tribunals. I have framed this as their *auctoritas* without *potestas*, their ability to issue rulings in a setting in which no *imperium* is attached to their *jurisdictio*. Unlike domestic courts, international adjudicators do not have hierarchical authority over agents with the means to take measures of constraint against recalcitrant wrongdoers (*potestas*). These agents, who ultimately exert coercion on behalf of their domestic legal order, may reliably act upon an order by a domestic court, but will demand an in-hierarchy confirmation, by a domestic political or judicial authority, before acting upon the pronouncements of an international court. This limitation precludes international courts and tribunals from decisively ordering, in response to non-compliance, measures of 'enforcement' or 'execution', such as the seizing of assets, the arrest of individuals, or even the adoption of political and economic measures aimed at exerting pressure on wrongdoers to change their conduct.

However, when assessing the role of adjudication, focusing excessively on this limitation misses two crucial points. First, at least to some extent, the matter is one of the applicable substantive law, in particular the law of state immunity. Traditionally, no actor – domestic or international – was given authority to apply coercion over state assets or the highest state representatives. The recognition of state immunities, deriving from the principle of sovereign equality, historically prevented states from applying measures of constraint against each other's assets, as well as against high state officials, whether or not a court was involved. This law, however, increasingly features limitations, as a matter of the internationally agreed rules and, perhaps even more significantly, as a matter of domestic judicial practice.[9]

State assets involved in commercial transactions can now be seized, and states can validly waive their immunity from enforcement. Cunning lawyers have seized the opportunity to establish a quasi-worldwide enforcement mechanism for international investment law. In the same vein, the International Criminal Court has affirmed a number of times its view that state immunity does not apply to the crimes subject to its

[9] See Section 5.5.

jurisdiction, not only vertically (i.e. between the ICC and the state of nationality of an accused) but also horizontally (i.e. between two states parties to the Rome Statute, or in situations referred to the ICC by the Security Council). The next frontier – the seizing of state assets by other states in case of flagrant breaches of core rules of international law – is, at the time of the conclusion of this book, being actively explored by academics[10] and has begun being implemented by policymakers.[11]

Second, when states have recourse to international courts, it is generally not because they must do so prior to taking measures identified as 'of enforcement' but precisely as an alternative to adopting coercive, forceful, or confrontational measures. States may act upon their own understanding of the law, and may have recourse to measures of self-help to enforce this understanding, without prior recourse to adjudication. Conversely, prevailing before an international court does not add to the array of possibilities (including recourse to bodies such as the Security Council) that a state may employ to affirm its rights against another state. If anything, taking a dispute before an international adjudicator may prevent a state from lawfully affirming, or continuing to affirm, its rights through countermeasures.[12]

In other words, adjudication is not perceived as a prerequisite for states to engage in the inter-state enforcement of obligations but as an alternative means of enforcement. In particular in situations where states are least capable of meaningfully having recourse to self-help or of exerting pressure within political organs, adjudication often represents

[10] See Menno T. Kamminga, 'Confiscating Russia's Frozen Central Bank Assets: A Permissible Third-Party Countermeasure?' (2023) 70 *Netherlands International Law Review* 1; Anton Moiseienko, 'Legal: The Freezing of the Russian Central Bank's Assets' (2023) 34 *European Journal of International Law* 1007; Joseph E. Stiglitz and Andrew Kosenko, *A Proposal for Russian Asset Seizure* (Economic Studies at Brookings, July 2024).

[11] European Commission, 'First Transfer of €1.5 Billion of Proceeds from Immobilised Russian Assets Made Available in Support of Ukraine Today', 24 July 2024; G7 Leaders' Statement, 24 February 2024, available at www.consilium.europa.eu/media/70462/g7-leaders-statement.pdf, 4 ('immobilized Russian sovereign assets could be made use of to support Ukraine, consistent with our respective legal systems and international law').

[12] International Law Commission, Articles on Responsibility of States for Internationally Wrongful Acts, UN Doc. A/56/49(Vol. I)/Corr.4., Article 52.3(b) ('Countermeasures may not be taken, and if already taken must be suspended without undue delay if: (a) the internationally wrongful act has ceased; and (b) the dispute is pending before a court or tribunal which has the authority to make decisions binding on the parties'). See *United States Diplomatic and Consular Staff in Tehran, United States of America* v. *Iran*, Judgment, [1980] ICJ Reports 3, p. 43–44.

the most effective means of pressure against wrongdoing at the disposal of an aggrieved party. As the experience of the World Trade Organization (WTO) examined in Chapter 6 reveals, even express permissions to have recourse to self-help measures rarely translate into concrete measures, except by those members that could have employed these measures even in the absence of adjudication.

Despite its limitations, therefore, recourse to adjudication is an essential – sometimes the only – means available to claimants to press for compliance with international law. To consider implementation of judicial decisions as a 'post-adjudication', 'political' issue, and to discourage recourse to courts to settle matters of compliance, reduces the subsequent options of claimants, following a judicial decision, to those that they would have had in the absence of any avenue permitting bringing the dispute to adjudication.

The analysis of judicial practice in Chapters 6, 7, 8, and 9 provides evidence that, contrary to a common perception, neither the absence of centralised enforcement mechanisms in the international society nor the limits on the remedial powers of international courts and tribunals prevent adjudicators from taking a strategic approach to the deployment of their remedial powers. The role of international adjudicators does not exclude assessments of compliance with their own rulings, or providing remedies for non-compliance. The highly regulated, and frequently used, mechanism for compliance adjudication available under WTO law is evidence that there is ample scope for the development of judicial remedies for non-compliance in international law. Though some ICs have refused to perform an equivalent role, others have, using the instruments at their disposal and within the confines of their assigned role, sought to employ their judicial authority to offer, in one form or another, adjudication on compliance with rulings.

In many international adjudication systems, claims directly requesting adjudication on compliance with final rulings remain the exception. International courts such as the International Court of Justice (ICJ), the European Court of Human Rights (ECtHR), and the African Court of Human and People's Rights (AfCHPR) have openly hesitated to take this step; others, such as the ECOWAS Community Court of Justice (ECCJ) and the Central American Court of Justice (CACJ), have rejected it entirely. In part, this may be due to a lingering perception that a new recourse to adjudication is not an appropriate response to non-compliance. There are nonetheless a number of instances in which compliance adjudication has been sought, and sometimes provided, through legal instruments such as new requests for adjudication, requests for interpretation, assessment of compliance with provisional measures, or deferral of key determinations to the merits or quantification stages of disputes. Though it is beyond the scope of this book to establish causal connection in individual cases, on many instances a ruling establishing legal parameters while deferring remedies has been followed by either compliance or a settlement obviating the need for further judicial intervention.

International courts are sometimes given a role at the compliance stage through specific treaty provisions permitting adjudication on compliance with, or execution or implementation of, final rulings. Some of these provisions appear in treaties dating from the early twentieth century. Others are more recent, included in bilateral *compromis* for the solution of specific disputes or in multilateral conventions establishing broad regimes, such as United Nations Convention on the Law of the Sea (UNCLOS). These provisions set out an unequivocal path to request international courts and tribunals to adjudicate on matters of compliance. Besides the now-maimed WTO dispute settlement system, the Andean Court of Justice (ACJ) has developed a jurisprudence on compliance adjudication based on such provisions.

Absent a clear provision to this effect, other paths have been used to seek, and provide, judicial remedies for non-compliance with rulings. Some of these paths involve legal instruments, such as bifurcation of proceedings and requests for interpretation, not aimed at permitting adjudication on compliance. These instruments nonetheless ensure that judicial intervention is not restricted to a single pronouncement, which might settle disputes as a matter of law while leaving claimants with no other option but to resort to self-help and political means of persuasion and enforcement. In other cases still, ICs themselves have established procedures for compliance adjudication, including sometimes by codifying entire legal mechanisms in their procedural rules, as the Inter-American Court of Human Rights (IACtHR) and AfCHPR have done.

International adjudicators may also hear claims of non-compliance as fresh claims of breach. Practice of compliance adjudication within new claims goes back to the *Chorzów Factory* case before the Permanent Court of International Justice and the *Junghans* arbitrations. More recently, the ECtHR has established a significant jurisprudence allowing complainants new recourse to the court in case of non-compliance. While nominally new complaints do not target compliance itself but merely the continuation of the breach, non-compliance is almost unavoidably factored in in the determination of remedies. Thus, in

Wasserman v. *Russia (No 2)*, the ECtHR condemned Russia to pay pecuniary compensation where previously it had only ordered the performance of a substantive obligation; and, in *Ivanţoc* v. *Moldova and Russia*, the ECtHR condemned Russia for an 'aggravated violation' of the European Convention.

The final frontier of judicial remedies, explored in Chapter 5, currently remains largely untapped: the awarding of Permissible Responses, that is, an authoritative judicial determination that the circumstances of the dispute warrant the adoption of one or more of international law's traditional means of tangible response to wrongful conduct. The scholarship and broader discourse around sanctions and adjudication usually consider them as separate means of enforcing international commitments. Adjudication is often dissociated from sanctioning, the latter considered a political activity. However, like other aspects of the international order, sanctioning exists at once as a political decision and as legally ascertainable conduct. Sanctioning is legally permissible in some instances and prohibited in others. Even where permissible, it is subject to legal limitations. Sanctions therefore do not exist on a 'political plane' that can be separated from legal considerations. Like any other state conduct, sanctions are assessed, by the sanctioning actor as well as by other actors, as a permitted enforcement or a legal violation. Applied to sanctions, adjudication can perform the same role it performs in international relations more broadly: declaring conduct obligatory, permissible, or prohibited, and thereby legitimising or de-legitimising its adoption.

A particularly challenging type of permissible responses is the deployment of coercive measures against the assets of a wrongdoing state, or against the freedom of its leaders. While international adjudicators are unable to coercively impose on states a change of conduct, it is at least conceivable that they can make *legal* determinations concerning the permissibility of applying coercive measures. Although the logical next step following these determinations – the seizing of assets or taking of measures in response to a breach, or to non-compliance with rulings – remains the preserve of *imperium*-holding states, the determination of the lawfulness of conduct, and of the legal consequences of unlawful conduct, falls entirely within the sphere of *jurisdictio*. In the case of a dispute regarding the permissibility of measures adopted in response to an alleged unlawful conduct, a court or tribunal may be able to settle the matter in light of the applicable legal rules.

In sum, the potential for judicial remedies to address non-compliance and lead to enforcement through coercive measures hinges less on the existence of dedicated legal provisions (although it will benefit from such provisions) than on the broader issue of the perceived role of adjudicators in international law. While ICs retain their role as final decision-makers and providers of reparation, they may also offer continued legal guidance within the interactional process of applying, enforcing, and renegotiating rights and obligations. There is no contradiction between permitting and even demanding post-judgment negotiations for implementation, whether inter-state or institutionalised, and permitting adjudicators to intervene, within the limits of their jurisdiction, to verify compliance with rulings and settle legal disputes, including at the implementation stage, or by establishing Permissible Responses.

Adopting measures of constraint – whether before or after adjudication – remains an essential prerogative of states, as the entities capable of mobilising resources and key agent to induce compliance with international obligations. At the same time, international courts and tribunals may play an essential role in the underlying process. Adjudication provides a means for authoritatively distinguishing obligatory from non-obligatory behaviour, lawful from unlawful conduct, well-founded from ill-founded demands, and permissible from impermissible responses. While it can never ensure compliance with the law, international adjudication empowers those whose rights have been infringed, providing their demands with the imprint of legality.

Some of the remedies and approaches surveyed in this book may require ICs awarding them to embrace a conception of their role that departs from more traditional views of international adjudication. These traditional views are rooted in the late nineteenth-century vision of international law articulated by Frederic de Martens, one marked by minimal institutionalisation, in which adjudicators acted only at the behest of pairs of states and played a marginal role, rather than operating under an *ex ante* mandate designed to enable coordination and cooperation in the international order.

In the contemporary international legal landscape, the role of international adjudication is no longer limited to the retrospective clarification of obligations; it increasingly involves upholding and preserving the integrity of legal regimes. By articulating the legal consequences of continued or renewed violations, international courts and tribunals reinforce the authority of the norms they are mandated to apply. Though their rulings will not be backed by centralised coercive enforcement in the foreseeable future, they shape expectations, influence state behaviour, and provide an authoritative foundation fostering permissible responses to breaches. In doing so, international adjudicators do not encroach upon the prerogatives of states but contribute to a more stable and rule-oriented international order – one in which law and adjudication retain their relevance beyond the moment of a judgment or award, guiding interactions among states and shaping behaviour within them over time.

BIBLIOGRAPHY

Disputes and Cases

Permanent Court of International Justice

Appeal from a Judgment of the Hungaro-Czechoslovak Mixed Arbitral Tribunal (the Peter Pázmány University *v.* the State of Czechoslovakia), (1933) PCIJ Ser A/B No 61

Certain German Interests in Polish Upper Silesia, Germany *v.* Poland, Judgment, (1926) PCIJ Ser A No 7

Certain German Interests in Polish Upper Silesia, Germany *v.* Poland, Preliminary Objections, (1925) PCIJ Ser A No 6

Certain German Interests in Polish Upper Silesia, Jurisdiction, Germany *v.* Poland, Preliminary Objections, (1925) PCIJ Ser A No. 5

Diversion of Waters from the Meuse, Netherlands *v.* Belgium, Judgment, (1937) PCIJ Ser A/B No 70

Electricity Company of Sofia, Belgium *v.* Bulgaria, Preliminary Objections, (1939) PCIJ Ser A/B No 77

Factory at Chorzów (Indemnities), Germany *v.* Poland, Provisional Measures, (1927) PCIJ Ser A No 12

Factory at Chorzów (Interpretation of Judgments Nos 7 and 8), Germany *v.* Poland, Judgment, (1925) PCIJ Ser A No 11

Factory at Chorzów (Order of 16 October 1928), (1928–1929) PCIJ Ser E

Factory at Chorzów (Jurisdiction), Germany *v.* Poland, Judgment, (1927) PCIJ Ser A No 9

Factory at Chorzów (Merits), Germany *v.* Poland, Judgment, (1928) PCIJ Ser A No 17

Factory at Chorzów (Order of 13 September 1928), (1928) PCIJ Ser A No 17

Factory at Chorzów (Order of 25 May 1929), (1929) PCIJ Ser A No 19

Free Zones of Upper Savoy and the District of Gex (First Phase) (Order), France *v.* Switzerland, Judgment, (1929) PCIJ Ser A No 22

Free Zones of Upper Savoy and the District of Gex (Second Phase) (Order), France *v.* Switzerland, Judgment, (1930) PCIJ Ser A No 24

Free Zones of Upper Savoy and the District of Gex, France *v.* Switzerland, Judgment, (1932) PCIJ Ser A/B No 46

Interpretation of Judgments Nos 7 and 8 (Chorzów Factory), Germany *v.* Poland, Judgment, (1927) PCIJ Ser A No 13
Lighthouses in Crete and Samos, France *v.* Greece, Judgment, (1934) PCIJ Ser A/B No 62
Lighthouses in Crete and Samos, France *v.* Greece, Judgment, (1937) PCIJ Ser A/B No 71
Mavrommatis Jerusalem Concessions (Readaptation), Greece *v.* Great Britain, Judgment, (1927) PCIJ Ser A No 11
Mavrommatis Palestine Concessions, Greece *v.* Great Britain, Preliminary Objections, (1924) PCIJ Ser A No 2
Monastery of Saint Naoum, Advisory Opinion, (1924) PCIJ Ser B No 9
Phosphates in Morocco (Preliminary Objections), (1938) PCIJ Ser A/B No 74
Polish Postal Service in Danzig, Advisory Opinion, (1925) PCIJ Ser B No 11
Question of Jaworzina, Advisory Opinion, (1923) PCIJ Ser B No 8
Société Commerciale de Belgique, Belgium *v.* Greece, Judgment, (1939) PCIJ Ser A/B No 78
S.S. Lotus, France *v.* Turkey, Judgment, (1927) PCIJ Ser A No 10
S.S. Wimbledon, United Kingdom, France, Italy and Japan *v.* Germany, Judgment, (1923) PCIJ Ser A No 1

International Court of Justice

Aerial Incident of 10 August 1999, Pakistan *v.* India, Judgment, [2000] ICJ Reports 12
Ahmadou Sadio Diallo (Compensation), Republic of Guinea *v.* Democratic Republic of the Congo, [2012] ICJ Reports 324
Ahmadou Sadio Diallo (Merits), Republic of Guinea *v.* Democratic Republic of the Congo, [2010] ICJ Reports 639
Allegations of Genocide under the Convention on the Prevention and Punishment of the Crime of Genocide, Ukraine *v.* Russian Federation: 32 States Intervening, Preliminary Objections, [2024] ICJ
Allegations of Genocide under the Convention on the Prevention and Punishment of the Crime of Genocide, Ukraine *v.* Russian Federation, Provisional Measures, [2022] ICJ Reports 211
Alleged Violations of Sovereign Rights and Maritime Spaces in the Caribbean Sea, Nicaragua *v.* Colombia, Preliminary Objections, [2016] ICJ Reports 3
Alleged Violations of Sovereign Rights and Maritime Spaces in the Caribbean Sea, Nicaragua *v.* Colombia, [2022], ICJ Reports 226
Appeal Relating to the Jurisdiction of the ICAO Council, India *v.* Pakistan [1972] ICJ Reports 46
Appeal relating to the Jurisdiction of the ICAO Council under Article II, Section 2, of the 1944 International Air Services Transit Agreement, Bahrain, Egypt and United Arab Emirates *v.* Qatar, Judgment, [2020] ICJ Reports 172

Appeal relating to the Jurisdiction of the ICAO Council under Article 84 of the Convention on International Civil Aviation, Bahrain, Egypt, Saudi Arabia and United Arab Emirates *v.* Qatar, Judgment, [2020] ICJ Reports 81

Applicability of the Obligation to Arbitrate under Section 21 of the United Nations Headquarters Agreement of 26 June 1947, Advisory Opinion, [1988] ICJ Reports 12

Application for Revision of the Judgment of 11 September 1992 in the Case concerning the Land, Island and Maritime Frontier Dispute (El Salvador/Honduras: Nicaragua intervening) (El Salvador *v.* Honduras, Judgment [2003] ICJ Reports 329

Application of the Convention on the Prevention and Punishment of the Crime of Genocide (Croatia *v.* Serbia), Preliminary Objections, Judgment, [2008] ICJ Reports 412

Application of the Convention on the Prevention and Punishment of the Crime of Genocide, Bosnia and Herzegovina *v.* Yugoslavia (Serbia and Montenegro), Provisional Measures, Order of 13 September 1993, ICJ Reports 1993

Application of the International Convention on the Elimination of All Forms of Racial Discrimination (Qatar *v.* United Arab Emirates), Preliminary Objections, Judgment, [2021] ICJ Reports 71

Application of the International Convention on the Elimination of All Forms of Racial Discrimination (Georgia *v.* Russian Federation), Preliminary Objections, Judgment, [2011] ICJ Reports 70

Application of the Convention on the Prevention and Punishment of the Crime of Genocide, Bosnia and Herzegovina *v.* Serbia and Montenegro, Judgment, [2007] ICJ Reports 43

Application of the Convention on the Prevention and Punishment of the Crime of Genocide, Bosnia and Herzegovina *v.* Serbia and Montenegro, Counter-Claims, [1997] ICJ Reports 243

Application of the Convention on the Prevention and Punishment of the Crime of Genocide in the Gaza Strip, South Africa *v.* Israel, Order of 28 March 2024

Application of the Interim Accord of 13 September 1995, Macedonia *v.* Greece, Judgment, [2011] ICJ Reports 644

Arbitral Award made by the King of Spain on 23 December 1906, Honduras *v.* Nicaragua, [1960] ICJ Reports 192

Arbitral Award of 31 July 1989, Guinea-Bissau *v.* Senegal, Judgment, [1991] ICJ Reports 53

Arbitral Award of 3 October 1899, Guyana *v.* Venezuela, Jurisdiction of the Court, Judgment, [2020] ICJ Reports 455

Armed Activities in the Territory of the Congo, Democratic Republic of the Congo *v.* Uganda, Judgment, [2005] ICJ Reports 168

Armed Activities in the Territory of the Congo (New Application: 2002), Democratic Republic of the Congo *v.* Rwanda [2006] ICJ Reports 6
Arrest Warrant, Democratic Republic of the Congo *v.* Belgium, Judgment, [2002] ICJ Reports 3
Asylum Case, Colombia *v.* Peru, [1950] ICJ Reports 266
Avena and Other Mexican Nationals, Mexico *v.* United States of America, Judgment, [2004] ICJ Reports 12
Avena and Other Mexican Nationals (Interpretation), Mexico *v.* United States of America, [2009] ICJ Reports 3
Barcelona Traction, Light and Power Company, Limited, Belgium *v.* Spain, Judgment, [1970] ICJ Reports 3
Border and Transborder Armed Actions, Nicaragua *v.* Honduras, Jurisdiction and Admissibility, [1988] ICJ Reports 69
Certain Activities Carried Out by Nicaragua in the Border Area (Compensation), Costa Rica *v.* Nicaragua, [2018] ICJ Reports 15
Certain Activities Carried Out by Nicaragua in the Border Area and Construction of a Road in Costa Rica along the San Juan River (Merits), Costa Rica *v.* Nicaragua and Nicaragua *v.* Costa Rica, [2015] ICJ Reports 665
Certain Iranian Assets, Islamic Republic of Iran *v.* United States of America (Merits), [2013] ICJ Reports 51
Certain Iranian Assets (Islamic Republic of Iran *v.* United States of America), Judgment (Merits), [2023] ICJ Reports 224
Certain Phosphate Lands in Nauru (Nauru *v.* Australia), Preliminary Objections, Judgment, [1992] ICJ Reports 240
Certain Property, Liechtenstein *v.* Germany, Preliminary Objections, [2005] ICJ Reports 6
Certain Property, Liechtenstein *v.* Germany, Judgment, [2005] ICJ Reports 6
Continental Shelf, Tunisia/Libya, Revision and Interpretation, [1985] ICJ Reports 192
Corfu Channel (Compensation), United Kingdom *v.* Albania, Judgment, [1949] ICJ Reports 244
Corfu Channel (Merits), United Kingdom of Great Britain and Northern Ireland *v.* Albania, Judgment, [1949] ICJ Reports 4
Delimitation of the Continental Shelf beyond 200 Nautical Miles, Nicaragua *v.* Colombia, Preliminary Objections, [2016] ICJ Reports 100
Dispute over the Status and Use of the Waters of the Silala, Chile *v.* Bolivia, Judgment, [2022] ICJ Reports 614
East Timor, Portugal *v.* Australia, Judgment, ICJ Reports 1995
Effect of Awards of Compensation made by the UN Administrative Tribunal, Advisory Opinion, [1954] ICJ Reports 47
Fisheries Jurisdiction, Germany *v.* Iceland, Judgment, [1974] ICJ Reports 175
Fisheries Jurisdiction, United Kingdom *v.* Iceland, Judgment, [1974] ICJ Reports 3

Frontier Dispute, Benin/Niger, Judgment, [2005] ICJ Reports 90

Frontier Dispute, Burkina Faso/Niger, Judgment, [2013] ICJ Reports 441

Gabčíkovo-Nagymaros Project, Hungary/Slovakia, Judgment, [1997] ICJ Reports 7

Great Belt (Provisional Measures), Finland *v.* Denmark, Judgment, [1991] ICJ Reports 12

Haya de la Torre, Peru *v.* Colombia, [1951] ICJ Reports 71

Immunities and Criminal Proceedings, Equatorial Guinea *v.* France, Preliminary Objections, [2018] ICJ Reports 292

Interpretation of Peace Treaties with Bulgaria, Hungary and Romania, Advisory Opinion (First Phase), [1950] ICJ Reports 65

Interpretation of Peace Treaties with Bulgaria, Hungary and Romania, Advisory Opinion (Second Phase), [1950] ICJ Reports 221

Jadhav (India *v.* Pakistan), Judgment, [2019] ICJ Reports 418

Jurisdictional Immunities of the State, Italy *v.* Germany, [2012] ICJ Reports 9

Kasikili/Sedudu Island, Botswana/Namibia, Judgment, [1999] ICJ Reports 1045

LaGrand, Germany *v.* United States of America, Judgment, [2001] ICJ Reports 466

Land and Maritime Boundary between Cameroon and Nigeria, Cameroon *v.* Nigeria: Equatorial Guinea intervening, Judgment, [2002] ICJ Reports 303

Land and Maritime Boundary between Cameroon and Nigeria, Nigeria *v.* Cameroon, Preliminary Objections, [1998] ICJ Reports 275

Land, Island and Maritime Frontier Dispute, El Salvador and Nicaragua (intervening) *v.* Honduras, Judgment, [1990] ICJ Reports 92

Legal Consequences for States of the Continued Presence of South Africa in Namibia (South West Africa) notwithstanding Security Council Resolution 276 (1970), Advisory Opinion, [1971] ICJ Reports 16

Legal Consequences arising from the Policies and Practices of Israel in the Occupied Palestinian Territory, including East Jerusalem, Advisory Opinion of 19 July 2024

Legal Consequences of the Construction of a Wall in the Occupied Palestinian Territory, Advisory Opinion, [2004] ICJ Reports 136

Legality of the Threat or Use of Nuclear Weapons, Advisory Opinion, [1996] ICJ Reports 226

Legality of Use of Force, Serbia and Montenegro *v.* United Kingdom, [2004] ICJ Reports 1307

Maritime Delimitation and Territorial Questions between Qatar and Bahrain, Qatar *v.* Bahrain, Jurisdiction and Admissibility, [1994] ICJ Reports 112

Military Activities in Congo, Democratic Republic of the Congo *v.* Uganda, Judgment, [2005] ICJ Reports 168

Military Activities in Congo, Democratic Republic of the Congo *v.* Uganda (Reparations), [2022] ICJ Reports 13

Military and Paramilitary Activities in and against Nicaragua (Jurisdiction), Nicaragua *v.* United States of America, [1984] ICJ Reports 392

Military and Paramilitary Activities in and against Nicaragua, Nicaragua *v.* United States of America (Merits), Judgment, [1986] ICJ Reports 14
Mutual Assistance in Criminal Matters, Djibouti *v.* France, [2008] ICJ Reports 177
Navigational and Related Rights, Costa Rica *v.* Nicaragua, [2009] ICJ Reports 213
North Sea Continental Shelf, Federal Republic of Germany/Netherlands, [1969] ICJ Reports 3
Northern Cameroons, Cameroon *v.* United Kingdom, Preliminary Objections, [1963] ICJ Reports 15
Nuclear Tests, Australia *v.* France, [1974] ICJ Reports 253
Nuclear Tests, New Zealand *v.* France, [1974] ICJ Reports 457
Obligation to Negotiate Access to the Pacific (Bolivia *v.* Chile), Judgment, ICJ Reports 2018, p. 507, 563
Oil Platforms (Merits), Iran *v.* United States, Judgment, [2003] ICJ Reports 161
Pedra Branca/Pulau Batu Puteh, Middle Rocks and South Ledge, Malaysia/Singapore, Judgment, [2008] ICJ Reports 12
Pulau Litigan and Pulau Sipadan, Indonesia/Malaysia, Judgment, [2002] ICJ Reports 62
Pulp Mills on the River Uruguay, Argentina *v.* Uruguay, Judgment [2010] ICJ Reports 14
Questions of Interpretation and Application of the 1971 Montreal Convention Arising from the Aerial Incident at Lockerbie, Libya *v.* United Kingdom, Preliminary Objections, [1998] ICJ Reports 115
Reparation for injuries suffered in the service of the Nations, Advisory Opinion, [1949] ICJ Reports 174
Request for an Examination of the Situation (Nuclear Tests), New Zealand *v.* France, [1995] ICJ Reports 288
Request for Interpretation of the Judgment of 11 June 1998 in the Case concerning the Land and Maritime Boundary between Cameroon and Nigeria, Cameroon *v.* Nigeria, Preliminary Objections, [1999] ICJ Reports 31
Request for Interpretation of the Judgment of 20 November 1950 in the Asylum Case, Colombia *v.* Peru, Judgment, [1950] ICJ Reports 395
Request for Interpretation of the Judgment of 31 March 2004 in the Case concerning Avena and Other Mexican Nationals, Mexico *v.* United States of America, Judgment, [2009] ICJ Reports 3
Request for Interpretation of the Judgment of 31 March 2004 in the Case concerning Avena and Other Mexican Nationals, Mexico *v.* United States of America, Provisional Measures, [2008] ICJ Reports 311
Rights of Nationals of the United States of America in Morocco, France *v.* United States, Judgment, [1952] ICJ Reports 176
South West Africa, Ethiopia *v.* South Africa, Judgment, [1966] ICJ Reports 6
South West Africa, Ethiopia *v.* South Africa, Preliminary Objections, [1962] ICJ Reports 319

Temple of Preah Vihear, Cambodia *v.* Thailand, Judgment, [1962] ICJ Reports 6
Temple of Preah Vihear (Interpretation), Cambodia *v.* Thailand, Judgment, [2013] ICJ Reports 28
Territorial and Maritime Dispute in the Caribbean Sea, Nicaragua *v.* Honduras, [2007] ICJ Reports 659
Territorial and Maritime Dispute, Nicaragua *v.* Colombia, Preliminary Objections, [2007] ICJ Reports 832
Territorial and Maritime Dispute, Nicaragua *v.* Colombia, Judgment, [2012] ICJ Reports 624
United States Diplomatic and Consular Staff in Tehran, Iran *v.* United States of America, Provisional Measures, [1979] ICJ Reports 7
United States Diplomatic and Consular Staff in Tehran, United States of America *v.* Iran, Judgment, [1980] ICJ Reports 3
Whaling in the Antarctic, Australia *v.* Japan, Judgment, [2014] ICJ Reports 226

International Centre for Settlement of Investment Disputes

ADC Affiliated Limited and ADC & ADMC Management Limited *v.* Hungary, [2006] ICSID Case No. ARB/03/16
AGIP S.p.A. *v.* People's Republic of the Congo, [1982] ICSID Case No. ARB/77/1
Apotex Holdings Inc. and Apotex Inc. *v.* United States of America, [2013] ICSID Case No. ARB(AF)/12/1
Archer Daniels Midland Company *v.* Mexico, [2007] ICSID Case No. ARB(AF)/04/05
Arif *v.* Moldova, [2013] ICSID Case No. ARB/11/23
BIVAC *v.* Paraguay, [2012] ICSID Case No. ARB/07/9
BIVAC *v.* Paraguay, [2014] ICSID Case No. ARB/07/9
Burlington Resources Inc. *v.* Ecuador, [2012] ICSID Case No. ARB/08/5
Cargill, Inc. *v.* Mexico, [2009] ICSID Case No. ARB(AF)/05/2
Cementownia *v.* Turkey (I), [2009] ICSID Case No. ARB(AF)/06/2
CMS Gas Transmission Co. *v.* Argentine Republic, [2005] ICSID Case No. ARB/01/8
ConocoPhillips Petrozuata B.V., ConocoPhillips Hamaca B.V. and ConocoPhillips Gulf of Paria B.V. *v.* Venezuela, [2014] ICSID Case No. ARB/07/30
Corn Products International (CPI) *v.* Mexico, [2008] ICSID Case No. ARB(AF)/04/01
Enron *v.* Argentina, ICSID Case No. ARB/01/3
Goetz and Others *v.* Burundi, [1998] ICSID Case No. ARB/95/3
Goetz and Others *v.* Burundi, [1999] ICSID Case No. ARB/95/3
Goetz and Others *v.* Burundi, [2012] ICSID Case No. ARB/01/2
Klöckner *v.* Cameroon, [1983] ICSID Case No. ARB/81/2
Klöckner *v.* Cameroon (Annulment), [1985] ICSID Case No. ARB/81/2

LG&E *v.* Argentina, [2006] ICSID Case No. ARB/02/1
Quiborax S.A. *v.* Bolivia, ICSID Case No. ARB/06/2
RWE Innogy GmbH and RWE Innogy Aersa S.A.U. *v.* Kingdom of Spain, [2019] ICSID Case No. ARB/14/34
Saluka Investments BV *v.* Czech Republic, (2006) PCA IIC 210
SGS *v.* Pakistan, [2003] ICSID Case No. ARB/01/13
SGS *v.* Philippines, [2004] ICSID Case No. ARB/02/6
Siemens A.G. *v.* Argentina, [2007] ICSID Case No. ARB/02/8
Suez, Sociedad General de Aguas de Barcelona S.A. *v.* Argentina, [2010] ICSID Case No. ARB/03/19
Telefónica S.A. *v.* Argentina, [2006] ICSID Case No. ARB/03/20, Decision on Objections to Jurisdiction, 25 May 2006
Tethyan Copper *v.* Pakistan, [2019] ICSID Case No. ARB/12/1
Texaco Overseas Petroleum Co. *v.* Government of the Libyan Arab Republic, (1979) 53 ILR 389
Trans-Global Petroleum, Inc. *v.* Jordan, [2008] ICSID Case No. ARB/07/25
Total S.A. *v.* Argentina, [2010] ICSID Case No. ARB/04/1
Waste Management, Inc. *v.* Mexico, [2000] ICSID Case No. ARB(AF)/98/2
Waste Management, Inc. *v.* Mexico ('Number 2'), [2002] ICSID Case No. ARB (AF)/00/3

International Tribunal for the Law of the Sea

'ARA Libertad', Argentina *v.* Ghana, Provisional Measures, ITLOS, (2012) ITLOS Case No. 20
Arctic Sunrise, Netherlands *v.* Russia, Provisional Measures, ITLOS, (2013) ITLOS Case No. 22
Case concerning the detention of three Ukrainian naval vessels, Ukraine *v.* Russian Federation, Provisional Measures, ITLOS, (2019) ITLOS Case No. 26
Dispute concerning delimitation of the maritime boundary between Ghana and Côte d'Ivoire in the Atlantic Ocean (Ghana/Côte d'Ivoire), ITLOS, (2017), ITLOS Case No. 23
Land Reclamation by Singapore in and around the Straits of Johor, Malaysia *v.* Singapore, (2005) PCA XXVII RIAA 133
Land Reclamation by Singapore in and around the Straits of Johor, Malaysia *v.* Singapore (Provisional Measures), ITLOS, (2003) 126 ILR 487
M/V 'Saiga' (Prompt Release), Saint Vincent and the Grenadines *v.* Guinea, (1997) ITLOS Case No. 1
M/V 'SAIGA' (No. 2), Saint Vincent and the Grenadines *v.* Guinea, ITLOS, ITLOS Reports 1999, p. 10, (1998) 120 ILR 144
M/V 'Virginia G', Panama *v.* Guinea-Bissau, Judgment, ITLOS Reports 2014, p. 4
Request for Advisory Opinion submitted by the Sub-Regional Fisheries Commission, Advisory Opinion, ITLOS Reports 2015, p. 463

Southern Bluefin Tuna, New Zealand – Japan, Australia – Japan, ITLOS, (2000) 119 ILR 508

Southern Bluefin Tuna, New Zealand – Japan, Australia – Japan (Provisional Measures), ITLOS, (1999) 38 ILM 1624

African Court on Human and Peoples' Rights (AfCHPR)

Application 006/2012 (The African Commission on Human and Peoples' Rights vs Republic of Kenya), Judgment (Reparations), 23 June 2022

Application 003/2020 (Houngue Eric Noudehouenou *v.* Republic of Benin), Judgment, 4 December 2020

Application 028/2020 (Houngue Eric Noudehouenou *v.* Republic of Benin), Judgment, 1 December 2022

Andean Court of Justice

Case No. 13-AI-2002 (Non-compliance with Judgment) (Summary Procedure), Order, 26 February 2003

Case No. 118-AI-2003 (Secretary-General of the Andean Community *v.* Colombia), Judgment, 14 April 2005

Case No. 118-AI-2003 (Non-compliance with Judgment of 14 April 2005) (Summary Procedure), Order, 26 October 2006

Case No. 118-AI-2003 (Non-compliance with Judgment of 14 April 2005) (Second Summary Procedure), Order, 18 July 2012

Case No. 118-AI-2003 (Non-compliance with Judgment of 14 April 2005) (Second Summary Procedure), Order, 28 June 2018

Case No. 118-AI-2003 (Non-compliance with Judgment of 14 April 2005) (Second Summary Procedure), Order, 28 November 2022

Case No. 118-AI-2003 (Non-compliance with Judgment of 14 April 2005) (Second Summary Procedure), Order, 10 October 2023

Case No. 118-AI-2003 (Non-compliance with Judgment of 14 April 2005) (Second Summary Procedure), Request for Interpretation, 24 October 2023

Case No. 118-AI-2003 (Non-compliance with Judgment of 14 April 2005) (Second Summary Procedure), Judgment, 12 July 2023

Case No. 05-AI-2021 (Peru *v.* Ecuador), Judgment, 17 July 2023

Case No. 02-AI-2020 (Peru *v.* Bolivia), Judgment, 17 July 2023

Case No. 02-AI-2019 (SugarLatam *v.* Ecuador), Judgment, 18 July 2023

Caribbean Court of Justice (CCJ)

Rudisa Beverages & Juices N.V. and Caribbean International Distributors Inc. *v.* The Co-operative Republic of Guyana, App. No. OA 003 of 2013 (Original Jurisdiction), Judgment, 8 May 2014

SM Jaleel & Co Ltd & Guyana Beverages Inc Claimants and The Co-Operative Republic of Guyana, CCJ Application No. TTOJ2016/001 (Original Jurisdiction), Judgment, 9 May 2017

Trinidad Cement Limited *v.* the Caribbean Community, CCJ App No. 3 of 2008 (Original Jurisdiction), Judgment, 5 February 2009

Trinidad Cement Limited and TCL Guyana Incorporated *v.* Guyana (Non-compliance/Contempt), CCJ App. No. 2 of 2009 (Original Jurisdiction), Judgment, 29 March 2010

Central American Court of Justice

Case No. 2-23-3-2018 (Gilmar Othmar Sánchez Herrera *v.* Guatemala) (Contempt of Court and Non-compliance), Judgment, 17 July 2019

Central American Integration System (SICA)

Case MSC-01-16, Guatemala – Importation of Juices in Panama, Award of the Arbitral Tribunal, 16 February 2017

Common Market of the South (Mercosur)

Award No 1/2005, Mercosur Court, 20 December 2005

Award No 1/2006, Mercosur Court, 13 January 2006

Award No 2/2006, Mercosur Court, 6 July 2006

Award No 1/2007, Mercosur Court, 8 June 2007

Award No 1/2008, Mercosur Court, 25 April 2008

Award No 9/2006, Mercosur Ad-Hoc Tribunal, 6 September 2006

Award No 1/2012, Mercosur Court, 21 July 2012

Decision No 28/2012, Mercosur Court, 29 June 2012

Court of Justice of the European Union

Commission *v.* France (1997) C-265/95 (CJEU)

Commission *v.* Luxemburg and Belgium [1964] ECR 625 (CJEU)

Flaminio Costa *v.* ENEL [1964] Case 6/64, ECR (English Spec Ed) 585 (CJEU)

Francovich *v.* Italy [1991] Case No. C-6/90, ECR I-5357 (CJEU)

Kadi and Al Barakaat International Foundation *v.* Council and Commission [2008] Joined Cases C-402/05 P and C-415/05 P, ECR I-2685 (CJEU)

Moldova *v.* Komstroy [2021] ECLI:EU:C:2021:655 (CJEU)

Opinion 2/15, The Free Trade Agreement with Singapore, [2017] ECLI:EU:C:2017:376

PL Holdings *v.* Poland [2021] ECLI:EU:C:2021:875 (CJEU)
Slovakia *v.* Achmea BV [2018] ECLI:EU:C:2018:158; [2018] 2 CMLR 40 (CJEU)
Van Gend en Loos *v.* Nederlandse administratie der belastingen [1963] Case 26/62, ECR (English Spec Ed) 1 (CJEU)
Yassin Abdullah Kadi and Al Barakaat International Foundation *v.* Council of the European Union and Commission of the European Communities [2008] ECR I-6351 (CJEU)

East African Court of Justice

Sitenda Sebalu *v.* EAC Secretary General, Reference No. 8 of 2012, Judgment, 22 November 2013

Eritrea-Ethiopia Claims Commission

Eritrea-Ethiopia Claims Commission, Partial Award – Jus Ad Bellum – Ethiopia's Claims 1–8, (2005) 27 RIAA 457
Eritrea-Ethiopia Claims Commission, Final Award – Ethiopia's Damages Claims, (2009) 26 RIAA 631
Eritrea-Ethiopia Claims Commission, Final Award – Eritrea's Damages Claims (2009) 26 RIAA 505

Economic Community of West African States (ECOWAS) Community Court of Justice

Application no. ECW/CCJ/APP/12/15, Aziagbede and Others *v.* Republic of Togo, Judgment, 6 December 2016 (ECW/CCJ/JUD/29/16)
Application no. ECW/CCJIAPP/20/21, Sambo Dasuki *v.* Federal Republic of Nigeria, Judgment, 6 June 2024 (ECW/CCJ/JUD/19/24)
Application no. ECW/CCJ/APP/22/16, Chude Mba *v.* Republic of Ghana and Others, Judgment, 12 March 2019 (ECW/CCJ/JUD/30/18)
Application no. ECW/CCJ/APP/08/09, SERAP *v.* Nigeria, Judgment, 14 December 2012 (ECW/CCJ/JUD/18/12)
Application no. ECW/CCJ/APP/09/13, Karim Meissa Wade *v.* Republic of Senegal, Judgment, 19 July 2013 (ECW/CCJ/JUD/19/13)

European Court of Human Rights (ECtHR)

Application No. 71503/01, Assanidze *v.* Georgia, [2004]
Application No. 16574/08, Fabris *v.* France, [2013]
Application No. 6833/74, Marckx *v.* Belgium, [1979]

Application No. 15511/89, Scopelliti *v.* Italy, [1993]
Application No. 2614/65, Ringeisen *v.* Austria, [1972]
Application Nos. 2832/66, 2835/66, 2899/66, De Wilde, Ooms and Versyp *v.* Belgium, [1971]
Application No. 14556/89, Papamichalopoulos and Others *v.* Greece, [1995]
Application No. 15012/02, Wasserman *v.* Russia, [2004]
Application No. 15227/03, Lyons and Others *v.* United Kingdom, [2003]
Application No. 153118/89, Loizidou *v.* Turkey, [1996]
Application No. 21071/05, Wasserman *v.* Russia (No. 2), [2008]
Application No. 23687/05, Ivanţoc *v.* Moldova and Russia, [2012]
Application No. 24699/94, Verein gegen Tierfabriken Schweiz (VgT) *v.* Switzerland, [2001]
Application No. 25701/94, Former King of Greece *v.* Greece (Merits), [2000]
Application No. 25701/94, Former King of Greece *v.* Greece (Just Satisfaction), [2002]
Application No. 25781/94, Cyprus *v.* Turkey (Merits), [2001]
Application No. 25781/94, Cyprus *v.* Turkey (Just Satisfaction), [2014]
Application No. 28342/95, Brumarescu *v.* Romania (Merits), [1999]
Application No. 28342/95, Brumarescu *v.* Romania (Just Satisfaction), [2001]
Application No. 29522/95, IJL, GMR and AKP *v.* United Kingdom, [2000]
Application No. 32772/02, Verein gegen Tierfabriken Schweiz *v.* Switzerland (No. 2), [2009]
Application No. 35763/97, Al-Adsani *v.* United Kingdom, [2001]
Application No. 48787/99, Ilaşcu *v.* Moldova and Russia, [2004]
Application No. 14902/04, Yukos *v.* Russia (Just Satisfaction), [2014]
Application No. 13255/07, Georgia *v.* Russia (I) [2019]
Application No. 5310/71, Ireland *v.* United Kingdom (Merits and Just Satisfaction) [1978]
Application No. 39630/09, El-Masri *v.* The Former Yugoslav Republic of Macedonia, Judgment [2012]

Inter-American Court of Human Rights

Aloeboetoe *v.* Suriname (Reparation and Costs, Judgment) IACtHR, (1993) Ser. C No. 11
Apitz Barbera et al. *v.* Venezuela (Compliance with Judgment), IACtHR, 23 November 2012
Apitz Barbera et al. *v.* Venezuela (Preliminary Objection, Merits, Reparations and Costs), IACtHR, (2008) Ser C No 182
Applicability of Article 65 of the American Convention on Human Rights (Order), IACtHR, 29 June 2005

Baena Ricardo et al. *v.* Panama (Monitoring Compliance with Judgment), IACtHR, 21 June 2002

Baena Ricardo et al. *v.* Panama (Monitoring Compliance with Judgment), IACtHR, 22 November 2002

Baena Ricardo et al. *v.* Panama (Monitoring Compliance with Judgment), IACtHR, 28 November 2003

Barrios Altos *v.* Peru (Reparation and Costs), IACtHR, (2001) Ser C No 87

Case of the 19 Merchants *v.* Colombia (Merits, Reparations and Costs, Judgment), IACtHR, (2004) Ser. C No. 109

Castillo Pérez, Loaza Tamayo, Castillo Petruzzi et al., Ivcher Bronstein and Constitutional Court (Monitoring Compliance with Judgment), IACtHR, Order, 1 June 2001

Castillo Petruzzi et al. *v.* Peru (Merits, Reparation and Costs), IACtHR, (1999) Ser C No 52

Castillo Petruzzi et al. *v.* Peru (Compliance with Judgment), IACtHR, (1999) Ser C No 59

Claude Reyes et al. *v.* Chile (Compliance with Judgment), IACtHR, 24 November 2008

Constitutional Court (Aguirre Roca, Rey Ferry and Revoredo Marsano) *v.* Peru (Compliance with Judgment), IACtHR, 5 August 2008

Durand and Ugarte *v.* Peru (Reparations), IACtHR, (2001) Ser C No 89

Fleury et al. *v.* Haiti (Compliance with Judgment), IACtHR, 22 November 2019

Godínez Cruz *v.* Honduras (Interpretation), IACtHR, (1990) Ser C No 10

Godínez Cruz *v.* Honduras (Merits), IACtHR, (1989) Ser C No 5

Godínez Cruz *v.* Honduras (Reparation and Costs), IACtHR, (1989) Ser C No 8

González and others *v.* Mexico, Preliminary objections, merits, reparations and costs, Judgment, 16 September 2009, IACHR Ser C No 205

Gómez-Palomino *v.* Peru (Merits, Reparations and Costs, Judgment) 22 November 2005, IACHR Ser. C No. 136

Gutiérrez-Soler *v.* Colombia (Compliance with Judgment), IACtHR, 30 June 2009

Gutiérrez-Soler *v.* Colombia, Merits, Reparations and Costs, Judgment, 12 September 2005, IACHR Ser C No 132

Interpretation of the American Declaration of the Rights and Duties of Man, Advisory Opinion OC-10/89, 14 July 1989, Ser. A No. 10

Ivcher Bronstein *v.* Peru (Competence), IACtHR, (1999) Ser C No 54

José Miguel Gudiel Alvarez and others *v.* Guatemala, Merits, Reparations and Costs, Judgment, 20 November 2012, IACHR Ser C No 253

Juvenile Reeducation Institute *v.* Paraguay, Preliminary Objections, Merits, Reparations and Costs, Judgment, 2 September 2005, IACHR Ser C No 112

Loayza Tamayo *v.* Peru (Compliance with Judgment), IACtHR, (1999) Ser C No 60

Mack Chang *v.* Guatemala, Merits, Reparation and Costs, Judgment, 25 November 2003, IACHR Ser C No 101

Velásquez-Rodríguez *v.* Honduras (Interpretation of the Judgment on Reparations and Costs), IACtHR, (1990) Ser C No 9

Velásquez-Rodríguez *v.* Honduras (Merits), IACtHR, (1988) Ser C No 4

Velásquez-Rodríguez *v.* Honduras (Reparation and Costs), IACHR, (1989) Ser C No 7

YATAMA *v.* Nicaragua, Preliminary Objections, Merits, Reparations and Costs, Judgment, 23 June 2005, IACHR Ser C No 127

Yvon Neptune *v.* Haiti (Compliance with Judgment), IACtHR, 20 November 2015

International Criminal Court (ICC)

ICC, Appeals Chamber, *Judgment in the Jordan Referral re Al-Bashir Appeal*, 6 May 2019, (ICC-02/05-01/09 OA2), para. 114

ICC, Pre-trial Chamber II, *Decision on the Prosecutor's Request for a Finding of Non-Compliance against the Republic of the Sudan*, 9 March 2015 (ICC-02/05-01/09-227)

ICC, Pre-trial Chamber II, *Decision under Article 87(7) of the Rome Statute on the non-compliance by South Africa with the request by the Court for the arrest and surrender of Omar Al-Bashir*, 6 July 2017 (ICC-02/05-01/09-302), para. 31

ICC, Pre-trial Chamber I, *Second Warrant of Arrest for Omar Hassan Ahmad Al Bashir*, 12 July 2010 (ICC-02/05-01/09-94), p. 8–9 (genocide)

ICC, Pre-trial Chamber I, *Warrant of Arrest for Omar Hassan Ahmad Al Bashir*, 4 March 2009 (ICC-02/05-01/09-1), p. 7–8

ICC, *Prosecutor vs Al-Bashir*, Pre-Trial Chamber 1, Case No ICC-02/05-01/09, *Decision of the Prosecution's Application for a Warrant of Arrest*, 4 March 2009 (ICC-02/05-01/09-3)

Iran–U.S. Claims Tribunal

Burton Marks and Harry Umann v. Republic of Iran, IUCT, (1985) 8 Iran–US CTR 290, 297

Case No. A21, IUCT, (1987) Decision No 62-A21-FT

Case No. A27, IUCT, (1995) Award No 586-A27-FT

North American Free Trade Agreement (NAFTA)

NAFTA Panel Report, Tariffs Applied by Canada to Certain U.S.-Origin Agricultural Products, (1996) CDA-USA-1995-2008-01

NAFTA Panel Report, U.S. Safeguard Action Taken on Broom Corn Brooms from Mexico, (1997) USA-MEX-1997-2008-01

NAFTA Panel Report, Cross-Border Trucking Services, (1998) USA-MEX-1998-2008-01

Tribunal of the Southern African Development Community (SADC)

Gongo *v.* Zimbabwe, Judgment, Case No. SADCT: 05/2008 (SADC, 9 December 2010)
Campbell *v.* Zimbabwe, Ruling, Case No. SADCT: 11/18 (SADC, 18 July 2008)
Campbell *v.* Zimbabwe, Ruling, Case No. SADCT: 03/2009 (SADC, 18 July 2009)
Fick *v.* Zimbabwe, Ruling, Case No. SADCT: 01/2010 (SADC, 16 July 2010)

Miscellaneous

Achmea B.V. *v.* Slovakia, (2014) PCA Case No. 2013-12
Affaire Junghans (Première Partie), Allemagne contre Roumanie, (1939) 3 RIAA 1845
Affaire Junghans (Deuxième Partie), Allemagne contre Roumanie, (1940) 3 RIAA 1883
Air Service Agreement of 27 March 1946, (1978) 18 RIAA 417
Argentina/Chile Beagle Channel Arbitration Agreement, (1971) 21 RIAA 53
Argentine-Chile Frontier Case, Argentina/Chile, (1966) 16 RIAA 109
Arbitration for the Brcko Area (Supplemental Award), Republika Srpska *v.* the Federation of Bosnia and Herzegovina (1998) UN Doc. S/1998/248
Arrest and Return of Savarkar (France *v.* Great Britain), PCA Case No. 1910-03, Award, 23 February 1911, (1911) XI RIAA 243
Award in the Arbitration regarding the Indus Waters Kishenganga between Pakistan and India, Pakistan *v.* India, (2013) 31 RIAA 1
Beagle Channel Arbitration, Argentina/Chile, (2006) 21 RIAA 190
Beagle Channel Arbitration, Act of Montevideo, Argentina/Chile, (1979) 21 RIAA 240
Beagle Channel Arbitration, Communication of the Court of Arbitration to the Parties, Argentina/Chile, (1978) 17 ILM 1203
Beagle Channel Arbitration, Declaration of Her Majesty, Argentina/Chile, (1977) 21 RIAA 224
Beagle Channel Arbitration, Declaration of Nullity, Argentina/Chile, (2006) 21 RIAA 227
Beagle Channel Arbitration, Further Communication to the Parties, Argentina/Chile, (1978) 17 ILM 1204
Beagle Channel Arbitration, Note of the President of the Court of Arbitration to the United Kingdom, Argentina/Chile, (1978) 17 ILM 1198
Beagle Channel Arbitration, Treaty of Peace and Friendship, Argentina/Chile, (1984) 21 RIAA 250
BP Exploration Company (Libya) Ltd *v.* Government of Libyan Arab Republic (1973) 53 ILR 297
Channel Arbitration (Interpretation), United Kingdom *v.* France, (1978) 54 ILR 139

Chen (No 2), ILO Administrative Tribunal, (1983) Judgment No. 547
Chevron Corporation and Texaco Petroleum Company *v.* The Republic of Ecuador, PCA Case No. 2009-23
Colonies Portugaises (Naulilaa), Portugal *v.* Germany, (1928) 2 UNRIAA 1011
Company General of the Orinoco, United States of America *v.* Venezuela, (1905) 10 RIAA 184
Control over the Brčko Corridor, Republika Srpska *v.* the Federation of Bosnia and Herzegovina, (1997) 36 ILM 396
Cordillera of the Andes Boundary, Argentina/Chile, (1902) 20 RIAA 37
Cosmos 954 (1979) 18 ILM 899
Cysne Case, Portugal *v.* Germany, (1930) 2 UNRIAA 1035
Delimitation of the Exclusive Economic Zone and the Continental Shelf between Barbados and Trinidad and Tobago, Barbados *v.* Trinidad and Tobago, (2006) PCA 45 ILM 839
Danford Knowlton & Co (1881), Spanish-United States Claims Commission
Delgado (1881), Spanish-United States Claims Commission
Delimitation of the Maritime Boundary between Guyana and Suriname, Guyana *v.* Suriname, PCA Case No. 2004-04, Award, (2007) 30 RIAA 1, (2008) PCA 47 ILM 166
Detention of Ukrainian Naval Vessels and Servicemen Ukraine *v.* Russia, Award on Preliminary Objections (2022) PCA Case No. 2019-28
Dickson Car Wheel Co, United States of America *v.* United Mexican States, (1931) 4 RIAA 669
Dispute between Argentina and Chile concerning the Beagle Channel, Argentina/ Chile, (2006) 21 RIAA 53
Dispute Concerning Access to Information under Article 9 of the OSPAR Convention, Ireland *v.* United Kingdom, (2003) 23 RIAA 59
Dispute over Inter-Entity Boundary in Brčko (Final Award), Federation of Bosnia and Herzegovina *v.* Republika Srpska, (1999) 38 ILM 534
Duzgit Integrity Arbitration, Malta *v.* São Tomé and Príncipe, PCA Case No. 2014-07
Ecuador *v.* United States, (2012) PCA Case No. 2012-05
Eurotunnel, France *v.* United Kingdom, (2007) PCA, Partial Award
Forests of Central Rhodope (Merits), Greece *v.* Bulgaria, (1933) 3 RIAA 1405
Free Zones of Upper Savoy and the District of Gex, France *v.* Switzerland, Award, (1933) 3 RIAA 1455
Hernández de Agüero *v.* Secretary General of the Organization of American States, (1980) OASAT, Judgment No. 51
Indus Waters Treaty Arbitration, Pakistan *v.* India, (2023) PCA Case No. 2023-01, Award on the Competence of the Court
Lac Lanoux, France *v.* Spain, (1957) 12 RIAA 281, 316
Laguna del Desierto, Argentina/Chile, (1991) 113 ILR 1

Laguna del Desierto, Argentina/Chile, (1994) 113 ILR 1
Laguna del Desierto, Argentina/Chile, (1995) 113 ILR 194
Laguna del Desierto, Argentina/Chile, Resolution of 13 October 1995, (1995) 113 ILR 257
Laguna del Desierto, Argentina/Chile, Statement of the Government of Chile, (1995) 113 ILR 259
LIAMCO *v.* Government of Libyan Arab Republic (1982) 62 ILR 140
Lusitania, Germany *v.* United States of America, (1923) 7 RIAA 32
Machado, (1881) Spanish-United States Claims Commission
Manouba, France *v.* Italy (1913) 11 UNRIAA 463
Morgenstern et al. *v.* Germany, (1928) 7 Recueil des Décisions des Tribunaux Arbitraux Mixtes 725
MOX Plant (UNCLOS), Ireland *v.* United Kingdom, (2003) PCA Order No 3
Norwegian Shipowners, Norway *v.* United States of America, (1922) 1 RIAA 307
Pious Fund Case, Sir Edward Thornton, 11 November 1875
Pious Fund of the Californias, United States of America *v.* United Mexican States, (1902) 9 RIAA 1
Pious Fund of the Californias, Award, (1908) 2 AJIL 893
Rainbow Warrior (New Zealand *v.* France) (1990) 20 RIAA 215
Saar Papier Vertriebs GmbH *v.* Poland, (1994) UNCITRAL, Interim Award (Jurisdiction)
Sergei Paushok et al. *v.* Mongolia, (2011) UNCITRAL, Award on Jurisdiction and Liability
S.S. 'I'm Alone', United States of America *v.* Canada, (1935) 3 RIAA 1616
Tacna-Arica Question, Chile/Peru, (1925) 2 UNRIAA 921
The Agreement to Arbitration in Boundary dispute between Argentina and Chile concerning the frontier line between Boundary Post 62 and Mount Fitzroy, Chile *v.* Argentina, (1995) 113 ILR 1
The 'Enrica Lexie' Incident, Italy *v.* India, (2020) PCA Case No. 2015-28
The South China Sea Arbitration (The Republic of Philippines *v.* The People's Republic of China), PCA Case No. 2013-19, Award, 12 July 2016
Trail Smelter, United States of America *v.* Canada, (1941) 3 RIAA 1905
Trail Smelter, United States of America *v.* Canada, (1941) 3 RIAA 1952
Walter Fletcher Smith, Cuba/United States of America, (1929) 2 UNRIAA 913
Young Loan Arbitration, Belgium and Ors. *v.* Germany, (1980) 59 ILR 494
Yukos Universal *v.* Russia, PCA Case No. AA 227, Final Award, 18 July 2014

World Trade Organization (WTO)

ACP-EC Partnership Arbitration, WT/L/616, adopted 1 August 2015

Agreement between Antigua and Barbuda and the United States Regarding Procedures under Articles 21 and 22 of the DSU (US – Gambling), WT/285/16, 26 May 2006

Appellate Body Report, Canada – Aircraft (21.5), WT/DS70/AB/RW, adopted 4 August 2000

Appellate Body Report, Chile – Price Band System, WT/DS207/AB/R, adopted 22 October 2002

Appellate Body Report, Chile – Price Band System (21.5), WT/DS207/AB/RW, adopted 22 May 2007

Appellate Body Report, China – Measures Related to the Exportation of Various Raw Materials, WT/DS395/AB/R, adopted 30 January 2012

Appellate Body Report, China – Raw Materials, WT/DS395/AB/R, adopted 22 February 2012

Appellate Body Report, EC – Bananas III (21.5 – Ecuador II), WT/DS27/AB/RW2/ECU, adopted 11 December 2008

Appellate Body Report, EC – Bananas III (21.5 – US), WT/DS27/AB/RW/USA, adopted 22 December 2008

Appellate Body Report, EC – Bed Linen (21.5), WT/DS141/AB/RW, adopted 24 April 2003

Appellate Body Report, EC – Continued Suspension, WT/DS320/AB/R, adopted 14 November 2008

Appellate Body Report, Mexico – Soft Drinks, WT/DS308/AB/R, adopted 26 March 2006

Appellate Body Report, US – Certain EC Products, WT/DS165/AB/R, adopted 10 January 2001

Appellate Body Report, US – Clove Cigarettes, WT/DS406/AB/R, adopted 24 April 2012

Appellate Body Report, US – Continued Suspension, WT/DS320/AB/R, WT/DS321/AB/R, adopted 14 November 2008

Appellate Body Report, US – Cotton (21.5), WT/DS267/AB/RW, adopted 20 June 2008

Appellate Body Report, US – FSC (21.5 II), WT/DS108/AB/RW2, adopted 14 March 2006

Appellate Body Report, US – OCTG Sunset (21.5), WT/DS268/AB/RW, adopted 17 December 2004

Appellate Body Report, US – Stainless Steel from Mexico, WT/DS344/AB/R, adopted 20 May 2008

Appellate Body Report, US – Softwood Lumber IV (21.5), WT/DS257/AB/RW, adopted 20 December 2005

Appellate Body Report, US – Tuna II (21.5 II), WT/DS381/AB/RW/USA, WT/DS381/AB/RW2, adopted 11 January 2019

Appellate Body Report, US – Zeroing (21.5), WT/DS294/AB/RW, adopted 11 June 2009

Appellate Body Report, US/Canada – Continued Suspension, WT/DS320/R, WT/DS321/R, adopted 14 November 2008

Arbitration Award, ACP-EC Partnership Arbitration, WT/L/616, adopted 1 August 2015

Arbitration Award, Brazil – Aircraft (22.6), WT/DS46/ARB, 28 August 2000

Arbitration Award, Canada – Aircraft II (22.6), WT/DS222/ARB, 17 February 2003

Arbitration Award, Canada – Export Credits and Loan Guarantees for Regional Aircraft (22.6, 4.11), WT/DS222/ARB, 17 February 2003

Arbitration Award, EC – Bananas (22.6 – US), WT/DS27/ARB, 9 April 1999

Arbitration Award, EC – Bananas III (22.6 – ECU), WT/DS27/ARB/ECU, 24 March 2000

Arbitration Award, EC – Hormones (22.6), WT/DS26/ARB, WT/DS48/AB/R, adopted 13 February 1998

Arbitration Award, Second ACP-EC Partnership Arbitration, WT/L/625, adopted 27 October 2005

Arbitration Award, US – 1916 Act (22.6), WT/DS136/ARB, 24 August 2004

Arbitration Award, US – Byrd Amendment (22.6), WT/DS217/ARB, WT/DS234/ARB, 31 August 2004

Arbitration Award, US – Cotton (22.6, 4.11), WT/DS267/ARB/1, 31 August 2009

Arbitration Award, US – Cotton (22.6, 7.10), WT/DS267/ARB/2, 31 August 2009

Arbitration Award, US – FSC (22.6), WT/DS108/ARB, 30 August 2002

Arbitration Award, US – Gambling (22.6), WT/DS285/ARB, 21 December 2007

GATT Panel Report, EEC – Quantitative Restrictions against Imports of Certain Products from Hong Kong, L/5511 – 30S/129, adopted 12 July 1983

GATT Panel Report, France – Assistance to Exports of Wheat and Wheat Flour, L/924, 7S/46, adopted 21 November 1958

GATT Panel Report, France – Import Restrictions, L/1921 – 11S/94, adopted 14 November 1962

GATT Panel Report, Italian Discrimination against Imported Agricultural Machinery, L/833 – 7S/60, adopted 23 October 1958

GATT Panel Report, Jamaica – Margins of Preference, L/3485 – 18S/183, adopted 2 February 1971

GATT Panel Report, Panel on Poultry, L/2088, 21 November 1965

GATT Panel Report, Uruguay – Margins of Preference, L/3485 – 18S/183, adopted 2 February 1971

GATT Panel Report, Uruguay Recourse to Article XXIII (1962), L/1923 – 11S/95, adopted 16 November 1962

GATT Panel Report, Uruguay Recourse to Article XXIII (1963), L/2074 – 13S/35, adopted 3 March 1965

GATT Panel Report, Uruguay Recourse to Article XXIII (1964), L/2278 – 13S/45, adopted 3 March 1965

Panel Report, Argentina – Hides and Leather, WT/DS155/R, adopted 16 February 2001

Panel Report, Argentina – Poultry Anti-Dumping Duties, WT/DS241/R, adopted 19 May 2003

Panel Report, Brazil – Aircraft (21.5 II), WT/DS46/RW/2, adopted 23 August 2001

Panel Report, China – Raw Materials, WT/DS394/R, WT/DS395/R, WT/DS398/R, adopted 22 February 2012

Panel Report, EC – Commercial Vessels, WT/DS301/R, adopted 20 June 2005

Panel Report, EC – Trademarks and Geographical Indications, WT/DS174/R, adopted 20 April 2005

Panel Report, US – Anti-Dumping Measures on PET Bags, WT/DS383/R, adopted 18 February 2010

Panel Report, US – Byrd Amendment, WT/DS217/R, WT/DS234/R, adopted 27 January 2003

Panel Report, US – Cotton, WT/DS267/R, adopted 21 March 2005

Panel Report, US – Sections 301–310 of the Trade Act of 1974, WT/DS152/R, adopted 27 January 2000

Panel Report, US – Underwear, WT/DS24/R, adopted 25 February 1997

WTO Decision, Decision of 5 April 1966 on Procedures under Article XXIII, BISD 14S/18

Decisions of National Courts and Tribunals

Australia

Eiser Infrastructure Ltd. v. Kingdom of Spain (Case No. NSD 601 of 2019 and NSD 602 of 2019), Judgment, 24 February 2020 (Federal Court of Australia)

Kingdom of Spain *v.* Infrastructure Services Luxembourg S.à.r.l. (Case No. NSD 602 of 2019), Judgment, 12 April 2023 (High Court of Australia)

France

Komstroy LLC *v.* Republic of Moldova (Case No. 15/21703), Judgment, 10 January 2023 (Paris Court of Appeal)

Germany

RWE AG and RWE Eemshaven Holding II BV *v.* Kingdom of the Netherlands (Case No. OLG Köln, 19 U 63/21, 2022), Judgment, 1 September 2022 (Higher Regional Court of Cologne)

Uniper SE, Uniper Benelux Holding B.V. and Uniper Benelux N.V. *v*. Kingdom of the Netherlands (Case No. 19 SchH 14/21), Judgment, 1 September 2022 (Higher Regional Court of Cologne)

Ghana

The Republic *v*. High Court (Comm Div) Accra, Judgment No. J5/10/2013 (Supreme Court of Ghana)

Greece

Prefecture of Voiotia *v*. Federal Republic of Germany, Case No. 11/2000, 4 May 2000 (Areios Pagos/Hellenic Supreme Court)

Italy

Ferrini *v*. Federal Republic of Germany, Judgment No. 5044, 6 November 2003 (Corte di Cassazione)

Luxembourg

Ioan Micula, Viorel Micula, S.C. European Food S.A, S.C. Starmill S.R.L. and S.C. Multipack S.R.L. *v*. Romania (Case No. 6/2022, Cas-2021-00061), 14 July 2022 (Court of Cassation)

Netherlands

Republic of Poland *v*. LC Corp BV (Case No. C/13/721410/HA ZA 22-614), Judgment, 8 March 2023 (Amsterdam Court of Appeals)

The Kingdom of Spain *v*. AES Solar Energy Cooperative UA and Ampere Equity Fund BV (Case No. C/13/730418 / KG ZA 23-164 EAM/MV), Judgment, 4 March 2023 (Amsterdam Court of Appeals)

Yukos Capital s.a.r.l. (Luxembourg) *v*. OAO Rosneft (Russian Federation) (Case No. 200.005.269/01), Decision, 28 April 2009 (Amsterdam Court of Appeals)

Yukos Universal Limited and Hulley Enterprses Limited *v*. The Russian Federation (Case No. C/09/477160 / HA ZA 15-1, C/09/477162 / HA ZA 15-2, C/09/481619 / HA ZA 15-112), Judgment, 20 February 2024 (Amsterdam Court of Appeals)

South Africa

Democratic Alliance *v*. Minister of International Relations and Cooperation and Others (Council for the Advancement of the South African Constitution Intervening) (83145/2016) [2017] ZAGPPHC 53 (High Court)

Southern Africa Litigation Centre *v.* Minister of Justice and Constitutional Development & others, 2015 (5) SA 1 (GP) (ZASCA)

Sweden

Franz Sedelmayer *v.* The Russian Federation (Case No. Ö 170-10), Decision, 1 July 2011 (Swedish Supreme Court)
Novenergia II – Energy & Environment (SCA) *v.* Kingdom of Spain (Case No. T 4658-18), Judgment, 13 December 2022 (Svea Court of Appeal)
PL Holdings S.à.r.l. *v.* Republic of Poland (Case No. T 1569-19), Judgment, 14 December 2022 (Swedish Supreme Court)

Ukraine

Case No. 308/9708/19 of 14 April 2022 (Ukrainian Supreme Court)
Case No. 428/11673/19 of 18 May 2022 (Ukrainian Supreme Court)

United Kingdom

17 House of Lords Journal 526–536 (27 March 1704) (House of Lords)
Ashby *v.* White (1703) 92 ER 126 (King's Bench)
Border Timbers Ltd *v.* Republic of Zimbabwe [2024] EWHC 58 (Comm) (High Court)
Infrastructure Services Luxembourg Sarl *v.* Spain [2023] EWHC 1226 (Comm) (High Court)
Ioan Micula et al. *v.* Romania [2018] EWCA Civ 1801 (Court of Appeal)

United States

Ioan Micula et al. *v.* Government of Romania (Case No. 23-7008), Judgment, 14 May 2024 (District Court of Columbia Court of Appeals)
Kendall *v.* United States, 37 US 524 (1838) (Supreme Court)
Marbury *v.* Madison, 5 US 137 (1803) (Supreme Court)
Yukos Universal Limited and Hulley Enterprses Limited *v.* The Russian Federation (Civil Action No. 14-1996), Memorandum Opinion, 17 November 2023 (District Court DC)

Books

Abass, Ademola, *Regional Organisations and the Development of Collective Security* (London: Hart Publishing, 2004)

Adler, Emanuel, *Communitarian International Relations: The Epistemic Foundations of International Relations* (New York: Routledge, 2005)

Alder, Murray Colin, *The Inherent Right of Self-Defence in International Law* (Dordrecht: Springer, 2012)

Alland, Dennis, *Justice privée et ordre juridique international* (Paris: Pedone, 1994)

Alter, Karen J., *The New Terrain of International Law: Courts, Politics, Rights* (Princeton, NJ: Princeton University Press, 2014)

Alter, Karen J., and Laurence R. Helfer, *Transplanting International Courts – The Law and Politics of the Andean Tribunal of Justice* (Oxford: Oxford University Press, 2017)

Alter, Karen J., Laurence R. Helfer, and Mikael Rask Madsen, *International Court Authority* (Oxford: Oxford University Press, 2018)

Alvarez, Jose E., *International Organizations as Law-Makers* (Oxford: Oxford University Press, 2006)

Amerasinghe, Chittharanjan F., *Jurisdiction of International Tribunals* (The Hague: Kluwer, 2003)

Local Remedies in International Law, 2nd edn (Cambridge: Cambridge University Press, 2004)

Amerasinghe, Chittharanjan Felix, *Jurisdiction of Specific International Tribunals* (Leiden: Martinus Nijhoff, 2009)

International Arbitral Jurisdiction (Leiden: Martinus Nijhoff, 2009)

Amr, Mohamed Sameh M., *The Role of the International Court of Justice as the Principal Judicial Organ of the United Nations* (The Hague: Kluwer, 2003)

Anzilotti, Dionisio, *Teoria generale della responsabilità dello stato nel diritto internazionale* (Firenze: F. Iumachi, 1902)

Armstrong, David, Theo Farrell, and Hélène Lambert, *International Law and International Relations* (Cambridge: Cambridge University Press, 2012)

Aron, Raymond, *Peace and War: A Theory of International Relations* (New Jersey: Transaction Publishers, 2003)

Austin, John, *The Province of Jurisprudence Determined* (London: John Murray, 1832)

Axelrod, Robert, *The Evolution of Cooperation* (New York: Basic, 1984)

The Evolution of Cooperation, Revised Edition (New York: Basic, 2006)

Babu, Rajesh, *Remedies under the WTO Legal System* (Leiden: Martinus Nijhoff, 2012)

Bankas, Ernest K., *The State Immunity Controversy in International Law: Private Suits against Sovereign States in Domestic Courts*, 2nd edn (Berlin: Springer, 2022)

Barents, René, *Remedies and Procedures before the EU Courts*, 2nd edn (Alphen aan den Rijn: Wolters Kluwer, 2016)

Bentham, Jeremy, *An Introduction to the Principles of Morals and Legislation* (London: T. Payne and Son, 1780)

Bhagwati, Jagadish N., and Hugh T. Patrick (eds.), *Aggressive Unilateralism: America's 301 Trade Policy and the World Trading System* (Ann Arbor: University of Michigan Press, 1990)

Black, Henry Campbell, *Black's Law Dictionary*, 6th edn (Saint Paul: West, 1991)

Blaeu, Johannes, and others, *Corpus Iuris Civilis* (Amsterdam: Blaeu and Elsevier, 1659)

Borchard, Edwin M., *Diplomatic Protection of Citizens Abroad* (New York: Banks Law, 1928)

Bower, Adam, *Norms without the Great Powers: International Law and Changing Social Standards in World Politics* (Oxford: Oxford University Press, 2017)

Brierly, James, *The Law of Nations* (Oxford: Clarendon Press, 1928)

Broude, Tomer, and Yuval Shany, *Multi-Sourced Equivalent Norms in International Law* (Oxford: Hart Publishing, 2011)

Brown, Chester, *A Common Law of International Adjudication* (New York: Oxford University Press, 2007)

Brunée, Jutta, and Stephen J. Toope, *Legitimacy and Legality in International Law: An Interactional Account* (Cambridge: Cambridge University Press, 2010)

Bull, Hedley, *The Anarchical Society: A Study of Order in World Politics* (Basingstoke: Macmillan, 1995)

The Anarchical Society: A Study of Order in World Politics (Houndmills: Palgrave Macmillan, 2002)

Burgorgue-Larsen, Laurence, *The 3 Regional Human Rights Courts in Context – Justice That Cannot Be Taken for Granted* (Oxford: Oxford University Press, 2024)

Burgorgue-Larsen, Laurence, and Amaya Ubeda de Torres, *The Inter-American Court of Human Rights – Case Law and Commentary* (Oxford: Oxford University Press, 2011)

Burgstaller, Markus, *Theories of Compliance with International Law* (Leiden: Brill, 1995)

Burke, John (ed.), *Jowitt's Dictionary of English Law*, 2nd edn (London: Sweet & Maxwell, 1977)

Buzan, Barry, Charles Jones, and Richard Little, *The Logic of Anarchy: Neorealism to Structural Realism* (New York: Columbia University Press, 1993)

Çali, Başak, *The Authority of International Law: Obedience, Respect, and Rebuttal* (Oxford: Oxford University Press, 2015)

Carr, Eric H., *Twenty Years' Crisis, 1919–1939: An Introduction to the Study of International Relations* (London: MacMillan, 1939/1946)

Chayes, Abram, and Antonia Handler Chayes, *The New Sovereignty: Compliance with International Regulatory Agreements* (Cambridge, MA: Harvard University Press, 1998)

Cheng, Bin, *General Principles of Law as Applied by International Courts and Tribunals* (London: Stevens, 1953)

Collier, John G., and Vaughan Lowe, *The Settlement of Disputes in International Law: Institutions and Procedures* (Oxford: Oxford University Press, 2000)

Combacau, Jean, *Le pouvoir de sanction de l'ONU: étude théorique de la coercition non militaire* (Paris: A. Pedone, 1974)

Corten, Olivier, *The Law against War: The Prohibition on the Use of Force in Contemporary International Law*, 2nd edn (Oxford: Hart Publishing, 2021)

Craig, Paul, and Gráinne De Búrca, *EU Law, Texts, Cases and Materials*, 6th edn (Oxford: Oxford University Press, 2015)

Crawford, James, *Brownlie's Principles of Public International Law*, 8th edn (Oxford: Oxford University Press, 2012)

State Responsibility: The General Part (Cambridge: Cambridge University Press, 2013)

The Law of State Responsibility: The General Part (Cambridge: Cambridge University Press, 2013)

Dam, Kenneth W., *The GATT: Law and International Economic Organization* (Chicago: University of Chicago Press, 1970)

Davis, Christina L., *Why Adjudicate? Enforcing Trade Rules in the WTO* (Princeton, NJ: Princeton University Press, 2011)

Dawidowicz, Martin, *Third-Party Countermeasures in International Law* (Cambridge: Cambridge University Press, 2017)

Domingo, Rafael, *The New Global Law* (Cambridge: Cambridge University Press, 2010)

Dörfler, Thomas, *Security Council Sanctions Governance: The Power and Limits of Rules* (Oxford: Routledge, 2019)

Douglas, Zachary, *The International Law of Investment Claims* (New York: Cambridge University Press, 2009)

Drezner, Daniel W., *The Sanctions Paradox: Economic Statecraft and International Relations* (Cambridge: Cambridge University Press, 1999)

All Politics Is Global: Explaining International Regulatory Regimes (Princeton, NJ: Princeton University Press, 2007)

Eagleton-Pierce, Matthew, *Symbolic Power in the World Trade Organization* (Oxford: Oxford University Press, 2013)

Ebers, Martin, *Rechte, Rechtsbehelfe und Sanktionen im Unionsprivatrecht* (Tübingen: Mohr Siebeck, 2016)

Ellickson, Robert, *Order without Law: How Neighbors Settle Disputes* (Cambridge: Harvard University Press, 1991)

Farrall, Jeremy Matam, *United Nations Sanctions and the Rule of Law* (Cambridge: Cambridge University Press, 2007)

Fisher, Roger, *Improving Compliance with International Law* (Charlottesville, VA: University Press of Virginia, 1981)

Fitzmaurice, Gerald, *The Law and Procedure of the International Court of Justice* (Cambridge: Cambridge University Press, 1986)

Fonteles, Samuel Sales, *Remédios Constitucionais*, 5th edn (Salvador: Juspodivm, 2023)

Fox, Hazel, and Philippa Webb, *The Law of State Immunity*, 3rd edn (Oxford: Oxford University Press, 2015)

Francioni, Francesco, and James Gordley (eds.), *Enforcing International Cultural Heritage Law, Cultural Heritage Law and Policy* (Oxford: Oxford University Press, 2013)

Franck, Thomas M., *Fairness in International Law and Institutions* (Oxford: Oxford University Press, 1998)

The Power of Legitimacy among Nations (Oxford: Oxford University Press, 1990)

Fuller, Lon L., *The Morality of Law*, Revised Edition (New Haven: Yale University Press, 1969)

Furedi, Frank, *Authority: A Sociological History* (Cambridge: Cambridge University Press, 2013)

Gaillard, Emmanuel, and John Savage, *Fouchard, Gaillars, Goldman on International Commercial Arbitration* (The Hague: Kluwer, 1999)

Gaillard, Emmanuel, and Yas Banifatemi (eds.), *Annulment of ICSID Awards* (New York: Juris, 2004)

García-Amador, F.V., *The Changing Law of International Claims*, vol. 575 (Dobbs Ferry: Oceana, 1984)

Garner, Brian A. (ed.), *Black's Law Dictionary*, 9th edn (Saint Paul: West, 2004)

Gateva, Eli, *European Union Enlargement Conditionality* (New York: Palgrave, 2015)

Goldsmith, Jack L., and Eric A. Posner, *The Limits of International Law* (Oxford: Oxford University Press, 2005)

Gray, Christine, *International Law and the Use of Force*, 4th edn (Oxford: Oxford University Press, 2018)

Judicial Remedies in International Law (Oxford: Clarendon, 1987)

Green, James A., *Collective Self-Defence in International Law* (Cambridge: Cambridge University Press, 2024)

Grewe, Wilhelm G., *The Epochs of International Law* (Berlin and New York: de Gruyter, 2000)

Grossman, Nienke, Harlan Grant Cohen, Andreas Føllesdal, and Geir Ulfstein (eds.), *Legitimacy and International Courts* (Cambridge: Cambridge University Press, 2018)

Grotius, Hugo, *The Law of War and Peace* (Indianapolis: Liberty Fund, 2005)

The Rights of War and Peace (transl. A.C. Campbell) (Clark: Lawbook Exchange, 1901)

The Rights of War and Peace: Including the Law of Nature and of Nations (transl. A.C. Campbell) (New York: Nabu, 2011)

Guzman, Andrew, *How International Law Works: A Rational Choice Theory* (Oxford: Oxford University Press, 2008)

Hambro, Edvard, *L'Exécution des Sentences Internationales* (Liège: Vaillant-Carmanne, 1936)

Hart, H.L.A., *The Concept of Law* (Oxford: Clarendon Press, 1961)

Henkin, Louis, *How Nations Behave: Law and Foreign Policy*, 2nd edn (New York: Columbia University Press, 1979 [1968])

Hillebrecht, *Courtney, Domestic Politics and International Human Rights Tribunals: The Problem of Compliance* (Cambridge: Cambridge University Press, 2014)

Hovell, Devika, *The Power of Process: The Value of Due Process in Security Council Sanctions Decision-Making* (Oxford: Oxford University Press, 2016)

Howse, Robert, Hélène Ruiz Fabri, Geir Ulfstein, and Michelle Q. Zang (eds.), *The Legitimacy of International Trade Courts and Tribunals* (Cambridge: Cambridge University Press, 2018)

Hudec, Robert E., *Adjudication of International Trade Disputes*, Thames Essay No. 16 (London: Trade Policy Research Center, 1978)

Enforcing International Trade Law: The Evolution of the Modern GATT Legal System (Salem, NH: Butterworth, 1991)

Hurrell, Andrew, *On Global Order: Power, Values, and the Constitution of International Society* (Oxford: Oxford University Press, 2007)

Iovane, Massimo, *La Riparazione nella Teoria e nella Prassi dell'Illecito Internazionale* (Milan: Giuffrè, 1990)

Jha, Green B.P., *International Nuclear Law and Nuclear Liability* (The Hague: Kluwer, 1998)

Jhering, Rudolf von, *L'esprit du droit romain dans ses diverses phases de son développement*, 3rd edn (Paris: A. Marescq, 1878)

Johns, Leslie, *Strengthening International Courts: The Hidden Costs of Legalization* (Ann Arbor, MI: University of Michigan Press, 2015)

Kahneman, Daniel, Paul Slovic, and Amos Tversky (eds.), *Judgment under Uncertainty: Heuristics and Biases* (Cambridge: Cambridge University Press, 1982/2013)

Kaikobad, Kaiyan Homi, *Interpretation and Revision of International Boundary Decisions* (Cambridge: Cambridge University Press, 2012)

Kelsen, Hans, *Principles of International Law* (New York: Rinehart, 1952)

The Law of the United Nations (London: Stevens & Sons, 1951)

The Law of the United Nations: A Critical Analysis of Its Fundamental Problems (Clark: Lawbook Exchange, 2011)

The Pure Theory of Law (transl. Max Knight) (Clark: Lawbook Exchange, 2005)

Kennedy, Duncan, *A Critique of Adjudication (fin de siècle)* (Cambridge, MA: Harvard University Press, 1998)

Keohane, Robert O., *After Hegemony: Cooperation and Discord in the World Political Economy* (Princeton, NJ: Princeton University Press, 1984)

Klein, Natalie, *Dispute Settlement in the UN Convention on the Law of the Sea* (Cambridge: Cambridge University Press, 2004)

Krasner, Stephen D., *International Regimes* (Ithaca: Cornell University Press, 1983)

Kratochwil, Friedrich V., *Rules, Norms, and Decisions: On the Conditions of Practical and Legal Reasoning in International Relations and Domestic Affairs* (Cambridge: Cambridge University Press, 1991)

Lauterpacht, Hersch, *The Development of International Law by the International Court* (London: Steven, 1958)

The Function of Law in the International Community (Oxford: Oxford University Press, 2011 [1933])

Law, Jonathan, and Elizabeth A. Martin (eds.), *Oxford Dictionary of Law*, 7th edn (Oxford: Oxford University Press, 2009)

Laycock, Douglas, *Modern American Remedies*, 3rd edn (New York: Aspen, 2002)

Modern American Remedies, 4th edn (New York: Aspen, 2010)

Leben, Charles, *Les sanctions privatives de droits ou de qualité dans les organisations internationales spécialisées: recherches sur les sanctions internationales et l'évolution du droit des gens* (Bruxelles: Bruylant, 1979)

Lebow, Richard Ned, *A Cultural Theory of International Relations* (Cambridge: Cambridge University Press, 2009)

Lucy, William, *Understanding and Explaining Adjudication* (Oxford: Oxford University Press, 1999)

Marcuse, Herbert, *A Study on Authority* (transl. Joris de Bres) (London: Verso, 2008)

Martin, Lisa L., *Coercive Cooperation: Explaining Multilateral Economic Sanctions* (Princeton, NJ: Princeton University Press, 1992)

Merrills, J.G., *International Dispute Settlement*, 5th edn (Cambridge: Cambridge University Press, 2011)

Miéville, China, *Between Equal Rights: A Marxist Theory of International Law* (Leiden: Brill, 2005)

Milde, Michael, *International Air Law and ICAO*, 3rd edn (The Hague: Eleven, 2016)

Miles, Cameron A., *Provisional Measures before International Courts and Tribunals* (Cambridge: Cambridge University Press, 2017)

Miles, Kate, *The Origins of International Investment Law: Empire, Environment and the Safeguarding of Capital* (Cambridge; Cambridge University Press, 2013)

Milner, Helen V., *Interests, Institutions, and Information: Domestic Politics and International Relations* (Princeton, NJ: Princeton University Press, 1997)

Möhrlein, Rosa, *The Multiplicity of Judicial Functions of International Courts and Tribunals. An Inquiry with a Focus on the International Court of Justice* (Groningen: Chimaira, 2024)

Mommsen, Theodor, *Römisches Staatsrecht*, 3rd edn (Leipzig: S. Hirzel, 1888)

Montaldo, Stefano, Francesco Costamagna, and Alberto Miglio (eds.), *EU Law Enforcement: The Evolution of Sanctioning Powers* (London: Routlege, 2021)

Moore, John Bassett, *History and Digest of the International Arbitrations to Which the United States Has Been a Party* (Washington, DC: US Government, 1989)

Morgenthau, Hans J., *Politics among Nations: The Struggle for Power and Peace*, 5th edn (New York: Alfred A. Knopf, 1978)

Morrisson, Wayne (ed.), *Blackstone's Commentaries on the Laws of England* (London: Cavendish, 2013)

Nantwi, E.K., *The Enforcement of International Judicial Decisions and Arbitral Awards in Public International Law* (Leiden: Sijthoff, 1966)

Nordquist, Myron H. (ed.), *United Nations Convention on the Law of the Sea 1982 – A Commentary* (Netherlands: Martinus Nijhoff, 1989)

North, Douglass C., *Institutions, Institutional Change and Economic Performance* (Cambridge: Cambridge University Press, 1990/2012)

O'Connell, Mary Ellen, *International Dispute Resolution: Cases and Materials* (Durham, NC: Carolina Academic, 2012)

Onuf, Nicholas, *World of Our Making: Rules and Rule in Social Theory and International Relations* (New York: Routledge, 1989/2012)

Oppenheim, Lassa, *International Law: A Treatise* (New York: Longmans Green, 1905)

Özsu, Umut, *Completing Humanity: The International Law of Decolonization, 1960–82* (Cambridge: Cambridge University Press, 2024)

Paddeu, Federica, *Justification and Excuse in International Law: Concept and Theory of General Defences* (Cambridge: Cambridge University Press, 2018)

Paine, Joshua, *The Functions of International Adjudication and International Environmental Litigation* (Cambridge: Cambridge University Press, 2024)

Palazón Garrido, María Luisa, *Los Remedios Frente al Incumplimiento en el Derecho Comparado* (Navarra: Aranzadi, 2014)

Pauwelyn, Joost, *Conflict of Norms in Public International Law: How WTO Law Relates to Other Rules of International Law* (Cambridge: Cambridge University Press, 2003)

Optimal Protection of International Law: Navigating between European Absolutism and American Voluntarism (Cambridge: Cambridge University Press, 2008)

Ralston, Jackson H., *International Arbitration from Athens to Locarno* (Standford: Stanford University Press, 1929)

Reece Thomas, Katherine, *The Commercial Activity Exception to State Immunity: An Introduction* (Cheltenham: Edward Elgar, 2024)

Reiners, Nina, *Transnational Lawmaking Coalitions for Human Rights* (Cambridge: Cambridge University Press, 2021)

Reisman, William M., *Systems of Control in International Adjudication and Arbitration: Breakdown and Repair* (Durham, NC: Duke University Press, 1992)

Reisman, William Michael, *Nullity and Revision – The Review and Enforcement of International Judgments and Awards* (New Haven: Yale University Press, 1971)

Roach, Kent, *Remedies for Human Rights Violations: A Two-Track Approach to Supra-national and National Law* (Cambridge: Cambridge University Press, 2021)

Romani, Francesco, *Belligerent Reprisals from Enforcement to Reciprocity: A New Theory of Retaliation in Conflict* (Cambridge: Cambridge University Press, 2024)

Rosenne, Shabtai, *Breach of Treaty* (Cambridge: Grotius, 1985)

Interpretation, Revision and Other Recourse from International Judgments and Awards (Leiden: Martinus Nijhoff, 2007)

Provisional Measures in International Law: The International Court of Justice and the International Tribunal for the Law of the Sea (Oxford: Oxford University Press, 2005)

The Law and Practice of the International Court, 1920–2005, 4th edn (Leiden: Martinus Nijhoff, 2006)

Ruiz Fabri, Hélène, and Michel Erpelding, *The Mixed Arbitral Tribunals, 1919–1939 – An Experiment in the International Adjudication of Private Rights* (Baden-Baden: Nomos, 2023)

Ruys, Tom, *'Armed Attack' and Article 51 of the UN Charter: Evolutions in Customary Law and Practice* (Cambridge: Cambridge University Press, 2011)

Sabahi, Burzu, *Compensation and Restitution in Investor-State Arbitration: Principles and Practice* (Oxford: Oxford University Press, 2011)

Sarooshi, Dan, *International Organizations and Their Exercise of Sovereign Powers* (Oxford: Oxford University Press, 2005)

Schill, Stephan W., *The Multilateralization of International Investment Law* (Cambridge: Cambridge University Press, 2009)

Schreuer, Christoph, *The ICSID Convention: A Commentary*, 2nd edn (Cambridge: Cambridge University Press, 2009)

Schulte, Constanze, *Compliance with Decisions of the International Court of Justice* (Oxford: Oxford University Press, 2004)

Scott, James B. (ed.), *Reports to the Hague Conferences of 1899 and 1907* (Carnegie Endowment for International Peace, 1917)

(ed.), *The Proceedings of the Hague Peace Conferences: The Conference of 1907: Translation of the Official Texts*, vol. II (Hague: Carnegie Endowment for International Peace, 1921)

(dir.), *The Proceedings of the Hague Peace Conferences – The Conference of 1899* (New York: Oxford University Press, 1920)

Shapiro, Martin, *Courts: A Comparative and Political Analysis* (Chicago: University of Chicago Press, 1981)

Shaw, Malcolm N., *International Law*, 6th edn (Cambridge: Cambridge University Press, 2008)

Shelton, Dinah, *Remedies in International Human Rights Law*, 2nd edn (Oxford: Oxford University Press, 2005)

Simmons, Beth A., *Mobilizing for Human Rights: International Law in Domestic Politics* (Cambridge: Cambridge University Press, 2009)

Sinha, Bhek P., *Unilateral Denunciation of Treaty Because of Prior Violations of Obligations by Other Party* (The Hague: M. Nijhoff, 1966)

Smith, William (ed.), *Dictionary of Greek and Roman Antiquities* (Boston: Little Brown, 1870)

Squatrito, Theresa, Oran R. Young, Andreas Føllesdal, and Geir Ulfstein (eds.), *The Performance of International Courts and Tribunals* (Cambridge: Cambridge University Press, 2018)

St John, Taylor, *The Rise of Investor-State Arbitration: Politics, Law, and Unintended Consequences* (Oxford: Oxford University Press, 2018)

Stoica, Victor, *Remedies before the International Court of Justice: A Systemic Analysis* (Cambridge: Cambridge University Press, 2021)

Stone Sweet, Alec, *The Judicial Construction of Europe* (Oxford: Oxford University Press, 2004)

Tams, Christian J., *Enforcing Obligations Erga Omnes in International Law* (Cambridge: Cambridge University Press, 2005)

Thirlway, Hugh, *The Law and Procedure of the International Court of Justice* (Oxford: Oxford University Press, 2013)

Tistounet, Eric, *The UN Human Rights Council: A Practical Anatomy* (Cheltenham: Edward Elgar, 2020)

Trachtman, Joel P., *The Economic Structure of International Law* (Cambridge: Harvard University Press, 2008)

Treves, Tullio, et al. (eds.), *Non-Compliance Procedures and Mechanisms and the Effectiveness of International Environmental Agreements* (The Hague: TMC Asser, 2009)

Tyler, Tom R., *Why People Obey the Law* (Princeton, NJ: Princeton University Press, 2006)

Tzanakopoulos, Antonios, *Disobeying the Security Council: Countermeasures against Wrongful Sanctions* (Oxford: Oxford University Press, 2011)

Vattel, Emmerich de, *Le Droit des Gens ou Principes de la loi naturelle, appliqués à la conduite et aux affaires des Nations et des Souverains* (Neuchâtel: A. Londres, 1758)

Venzke, Ingo, *How Interpretation Makes International Law: On Semantic Change and Normative Twists* (Oxford: Oxford University Press, 2012)

Villiger, Mark E., *Commentary on the 1969 Vienna Convention on the Law of Treaties* (Boston, MA: Martinus Nijhoff, 2009)

Villiger, Mark Eugen, *Customary International Law and Treaties: A Manual on the Theory and Practice of the Interrelation of Sources*, 2nd edn (Hague: Kluwer, 1997)

von Bogdandy, Armin, and Ingo Venzke, *In Whose Name? A Public Law Theory of International Adjudication* (Oxford: Oxford University Press, 2012)

Vrdoljak, Ana Filipa, *International Law, Museums and the Return of Cultural Objects* (Cambridge: Cambridge University Press, 2006)

Waibel, Michael, *Sovereign Defaults before International Courts and Tribunals* (Cambridge: Cambridge University Press, 2011)

Weatherall, Thomas, *Jus Cogens: International Law and Social Contract* (Cambridge: Cambridge University Press, 2015)

Weiler, Joseph H.H., Antonio Cassese, and Marina Spinedi, *International Crimes of State: A Critical Analysis of the ILC's Draft Article 19 on State Responsibility* (Berlin: Walter de Gruyter, 1989)

Wendt, Alexander, *Social Theory of International Politics* (Cambridge: Cambridge University Press, 1999)

Whiteman, Marjorie M. (ed.), *Digest of International Law* (Washington: US Government Printing Office, 1970)

Wilcox, Clair, *A Charter for World Trade* (New York: MacMillan, 1949)

WTO, *GATT Disputes: 1948–1995 Volume 1: Overview and One-Page Case Summaries* (Geneva: WTO, 2018)

Wunderlich, Carmen, *Rogue States as Norm Entrepreneurs: Black Sheep or Sheep in Wolves' Clothing?* (Cham: Springer, 2020)

Wyatt, Tanya, *Is CITES Protecting Wildlife? Assessing Implementation and Compliance* (Oxon: Routledge, 2021)

Xiouri, Maria, *The Breach of a Treaty: State Responses in International Law* (Leiden: Brill | Nijhoff, 2021)

Young, Oran R., *Compliance and Public Authority: A Theory with International Application* (Baltimore: Johns Hopkins University Press, 1979)

Governance in World Affairs (Ithaca: Cornell University Press, 1999)

International Governance: Protecting the Environment in a Stateless Society (Ithaca: Cornell University Press, 1994)

Zoller, Elisabeth, *Peacetime Unilateral Remedies: An Analysis of Countermeasures* (Dobbs Ferry, NY: Transnational Publishers, 1984)

Articles

Abbott, Kenneth W., Robert O. Keohane, Andrew Moravcsik, Anne-Marie Slaughter, and Duncan Snidal, 'The Concept of Legalization' (2000) 54(3) *International Organization* 401–433

Abdulqawi, Yusuf, 'The Notion of "Armed Attack" in the Nicaragua Judgment and Its Influence on Subsequent Case Law' (2012) 25(2) *Leiden Journal of International Law* 461–470

Abizadeh, Arash, 'The Grammar of Social Power: Power-To, Power-With, Power-Despite and Power-Over' (2023) 71(1) *Political Studies* 3–19

Adler, Emanuel, 'Seizing the Middle Ground: Constructivism in World Politics' (1997) 3(3) *European Journal of International Relations* 319–363

Ago, Roberto, 'Binding Advisory Opinions of the International Court of Justice' (1991) 85(3) *American Journal of International Law* 439–451

'Le délit International' (1939) 68 *Hague Recueil* 415–554

Alexander, Klint W., and Bryan J. Soukup, 'Obama's First Trade War: The US-Mexico Cross-Border Trucking Dispute and the Implications of Strategic Cross-Sector Retaliation on U.S. Compliance under NAFTA' (2010) 28(2) *Berkeley Journal of International Law* 313–364

Al-Qahtani, Mutlaq, 'The Role of the International Court of Justice in the Enforcement of Its Judicial Decisions' (2002) 15(4) *Leiden Journal of International Law* 781–802

Alschner, Wolfgang, 'Amicable Settlements of WTO Disputes: Bilateral Solutions in a Multilateral System' (2014) 13(1) *World Trade Review* 65–102

Alston, Philip, 'Resisting the Merger and Acquisition of Human Rights by Trade Law: A Reply to Petersmann' (2002) 13(4) *European Journal of International Law* 815–844

Alter, Karen J., 'Agents or Trustees? International Courts in Their Political Context' (2008) 14(1) *European Journal of International Relations* 33–63

'*The European Court's Political Power*' (1996) 19(3) *West European Politics* 458–487

Alter, Karen J., Emilie M. Hafner-Burton, and Laurence R. Helfer, 'Theorizing the Judicialization of International Relations' (2019) 63(3) *International Studies Quarterly* 449–463, 450–451

Alter, Karen J., James T. Gathii, and Lawrence R. Helfer, 'Backlash against International Courts in West, East and Southern Africa: Causes and Consequences' (2016) 27(2) *European Journal of International Law* 293–328

Alter, Karen J., Laurence R. Helfer, and Mikael Rask Madsen 'How Context Shapes the Authority of International Courts' (2016) 79(1) *Law and Contemporary Problems* 1–36

Ambos, Kai, 'International Criminal Procedure: "Adversarial", "Inquisitorial" or Mixed?' 3 *International Criminal Law Review* (2003) 1

Andersen, Scott D., and Justine Blanchet, 'The United States' Experience and Practice in Suspending WTO Obligations', in Chad P. Bown and Joost Pauwelyn (eds.), *The Law, Economics and Politics of Retaliation in WTO Dispute Settlement* (Cambridge: Cambridge University Press, 2010), 172–202

Anderson, Kenneth, 'The Ottawa Convention Banning Landmines, the Role of International Non-Governmental Organizations and the Idea of International Civil Society' (2000) 11(1) *European Journal of International Law* 91–120

Antkowiak, Thomas M., 'Remedial Approaches to Human Rights Violations: The Inter-American Court of Human Rights and Beyond' (2008) 46(2) *Columbia Journal of Transnational Law* 351–419

Arato, Julian, 'Subsequent Practice and Evolutive Interpretation: Techniques of Treaty Interpretation over Time and Their Diverse Consequences' (2010) 9 *The Law & Practice of International Courts and Tribunals* 443–494

Arendt, Hannah, '*What Is Authority?', in Hannah Arendt, between Past and Future* (New York: Penguin, 1968), 91–141

Ascensio, Hervé, '*La notion de juridiction internationale en question', in Société Française de Droit International, La Juridictionnalisation du Droit International* (Paris: Pedone, 2003), 163–202

Azaria, Danae, 'The Legal Significance of Expert Treaty Bodies Pronouncements for the Purpose of the Interpretation of Treaties' (2020) 22(1) *International Community Law Review* 33

'Trade Countermeasures for Breaches of International Law outside the WTO' (2022) 71(2) *International and Comparative Law Quarterly* 389–421

Badanova, Ielyzaveta, 'Jurisdictional Immunities v Grave Crimes: Reflections on New Developments from Ukraine' (8 September 2022) *EJIL: Talk!*, available at www.ejiltalk.org/jurisdictional-immunities-v-grave-crimes-reflections-on-new-developments-from-ukraine

Bagwell, Kyle, 'Remedies in the WTO: An Economic Perspective', in Merit E. Janow, Victoria J. Donaldson, and Alan Yanovitch (eds.), *The WTO Governance, Dispute Settlement and Developing Countries* (New York: Juris, 2008), 733–770

Baluarte, David C., '*Strategizing for Compliance: The Evolution of the Compliance Phase of Inter-American Court Litigation and the Strategic Imperative for Victims' Representatives*' (2012) 27(2) *American University International Law Review* 263–321

Barber, Rebecca, 'An Exploration of the General Assembly's Troubled Relationship with Unilateral Sanctions' (2021) 70(2) *International and Comparative Law Quarterly* 343–375

Barboza, Julio, 'The Beagle Channel Dispute: Reflections of the Agent of Argentina' (2014) 13(1) *Chinese Journal of International Law* 147–170

Barker, John, 'The Different Forms of Reparation: Compensation', in James Crawford, Alain Pellet, and Simon Olleson (eds.), *The Law of International Responsibility* (Oxford: Oxford University Press, 2010), 599–611

Bartels, Lorand, 'Applicable Law in WTO Dispute Settlement Proceedings' (2001) 35(3) *Journal of World Trade* 499–519

'Jurisdiction and Applicable Law Clauses in International Law: Where Does a Tribunal Find the Principal Norms Applicable to the Case before It?', in Tomer Broude and Yuval Shany (eds.), *Multi-Sourced Equivalent Norms in International Law* (Oxford: Hart, 2011), 115–140

Batselé, Filip, 'Foreign Investors of the World, Unite! The International Association for the Promotion and Protection of Private Foreign Investments (APPI) 1958–1968' (2023) 34(2) *European Journal of International Law* 415–447

Baum, Matthew A., 'The Constituent Foundations of the Rally-Round-the-Flag Phenomenon' (2002) 46(2) *International Studies Quarterly* 263–298

Baxter, R.R., 'International Law in "Her Infinite Variety"' (1980) 23 *International and Comparative Law Quarterly* 549

Bederman, David J., 'Constructivism, Positivism, and Empiricism in International Law' (2001) 89(2) *Georgetown Law Journal* 469–540

Bederman, David, 'Counterintuiting Countermeasures' (2002) 96(4) *American Journal of International Law* 817–832

Beer, Yishai, 'Regulating Armed Reprisals: Revisiting the Scope of Lawful Self-Defense' (2020) 59(1) *Columbia Journal of Transnational Law* 117

Bello, Judith H., 'The WTO Dispute Settlement Understanding: Less is More' (1996) 90(3) *American Journal of International Law* 416–418

Bermann, George A., 'Understanding ICSID Article 54' (2020) 35(2) *ICSID Review – Foreign Investment Law Journal* 311–342

Bernstein, Lisa, 'Opting Out of the Legal System: Extralegal Contractual Relations in the Diamond Industry' (1992) 21(1) *The Journal of Legal Studies* 115–157

Besson, Samantha, 'European Legal Pluralism After Kadi' (2009) 5(2) *European Constitutional Law Review* 237–264

Bianchi, Andrea, 'Human Rights and the Magic of Jus Cogens' (2008) 19(3) *European Journal of International Law* 491–508

Bilder, Richard B., 'International Third Party Dispute Settlement' (1989) 17(3) *Denver Journal of International Law & Policy* 471

Bjorge, Eirik, '*Opposability and Non-Opposability in International Law*' (2021) *British Yearbook of International Law Online*

Bondar, Kateryna, 'Annulment of ICSID and Non-ICSID Investment Awards: Differences in the Extent of Review' (2015) 32(6) *Journal of International Arbitration* 621–640

Borchard, Edwin M., 'Editorial Comment – Declaratory Judgments in International Law' (1935) 29(3) *American Journal of International Law* 488–492

Borger, Julian, 'South Africa's President and ANC Sow Confusion over Leaving ICC' (25 April 2023) *The Guardian*, available at www.theguardian.com/world/2023/apr/25/south-africas-president-and-party-sow-confusion-over-leaving-icc

Born, Gary, 'A New Generation of International Adjudication' (2012) 61(4) *Duke Law Journal* 775–879

Bourdieu, Pierre, 'Social Space and Symbolic Power' (1989) 7(1) *Sociological Theory* 14–25

Bourdon, Pierre, and Pauline Marcou, *Aux Origines de la Notion de Remède pour Traiter les Vices de la Formation des Contrats Civils et Administratifs* (2022) 4 *Revue des Contrats* 92

Boyes, Christina, Cody D. Eldredge, Megan Shannon, and Kelebogile Zvobgo, 'Social Pressure in the International Human Rights Regime: Why States Withdraw Treaty Reservations' (2023) 54(1) *British Journal of Political Science* 241–258

Breuss, Fritz, 'WTO Dispute Settlement: An Economic Analysis of Four EU–US Mini Trade Wars – A Survey' (2004) 4(3) *Journal of Industry, Competition and Trade* 275–317

Brewster, Rachel, '*The Remedy Gap: Institutional Design, Retaliation, and Trade Law Enforcement*' (2011) 80(1) *George Washington Law Review* 102–158

Briggs, Herbert, 'Unilateral Denunciation of Treaties: The Vienna Convention and the International Court of Justice' (1974) 68(1) *American Journal of International Law* 51–58

Bronckers, Marco, and Freya Baetens, 'Reconsidering Financial Remedies in WTO Dispute Settlement' (2013) 16(2) *Journal of International Economic Law* 281

Bronckers, Marco, and Giovanni Gruni, 'Retooling the Sustainability Standards in EU Free Trade Agreements' (2021) 24(1) *Journal of International Economic Law* 25–54

Broude, Tomer, 'Behavioral International Law' (2015) 163(4) *University of Pennsylvania Law Review* 1099–1157

Brown, Chester, '*The Inherent Powers of International Courts and Tribunals*' (2005) 76(1) *British Yearbook of International Law* 195–244

Brownlie, Ian, 'Remedies in the International Court of Justice', in Vaughan Lowe and Malgosia Fitzmaurice (eds.), *Fifty Years of the International Court of Justice* (Cambridge: Cambridge University Press, 1996), 566–580

Brunnée, Jutta, 'Enforcement Mechanisms in International Law and International Environmental Law', in Ulrich Beyerlin, Peter-Tobias Stoll, and Rüdiger Wolfrum (eds.), *Ensuring Compliance with Multilateral Environmental Agreements* (Leiden: Martinus Nijhoff, 2006), 1–23

'Compliance Control', in Geir Ulfstein, Thilo Marauhn, and Andreas Zimmermann (eds.), *Making Treaties Work: Human Rights, Environment and Arms Control* (Cambridge: Cambridge University Press, 2007), 373–390

Brunnée, Jutta, and Stephen J. Toope, '*International Law and the Practice of Legality: Stability and Change*' (2018) 49(4) *Victoria University of Wellington Law Review* 429–456

Brunnée, Jutta, 'Promoting Compliance with Multilateral Environmental Agreements', in Jutta Brunnée, Meinhard Doelle, and Lavanya Rajamani (eds.), *Promoting Compliance in an Evolving Climate Regime* (Cambridge: Cambridge University Press, 2011), 38–66

Buergenthal, Thomas, 'Proliferation of International Courts and Tribunals: Is It Good or Bad?' (2001) 14(2) *Leiden Journal of International Law* 267–275

Burelli, Camilla, 'The Deterrent Effect of Financial Sanctions Pursuant to Article 260(2) TFEU in the Context of Violations of Environmental Obligations' (2023) 3(3) *Italian Review of International and Comparative Law* 367–395

Burgorgue-Larsen, Laurence, 'The Powers of the Court to Monitor Compliance with Its Judgments', in Laurence Burgorgue-Larsen and Amaya Ubeda de Torres (eds.), *The Inter-American Court of Human Rights – Case Law and Commentary* (Oxford: Oxford University Press, 2011), 171–210

Busse, Dietrich, 'Semantic Strategies as a Means of Politics: Linguistic Approaches to the Analysis of "Semantic Struggles"', in Pertti Ahonen (ed.), *Tracing the Semiotic Boundaries of Politics* (Berlin: de Gruyter, 1993), 121–147

Byers, Michael, '*Terrorism, the Use of Force and International Law After 11 September*' (2002) 51(2) *International & Comparative Law Quarterly* 401–414

Cançado Trindade, Antonio Augusto, 'Exhaustion of Local Remedies in International Law and the Role of National Courts' (1986) 17(3/4) *Archiv des Völkerrechts* 333–370

Canizzarro, Enzo, and Paolo Palchetti, 'Ultra Vires Acts of International Organizations', in Jan Klabbers and Asa Wallendahl (eds.), *Research Handbook on the Law of International Organizations* (Cheltenham: Elgar, 2011), 365–388

Caroli, Paolo, 'Compensation without Recognition: The German-Italian Dispute over War Crime Compensation and Transnational Justice' (6 June 2022) *Verfassungsblog*, available at https://verfassungsblog.de/compensation-without-recognition

Caron, David D., 'Towards a Political Theory of International Courts and Tribunals' (2006) 24(2) *Berkeley Journal of International Law* 401–422

Caserta, Salvatore, and Mikael Rask Madsen, 'Between Community Law and Common Law: The Rise of the Caribbean Court of Justice at the Intersection of Regional Integration and Post-Colonial Legacies' (2016) 79(1) *Law and Contemporary Problems* 89–115

Cassese, Antonio, 'Remarks on Scelle's Theory of 'Role Splitting' (Dédoublement Fonctionnel) in International Law' (1990) 1(1) *European Journal of International Law* 210–231

Charney, Jonathan, 'Third Party Dispute Settlement and International Law' (1998) 36(1) *Columbia Journal of Transnational Law* 65–126

'Third State Remedies in International Law' (1989) 10(1) *Michigan Journal of International Law* 57–101

Charnovitz, Steve, 'Should the Teeth Be Pulled? An Analysis of WTO Sanctions', in Daniel L. M. Kennedy and James D. Southwick (eds.), *The Political Economy of International Trade – Essays in Honour of Robert E. Hudec* (Cambridge: Cambridge University Press, 2002), 602–635

'The WTO's Problematic "Last Resort" against Noncompliance' (2002) 57(3) *Aussenwirtschaft* 409–434

Chinese Society of International Law, 'The South China Sea Arbitration Awards: A Critical Study' (2018) 17(2) *Chinese Journal of International Law* 207–268

Choi, Susan, 'Judicial Enforcement of Arbitration Awards under the ICSID and New York Conventions' (1995) 28 *NYU Journal of International Law & Politics* 175–216

Christiano, Tom, 'Authority', in Edward N. Zalta (ed.), *The Stanford Encyclopedia of Philosophy* (2020)

Claes, Monica, 'The Primacy of EU Law in European and National Law', in Anthony Arnull and Damian Chalmers (eds.), *Oxford Handbook of European Union Law* (Oxford: Oxford University Press, 2015), 178–202

Closa, Carlos, and Gisela Hernández, 'Defining and Operationalising Defiant Non-Compliance in the EU: The Rule of Law Case' (2025) 63(3) *Journal of Common Market Studies* 964–986

Cohen, Harlan Grant, 'Can International Law Work? A Constructivist Expansion' (2009) 27(2) *Berkeley Journal of International Law* 636–678

'International Law's Erie Moment' (2013) 34(3) *Michigan Journal of International Law* 249–302

'Theorizing Precedent in International Law', in Andrea Bianchi, Daniel Peat, and Matthew Windsor (eds.), *Interpretation in International Law* (Oxford: Oxford University Press, 2015), 268–289

Combacau, Jean, 'Le chapitre VII de la Charte des Nations Unies: résurrection ou métamorphose ?', in Rafâa Ben Achour and Slim Laghani (eds.), *Les nouveaux aspects du droit international – Colloque des 14, 15 et 16 avril 1994* (Pedone, 1994), 139–162

Contesse, Jorge, 'Contestation and Deference in the Inter-American Human Rights System' (2016) 79(1) *Law & Contemporary Problems* 123–170

Costa, Oriol, 'The Unexpected EU Leadership on Landmines: The Influence of the Ottawa Convention on the EU' (2009) 18(3) *European Security* 245–261

Cover, Robert M., '*The Bonds of Constitutional Interpretation: Of the Word, the Deed, and the Role*' (1986) 20(4) *Georgia Law Review* 815–833

'*The Supreme Court, 1982 Term-Foreword: Nomos and Narrative*' (1983) 97(1) *Harvard Law Review* 1–68

'Violence and the Word' (1986) 95(8) *Yale Law Journal* 1601–1629

Crawford, James, 'The Relationship between Sanctions and Countermeasures', in Gowlland-Debbas (ed.), *United Nations Sanctions and International Law* (The Hague: Kluwer Law, 2007), 57–68

Crawford, James, and Simon Olleson, 'The Exception of Non-Performance: Links between the Law of Treaties and the Law of State Responsibility' (2000) 21(1) *Australian Yearbook of International Law* 55–85

'Multilateral Rights and Obligations in International Law' (2006) 319 *RdC* 325–482

d'Argent, Pierre, 'Reparations and Compliance', in Karine Bannelier, Theodore Christakis, and Sarah Heathcote (eds.), *The ICJ and the Evolution of International Law – The Enduring Impact of the Corfu Channel Case* (London: Routledge, 2012), 335–356

Dai, Xinyuan, 'Why Comply? The Domestic Constituency Mechanism' (2005) 59(2) *International Organization* 363–398

Davey, William J., 'Compliance Problems in WTO Dispute Settlement' (2009) 42(1) *Cornell International Law Journal* 120–162

de Chazournes, Laurence Boisson, and Antonella Angelini, '*After "The Court Rose": The Rise of Diplomatic Means to Implement the Pronouncements of the International Court of Justice*' (2012) 11(1) *Law and Practice of International Courts and Tribunals* 1–34

Dempsey, Michelle Madden, '*Authority, Obedience, and Justification*' (2021) 90(2) *University of Cincinnati Law Review* 408–453

De Silva, Nicole, and Misha Ariana Plagis, '*NGOs, International Courts, and State Backlash against Human Rights Accountability: Evidence from NGO Mobilization against Tanzania at the African Court on Human and Peoples' Rights*' (2023) 57(1) *Law & Society Review* 36–60

Diakité, Maïmouna, and Zoé Baize, 'Sanctions by International Organizations and Judicial Review: The Case of Mali vs the Conference of Heads of States and Government of the WAEMU' (2024) 51(2) *Legal Issues of Economic Integration* 171–194

Dodge, William, '*Res Judicata*', *in Max Planck Encyclopedia of Public International Law* (Oxford: Oxford University Press, 2006)

Domingo, Rafael, 'Das Binom auctoritas-potestas im römischen und modernen Recht' (1998) 4 *Orbis Iuris Romani* 7

Domínguez Redondo, Elvira, 'The Universal Periodic Review of the UN Human Rights Council: An Assessment of the First Session' (2008) 7(3) *Chinese Journal of International Law* 721–734

Downs, George W., 'Enforcement and the Evolution of Cooperation' (1997) 19(2) *Michigan Journal of International Law* 319–344

Downs, George W., David M. Rocke, and Peter N. Barsoom, '*Is the Good News about Compliance Good News about Cooperation?*' (1996) 50(3) *International Organization* 379–406

Downs, George W., and Michael A. Jones, 'Reputation, Compliance, and International Law' (2002) 31(S1) *The Journal of Legal Studies* S95–S114

Drezner, Daniel W., 'Bargaining, Enforcement, and Multilateral Sanctions: When Is Cooperation Counterproductive?' (2000) 54(1) *International Organization* 73–102

'The Hidden Hand of Economic Coercion' (2003) 57(3) *International Organization* 643–659

Drogula, Fred K., '*Imperium, Potestas, and the Pomerium in the Roman Republic*' (2007) 56(4) *Historia: Zeitschrift für Alte Geschichte* 419–452

Dworkin, Ronald, '*The Model of Rules I*' (1967) 35(1) *University of Chicago Law Review* 14–46

Ehring, Lothar, 'The European Community's Experience and Practice in Suspending WTO Obligations', in Chad P. Bown and Joost Pauwelyn (eds.), *The Law, Economics and Politics of Retaliation in WTO Dispute Settlement* (Cambridge: Cambridge University Press, 2010), 244–280

Eichberger, Fabian Simon, '*Give a Court an Inch and It Will Take a Yard? The Exercise of Jurisdiction over Incidental Issues*' (2021) 81(1) ZaöRV 235–264

Fassbender, Bardo, 'Targeted Sanctions Imposed by the UN Security Council and Due Process Rights' (2006) 3(2) *International Organizations Law Review* 437–448

Fikfak, Veronika, 'Compliance and Compensation: Money as a Currency of Human Rights', in Rachel Murray and Debra Long (eds.), *Research Handbook on Implementation of Human Rights in Practice* (Cheltenham: Elgar, 2022), 45–67

Finnemore, Martha, and Kathryn Sikkink, 'International Norm Dynamics and Political Change' (1998) 52(4) *International Organization* 887–917

Fitzmaurice, Gerald, 'The Law and Procedure of International Court of Justice, 1951–4: Questions of Jurisdiction, Competence and Procedure' (1958) 34(1) *British Yearbook of International Law* 1–69

Fitzmaurice, Malgosia A., and Catherine Redgwell, 'Environmental Non-Compliance Procedures and International Law' (2000) 31 *Netherlands Yearbook of International Law* 35–65

Fitzmaurice, Malgosia 'Angst of the *Exceptio Inadimplenti Non Est Adimplendum* in International Law', in Lorand Bartels and Federica Paddeu (eds.), *Exceptions in International Law* (Oxford: Oxford University Press, 2020), 285–304

Forlati, Serena, 'Reactions to Non-Performance of Treaties in International Law' (2012) 25(4) *Leiden Journal of International Law* 759–790

Fox-Decent, Evan, 'Fiduciary Authority and the Service Conception', in Andrew S. Gold and Paul B. Miller (eds.), *Philosophical Foundations of Fiduciary Law* (Oxford: Oxford University Press, 2014), 363–387

Franck, Thomas M., 'Icy Day at the ICJ' (1985) 79(2) *American Journal of International Law* 379–384

'The Power of Legitimacy and the Legitimacy of Power' (2006) 100(1) *American Journal of International Law* 88–106

Fuller, Lon L., 'Human Interaction and the Law' (1969) 14 *American Journal of Jurisprudence* 1–36

'Law as an Instrument of Social Control and Law as a Facilitation of Human Interaction' (1975) 1(1) *BYU Law Review* 89–96

Gaeta, Paola, and Patryk I. Labuda, 'Trying Sitting Heads of State: The African Union versus the ICC in the Al Bashir and Kenyatta Cases', in Charles Chernor Jalloh and Ilias Bantekas (eds.), *The International Criminal Court and Africa* (Oxford: Oxford University Press, 2017), 48–79

Gallie, W.B., 'Essentially Contested Concepts' (1956) 56 *Proceedings of the Aristotelian Society* 167–198

Gantz, David A., 'Dispute Settlement under the NAFTA and the WTO: Choice of Forum Opportunities and Risks for the NAFTA Parties' (1999) 14(4) *American University International Law Review* 1025–1106

Garcia Blesa, Juan J., 'Indeterminacy, Ideology and Legitimacy in International Investment Arbitration: Controlling International Private Networks of Legal Governance?' (2022) 35(5) *International Journal for the Semiotics of Law* 1967–1194

Gattini, Andrea, 'Breach of the Obligation to Prevent and Reparation Thereof in the ICJ's Genocide Judgment' (2007) 18(4) *European Journal of International Law* 695–713

Gazzini, Tarcisio, and Attila Tanzi, 'Handle with Care: Umbrella Clauses and MFN Treatment in Investment Arbitration' (2013) 14(6) *Journal of World Investment & Trade* 978–1008

Georgiev, George Stephanov, 'The Award in Saluka Investments v Czech Republic', in W. Michael Reisman (ed.), *The Reasons Requirement in International Investment Arbitration* (Leiden: Martinus Nijhoff, 2008), 149–171

Ginsburg, Tom, and Richard H. McAdams, 'Adjudicating in Anarchy: An Expressive Theory of International Law' (2004) 45(4) *William and Mary Law Review* 1229–1339

Gneezy, Uri, and Aldo Rustichini, 'A Fine Is a Price' (2000) 29(1) *Journal of Legal Studies* 1–17

Goldsmith, Jack L., and Eric A. Posner, 'A Theory of Customary International Law' (1999) 66(4) *University of Chicago Law Review* 1113–1177

Gorobets, Kostiantyn, 'Peaks and Valleys: Contemplating the Authority of International Law', in Pauline Westerman et al. (eds.), *Conceptual (Re) Constructions of International Law* (Cheltenham: Elgar, 2022), 171–194

Gray, Christine, 'Is There an International Law of Remedies?' (1985) 56(1) *British Yearbook of International Law* 25–79

'Remedies in International Dispute Settlement', in Cesare P. R. Romano, Karen J. Alter, and Yuval Shany (eds.), *The Oxford Handbook of International Adjudication* (Oxford: Oxford University Press, 2014), 871–889

'The Choice between Restitution and Compensation' (1999) 10(2) *European Journal of International Law* 413–423

'Types of Remedies in ICJ Cases: Lessons for the WTO', in Friedl Weiss and Jochem Wiers (eds.), *Improving WTO Dispute Settlement Procedures* (London: Cameron May, 2000), 401–415

Greenwood, Lucy, 'Does Bifurcation Really Promote Efficiency?' (2011) 28(2) *Journal of International Arbitration* 105–111

Guilfoyle, Douglas, and Cameron Miles, 'Provisional Measures and the MV Arctic Sunrise' (2014) 108(2) *American Journal of International Law* 271–287

Guzman, Andrew T., 'A Compliance-Based Theory of International Law' (2002) 90(6) *California Law Review* 1823–1887

'International Tribunals: A Rational Choice Analysis' (2008) 157 *University of Pennsylvania Law Review* 171

Hakimi, Monica, 'Making Sense of Customary International Law' (2020) 118(8) *Michigan Law Review* 1487–1537

'*The Work of International Law*' (2017) 58(1) *Harvard International Law Journal* 1–46

Hammond, Felicity, '*A Balancing Act: Using WTO Dispute Settlement to Resolve Regional Trade Agreement Disputes*' (2012) 4(2) *Trade, Law and Development* 421–452

Harvard Research on 'Responsibility of States for Damage Done in Their Territory to the Person or Property of Foreigners' (1929) 20 *American Journal of International Law Special Supplement* 133–239

Hathaway, Oona, and Scott J. Shapiro, 'Outcasting: Enforcement in Domestic and International Law' (2011) 121(2) *Yale Law Journal* 252–349

Helfer, Laurence R., and Anne-Marie Slaughter, 'Toward a Theory of Effective Supranational Adjudication' (1997) 107(2) *Yale Law Journal* 273–391

'*Why States Create International Tribunals: A Response to Professors Posner and Yoo*' (2005) 93(3) *California Law Review* 899–956

Hellquist, Elin. "Regional Organizations and Sanctions against Members: Explaining the Different Trajectories of the African Union, the League of Arab States, and the Association of Southeast Asian Nations." (2014) KFG Working Paper Series, No. 59. Berlin: Free University Berlin

Hess, Burkard, 'The International Law Commission's Draft Convention on the Jurisdictional Immunities of States and Their Property' (1993) 4(2) *European Journal of International Law* 269–282

Higgins, Rosalyn, 'Policy Considerations and the International Judicial Process' (1968) 17(1) *International and Comparative Law Quarterly* 58–84

'The Place of International Law in the Settlement of Disputes by the Security Council' (1970) 64(1) *American Journal of International Law* 1–18

Horlick, Gary N., 'Problems with the Compliance Structure of the WTO Dispute Resolution Process', in Daniel L. M. Kennedy and James D. Southwick (eds.), *The Political Economy of International Trade Law* (Cambridge: Cambridge University Press, 2002), 636–645

Hovell, Devika, 'Unfinished Business of International Law: The Questionable Legality of Autonomous Sanctions' (2019) 113 *American Journal of International Law Unbound* 140–145

Howse, Robert, and Ruti G. Teitel, 'Beyond Compliance: Rethinking Why International Law Really Matters' (2010) 1(2) *Global Policy* 127–136

Hudec, Robert E., 'Broadening the Scope of Remedies in WTO Dispute Settlement', in Friedl Weiss and Jochem Wiers (eds.), *Improving WTO Dispute Settlement Procedures* (London: Cameron May, 2000), 345–376

Hudec, Robert E., Daniel L.M. Kennedy, and Mark Sgarbossa, 'A Statistical Profile of GATT Dispute Settlement Cases: 1948–1989', 2 *Minnesota Journal of International Law* (1993) 1

Hudson, Manley O., 'The Central American Court of Justice' (1932) 26(4) *American Journal of International Law* 759–786

Huerta-Goldman, Jorge A., 'Is Retaliation Useful? Observations and Analysis of Mexico's Experience', in Chad P. Bown and Joost Pauwelyn (eds.), *The Law, Economics and Politics of Retaliation in WTO Dispute Settlement* (Cambridge: Cambridge University Press, 2010), 281–309

Huneeus, Alexandra, 'Constitutional Lawyers and the Inter-American Court's Varied Authority' (2016) 79(1) *Law & Contemporary Problems* 179–207

Jackson, John H., 'International Law Status of WTO Dispute Settlement Reports: Obligation to Comply or Option to "Buy Out"?' (2004) 98(1) *American Journal of International Law* 109–125

'*The Birth of the GATT-MTN System: A Constitutional Appraisal*' (1980) 12(1) *Law & Policy in International Business* 21–58

'The WTO Dispute Settlement Understanding – Misunderstandings on the Nature of Legal Obligation' (1997) 91(1) *American Journal of International Law* 60–64

Jacur, Francesca Romanin, 'The Non-Compliance Procedure of the 1987 Montreal Protocol to the 1985 Vienna Convention on Substances that Deplete the Ozone Layer', in Tullio Treves et al. (eds.), *Non-Compliance Procedures and Mechanisms and the Effectiveness of International Environmental Agreements* (The Hague: TMC Asser, 2009), 11–43

Janig, Phillip, 'State Immunity from Non-Judicial Measures of Constraint' (2025) 74(1) *International and Comparative Law Quarterly* 179–204

Janeba, Eckhard, 'Regulatory Chill and the Effect of Investor State Dispute Settlements' (2019) 27(4) *Review of International Economics* 1172–1198

Jarrosson, Charles, *'Réflexions sur l'imperium', in Etudes offertes à Pierre Bellet* (Paris: Litec, 1991), 245–268

Jay, Zoe, and Matt Killingsworth, 'To Arrest or Not Arrest? South Africa, the International Criminal Court, and New Frameworks for Assessing Noncompliance' (2024) 68(2) *International Studies Quarterly* 10–28

Jennings, Robert, '*The Judicial Enforcement of International Obligations*' (1987) 47(1) *ZaöRV* 3–24

Jónsdóttir, Helga, '*The Kyoto Protocol Compliance System: Is the System Effective Enough to Ensure Compliance?*', Thesis, Stockholms universitet, 2013

Joyce, Edward J., and Gary C. Biddle, '*Anchoring and Adjustment in Probabilistic Inference in Auditing*' (1981) 19(1) *Journal of Accounting Research* 120–145

Kaempfer, William H., and Anton D. Lowenberg, '*Unilateral Versus Multilateral International Sanctions: A Public Choice Perspective*' (1999) 43(1) *International Studies Quarterly* 37–58

Kalala, Tshibangu, '*La décision de l'O.U.A. de ne plus respecter les sanctions décrétées par l'O.N.U. Contre la Libye: désobéissance civile des États africains à l'égard de l'O.N.U.*' (1999) 32(2) *Revue Belge de Droit International* 545–568

Kammerhofer, Jörg, 'Uncertainty in the Formal Sources of International Law: Customary International Law and Some of Its Problems' (2004) 15(3) *European Journal of International Law* 523–553

Kamminga, Menno T., 'Confiscating Russia's Frozen Central Bank Assets: A Permissible Third-Party Countermeasure?' (2023) 70(1) *Netherlands International Law Review* 1–17

Kearns, Jason E., and Steve Charnovitz, 'Adjudicating Compliance in the WTO: A Review of DSU Article 21.5' (2002) 5(2) *Journal of International Economic Law* 331–352

Keller, Helen, Corina Heri, and Réka Piskóty, 'Something Ventured, Nothing Gained? – Remedies before the ECtHR and Their Potential for Climate Change Cases' (2022) 22(3) *Human Rights Law Review* 1–32

Kelsen, Hans, 'Sanctions under the Charter of the United Nations' (1946) 12(4) *Canadian Journal of Economics and Political Science* 429–441

'Compulsory Adjudication of International Disputes' (1943) 37(3) *American Journal of International Law* 397–406

'*The Pure Theory of Law and Analytical Jurisprudence*' (1941) 55(1) *Harvard Law Review* 44–70

Khachvani, David, '*Compensation for Unlawful Expropriation: Targeting the Illegality*' (2017) 32(2) *ICSID Review* 385–403

Kindji, Kévine, and Michael Faure, 'Assessing Reparation of Environmental Damage by the ICJ: A Lost Opportunity?' (2019) 57 *Questions of International Law* 5–33

Kingsbury, Benedict, 'Foreword: Is the Proliferation of International Courts and Tribunals a Systemic Problem' (1999) 31(4) *New York University Journal of International Law and Politics* 679–696

'The Concept of Compliance as a Function of Competing Conceptions of International Law' (1998) 19(2) *Michigan Journal of International Law* 345

Kiššová, Sára, '*An Overview of the Doctrine of Ultra Vires from the Perspective of the German Federal Constitutional Court and the Polish Constitutional Court*' (2022) 2(1) *Slovak Yearbook of European Union Law* 33–58

Koh, Harold Hongju, 'Internalization through Socialization' (2005) 54(4) *Duke Law Journal* 975–982

'*The Future of Lou Henkin's Human Rights Movement*' (2007) 38(2) *Columbia Human Rights Law Review* 487–504

Koskenniemi, Martti, '*Case Concerning Passage through the Great Belt*' (1996) 27(3) *Ocean Development & International Law* 255–269

'The Place of Law in Collective Security' (1996) 17(2) *Michigan Journal of International Law* 455–490

Krasner, Stephen D., 'Structural Causes and Regime Consequences: Regimes as Intervening Variables' (1982) 36(2) *International Organization* 185–205

Kriebaum, Ursula, 'Evaluating Social Benefits and Costs of Investment Treaties: Depoliticization of Investment Disputes', in *Katia Fach Gómez*, Anastasios Gourgourinis, and Catherine Titi (eds.), *International Investment Law and the Law of Armed Conflict* (Cham: Springer, 2020), 231–254

'Why Do Nations Obey International Law?' (1997) 106(8) *Yale Law Journal* 2599–2659

Kronman, Anthony, 'Hart, Austin, and the Concept of a Legal System: The Primacy of Sanctions' (1974–1975) 84(3) *Yale Law Journal* 584–607

Kubálková, Vendulka, 'Foreign Policy, International Politics, and Constructivism', in Vendulka Kubálková (ed.), *Foreign Policy in a Constructed World* (New York: M.E. Sharpe, 2001), 15–37

Kulick, Andreas, 'Article 60 ICJ Statute, Interpretation Proceedings, and the Competing Concepts of Res Judicata' (2015) 28(1) *Leiden Journal of International Law* 73–100

Kwiatkowska, Barbara, 'Southern Bluefin Tuna (New Zealand v. Japan; Australia v. Japan), Order on Provisional Measures (ITLOS Cases Nos. 3 and 4)' (2000) 94(1) *American Journal of International Law* 150–159

Lafer, Celso, 'The Dispute Settlement System in the World Trade Organization', *Gilberto Amado Memorial Lecture*, 18 June 1996

Lamp, Nicolas, 'How Some Countries Became 'Special': Developing Countries and the Construction of Difference in Multilateral Trade Lawmaking' (2015) 18(4) *Journal of International Economic Law* 743–771

Langford, Malcolm, Daniel Behn, and Runar Hilleren Lie, 'The Revolving Door in International Investment Arbitration' (2017) 20(2) *Journal of International Economic Law* 301–331

Lanzoni, Niccolò, 'The Authority of ICJ Advisory Opinions as Precedents: The Mauritius/Maldives Case' (2022) 2(1) *Italian Review of International and Comparative Law* 1–25

Lauterpacht, Elihu, 'Partial Judgments and the Inherent Jurisdiction of the International Court of Justice', in Vaughan Lowe and Malgosia Fitzmaurice (eds.), *Fifty Years of the International Court of Justice – Essays in Honour of Sir Robert Jennings* (Cambridge: Cambridge University Press, 1996), 465–486

Laycock, Douglas, 'How Remedies Became a Field: A History' (2008) 27 *Review of Litigation* 161, 165

Leach, Philip, 'Beyond the Bug River – A New Dawn for Redress before the European Court of Human Rights?' (2005) 10(2) *European Human Rights Law Review* 148

Leczykiewicz, Dorota, 'Effectiveness of EU Law before National Courts: Direct Effect, Effective Judicial Protection, and State Liability', in Anthony Arnull and Damian Chalmers (eds.), *The Oxford Handbook of European Union Law* (Oxford: Oxford University Press, 2015), 212–239

Lieblich, Eliav, 'The Death and Life of the Prohibition on Forcible Reprisals', (2025) 51 *Yale Journal of International Law* [forthcoming]

Lipson, Michael, 'Transaction Cost Estimation and International Regimes: Of Crystal Balls and Sheriff's Posses' (2004) 6(1) *International Studies Review* 1–22

Lixinski, Lucas, 'Mechanisms of Systemic Change in Regional Human Rights Courts: Switching between Legitimacy and Impact' (2019) 8(1) *Cambridge International Law Journal* 60

Longobardo, Marco, 'The Italian Constitutional Court's Ruling against State Immunity When International Crimes Occur: Thoughts on Decision No 238 of 2014' (2015) 16(1) *Melbourne Journal of International Law* 255

'State Immunity and Judicial Countermeasures' (2021) 32(2) *European Journal of International Law* 457–484

Lowe, Vaughan, 'Res Judicata and the Rule of Law in International Arbitration' (1996) 8(1) *African Journal of International and Comparative Law* 38–58

Maggi, Giovanni, 'The Role of Multilateral Institutions in International Trade Cooperation' (1999) 89(1) *The American Economic Review* 190–214

Magid, Per, 'The Post-Adjudicative Phase', in Connie Pack and Roy S. Lee (eds.), *Increasing the Effectiveness of the International Court of Justice – Proceedings of the ICJ/UNITAR Colloquium to Celebrate the 50th Anniversary of the Court* (Leiden: Martinus Nijhoff, 1997), 324–347

Magliveras, Konstantinos D., 'Legal and Procedural Issues Arising from the Expulsion of the Russian Federation from the Council of Europe' (2023) 23(1) *International and Comparative Law Review* 95–116

Mann, F.A., 'The Consequences of an International Wrong in International and National Law' (1976) 48(1) *British Yearbook of International Law* 1–65

Marceau, Gabrielle, and Anastasios Tomazos, 'Comments on Joost Pauwelyn's Paper: "How to Win a WTO Dispute Based on Non-WTO Law?"', in Stefan Griller (ed.), *At the Crossroads* (Wien: Springer, 2008), 55–85

March, James G., and Johan P. Olsen, 'The Institutional Dynamics of International Political Orders' (2005) 52(4) *International Organization* 943–969

Marsden, Simon, 'Non-Compliance Procedures' (2016) 27 *Yearbook of International Environmental Law* 131–136

Martin, Lisa L., 'against Compliance', in Jeffrey L. Dunoff and Mark A. Pollack (eds.), *Interdisciplinary Perspectives on International Law and International Relations: The State of the Art* (Cambridge: Cambridge University Press, 2013), 591–610

'Credibility, Costs, and Institutions: Cooperation on Economic Sanctions' (1993) 45(3) *World Politics* 406–432

Mavroidis, Petros C., 'Remedies in the WTO Legal System: Between a Rock and a Hard Place' (2000) 11(4) *European Journal of International Law* 763–813

Mayer, Pierre, 'Imperium et mesures provisoires', in Jacques Haldy, Jean-Marie Rapp, and Phidias Ferrari (eds.), *Mélanges de procédure et d'arbitrage en l'honneur de Jean-François Poudret* (Lausanne: Université de Lausanne, 1999), 437–456

McAdams, Richard H., 'The Expressive Power of Adjudication' (2005) 2005(5) *University of Illinois Law Review* 1043–1121

McGregor, Lorna, 'State Immunity and Human Rights: Is There a Future after Germany v. *Italy?*' (2013) 11(1) *Journal of International Criminal Justice* 125–145

McIntyre, Juliette, 'Declaratory Judgments of the International Court of Justice' (2012) 25 *Hague Yearbook of International Law* 107–158

'Rules Are Rules: Reconceiving Monetary Gold as a Rule of Procedure, (2021) 115 *AJIL Unbound* 144–148

McLachlan, Campbell, 'The Principle of Systemic Integration and Article 31(3)(C) of the Vienna Convention' (2005) 54(2) *International & Comparative Law Quarterly* 279–319

Mearsheimer, John J., 'The False Promise of International Institutions' (1995) 19(3) *International Security* 5–49

Mégret, Frédéric, 'Mixed Claim Commissions and the Once Centrality of the Protection of Aliens', in Ignacio De la Rasilla and Jorge Viñuales (eds.), *Experiments in International Adjudication: Historical Accounts* (Cambridge: Cambridge University Press, 2019), 89–117

Mendel, Mark E., 'Retaliation in the WTO: The Experience of Antigua and Barbuda in US – Gambling', in Chad P. Bown and Joost Pauwelyn (eds.), *The Law, Economics and Politics of Retaliation in WTO Dispute Settlement* (Cambridge: Cambridge University Press, 2010), 310–318

Mercurio, Bryan, 'Why Compensation Cannot Replace Trade Retaliation in the WTO Dispute Settlement Understanding' (2009) 8(2) *World Trade Review* 315–338

Meshel, Tamar, '225 Years to the Jay Treaty: Interstate Arbitration between Progress and Stagnation' (2020) 3(1) *International Comparative, Policy & Ethics Law Review* 1–34

Methymaki, Eleni, and Antonios Tzanakopoulos, 'Freedom with Their Exception: Jurisdiction and Immunity as Rule and Exception', in Lorand Bartels and Federica Paddeu (eds.), *Exceptions in International Law* (Oxford: Oxford University Press, 2020), 158–181

'Mechanisms of Systemic Change in Regional Human Rights Courts: Swinging the Pendulum between Legitimacy and Impact' (2019) 8(1) *Cambridge International Law Journal* 60–83

Michaels, Ralf, and Joost Pauwelyn, 'Conflict of Norms or Conflict of Laws: Different Techniques in the Fragmentation of Public International Law' (2012) 22(3) *Duke Journal of Comparative & International Law* 349–376

Milanovic, Marko, 'State Responsibility for Genocide: A Follow-Up' (2007) 18(4) *European Journal of International Law* 669–694

Miles, Cameron, 'Provisional Measures and the "New" Plausibility in the Jurisprudence of the International Court of Justice' (2018) 88(1) *British Yearbook of International Law* 1–49

Miron, M.C., 'International Law and Religion in Latin America: The Beagle Channel Dispute' (2005) 28(1) *Suffolk Transnational Law Review* 1–34

Mitchell, Ronald B., 'Compliance Theory: An Overview', in James Cameron, Jacob Werksman, and Peter Roderick (eds.), *Improving Compliance with International Environmental Law* (London: Earthscan, 1996), 3–28

Moehlecke, Carolina, 'The Chilling Effect of International Investment Disputes: Limited Challenges to State Sovereignty' (2020) 64(1) *International Studies Quarterly* 125–145

Moiseienko, Anton, 'Legal: The Freezing of the Russian Central Bank's Assets' (2023) 34(4) *European Journal of International Law* 1007–1020

Montana i Mora, Miguel, 'A GATT With Teeth: Law Wins over Politics in the Resolution of International Trade Disputes' (1993) 31(1) *Columbia Journal of Transnational Law* 131–195

Moore, John Norton, 'Enhancing Compliance with International Law: A Neglected Remedy' (1999) 39(4) *Virginia Journal of International Law* 881–1016

Moser, Patricia Tarre, 'Non-Recognition of State Immunity as a Judicial Countermeasure to Jus Cogens Violations: The Human Rights Answer to the ICJ Decision on the Ferrini Case' (2012) 4(3) *Gottingen Journal of International Law* 809–852

Mutangi, Tarisai, 'Enforcing Compliance with the Judgments of the African Court on Human and Peoples' Rights: Prospects and Challenges', in Adeola Aderomola (ed.), *Compliance with International Human Rights Law in Africa* (Oxford: Oxford University Press, 2022), 183–232

Myers, Steven Lee, '*Russia Releases Greenpeace Ship*' (6 June 2014) *New York Times*

Negm, Namira, 'The Sanctions Regime of the African Union in Response to Unconstitutional Changes of Government', in Ian Johnstone and Steven Ratner (eds.), *Talking International Law: Legal Argumentation outside the Courtroom* (New York: Oxford University Press, 2022), 218–245

Newton, Michael, 'Reconsidering Reprisals' (2010) 20(3) *Duke Journal of Comparative & International Law* 361–388

Nollkaemper, André, 'The Role of National Courts in Inducing Compliance with International and European Law: A Comparison', in Marise Cremona (ed.), *Compliance and the Enforcement of EU Law* (Oxford: Oxford University Press, 2012), 125–147

Norman, George, and Joel P. Trachtman, 'The Customary International Law Game' (2005) 99(3) *American Journal of International Law* 541–580

Nossal, Kim Richard, 'International Sanctions as International Punishment' (1989) 43(2) *International Organization* 301–322

Nottage, Hunter, 'Evaluating the Criticism That WTO Retaliation Rules Undermine the Utility of WTO Dispute Settlement for Developing Countries', in Chad P. Bown and Joost Pauwelyn (eds.), *The Law, Economics and Politics of Retaliation in WTO Dispute Settlement* (Cambridge: Cambridge University Press, 2010), 319–338

Nzelibe, Jide, 'The Case against Reforming the WTO Enforcement Mechanism' (2008) 1(1) *University of Illinois Law Review* 319–363

'The Credibility Imperative: The Political Dynamics of Retaliation in the World Trade Organization's Dispute Resolution Mechanism' (2005) 6(1) *Theoretical Inquiries in Law* 215–254

Oberthür, Sebastian, and René Lefeber, 'Holding Countries to Account: The Kyoto Protocol's Compliance System Revisited After Four Years of Experience' (2010) 1(1) *Climate Law* 133–158

O'Connell, Mary Ellen, 'Debating the Law of Sanctions' (2002) 13(1) *European Journal of International Law* 63–79

'The Popular But Unlawful Armed Reprisal' (2018) 44 *Ohio Northern University Law Review* 325

O'Connor, Bernard, and Margareta Djordjevic, 'Practical Aspects of Monetary Compensation: The US – Copyright Case' (2005) 8(1) *Journal of International Economic Law* 127–154

Oellers-Frahm, Karin, 'Article 94 UN Charter', in Andreas Zimmerman et al. (eds.), *The Statute of the International Court of Justice: A Commentary* (Oxford: Oxford University Press, 2012), 159–181

'*Multiplication of International Courts and Tribunals and Conflicting Jurisdiction – Problems and Possible Solutions*' (2001) 5(1) *Max Planck Yearbook of United Nations Law Online* 67–104

Orakhelashvili, Alexander, 'Political Life of Treaties: Indeterminacy, Interpretation and Political Consequences' (2021) 20(3) *Chinese Journal of International Law* 545–560

Osiander, Andreas, 'Sovereignty, International Relations, and the Westphalian Myth' (2001) 55(2) *International Organization* 251–287

Palestini, Stefano, 'Regional Organizations and the Politics of Sanctions against Undemocratic Behaviour in the Americas' (2021) 42(4) *International Political Science Review* 469–483

Palmeter, David, and Stanimir A. Alexandrov, '"Inducing Compliance" in WTO Dispute Settlement', in Daniel L. M. Kennedy and James D. Southwick (eds.), *The Political Economy of International Trade – Essays in Honour of Robert E. Hudec* (Cambridge: Cambridge University Press, 2002), 646–670

Papanicolopulu, Irini, 'Procedures and Mechanisms on Compliance under the 1976/1995 Barcelona Convention on the Protection of the Mediterranean Sea and its Protocols', in Tullio Treves et al. (eds.), *Non-Compliance Procedures and Mechanisms and the Effectiveness of International Environmental Agreements* (Cambridge: Cambridge University Press, 2009), 165–182

Paparinskis, Martins, 'A Case against Crippling Compensation in International Law of State Responsibility' (2020) 83(6) *Modern Law Review* 1246–1286

'Investors' Remedies under EU Law and International Investment Law' (2016) 17(6) *Journal of World Investment & Trade* 919–945

Parisi, Francesco, and Nita Ghei, 'The Role of Reciprocity in International Law' (2004) 36(1) *Cornell Journal of International Law* 93–123

Paulsson, Jan, 'Arbitration without Privity' (1995) 10(2) *ICSID Review – Foreign Investment Law Journal* 232–257

'Jurisdiction and Admissibility', in Global Reflections on International Law: Commerce and Dispute Resolution: Liber Amicorum in Honour of Robert Briner (Paris: ICC Publishing, 2005), 601–617

Pauwelyn, Joost, 'Editorial Comment: Adding Sweeteners to Softwood Lumber: The WTO–NAFTA "Spaghetti Bowl" is Cooking' (2006) 9(1) *Journal of International Economic Law* 197–206

'Enforcement and Countermeasures in the WTO: Rules Are Rules – Toward a More Collective Approach' (2000) 94(2) *American Journal of International Law* 335–347

Pavel, Carmen E., 'Is International Law a Hartian Legal System?' (2018) 31(3) *Ratio Juris* 307–325

Pavone, Tommaso, and R. Daniel Kelemen, 'The Evolving Judicial Politics of European Integration: The European Court of Justice and National Courts Revisited' (2019) 25(4) *European Law Journal* 352–373

Peat, Daniel C., 'Perception and Process: Towards a Behavioural Theory of Compliance' (2022) 13(2) *Journal of International Dispute Settlement* 179–203

Peat, Daniel, Veronika Fikfak, and Eva van der Zee, 'Behavioural Compliance Theory' (2022) 13(2) *Journal of International Dispute Settlement* 167–178

Pelc, Krzysztof J., 'The Politics of Precedent in International Law: A Social Network Application' (2014) 108(3) *American Political Science Review* 547–564

Pellet, Alain, 'The ILC's Articles on State Responsibility for Internationally Wrongful Acts and Related Texts', in James Crawford, Alain Pellet, and Simon Olleson (eds.), *The Law of International Responsibility* (Oxford: Oxford University Press, 2010), 75–94

Pellet, Alain, and Daniel Müller, 'Article 38', in Andreas Zimmermann, Christian J. Tams, Karin Oellers-Frahm, and Christian Tomuschat (eds.), *The Statute of the International Court of Justice: A Commentary*, 3rd edn (Oxford: Oxford University Press, 2019), 924–1008

Pollack, Mark A., 'Political Science in International Adjudication', in Cesare P. R. Romano, Karen J. Alter, and Yuval Shany (eds.), *The Oxford Handbook of International Adjudication* (Oxford: Oxford University Press, 2014), 388–407

Prete, Luca, 'The Systemic Criterion in the Use of Infringement Proceedings' (2023) 24(5) *German Law Journal* 1011–1032

Priem, Claudia, 'International Investment Treaty Arbitration as a Potential Check for Domestic Courts Refusing Enforcement of Foreign Arbitration Awards' (2013) 10 *NYU Journal of Law & Business* 189–221

Putnam, Robert D., 'Diplomacy and Domestic Politics: The Logic of Two-Level Games' (1988) 42(2) *International Organization* 427–460

Puig, Sergio, 'No Right without a Remedy: Foundations of Investor-State Arbitration' (2014) 35(3) *University of Pennsylvania Journal of International Law* 829–861

Raustiala, Kal, and Anne-Marie Slaughter, 'International Law, International Relations and Compliance', in Walter Carlsnaes, Thomas Risse, and Beth A. Simmons (eds.), *The Handbook of International Relations* (Thousand Oaks, CA: Sage Publications, 2002), 538–558

Raz, Joseph, 'Authority and Justification' (1985) 14(1) *Philosophy & Public Affairs* 3–29

'Authority, Morality and Law' (1985) 68(3) *Monist* 195–324

'The Problem of Authority: Revisiting the Service Conception' (2006) 90(4) *Minnesota Law Review* 1003–1044

Reinisch, August, 'The Use and Limits of Res Judicata and Lis Pendens as Procedural Tools to Avoid Conflicting Dispute Settlement Outcomes' (2004) 3 *Law and Practice of International Courts and Tribunals* 37–77

Reisman, W. Michael, 'The Enforcement of International Judgments' (1969) 63 *American Journal of International Law* 1–27

Rhodes, Sylvia A., 'The Article 21.5/22 Problem: Clarification through Bilateral Agreements?' (2000) 3(4) *Journal of International Economic Law* 553–568

Rigaux, Francois, 'Hans Kelsen on International Law' (1998) 9 *European Journal of International Law* 381–408

Ripley, Charles, 'The Central American Court of Justice (1907–1918): Rethinking the World's First Court' (2018) 19(1) *Diálogos* 47–72

Rogstad, Adrian, 'When Stigmatization Fails: Russia and Aggression in Ukraine' (2022) 7(4) *Journal of Global Security Studies* 1–20

Romano, Cesare P.R., 'Legitimacy, Authority, and Performance: Contemporary Anxieties of International Courts and Tribunals' (2020) 114(1) *American Journal of International Law* 149–163

'The Proliferation of International Judicial Bodies: The Pieces of the Puzzle' (1999) 31(4) *N.Y.U. Journal of International Law & Policy* 709

Root, Elihu, 'The Sanction of International Law' (1908) 2 *ASIL Proceedings* 14–27

Rose, Cecily, 'Appeal Relating to the Jurisdiction of the ICAO Council' (2021) 115(2) *American Journal of International Law* 301–316

Rowe, Gregory, 'Reconsidering the Auctoritas of Augustus' (2013) 103 *Journal of Roman Studies* 115

Ruse-Khan, Henning Grosse, 'A Pirate of the Caribbean? The Attraction of Suspending TRIPS Obligations' (2008) 11(2) *Journal of International Economic Law* 313–357

Ruys, Tom, 'Sanctions, Retortions and Countermeasures: Concepts and International Legal Framework', in Larissa van den Herik (ed.), *Research Handbook on UN Sanctions and International Law* (Cheltenham: Elgar, 2017), 19–50

Sand, Peter H., '*Enforcing CITES: The Rise and Fall of Trade Sanctions*' (2013) 22(3) *Review of European, Comparative & International Environmental Law* 251–263

Sarkin, Jeremy Julian, 'Will the International Criminal Court (ICC) Be Able to Secure the Arrest of Vladimir Putin When He Travels? Understanding State Cooperation through Other ICC Non-Arrest Cases against Malawi, Chad, Nigeria, the Democratic Republic of Congo, South Africa, Djibouti, Uganda, and Jordan' (2023) 12(1) *International Human Rights Law Review* 26–68

Scelle, Georges, 'Le phénomène juridique du dédoublement fonctionnel', in Walter Schätzel (ed.), *Rechtsfragen der Internationalen Organisation – Festschriftfir H. Wehberg* (Frankfurt: Klostermann, 1956), 324–342

Schachter, Oscar, 'Compensation for Expropriation' (1984) 78(1) *American Journal of International Law* 121–130

'The Enforcement of International Judicial and Arbitral Decisions' (1960) 54(1) *American Journal of International Law* 1–24

'The Quasi-Judicial Role of the Security Council and the General Assembly' (1964) 58(4) *American Journal of International Law* 962–984

Schauer, Frederick, 'Was Austin Right After All? On the Role of Sanctions in a Theory of Law' (2010) 22 *Ratio Juris* 1

Schimmelfennig, Frank, and Ulrich Sedelmeier, 'Governance by Conditionality: EU Rule Transfer to the Candidate Countries of Central and Eastern Europe' (2004) 11(5) *Journal of European Public Policy* 661–679

Schmitt, Michael N., 'Below the Threshold Cyber Operations: The Countermeasures Response Option and International Law' (2014) 54(3) *Virginia Journal of International Law* 697–732

Schreuer, Christoph, 'Non-Pecuniary Remedies in ICSID Arbitration' (2004) 20(4) *International Arbitration* 325–332

'The Brčko Award of 14 February 1997' (1998) 11(1) *Leiden Journal of International Law* 71–84

Schwartz, Warren F., and Alan O. Sykes, 'The Economic Structure of Renegotiation and Dispute Resolution in the World Trade Organization' (2002) 31(S1) *The Journal of Legal Studies* S179–S204

Scobbie, Ian, 'Res Judicata, Precedent and the International Court: A Preliminary Sketch' (1999) 20 *Australian Yearbook of International Law* 299–317

Scott, James Brown, '*The Hague Court Reports*' (Hague: Carnegie Endowment for International Peace, 1916)

Sending, Ole Jacob, 'Constitution, Choice and Change: Problems with the "Logic of Appropriateness" and Its Use in Constructivist Theory' (2002) 8(4) *European Journal of International Relations* 443–470

Shaffer, Gregory, and Daniel Ganin, 'Extrapolating Purpose from Practice: Rebalancing or Inducing Compliance', in Chad P. Bown and Joost Pauwelyn (eds.), *The Law, Economics and Politics of Retaliation in WTO Dispute Settlement* (Cambridge: Cambridge University Press, 2010), 73–108

Shany, Yuval, 'Jurisdiction and Admissibility', in Cesare P. R. Romano, Karen J. Alter, and Yuval Shany (eds.), *The Oxford Handbook of International Adjudication* (Oxford: Oxford University Press, 2014), 779–804

Shapiro, Scott J., 'Authority', in *Jules L.* Coleman, Kenneth Einar Himma, and Scott J. Shapiro (eds.), *The Oxford Handbook of Jurisprudence and Philosophy of Law* (Oxford: Oxford University Press, 2012), 382–439

Shaw, Malcolm N., 'A Practical Look at the International Court of Justice', in Malcolm D. Evans (ed.), *Remedies in International Law: The Institutional Dilemma* (Oxford: Hart Publishing, 1998), 201–221

Sikkink, Kathryn, and Martha Finnemore, 'Taking Stock: The Constructivist Research Program in International Relations and Comparative Politics' (2001) 4 *Annual Review of Political Science* 391–416

Simma, Bruno, 'From Bilateralism to Community Interests' (1994) 250 *RdC* 217–384

'*Reciprocity*' (2008) *Max Planck Encyclopedia of International Law* para. 1–15

Simma, Bruno, and Christian J. Tams, '1969 Vienna Convention: Article 60 – Termination or Suspension of the Operation of a Treaty as a Consequence of Its Breach', in Olivier Corten and Pierre Klein (eds.), *The Vienna Conventions on the Law of Treaties: A Commentary* (Oxford: Oxford University Press, 2011), 1351–1378

Simmons, Beth A., 'Compliance with International Agreements' (1998) 1 *Annual Review of Political Science* 75–93

Slaughter Burley, Anne-Marie, 'International Law and International Relations: A Dual Agenda' (1993) 87(2) *American Journal of International Law* 205–239

Smith-van Lin, Lorraine, 'Non-Compliance and the Law and Politics of State Cooperation: Lessons from the Al Bashir and Kenyatta Cases', in Olympia Bekou and Daley Birkett (eds.), *Cooperation and the International Criminal Court: Perspectives from Theory and Practice* (Leiden: Brill/Nijhoff, 2016), 114–140

Snyder, Franklin G., 'Nomos, Narrative, and Adjudication: Toward a Jurisgenetic Theory of Law' (1999) 40(5) *William and Mary Law Review* 1623–1725

Steinberg, Richard, 'Wanted – Dead or Alive: Realism in International Law', in Jeffrey L. Dunoff and Mark A. Pollack (eds.), *Interdisciplinary Perspectives on International Law and International Relations: The State of the Art* (Cambridge: Cambridge University Press, 2013), 146–172

Stevenson, Drury D., '*Reverse Bifurcation*' (2008) 75(4) *University of Cincinnati Law Review* 213–261

Stiglitz, Joseph E. and Andrew Kosenko, A Proposal for Russian Asset Seizure, (2024) *Economic Studies at Brookings*

Stoler, Andrew L., 'The WTO Dispute Settlement Process: Did the Negotiators Get What They Wanted?' (2004) 3(1) *World Trade Review* 99–118

Stoltz, Daniella, and Beth Van Schaack, 'It's Never Too Late to Say "I'm Sorry": Sovereign Apologies over the Years', Just *Security* (2021)

Sunstein, Cass R., 'Social Norms and Social Roles' (1996) 96 *Columbia Law Review* 903–968

'On the Expressive Function of Law' (1996) 144(5) *University of Pennsylvania Law Review* 2021–2053

Sykes, Alan O., 'Constructive Unilateral Threats in International Commercial Relations: The Limited Case for Section 301' (1992) 23(2) *Law and Policy in International Business* 263–330

'Optimal Sanctions in the WTO: The Case for Decoupling' (2019) 14 *Journal of International Economic Law* 545–570

'Optimal Sanctions in the WTO: The Case for Decoupling (and the Uneasy Case for the Status Quo)', in Chad P. Bown and Joost Pauwelyn (eds.), *The Law, Economics and Politics of Retaliation in WTO Dispute Settlement* (Cambridge: Cambridge University Press, 2010), 339–371

'Public Versus Private Enforcement of International Economic Law: Standing and Remedy' (2005) 34(2) *Journal of Legal Studies* 631–666

'The Remedy for Breach of Obligations under the WTO Dispute Settlement Understanding: Damages or Specific Performance?', in Marco Bronckers and Reinhard Quick (eds.), *New Directions in International Economic Law: Essays in Honour of John H. Jackson* (The Hague: Kluwer, 2000), 347–357

Szabó, Marcel, '*The Implementation of the Judgment of the ICJ in the Gabčíkovo-Nagymaros Dispute*' (2009) 39(4) *Environmental Policy and Law* 97–103

Tallerico, Thomas J., and J. Adam Behrendt, 'The Use of Bifurcation and Direct Testimony Witness Statements in International Commercial Arbitration Proceedings' (2003) 3(1) *Journal of International Arbitration* 20–45

Talmon, Stefan A. G., 'The South China Sea Arbitration: Is There a Case to Answer?', in Stefan Talmon and Bing Bing Jia (eds.), *The South China Sea Arbitration: A Chinese Perspective* (Oxford: Hart, 2014), 15–58

Thirlway, Hugh, 'The Indication of Provisional Measures by the International Court of Justice', in Rudolf Bernhardt (ed.), *Interim Measures indicated by International Courts* (New York: Springer-Verlag, 1994), 1–35

'*The Law and Procedure of the International Court of Justice 1960–1989*' (2011) 81(1) *British Yearbook of International Law* 13–170

Thompson, Alexander, 'The Rational Enforcement of International Law: Solving the Sanctioners' Dilemma' (2009) 1(2) *International Theory* 307–321

Thouvenin, Jean-Marc, 'Articulating UN Sanctions with Unilateral Restrictive Measures', in Charlotte Beaucillon (ed.), *Research Handbook on Unilateral and Extraterritorial Sanctions* (Cheltenham: Elgar, 2021), 152–174

Tomuschat, Christian, 'Article 19', in Bruno Simma et al. (eds.), *The Charter of the United Nations: A Commentary, Volume I*, 3rd (Oxford: Oxford University Press, 2012), 650–681

'Obligations Arising for States without or against Their Will' (1993) 241 *RdC* 269–374

Torterola, Ignacio, and Diego Brian Gosis, 'Argentina', in Jonathan C. Hamilton, Omar E. Garía-Bolívar, and Hernando Otero (eds.), *Latin American Arbitration and Investment Protection* (Leiden: Brill, 2012), 5–43

Townsend, Jesse, 'Medellín Stands Alone: Common Law Nations Do Not Show a Shared Postratification Understanding of the ICJ' (2009) 34(2) *Yale Journal of International Law* 463–495

Trachtman, Joel P., 'The WTO Cathedral' (2007) 43(1) *Stanford Journal of International Law* 127–167

Triepel, Heinrich, *Droit international et droit interne* (Paris: Pédone, 1920)

Tversky, Amos, and Daniel Kahneman, 'Judgment under Uncertainty: Heuristics and Biases' (1974) 185(4157) *Science* 1124–1131

'The Framing of Decisions and the Psychology of Choice' (1981) 211(4481) *Science* 453–458

Tzanakopoulos, Antonios, 'The Right to Be Free from Economic Coercion' (2015) 4(3) *Cambridge Journal of International and Comparative Law* 616–633

Urs, Priya, 'Obligations Erga Omnes and the Question of Standing before the International Court of Justice' (2021) 34(2) *Leiden Journal of International Law* 505–525

'The Elusiveness of "Interdependent Obligations" and the Invocation of Responsibility for Their Breach' (2024) *British Yearbook of International Law* 1–48

Valles, Cherise M., and Brendan McGivern, 'The Right to Retaliate under the WTO Agreement: The "Sequencing Problem"' (2000) 34(3) *Journal of World Trade* 63–84

van Aaken, Anne, 'Behavioral International Law and Economics' (2014) 55(2) *Harvard International Law Journal* 421–481

'Primary and Secondary Remedies in International Investment Law and National State Liability: A Functional and Comparative View', in Stephan W. Schill (ed.), *International Investment Law and Comparative Public Law* (Oxford: Oxford University Press, 2010), 721–756

van Aaken, Anne, and Betül Simsek, 'Rewarding in International Law' (2021) 115(2) *American Journal of International Law* 195–241

van Erp, Judith, 'Shaming and Compliance', in Benjamin van Rooij and Daniel Sokol (eds.), *The Cambridge Handbook of Compliance* (Cambridge: Cambridge University Press, 2021), 438–460

van Rooij, Benjamin, 'Behavioral Jurisprudence: The Quest for Knowledge about the Ex-Ante Function of Law and Behavior' (2020) 22(1) *Jerusalem Review of Legal Studies* 57–77

Venzke, Ingo, 'Between Power and Persuasion: On International Institutions' Authority in Making Law' (2013) 4(3) *Transnational Legal Theory* 354–373

Vermeer-Künzli, Annemarieke, 'Diallo: Between Diplomatic Protection and Human Rights' (2013) 4(3) *Journal of International Dispute Settlement* 487–514

Vidigal, Geraldo, 'Enforcing Democracy at the Regional Level: Paraguay's Suspension before the Mercosur Court' (2013) 2(2) *Cambridge International Law Journal* 337–349

'Living without the Appellate Body: Multilateral, Bilateral and Plurilateral Solutions to the WTO Dispute Settlement Crisis' (2019) 20(6) *Journal of World Investment & Trade* 862–890

'Re-Assessing WTO Remedies: The Prospective and the Retrospective' (2013) 16(3) *Journal of International Economic Law* 505–534

'Regional Trade Adjudication and the Rise of Sustainability Disputes: Korea – Labor Commitments and Ukraine – Wood Export Bans' (2022) 116(3) *American Journal of International Law* 567–590

'Remedies and Compliance', in Daniel Bethlehem, Donald McRae, Rodney Neufeld, and Isabelle Van Damme (eds.), *The Oxford Handbook of International Trade Law*, 2nd edn (Oxford: Oxford University Press, 2022), 967–990

'Why Is There So Little Litigation under Free Trade Agreements? Retaliation and Adjudication in International Dispute Settlement' (2017) 20(4) *Journal of International Economic Law* 927–956

Viñuales, Jorge E., and Dolores Bentolila, 'The Use of Alternative (Non-Judicial) Means to Enforce Investment Awards against States', in *Laurence Boisson de Chazournes*, Marcelo Kohen, and Jorge E. Viñuales (eds.), *Diplomatic and Judicial Means of Dispute Settlement* (Leiden: Brill, 2012), 247–272

von Stein, Jana, 'The Engines of Compliance', in Jeffrey L. Dunoff and Mark A. Pollack (eds.), *Interdisciplinary Perspectives on International Law and International Relations: The State of the Art* (Cambridge: Cambridge University Press, 2013), 477–501

Walker, Herman, 'The Chicken War' (1964) 58(3) *American Journal of International Law* 671–685

Webber, Jeremy, 'The Grammar of Customary Law' (2009) 54(4) *McGill Law Journal* 579–626

Weil, Prosper, 'Towards Relative Normativity in International Law?' (1983) 77(3) *American Journal of International Law* 413–442

Weiler, Joseph H. H., 'The Transformation of Europe' (1991) 100(8) *Yale Law Journal* 2403–2483

Wendt, Alexander, 'Anarchy Is What States Make of It: The Social Construction of Power Politics' (1992) 46(2) *International Organization* 391–425

Wendtlandt, Matthew, 'SGS v Philippines and the Role of ICSID Tribunals in Investor-State Contract Disputes' (2008) 43(3) *Texas International Law Journal* 523–564

White, Nigel, and Ademola Abass, 'Countermeasures and Sanctions', in Malcolm Evans (ed.), *International Law*, 3rd edn (Oxford: Oxford University Press, 2010), 521–547

Wuerth, Ingrid, 'Compliance', in Jean d'Aspremont and Sahib Singh (eds.), *Concepts for International Law: Contributions to Disciplinary Thought* (Cheltenham: Elgar, 2019), 117–134

Yannaca-Small, Katia, 'Case Comment – BIVAC v Paraguay versus SGS v Paraguay – The Umbrella Clause Still in Search of One Identity' (2013) 28(2) *ICSID Review* 307–340

Yoo, John C., and Eric Posner, '*Judicial Independence in International Tribunals*' (2005) 93(1) *California Law Review* 1–74

Yoshida, O., 'Soft Enforcement of Treaties: The Montreal Protocol's Noncompliance Procedure and the Functions of Internal International Institutions' (1999) 10(2) *Colorado Journal of International Environmental Law and Policy* 95–142

Zarbiyev, Fuad, 'International Law in an Age of Post-Shame' (2020) 9(3) *ESIL Reflections* 1–15

Ziemele, Ineta, 'International Courts and Ultra Vires Acts', in Caflisch et al. (eds.), *Droits de l'Homme – Regards de Strasbourg. Liber Amicorum Luzius Wildhaber* (Kehl am Rhein: N.P. Engel, 2007), 537–558

Zimmerman, Wim, Beyond Indeterminacy: On Reputation and Interpretation in International Law' (PhD Thesis defended at the University of Amsterdam, 2023, on file with author)

UN and Other Documents

Advisory Committee of Jurists, Procès-Verbaux of the Advisory Committee of Jurists, June 16–July 24, 1920 with Annexes (The Hague: Van Langenhuysen, 1920)

AfCHPR, 'African Court Sets Deadline for Kenya to Comply With the Ogiek Judgment', Press Release, 12 November 2024

AfCHPR, Rules of Court (1 September 2020)

Agreement between Argentina and Ghana (27 September 2013), available at https://pcacases.com/web/sendAttach/429

Application Instituting Proceedings, *Alleged Violations of State Immunities, Islamic Republic of Iran v. Canada*, 27 June 2023

Application Instituting Proceedings, *Questions of Jurisdictional Immunities of the State and Measures of Constraint against State-Owned Property, Germany v. Italy*, 29 April 2022

Brazil Law No. 12270 of 24 June 2010

CoE Committee of Ministers, Interim Resolution CM/ResDH(2007)106, 12 July 2007

CoE Committee of Ministers, Execution of Brumarescu and 30 other cases against Romania, CM/ResDH(2007)90, 20 July 2007

CoE Committee of Ministers, Execution of Former King of Greece and Others against Greece, CM/ResDH, 5, 22 February 2006

Committee Document, Committee on Trade and Development, Compensation to Less-Developed Contracting Parties for Loss of Trading Opportunities Resulting From the Application of Residual Restrictions, COM.TD/5, 2 March 1965

Committee of Ministers. Consequences of the aggression of the Russian Federation against Ukraine, CM/Del/Dec(2022)1426ter/2.3, 25 February 2022

Committee of Ministers. Resolution CM/Res(2022)2 on the cessation of the membership of the Russian Federation to the Council of Europe. CM/Res(2022)2, 16 March 2022

Communication, Brazil – Aircraft, WT/DS46/13, 23 November 1999

Communication, European Communities, United States – Taxes on Petroleum and Certain Imported Substances: Follow-Up on the Panel Report, C/W/540, 14 March 1988

Documents of the United Nations Conference on International Organization (1945) 14 UNCIO 853

Documents Presented to the Committee Relating to Existing Plans for the Establishment of a Permanent Court of International Justice (League of Nations, 1920)

DSB Minutes, EC – Bananas, WT/DSB/M/54, 20 April 1999

DSB Minutes, WT/DSB/M/183, 17 February 2005

DSB Minutes, WT/DSB/M/212, 20 June 2006

DSB Minutes, WT/DSB/M/335, 23 August 2013

DSB Minutes, WT/DSB/M/41, 22 January 1998

DSB Minutes, WT/DSB/M/486, 18 December 2023

ECOWAS, Supplementary Act A/SP.13/02/12 on Sanctions against Member States that Fail to Honour their Obligations to ECOWAS (Act 2-SP13 of 2012), 17 February 2012

European Commission, 'First Transfer of €1.5 Billion of Proceeds from Immobilised Russian Assets Made Available in Support of Ukraine Today', 24 July 2024

European Court of Human Rights, Rules of Court, 1 January 2014

Fransisco V. García-Amador, 'First Report on State Responsibility', ILC Ybk 1956, II.2 (1956).

G7 Leaders' Statement, 24 February 2024, available at www.consilium.europa.eu/media/70462/g7-leaders-statement.pdf

GATT Council Minutes, C/M/236, 11 October 1989

GATT Resolution, United States Import Restrictions on Dairy Products, GATT/CP/130 – BISDII/16, 26 October 1951

GATT Summary Record, SR.7/10, 31 October 1952

GATT Summary Record, SR.7/16, 11 November 1952

GATT Working Party Report, Netherlands Action under Article XXIII:2, L/61, 7 November 1952

General Assembly, UNCITRAL Arbitration Rules – Resolution 31/98, (1976) UN Doc A/RES/31/98, 15 December 1976

Gerald Fitzmaurice, 'Fourth Report on the Law of Treaties', ILC Ybk II.2 (1956)

Humphrey Waldock, 'Second Report on the Law of Treaties', ILC Ybk 1963 II (1963)

ICC, Finding under article 87(7) of the Rome Statute on the non-compliance by Mongolia with the request by the Court to cooperate in the arrest and surrender of Vladimir Vladimirovich Putin and referral to the Assembly of States Parties, 24 October 2024 (ICC-01/22)

ICC, 'Situation in the State of Palestine: ICC Pre-Trial Chamber I rejects the State of Israel's challenges to jurisdiction and issues warrants of arrest for Benjamin Netanyahu and Yoav Gallant', *Press Release*, 21 November 2024

ICC, Transmission of Hungary's submission in response to Pre-Trial Chamber I's 'Invitation to Hungary to provide submissions for the purposes of proceedings under article 87(7) of the Rome Statute', 16 April 2025 (ICC-01/18-433)

ICC, Warrant of Arrest for Vladimir Vladimirovich Putin, ICC-01/22-18-SECRET

ICJ Press Release No. 2017/31 (21 July 2017)

ICSID Secretariat, 25(1) News from ICSID (2008)

Inter-American Juridical Committee of the Organization of American States, Draft Inter-American Convention on Jurisdictional Immunity of the States, adopted 21 January 1983, 22 (2) ILM 292

International Law Association, Committee on International Commercial Arbitration, Resolution No 1/2006, Annex 2

International Law Association, International Commercial Arbitration, Interim Report: 'Res Judicata' and Arbitration (ILA, 2004)

International Law Commission, 'Draft Conclusions on Identification', ILC Ybk 2018/II.2 (2018)

International Law Commission, 'Fragmentation of International Law: Difficulties Arising from the Diversification and Expansion of International Law – Report of the ILC Study Group finalized by Martti Koskenniemi', A/CN.4/L.682 (2006)

International Law Commission, 'Jurisdictional Immunities of States and Their Property', ILC Ybk 1980/II.2 (1980)

International Law Commission, 'Report of the International Law Commission', ILC Ybk 1966/II (1996)

International Law Commission, 'Report of the International Law Commission', ILC Ybk 2001/I (2001)

International Law Commission, 'Report of the International Law Commission', ILC Ybk 2001/II (2001)

International Law Commission, 'Draft Articles on Responsibility of States for Internationally Wrongful Acts, with commentaries', A/56/10, 2001 (2001)

International Law Commission, 'Articles on Responsibility of States for Internationally Wrongful Acts', UN Doc. A/56/49(Vol. I)/Corr.4

Joint Communication, European Union and United States, WT/DS26/29, 17 April 2014

Meeting of the Parties to the Montreal Protocol, Decision IV/5 (25 November 1992)

Meeting of the Parties to the Montreal Protocol, *Decision VII/18: Compliance with the Montreal Protocol by the Russian Federation* (27 December 1995)

Mutually Agreed Solution, Agreement between Antigua and Barbuda and the United States Regarding Procedures under Articles 21 and 22 of the DSU (US – Gambling), WT/285/16, 26 May 2006

Mutually Agreed Solution, EC – Bananas III, WT/DS27/98, 8 November 2012

Mutually Agreed Solution, Turkey, WT/DS34/14, 19 July 2001

Mutually Agreed Solution, WT/DS105/11, 12 November 2012

Notice (2006/C 104/08), OJEU 3.5.2006 C 104/18

Notice (2006/C 126/07), OJEU 30.5.2006 C 126/7

Notification, China – Canola Seed (Canada), WT/DS589/7, WT/DS589/8, WT/DS589/9

Notification, DSU, WT/DS413/10, 21 August 2013

Notification, Japan – Quotas on Laver, WT/DS323/4, WT/DS323/5

Notification, SCM Agreement (US – Cotton), WT/267/22, 8 July 2007

Notification, SCM Agreement (US – FSC), WT/DS108/12, 5 October 2000

Notification, US – Copyright, WT/DS160/23, WT/DS160/24/Add.111

Notification, US – Cotton, WT/DS267/43, WT/DS267/44, WT/DS267/45, WT/DS267/4

Notification, US – Hormones, WT/DS26/23, WT/DS26/28

Office of the High Representative, 'Brčko District is a testament to the power of reconciliation and coexistence, authorities must use the opportunities ahead', Speech by Brčko Supervisor Jonathan Mennuti, 8 March 2024

Papers Relating to the Foreign Relations of the United States 1926, (Washington: Government Printing Office, 1941), vol. I, p. 459

President of the Security Council, UN Doc. S/2002/108, 23 January 2002

Presidential Decree, Diario Oficial de la Federación, 18 March 2009

Règlement de Procédure, Tribunal Arbitral Mixte Germano-Polonais, (1922) 1 Tribunaux Arbitraux Mixtes 687

Statute and Rules of the Court, PCIJ Ser D No 1, 4th edn (April 1940)

Submission, Contribution of Ecuador to the Improvement of the DSU, WT/DS/W/9, 28 June 2002

The Declaration of London is the Declaration concerning the Laws of Naval War, (1909) 208 Consol. T.S. 338

UN Security Council, Resolution S/RES/1103, adopted 31 March 1997
UN Security Council, Resolution S/RES/1593 (2005), adopted 31 March 2005, p. 1
UN, 'South Africa: Withdrawal of notification of withdrawal, 7 March 2017 (C.N.121.2017.TREATIES-XVIII.10 (Depositary Notification)
Understanding Regarding Notification, Consultation, Dispute Settlement and Surveillance, L/4907, adopted 28 November 1979
UNFCCC, Enforcement branch of the Compliance Committee. CC-2009-1-6/ Croatia/EB (13 October 2009) Preliminary finding, para. 23
UNFCCC. Enforcement branch of the Compliance Committee. CC-2007-1-6/ Greece/EB (6 March 2008) Preliminary finding, para. 18
UNGA Res. 2758/XXVI of 25 October 1971 ('Restoration of the lawful rights of the People's Republic of China in the United Nations')
UNGA Res. 377 (V) ('Uniting for Peace'), 3 November 1950
UNGA Res. 498 (V) ('Intervention of the Central People's Government of People's Republic of China in Korea'), 1 February 1951, paras. 1, 3, 4, 5
UNGA Res. 60/251 of 3 April 2006 ('Human Rights Council'), para. 8
UNGA Res. 65/265 of 1 March 2011 ('Suspension of the rights of membership of the Libyan Arab Jamahiriya in the Human Rights Council')
UNGA Res. ES-11/3 of 7 April 2022 ('Suspension of the rights of membership of the Russian Federation in the Human Rights Council')
UNGA Resolutions A/RES/36/172, of 17 December 1981
United Nations Environment Program, Report of the Implementation Committee under the Non-Compliance Procedure for the Montreal Protocol on the Work of its Tenth Meeting, UN Doc. UNEP/OzL.Pro/ImpCom/lO/4 (30 August 1995)
United Nations Environment Program, Report on the Seventh Meeting of the Parties to the Montreal Protocol, UN Doc. UNEP/OzL.Pro.7/12 (27 December 1995)
USTR Press Release, Statement on Internet Gambling, 21 December 2007, Office of the United States Trade Representative, available at https://ustr.gov/archive/Document_Library/Press_Releases/2007/December/Statement_on_Internet_Gambling.html
Working Party Report, Working Party IV on Organization and Functional Questions, L/327/Reb.1, 4 April 1955

Treaties and Agreements

1899 Hague Convention on the Pacific Settlement of International Disputes, adopted 29 July 1899, in Force 4 September 1900
American Convention on Human Rights, San Jose, 22 November 1969, in force 18 July 1978, 1144 UNTS 123

American Treaty on Pacific Settlement 'Pact of Bogotá', Bogota, 30 April 1948, 30 UNTS 55

Charter of the United Nations, San Francisco, 26 June 1945, in force 24 October 1945, XV UNCIO 335, amendments in 557 UNTS 143, 638 UNTS 308 and 892 UNTS 119

Chicago Convention on International Civil Aviation, Chicago, 7 December 1944, in force 4 April 1947, 15 UNTS 295

Chicago International Air Services Transit Agreement, Chicago, 7 December 1944, in force 20 January 1945, 171 UNTS 387

Convention for the Conservation of Southern Bluefin Tuna, Canberra, 10 May 1993, 1819 UNTS 359

Convention for the Establishment of a Central American Court of Justice, (1908) 2(1) Special Suppl. AJIL 231

Convention for the Pacific Settlement of International Disputes, Hague, 29 July 1899, in force 04 September 1900, 1 AJIL 103

Convention for the Pacific Settlement of International Disputes, Hague, 18 October 1907, UKTS 6 (1971) Cmnd 4575

Convention for the Prevention and Punishment of the Crime of Genocide, Paris, 9 December 1948, in force 12 January 1951, 78 UNTS 276

Convention on the Elimination of All Forms of Racial Discrimination

Convention on the Prevention and Punishment of the Crime of Genocide, Montego Bay, 10 December 1982, in force 16 November 1994, 1833 UNTS 39

Convention on the Recognition and Enforcement of Foreign Arbitral Awards, New York, 10 June 1958, in force 7 June 1959, 330 UNTS 3

Convention on the Settlement of Investment Disputes between States and Nationals of other States, Washington, 18 March 1965, in force 14 October 1966, 575 UNTS 159

Covenant of the League of Nations, Paris, 28 April 1919, in force 10 January 1920, (1919) UKTS 4 (Cmd. 153)

Declaration of the Government of the Democratic and Popular Republic of Algeria Concerning the Settlement of Claims by the Government of the United States of America and the Government of the Islamic Republic of Iran, (1981) 20 ILM 230

European Convention for the Peaceful Settlement of Disputes, Strasbourg, 29 April 1957, in force 30 April 1958, 320 UNTS 243

European Convention for the Protection of Human Rights and Fundamental Freedoms, as amended by Protocols Nos. 11 and 14, ETS 5, 4 November 1950

European Convention on State Immunity, Basel, 16 May 1972, in force 11 June 1976, 11 ILM 470

Free Trade Agreement between the European Union and its Member States, of the one part, and the Republic of Korea, of the other part, 6 October 2010, OJ L 127, 14 May 2011

General Act for the Pacific Settlement of International Disputes, Geneva, in force 26 September 1928, 93 LNTS 344

General Agreement on Tariffs and Trade 1947, Geneva, 30 November 1947, in force 1 January 1948, 55 UNTS 194

General Agreement on Trade in Services, Uruguay, 15 April 1994, in force 1 January 1995, 1869 UNTS 183

General Framework Agreement for Peace in Bosnia and Herzegovina with Annexes, Paris, 14 December 1995, (1996) 35 ILM 75 ('Dayton Accords')

Interim Agreement on trade and trade-related matters between the European Community, of the one part, and the Republic of Serbia, of the one part, and the Republic of Serbia, of the other part, 24 April 2008, OJ L 28, 30 January 2010

Montreal Protocol on Substances that Deplete the Ozone Layer, 16 September 1987, in force 1 January 1989, 1522 UNTS 3

North American Free Trade Agreement, Washington and Mexico City and Ottawa, 17 December 1992, in force 1 January 1994, 32 ILM 289

OECD Convention on Combating Bribery of Foreign Public Officials in International Business Transactions, 21 November 1997, OECD/LEGAL/0293

Olivos Protocol for the Solution of Controversies in the Mercosur, Olivos, 18 February 2002, 2251 UNTS 244

OSCE Convention on Conciliation and Arbitration, Stockholm, 15 December 1992, in force 5 December 1994

Protocol A/P.l/7/91 of 6 July 1991 on the Community Court of Justice, as amended by Supplementary Protocol A/P.1/01/05 of 19 January 2005

Protocol on the Tribunal in the Southern African Development Community and Rules thereof (in force 7 August 2001, as amended up until 17 August 2008)

Protocol to the Association of Southeast Asian Nations (ASEAN) Charter on Dispute Settlement Mechanisms, 8 April 2010, in force 28 July 2017

Revised General Act for the Pacific Settlement of International Disputes, in force 28 April 1949, 71 UNTS 101

Revised Treaty of the Economic Community of West African States (ECOWAS), signed 24 July 1993, in force 23 August 1995, 2373 U.N.T.S. 233

Rome Statute of the International Criminal Court, Rome, 17 July 1998, in force July 1, 2002, 2187 UNTS 90

Statute of the International Court of Justice, San Francisco, 24 October 1945, in force 18 April 1946, XV UNCIO 355

Statute of the International Tribunal for the Law of the Sea, signed 10 December 1982, in force 16 November 1994, 1833 UNTS 561, UNCLOS, Annex VI

Trade Agreement between the European Union and its Member States, of the one part, and Colombia and Peru, of the other part, 26 June 2012, OJ L 354, 21 December 2012

Treaty of Arbitration concluded between Argentina and Chile, signed 28 May, 1902, (1907) 1 AJIL, 3 Special Suppl 290

Treaty Creating the Court of Justice of the Cartagena Agreement, adopted 28 May 1979, in force 19 May 1983, as amended

Treaty Establishing the Court of Justice of the Cartagena Agreement, as amended, in force 29 August 1999 (Official Gazette of the Cartagena Agreement no 483, 17 September 1999)

Understanding on Rules and Procedures Governing the Settlement of Disputes, Marrakesh, 15 April 1994, 1869 UNTS 401

United Nations Convention on Jurisdictional Immunities of States and their Property, UNGA Res 59/38, 2 December 2004, UN Doc. A/59/508

United Nations Convention on the Law of the Sea, Montego Bay, 10 December 1982, in force 16 November 1994, 1833 UNTS 39

United States-Australia Free Trade Agreement, 18 May 2004

United States-Bahrain Free Trade Agreement, 14 September 2014

United States-CAFTA-DR Free Trade Agreement, 5 August 2004

United States-Chile Free Trade Agreement, 6 June 2003

United States-Korea Free Trade Agreement, 30 June 2007

United States and Morocco Free Trade Agreement, 15 June 2004

United States-Oman Free Trade Agreement, 19 January 2006

United States-Panama Trade Promotion Agreement, 28 June 2007

United States-Peru Trade Promotion Agreement, 12 April 2006

United States-Singapore Free Trade Agreement, 6 May 2003

Vienna Convention on Diplomatic Relations, Vienna, 18 April 1961, in force 24 April 1964, 500 UNTS 95

Vienna Convention on the Law of Treaties, Vienna, 23 May 1969, in force 27 January 1980, 1155 UNTS 331

INDEX

CAMBRIDGE STUDIES IN INTERNATIONAL AND COMPARATIVE LAW

Recent Books in the Series

195 *Adjudicating over Anarchy: Judicial Remedies, Compliance, and Enforcement in International Law*
Geraldo Vidigal

194 *Regional Trade Agreements, Prosperity and the Global South: Normative Beliefs and Interests*
Yenkong Ngangjoh Hodu and Collins Chikodili Ajibo

193 *A Theory of International Organizations in Public International Law*
Orfeas Chasapis Tassinis

192 *The Individual in the Law and Practice of the International Court of Justice*
Yusra Suedi

191 *Ghosts of International Law: The Figure of the Foreign Fighter in a Cultural Perspective*
Alberto Rinaldi

190 *Merchants of Legalism: A History of State Responsibility (1870–1960)*
Alan Tzvika Nissel

189 *The Functions of International Adjudication and International Environmental Litigation*
Joshua Paine

188 *Demystifying Treaty Interpretation*
Andrea Bianchi and Fuad Zarbiyev

187 *International Law-Making by the International Court of Justice and International Law Commission: Partnership for Purpose in a Decentralized Legal Order*
Omri Sender

186 *The Rebirth of Territory*
Gail Lythgoe

185 *Reimagining Sustainable Development in International Law: Perspectives from African Legal Cosmologies*
Godwin Eli Kwadzo Dzah

184 *Collective Self-Defence in International Law*
James A. Green

183 *Weaponising Evidence: A History of Tobacco Control in International Law*
Margherita Melillo

182 *The Justice Factory: Management Practices at the International Criminal Court*
Richard Clements

181 *A Communitarian Theory of WTO Law*
Chi Carmody

For EU product safety concerns, contact us at Calle de José Abascal, 56–1°,
28003 Madrid, Spain or eugpsr@cambridge.org.

www.ingramcontent.com/pod-product-compliance
Lightning Source LLC
Chambersburg PA
CBHW071534240226
40197CB00004B/36
9781107160255